Roman Virtue in the Early Christian Thought of Lactantius

OXFORD STUDIES IN HISTORICAL THEOLOGY

Series Editor
Richard A. Muller, Calvin Theological Seminary

Founding Editor
David C. Steinmetz †

Editorial Board
Robert C. Gregg, Stanford University
George M. Marsden, University of Notre Dame
Wayne A. Meeks, Yale University
Gerhard Sauter, Rheinische Friedrich-Wilhelms-Universität Bonn
Susan E. Schreiner, University of Chicago
John Van Engen, University of Notre Dame
Robert L. Wilken, University of Virginia

THE REGENSBURG ARTICLE 5 ON
JUSTIFICATION
*Inconsistent Patchwork or Substance of
True Doctrine?*
Anthony N. S. Lane

AUGUSTINE ON THE WILL
A Theological Account
Han-luen Kantzer Komline

THE SYNOD OF PISTORIA AND
VATICAN II
*Jansenism and the Struggle for
Catholic Reform*
Shaun Blanchard

CATHOLICITY AND THE
COVENANT OF WORKS
*James Ussher and the Reformed
Tradition*
Harrison Perkins

THE COVENANT OF WORKS
*The Origins, Development, and
Reception of the Doctrine*
J. V. Fesko

RINGLEADERS OF REDEMPTION
How Medieval Dance Became Sacred
Kathryn Dickason

REFUSING TO KISS THE SLIPPER
*Opposition to Calvinism in the
Francophone Reformation*
Michael W. Bruening

FONT OF PARDON AND NEW LIFE
John Calvin and the Efficacy of Baptism
Lyle D. Bierma

THE FLESH OF THE WORD
The extra Calvinisticum *from Zwingli to
Early Orthodoxy*
K. J. Drake

JOHN DAVENANT'S
HYPOTHETICAL UNIVERSALISM
*A Defense of Catholic and Reformed
Orthodoxy*
Michael J. Lynch

RHETORICAL ECONOMY IN
AUGUSTINE'S THEOLOGY
Brian Gronewoller

GRACE AND CONFORMITY
*The Reformed Conformist Tradition and
the Early Stuart Church of England*
Stephen Hampton

MAKING ITALY ANGLICAN
*Why the Book of Common Prayer Was
Translated into Italian*
Stefano Villani

AUGUSTINE ON MEMORY
Kevin G. Grove

UNITY AND CATHOLICITY
IN CHRIST
The Ecclesiology of Francisco Suarez, S.J.
Eric J. DeMeuse

CALVINIST CONFORMITY IN POST-REFORMATION ENGLAND *The Theology and Career of Daniel Featley* Gregory A. Salazar

RETAINING THE OLD EPISCOPAL DIVINITY *John Edwards of Cambridge and Reformed Orthodoxy in the Later Stuart Church* Jake Griesel

BEARDS, AZYMES, AND PURGATORY *The Other Issues that Divided East and West* A. Edward Siecienski

BISSCHOP'S BENCH *Contours of Arminian Conformity in the Church of England, c.1674–1742* Samuel Fornecker

JOHN LOCKE'S THEOLOGY *An Ecumenical, Irenic, and Controversial Project* Jonathan S. Marko

THEOLOGY AND HISTORY IN THE METHODOLOGY OF HERMAN BAVINCK *Revelation, Confession, and Christian Consciousness* Cameron D. Clausing

CHRIST, THE SPIRIT, AND HUMAN TRANSFORMATION IN GREGORY OF NYSSA'S *IN CANTICUM CANTICORUM* Alexander L. Abecina

AUGUSTINE ON THE WILL *A Theological Account* Han-luen Kantzer Komline

THE ZURICH ORIGINS OF REFORMED COVENANT THEOLOGY Pierrick Hildebrand

RAMISM AND THE REFORMATION OF METHOD *The Franciscan Legacy in Early Modernity* Simon J. G. Burton

GENEVA'S USE OF LIES, DECEIT, AND SUBTERFUGE, 1536–1563 *Telling the Old, Old Story in Reformation France* Jon Balserak

ROMAN VIRTUE IN THE EARLY CHRISTIAN THOUGHT OF LACTANTIUS Jason M. Gehrke

Roman Virtue in the Early Christian Thought of Lactantius

JASON M. GEHRKE

OXFORD
UNIVERSITY PRESS

Oxford University Press is a department of the University of Oxford.
It furthers the University's objective of excellence in research, scholarship,
and education by publishing worldwide. Oxford is a registered trade mark of
Oxford University Press in the UK and in certain other countries.

Published in the United States of America by Oxford University Press
198 Madison Avenue, New York, NY 10016, United States of America.

© Oxford University Press 2025

All rights reserved. No part of this publication may be reproduced, stored in a retrieval system, transmitted, used for text and data mining, or used for training artificial intelligence, in any form or by any means, without the prior permission in writing of Oxford University Press, or as expressly permitted by law, by license or under terms agreed with the appropriate reprographics rights organization. Inquiries concerning reproduction outside the scope of the above should be sent to the Rights Department, Oxford University Press, at the address above.

You must not circulate this work in any other form
and you must impose this same condition on any acquirer.

Library of Congress Cataloging-in-Publication Data
Names: Gehrke, Jason M., author.
Title: Roman virtue in the early Christian thought of Lactantius / Jason M. Gehrke.
Description: 1. | New York, NY : Oxford University Press, [2025] |
Series: Oxford studies in historical theology series |
Includes bibliographical references and index.
Identifiers: LCCN 2024060241 (print) | LCCN 2024060242 (ebook) |
ISBN 9780197667750 (hardback) | ISBN 9780197667781 |
ISBN 9780197667774 (epub)
Subjects: LCSH: Lactantius, approximately 240-approximately 320. | Virtues.
Classification: LCC BR65.L26 G44 2025 (print) | LCC BR65.L26 (ebook) |
DDC 241/.4—dc23/eng/20250215
LC record available at https://lccn.loc.gov/2024060241
LC ebook record available at https://lccn.loc.gov/2024060242

DOI: 10.1093/9780197667781.001.0001

Printed by Marquis Book Printing, Canada

In memory of Rev. Klemet Preus

Contents

Foreword	xi
Acknowledgments	xv
Most Commonly Cited Primary Sources	xix
Introduction	1
1. *Virtus* in Roman Life and Literature	24
2. Power and *Virtus* from Republic to Principate	55
3. *Virtus* in Early Latin Christian Apologetic	109
4. *Virtus:* The Power of God in Lactantius	146
5. The Power of the Son	166
6. *Virtus* Revealed in Christ	206
7. *Virtus:* Christ's Precepts of Justice	240
Conclusion	284
Bibliography	289
Index	317

Foreword

All too often studies of early Christian theology fail to achieve the aim of elucidating the complexity of their subjects. Such failures usually result from a faulty method that manifests itself either as a focus on the ideas of an author, to the exclusion of that author's historical context; a focus on historical context, to the exclusion of how that context is appropriated by an author; or a focus on the latent meanings of a text, to the exclusion of its ostensible meanings.[1] None of these faults may be laid at the foot of this study. Indeed, its great strength is the way in which it locates Lactantius in his broader historical and cultural context. The result is a study that sheds light on Roman society, Roman Christians generally, and the way that the ethical and political preoccupations of Roman society set the stage for one Roman Christian's identification of Christ as the proper exemplar of Roman virtue.

The portrait of Lactantius that appears in the following pages draws some of its lines from a rich palette of previous scholarship. For instance, we see the initial sketch for this study in Peter Garnsey's observation that Lactantius strove to construct a Christian moral philosophy that could supplant classical ethical systems.[2] Lewis Ayres questioned the scholarly narrative that Lactantius authored an idiosyncratic theology that betrays no awareness of his Latin theological context but rather draws on philosophical sources. Ayres, instead, reads Lactantius as adapting Tertullian's theology in accordance with the polemical concerns of his own day.[3] Clifford Ando, for his part, argued that the Roman imperial government promoted the notion of a political theology focused upon the emperor.[4] The emperor was depicted—and, indeed, viewed—as a deified figure who was invested with and, in turn, mediated divine power.[5] This imperial theology, Ando maintains, explains Christian opposition to the imperial cult.[6] But

---

[1] For more on such matters, see A. Briggman and E. Scully, "Historical Theology: Aim and Methodology," pp. 1–24, in *New Narratives for Old: The Historical Method of Reading Early Christian Theology. Essays in Honor of Michel René Barnes* (Washington, DC: Catholic University of America Press, 2022).

[2] P. Garnsey, "Introduction," in Lactantius, *The Divine Institutes*, translated with an introduction and notes by Anthony Bowen and Peter Garnsey (Translated Texts for Historians, volume 40; Liverpool: Liverpool University Press, 2003), pp. 33–35.

[3] L. Ayres, *Nicaea and Its Legacy: An Approach to Fourth-Century Trinitarian Theology* (Oxford: Oxford University Press, 2004), pp. 71–75.

[4] C. Ando, *Imperial Ideology and Provincial Loyalty in the Roman Empire* (Berkeley: University of California Press, 2000), pp. 23–24.

[5] Ando, *Imperial Ideology*, esp. pp. 37–39 and pp. 386–393.

[6] Ando, *Imperial Ideology*, p. 394.

xii FOREWORD

rather than simply disavowing the ideas of Roman political theology, Christians appropriated its ideas and terms in ways that advanced their own apologetic and theological goals.[7]

The research of Garnsey, Ayres, and Ando lays the groundwork for Gehrke to identify the concept of power in Latin theologies—imperial, philosophical, and Christian—as key to Lactantius's thought. Lactantius's use of power language reveals the ways in which his ethical and Christological accounts draw upon—and to some extent belong to—both pagan and Christian traditions. At the same time, the manner in which he uses power language reveals how Lactantius challenges Roman ethical systems of his day. His approach to power language also instantiates the influence—both positive and negative—of imperial theology upon Christian theology.

Gehrke, however, is not the first to highlight the significance of philosophical notions of power—expressed by several terms, including, *vis, virtus, potestas,* and *potentia*—to early Christian theology. In exploring these matters, he very much travels the path explored by Michel René Barnes, who charted the concept of δύναμις (power) from the pre-Socratic philosophers, through Plato, to various early Christian theologies. Plato, Barnes writes, drew upon the concept of δύναμις in medical theories to fashion an understanding of causation and existence that loomed large in early Christian theology, especially Trinitarian theology.[8] In identifying the significance of the philosophical notion of power for imperial theology and early Christian theology, Gehrke fittingly assumes from Barnes this mantle of scholarly inquiry. Not just because—by documenting its significance to both Latin imperial and ecclesial theologies—Gehrke expands our understanding of the philosophical and theological importance of the language of power, but also because, with Barnes, he derives meaning from the philosophical and theological traditions that functioned as historical contexts for the subjects under study.

When Lactantius is read in the light of his cultural, philosophical, and Christian contexts, as this study reveals, a new picture emerges. Attention to his imperial and Christian theological contexts brings out the ways in which Lactantius founds his moral convictions upon his conception of the divine nature revealed in the person and work of Christ. Thus, once viewed as morally sophisticated but doctrinally naïve—disjointed at best, incoherent at worst—Lactantius's thought now appears as coherent and compelling. Attention to these contexts also demonstrates the way in which Lactantius stands in the Roman tradition—as seen in Cicero, Lucretius, Vergil, Seneca, et al.—of criticizing

---

[7] Ando, *Imperial Ideology*, pp. 390–391.
[8] M. R. Barnes, *Power of God: Δύναμις in Gregory of Nyssa's Trinitarian Theology* (Washington, DC: Catholic University of America Press, 2001).

ideals promulgated by Roman imperial theology and of reflecting on the civic value of the concept of *virtus*. Over time *virtus* came to be seen in this tradition as not just connoting the martial force embodied by the emperor but also ethical perfections and divine power. This shift in thinking finds a home in Lactantius's own thought. These contexts also reveal the ways in which Lactantius stands in the tradition of Christian apologists who sought to carve out a place for the adherents of their new religion in Roman society. Heirs to some of the Roman critiques of imperial theology just mentioned, Christian apologists developed their own understanding of power in the Christian theological context and redefined ideal virtue in light of the life and work of Christ. Lactantius, himself, finds in Jesus Christ the exemplar of virtue long sought by Roman philosophers. Christ, Lactantius maintains, offers Rome a moral standard able to sustain social order.

As this new picture of Lactantius emerges, so too do new understandings about more general matters. Three merit mention here. First, we are reminded anew that the simplistic binary of Christian versus pagan fails to encapsulate the historical reality of life in ancient Rome. Early Christians received, criticized, and developed Roman imperial ideologies long construed by scholars as strictly pagan. Reality—historical and contemporary—is never simple, always complex. Second, as Gehrke observes, scholarly accounts of the development of Trinitarian theology have given little attention to imperial theology as a cultural and theological context. A context, however, it was—and an important one at that. We now have eyes to see that Latin theological convictions about God and ethical living partly developed as a result of critical engagement with imperial theology. Finally, a few years ago Dan Williams argued that the moral and doctrinal instruction offered in early Christian apologies was more significant than their defensive role.[9] But another scholarly trope persists; that Latin apologetic literature is concerned with the construction of identity and not theology. Not so, this study avers: in both the imperial discourse of pagan Rome and the Latin apologetical literature of early Christianity, theological developments and construction of identity go hand in hand.

Take and read, of ancient Rome and ancient Christians, of power and virtue, each brought to life and to our understanding by careful attention to the complexity of historical reality.

Anthony Briggman
Lent 2024

---

[9] D. H. Williams, *Defending and Defining the Faith: An Introduction to Early Christian Apologetic Literature* (New York: Oxford University Press, 2020).

Acknowledgments

The writing and publication of any book is a serious undertaking that requires long-term focus, determination, and effort. In the case of a first book, that challenge is increased as the author begins as a novice and learns through the process. Which also means that no first book comes to light without an enormous amount of teaching, guidance, correction, support, and encouragement from others. My case is no exception. I could never have done this on my own, without the help of institutions, teachers, mentors, friends, and family. It is a pleasure to acknowledge them here, in something that approximates a chronological order.

My interest in this field began with the patient teaching and mentorship of my undergraduate faculty at Hillsdale College. Prof. Harold Siegel first introduced me to the fascinating study of the Later Roman Empire and the world of early Christianity. Even more, Dr. Mark Kalthoff has been a constant friend and mentor since my undergraduate education. I cannot begin to name or recompense the gift of time, teaching, conversation, encouragement, and wisdom that he and Christy provided me over the years. In a most fundamental way, all my scholarly accomplishments are due to them.

At Marquette University, Michel R. Barnes was a true friend and mentor. He was a captivating teacher, committed unwaveringly to a rigorous historical method and always willing to let a student go where interest and the sources might lead. Michel invited vigorous dialogue and never feared to open a new text that might shed light on anything. His work on the technical sense of "power" is, of course, fundamental to my own, but his teaching and conversation have been an even greater contribution. He remains a true friend. Still, this research and writing would have failed except for the generosity of Dr. Michael Cover, who brought his great expertise in classical Roman literature and New Testament scholarship to the project. Michael helped me to conceive and reconceive the work, faithfully read many drafts, and showed constant patience all the way. He represents everything I would hope to be in a colleague, a dissertation director, and friend. Likewise, fellow students from Marquette, Phillip Anderas, Daniel Lloyd, Andrew Harmon, and Kellen Plaxco, all encouraged and supported me over the years. Adam Ployd was the first to recommend that I submit this work to Oxford, and I am grateful for his encouragement.

Mickey Mattox did not directly supervise my earlier work, but his friendship and conversation have been constant since 2011. In 2012–2013, I deployed to Afghanistan as a reservist in the United States Army. The year interrupted my

xvi ACKNOWLEDGMENTS

study and impacted me deeply. Mickey and his beloved Pam helped me come home, in ways that I can neither explain nor adequately recompense. I would not have continued without them. I owe a similar debt of gratitude to Jeanne-Nicole Mellon Saint-Laurent, who encouraged and guided me into previously unknown scholarly landscapes in the later years of my career as a graduate student.

Several institutions supported the research that went into this project. Marquette University awarded a Dissertation Research Fellowship that brought the project to its first form as a doctoral dissertation. Research and writing was made possible by a Rotary Global Ambassador Fellowship, which allowed me to spend a year as an invited researcher at Strasbourg University's Center for the Analysis of Patristic Documents, where Dr. Rémi Gounelle generously received me, despite my then barely existent French, and never wavered in his support and collegiality. I will be always grateful for an experience that has proven pivotal to my personal and professional journey.

Although this book began as a dissertation, deeply insightful and serious comments of an anonymous Oxford Reader helped me to remake that work into this book, while I was teaching as a Lilly Fellow in Christ College, the Honors College of Valparaiso University. There, a generous circle of friends and colleagues provided an ideal community for this work to continue. Dr. Mehl Piehl read every chapter and made recommendations the whole way. Matt Puffer was a daily conversation partner, who challenged and improved my thinking on so many things. Among other Lilly Fellows, Daniel Silliman, Ashleigh Elser, Chris Hedlin, and Jillian Snyder were all constant in their friendship, challenges, and support. Likewise, senior faculty mentors were instrumental: Kevin Gary, Tal and Agnes Howard, Joe Creech, and Heath Carter all contributed.

Another platoon of colleagues and friends must be acknowledged. Oliver Nicholson, Blandine Colot, and the 2019 Oxford Working Group on Lactantius were a great encouragement that kept me going at a pivotal juncture in this project. Oliver has remained always ready with helpful criticism or a resource overlooked, and he has been a steady encouragement whenever asked. Mattias Gassman has become a true friend in the discipline. He provided expert criticism on each chapter, which saved me from many errors.

Anthony Briggman has made himself a mentor in the field to many of us junior patrologists. I know that I am not alone in expressing gratitude for his example and friendship. Several years ago, he generously invited my contribution to *New Narratives for Old: Reading Early Christian Theology Using the Historical Method*. Since then, he has given advice and generously provided a foreword for this work. Although he bears no responsibility for my mistakes, I am sincerely grateful for his encouragement at this late stage of the race.

If conceiving and drafting a book requires long-term vision and focus, completing a book requires both meticulous editing and a little faith. For that,

I am most grateful to Ms. Kristin Malcolm, who edited the text and notes prior to submission and produced the index. Her editorial insight has improved it much, and she saved me the embarrassment of numerous mistakes. I could not have finished without her aid. Likewise, my brother Joel read several drafts and provided useful criticism—sometimes happy insults—that greatly improved the writing. His comments have encouraged and sustained my work since the beginning.

At Hillsdale College, Matthew Gaetano improved the work by his generous reading and commentary. Anna Vincenzi, Miles Smith, Cody Strecker, Korey Maas, Brad Birzer, Dave Stewart, Paul Rahe, Paul Moreno, and so many others have given constant encouragement. Likewise, the History Department, the community, and the administration at Hillsdale College have welcomed me to a life of teaching and reading that no one can really deserve. I hope this work and future scholarship will, at least, reflect my sincere gratitude for all their grace and friendship.

Elements of previously published materials have been incorporated into this work, and I am grateful to the institutions who have granted permission to re-work and republish them here. Elements of Chapters 2 and 3 appeared previously in Jason M. Gehrke, "*Singulare et Unicum Imperium*: Monarchianism and Latin Apologetic in Rome," in Anthony Briggman and Ellen Scully (eds.), *New Narratives for Old: Reading Early Christian Theology Using the Historical Method*, Studies in Early Christianity Series (Catholic University of America Press, 2022). An earlier form of arguments contained in Chapters 4 and 5 appears in Jason Gehrke, "Lactantius's Power Theology," *Nova et Vetera* 17(3) (Summer, 2019): pp. 683–715. Finally, elements of Chapters 6 and 7 appear in Jason M. Gehrke, "*Rectus Status, Cultor Dei*: Lactantius' Pre-Nicene Latin Theology," *Studia Patristica* 127 (2019): pp. 235–246. I am grateful to each of these publishers for their support of this work as well.

All of these institutions and friends have encouraged and improved this book. Whatever errors do remain are entirely mine.

Most of all, I give thanks here for my wife Erika, my most faithful friend, the mother of Maren, Theodore, Klemet, Michael Christian, Aaron, and Andreas. It is a gross injustice to say that this book would never have been written without her. This work is dedicated to her.

Most Commonly Cited Primary Sources

Origen Adamantius[1]

    Prin.   *De principiis*

Lucius Aeneus Seneca

    Ben.   *De beneficiis*
    Ep.   *Epistulae*
    Nat. q.   *Quaetiones Naturales*
    Prov.   *De providentia*

Marcus Aeneus Lucanus

    Phar.   *Pharsalia*

Thascus Caecilius Cyprianus
(Cyprian of Carthage)

    Dem.   *Ad Demetrianum*
    Fort.   *Ad Fortunatum*
    Bon.Pat. *De bono patientiae*
    Unit.   *De unitate ecclesiae*

Lucius Caecilius Firmianus,
qui est Lactantius

    Epit.   *Epitome divinarum institutionum*
    Inst.   *Divinarum institutionum libri septem*
    Ir.   *De ira Dei*
    Mort.   *De mortibus persecutorum*
    Opif.   *De opificio Dei*

---

[1] This table is listed alphabetically by the second name (*nomen*), which names the *gens* or *clan* to which a person belongs.

XX MOST COMMONLY CITED PRIMARY SOURCES

Collator Obscurus

Legum collatio   *Mosaicarum et romanarum legum collatio*

Aulus Cornelius Celsus

Med.   *De medicina antiqua*

Titus Livius

Liv.   *Ab urbe condita*

Titus Lucretius Carus

Nat. r.   *De rerum natura*

Marcus Minucius Felix

Oct.   *Octavius*

Novatianus

Trin.   *De Trinitate*

Publius Ovidius Naso

Met.   *Metamorphoses*

Gaius Sallustius Crispus

BC   *Bellum Catalinae*
Bel.Iug.   *Bellum Iugurthinum*

Quintus Septimius Florens Tertullianus

Apol.   *Apologeticus*
Adv.Iud.   *Adversus Iudaeos*
Carn.   *De carne Christi*
Prax.   *Adversus Praxean*
Pat.   *De patientia*

MOST COMMONLY CITED PRIMARY SOURCES   xxi

Gaius Suetonius Tranquillus

    Aug.   *Historia Augusta*

Marcus Tullius Cicero

    Acad.   *Academica*
    Arat.   *Aratea*
    Fin.   *De finibus bonorum et malorum*
    Har. Rep. *De haruspicum reponsis*
    Nat. d.   *De natura deorum*
    Inv.   *De inventione*
    Leg.   *De legibus*
    Rep.   *De re publica*
    Sest.   *Pro Sestio*
    Tusc.   *Disputationes Tusculanae*
    Orat.   *De oratore*

Publius Vergilius Maro

    Aen.   *Aeneid*
    Georg.   *Georgica*

Introduction

This study arises from a long-standing interest in theology and politics. I have wanted to understand how Christian thinking about the person of Jesus has informed Christian thinking about political order. Because differing views of Constantine often shape modern discourse on that question, Lactantius's *Divine Institutes* drew my attention. His reputation as the "Christian Cicero," his proximity to Diocletian and Constantine, and his engagement with classical literature all seemed promising.[1] But Lactantius surprised me. His *Divine Institutes* does not engage in the sort of legal adjudication one might expect from an orator responding to persecution. Instead, he starts an argument about "virtue" (*virtus*), which criticizes the traditional Roman gods (*Inst.*, 1–3), and later advocates Christian moral practices like almsgiving, chastity, and forbearance (*Inst.*, 5–6). A Christological treatise (*Inst.*, 4) serves as a bridge between a lengthy critique of traditional Roman ideas of divine *virtus* (*Inst.*, 1–3) and Lactantius's own construction of a Christian ethics (*Inst.*, 5–6). The structure of this arrangement suggests that the argument turns upon the author's view of Jesus and that some notion of *virtus* unifies the whole. Yet the content of Lactantius's Christology and the notion of *virtus* it entails are not immediately evident.

Lactantius's *Divine Institutes* thus prodded me to restate my original question in a new textually and historically oriented way: How did Rome's long tradition of discourse about "virtue" (*virtus*) lead Lactantius to argue that the revelation of God's "power" (Lat. *virtus*) in Jesus Christ was the only true foundation for "virtue" (Lat. *virtus*) in society? The question involves no small degree of equivocation, since Romans often used the same term for a wide range of topics and ideas. As shall be seen, the term *virtus* could figure alongside synonyms like *vis*, *potestas*, and *potentia* to signify a bare causal notion of "power," or it could capture inherited social ideals of "manliness" and later the more familiar philosophical notion of "moral excellence."[2] Exploring the traditions of discourse that

---

[1] Despite gaps in our knowledge of Lactantius's life, scholars generally agree that he was known to Constantine prior to 305 and influenced Constantine between 311 and 315. T. D. Barnes, *Constantine: Dynasty, Religion, and Power in the Later Roman Empire* (Oxford: Wiley-Blackwell, 2011), pp. 118–119, also observes that Constantine knew Lactantius prior to 305, employed him as tutor to his son Crispus, and relied on Lactantius's arguments in his *Speech to the Assembly of the Saints* on 17 April 325.

[2] See Chapters 1 and 2, this volume.

Roman Virtue in the Early Christian Thought of Lactantius. Jason M. Gehrke, Oxford University Press.
© Oxford University Press 2025. DOI: 10.1093/9780197667781.003.0001

2 ROMAN VIRTUE IN THE EARLY CHRISTIAN THOUGHT OF LACTANTIUS

explain this breadth of expression reveals Lactantius's distinctive position on a wider intellectual arc in the Roman world. In the *Divine Institutes*, he argues that the life and work of Jesus Christ provide the eternal definition and paradigm of divine *virtus* revealed in the actions of a human being. That paradigm discloses the ultimate orientation of human life, the character of any admirable action, and therefore the moral order of a just society. Lactantius's claim reflects an ancient Roman way of thinking about divine power, human action, and a society's collective ideals—*exempla virtutis*—which had already been integrated into Latin Christian theology in the third century. His argument, distinctive as it might seem, represents a traditional Latin Christian position within a larger social and philosophical debate in which earlier Latin Christians writers had also engaged. To grasp his argument and perceive its historical character, I came to believe that modern scholarship required a fuller account of the way Roman discourse about *virtus* shaped early Latin Christian thought between Caesar Augustus (27 B.C.–14 A.D.) and Diocletian (284–311 A.D.).

Lactantius: His Life and Works

Relatively little is known about Lactantius's life and career, but the scant biography scholars glean from his writings and from the testimony of Jerome helps to explain his concern with Roman arguments about *virtus* and its implications for Roman society. Through a process of calculation and inference, scholars agree that L. Cae[ci]lius,[3] "*Firmianus, qui et Lactantius*" was born in the last years of Cyprian's ministry (250–322 A.D.) and lived until perhaps 324, the year Constantine defeated Licinius.[4] No firm witness to Lactantius's childhood or parentage remains. St. Jerome, the major source for his biography, praised him as "the most eloquent man of his time" but also expressed disappointment that he could not represent "our [Christian teaching] as easily as he had demolished

---

[3] Scholars have debated the form of Lactantius's second name. The manuscripts witness either to *Caelius* or *Caecilius*, but Wlosok argued for the latter. See A. Wlosok, "Lactance (L. Caelius *ou* Caec(il)ius Firmianus Lactantius)," in *Nouvelle histoire de La Litterature Latine*, vol. 5, ed. R. Herzog and P. L. Schmidt (Paris: Brepols, 1993), pp. 426–459. Anthony Bowen and Peter Garnsey, "Introduction," p. 3, in *The Divine Institutes of Lactantius* (Liverpool: Liverpool University Press, 2003), retains *Caecilius*, following M. Schanz, *Geschichte der römischen Litteratur bis zur Gesetzgebungswerk des Kaisers Justinian*, vol. 3 (Munich, 1922), although Perrin, "Introduction," p. 12, fn. 1, in Michel Perrin, *Lactantius: Dieu le Créateur, SC* 213–214 notes Schanz's adoption of *Caecilius* "sans en donner la raison." The starting place for any research on Lactantius is Jackson Bryce's *Bibliography of Lactantius*, www.carleton.edu/classics/lactantius/.

[4] For Cyprian's martyrdom, see François Decret, *Early Christianity in North Africa*, trans. Edward L. Smither (Eugene, OR: Cascade Books, 2009), p. 80. Cyprian was beheaded 14 September 258 under Emperors Valerian and Gallienus. If Lactantius was indeed older than seventy years in 315–317 and lived until c. 324 (see below), then he might have been eleven at Cyprian's death.

their [pagan ideas]."[5] Jerome's brief entry in *De viris illustribus* also calls Lactantius "the student of Arnobius [*Arnobi discipulus*]" and records that he was appointed "under Diocletian [*sub Diocletiano*]," to teach rhetoric at Nicomedia.[6] Lactantius would then have trained as an orator in Sicca Proconsularis (El Kef, Tunisia) and earned notoriety as an orator in North Africa, perhaps even at Carthage.[7] Although a student of Arnobius, Lactantius shows no knowledge of Arnobius's major apologetic work. Sometime in the early 290s, Lactantius traveled in the company of "Flavius the Grammarian, who wrote two books *On Medicine*" to Nicomedia, where he assumed his post as professor of Latin rhetoric in Diocletian's new court, where the future emperor Constantine was then serving as a military tribune of the first rank.[8]

Lactantius's rhetorical prowess thus elevated him to the privileged company of the two men who most defined the age. Like Constantine, Lactantius was present in Nicomedia during the winter of 302–303, as Diocletian's consistory debated a policy of persecution subsequently enacted on 23 February 303.[9] Although he suffered no bodily harm in the persecution, Lactantius preferred to relinquish his status rather than compromise his faith. How long he remained in Nicomedia is a matter of debate, but he must have stayed until 305, when he personally witnessed his former colleagues burned and drowned, jailed, and

[5] Jerome, *Ep.*, 58.10, in Bowen and Garnsey, "Introduction," in *Lactantius: The Divine Institutes*, p. 4.

[6] Jerome, *Vir. ill.*, 80. For clarity and ease of reference: "Firmianus, who also [is called] Lactantius, was a student of Arnobius [*Firmianus, qui et Lactantius, Arnobii discipulus*]. Appointed under Diocletian the *princeps* [*sub Diocletiano principe accitus*], he taught rhetoric at Nicomedia with Flavius the Grammarian, whose books, *On Medicine*, composed in verse are still extant [*sub Diocletiano principe accitus cum flauio grammatico, cuius 'de medicinalibus' uersu compositi extant libri*]. For lack of students, as it was a Greek city, he took up writing. We have his *Symposium*, which he wrote as a youth in Africa, an *itinerarium* [Ὁδοιπορικόν] of his journey from Africa to Nicomedia written in hexameter verses, as well as another book entitled *Grammarian*, also a very beautiful work, *On God's Wrath* [*et pulcherrimum de ira dei*], and *Seven Books of Divine Institutes Against the Pagans*, as well as an *Epitome* of this same work in one book without a title [*in libro uno ἀκεφάλῳ*], also two books *To Asclepides*, one book *On the persecution* [*de persecutione librum unum*], four books of letters *To Probus*, two books of letters *To Severus*, and *To Demetrianus*, his student [*ad Demetrianum, auditorem suum*]. [In addition, we have] two books of letters and to the same person, one book, *On the Workmanship of God* [*De opificio Dei*] or *On the fashioning of the person* [*formatione hominis*]. In his extreme old age, he was in Gaul as teacher of Crispus Caesar, the son of Constantine, who later was killed by his father."

[7] For Arnobius's school in *Sicca Proconsularis*, see Michael Bland Simmons, *Arnobius of Sicca: Religious Conflict and Competition in the Age of Diocletian* (Oxford: Clarendon Press, 1995). Lactantius made no mention of Arnobius or his apology.

[8] I have followed the chronology of Timothy David Barnes, *Constantine: Dynasty, Religion, and Power in the Later Roman Empire*, pp. 51–56.

[9] Lactantius, *Inst.*, 5.2, *Mort.*, 11.4–5, 6–7. See Elizabeth DePalma Digeser, *The Making of a Christian Empire: Lactantius and Rome* (Ithaca, NY: Cornell University Press, 2000), pp. 7–13. Lactantius's eye-witness account remains a principal source for scholarship on the period. See J. L. Creed, *Lactantius: De mortibus persecutorum* (Oxford: Clarendon Press, 1984); T. D. Barnes, "Lactantius and Constantine," *Journal of Roman Studies* 63 (1973): pp. 29–46; also, T. D. Barnes, *Constantine and Eusebius* (Cambridge, MA: Harvard University Press, 1981), pp. 13–14, 149.

4   ROMAN VIRTUE IN THE EARLY CHRISTIAN THOUGHT OF LACTANTIUS

put to trial by torture.[10] After the persecution, Jerome places Lactantius with Constantine in Trier serving as "the teacher [*magister*] of Crispus Caesar in extreme old age."[11] Jerome's comment might have come from clear evidence in a now lost collection of Lactantius's correspondence. If so, his remarks place Lactantius at Constantine's western court around the year 317. T. D. Barnes, however, has argued for an earlier date, 311–313.[12] Whatever the case may be, scholars generally agree that the appointment as tutor to the emperor's son marks Lactantius as a close and influential person in Constantine's life, and quite possibly from an early period, when Constantine was serving under Diocletian in Nicomedia. The Latin phrase "in extreme old age" usually indicates a lifespan greater than seventy years and thus provides an important coordinate for Lactantius's age.[13] Still, our evidence is a single line. Based on textual analysis of the *Divine Institutes*, the Teubner editors suggest he altered his *Institutes* sometime after 324.[14] There is no extant account of Lactantius's death. He fades from the historical scene just prior to the curtain call at Nicaea.

The above portrait omits a common trope of Lactantius's modern biography: his "conversion." Although some make it an important feature in the story of his character and work, there is little evidence to support it. Scholars usually infer the conversion from Lactantius's remarks at *Opif.* 1.1 paired with his *Inst.* 1.1.8. The former passage contrasts the pride and vanity of his work as a teacher of rhetoric with his apologetic enterprise. As a rhetoric professor, he was not educating young men "for virtue [*ad virtutem*]," but simply for "demonstrated malice [*ad argutam malitiam*]," he reports.[15] A modern tradition inferred from

---

[10]   See Lactantius, *Inst.*, 5.2; *Mort.*, 11.4–5, 6–7, 13.1, 14.3–4, 15.3. Although Jerome says Lactantius lacked students, Perrin, "Introduction," observes that he must have lost his position when the persecution began. Barnes, *Constantine and Eusebius*, p. 13, says that he "lost or resigned his chair and began to compose works of Christian apologetic." For Lactantius's whereabouts during the persecution, see Eberhard Heck, "Constantin und Lactanz in Trier," *Historia: Zeitschrift für Alte Geschichte* 58.1 (2009): pp. 118–130. Heck writes *contra* Digeser, *The Making of a Christian Empire*, pp. 135ff., who placed Lactantius in Trier as early as 305 in order to argue that he presented his first edition of the *Divine Institutes* to the imperial court at Trier between 310 and 313. Still, Lactantius lived in close proximity to Constantine both at Nicomedia (c. late 290s–311) and again in the western capital of Trier (c. 313–324).

[11]   Jerome, *Vir. ill.*, 80.

[12]   See T. D. Barnes, "Appendix A: The Career of Lactantius," in Barnes, *Constantine: Dynasty, Religion, and Power in the Later Roman Empire*, pp. 176–178, who reviews the whole question and concludes that "it was in 311 and 312 that Lactantius was teaching Crispus and doubtless conversing frequently with his pupil's father."

[13]   Jerome, *Vir. ill.*, 80. For discussion of Lactantius's age and Jerome's information, see Mattias Gassman, "Arnobius' Scythians and the Dating of *Adversus Nationes*," *Journal of Theological Studies* 72.2 (2021): pp. 838–841. Also, Michel Perrin, *L'ouvrage du dieu créateur vol 1*. (Paris: Éditions du Cerf, 1974), p. 12, fn. 20.

[14]   Heck and Wlosok, "Introduction," in *Divinarum Institutionum Libri Septem*, fasc I–IV, ed. Eberhard Heck et Antonie Wlosok (Berlin: De Gruyter, 2005–2011), p. viii.

[15]   See Lactantius, *Opif.*, 1.1: "*nam si te in litteris nihil aliud quam linguam instruentibus auditorem satis strenuum praebuisti, quanto magis in his ueris et ad uitam pertinentibus docilior esse debebis.*" Also *Inst.*, 1.1.8, "*professio multo melior . . . putanda est quam illa oratoria, in qua diu versati non ad virtutem, sed plane ad argutam malitiam iuvenes erudiebamus.*" This vision of Lactantius's conversion

INTRODUCTION 5

these lines that Lactantius's criticism of his former occupation denotes his turn to Christianity—he must have been a pagan in his former career but left his position upon conversion and thus became an apologist.[16] By another inference, Lactantius must have begun serious engagement with Christian theology *after* his "conversion," and so rather late in life, perhaps when he began drafting the *Divine Institutes*.[17] John McGuckin noted long ago, however, that neither text relates any conversion explicitly: "The 'conversion' is a reference to the political climate in Nicomedia which had forced [Lactantius] out of his rhetorical position."[18] Hence, Anthony Coleman has reiterated alternatives. Lactantius's familiarity with other Latin writers, his use of the Scriptures, his appearance in Nicomedia as a Christian, his knowledge of the African Novatianists, and Jerome's silence on any conversion might all suggest that "after being reared in the traditional cults, his catechesis began sometime during his youth in Africa."[19] The range of possible judgments ultimately makes the "conversion" unhelpful to the historical analysis of Lactantius's major works. His own writings are a far better source for evaluating the character and sophistication of his Christianity.

Lactantius's literary corpus has made him an important witness to the interaction of religion and politics in the first quarter of the fourth century. His earliest surviving work is the short treatise, *De opificio dei* (303–304), written perhaps in the first year of the Great Persecution (303–311).[20] Between 304 and 311,

derives ultimately from A. Wlosok, *Laktanz und die philosophische Gnosis: Untersuchungen zu Geschichte und Terminologie der gnostischen Erlösungsvorstellung* (Heidelberg: Carl Winter, 1960), p. 191, fn. 28. Wlosok rejected J. Stevenson, "The Life and Literary Activity of Lactantius," *Studia Patristica* 1 (1955): pp. 61–67, who argued that Lactantius had been already a Christian in Africa. Perrin, "Introduction," p. 14, follows Wlosok.

[16] See Blandine Colot, *Penser la conversion de Rome au Temps de Constantin* (Firenze: Leo S. Olschki Editore, 2016), xii–xiii. In English, Bowen and Garnsey, "Introduction," in *The Divine Institutes*, pp. 3–4. Cf. Heck, "Constantin und Laktanz in Trier," p. 118.

[17] E.g., Bowen and Garnsey, "Introduction," in *The Divine Institutes*, p. 48, "Lactantius until his late middle age was a faithful servant of Rome, a prime witness to the success of the Romans in spreading their culture and values among the provincial elites of the west. Conversion to Christianity . . . followed within a short space of time by the shock of the Great Persecution, profoundly transformed his outlook and attitudes. . . . Of course, Lactantius as a Christian convert had not lost contact altogether with the *Romanitas* that had formed him." Barnes, *Constantine and Eusebius*, p. 13, cites Wlosok, *Laktanz und die philosophische Gnosis*, pp. 191ff. and suggests a certain opportunism: "In Nicomedia, Lactantius was converted to Christianity while it was not only fashionable but also safe." In historical theology, Aloys Grillmeier, *Christ in the Christian Tradition*, vol. 1, *From the Apostolic Age to Chalcedon (451)*, 2nd rev. ed. (London: Mowbrays, 1976), p. 191, used the conversion to explain Lactantius's attempt to wed Hermetic theory with Christian *praxis*: "Lactantius did not acquire his concept of religion from Christianity, but brought it over from his pagan period."

[18] J. A. McGuckin, *Researches into the Divine Institutes* (Unpublished dissertation: Durham, 1980), p. 22. Stevenson, "The Life and Literary Activity of Lactantius," and Ogilvie, *The Library of Lactantius*, also objected to the conversion.

[19] Anthony P. Coleman, *Lactantius the Theologian: Lactantius and the Doctrine of Providence* (Piscataway, NJ: Gorgias Press, 2017), p. 11, fn. 14.

[20] For dates and internal development of Lactantius's writing, see Michel Perrin, *De Opificio Dei* (Paris: Éditions du Cerf, 1974); Eberhard Heck, *Die dualistischen Zusätze und die Kaiseranreden bei Lactantius: Untersuchungen zur Testgeschichte der Divinae institutiones und der Schrift De*

6 ROMAN VIRTUE IN THE EARLY CHRISTIAN THOUGHT OF LACTANTIUS

he composed his major work, *Divinarum institutionum septem libri adversus gentes*, commonly known as *Divine Institutes*. Lactantius later redacted that work, adding lengthy dedications to Constantine and much-expanded sections known as the "dualistic passages," perhaps just after Constantine's defeat of Licinius on 18 September 324.[21] His *Divine Institutes* has thus come down to us in two editions.

Between those editions, he also composed three other surviving works. A historical and protreptic treatise, *De mortibus persecutorum* (314–315) is the most significant contemporaneous account of the Tetrarchy and Great Persecution. Shaped by the author's theological understanding of history, the work revels in sometimes gruesome detail in God's providential judgment on the persecuting emperors—Diocletian, Maximian, Galerius, and Maximin Daza.[22] Previewed already in his *Divine Institutes*, *De ira dei* (316) expands an early defense of divine emotion in remarks that address political authority as well.[23] One further work, an elegiac poem, *On the Phoenix* (*De ave phoenice*), is uncertain, but often attributed to him.[24]

Lactantius eventually redacted his *Divine Institutes* into a one-volume *Epitome* that notably reverses his earlier categorical injunction against any form of violence.[25] Such redactions mean that Lactantius's literary corpus bears the marks of a theological development that occurs in the course of his experience of Constantine's rise between 313 and 324. And yet, extant in two editions, *Divine Institutes* remains the central witness to Lactantius's theological understanding. Keenly aware of his times, he interpreted history from the perspective of his theological commitments. This fact makes his theology in the *Divine Institutes* all the more significant for understanding the dynamic interrelationship between Christian tradition and Constantine's actions in this era.

opificio dei (Heidelberg: Carl Winter, 1972). Also, Digeser, "Casinensis 595, Parisinus Lat. 1664, Palatino-Vaticanus 161 and the 'Divine Institutes' Second Edition," *Hermes* 127, 1 (1999): pp. 75–98; Elizabeth DePalma Digeser, "Lactantius and Constantine's Letter to Arles: Dating the Divine Institutes," *Journal of Early Christian Studies* 21 (1994): pp. 33–52. Heck and Wlosok, "Introduction," in *Divinarum Institutionum*, xxx, takes the position that Lactantius composed the short form first and then edited it into the longer unfinished version in the early 320s.

[21] See Stefan Freund, *Laktanz, Divinae institutiones, Buch 7, De vita beata: Einleitung, Text, Übersetzung und Kommentar. Texte und Kommentare* (Berlin: Walter DeGruyter, 2009), esp. pp. 598–599.

[22] See Gianna Zipp, *Gewalt in Laktanz' De mortibus persecutorum* (Berlin: DeGruyter, 2021). The standard edition in English is J. L. Creed, *Lactantius: De mortibus persecutorum*, ed. and trans. J. L. Creed (Oxford: Clarendon Press, 1984).

[23] See Chapter 7, this volume. Critical edition and introduction to this work is Christian Ingremeau, *La Colère de Dieu* (Paris: Les Éditions du Cerf, 1982).

[24] See Sister Mary Francis McDonald, *Lactantius: the Minor Works* (Washington, DC: Catholic University of America Press, 1965).

[25] Lactantius, *Epitome Divinarum Institutionum*, ed. Eberhard Heck and Antonie Wlosok (Stuttgart: Teubner, 1994). For discussion, see Chapter 7, this volume.

INTRODUCTION 7

Although prompted by Diocletian's persecution, Lactantius did not restrict himself to a narrow rebuttal of the jurist Sossianus Hierocles and an unknown orator—the two opponents he names as advocates of Diocletian's policy.[26] Instead, his *Divine Institutes* aims to address and refute "every critic, past, present, and future," by proving the truth of Christianity, even from non-Christian sources.[27] Such breadth of vision requires that he reconcile widely disparate elements of Roman culture and philosophy, ancient oracles, and Christian tradition in ways that can obscure his basic convictions. Lactantius presents himself as the defender of third-century Latin Christianity. At *Inst.* 5.1.22–28, he situates the *Divine Institutes* as the culminating expression of a Latin apologetic tradition. Scholars have often viewed his remarks in this passage as primarily critical of earlier apologists, but Lactantius identifies with his predecessor apologists, while distinguishing his contributions to the tradition they created. He first describes the well-known advocate Minucius Felix as a model apologist, inadequate only because his work was incomplete.[28] Tertullian comes in second place, "learned in every kind of literature, but his speech was blunt, not properly arranged, and often unclear."[29] The phrase "*in omne genere litterarum*" suggests that Lactantius knew Tertullian's non-apologetic works but saw their occasional character, advanced theological content, and acerbic tone as poorly suited to the task of introducing Christianity to a broad Roman audience. Cyprian, by contrast, deserved the fame he earned as an orator prior to his conversion; his eloquence was rivaled only by his depth of understanding and clarity as a teacher. However, Cyprian could not persuade outsiders because "the mystical things he spoke were meant to be heard only by the faithful."[30] The context makes Lactantius's meaning clear: Cyprian wrote mainly for Christian audiences and relied heavily on Scriptural exegesis that could never win over the Roman administrative class.[31] Hence, Lactantius notes with a nod to 1 Cor. 1:20 that "[Cyprian] is usually mocked 'by the learned of this age [*a doctis huius saeculi*],' when they come to know his writings."[32] The reference makes Cyprian

---

[26] Elizabeth DePalma Digeser, *A Threat to Public Piety: Christians, Platonists, and the Great Persecution* (Ithaca, NY: Cornell University Press, 2012), identifies Porphyry of Tyre as the anonymous philosopher; also, Jeremy Schott, *Christianity, Empire, and the Making of Religion in Late Antiquity* (Philadelphia: University of Pennsylvania Press, 2008). However, see T. D. Barnes, "Review: Christianity, Empire, and the Making of Religion in Late Antiquity. By Jeremy Schott" (Philadelphia: University of Pennsylvania Press, 2008), *Journal of Theological Studies* 61.1 (2010): pp. 337–340.

[27] Oliver Nicholson, "Lactantius: A Man of His Own Time?" *Studia Patristica* 127.24 (2021).

[28] Lactantius, *Inst.*, 5.1.22. Lactantius calls him "*idoneus adsertor veritatis.*"

[29] Lactantius, *Inst.*, 5.1.23, "*Septimius Tertullianus in omne genere litterarum peritus fuit, sed in eloquendo parum facilis et minus comptus et multum obscurus fuit.*"

[30] Lactantius, *Inst.*, 5.1.24–26, "*mystica sunt quae locutus est et ad id praeparata, ut a solis fidelibus audiantur.*"

[31] Lactantius, *Inst.*, 5.1.10–22.

[32] Lactantius, *Inst.*, 5.1.26. I suggest a nod to 1 Cor. 1:18–23 in the phrase "*a doctis huius saeculi.*"

8 ROMAN VIRTUE IN THE EARLY CHRISTIAN THOUGHT OF LACTANTIUS

an heir to Paul, nonetheless. These lines also explain Lactantius's apologetic contribution. His *Divine Institutes* seeks to combine Minucius's erudite criticism and Tertullian's depth and learning with Cyprian's faithful clarity, in order to form a complete synthesis that will confound Roman errors while leading cultivated Romans gradually toward the Christian tradition.

Lactantius may not have pulled off such an ambitious project. As a representative of ancient Christianity, he has often perplexed readers, who saw little of the Christianity they knew in his writings. Although he claimed continuity with earlier Christian writers, his *Divine Institutes* can seem like an unlikely combination of texts and traditions connected only by the author's famous Ciceronian rhetoric. The influence of Roman jurisprudence appears in the work's genre and structure.[33] The title proposes a systematic address modeled on handbooks of Roman law—*Institutiones iuris civilis*—such as Ulpian's *De officio proconsulis*.[34] *Institutio* 1, *De falsa religione*, and *Institutio* 2, *De origine erroris*, provide a Ciceronian euhemerist critique of Rome's traditional *cultus deorum*. Drawing on pseudepigraphic and biblical literature, Lactantius's creation-narrative appears in this context. Citing the Egyptian Hermes Trismegistus, alongside Sybilline Oracles, Cicero, Ovid, and Lucretius (among others), Lactantius updates the biblical rejection of idol worship and argues that *cultus deorum* is the origin of every other kind of human error.[35] Now famous "dualistic passages" combine ancient elemental theory with a Jewish-Christian protology that reflects the Genesis account of creation but never cites it. Yet another ingredient appears in *Institutio* 3, *De falsa sapientia*, which turns to confound the philosophers. Lactantius says they compromised with a religious praxis they knew to be absurd while obscuring the true meaning of the *virtus* they purported to seek. The philosophers' errors exemplify the futility of human speculation disconnected from knowledge of the One God. Three books of nearly complete polemic nonetheless articulate a doctrine of God and an innovative concept of *religio*, as Lactantius develops traditional Roman discourses in ways that anticipate and eventually influenced definitively modern ideas.[36]

---

[33] For overview, see *The Divine Institutes of Lactantius*, ed. Anthony Bowen and Peter Garnsey (Liverpool: Liverpool University Press, 2003), pp. 1–57. Also, a lucid and succinct discussion is Christiane Ingremeau, "Les Institutions Divines de Lactance: une composition architecturale," *Vita Latina* 132 (1993): pp. 33–40.

[34] Lactantius, *Inst.*, 1.1.12 for "*Institutiones iuris civilis*." Ulpian identified as "Domitianus" at *Inst.*, 5.11.19.

[35] See Chapters 4 and 5, this volume.

[36] For introduction of Lactantius in the context of Roman religion, see Mattias Gassman, *Worshippers of the Gods: Debating Paganism in the Fourth Century West.* Oxford Studies in Late Antiquity Series (Oxford: Oxford University Press, 2020); Colot, *Penser la Conversion de Rome au temps de Constantin*, pp. 263–210. Toni Alimi, "Lactantius' Modern Concept of Religion," *Journal of Religious History* (2023): pp. 1–23.

INTRODUCTION 9

Lactantius nonetheless begins to fill the void left by his demolition of Roman traditional cultures in *Institutio* 4, *De vera sapientia et religione*. Tellingly, this book is his major Christological treatise. He relies for the first time on lengthy scriptural exegesis shaped by Cyprian, but also describes Christ in categories drawn from Vergil and from the oratorical tradition. His narrative weaves the imagery of illumination into a Christology that emphasizes pedagogical and exemplary themes. In this, Lactantius can also seem disconnected from Christian theological discourse, for example, when he gives the Roman notion of *paterfamilias* a central place in his doctrine of God. Already in antiquity, Jerome claimed that his representations of the Holy Spirit indicated a poor doctrinal understanding.[37] *Institutio* 5, *De iustitia*, and *Institutio* 6, *De vera cultu*, have been called a kind of literary diptych. Lactantius aims to correct Cicero by advancing his own Christian vision of justice, both in theory and practice. *Institutio* 7, *De vita beata*, places all the preceding into the context of a chiliastic eschatology rooted in the early Christian idea of the cosmic week, which Lactantius found in Theophilus of Antioch.[38] This discussion contains redactions that expand on Lactantius's earlier "dualism" to dramatize human history as a theater of conflict between God and the devil. Lactantius everywhere adheres to the forms of a classical rhetoric he had once taught.[39]

Measured by its component parts, *Divine Institutes* can seem to modern scholars like a massive compilation of unreconcilable sources testifying to a shallow and archaic theological understanding. In the search for a unifying thought, modern scholars have mainly observed one significant idea. As the book titles suggest, Lactantius develops a connection between *sapientia* and *religio*, which provides both structural and conceptual unity to the work. The separation of philosophic wisdom from Roman *cultus deorum*, he argues, distorted both wisdom and worship. Greco-Roman civilization unmoored speculation from piety while stultifying common understanding of the divine nature; the political and moral effects of the schism were disastrous.[40] Lactantius thus presents concomitantly the ancient topos of the "upright stance [*rectus status*]" as a corrective to humanity's false worship and foolish speculation.[41] Only by raising their eyes from the dirt and looking up to heaven can people remember their own status as immortal beings made for virtue and its reward, the blessedness of eternal life.[42]

---

[37] Jerome, *Ep.* 84.7 criticized Lactantius's understanding of the Holy Spirit. See Chapter 5, this volume.

[38] See Oliver Nicholson, "The Sources of the Dates in Lactantius' *Divine Institutes,*" *JTS* 36. 2 (1985): pp. 291–310. For the Golden Age, see Arthur Fisher, "Lactantius' Ideas Relating Christian Truth and Christian Society," *Journal of the History of Ideas* 43.3 (1982): pp. 355–377.

[39] On L.'s rhetoric, Colot, *Penser la Conversion de Rome au temps de Constantin*, esp. pp. 1–56. Also Kristina A. Meinking, "*Sic Traditur a Platone*: Plato and the Philosophers in Lactantius," in *Plato in the Third Sophistic*, ed. Ryan C. Fowler (Boston: De Gruyter, 2014), pp. 101–121.

[40] Lactantius, *Inst.*, 6.2.

[41] See Colot, *Penser la Conversion de Rome*, pp. 1–56.

[42] See Chapter 5, this volume.

Lactantius's early work, *De opificio dei*, first developed this *rectus status* theme, which remains a persistent thread running from his polemical arguments into his presentation of Christian doctrine and ethics. The *rectus status* topos even informs his peculiar portrait of Jesus: Christ reveals the eternal law of God and by his teaching and example leads human beings to look upward again to the immaterial divinity.[43] And yet, scholars have noted, no mere "concept of religion" (*religionsBegriff*) can fully express, much less advocate, the teaching and practice of ancient Christianity. Lactantius's reliance upon such a philosophic generalization thus makes him seem like a peculiar witness to the early Christian tradition for which he advocates.

Lactantius in Modern Scholarship

Given the size and ambition of the *Divine Institutes*, scholars of Lactantius spent a long time mapping his sources and weighing their relative authority. Modern studies find their point of origin in two major accomplishments—Samuel Brandt's edition of the *Divine Institutes* and René Pichon's subsequent monograph, which remained the standard narrative until the 1960s. Brandt and Pichon provided critical texts of Lactantius's works, established his importance for the social and political history of the Constantinian Era, and provided an initial narrative of his life and work.[44] They generally saw Lactantius as a middling intellect working in a decaying Roman Empire. As a stylist, he imitated Cicero. As a Christian, he was a new convert who, like his teacher Arnobius, threw rhetorical weight behind the Christian cause before acquiring a sophisticated knowledge of its teaching. Lactantius's use of Scripture was thought limited to Cyprian's compilation of scriptural testimonies, *Ad Quirinum*. From the year 312, Lactantius fell under the spell of Constantine and assumed the role of panegyrist in the new regime. Although much has changed since 1903, Lactantius's reputation never entirely recovered from Pichon's description of him as an orator whose intellectual capacity and theological formation were unequal to his apologetic ambition.[45]

---

[43] See Chapter 5, this volume.

[44] See Samuel Brandt and Georg Laubmann, *L. Caeli Firmiani Lactanti Opera Omnia*. CSEL, vols. 19 and 27 (Prague, Vienna, Leipzig: 1890–1897). Also, René Pichon, *Lactance: étude sur le mouvement philosophique et religieux sous le règne de Constantin* (Paris, 1901), was the first modern monograph on Lactantius and demonstrated Lactantius's authorship of *De mortibus persecutorum*. Also, P. Monceaux, *Histoire littéraire de l'Afrique Chrétienne depuis les origins jusqu'à l'invasion arabe*, 7 vols (Paris: E. Leroux, 1901–1923).

[45] J. Siegert, *Die Theologie des Apologeten Lactantius in ihrem Verhältnis zur Stoa* (Bonn: Rhenania-Druckerei, 1921), p. 5, writes, "Wir werden in ihm einen Schriftsteller kennen lernen, der mehr Philosoph als Theologe ist, und es ist nur zu begreiflich, wenn das eigentlich Christliche bei ihm häufig in den Hintergrund gerückt ist (vergl, Pichon S. 89; Brandt, Dualist. Zusätze, III S. 16)." Thus, Richard Gibson, "Lactantius on Anger," pp. 1–27, in *The Consolations of Theology*, ed. Brian

INTRODUCTION 11

For a time, it was common to approach the *Divine Institutes* only after acknowledging Pichon's criticism.[46] Pierre de Labriolle put it bluntly: "As a theologian, he does not count. . . . We must understand that Lactantius was possessed of an intelligence of no very great compass."[47] Mid-century scholars thus regarded Lactantius's work as a treasury of classical material and mined his corpus for the literature it preserved; they appreciated the fact of his compilation more than its argument. Their research eventually adjudicated the extent of his sources and produced nuanced studies of his acquaintance with Roman texts.[48] In the process, scholars came to recognize that *Divine Institutes* is not an incoherent compilation. Lactantius used a significant body of material—above all, Cicero—to bolster his apologetic, but the character of his usage was critical and dialectical.[49]

Antonie Wlosok decisively redirected scholarly interest toward the character of Lactantius's thought rather than just the sources he preserved. When it appeared in 1960, Wlosok's study was the first major monograph on Lactantius since Pichon.[50] She recognized the centrality of the *religio-sapientia* dyad in his *Divine Institutes* and traced its relationship to the *rectus status* theme. Wlosok argued that Lactantius's insistence upon both true knowledge of God and true

S. Rosner (Grand Rapids, MI: William B. Eerdmans, 2008), pp. 4–5, notes, "Nearly everyone who writes about Lactantius feels obliged to point out his intellectual limitations. . . . These perceptions . . . warn against expecting too much from him." Benjamin Hansen, "Preaching to Seneca: Christ as Stoic *Sapiens* in *Divinae Institutiones IV*," *Harvard Theological Review* 111.4 (2018): pp. 541–558, "Lactantius, for his part, was no theologian or philosopher—and we must be clear on this."

[46] Pichon, *Lactance*, viii–ix.

[47] Pierre de Labriolle, *History and Literature of Christianity from Tertullian to Boethius*, trans. Herbert Wilson (New York: Alfred A. Knopf, 1925), p. 207.

[48] Harald Hagendahl, *Latin Fathers and the Classics: A Study in the Apologists, Jerome, and Other Christians Writers* (Stockholm: Almquist & Wiksell, 1958), Jackson Bryce, *The Library of Lactantius* (New York: Garland, 1990), Ogilvie, *The Library of Lactantius*.

[49] E.g., Hagendahl, *Latin Fathers and the Classics*, Alain Goulon, "Les citations des poètes latines dans l'oeuvre de Lactance," in *Lactance et Son Temps: Recherches Actuelles: Actes Du IVe Colloque d'Etudes Historiques et Patristiques, Chantilly, 1976*, ed. J. Fontaine and M. Perrin (Paris: Editions Beauchesne, 1978), pp. 107–156. Also R. M. Ogilvie, *The Library of Lactantius* (Oxford: Clarendon Press, 1978). Jackson Bryce, *The Library of Lactantius* (New York: Garland, 1990); reprint of Harvard Dissertation, 1973.

[50] Two important caveats come from Thomas Leonhard, *Die Sapientia als Schlüsselbegriff zu den Divinae Institutiones des Laktanz: mit besonderer Berücksichtigung seiner Ethik* (Freiburg, Schweiz: Paulusdruckerei, 1959), who offered an excellent if not final reading of Lactantius's theology. Leonhard acknowledged the Hermetic influence but also recognized an early Christian reception of Hermetic trajectories prior to Lactantius. Second, J. A. McGuckin, *Researches into the Divine Institutes of Lactantius*, dissented strongly to the larger narratives shaped by A. Wlosok (*Laktanz und die philosophische Gnosis*). Vincenzo Loi (*Lattanzio nella storia del linguaggio e del pensiero teologico pre-niceno* [Zurich: Pas-Verlag, 1970]) noted important parallels with Cyprian, Novatian, and Tertullian. Major histories of Christian doctrine left Lactantius out of the picture. E.g., Jean Daniélou, *The Origins of Latin Christianity* (Philadelphia: Westminster Press, 1977); Jaroslav Pelikan, *The Christian Tradition: A History of the Development of Doctrine: The Emergence of the Catholic Tradition (100–600)* (Chicago: University of Chicago Press, 1975).

12   ROMAN VIRTUE IN THE EARLY CHRISTIAN THOUGHT OF LACTANTIUS

worship expressed a Hermetic-Gnostic concept of religion. Particularly, the phrases *cognitio Dei / agnitio Dei* and his pairing of *sapientia-religio* directly translated the Hermetic equivalent, γνῶσις θεοῦ-εὐσέβεια.[51] Likewise, his use of the term *cultor dei* described Christians in terms taken over from the literature of Hermetic gnosis. Lactantius's apparently eastern notion of baptism and his use of the same themes in the early *De opificio dei* seemed to clinch her case. She thus determined that Lactantius, a recent convert, developed his fundamental religious concept during a pre-Christian period and brought that concept with him into Christianity. More than a mere compiler, he sought a marriage of Gnostic insights with Christian praxis as he urged true knowledge of God and sincere religious obligation upon his Roman audience.[52]

Wlosok's research inspired two kinds of responses from scholars interested in the character of Lactantius's Christianity—a topic fundamentally involved with his relationship to the Scriptures. Vincenzo Loi made the first contributions. He agreed with Pichon's judgments about Lactantius's theological mediocrity, but applied the linguistic-analytical method of René Braun to explore the *Divine Institutes'* witness to the Christianity of the day. Although Loi offered a more complete portrait of Lactantius's relationship to early Christianity, he confirmed Wlosok's description of Lactantius's concept of religion and sought the distinctly Christian elements of Lactantius's thought in his moral ideas.[53] Wlosok and Loi thus developed an influential portrait of Lactantius as a morally serious Christian unacquainted with specialized Christian theology but working to unify his Hermetic notion of religion with Christian moral insight. Aloys Grillmeier later popularized this reputation among scholars of early Christianity.[54]

Scholars less persuaded by Wlosok's portrait sought a fuller understanding of Lactantius's relationship to the Scriptures and other early Christian writers.[55] Pierre Monat produced the best single study of Lactantius's biblical citations; John McGuckin provided much-expanded tabulations of his references.

---

[51]   Wlosok, *Laktanz und die philosophische Gnosis*, esp. pp. 180ff. See also Chapter 6, this volume.

[52]   Wlosok, *Laktanz und die philosophische Gnosis*, p. 230.

[53]   Loi, *Lattanzio nella storia del linguaggio e del pensiero teologico pre-niceno*, xv: "We are convinced with Pichon of Lactantius' '*mediocritas*' and his lack of metaphysical and theological genius (*genialità*). He is essentially a master of rhetoric with significant philosophic and theological information, but not an original thinker. But precisely because he is mediocre, because he is not original, he can be a precious witness to the cultural movements of his time and can faithfully (*fedelmente*) reflect the religious context in which he encountered Christianity." See also Vincenzo Loi, "Il concetto di iustitia e i fattori culturali dell'etica di Lattanzio," *Salesianum* 28 (1966): pp. 583–625; Vincenzo Loi, "I valori etici e politici della romanità negli scritti di Lattanzio," *Salesianum* 27 (1965): pp. 65–133.

[54]   See Aloys Grillmeier, *Christ in the Christian Tradition*, vol. 1, *From the Apostolic Age to Chalcedon (451)*, 2nd ed. (London: Mowbrays, 1975), p. 119.

[55]   E.g., Stefan Freund, "Christian Use and Valuation of Theological Oracles: The Case of Lactantius' Divine Institutes," *Vigilae Christianae* 60.3 (2006); Buchheit (1978, 1979, 1990), Walter, in *Pagane Texte und Wertvorstellungen bei Laktanz*, put the issue to rest showing that Lactantius gives superior authority to Scripture.

INTRODUCTION   13

Lactantius's knowledge of the Scriptures was not limited to Cyprian's *Ad Quirinum* after all.[56] Moreover, Vinzenz Buchheit questioned the idea that Lactantius viewed pagan *testimonia* as equal to the Scriptures. He showed that by pairing the notions of *pietas* and *aequitas* (fundamentally linked to the *sapientia-religio* dyad) to express his concept of justice, Lactantius translated Christ's double-love commandment and the text of Matt. 22:36–40 into the terms of classical philosophy.[57] Subsequently, Jochen Walter proved that Lactantius regarded Scripture as an authority beyond any other text and thus subordinated classical sources to his Christian understanding.[58]

Following Buchheit and Walter, Blandine Colot has more recently shown that Lactantius's rhetorical art progressively insinuates biblical language and ideas into an argument couched in the terms of classical rhetoric and philosophy. In the process, Lactantius gradually leads his audiences back to the reading of the Scriptures. His thought therefore rests not only upon the sources he cites, but rather upon a body of theology and scriptural exegesis that his apologetic method works to synthesize and conceal.[59] Colot further emphasizes that Lactantius's textual, rhetorical, and philosophical choices do not express a simplistic oratorical training. Rather, they are calculated to address a social and political ideology coming from the tradition he aims to correct. Lactantius engages not just with Diocletian's Persecution but also with an established Roman ideology ("*Romeideologie*") propagated by his opponents and grounded in classical literature.[60] In light of these developments, Stefan Freund has recently called for a new direction in research. He observes that, in contrast to our understanding

[56] See especially Pierre Monat, *Lactance et la Bible: une propédeutique latine à la lecture de La Bible dans l'Occident constantinen* (Paris: Études Augustiniénnes, 1982). Also, J. A. McGuckin, "The Non-Cyprianic Scripture-Texts in Lactantius," *Vigiliae Christianae* 36.2 (1982): pp. 145–163. In some sense, the need to search beyond Cyprian overlooked the doctrinal nature of Cyprian's *Ad Quirinum*. No one has fully considered the extent to which Cyprian's *Ad quirinum* conveyed a doctrinal content that frames Lactantius's work.

[57] Vinzenz Buchheit, "Cicero Inspiratus: Vergilius Propheta? Zur Wertung paganer Autoren bei Laktanz," *Hermes* 118.3 (1990): pp. 357–372; Vinzenz Buchheit, "Die Definition der Gerechtigkeit bei Laktanz und seinen Vorgängern," *Vigiliae Christianae* 33 (1979): pp. 356–374.

[58] J. Walter, *Pagane Texte und Wertvorstellungen bei Laktanz* (Göttingen: Vandenhoek & Ruprecht, 2006). Also fundamental is Andreas Löw, *Hermes Trismegistos alz Zeuge der Warheit: Die christliche Hermetikrezeption von Athenagoras bis Laktanz* (Berlin: Philo Verlagsgesellchaft, 2002). By concluding that Lactantius's use of Hermes was strategic and apologetic, his work also calls into question the basis of the view that Hermetic gnosis is the real source of his Christian understanding.

[59] Lewis J. Swift, "Lactantius and the Golden Age," *American Journal of Philology* 89 (1968), pp. 144–156; Goulon, "Les citations des poètes latines dans l'oeuvre de Lactance"; Buchheit, "Cicero Inspiratus: Vergilius Propheta?"; Walter, *Pagane Texte und Wertvorstellungen bei Laktanz*; Freund, "Christian Use and Valuation of Theological Oracles"; Colot, *Penser la conversion de Rome*.

[60] Colot, *Penser la conversion de Rome au temps de Constantin*, pp. 3–57. Nicholson, "Lactantius: Man of His Own Time?" p. 177, makes the same point differently: "For Lactantius was not wasting his time with dead men. Cicero had many readers among his contemporaries, and it was surely these middle-brow readers, rather than high-brow Greek intellectuals that Lactantius was hoping to reach with his writings."

14   ROMAN VIRTUE IN THE EARLY CHRISTIAN THOUGHT OF LACTANTIUS

of Lactantius's reading of non-Christian writers, "We know regrettably little about Lactantius' Christianity."[61]

Freund's observation has broader implications for our understanding of Christianity in the Constantinian Era. As a figure close to Constantine, Lactantius holds a prominent place in historical accounts of Constantine's rise and self-representation as a Christian.[62] Those historical accounts, however, presuppose more specialized narratives of Lactantius's thought. A primary example is Elizabeth DePalma Digeser's *Lactantius and Rome: The Making of a Christian Empire*. Among English-speaking readers, Digeser's monograph has served as a standard introduction to Lactantius's Christianity in its connection with Constantine's regime. She explores the dialogical nature of Lactantius's *Divine Institutes* as a source debating contemporary Neoplatonist political philosophy, one that "influenced the emperor Constantine's description of the Christian polity that he governed."[63] Digeser presents *Divine Institutes* as a "blueprint for building a new Rome out of the ashes of the tetrarchy."[64] Her vision of Lactantius's Christianity relies, quite rightly, upon more specialized twentieth-century narratives. She thus presupposes the idea that Lactantius was theologically idiosyncratic and seeks to explain that idiosyncrasy as evidence of a distinctive political project.[65] Amalgamating ideas taken from early Christianity and "philosophic monotheism," the *Divine Institutes* advocates a new kind of "inclusive Christianity."[66] This political context explains much

[61]   Stefan Freund, "The Hidden Library of Lactantius," *Studia Patristica* 24 (2012): p. 187.

[62]   E.g., *Constantine: Religious Faith and Imperial Policy*, ed. A. Edward Siecienski (New York: Routledge, 2017); Noel Lenski, *Constantine and the Cities: Imperial Authority and Civic Politics* (Philadelphia: University of Pennsylvania Press, 2016). Also Barnes, *Constantine: Dynasty, Religion, and Power in the Later Roman Empire*; H. A. Drake, *Constantine and the Bishops: The Politics of Intolerance* (Baltimore: Johns Hopkins University Press, 2002); J. E. Grubbs, *Law and Family in Late Antiquity: The Emperor Constantine's Marriage Legislation* (Oxford: Oxford University Press, 1995); earlier, F. Amarelli, *Vetustas-Innovatio: Un'antitesi apparente nella legislazione di Costantino* (Naples, Italy: E. Jovene, 1978), pp. 113–133.

[63]   Elizabeth DePalma Digeser, "Religion, Law, and the Roman Polity: The Era of the Great Persecution," in *Religion and Law in Classical and Christiane Rome*, ed. Clifford Ando and J. Rupke (Munich: F. Steiner, 2006), pp. 68–84; also, Elizabeth DePalma Digeser, "Lactantius," in *Great Christian Jurists and Legal Collections in the First Millenium*, ed. Philip L. Reynolds (Cambridge: Cambridge University Press, 2019). Noel Lenski, *Constantine and the Cities*, pp. 255–259, affirms Digeser's claim that Constantine had the *Divine Institutes* at hand when he wrote his *Letter to Arles* and in his dealings with the Donatists.

[64]   Digeser, *Lactantius and Rome*, p. 13. See also, Digeser, "Religion, Law, and the Roman Polity: The Era of the Great Persecution," pp. 68–84, which provides nuance by exploring Lactantius's dialogue with Neoplatonism.

[65]   Digeser, *Lactantius and Rome*, pp. 64–70, 84ff. and endnotes, rely on Wlosok and Loi. For response on grounds of Lactantius's use of sources, J. Walter, *Pagane Texte und Wertvorstellungen bei Laktanz*, pp. 214ff. Also, Colot, *Penser la conversion de Rome*, pp. 19–21, 182–186, *passim*. The argument leaves unanswered the question of which Christian exegetical and theological traditions shaped Lactantius's reading of the Scriptures and hence his apologetic.

[66]   Digeser, *Lactantius and Rome*, pp. 64–90, 115–144. Also, David Potter, *Constantine the Emperor* (Oxford: Oxford University Press, 2012), p. 343, fn. 7, cites Digeser, *Lactantius and Rome*, pp. 125–133, for its summary of Constantine's dealings with pagans and Jews.

that puzzled earlier readers. Lactantius's use of pagan sources, his Christology emphasizing pedagogical rather than sacrificial themes, and his elaborate use of Cicero, all sought to forge an alliance between Christians and traditional elites in the Constantinian empire. Hence, in Digeser's work, historical theology and political history have come into immediate connection, since historical accounts of Lactantius's theology become the basis for much wider judgments about Constantine's politics and the nature of the Christianity promoted under his reign. And yet, as observed above, major developments in scholarship on Lactantius's theology have overturned the presuppositions that shaped Pichon, Wlosok, Loi, and those they influenced. By extension, a new account of Lactantius's theology holds significant implications for broader accounts of Christianity in the reign of Constantine.

A New Approach to Lactantius

Recent developments in modern scholarship confirmed my sense that historical understanding of Lactantius's Christianity would benefit from a nuanced account of *virtus* in his thought. Lewis Ayres has provided a significant lead in this respect. In his influential study of early Trinitarian theology, Ayres notes, "Modern scholars have treated Lactantius' theology as idiosyncratic and Lactantius as ignorant of other Latin theology. . . . The standard scholarly account of Lactantius as indebted primarily to non-Christian philosophy has long needed reconsideration."[67] In his brief treatment, Lactantius appears alongside Novatian as an inheritor of Tertullian's thought.[68] However, the central term Ayres examines is not *sapientia* or *religio*, but various terms for "power"—*virtus, vis, potestas, dynamis,* and its cognates. Ayres interprets these terms as expressions of a theological grammar well known to early Christian writers.[69] He does not provide a complete study of Lactantius, but his treatment marks a striking contrast to most studies, which consider the notion of *virtus* as a moral term rooted in rhetoric and cultural history, but not as a technical theological term.[70]

Ayres's focus upon the notion of "power" is especially striking because modern scholarship generally regarded this vocabulary as lacking technical theological content. Scholars regarded Lactantius's critique of Roman *virtus* and his portrait of Christ as a "revealer of *virtus*" as a sign of his status as a theological novice. *Virtus*, with its variety of potential meanings (e.g., power, strength, moral

---

[67] See Lewis Ayres, *Nicaea and Its Legacy: An Approach to Fourth Century Trinitarian Theology* (Oxford: Oxford University Press, 2004), p. 71.

[68] Ayres, *Nicaea and Its Legacy*, pp. 72–73. See Chapter 5, this volume.

[69] For discussion, see Chapter 2, this volume.

[70] Colot, *Lactance: penser la conversion de Rome*, xii, on virtue, pp. 103–158.

16 ROMAN VIRTUE IN THE EARLY CHRISTIAN THOUGHT OF LACTANTIUS

excellence, manliness, courage) seemed ill-suited to the technical debates of early Christian discourse.[71] Pichon thus observed Lactantius's use of *virtus* and his image of God as a *paterfamilias* as evidence that he "expresses the unity of the Father and Son by an analogy drawn from Roman law."[72] Grillmeier numbered Lactantius's notion of Christ as "himself the convincing model of virtue" among the "strange emphases" in a proto-Arian Christology that makes Christ a "super-human being."[73] Citing Pichon, Basil Studer criticized the language of *virtus* as insufficient to the subject: "[Lactantius] had no success at defining precisely the relationship between the Father and the Son. . . . He conceives the unity between Father and Son in a merely moral sense."[74] François Heim drew parallels with Constantine's rhetoric, where *virtus* figured as a "nom divin," alongside terms like δύναμις, ἀρετή, ἀνδρεία, ἐξουσία, and *potentia superna*.[75] For Heim, Lactantius's use of *virtus* reflected the efforts of an impressionable Christian orator adapting Rome's ancient *"théologie de victoire"* for Constantine's new regime.[76] Heim thus observed parallels between Christian theology and Roman imperial discourse, but regarded Lactantius's focus upon *virtus* as a merely political effort to place Roman political and moral traditions in the service of Christian thought.[77] All of these writers recognized the centrality of *virtus* in Lactantius's portrait of Christ. The fact that modern criticism gives *virtus* a central place in Lactantius's thought also suggests that misunderstanding of *virtus* would obscure our comprehension of his theology.

---

[71] On the polyvalence of *virtus,* see Catalina Balmaceda, *Virtus Romana: Politics and Morality in the Roman Historians* (Chapel Hill: University of North Carolina Press, 2017); Myles McDonnell, *Roman Manliness:* Virtus *and the Roman Republic* (Cambridge: Cambridge University Press, 2006); Donald Earl, *Moral and Political Tradition of Rome* (Ithaca, NY: Cornell University Press, 1967). Also, Bowen and Garnsey, *Divine Institutes,* xi, pp. 26–28, echoed Pichon et al. in connection with this term: "*Virtus,* here mostly translated as 'virtue' is a particular problem. Lactantius was more of a moralist than a theologian and the worth of his arguments varies greatly, even within a paragraph, for he measured worth more on a rhetorical than on an intellectual scale."

[72] Pichon, *Lactance,* pp. 117–118.

[73] Grillmeier, *Christ in the Christian Tradition,* p. 204. Cf. Hans F. Von Campenhausen, *The Fathers of the Latin Church,* trans. Manfred Hoffman (London: A&C Black, 1972), pp. 60–86.

[74] Studer, "La Soteriologie de Lactance," p. 259, in *Lactance et son Temps: Recherches Actuelles: Actes du IVe Colloque d'Etudes Historiques et Patristiques,* pp. 258–259. Studer relied on Loi, *Lattanzio nella storia del linguaggio e del pensiero teologico pre-niceno,* pp. 203, 252–253. Loi does note that the Apostolic Fathers, Clement and Origen, also reflected on Christ as Teacher, but characterizes Lactantius as the only Latin writer who made this idea "nearly exclusive" in his doctrinal exposition. Loi notes the absence of terms such as *reconciliare, reconciliatio, iustificare, iustificatio*; and only the "sporadic appearance" of terms like *salvare, salvator,* and *salus.* Cf. Wlosok, *Laktanz und die philosophische Gnosis,* pp. 188–195, 211–214, 224.

[75] Heim, "L'influence exercée par Constantin sur Lactance: sa Théologie de la Victoire," pp. 55–70, in *Lactance et Son Temps: Recherches Actuelles: Actes Du IVe Colloque d'Etudes Historiques et Patristiques,* pp. 58–59.

[76] François Heim, *La Théologie de Victoire de Constantin á Théodose* (Paris: Beauchesne, 1992), pp. 51–57.

[77] François Heim, "*Virtus* chez Lactance: du *bonus vir* au Martyr," *Augustinianum* 36 (1996): pp. 361–375.

INTRODUCTION 17

Lewis Ayres's emphasis upon the language of power provides essential direction for a field seeking a better account of Lactantius's Christianity. Ayres's work suggests that *virtus* merits the same kind of consideration that earlier scholarship gave to *sapientia* and *religio*. While the *sapientia-religio* dyad is a structural and organizing theme for Lactantius, as a term that expresses Lactantius's understanding of the divine nature, *virtus* is the content of what wisdom and religion know and worship. For that reason, Lactantius's positive elaboration of both terms—*sapientia-religio* and *virtus*—begins in his portrait of Christ at *Inst.* 4, which is also the basis for the moral and political themes that occupy his later books. Put otherwise, by exploring *virtus* in his thought, this work aims to move past the scholarly occupation with Lactantius's apologetic, in order to explore its basis in the theology he advocated. However, because Lactantius situates his work as the continuation of a more ancient Roman and Christian debate (*Inst.*, 5.22–28), his thought is best understood in its continuing engagement with classical arguments that were, for Lactantius and his interlocutors, a shared cultural tradition. Understanding his argument requires an integrated account of the historical, cultural, and theological discourses that concerned him and thus influenced the form and content of his writing.

To achieve an integrated view of Lactantius's debate with classical Roman thought and culture, this study draws upon an emergent body of scholarship that increasingly recognizes the mutual involvement of philosophic, religious, and political discourses in Roman society.[78] That recognition makes it possible to resituate Lactantius, not as an eccentric voice relative to early Christianity but rather as an apologist working in continuity with his predecessors. From the first century onward, Roman intellectuals reconciled their traditional pantheon with philosophical accounts of a single God. That intellectual work was integral to elite Roman attempts to rethink their inherited political and religious ideals in the aftermath of the Late Republic's civil wars. Under Augustus, Cicero's works became a fundamental touchstone for a public discourse about *virtus*, which was conducted across major works of Roman philosophy, history, and poetry.[79] Tertullian, Minucius Felix, Cyprian, and Novatian all received and developed their theology in dialogue with that older Roman philosophical tradition. Although scriptural exegesis determined their judgments, their works reveal a trajectory of Christian thought developing its central terms and logic in the course of a fierce debate

---

[78] E.g., Katharina Volk, *The Roman Republic of Letters: Scholarship, Philosophy, and Politics in the Age of Cicero and Caesar* (Princeton, NJ: Princeton University Press, 2021); Gassman, *Worshippers of the Gods*; Duncan McRae, *Legible Religion: Books, Gods, and Rituals in Roman Culture* (Cambridge, MA: Harvard University Press, 2016), pp. 28–52.

[79] Allen Brent, "The Political Theology of the Augustan Revolution: Cosmic Reconstruction," in *A Political History of Christianity*, ed. Allen Brent (New York: T&T Clark, 2009), pp. 78–128.

with Roman political and intellectual traditions that shaped all later theological discourse in the Latin language.

Against the background of early Roman and Latin Christian discourse, Lactantius's apologetic theology, and particularly his Christology, appears quite traditional and occasionally innovative. His *Divine Institutes* synthesizes Latin Christian apologetic and doctrinal theology into a comprehensive account of God's revelation in Christ and its consequences for Roman thinking about moral and political order. This objective governs the progress of Lactantius's argument across the *Institutes*. He first criticizes Rome's traditional gods as a false foundation for political order, arguing that the Romans' famous *pietas* is the source, not of social cohesion and unity, but of an ancient turmoil that Diocletian's persecution (303–311) unjustly reenacts in his own day. Lactantius thus proceeds to show that Christ's person and work reveal the ultimate ends of human life lived eternally with God. That revelation corrects Rome's defective Ciceronian vision of ideal virtue, which contained "only a shadow" of the true thing.[80] Expressing the character and content of that virtue which takes Christ as its foundational public image—its *species* and *exemplum*—is Lactantius's fundamental aim. He sets this revelation into a theological understanding of history that orients human life toward eternity with God. The argument builds from classical and early Christian texts, which constituted for him a continuous Roman tradition of discourse about divine and human order.

In this conversation, Lactantius develops his account of ideal virtue out of earlier Latin expressions of the Christian doctrine of God. His account responds to a perennial problem of natural law theory, as he himself says: although classical philosophy described the fact of a *lex naturae*, no one knew or could agree on its specific requirements. Lactantius presents the Incarnation as the solution to this epistemic and ethical problem. He argues that the Christian vision of divine relations revealed in Christ provides the eternal model of a good society; the dictates of the natural law become visible in the example of Christ's public life and ministry. This argument allows Lactantius to reimagine classical notions of *virtus*. He argues that, like the Father and Son, human beings have a common dignity because they share a common *virtus*, which discloses their common nature. The specific moral obligations to that nature are expressed in Christ's public ministry and revealed in the Synoptic Gospels, which Lactantius reads through a theological prism inherited from Cyprian. Because he takes Jesus Christ as the one true historical *exemplum virtutis*, Lactantius refashions classical thinking about power and justice according to the Christian image of God. Lactantius's more famous ideas about toleration—rooted in *humanitas* and *patientia*—express this Christian understanding. Although his thinking develops from the theology of

---

[80] Lactantius, *Inst.*, 1.20.

INTRODUCTION   19

Tertullian, Cyprian, Minucius Felix, and Novatian, his argument observes the rules of classical Roman exemplary discourse. In good Ciceronian fashion, he sees historical exemplars as revelatory of divine *virtus* and thus develops an account of the divine nature out of Christ's historical actions.[81] The argument is predicated upon technical notions of "power" (*vis, virtus, potestas, dynamis*) that provided a shared medium for public discourse among cultivated Romans and, later, in early Christian theology. Lactantius differs from traditional Roman accounts of divinity precisely by selecting Christ rather than Roman heroes as the true model of ideal virtue.

Outline of the Work

It remains for me to outline this work. The early chapters characterize a philosophical grammar that emerged in the Roman imperial milieu and came to shape early Latin Christianity. By expanding our conception of Latin Christianity's relationship to Roman imperial literature and political discourse, these chapters shift the conceptual horizon that governs our sense of Lactantius's use and representation of early Latin Christianity as a whole.

Chapter 1 establishes the social context that informed philosophical and theological discourse about *virtus* in the age of the Roman Revolution. This chapter argues that Roman imperial ideology built upon Late Republican philosophical arguments about *virtus*, which it appropriated for ideological aims. The discussion shows that the most famous sources of imperial Roman ideological claims were also, arguably, its most skillful critics. Latin literature and historiography witness to pervasive objections latent in the empire's chief literary works. Many criticized the imperial reconstruction of *virtus* and rejected its façade. Their works set a precedent for Lactantius and his Christian predecessors, who drew upon earlier critiques.

Chapter 2 attempts to resolve the knotty question of precisely how philosophical notions of *virtus* as "virtue" relate to the early and basic sense of *virtus* as *power*, or even *courage* and *manliness*. Studies uniformly identify the ethical notion of "virtue" with some influence from Greek philosophy, but philologists have not aimed to connect the traditional notion of *virtus* to the specific philosophical discourses that transformed the term. By my reading, Roman philosophical redefinitions of *virtus* were intimately connected to Rome's traditional ideals and the politics such ideals created. Cicero takes pride of place, in my

---

[81] Literature on exemplarity is vast. Still fundamental is Matthew Roller, "Exemplarity in Roman Culture: The Cases of Horatius Cocles and Cloelia," *Classical Philology* 99.1 (2004): pp. 1–56; Jane Chaplin, *Livy's Exemplary History* (Oxford: Oxford University Press, 2001); Rebecca Langlands, *Exemplary Ethics in Ancient Rome* (Cambridge: Cambridge University Press, 2018).

account, as the one who first interpreted traditional Roman *virtus* in terms of Hellenistic theories of mixture, which gave technical notions of "power" a fundamental role. His efforts provided a Latin vocabulary for later writers. By its immense rhetorical and philosophical influence, Cicero's corpus became both directly and indirectly a major touchstone for later Roman discourse about the divine character and basis of Roman imperial rule. Although Cicero was not the only writer, later authors praising the imperial divinity plundered a treasure of concepts and language that he first introduced to the Latin world. Hence also, Cicero's philosophical vocabulary came to shape early Latin Christian theology as Christian writers advocated for Christians' place in an imperial order that had long been constructed and debated in ideological terms.

Chapter 3 establishes the historical and textual connection between early Latin Trinitarian theology and the Roman imperial theology outlined in the preceding chapters. I argue that the Latin apologists positioned themselves as the political heirs of Rome's most vehement critics of Augustus and the principate. Criticism that remained only ambivalent in classical Latin literature becomes explicit in Latin Christian apologetic. And the foundational vocabulary of Latin Trinitarian thought emerges from within this apologetic context. Only later does that vocabulary migrate to major statements of third-century Latin Trinitarian thought, such as Tertullian's *Against Praxeas* and Novatian's *De Trinitate*. These combined observations amount to a new account of the way early Latin theology was built. Apologetic, as a genre, was an engine of theological production in the Latin milieu. Early Latin Christian writers constructed their theology out of the same sources and discourses in which Latin Christians articulated their identity. In this respect, Chapters 1–3 argue that Roman imperial theology provided terms and grammar for third-century Latin Christian theology. The influence of apologetic discourses witnesses, in turn, to the fact that even elite Christian theology developed in intimate connection with cultural and political debates that necessarily concerned persecuted Roman Christians like Perpetua, Cyprian of Carthage, and Lactantius.

Against the background of elite Roman discourse, the later chapters establish the technical content of Lactantius's language and then explore his doctrine of God, Christology, and ethics in order ultimately to argue that Lactantius's theology is typical of earlier Latin writers and should be recognized as a point of continuity with writers like Tertullian, Cyprian, and Novatian.

Chapters 4–5 show that Lactantius's use of *virtus* reflects the standard theological grammar of his Latin Christian predecessors; and he is often citing or alluding to them. Lactantius understands *virtus* in the technical sense common to Latin Christian and Latin philosophical discourses since Cicero. Tertullian's famous claim that Christ's historical actions reveal the Father is foundational to Lactantius's thinking. In this respect, his theology is traditional both in early

Christian and in Roman terms. Chapter 4 establishes the theological basis of his critique of the Roman gods by connecting his moral criticisms to the underlying grammar that sustains his argument. Chapter 5 proceeds to a new account of Lactantius's Christology. Pursuing an insight first argued by Lewis Ayres, I present Lactantius as a point of continuity with earlier Latin authors. At the same time, I argue that Lactantius draws on third-century Latin theology in order to redefine Rome's own highest ideals according to the example of Jesus Christ. By offering Christ as a new exemplary model, Lactantius redefines ideal virtue as forbearance (*patientia*) and locates its highest expression in the works of equity. His argument amounts to a significant reimagination of classical ideals of virtue in the later Roman Empire.

Chapters 6–7 explore the relationship between Lactantius's Christology and his moral theory. I argue that he rewrites classical notions of virtue according to a traditional vision of the Father's relationship to the Son, which is rooted mainly in the Trinitarian thought of Tertullian and Cyprian but also comparable to the work of Novatian. As a result, Lactantius develops a notion of justice as equality that directly expresses his Christology. The coherence of his thought is apparent at both literary and conceptual levels. Hence, I outline the theological model that grounds Lactantius's moral thought in his Christology and explore his theological language and idiom. Chapter 7 concludes by examining the specific ethical applications Lactantius finds for his understanding of justice defined by God's revelation in Christ. Lactantius's comments on property, sexuality, and warfare express a moral vision that ultimately theorizes Christ's public teaching as a new revelation of the true content of the natural law. In this context, I treat the vexed question of whether or not Lactantius compromised his commitment to nonviolence in his later work. The resulting portrait shows Lactantius as a mainstream Christian thinker, who expresses the central moral and political insights of early Latin Christianity.

My interest in the fundamental grammar of Lactantius's theology requires that certain topics important for his work receive much less attention than they might deserve. The *sapientia-religio* dyad is a major feature in *Divine Institutes* and normally garners a great deal of attention, but because I regard that theme as an organizing structural component, rather than the content itself of Lactantius's theology, *sapientia-religio* has only a secondary role in my account. Likewise, the traditional question of Lactantius's "dualism" receives scant treatment, though my understanding of *virtus* impinges on any reading of the "dualistic passages." Fuller treatment of his understanding of the Holy Spirit is much needed and deserves attention, but that does not occur in this work. Likewise, Lactantius's eschatology and sacramental theology go mainly unaddressed, as does the famous Lactantian "*summa*" of *Inst.* 7.5, since its fundamental meaning is determined by whatever theology is to be found in the earlier books. I do not devote major efforts to debating the character of Lactantius's use of non-Christian sources because my account presumes the findings of Vinzenz Buchheit, Oliver Nicholson, Jochen Walter, Blandine Colot, and others, who have shown that Lactantius's use of non-Christian oracles is controlled by his experience of persecution and his reading of Christian Scriptures. Hence, I explore the underlying Christian literature and tradition that informs his apologetic theology. By focusing on the sources and logic of Lactantius's Christology and moral theology, I hope to provide a new starting point for judgments about his theological understanding and its relationship to other Christian writers.

A new account of Lactantius's theology suggests that Christian reflection upon Christ's example provided a foundation for early Christian thinking about the ends of politics and the nature of a good society, particularly in the third-century Latin west. Lactantius represented that tradition. To the extent that he was a political actor in his time, he represents an attempt to correct Roman politics by drawing upon third-century Latin Christian understanding of Christ's person and work. Of course, assessing the degree to which Lactantius's ideas might have been expressed in Constantine's policy, or even later Roman law, is a task that falls beyond the scope of this work.[82] Still, my account of Lactantius shows that in the uncertain era of Constantine's rise, the foundational claims of third-century Latin Christian tradition profoundly influenced Christian Romans close to the new imperial administration. Lactantius is an important reference for understanding their early Christian vision of Christ and his impact upon their inherited notions of the moral and political order.

---

[82] See Carmen Macarena Palomo Pinel, *Nec Inmerito Paterfamilias Dicitur: el paterfamilias en el pensamiento de Lactantio* (Madrid: Dykinson S.L., 2017), which examines Roman legal concepts in Lactantius and includes substantial comparison of his and other Church Fathers' influence in Roman law after Constantine.

Lactantius, *Divine Institutes*, 1.1.1–6

When men of great and outstanding ability had come to despise all their public and private actions, they gave themselves over entirely to learning and expended all the labor they could in their desire for seeking the truth, esteeming it much better to investigate and know the meaning [*rationem*] of matters human and divine than to cling to the accumulation of wealth and the gaining of honors. For by such things no one is made better or more just, because they are fragile and earthly and pertain to the worship [*cultum*] of the body alone. These men were indeed worthy of the knowledge of the truth, for they longed to know it so much that they placed it before all other things. Some even cast aside their inherited possessions, as is well known, and renounced all pleasures, so that naked and unencumbered they could pursue naked *virtus* alone. So much did the name and authority of *virtus* avail with them that they judged that the prize [*praemium*] of the highest good was in it. But they did not obtain what they wanted. They wasted all their work and industry as well, because truth - the secret of the Most High God who made all things - cannot be grasped by human ability and faculties. For nothing would separate God and man, if human thought could grasp the counsel and dispositions of that eternal majesty. And so, because it was impossible that the divine reason should become known to man on his own, God did not suffer [*non passus est*] him seeking the light of wisdom [*lumen sapientiae*] to wander any longer lost in inextricable darkness without any product from his labor. At some point in time, God opened his eyes and made knowledge of the truth [*notionem veritatis*] his own gift, in order to show that there is no human wisdom [*ut humanam sapientiam esse nullam montraret*] and to make known to man wandering and lost the way of obtaining immortality.

1

Virtus in Roman Life and Literature

Nothing indicates Lactantius's concern for politics so boldly as the opening lines of the *Divine Institutes*, which introduce his intent to engage and criticize classical Roman ideals of *virtus* and the literature that preserved them. Lactantius's seven lengthy books are replete with references to Cicero and Lucretius, Vergil, Seneca, and the Roman historians.[1] By focusing on *virtus* in these writers, Lactantius entered into argument with a political and philosophical tradition that had shaped public life since the Late Republic (50s B.C.). As Catalina Balmaceda explains, "For the Romans it was difficult to approach any important topic without referring to *virtus*."[2] Literary constructions of *virtus* provided authoritative forces for a broader social discourse that appears in ancient inscriptions, public monuments, and Rome's political iconography.[3] *Virtus* was not simply an important value. It came to signify the way Romans thought of themselves and their ancestors. Myles McDonnell thus notes that "*Virtus* played a central part in war, politics, and religion. . . . *Virtus* was regarded as nothing less than the quality associated with, and responsible for, Roman greatness and was central to . . . the ancient Roman self-image."[4] For that reason, any ancient discussion of *virtus* involved the writer in an ancient debate about the character of Roman society and the authority of its fundamental myths. The political valence of discourse about *virtus* became only more pronounced after Caesar Augustus claimed to have rescued the Republic and ushered in a new age of peace by restoring to the Roman people their ancestral mores. Augustus's successors followed suit, broadcasting their distinctive *virtutes* in order to characterize their regimes. This historical and social context provides the broadest frame of reference for reading

---

[1] Lactantius, *Inst.* 1.1.1–6 is laden with allusions to Cicero's *Republic* and *Laws*. See Jochen Walter, *Pagane Texte und Wertvorstellungen bei Laktanz* (Goettingen: Vandenhoeck and Ruprecht, 2006). In English, Jackson Bryce, *The Library of Lactantius* (New York: Garland, 1990) R. M. Ogilvie, *The Library of Lactantius* (Oxford: Clarendon Press, 1978). Harald Hagendahl, *The Latin Fathers and the Classics: A Study on the Apologists, Jerome, and Other Christian Writers* (Stockholm: Almquist & Wiksell, 1958), pp. 48–77. Lactantius, *Divinarum Institutionum Libri Septem*, fasc I–IV, ed. Eberhard Heck et Antonie Wlosok (Berlin: De Gruyter, 2005–2011), p. 4.

[2] Catalina Balmaceda, *Virtus Romana: Politics and Morality in the Roman Historians* (Chapel Hill: University of North Carolina Press, 2017), p. 1.

[3] Denis C. Feeney, *Literature and Religion at Rome: Cultures, Contexts, and Beliefs* (Cambridge: Cambridge University Press, 1998), p. 1.

[4] Myles McDonnell, *Roman Manliness:* Virtus *and the Roman Republic* (Cambridge: Cambridge University Press, 2006), p. 3.

Roman Virtue in the Early Christian Thought of Lactantius. Jason M. Gehrke, Oxford University Press.
© Oxford University Press 2025. DOI: 10.1093/9780197667781.003.0002

Lactantius and understanding his argumentative choices. When Lactantius opened his defense of Christianity with a broad critique of Roman ideas of *virtus*, he took aim at a long-standing Roman self-image. Lactantius engaged classical writers throughout his work because their literature was a primary medium for articulating the Roman self-image as it had been constructed and reconstructed since the days of Cicero. To appreciate Lactantius's approach, we must recall the social significance of *virtus* in the Roman world and the authority that classical Roman literature continued to exert as a source of elite Roman self-understanding, even at the turn of the fourth century A.D.

Virtus from Republic to Principate

Clifford Ando's learned study, *Imperial Ideology and Provincial Loyalty in the Roman Empire*, outlines the central tropes of an imperial ideology that Lactantius would eventually confront under Diocletian's Tetrarchy.[5] "At a superficial level," Ando writes, "the Roman imperial government advertised to its subjects the existence of a shared history and a common political theology: the history was that of Rome in the era of her empire, and the one constant in the religious firmament was the emperor."[6] After Augustus, imperial society found its stability "in the fiction of dynastic continuity on the throne that became so prevalent in the second century; and every pagan religion . . . allowed its practitioners to accommodate the extraordinary power of the emperor in their individual theologies."[7] As the centerpiece of Roman stability, the imperial office appropriated an older martial ideal, which was purportedly renewed in the military prowess of each new successor. First Julius Caesar and then his adopted son, Octavian (hereafter, Caesar Augustus), secured their positions through victory in battle. Each credited his success to the power and favor of the gods. Following Augustus, later Roman emperors often ascended the throne after defeating rivals. The victor claimed a "divine charisma" originating in Augustus, whose honorific he assumed as a title.[8] Each saw the consummate expression of that charisma in the altar of Victory—*Victoria Augusti*—consecrated in the Senate at Rome.[9]

Augustus cloaked the martial ideal in another layer of tradition refashioned for the new age. Toward the end of his reign, the Senate awarded Augustus the title *pater patriae*. This action appropriated a traditional Roman honor dating

---

[5] Clifford Ando, *Imperial Ideology and Provincial Loyalty in the Roman Empire* (Berkeley: University of California Press, 2000), pp. 19–49, 73–131.

[6] Ando, *Imperial Ideology and Provincial Loyalty*, p. 23.

[7] Ando, *Imperial Ideology and Provincial Loyalty*, p. 24.

[8] Ando, *Imperial Ideology and Provincial Loyalty*, pp. 24–33, *passim*.

[9] See Stefan Weinstock, *Divus Julius* (Oxford: Clarendon Press, 1971), p. 230; McDonnell, *Roman Manliness*.

26 ROMAN VIRTUE IN THE EARLY CHRISTIAN THOUGHT OF LACTANTIUS

to the early Republic while preserving the image of continuity with Rome's legendary founders, Romulus and Numa Pompilius—the former a military hero, the latter, an inspired founder of Roman law and civic cult. In this capacity, Augustus and his heirs exercised the ancient censorial function as guardian of the laws and mores of the people (*curator legum et morum*). As a father raised his children by cultivating their character, so the emperor cultivated his people by tending their virtue. His *pietas* preserved traditional Roman rites; his legislation guaranteed traditional mores as the new regime reimagined them.[10] In tending to the particulars of such moral legislation and updating a theology of deification for *virtus*, imperial ideology maintained a façade of continuity with the past. That claim of continuity sought to root imperial discourse about *virtus* in even more ancient Republican ideals.

The Augustan refashioning of Republican ideals of *virtus* was part of a larger cultural shift that effected a significant change in the Latin language. In its earlier usage (i.e., 4th–3rd centuries B.C.) the term *virtus* signified the martial capacity of a warrior, a victor in battle.[11] In this sense, *virtus* has often been rendered as "power" or "courage," even "courageous deeds" in the plural (*virtutes*). Romans associated this notion of courage with the gods' favor, and heroes were thought to be patronized by the powers (*virtutes*) of specific deities. Over time, the martial notion expanded to encompass an idea of moral excellence, which reflects the influence of Greek philosophy in the middle-Republic and the use of such philosophy in elite political competition.[12] Still, even as the definition was adapted, *virtus* continued to serve as the basis of political assertion and evoke claims about divinity. Whatever else it might be, *virtus* was a quality that earns divine favor on behalf of the Roman people.

The religious association of *virtus* with victory is evident from some of the earliest Latin literature. And it undergirds the Roman habit of developing literary *exempla* for use in moral and civic instruction. For example, M. Porcius Cato (234–149 B.C.) wrote of Q. Caedicius: "The immortal gods gave fortune to the tribune of the soldiers because of his *virtus*."[13] The remark contains a compressed political theology. Cato's comment implies that ancestral *virtus* was a unique property of Rome's forebears, one that merits favorable *fortuna*. He evokes Caedicius's *virtus* not simply to praise Roman bravery but to praise that quality which the gods reward. His thought contains a political doctrine that is simultaneously theological, moral, and military—one man's *virtus* wins divine favor for the benefit of the commonwealth. The Roman phenomenon

---

[10] Ando, *Imperial Ideology and Provincial Loyalty*, pp. 399–404.

[11] McDonnell, *Roman Manliness*, pp. 12–59.

[12] For the philosophical dimension of Roman virtue discourse, see Chapter 2, this volume.

[13] Cato, *Origines*, 4.7, quoted in McDonnell, *Roman Manliness*, p. 51: "*Dii immortales tribuno militum fortunam ex virtute eius dedere.*" See Quintus Ennius and Otto Skutsch, *The Annals of Q. Ennius* (Oxford: Oxford University Press, 1985), pp. 316–317.

of exemplarity is latent in the claim. Cato elevates Caedicius as an example of how Rome, in its ideal past, secured the prosperity of its people. Hence, Cato presumes, Caedicius merits imitation.

After Cato, assertions about *virtus* became a constant vehicle of political self-promotion in Republican Rome. Charismatic leaders associated themselves with personified *Virtus*. M. Claudius Marcellus set an early precedent by vowing to build a temple to *Honos et Virtus* after the battle of Clastidium in 222 B.C. His temple would serve as a monument to Marcellus's own *virtus* and to the divine favor demonstrated by its exercise in victory. The Senate blocked the temple's construction because its presence would serve as a monument to Marcellus's claim about himself. Senatorial elites understood the political assertion conveyed through such a pious monument. Marcellus's son and namesake persisted and fulfilled the vow for the same reason. Later, Marius built a new temple to the same deities, *Honos* and *Virtus*, which Marcellus had commemorated. Such actions expressed a foundational principle: demonstrable *virtus* constituted the basis for claims about political legitimacy and leadership. Marius's consecration was an act both of piety and competition. He was signaling that Marcellus's *honos et virtus* were now rightfully his own. The action placed Marius in competition with Marcellus just as Marcellus's earlier dedication had placed him in competition with an earlier set of senatorial rivals.[14]

Such rivalry over *virtus* characterized the political climate that led to the collapse of the Roman Republic and Caesar Augustus's eventual rise. By the Late Republican period, *virtus* had become a crucial concept in political competition between the "new men" (*novi homines*) and the "nobles" (*nobiles*), the old patrician senatorial families. By all accounts, *virtus* provided the terms in which any political newcomer could justify his membership in elite circles.[15] Marius is a prime example. He was the uncle by marriage of Julius Caesar and thus the adoptive great-uncle of Caesar Augustus. A *novus homo*, Marius laid claim to the high office of consul five times by touting his *virtus*. For him, *virtus* demonstrated his worthiness for leadership proven through military achievement. Marius's boast reflects both the traditional martial notion of *virtus* and its operation as a first principle in Roman politics:

> Compare me now, Quirites, a "new man" with their pride. What they are accustomed to hear or read about . . . I myself have done. . . . Determine for yourselves

---

[14] Weinstock, *Divus Julius*, pp. 92, 177–178, 231; McDonnell, *Roman Manliness*, pp. 241–243, 267 ff.

[15] See Matthias Gelzer, *The Roman Nobility*, trans. Robin Seager (Oxford: Blackwell, 1969), p. 52. For further debate, Joseph Vogt, *Homo Novus, Ein Typus des römischen Republik* (Stuttgart, 1926); H. Strasburger, "Novus Homo," *Realencyclopädie der classischen Altertumswissenschaft* 17.1 (1937): pp. 1–17; sed contra Shackleton Bailey, "Nobiles and Novi Reconsidered," *American Journal of Philology* 107 (1986): pp. 255–260; Donald Earl, *The Moral and Political Tradition of Rome* (Ithaca, NY: Cornell University Press, 1967); T. P. Wiseman, *New Men in the Roman Senate* (London: Oxford University Press, 1971).

whether words or deeds are more important. . . . And if they are right to look down on me, let them do the same to their own ancestors, whose nobility, like mine, began from *virtus*.[16]

Marius's claim illustrates the way that argument about *virtus* allowed political actors to present themselves as heirs to the ancestors, whatever their social position.[17] His claim anticipates an approach that Augustus would also follow. Marius was asserting that the *virtus* claimed by Rome's most ancient patrician families was, by rights, his own. Notably, Marius was not arguing for some kind of revolutionary action. Rather, as a "new man," he advanced by showing that his own *virtus* equaled the ancestors from whom the *nobiles* derived their own legitimacy. Superiority in *virtus* thus made him a better heir to the *mos maiorum*. In this respect, *virtus* replaced bloodline as the principle of continuity with the past. Still, the principle was continuity.

Pompey the Great and Julius Caesar acted in the same way that Marius had. Each asserted himself by demonstrating his *virtus* and taking that *virtus* as proof of divine favor. And this is a key point for later theological debate. All of these figures understood *virtus* as evidence for claims that were ultimately religious. As Weinstock relates, "Pompey's principal deities were . . . *Venus Victrix* and *Hercules Invictus*; but he also combined the tradition of Marius and Sulla by dedicating shrines both to *Honos* and *Virtus*."[18] Pompey's rival, Julius Caesar, had his own *virtus* acclaimed in several public ways. After him, *virtus* became the name of more than one city in the province of Africa. Thus, as J. Rufus Fears explained, "By the end of the Republic there existed a well-developed tradition at Rome of associating specific Virtues closely with the person of individual charismatic Roman statesmen."[19] Such competition affected not only the politics of Roman *virtus* but the very definition of the term. As elite Romans drew upon philosophical resources to redefine *virtus*, public actors claimed these new forms of *virtus* for themselves. Hence, Caesar Augustus claimed to restore the republic by renewing

[16] Sallust, *BJ*, 85.13–17, *passim* in *The War with Catiline; The War with Jugurtha*, trans. J. C. Rolfe, revised John T. Ramsey (Cambridge, MA: Harvard University Press, 2013). See Balmaceda, *Virtus Romana*, pp. 48–82.

[17] McDonnell, *Roman Manliness*, p. 329. As McDonnell argues, "The martial excellence that *virtus* denoted was a quality prized by all Roman citizens, and one that Roman nobles sought to demonstrate and advertise, which is precisely why a reputation for *virtus* was the best way for a new man to make his entry into the Senate. The new man's claim of *virtus* mimicked that of the established nobleman." Contra Earl, *Moral and Political Tradition of Rome*, p. 47. Cf. Wiseman, *New Men in the Roman Senate*, p. 109.

[18] Weinstock, *Divus Julius*, pp. 232–233.

[19] J. Rufus Fears, "The Cult of Virtues and Roman Imperial Ideology," *Aufstieg und Niedergang der Römischen Welt* 17.2 (1986): pp. 827–947, esp. p. 877. According to Fears, Sulla's tyranny marks how "Roman statesmen sought to associate a particular Virtue closely with themselves by adopting it as a *cognomen* . . . [This was a] forerunner of the imperial image of the emperor as savior of the commonwealth and earthly incarnation of specific Virtues."

VIRTUS IN ROMAN LIFE AND LITERATURE   29

Roman *virtus*, but his boasts reinterpreted *virtus* in philosophical terms that had developed in the preceding generation. Augustus placed his famous "Shield of Virtue" (*clupeus virtutis*) on display in Rome and throughout the Empire. Like the "Altar of Peace" (*ara pacis*), which touted Augustus's restoration of ancestral *mores*, the shield commemorated his ethical as well as martial qualities. On it, Augustus inscribed his "clemency, justice, and *pietas* toward the gods and fatherland [*clementia, iustitia,* and *pietas erga deos patriamque*]."[20] As Myles McDonnell has argued, by placing ethical virtues on the traditional symbol of martial prowess, Augustus united the martial and ethical ideals of *virtus* developed in the preceding century.[21] The "Shield of Virtue" presents Augustus as an exemplary leader of the Roman people, most especially in his religious devotion (i.e., *pietas*) and moral quality. The shield marks a shift. By Augustus's day, the narrow martial notion of *virtus* had expanded to include a variety of ethical connotations. The shield captures those several notions (*pietas, iustitia, bones artes,* among others) and reasserts them as the basis of a political theology (*erga deos patriamque*) touting ancestral mores as a way of life that merited the gods' reward and favor.

The moral language stamped on Augustus's shield witnesses to the interpenetration of philosophical, political, and traditional discourses in Rome. His invocation of "*pietas* towards gods and fatherland" reflects a traditional idea that the "customs of the ancestors [*mos maiorum*]" constituted an enduring norm for later Romans.[22] They imagined their actions as guided by a canon of ancestral precedent. The Augustan author Valerius Maximus (14–37 A.D.) attests to this traditional posture; he reports the elder Cato's (234–149 B.C.) claim about the ancestors' way of raising children. "To the [sound of a] flute, they sang the praises and *virtutes* of famous men," he writes.[23] In so doing, "they made the youth keener to imitate those deeds."[24] The line involves two levels of idealization.

---

[20] For an image of the *clupeus virtutis*, see Weinstock, *Divus Julius*, p. 233. See also Fears, "The Cult of Virtues and Roman Imperial Ideology," pp. 884–889; Karl Galinsky, *Augustan Culture: An Interpretive Introduction* (Princeton, NJ: Princeton University Press, 1996); McDonnell, *Roman Manliness*, pp. 385–389. Literature on the *ara pacis* is large, but the idea that it interacts with Roman literature and public life in the Augustan context is not controversial. See Paul Zanker, *The Power of Images in the Age of Augustus* (Ann Arbor: University of Michigan Press, 1988). More recently, Gail E. Armstrong, "Sacrificial Iconography: Creating History, Making Myth, and Negotiating Ideology on the Ara Pacis Augustae," *Religion & Theology* 15.3/4 (June 2008): pp. 340–356.

[21] McDonnell, *Roman Manliness*, pp. 385–389.

[22] Martin Goodman, *The Roman World: 44 BC–AD 180*, 2nd ed. (New York: Routledge, 2012), p. 25, "Any action that accorded with ancestral custom (*mos maiorum*) was praiseworthy. Alongside this notion went an idealization of an imaginary heroic past, when Roman peasant soldiers had embodied simple, sterling qualities."

[23] Valerius Maximus, *Factorum ac dictorum memorabilium libri IX*, 2.1.10 in McDonnell, *Roman Manliness*, p. 52: "*ad ea imitanda iuventutem alacriorem redderent.*" See Hans-Friedrich Mueller, *Roman Religion in Valerius Maximus* (New York: Routledge, 2002). Valerius Maximus belonged to a literary circle that included Ovid. He flourished under Tiberius (14–37 A.D.) and composed a compendium of *exempla* for moral instruction.

[24] Valerius Maximus, *Factorum ac dictorum memorabilium libri IX*, 2.1.10 in McDonnell, *Roman Manliness*, p. 52.

30 ROMAN VIRTUE IN THE EARLY CHRISTIAN THOUGHT OF LACTANTIUS

Valerius remembers the elder Cato, who himself remembers the ancestors, and lifts them up as a model. They not only exercised *virtutes*, but honored and commemorated *virtutes* in order to cultivate *virtus* in the young. That practice itself belongs to the *virtus* of *pietas*, which respects the *mos maiorum*.

Even while claiming fidelity to the *mos maiorum*, Augustus's shield also demonstrates the way that elite Romans could project later ideals of *virtus* onto their past. Written from exile, Cicero's *Republic* manifests this anachronistic tendency in elite Roman discourse of the Late Republic. Cicero echoes Cato's respect for the past by quoting a famous line of the poet Ennius (239–169 B.C.): "The Roman state stands upon ancient customs and heroes."[25] Cicero could also urge that "*virtus* is the badge of the Roman race and breed. Cling fast to it, I beg you men of Rome, as a heritage that your ancestors bequeathed to you."[26] And yet he himself was a principal architect of the philosophical ideals that Augustus's shield would claim. Even as Cicero urged the young toward ancestral *virtus*, he attached new philosophical notions to the ancient term:

> You, young men, who are *nobiles*, I will stir up to the imitation of your ancestors; and you who are able to obtain *nobilitas* by your character and virtue [*ingenio ac virtute*], I will urge to that method [*ad eam rationem*] by which many new men [*novi homines*] have flourished in both honor and glory. This is the one path, believe me, of praise and *dignitas* and honor, [the path] to being praised and loved by good men, wise and well constituted by nature: to know the pattern [*descriptionem*] of the State constituted so wisely [*sapientissime*] by our ancestors.[27]

Cicero's speech urges a traditional idea—imitate ancient *virtus* as the source of Rome's health and glory. But Cicero's term has taken on philosophical hues.[28] In place of military deeds, he exalts ancestral wisdom (*sapientissime*) and knowledge (*nosse*) in the art of politics. Coupled with *ingenium*, *virtus* is a matter of the soul, a point of character more than military prowess or courage in battle. Cicero thus reframes ancestral *virtus* in philosophic terms. His remarks exemplify the way the *mos maiorum* could set parameters for public discourse while being manipulated for the needs of the moment.

[25] Cicero, *Rep.*, 5.1 in Marcus Tullius Cicero, *De Re Publica; De Legibus; Cato Maior de Senectute; Laelius de Amicitia*, ed. J. G. F. Powell (Oxford: Oxford University Press, 2006), "*moribus antiquis res stat Romana virisque.*"
[26] Cicero, *Phil.*, 4.13 in Marcus Tullius Cicero, *Philippics 1–6*, ed. and trans. D. R. Shackleton Bailey, revised John T. Ramsey, Gesine Manuwald, Loeb Classical Library 189 (Cambridge, MA: Harvard University Press, 2010).
[27] Cicero, *Ses.*, 136 in Marcus Tullius Cicero, *Pro Sestio; In Vatinium*, trans. R. Gardner, Loeb Classical Library 309 (Cambridge, MA: Harvard University Press, 1958). McDonnell, *Roman Manliness*, p. 344.
[28] McDonnell, *Roman Manliness*, p. 330, "When contrasted to *nobilitas* by Cicero, *virtus* almost always has the meaning of general excellence, ability, or merit, and it sometimes comprises a wide range of other qualities and abilities—*labor, industria, frugalitas, sapientia*, etc. Such a general meaning of *virtus*, as we have seen, is rarely found in surviving pre-classical Latin, and the use of *virtus* or *virtutes* as a general or all-embracing term under which other qualities are subsumed, was based on the analogy of the common usage of ἀρετή."

VIRTUS IN ROMAN LIFE AND LITERATURE   31

Cicero's exhortation suggests an ambivalence about the ideal of Roman military glory, which also appears on the Shield of Augustus. Cicero honors the past even as he subverts it. Likewise, as an icon of traditional piety, the shield effects a purposeful anachronism. It appropriates traditional discourse about *virtus*, but only by assuming philosophical connotations that were decidedly contemporary, and perhaps originating in Greece, not Rome.[29] Roman discourse about *virtus* would continue to reflect a deep inner conflict about the meaning of the term and the ideal it represented. Augustus's shield inscribed that ambivalence onto an icon of the imperial order.

The central themes of Augustus's imperial self-presentation set a precedent for later emperors. Into the fourth century, Roman emperors thought of their regimes as extensions of Augustus's own charisma. Proclaiming the emperor's virtues became a central project of the imperial coinage.[30] By touting their *virtutes*, emperors articulated the distinctive character of their regimes in a manner that always claimed fundamental continuity with the past.[31] As Ando explains, "Many different men, from very disparate backgrounds, occupied the throne of the empire in its first four centuries. . . . [But] they all justified their rule in similar terms; they even expressed their desire to renew the state in wholly traditional terms."[32] The Tetrarchs, whom Lactantius first served and then confronted, were no exception.[33] As just one example, some Tetrarchic coinage proclaimed the "*Virtus Augustorum [Virtus AUGG]*" on the face. On the obverse was printed the image of a bearded Hercules, the mythic ancestor of Augustus.[34] By that image, the coin presented the *virtus* of Hercules as manifest in the Tetrarchs' actions.[35] Diocletian's edict persecuting the Manichees

---

[29] For more on this, see Chapter 2, this volume.

[30] Clare Rowan, *Under Divine Auspices: Divine Ideology and the Visualization of Imperial Power in the Severan Period* (Cambridge: Cambridge University Press, 2012), p. 5: "The Reka-Devnia hoard contains more than 80,000 silver coins from a variety of emperors. . . . For Trajan, Hadrian, Antoninus Pius, Marcus Aurelius and Commodus, personifications and virtues constitute a substantial part of the emperor's reverse types (52%, 61%, 67%, 56%, and 60%, respectively.) These types communicate the idea of a virtuous ruler whose reign brought manifold blessings to Rome and the empire."

[31] Fears, "The Cult of Virtues and Roman, Imperial Ideology," p. 901. More recently, Achim Lichtenberger, *Severus Pius Augustus: Student zur sakralen Repraesentation und Rezeption der Herrschaft des Spitimius Severus und seiner Familie* (Leiden: Brill, 2011), e.g., pp. 157–158, 161, 227, 314, etc.

[32] Ando, *Imperial Ideology and Provincial Loyalty*, p. 385.

[33] See also Andrew Wallace-Hadrill, "The Emperor and His Virtues," *Historia: Zeitschrift fur Alte Geschichte* 30.3 (3rd Qtr., 1981): pp. 298–323; C. H. V. Sutherland, "Two 'Virtues' of Tiberius: A Numismatic Contribution to the History of His Reign," *Journal of Roman Studies* 28.2 (1938): pp. 129–140; M. P. Charlesworth, "The Virtues of a Roman Emperor: Propaganda and the Creation of Belief," *Proceedings of the British Acacdemy* 23 (1937): pp. 105ff.

[34] R. Joy Littlewood, *A Commentary on Ovid's Fasti, Book 6* (Oxford: Clarendon Press, 2006); G. Karl Galinsky, *The Herakles Theme: The Adaptions of the Hero in Literature from Homer to the Twentieth Century* (Oxford: Basil Blackwell, 1972), pp. 126–149.

[35] Harold Mattingly, Edward Sydenham, and Percy Webb, *Roman Imperial Coinage*, vol. 5B (London: Spink and Son, 1984), pp. 204ff. Cf. *Panegyrici Latini*, II.3. See Frank Kolb, *Diocletian Und Die Erste Tetrarchie: Improvisation oder Experiment in der Organisation monarchischer Herrschaft* (Berlin: Walter de Gruyter, 1987); T. D. Barnes, *Constantine and Eusebius* (Cambridge,

32 ROMAN VIRTUE IN THE EARLY CHRISTIAN THOUGHT OF LACTANTIUS

amplified the message. In it, Diocletian justified the persecution by invoking the myth stamped on Augustus's shield:

> For there is no doubt that if we shall have seen to it that all under our rule [*sub imperio nostro*] lead a pious and religious life [*piam reliosamque*], both quiet and chaste [*quietam et castam*] in everything, the immortal gods themselves [*ipsos immortales deos*] will be pleased and favorable toward the Roman name, as they have always been.[36]

In the latter Roman Empire, no theologian, philosopher, panegyrist, or lawyer could speak of *virtus* without touching upon such public media and the political tradition they evoked. That tradition traced its roots to the literary and philosophical productions of the Augustan Age, when Rome's greatest literary stylists reimagined traditional *virtus* and wrote their new vision into an imperial narrative of Rome's past and the sources of its power. Their works demonstrate that Roman authors could reimagine and redefine *virtus* in order to offer their commentary upon imperial society and politics. In Roman literature, rival notions of *virtus* were contested and imperial claims criticized. In the Latin language, that traditional Roman public, literary, and historical context constituted the most basic frame of reference for any argument about God, humanity, and *virtus*. Early Latin Christian literature cannot be read without reference to this earlier Roman tradition.

Virtus and Politics in Roman Literature

Political competition over *virtus* often motivated and always informed the great literary productions of the Augustan Age, whether in poetry, prose, or philosophy.[37] Augustan literature (especially Cicero and Vergil) became the basis for Roman education and a constant source for articulating competing Roman identities. This is the period when Cicero, Vergil, and the Roman historians were composing seminal literary expressions of the idea that Romans were

MA: Harvard University Press, 1981), p. 11. The association with Hercules was itself traditional. See Galinsky, *The Herakles Theme*, pp. 126–231.

[36] *Legum collatio*, 6.4.1 in Robert M. Frakes, *Compiling the* Collatio Legum Mosaicarum et Romanarum *in Late Antiquity* (Oxford: Oxford University Press, 2012). Cf. Horace, *Carm.*, 3.6.1–5 in Horace, *Odes IV and Carmen Saeculare*, ed. Richard Thomas (Cambridge: Cambridge University Press, 2011).

[37] W. J. Dominik, J. Garthwaite, and P. A. Roche, *Writing Politics in Imperial Rome* (Leiden: Brill, 2009). The term "Augustan Age" and its parallels "Augustan literature" and "Augustanism" refer historically to Caesar Augustus's reign (14 B.C.–27 A.D.) and to the cultural and ideological production of that time. See Galinsky, *Augustan Culture*.

a people distinguished by their ancestral virtues and favored by the gods because of them.[38] The timing is important. A half-century of war and revolution caused the Roman upper classes to rethink their inherited ideals and draw upon philosophical accounts of *virtus* to do so.[39] The structures of traditional thought remained: leading authors still presented *virtus*, even martial *virtus*, as a sign of divine favor and evidence of a man's right to lead. However, Augustan writers registered their objections as well. Sallust and Livy produced crowning expressions of traditional Roman thinking about *virtus*, but their works also sounded bitter critical notes. No less did Vergil, Ovid, and Lucan satirize the story told on Augustus's shield and propagated in a culture shaped by new political circumstances.[40] Hence, the same authors who updated Rome's ancient myths also criticized the imperial narrative articulated by the Augustan regime. Their works set a precedent for later Christian apologists, who also criticized the imperial regime by attacking its founding mythologies.

Sallust's Disillusion

A younger contemporary of Cicero, the historian Sallust (86–34 B.C.) reflected on the tumult of his period. He is typical of a trend among elite Romans of the Late Republic. He grapples with an apparent conflict between the traditional lore that idealized Rome's ancestral *virtus* and the bitter realities of the Republic's collapse under the impetus of that *virtus* itself.[41] As Ronald Syme observed, "[Sallust] belongs to the company of searching and subversive writers, preoccupied with power and the play of chance in human affairs, who find their delectation in disillusionment."[42] Sallust's work marks an important moment in the redefinition of Roman *virtus* that his era brought about. McDonnell explains that "Sallust used ideas traditionally associated with ἀρετή to expand the references of the

[38] Technically, Cicero (106–43 B.C.) and Sallust were not Augustan authors, but their works shape the period.

[39] E.g., Lucretius, *On the Nature of the Universe: A Verse Translation by Sir Ronald Melville with Introduction and Notes by Don and Peta Fowler* (Oxford: Clarendon Press, 1997), x–xi. Fowler recalls that "a century like that between 133–31 B.C., which killed perhaps 200,000 men in 91–82 and perhaps 100,000 men in 49–42, in both cases out of a free population of Rome and Italy of 4,500,000 and which destroyed a system of government after 450 years was a cataclysm."

[40] R. J. Tarrant, "Aspects of Virgil's Reception in Antiquity," in *The Cambridge Companion to Virgil*, ed. Charles Martindale (Cambridge: Cambridge University Press, 1997), pp. 56–72.

[41] My reading of Sallust is indebted to McDonnell's discussion of the "dual nature of *virtus* in Sallust." Like William W. Batstone, "The Antithesis of Virtue: Sallust's 'Synkrisis' and the Crisis of the Late Republic," *Classical Antiquity* 7, 1 (1988): pp. 1–29; R. Sklenář, "La République des Signes: Caesar, Cato, and the Language of Sallustian Morality," *Transactions of the American Philological Association (1974–)* 128 (1998): pp. 205–220; and D. Levene, "Sallust's Catiline and Cato the Censor," *Classical Quarterly* 50 (2000): pp. 170–191, McDonnell recognizes that Sallust is critical both of the traditional martial ideal and of recent Republican pretensions of ethical *virtus*.

[42] Ronald Syme, *Sallust* (Berkeley: University of California Press, 1964), p. 264.

34 ROMAN VIRTUE IN THE EARLY CHRISTIAN THOUGHT OF LACTANTIUS

Latin word [*virtus*], and thereby to promote his apologetic and programmatic purposes."[43] Sallust is among the first in a tradition of historical writers who articulated Rome's traditional ideal of virtue only to criticize it. And in Sallust, that criticism takes shape as a rewriting of *virtus* in terms drawn from Hellenistic philosophical discourse.

The ancient logic of Roman *virtus* is everywhere assumed in Sallust. By a plain reading, he offers a glowing portrait of Rome's ancestral morals. At first, he seems to hold up the past as an enduring canon that judges his contemporaries:

> Since the occasion has raised [the topic] of the morals of the State [*de moribus civitatis*], the very subject matter seems to urge me to recall and discuss briefly the precedents [*statuta maiorum*] of the ancestors both in domestic and military matters [*domi militiaeque*], how they managed the commonwealth [*res publica*] and how great they left it, with the result that having been changed gradually from the most beautiful and best, it has become the worst and most wicked [*pessuma ac flagitiosissuma facta sit*].[44]

In the subsequent sections (*BC* 6–13), Sallust traces a tale of ancestral frugality, industry, and piety derived from the city's founder, Aeneas. Sallust's concept of traditional virtue, like Cato's, includes a core religious idea: "There is a great value, once you have taken stock of homes and villas built in the urban manner, to survey the temples of the gods, which our ancestors, most religious of mortals, built. Truly, those men decorated their shrines in piety for the gods, their own homes with glory."[45] By contrast with this ancient glory and piety, the text laments, the contemporary moral scene drags the best men into vice.[46]

Sallust's narrative quickly departs, however, from such a simple story of decline. His tale subverts the ancient ideal of *virtus* that it appears first to uphold.[47] In language reminiscent of Cicero, Sallust revises martial *virtus* in favor of a philosophical notion of character (*ingenio*):

> Our whole power [*vis*] has been placed in [the combination of] mind and body. We make use of the mind for rule [*animi imperio*], the body for [its] service; the former we have in common with the gods, the latter with the beasts. For that

---

[43] McDonnell, *Roman Manliness*, p. 370. See also Patrick McGushin, *C. Sallustius Crispus, Bellum Catilinae: A Commentary* (Lugduni Batavorum: Brill, 1977), esp. Appendix II, pp. 293–296; also, Thomas F. Scanlon, *The Influence of Thucydides on Sallust* (Heidelberg: Carl Winter, 1980).

[44] Sallust, *Bellum Catalinae*, 5.9 in *The War with Catiline; The War with Jugurtha*, trans. J. C. Rolfe, revised John T. Ramsey (Cambridge, MA: Harvard University Press, 2013).

[45] Sallust, *Bellum Catalinae*, 6.12.3.

[46] Sallust, *Bellum Catalinae*, 3.3–4. See also Catherine Edwards, *The Politics of Immorality in Ancient Rome* (Cambridge: Cambridge University Press, 1993).

[47] For a summary of recent scholarship on this point, see Levene, "Sallust's 'Catiline' and Cato the Censor."

VIRTUS IN ROMAN LIFE AND LITERATURE   35

reason, it seems better to me to pursue glory [*gloriam*] with the resources of character [*ingenio*] than of physical strength [*virium*].... For the glory of riches is fleeting and fragile, but *virtus* remains bright and eternal [*clara et aeterna habetur*].[48]

By preferring intellectual to military glory, Sallust revises the martial ideal of the Late Republic. In place of military prowess, he touts an intellectual and moral disposition whose power (*vis*) places human beings in the company of gods. In that respect, his philosophic agenda is the basis of a political critique. *Animi virtus* would rule human affairs far better than the volatile prowess of Rome's heroes, he says: "For if the intellectual virtue [*animi virtus*] of kings and generals would avail in peace as in war, you would not see . . . everything changed and confused."[49] In historical terms, we can say that Sallust invokes the Greek ideal of virtue as superior to the Roman one, which has caused upheaval and Revolution. It is worth noting that Sallust's reference to "power" (*vis*) draws from a philosophical discourse most fully articulated in Cicero.[50]

But Sallust does not therefore abandon the traditional Roman logic of *virtus*. For him, *virtus* is still the key notion in politics. It still involves piety toward the gods, and he still imagines *virtus* as the quality of his ancestors. The old Roman thought that unifies Sallust's Late Republican notion of *virtus* with Cato's or Marius's martial ideal rests in this religious presupposition. Sallust locates *virtus* at the center of a political theology:

For imperium is easily maintained by those good practices [*bonis artis*] that gave birth to it originally. But when hard work is replaced by sloth, self-restraint and equity by passion and pride, *Fortune* [*fortuna*] is at the same time changed with mores [*moribus*]. So, empire is always being transferred to whomever is best, from the lesser to the good man.[51]

The theological content of this statement should not be overlooked. Although Sallust projects a new ideal onto the old Roman canvas, imperium remains a divine reward for *virtus*.[52] He does not simply abandon traditional religious pieties toward the past.[53] Sallust still praises the ancestors: "Quarrels, disagreements,

---

[48] Sallust, *Bellum Catalinae*, 1.1–2.

[49] Sallust, *Bellum Catalinae*, 1.3–4.

[50] See Chapter 2. Sallust voices a Stoic commonplace. See Katja Maria Vogt, *Law, Reason, and the Cosmic City: Political Philosophy in the Early Stoa* (Oxford: Oxford University Press, 2008). Cf. Cicero, *Leg.*, 1.21–23 in Marcus Tullius Cicero, *De Re Publica; De Legibus; Cato Maior de Senectute; Laelius de Amicitia*, ed. J. G. F. Powell (Oxford: Oxford University Press, 2006).

[51] Sallust, *Bellum Catalinae*, 1.4.

[52] Sklenář, "La République des Signes," p. 209.

[53] Weinstock, *Divus Julius*, pp. 248–259. "The praetor M. Valerius maintained . . . in 193 B.C. . . . that *pietas* earned the benevolence of the gods for the Romans. . . . The next step was to ascribe all

36 ROMAN VIRTUE IN THE EARLY CHRISTIAN THOUGHT OF LACTANTIUS

rivalries they cultivated with enemies. Citizens vied with citizens for *virtus* [*de virtute*]. They were extravagant [*magnifici*] in offerings for the gods, at home frugal and faithful toward friends."[54] He thus overtly honors the past but reimagines Roman *virtus* as primarily ethical. In his work, military strength is just one element of a wider collection of noble qualities.

Despite this apparently laudatory tone, Sallust's criticism of traditional Roman *virtus* does not merely elevate martial *virtus* to an ethical register. More profoundly, *Bellum Catalinae* questions the ideal past that Sallust's preface seems to affirm. His portrait is laden with strategic contradiction. Immediately preceding his famous *synkrisis* of Cato and Caesar, Sallust reverses his earlier praise:

> While pondering [Rome's many great deeds of the past], it became clear to me that the outstanding virtue of just a few citizens accomplished all these things . . . but after the state was corrupted by soft-living and idleness, the commonwealth endured the vices of its generals and magistrates by its own great size; just as when the vitality [lit. *force, vi*] of parents is exhausted, in many times there was hardly anyone great in virtue at Rome [*haud sane quisquam Romae virtute magnus fuit*].[55]

This judgment revises Sallust's idealistic vision of the Roman past (cf. 53.5, *multis tempestatis*; 6.7, *ea tempestate*). He formerly imagined a period in which *virtus* and *ingenium* came together in the exemplary behavior of Rome's ancient citizens. "In that time, each man began more and more to elevate himself, and display his ability [*ingenium*] in public . . . *virtus* overcame all."[56] Upon further reflection, then, Sallust concludes that Rome's accomplishments were the work of only a few. *Virtus* never characterized the Roman people as a whole.

Sallust's judgment most evidently shapes his famous *synkresis* of Caesar and Cato, which enacts the very subversion that Sallust narrates. Caesar takes a philosophical position that would better fit the traditional image of Cato.[57] Promoting *ingenium* over *libido*, he invokes the precedent of the "*maiores*" who

---

the success to divine favor, which the Romans gained by their piety. This view was often held in the first century [B.C.], by Cicero, Varro, Horace, and Livy." Cf. Lactantius, *Inst.*, 3.29.9–10, specifically debates Sallust on this point.

[54] Sallust, *Bellum Catalinae*, 6.9. See also Daniel J. Kapust, *Republicanism, Rhetoric, and Roman Political Thought: Sallust, Livy, and Tacitus* (Cambridge: Cambridge University Press, 2011).

[55] Sallust, *Bellum Catalinae*, 53.2–5.

[56] Cf. Sallust, *Bellum Catalinae*, 6.7.1, "*virtus omnia domuerat.*"

[57] Sklenář, "La République des Signes," pp. 205–220. Caesar's speech draws deeply on the prologue (*BC*, 1.1–4), while Cato's depends upon Sallust's account of moral luxury and avarice (*BC*, 11–12). Also, Thomas F. Scanlon, *Spes Frustrata: A Reading of Sallust* (Heidelberg: Carl Winter, 1987), pp. 16–39.

often took counsel "against passion [*contra libidem*]" (51.4).[58] In an ironic turn, Julius Caesar, the archetypical man of martial *virtus* promotes *animi virtus* as the truest form.[59]

A second and perhaps greater irony reveals the way Rome's idea of ancestral precedent was subject to manipulation and renegotiation. Although Caesar invokes the *mos maiorum*, his argument turns the notion on its head. "All bad precedents [*exempla*]," he says, "have arisen from good practices; but when *imperium* passes to men unprepared for it, or to men of lesser character [*ad viros minus bonos*], that precedent is transferred from a worthy and fitting thing to an unworthy and inappropriate one."[60] Following good precedent is likely then to leave room for what is wrong. Caesar, paradoxically, upholds a precedent for no precedent at all:

> Our ancestors [*maiores nostri*], Senators, lacked neither judgment nor daring [*neque consili neque audaciae*] at any time; neither did pride prevent them from imitating foreign institutions [*aliena instituta*], when they were right. They always preferred to imitate rather than envy what was good [*imitari quam invidere bonis malebant*].[61]

Sallust's use of *imitari* evokes the Romans' traditional exemplary logic. He argues that the same *maiores* whose *exempla* provide models for imitation establish the precedent for the departure from Roman precedent. Caesar thus urges the Senate to follow customs found in foreign lands, not their own. Sallust's portrait of Caesar aims to expose the malleability of *virtus* and suggest that Roman tradition provides no stable guide at all.[62]

Cato's address reinforces the same critique from another angle. The man so famous for his philosophic habit makes no appeal to precedent at all. Instead, he implores the Senate by invoking their self-interest:

> By the immortal gods! I call upon you who have always regarded your homes, villas, statues, and paintings more highly than the commonwealth; if you want to keep those things which you embrace—whatever they are—if you want to spend leisure time in your pleasures, wake up and secure the commonwealth.... Our lives and liberty are at stake.[63]

---

[58] Syme, *Sallust*, pp. 112–113.

[59] Sklenář, "La République des Signes," p. 207.

[60] Sallust, *Bellum Catalinae*, 51.27.

[61] Sallust, *Bellum Catalinae*, 51.37.

[62] David James Christiansen, *Character and Morality in the Sallustian Monographs* (Unpublished dissertation: University of Wisconsin-Madison, 1990), p. 10.

[63] Sallust, *Bellum Catalinae*, 51.5.

38 ROMAN VIRTUE IN THE EARLY CHRISTIAN THOUGHT OF LACTANTIUS

Where Caesar promoted a plan of leniency in following philosophic reason and adherence to precedent, Cato appeals to a visceral self-interest. He recalls his many speeches exhorting the Senate to preserve ancestral virtue and reminding them that Roman power rests upon the virtue of its people; however, the time for all that is now gone:

> Very often, Senators, I have held forth at great length in this company; I have lamented the luxury and avarice of our citizens and have many mortals against me on account of it. . . . But now at stake is not whether we live by good or wicked morals, nor how great or magnificent the empire of the Roman people is, but whether this—whatever it seems to be—will belong to us or to our enemies along with ourselves. Does someone want to invoke lenience and compassion with me now? We have long lost the true names for things.[64]

Cato's famous statement echoes Sallust's diagnosis in the prologue.[65] For Cato, the verdict on Roman morals has already been rendered. Only lust and self-interest remain; the language of *virtus* is itself corrupt.[66] As a reflection on the Roman past, Sallust remembers the city's noblest lights acting in pragmatic calculation. The senators rule in Cato's favor, not out of some shared morality or desire for reform, but from concern for their own luxuries. Sallust thus undercuts the ancestral ideal. His technique echoes in Augustan literature.

Livy's Equivocation: Romulus

Sallust was not alone in his criticism of the traditional Roman self-image. The historian Livy (64 B.C.–17 A.D.) was a contemporary of Caesar Augustus and Vergil. He lived through the collapse of the Republic, saw Augustus's rise, and witnessed Tiberius Caesar's succession to the imperial purple. Livy's *History* makes a famous contribution to the Augustan project of retelling Rome's exemplary past.[67] Livy sifts the Roman past as a source of moral wisdom for a people living under a new regime in a new era.[68] He incorporates Sallust's sense of the

---

[64] Sallust, *Bellum Catalinae*, 52.7–8, 10–11.

[65] See McGushin, *C. Sallustius Crispus, Bellum Catilinae*, p. 259. Cato uses "terms which strongly recall the words and viewpoint of S. himself, e.g., *domos*, cf. 12.3; *villas*, cf. 13.1; *signa, tabulas*, cf. 11.6."

[66] Lydia Spielberg, "Language, Stasis and the Role of the Historian in Thucydides, Sallust and Tacitus," *American Journal of Philology* 138.2 (2017): pp. 331–373. Also Kapust, *Republicanism, Rhetoric, and Roman Political Thought*, pp. 55–61. Sklenář, "Language of Sallustian Morality," pp. 211–217, also deals at length with Cato's claim that words have lost their meanings.

[67] Ann Vasaly, *Livy's Political Philosophy: Power and Personality in Early Rome* (New York: Cambridge University Press, 2015).

[68] Ronald Syme, "Livy and Augustus," *Harvard Studies in Classical Philology* 64 (1959): pp. 27–87.

moral decline of Rome but presents his narrative as a series of literary *exempla virtutis*.[69]

Livy's history reports a traditional Roman sentiment, at the outset. Like Sallust, he contrasts ancient mores with the decline of his own day. His moralizing posture toward the decadent present serves a political aim. He voices traditional pieties toward the Roman past and imagines the ancestors as a people distinguished for their *virtus*, or so it seems:

> This is the particularly beneficial and fruitful result of historical study: that you reflect on the models of every example arrayed on a famous monument, from which you then select both for yourself and for your commonwealth, first what to imitate and then—shameful in its inception, shameful in its outcome—what to avoid. Furthermore, either love of the work undertaken deceives me, or there was never any commonwealth [*res publica*] greater nor more sacred [*sanctior*] nor richer in good examples [*bonis exemplis ditior*], nor did avarice and luxury immigrate to any city so late, nor was honor and office awarded to poverty and frugality so much nor so long. For with the absence of wealth came also the absence of cupidity; only recently did riches bring about avarice and abundant pleasures desire, through luxury and the passion for ruining and destroying everything.[70]

Livy thus seems to view antiquity as a sacred era when the ancestors established a glorious city on the basis of their unique character. He offers *exempla* as models of both virtue and vice fit for imitation. The religious element of Rome's traditional narrative is also prominent. Rome was "divinely sanctioned." In his account, the gods favored Rome because of its frugality, austerity, and religious piety.

Within this formally hagiographic portrait, Livy left ample reason to doubt the Roman political theology that would emerge in the imperial era. His narratives both present and question the myth of Rome's past, the story of its people's divine lineage and exemplary character. He tells the story of a city "which has grown from meager beginnings until now it labors under its own magnitude."[71]

---

[69] Roman *exemplarity* has a large and growing literature in modern scholarship. See Matthew Roller, "Exemplarity in Roman Culture," *Classical Philology* 99.1 (2004): pp. 1–56. For Livy, Jane D. Chaplin, *Livy's Exemplary History* (Oxford: Oxford University Press, 2000). Modern interest begins with Henry Litchfield, "National Exempla Virtvtis in Roman Literature," *Harvard Studies in Classical Philology* 25 (1914): pp. 1–71. For bibliography, see Ayelet Haimson Lushkov, *Magistracy and the Historiography of the Roman Republic: Politics in Prose* (Cambridge: Cambridge University Press, 2015). For Cicero, Henriette van der Blom, *Cicero's Role Models: The Political Strategy of a Newcomer* (Oxford: Oxford University Press, 2010).

[70] Livy, *Liv.*, 1.9–12 in Titus Livius, *Ab urbe condita vols. I–VI, recognovit et adnotatione critica Instruxit*, Robertus Maxwell Ogilvie and P. G. Walsh (Oxonii: E Typographeo Clarendoniano, 1974–1999).

[71] Livy, *Liv.*, 1.1.9, "*quae ab exiguis profecta initiis eo creverit ut iam magnitudine laboret sua.*"

40 ROMAN VIRTUE IN THE EARLY CHRISTIAN THOUGHT OF LACTANTIUS

The story of intensifying moral decline calls into question how early and how deeply rooted the collapse really was. Like Sallust, Livy offers ambivalent praise that suggests a subversive critique as much as any celebration.

Livy's rendition of Rome's founding by Romulus exemplifies this element in his prose. The timing of its publication is telling. On 16 July 27 B.C., the Roman Senate awarded Octavian the title "Augustus." The historian Suetonius reports that "some argued he should be called Romulus, as a second founder of the city."[72] Octavian had already assumed the title "Son of the Deified" (*Divi filius*) since Julius Caesar's deification by the Senate in the year 43 B.C. Octavian also boasted of himself as a "new Romulus" in the wake of his victory over Antony at the Battle of Actium in 31 B.C. However, Edmondson explains, "The glory of Romulus, much advertised after Actium, is allowed to fade into the background ... transcended by the achievements of the new regime."[73] During the time between Actium and Octavian's assumption of the title "Augustus" (31–27 B.C.), Livy was sorting through the various remaining strands of history and legend surrounding Romulus. His work was published sometime between 27 and 25 B.C., in the shade of Augustus's elevation.

Both academic exercise and political commentary, Livy's version of the tale comports with Augustan propaganda, and yet, at key moments, his report suggests that neither piety nor virtue, but rather violence and passion, explain Rome's mythic origins. Livy introduces Rome's founders as the offspring of gods, but disparages their maternal origins. His narrative casts a shadow over the *princeps*:

> The origin and beginning of so great a city, the greatest empire in the world, was determined by the fates, I think, through the help of the gods. After the Vestal had been raped and given birth to twins, she named Mars the father of her uncertain issue, either because she really thought it so, or because it was better [*honestior*] that a god be author [*auctor*] of the fault.[74]

Livy thus introduces Rome as the product of an ambiguous act of violence. As Stevenson explains, Rome's illegitimate founders are born in rape and a dubious story of their paternity, which "tends to undercut the innocence or moral purity of the *exemplum*."[75] Livy's comment foreshadows Rome's duplicity. The boys are soon found floating down a river in a basket, when the mythical

---

[72] Suetonius, *De vita XII Caesarum*, 7.2 in *Suetonius*, with an English translation by J. C. Rolfe (Cambridge, MA: Harvard University Press, 1997–1998).
[73] Jonathan Edmondson, *Augustus* (Edinburgh: Edinburgh University Press, 2009), p. 54.
[74] Livy, *Liv.*, 1.4.1–2.
[75] T. Stevenson, "Women of Early Rome as Exempla in Livy, *Ab Urbe Condita*, Book 1," *Classical World* 104.2 (2011): pp. 175–189, esp. p. 176.

she-wolf recovers them.[76] Livy reminds the reader of a perhaps common cynical view: "There are some who think that Larentia was called 'she-wolf', since she prostituted her body among the herdsmen, and that's what made room for this miraculous tale."[77] The detail impugns both mothers of Rome's founders, the first as a liar and the second as a prostitute—or at least, Livy leaves room for unnamed "some" to do so.

The twins' questionable beginnings are soon rivaled by Rome's own ambiguous start. The boys come to lead a band of robbers and learn that Numitor, king of Alba Longa, is their grandfather. Since he rules Alba Longa, they determine to conquer some new place. Livy's characterization foreshadows the coming violence: "The desire to found a city in that area where they themselves had been exposed (i.e., on the river) and raised soon seized them."[78] The twins, seeking a city to surpass Alba Longa and Lavinium, are overtaken by Rome's perpetual bane, "the passion for royal rule (1.6.4, *cupido regni*)." Disloyal to their grandfather, they set out to build a rival city.

A founding act of violence soon undermines all dreams of ancestral piety. As Livy relates, it was determined that "the gods by whose augury those regions were kept safe should determine, who would give his name to the city and rule it, once founded, under his authority [*imperium*]."[79] In Livy's prose, the twins' show of piety reinforces the reader's certainty of conflict. A failed augury leads to civil conflict that Livy's Roman audience would recognize as a stock narrative.[80] Opposing mobs claim rival leaders and the outcome is all too predictable:

> Thus, having clashed in argument they turned from an angry fight to bloodshed; there Remus fell, struck down in the fray. There is a more common story that Remus in mockery of his brother stepped over and then was killed by his angered brother, who also added these words, "Thus also for anyone who crosses my walls." Thus, Romulus alone gained the imperium; when the city was founded, it was called by the name of the founder. He built walls first on the Palatine where he had been reared. He performs rites [*sacra*] to some gods by the Alban rite, for Hercules in the Greek rite, as they had been instituted by Evander.[81]

Livy's report of the common fable of Remus's death undermines the dream of ancestral mores offered in the Preface. A cynical hue colors his story. Perhaps

---

[76] See Cristina Mazzoni, *She-Wolf: The Story of a Roman Icon* (Cambridge: Cambridge University Press, 2010).

[77] Livy, *Liv.*, 1.4.8.

[78] Livy, *Liv.*, 1.6.3.

[79] Livy, *Liv.*, 1.6.4.

[80] Livy, *Liv.*, 1.7.2.

[81] Livy, *Liv.*, 1.7.2.

42   ROMAN VIRTUE IN THE EARLY CHRISTIAN THOUGHT OF LACTANTIUS

Rome's founders were the illegitimate sons of a woman who was either raped, or just broke her vow (i.e., *auctor culpae*) and lied to cover it up. The passion (*cupido*) that seized their mother soon captures the twins. They also reject peace offered freely in a kingdom, preferring bloodshed to cooperation in government. And worse, Roman religion simply serves as a false mask for the truth of their behavior. Then, as now, political rivals stoke unruly mobs; fratricide belies false piety and portends dire days to come.

A deep hue of cynicism about the role of religion in Roman politics colors Livy's account. He relates that Romulus secured the city in a series of battles that qualified him for immortality, which was finally granted in Romulus's apotheosis. Livy's account drips with incredulity. One day, "after the completion of these immortal deeds [*his immortalibus editis operibus*]," a storm comes up and "Romulus was never again on the earth [*nec deinde Romulus in terris fuit*]." The senators, "who had been standing nearest [*qui proximi steterant*]," claim Romulus "was snatched up to heaven in the storm [*sublimem raptum procella*]." The people hail Romulus as "a god born from a god [*deum deo natum*]," and establish his cult. But Livy does not fail to recall another debunking view: "I believe there were some who quietly alleged that the king had actually been cut to pieces by the senators."[82] Livy's remark disparages the pious story of Roman leaders ascending to divinity. In so doing, he casts doubt on the current regime as well. His remark suggests that the Augustan theology of imperial deification could be a fiction covering over political violence. In point of fact, the people do not seem to accept Romulus's apotheosis until Proculus Iulius confirms it by a tale Livy obliquely characterizes as his "very obscure report [*perobscura fama*]." Proculus claims that an apparition of Romulus appeared to him in the early morning and prophesied Rome's destiny. Livy remarks sardonically: "How amazing that there was so much confidence [*fides*] in that man as he spoke."[83] In Livy's account, doubt dogs Rome's founders and, more important, the mythology of their divinely favored rule, from the beginning.

Vergil's Contradictions

Lucretius was perhaps the first poet to criticize Rome's political theology for the upheaval it promoted, but Vergil's *Aeneid* is the great literary icon of Augustan Rome and the counterpart to the physical monuments that proclaimed Augustus's achievements. Vergil (70–19 B.C.) reports the Augustan legend like no

[82] Livy, *Liv.*, 1.16.2, "*Fuisse credo tum quoque aliquos qui discerptum regem patrum manibus taciti arguerent.*"
[83] Livy, *Liv.*, 1.16.4, "*Mirum quantum illi viro nuntianti haec fides fuerit.*"

VIRTUS IN ROMAN LIFE AND LITERATURE   43

other; Augustus himself is said to have proposed the theme. The *Aeneid*'s composition coincides, notably, with the sculpting of Augustus's "Altar of Peace" (*ara pacis*), which portrayed Augustus as a descendant of Aeneas, Romulus, Mars, and the Romans of old. The *ara pacis* was dedicated in the Campus Martius at Rome on 30 January 9 B.C.[84] The impact of Vergil cannot be overstated. Yasmin Syed explains that "the *Aeneid* had a significant impact on its Roman readers' sense of self as Romans and that the poem articulated Roman identity for them through the reader's identification with . . . its fictional characters."[85] And yet, Vergil exhibits an ambivalence about the identity of Romans as people distinguished for *virtus* in general, and about the new imperial representations of *virtus* in particular.[86] Unsurprisingly, Vergil's lines furnished later critics with both the target and logic of their arguments.

Vergil dramatizes the distinctive claims of the Augustan political myth in the person of Aeneas, but two levels of criticism operate through his epic. Aeneas appears as the archetype of the imperial office, but that archetype revises Rome's traditional heroic ideal by projecting philosophical and religious qualities onto Rome's past. Vergil's Aeneas is distinguished not simply for strength at arms, but for his *pietas* toward home and hearth-gods. He exemplifies not only martial, but ethical *virtus*. At yet a deeper level, Vergil subverts such Augustan rewriting of Roman ideals of *virtus* by showing Aeneas, the founder of the Augustan line, as a contradictory figure whose work often descends from its noble ideal into naked violence.[87] Hence, Gian Biagio Conte summarizes a generation of scholarly debate about Vergil's intention: "Vergil was aiming at contradiction, deliberately and programmatically, in order to make it the very essence of his discourse. . . . This is the aspect of 'doubleness' . . . which comes from the ambiguous nature of the *Aeneid*, and its ambition to be simultaneously mythical and historical epic."[88] Vergil leaves startling impressions at precisely those places that most profoundly mark the political and historiographical character of his work. As a result, his poem dramatizes the Augustan political theology, while simultaneously registering compelling reasons for its critique.

---

[84] Edmondson, *Augustus*, p. 11.

[85] Yasmin Syed, *Vergil's Aeneid and the Roman Self: Subject and Nation in Literary Discourse* (Ann Arbor: University of Michigan Press, 2005), p. 11.

[86] Syed, *Virgil's Aeneid and the Roman Self*, p. 13.

[87] For critical voices in Vergil, see Richard F. Thomas, *Virgil and the Augustan Reception* (Cambridge: Cambridge University Press, 2001); Sabine Grebe, "Augustus's Divine Authority and Vergil's Aeneid," *Vergilius* 50 (2004): pp. 35–62. Michael C. J. Putnam, "Two Ways of Looking at the 'Aeneid,'" *The Classical World* 96.2 (2003): pp. 177–184; R. O. A. M. Lyne, *Further Voices in Vergil's Aeneid* (Oxford: Oxford University Press, 1987); sed contra Karl Galinsky, "Clothes for the Emperor," *Arion* 10 (January 2003): pp. 143–169; Anton Powell, *Virgil the Partisan: A Study in the Re-integration of Classics* (Oakville, CT: Distributed in the USA by David Brown, 2008).

[88] Gian Biagio Conte, *The Poetry of Pathos: Studies in Virgilian Epic* (Oxford: Oxford University Press, 2007), pp. 151, 166, *passim*.

44 ROMAN VIRTUE IN THE EARLY CHRISTIAN THOUGHT OF LACTANTIUS

"*Arma virumque cano*," Vergil's famous opening words, highlight the martial excellence of his hero. Vergil soon signals that Aeneas's distinctive virtue will be *pietas*: "O Muse, recount to me the causes, how was her divinity offended? / For what reason did the embittered queen of gods drive a man so marked by piety [*pietate*] to endure so many dangers / to undergo so many labors?"[89] Vergil's Aeneas will be distinguished not simply for valor (*arma*), but for his character. Aeneas soon embraces his identity as a hero marked by *pietas* toward his father, his household gods, and his fated mission: "I am *pius Aeneas* and carry in my fleet household gods snatched from the enemy. I am known above the heavens, and seek Italy for a fatherland and a race from Jupiter Highest."[90] Aeneas, like Augustus and his imperial successors, expects to win a place in the heavens for his heroism.

Vergil links Aeneas's *pietas* to a theology that promises divine care for the hero and the inevitable triumph of Rome.[91] The narrative is informed, broadly, by Stoic philosophical theology and, specifically, by Cicero.[92] In his first meeting with Dido, Aeneas expresses this perspective in a moving, if ultimately ironic, utterance: "If any divine powers [*numina*] look down on the pious [*pios*], if there is ever justice [*iustitia*] for anything, or any mind conscious of what is right [*mens sibi conscia recti*], may the gods reward you worthily."[93] Jupiter likewise promises distinctive favor for the pious at the beginning and end of the epic. Early in Book I he states, "Upon them I place neither limits of time or space, imperium without end I have given."[94] As Book XII approaches its climax, Jupiter associates Aeneas's *pietas* with the promised Roman descendants: "From here a race shall rise mixed with Ausonian blood which / you shall see surpass both men and gods

---

[89] Vergil, *Aen.*, 1.8–11 in Virgil, *Aeneis*, ed. Gian Biagio Conte (Berlin: Walter de Gruyter, 2009). Translations are my own. The narrator names him *pius* throughout the work. Cf. 1.220, 1.305, 5.26, 5.286, 5.685, 6.9, 6.176, 6.232, 7.5, 8.84, 10.591 (somewhat ironically), 10.783, 10.826, 12.175, 12.311.

[90] Vergil, *Aen.*, 1.378–380. Cf. 1.250–253, where Aeneas evokes his own *pietas*, while protesting that *pietas* is not rewarded: "*nos, tua progenies caeli quibus adnuis arcem, / navibus (infandum) amissis unius ob iram / prodimur atque Italis longe disiungimur oris. Hic pietatis honos?*" Also 1.544–545. Ilioneus to Dido: "*Rex erat Aeneas nobis, quo iustior alter, / nec pietate fuit, nec bello maior et armis.*" Aletes at 8.255, Evander, 11.170.

[91] Powell, *Virgil the Partisan*, p. 33: "Gods and men alike express the idea that human *pietas* can reasonably be expected to draw from divinity protection and favor on earth."

[92] E.g., Russell B. Sisson, "Roman Stoic Pre-Creation Discourse," *Religions and Theology* 18 (2011): pp. 227–243. Also, Nicholas Horsfall, *Virgil: Aeneid 6*, vol 2. (Berlin: Degruyter, 2013), p. 487. Commenting on 6.724ff—lines so important for the Latin Christian apologists—Horsfall attributes Vergil's thought directly to the *Somnium Scipionis*. Also, Edward B. Stevens, "Aeneid 6.724ff. and Cicero's Hortensius," *The Classical Weekly* 36.8 (1942): pp. 86–87. Cf. Servius, who understood Vergil's language as Stoic. Servius et al., *Servii Grammatici Qvi Fervntvr in Vergilii Carmina Commentarii* (Hildesheim: G. Olms, 1961), p. 178; "604. *SI QUI USQUAM IUSTITIAE EST: si valet apud homines iustitia. ET MENS CONSCIA RECTI secundum stoicos, qui dicunt, ipsam virtutem esse pro praemio, etiamsi nulla sint praemia.*" See J. D. Noonan, "*Sum Pius Aeneas*: Aeneas and the Leader as Conservator/σΩΤΗΡ," *Classical Bulletin* 83.1 (2007): pp. 65–91.

[93] Vergil, *Aen.*, 1.603–604. Compare *mens, numina* here to *Rep.* 1.56, *Leg.* 1.21.

[94] Vergil, *Aen.*, 1.278, "*His ego nec metas rerum nec tempora pono / imperium sine fine dedi.*"

VIRTUS IN ROMAN LIFE AND LITERATURE   45

in piety / and no people will celebrate your honors as they."[95] Rome still enjoys a distinctive divine favor, but the virtue rewarded is no longer martial. This "pro-Augustan" voice is critical of Republican valor and shifts the ideal qualities toward the realm of *mores*.[96]

Vergil's mythic narrative of Aeneas's *pietas* does not make him a mere herald and celebrator of the Augustan *pax Romana*. A second trajectory of criticism emerges in Vergil's portrait of Aeneas. The image of *pius Aeneas* comes into striking contradiction with the hero's own actions, which undermine the prophecies of a new Golden Age and of a political mission founded on Aeneas's distinct form of heroism.

Ancient and modern readers of the *Aeneid* have identified the first hint of irony in Vergil's portrait of the hero's flight from Troy. Venus complains to Jupiter of Aeneas's troubles: "O Great King, what end of labors are you giving? / Antenor, having escaped from the Greeks / was able to reach Illyric harbors and the inmost kingdoms of the Liburnians."[97] Antenor's fate contrasts with the wandering of Aeneas, her favored son. Rather, as Richard Thomas has argued, Servius heard the echo of another story in the pairing of Antenor and Aeneas.[98] For Servius, Vergil's pairing addresses a well-known calumny against Aeneas:

> The example of Antenor is not without cause, since many escaped the dangers that befell the Trojans. But for this reason: so that [Antenor] could not by some chance be rightly impugned [*iure vexari*] as a traitor to his country [*proditorem patriae*]. According to Livy, some say that these two betrayed Troy; and Vergil touches on this in passing [*per transitum*] when he says [at 1.485] "[Aeneas] recognized himself intermingled with Greek princes." Also, Horace excuses [Aeneas] when he says, "*ardentem sine fraude Troiam*," meaning, "without treachery [*proditione*]." This excuse is not unimportant, since no one offers excuses unless there is some serious [*rem plenam*] suspicion.[99]

For Servius, Vergil is addressing earlier accusations against the legendary hero. He notes that Horace does the same thing at *Carmen Saeculare* 41–44, when he writes of Aeneas escaping "through Troy burning without treachery [*per ardentem sine fraude Troiam*]."[100] The image of Aeneas running for his life as a traitor is perhaps reinforced by the puzzling moment when he directs his wife, Creusa, to follow the party fleeing Troy, "at a distance [*longe*]." That a man,

---

[95] Vergil, *Aen.*, 12.839.
[96] Kenneth Quinn, *Virgil's "Aeneid": A Critical Description* (London: Routledge & Kegan Paul, 1968).
[97] Vergil, *Aen.*, 1.224.
[98] Thomas, *Virgil and the Augustan Reception*, pp. 72–73.
[99] Servius et al., *Vergilii Carmina Commentarii*, 1.224.
[100] Horace, *Carmen Saeculare* 41, in Thomas, *Virgil and the Augustan Reception*, p. 71.

46 ROMAN VIRTUE IN THE EARLY CHRISTIAN THOUGHT OF LACTANTIUS

distinguished for his loyalty to hearth and home (*pietate insignis*), should direct his own wife to hang back in such a perilous moment has puzzled commentators. Aeneas ultimately loses Creusa, "maybe snatched by fate."[101] Turnus later echoes the indictment when he calls Aeneas "*desertorem Asiae*."[102] Vergil thus keeps the counter-narrative alive throughout.

Vergil's portrait of Augustan *virtus* continues in the Dido narrative. Through Dido, Vergil depicts Aeneas as a traitor, a coward, and a liar. Satisfied and refreshed by Dido's eager hospitality, Aeneas directs his officers to prepare their fleet in silence and not let anyone know about his plans. He tells them to "dissemble" (*dissimulare*).[103] "But the queen presages [*praesensit*] his trickery [*dolos*]," the narrator explains. Dido then accuses him of treachery, "You hoped to deceive me [*dissimulare*], faithless one, and depart my land in silence!?"[104] Her lines throw Aeneas's own words back in his face. By implication she also impugns the moral heritage of imperial Rome. Vergil's subversive voice leaves room for a double indictment, as the Dido tale intensifies a failing already evident in the account of Aeneas's flight from Troy. Not only has Aeneas fled martial conflict, but he has also failed the piety due to two noble women. *Domi militiaeque*, as Sallust would say, Vergil's Aeneas is a problem.

Aeneid 6 dramatizes the Augustan notion of a "dynastic continuity" that extends from Aeneas to Caesar Augustus and his heirs. From the underworld, Aeneas's father Anchises prophesies of the Roman heroes that will arise, from Aeneas himself to Augustus. In Anchises's prophecy, Vergil makes Aeneas the father and icon of Rome, and the archetype of all for later imperial history.[105] At first blush, his prognostications for Caesar Augustus appear glowing:

Behold this race, *your Romans*. This Caesar and all the offspring of the Iulii / who shall come to live under the great pole of heaven. This man, this is he, whom you have heard, I promised you so often. / Augustus Caesar, offspring of the Deified [*Augustus Caesar, divi genus*], who shall found again the Golden Age [*aurea condet / saecula*] in Latium, in fields where Saturn once reigned. He shall bear empire beyond Libyans and Indians.[106]

[101] Vergil, *Aen.*, 2.738.
[102] Vergil, *Aen.*, 12.15.
[103] Vergil, *Aen.*, 286–295.
[104] Vergil, *Aen.*, 4.305–306.
[105] Richard F. Thomas, "Torn between Jupiter and Saturn: Ideology, Rhetoric and Culture Wars in the 'Aeneid,'" *Classical Journal* 100.2 (2004): pp. 121–147. Also, Thomas, *Augustan Reception*, pp. 40–54, shows that Tibullus took the lines critically, much as Thomas does.
[106] Vergil, *Aen.*, 6.788–791. On the lines "*aurea condet / saecula*," see Thomas, *Augustan Reception*, pp. 1–7. Lucretius had used the exact phrase (*saecula condere*) in the sense of "conclude" or "close out," or "bring to an end." Paired with the portrait of Aeneas and Augustus as descendants of Jupiter, the line allows us to see Augustus as *ending* a Golden Age in Latium by conquering the rustic people.

Mythology and historiography merge in this utopian future, rendered more certain and vivid by its dramatic setting in Rome's unalterable past. But Vergil's setting actually accentuates the bankruptcy of Augustan morality. The prophecy identifies Augustus as the telos of Roman history. And yet, in so doing, Vergil actually mourns an inevitable history of corruption and then rebukes Caesar and Pompey, in the mouth of Augustus's mythic grandfather:

> These two souls now in harmony [*concordia*], whom you discern shining now in equal arms and while they are pressed by night, when they shall reach the lights of life, what great battle lines shall they draw up and slaughter! No, children [*pueri*], do not fashion in your minds such wars, nor turn the power and strength of your fatherland on its own flesh; and you first, you my own blood, who trace your race from Olympus, throw down your weapons from your hand.[107]

Several contradictions are at play in the juxtaposition of Anchises's two visions. The image of civil war stands in stark contrast to the Golden Age of peace; both will be the work of Aeneas's progeny. Julius Caesar and Pompey are, like Augustus, sons (*pueri*) of Aeneas; and Anchises will not let the reader forget that they will turn Roman power inward upon itself (*in viscera*). Aeneas is made, by implication, a cause of this bloodshed as well.

Notes of foreboding thus come to dominate the final lines of the prophecy. In the mouth of Anchises, Vergil articulates the doctrine that the gods had awarded to Rome the distinctive capacity and right to govern—what Ando calls "the Roman achievement in ancient thought."[108] Anchises gives Aeneas Rome's famous mandate: "Remember, O Roman, you shall rule peoples with imperium / these shall be your skills: to establish a way of life in peace, to spare the subject and in war subdue the proud."[109] With the vocative "*O Romane*," Vergil collapses the Augustan line into a single moment; he is addressing Caesar Augustus in the figure of Aeneas.[110] Anchises thus commands Aeneas, the Roman, (*tuque prior, tu parce . . .*) to set an example of peace for future generations. But every reader knows the true story. The admonition will ring futile as the books unfold. His words are more lament than prophecy.

---

[107] Vergil, *Aen.*, 6.826–830.

[108] Ando, *Imperial Ideology and Provincial Loyalty*, pp. 49ff.

[109] Vergil, *Aen.*, 6.851–852, "*tu regere imperio populos, Romane, memento / (hae tibi erunt artes) pacique imponere morem / Parcere subiectis et debellare superbos.*"

[110] Cf. Horace, *Carm.*, 3.6.2–5. Horace's *Carmen Saeculare* echoes the Augustan theology: "Though undeserved, you will pay for the transgressions of your ancestors / O Roman [*O Romane*], until you've rebuilt the temples of the gods and their dilapidated shrines / and their images filthy with black smoke. / You rule because you keep yourself below the gods. / Refer every beginning to this, and to it every ending.

The cracks in Vergil's portrait of Augustus sharpen with each passing book. Aeneas proves unable to fulfill Anchises's mandate. Aeneas's brutality often undermines the promise of Stoic piety sketched at the start. For example, at the death of his young protégé, Pallas, Aeneas cuts through the enemy line and captures four youths, whom he sacrifices to the lower deities (*Aen.*, 10.518–519). Magus, beaten down, approaches Aeneas "as a suppliant [*supplex*]," by "embracing his knees [*genua amplectens*]." Magus begs for mercy, just as Anchises prophesied would happen. His words actually invoke Anchises's prophecy (*parcere subiectis*, *Aen.*, 6.852). Reminding Aeneas of hearth and home, Anchises invokes Aeneas's distinct virtue of *pietas*: "by your household gods and the hope of rising Iulus / I pray you, may you save this soul for the sake of your child and father [*hanc animan serves*]."[111] Yet Aeneas mercilessly rejects him (*Aen.*, 10.530). Vergil glosses the whole episode as a fit of madness (*Dardanius torrentis aquae . . . more furens*, *Aen.*, 10.603–604); his portrait of bloodless cruelty remains vivid.

In the final scene as well, Vergil casts the founder of the Augustan race as a brutal man carried away by bloodlust. Aeneas again is swept along by his fury in a series of episodes that end in Turnus's death (*Aen.*, 12.498). Yet another hero invokes Anchises and his commands, even as he concedes defeat:

> Turnus, as a humble suppliant [*humilis supplex*] stretching out his right hand, praying "surely I have earned this, I do not pray more: / enjoy your fate. Still if any care for a parent can touch you, I pray (for you once had such a parent [*genitor*], Anchises), have mercy on the old age of Daunus, / and return me, or my body stripped of life if you prefer / to my family. You have conquered and the Ausonians have seen a conquered man stretch out his hands; Lavinia is your wife. Go no further in hatred [*ulterius ne tende odiis*]."[112]

Turnus acknowledges the entire doctrine of Aeneas's regime—his fated status, his piety, his rights to Lavinia. Once again, Aeneas is "consumed [*accensus*] with the furies and terrible wrath." Rather than extend clemency, he kills Turnus as a sacrifice: "'Pallas it is, Pallas slays you [*immolat*] by this wound and exacts the penalty from wicked blood.' So saying and hot with rage [*fervidus*], he thrusts his sword beneath the chest [*ferrum adverso sub pectore condit fervidus*]."[113] Turnus is the last of Latium's subjected heroes, whom Aeneas slaughters in violation of his father's mandate. Aeneas's final act thus betrays the myth of a Golden Age.

---

[111] Vergil, *Aen.*, 10.524–525.
[112] Vergil, *Aen.*, 12.930–938.
[113] Vergil, *Aen.*, 12.948–951.

Rather than restoring an *aurea saecula* (*Aen.*, 6.789–790), the death-blow literally "founds iron" (*ferrum condit*) in the breast of Turnus.[114]

By manipulating the language of Anchises's prophecy, Vergil's lines raise the question: Is Aeneas in fact Jupiter founding an age of iron in Latium rather than Saturn founding an age of gold? The unanswered question leaves the reader to decide by pondering Rome's story again and again. In effect, Vergil warns that the myth of empire sanctioned by a theology of virtue (e.g., *pietas, virtus*) may be used to sanction naked violence. Turnus's death, like the sacrifice of the four youths and the Latin wars—Rome's first civil wars—becomes a human sacrifice (*immolat*) on the altar of Jupiter and Fate. Conte notes that with the verb *immolat*, "Aeneas offers Turnus as a sacrificial victim and kills him like a priest who offers a sacrificial ritual."[115] Vergil's conclusion protests the whole doctrine of Roman *virtus* and thrusts its bloody consequences before the reader's eye. In so doing, Vergil criticizes not only Augustan politics, but the religious ideology that sanctioned it.

Ovid and Lucan: Outraged

After Vergil, Roman poets often rendered explicit the irony and ambivalence that was only latent or subtly inserted in Augustan literature. With particular attention to Vergil, Sergio Casali explains that "in post-Vergilian epic, the intertextual dialogue with Vergil is an act of interpretation in which the post-Vergilian epics attack and subvert the Vergilian text."[116] Ovid and Lucan represent sterling examples of this trend in post-Augustan writing. Both attack the regime and its doctrine by criticizing its mythic basis. Ovid was born in 43 B.C., the year after Julius Caesar's assassination. He lived through Augustus's victory and subsequent ushering in of the *pax Romana*. Ovid's poem *Ars amatoria*, however, ran

---

[114] See Lyne, *Further Voices in Virgil's Aeneid*, pp. 7–10. Cf. Cicero, *Nat. d.*, 2.159. "*Quibus cum terrae subigerentur fissione glebarum, ab illo aureo genere, ut poetae loquuntur, vis nulla umquam adferebatur: 'ferrea tum vero proles exorta repente est, / ausaque funestum prima est fabricarier ensem / et gustare manu vinctum domitumque iuvencum. / Tanta putabatur utilitas percipi e bubus ut eorum visceribus vesci scelus haberetur.'*"

[115] Gian Biagio Conte, "The Strategy of Contradiction," in Gian Biagio Conte, *The Poetry of Pathos: Studies in Virgilian Epic*, ed. S. J. Harrison (Oxford: Oxford University Press, 2007), p. 155.

[116] Sergio Casali, "The Bellum Civile as an Anti-Aeneid," in *Brill's Companion to Lucan*, ed. Paolo Asso (Leiden: Brill, 2010), p. 82. See also Paul Roche, *Lucan: De Bello Civili* (Oxford: Oxford University Press, 2009), pp. 21–22: "The Aeneid provides Lucan with the supreme poetic example of a foundation text of Augustan Rome . . . against which to situate his own poetic project. . . . This opposition takes the form of demystification and bitterly disillusioned re-writing of the Vergilian myth of Rome's past and future." For a broader picture of Silver Age criticism, see Phillip Hardie, *The Epic Successors of Virgil: A Study in the Dynamics of a Tradition* (Cambridge: Cambridge University Press, 1993); also Douglas Feeney, *The Gods in Epic: Poets and Criticism of the Classical Tradition* (Oxford: Oxford University Press, 1991).

50 ROMAN VIRTUE IN THE EARLY CHRISTIAN THOUGHT OF LACTANTIUS

directly counter to the broad program of moral reform which, consistent with his role as *curator legum et morum*, Augustus had vigorously enacted.[117] Exiled to the Black Sea region in 8 A.D., Ovid composed poetry bitterly criticizing the *princeps*. A generation later, Lucan (39–65 A.D.), the nephew of the Younger Seneca, would serve as mentor to Nero, the last of the Julio-Claudian emperors. Nero would force both Seneca and Lucan to commit voluntary suicide in the year 65, after both participated in the Pisonian conspiracy to have the lawless emperor assassinated. Lucan's last words are said to have been a recitation from his hostile poetry.[118] Their works exemplify the close relationship between literature and political competition in Rome. Each offers his attack as an endorsement of the anti-Augustan tradition preserved in the sources. Both authors take aim at the *virtus Augusti*.

As Richard Thomas showed, writing from exile, Ovid perceived the cynical potential latent in Vergil's account of Dido and Aeneas.[119] Ovid makes Dido a true wife and Aeneas the violator of familial *pietas*. In her voice, Ovid rejects the whole tragic yarn and the myth of Augustan piety it authorizes. Ovid's Dido connects Aeneas's night-time flight from Carthage to the earlier loss of Creusa:

> The image of your cheated wife will stand before your eyes / Grieving and hair-disheveled as she drips with blood . . . / You don't carry your gods with you, as you falsely boast / Neither did your gods and father weigh down your shoulders. / You're lying about all of it, and your tongue didn't just begin to deceive with us. / I am not the first one punished / If you ask, where is the mother of lovely Iulus? / She fell alone, abandoned by her hard-hearted husband . . . There's no doubt in my mind, your gods will damn you."[120]

Ovid makes explicit what Vergil left hidden. The political referent should not be overlooked either. In his effort to restore ancient *mores*, Augustus's legislation of 18 B.C. and then 9 A.D.—*Lex Julia de maritandis ordinibus* and *Lex Papia Poppaea*, respectively—encouraged marriage in the Roman upper classes and the production of children.[121] Ovid attacks the nostalgic project. His poem unmasks Augustus as the proponent of a *faux* morality based on a false myth.

---

[117] See Peter Green, *The Poems of Exile: Tristia and the Black Sea Letters* (Berkeley: University of California Press, 2005), xix.

[118] Tacitus, *Annals*, XV.70.1 in Tacitus, *Annals: Books 13–16*, trans. John Jackson, Loeb Classical Library 322 (Cambridge, MA: Harvard University Press, 1937).

[119] Thomas, *Virgil and the Augustan Reception*, pp. 78–80.

[120] Ovid, *Heroides*, 7.69–86, in Ovid, *Heroides; Amores*, trans. Grand Showerman, revised by G. P. Goold, Loeb Classical Library 41 (Cambridge, MA: Harvard University Press, 1914).

[121] Kristina Milnor, "Augustus, History, and the Landscape of the Law," *Arethusa* 40.1 (2007): pp. 7–23. Also, Adam M. Kemezis, "Augustus the Ironic Paradigm: Cassius Dio's Portrayal of the *Lex Julia* and *Lex Papia Poppaea*," *Phoenix* 61 (2007): pp. 273ff., notes that Augustus's actions were not received without criticism.

VIRTUS IN ROMAN LIFE AND LITERATURE   51

A generation later, Lucan further exemplifies the critical tradition that grew up after Augustus.[122] Like Ovid, he subverts Vergil's pro-Augustan voice in favor of the critical potential latent in Vergil's epic. Lucan satirizes the latest imperial "*Divus*" and the theology that had grown to anchor imperial ideology since 43 B.C.[123] He scoffs at the traditional narrative of Roman virtue and even more at its incarnation in the figure of a divinized emperor who could guarantee peace on earth.

Lucan's *Pharsalia* assaults the Roman imperial theology in its Vergilian form. In a web of intertextual allusions he attacks Augustus's descendant Nero by elevating the subversive voice in Vergil.[124] Where Vergil opened with Odysseus and sang of a "man," Lucan's ironic *Iliad* emphasizes the indiscriminate feuding of Rome's own leading clans:

> Of wars worse than civil across the Emathian plains / we sing, of law delivered unto crime [*iusque datum sceleri*] and a mighty people with its own conquering hand turned against its own flesh [*conversum viscera*] / of kindred battle lines [*cognatasque acies*], and after a broken compact / a struggle for dominion [*regni certatum*] by all the forces of the battered world, / of wickedness [*nefas*] in common, standards arrayed in opposition, eagles facing off, pikes threatening pikes.[125]

The facts of lawlessness, violence, war within families, and broken promises accuse the regime of failing every kind of virtue. Lucan goes on to satirize the notion of imperial apotheosis by mocking imperial panegyrics. In his edition, peace returns to Latium only after Nero's death, which will make the heavens rejoice. His mockery runs directly counter to the imperial story:

> When having turned over your post / you seek the stars at last, the kingdoms of glad heaven / shall receive you in [their] rejoicing pole / ... Then let the human race take comfort with arms laid down, / and let all peoples love one-another;

---

[122] E.g., Ovid, *Her.*, 7. For *Aen.* 4 as intertext see Howard Jacobson, *Ovid's Heroides* (Princeton, NJ: Princeton University Press, 1974), pp. 76ff. Also Joseph B. Solodow, *The World of Ovid's Metamorphoses* (Chapel Hill: University of North Carolina Press, 1988), pp. 154ff. See also Randall T. Ganiban, *Statius and Virgil: The Thebaid and the Reinterpretation of the Aeneid* (Cambridge: Cambridge University Press, 2009).

[123] Ando, *Imperial Ideology and Provincial Loyalty*, pp. 206ff.

[124] For discussion and bibliography, see Casali, "The *Bellum Civile* as an Anti-Aeneid," pp. 81–102. Also Roche, *Lucan: De Bello Civili*, pp. 21ff. For a summary of anti-Vergilian moments in Lucan, see Nicholas Horsfall, *A Companion to the Study of Virgil, Mnemosyne* (Leiden: Brill, 1995), pp. 268–272. Point of departure for modern discussion is E. Narducci, *Lucano: Un'epica Contra l'impero: Interpretazione della Pharsalia* (Rome: Laterza, 2002).

[125] Lucan, *Phars.*, 1.1–8 in *Lucan, The Civil War (Pharsalia)*, trans. J. D. Duff, Loeb Classical Library 220 (Cambridge, MA: Harvard University Press, 1928).

52   ROMAN VIRTUE IN THE EARLY CHRISTIAN THOUGHT OF LACTANTIUS

when peace has been sent throughout the world / let the iron gates of warlike Janus close.[126]

This statement of Lucan supports a broader critique of Roman virtue both in its traditional military and philosophical contexts. Lucan dwells most bitterly on the idea that Roman *virtus* had anything but a destructive role in Roman history. His scathing narrative moves from Nero to his predecessors, Julius Caesar and Pompey. Lucan argues that the Republic's false martial *virtus* led only to bloodshed. Referring to Caesar and Pompey, "rival *virtus* goaded them," he says.[127] But philosophical *virtus* did little better. Even the hero of Republican Stoicism does not escape his lashing. Cato's Stoic virtue is corrupted by the political concern that motivated it.[128] Taking a cue from Livy, Lucan ultimately singles out Romulus as the author of Rome's bloody cycle. *Pharsalia* 1.92–96 indicts the storied founder of Roman monarchy and predecessor to the Julio-Claudian line:

There will be no loyalty [*fides*] among neighbors when a kingdom is at stake, and supreme power / shall be impatient of a consort [*inpatiens consortis erit*] / Trust not in other peoples / nor let examples [*exempla*] of the fates be looked for abroad! / Rome's walls dripped first with a brother's blood. Nor then was earth and sea a prize for such great furor: a barren refugee-camp pitted lords against each other.[129]

Lucan inverts the theological implications of the ancient thought that *virtus* proves divine favor: if exemplary actions indicate the favor of the immortal gods, Romulus's fratricide was a prophecy of things to come. In Lucan's wake, what

[126] Cf. Lucan, *Phars.*, 1.45–47, 60–62.

[127] Cf. Lucan, *Phars.*, 2.120–121, "*stimulos dedit aemula virtus*," 1.161, "*rebus mores cessere secundis*," 1.175, "*mensuraque iuris / Vis erat.*" Also Roche, *Bellum Civile I*, p. 176: "Lucan imports the collocation *aemula virtus* from another classical civil war meditation, Horace, *Epod.*, 16.5, of the defection of Capua during the second Punic war. After Lucan, *V. Fl.* 5.86 and *Sil.* 1.510 redeploy the phrase in the same sense."

[128] Cf. Lucan, *Phars.*, 2.242–243 "[Brutus to Cato] *omnibus expulsae terris olimque fugatae Virtutis iam sola fides*," 2.258–260, "*Hoc solum longae pretium virtutis habebis: Accipient alios, facient te bella nocentem*"; and the truly ironic 2.323–325, where Cato's Stoic austerity stimulates passion: "*sic fatur, at acris / irarum movit stimulos iuvenisque calorem / excitat in nimios belli civilis amores.*" See W. R. Johnson, *Momentary Monsters: Lucan and His Heroes* (Ithaca, NY: Cornell University Press, 1987), esp. chapter 2, "Cato: The Delusions of Virtue," pp. 35–67; also R. Sklenář, *The Taste for Nothingness: A Study of Virtus and Related Themes in Lucan's Bellum Civile* (Ann Arbor: University of Michigan Press, 2003), pp. 59–101.

[129] Lucan, *Phars.*, 1.92–96, "*Nulla fides regni sociis, omnisque potestas / Inpatiens consortis erit. gentibus ullis / Credite nec longe fatorum exempla petantur: / Fraterno primi maduerunt sanguine muri. / Nec pretium tanti tellus pontusque furoris / Tunc erat: exiguum dominos commisit asylum.*"

remains is only the husk of a myth exposed as the true source and mask of imperial criminality and violence.

Conclusion

Before the coming of Jesus, before the New Testament or the writing of any Latin Christian text, there existed already a discourse about virtue (*virtus*) in Rome. The primary topic of that discourse was Rome and its people in their relationship with the ancestral divinities. Romans imagined themselves as a people distinguished by *virtus* and explained their political rise and dominion as a gift of the gods given because of that ancient and distinctive *virtus*. For that reason, they also traded claims in terms of *virtus*, negotiating and renegotiating its meaning in the rough and tumble of their bitter political rivalries. The great artistic and literary achievements of the Late Republic and of the Augustan era were a watershed in that conversation. They provided the hermeneutical lens by which Romans interpreted their ancient narratives to suit the new empire of Augustus and his heirs. With their help, Augustan society molded Rome's traditional self-portrait into a new imperial image. After Augustus, *virtus* became a mark of the Roman people by mediation and derivation from the imperial office.

Not everyone was happy. The Augustan myth of Rome's restoration papered over a history that was too violent and too recent to be forgotten by any thoughtful observer. Although Romans agreed that *virtus* was the vocabulary for expressing their ideal self-image, they never agreed on its basic definition. From the devastating civil wars of the late Republic, to the ham-fisted marriage laws of Augustus, to the divine absurdity of Nero ordering Seneca's suicide, elite Romans had ample reason to question the imperial order. And many did. Roman literature expresses their criticism at first obliquely, then ever more explicitly. What results is the image of an imperial Rome whose polished exterior poorly conceals deep and abiding fissures.

This history of celebratory discourse and its rhetorical subversion laid the foundation for an even more thoroughgoing reconfiguration of *virtus* among Latin Christians. Latin Christian apologists would exploit known cracks in the Roman imagination in order to divide their opposition and thus make room for a reconstruction of ideal *virtus* conformed to the image of Jesus. In linking this unlikely figure to long-standing ideas of divinely ordained imperial virtue, Latin Christianity developed a discernible tradition rooted in the arguments of its earliest advocates—but that is getting ahead of things. At this point, what must be grasped is that the primary referent for any talk of *virtus* in the Latin world was the history of Rome and her arguments about Roman virtue among Rome's leading families. Ideal notions of *virtus* were a primary subject of Rome's great literary epics, a preoccupation of philosophical discourse, and a central locus of political competition. Philosophical and theological discourse about *virtus* emerged under the pressure of that political competition and was shaped by its specifically social aims. Hence, talk of virtue in the Roman world always was a discussion of the meaning and nature of the Roman order itself.

2

Power and *Virtus* from Republic to Principate

Criticism of Rome's ancient self-image was not reserved to poets and historians. In the years that separate Cicero's youthful study in Athens (79–77 B.C.) from Lucan's mockery of Nero (61 A.D.), the Roman upper classes sought a new ideological basis for their traditional order in the philosophy and literature of the Hellenistic schools. As Katharina Volk explains, "Learned Romans of the late Republic were engaged in the project of Romanizing philosophy. . . . At the same time, members of the same class—and often the very same men—dedicated themselves to the study of what they perceived as fundamentally Roman: their own history, political and religious institutions, language, literature, and customs."[1] Their efforts involved substantial debate in both public oratory and literature about the content and worth of Rome's traditional ideals of *virtus*. That debate rendered traditional notions of *virtus* simultaneously more precise and more flexible by drawing technical terms and arguments from Hellenistic philosophy. Cicero and Lucretius were principal architects of the new Latin idiom. In their works, *virtus* could express not only the traditional capacities of a Roman warrior (*virtus*) but also his moral competencies and, later, the distinct powers (*virtutes/vires*) that named Rome's divinities and justified the elevation of great men to their number. After Cicero and Lucretius, Sallust, Vergil, Livy, Seneca, and Lucan all witness to the new developments in Roman thought and language.[2] Their writings shaped the Latin language that became a principal vehicle for Roman imperial discourse and, later, for early Latin Christian theology.

---

[1] This work by Katharina Volk, *The Roman Republic of Letters: Scholarship, Philosophy, and Politics in the Age of Cicero and Caesar* (Princeton, NJ: Princeton University Press, 2021), is among the latest in a growing body of research reconsidering the intersection of religious, philosophical, and political discourses in ancient Rome. See also Claudia Moatti, *The Birth of Critical Thinking in Republican Rome*, trans. Janet Lloyd (Cambridge University Press, 2015); Andrew Wallace-Hadrill, *Rome's Cultural Revolution* (Cambridge: Cambridge University Press, 2008); Denis Feeney, *Caesar's Calendar: Ancient Time and the Beginnings of History* (Berkeley: University of California Press, 2007).

[2] See Arnaldo Momigliano, "The Theological Efforts of the Roman Upper Classes in the First Century BC," in *Roman Religion*, ed. Clifford Ando (Edinburgh: Edinburgh University Press, 2003), pp. 157–161; also, Attilio Mastrocinque, "Creating One's Own Religion: Intellectual Choices," in *A Companion to Roman Religion*, ed. Jörg Rupke (Oxford: Wiley-Blackwell, 2011), pp. 378–392.

Roman Virtue in the Early Christian Thought of Lactantius. Jason M. Gehrke, Oxford University Press.
© Oxford University Press 2025. DOI: 10.1093/9780197667781.003.0003

56   ROMAN VIRTUE IN THE EARLY CHRISTIAN THOUGHT OF LACTANTIUS

In order to explore the roots of Latin Christian discourse about *virtus*, this chapter first draws upon the work of one classical historian, Clifford Ando, and one patrologist, Michel Barnes, to observe the intersection of Roman imperial and Christian theological discourses in the first centuries A.D. The chapter then proceeds to examine in Lucretius and Cicero the basic language and causal models that provided elite Romans with a set of shared terms and logic—a philosophical grammar[3]—appropriated from Hellenistic philosophical discourses for the sake of elite Roman arguments at the end of the first century B.C. I attempt to place these philosophical discourses in their historical context and highlight their political referents. After examining Lucretius, the discussion provides a detailed chronological study of Cicero's reliance upon Hellenistic theories of mixture to redefine *virtus* in his political thought and ethics. The argument concludes by showing the diffusion of Ciceronian language and content in a broader Latin literature that informed Augustan and later imperial ideology. What results is a precise account of the philosophical assumptions that led to an expansive use of the term *virtus* in elite Roman discourse about divine and political order between Cicero and Seneca. In the way that others have carefully examined the development and continuity of Roman and Christian discourse about *religio*, this chapter explores the central terms of a political and philosophical conversation that would come to shape later controversies between Christian and non-Christian Romans in the later Empire.[4]

---

[3] For my use of the term "philosophical grammar" to describe ancient philosophy and theology, I am indebted to Lewis Ayres, *Nicaea and Its Legacy: An Approach to Fourth Century Trinitarian Theology* (Oxford: Oxford University Press, 2004), pp. 14–15, which defines "'grammar' as a set of rules or principles intrinsic to theological discourse, whether or not they are formally articulated. . . . Embedded within exegetical and philosophical argument were different rules for speaking about divinity." A still helpful examination of language in theology is George Linbeck, *The Nature of Doctrine: Religion and Theology in a Post-Liberal Age* (Louisville, KY: John Knox Press, 1984).

[4] With special import for Lactantius, Mattias Gassman, *Worshippers of the Gods: Debating Paganism in the Fourth-Century Roman West* (Oxford: Oxford University Press, 2020). Earlier, Duncan MacRae, *Legible Religion: Books, Gods, and Rituals in Roman Culture* (Cambridge, MA: Harvard University Press, 2016), pp. 5–6: "In the late Republic, books created, for the first time, a 'Roman religion' from the huge variety of polytheistic practices in Rome and its empire. In the centuries that followed, they decisively formed Roman imperial and early Christian conceptions of 'traditional Roman religion.'" Also, see Spencer Cole, *Cicero and the Rise of Deification at Rome* (Cambridge: Cambridge University Press, 2014); Peter van Nuffelen, *Rethinking the Gods: Philosophical Readings of Religion in the Post-Hellenistic Period* (Cambridge: Cambridge University Press, 2011), esp. pp. 101–121; *One God: Pagan Monotheism in the Roman Empire*, ed. Peter van Nuffelen and Stephen Mitchell (Cambridge: Cambridge University Press, 2010); *Monotheism between Pagans and Christians in Late Antiquity*, ed. Peter van Nuffelen and Stephen Mitchell (Leuven: Peeters, 2010); Clifford Ando, *The Matter of the Gods: Religion and the Roman Empire* (Berkeley: University of California Press, 2008). Earlier, *Pagan Monotheism in Late Antiquity*, ed. Polymnia Athanassiadi and Michael Frede (Oxford: Oxford University Press, 2002).

Roman Imperial Ideology: Framing Narratives

Two recent scholarly contributions provide clear criteria for characterizing the continuity and influence of classical Roman discourse about *virtus* in early Latin Christian theology. The first comes from Clifford Ando's attempt to characterize what he identifies as a Roman "imperial ideology" in terms that avoid anachronism but capture the reality of a broadly shared discourse elite Romans used both to articulate a rational account of the divine sanction for their regime and participate in its development outside of the Roman center. Ando explains that through a combination of circulated texts, public images, and communicative actions, successive imperial regimes succeeded at curating consensus about the legitimacy of Roman rule, even over subjected provincial peoples: "The emperors and the governing class at Rome did not have to provide their world with Scripture, but merely with a system of concepts that could shape, and in so doing slowly unite, the cultural scripts of their subjects."[5] By examining that system of concepts and exploring the mechanisms for its creation and adaptation, Ando documents a discourse that was intentionally flexible, subject to revision and re-imagination, and yet consistent enough in its basic elements to cultivate a wide agreement about Rome and its authority to rule in the ancient Mediterranean.[6]

Central to the Roman imperial ideology, Ando argues, was a theological notion of divine power and a carefully curated historiography. "At a superficial level, the Roman imperial government advertised to its subjects the existence of a shared history and a common political theology: the history was that of Rome in the era of her empire, and the one constant in the religious firmament was the emperor."[7] The central tropes of this Roman ideological discourse—the emperor as victor, *pater patriae, curator legum et morum*—were grounded in a religious notion of the imperial office. Successive emperors regarded Caesar Augustus as the archetype of a theological vision of the emperor—a deified figure, who mediated divine power. Accepting the title *Divi filius*, Augustus received the honor of Julius Caesar's deification by the Senate in 42 B.C. while technically postponing his own divine honors. Later emperors presented themselves

---

[5] Clifford Ando, *Imperial Ideology and Provincial Loyalty in the Roman Empire* (Berkeley: University of California Press, 2000), p. 23. Ando's *Imperial Ideology* made an early contribution to an emerging scholarly trajectory emphasizing continuity between classical Roman and early Christian concepts of religion with increasing appreciation for the interpenetration of philosophical discourse, political order, and religious praxis (See Volk, *Roman Republic of Letters*, pp. 241–261).

[6] For Ando's later work on the mechanisms of imperial discourse, see Clifford Ando, *Law, Language, and Empire in the Roman Tradition* (Philadelphia: University of Pennsylvania Press, 2011).

[7] Ando, *Imperial Ideology*, p. 23, and the section, "Consensus in Theory and Practice," pp. 131–174, for the procedure of cultivating consensus.

as Augustus's heirs and imitators. A façade of continuity presented the divinized emperor as an element of traditional culture and piety, which guaranteed the continuity of Rome's ancient order.[8] Of course, Augustus did not invent the idea of divinization. Roman political rhetoric and pageantry had been introducing Hellenistic notions of deification into the Roman milieu long before.[9]

Ando identifies a definite theological notion as the foundation of the imperial ideology he traces. He understands imperial claims to divinity as predicated upon a "shared set of beliefs about the nature and extent of the emperor's power."[10] In this sense, "power" does not refer only to political authority but also to a technical notion. Ando says that imperial actions "implied . . . that the ruler was credited with potentialities operating beyond the range of his presence and even of his direction."[11] The emperor's "potentialities" were expressed first in his military prowess but extended beyond it. They included "a certain diffused power [*potestas diffusa*]" that could resupply gaps in the food supply, convey the emperor swiftly across the realm, and above all, establish justice and piety through his example.[12] Quoting Arthur Darby Nock, Ando argues that "from [an ancient] interest in 'ἡ τοῦ θεοῦ δύναμις' we could understand the habit 'of investing one deity with the attributes of others': By so representing the god you invested him with an accumulation of powers."[13] Ando argues that scholars should "use this framework to understand how emperors were assimilated to gods."[14] Among others, he finds in Diocletian, Lactantius's one-time employer, an example of an emperor whose divinity was expressed through "potentialities" that guaranteed Rome's military, agricultural, and moral harmony.[15]

Ando further argues that imperial ideological discourse penetrated deep into the thought-world of early Christianity. The notion of imperial divine powers, he suggests, expressed in a range of the emperor's "other qualities and deeds," can explain Christian opposition to the imperial cult.[16] In doing so, he warns

---

[8] See Ando, *Imperial Ideology*, pp. 37–39.

[9] See Chapter 1, this volume. Also, Spencer Cole, *Cicero and the Rise of Deification at Rome*; Stefan Weinstock, *Divus Julius* (Oxford: Clarendon Press, 1971).

[10] Ando, *Imperial Ideology*, p. 388: *maiestas*, divine majesty; θεότης (*theotes*), divinity, godhead. This term appears, for example, in Romans 1:20, referring to God's "invisible power and Godhead (ἥ τε ἀΐδιος αὐτοῦ δύναμις καὶ θειότης)." For δύναμις in Paul, see Jonathan Hill, "The Self-Giving Power of God: *Dunamis* in Early Christianity," in *Divine Powers in Late Antiquity*, ed. Anna Marmodoro and Irini-Fotini Viltanoiti (Oxford: Oxford University Press, 2017), pp. 127–140. Hill attempts to "fill the gap in [Michel] Barnes' overview" by focusing on the period from the New Testament to Justin Martyr, overlapping with imperial history between the Julio-Claudians up to the Antonine emperors.

[11] Ando, *Imperial Ideology*, p. 386.

[12] Ando, *Imperial Ideology*, pp. 387–389. He refers to Horace, Valerius Maximus, and Menander for the idea that "rains in season, abundance from the sea, unstinting harvests come happily to us because of the emperors' justice."

[13] Ando, *Imperial Ideology*, p. 387.

[14] Ando, *Imperial Ideology*, p. 387.

[15] Ando, *Imperial Ideology*, pp. 398–404.

[16] Ando, *Imperial Ideology*, p. 394.

that "unwillingness to countenance a scale of divine potentialities that included both Augustus and Christ can only impede attempts to understand the foreign thought-world of the ancient Mediterranean."[17] Hence also, understanding the scale of divine potentialities might explain why Christians could use language that also appeared in Roman imperial discourse about the relationship between traditional divinities and imperial claims to divinization. Ancient Christians could use terms like *numen* as a reference to the Christian God and the emperor interchangeably, while Greek-speaking subjects translated Latin political terms like *maiestas* as θεότης, which had a long life in Christian theology.[18] Still, Ando seems to think modern people may not be able to grasp the inner logic of this imperial discourse about human beings and divinity. He concedes that "even if we lack the apparatus to understand ancient belief and the terminology to describe it, we should not underestimate its power."[19] Ando thus points to the significance of an imperial discourse about gods and human beings, which shaped Roman political culture and self-understanding.

Recent scholarship in historical theology and philosophy has provided the conceptual apparatus needed to understand the ancient discourse that Ando regards as a "political theology."[20] In the last thirty years, historical scholars have sharpened our understanding of ancient metaphysical and theological discourses focused on the term "power" and their influence in the ancient Mediterranean. Most notable for this study is the work of Michel Barnes, who traced a technical sense of the term "power" (*virtus*, *vis*, *dynamis*) from its roots in pre-Socratic writers and Hippocrates, through Empedocles, Democritus, and most significantly Plato, to a range of ancient Christian theologies.[21] According to Barnes, Plato developed models of being and causation from medical notions of δύναμις that influenced a range of philosophical and early Christian theologies in the early Roman Empire. By the fourth century, "the technical sense of power" provided early Christian theology with "a scripturally-based term, authoritative in the tradition, given content and nuance by philosophy, and—by the fourth century—having a rich history in trinitarian theology."[22] Barnes coined the

---

[17] Ando, *Imperial Ideology*, p. 391.

[18] Ando, *Imperial Ideology*, p. 391.

[19] Ando, *Imperial Ideology*, p. 391.

[20] Ando, *Imperial Ideology*, p. 23.

[21] For a broader account of medical influences in Greek philosophic traditions at Alexandria and Rome, see Vivian Nutton, *Ancient Medicine*, 2nd ed. (New York: Routledge, 2013), pp. 116ff.

[22] Michel R. Barnes, *The Power of God: Dynamis in Gregory of Nyssa's Trinitarian Theology* (Washington, DC: Catholic University of America Press, 2001), p. 1. Barnes's work on δύναμις has influenced historical accounts of a range of early Christian authors and thus provides terms for identifying conceptual continuity across ancient writers. See Pui Him Ip, *Origen and the Origins of Divine Simplicity before Nicaea* (University of Notre Dame Press, 2022); Stephen E. Waers, *Monarchianism and Origen's Early Trinitarian Theology* (Leiden: Brill, 2022); Andy Radde-Gallwitz, *Gregory of Nyssa's Doctrinal Works: A Literary Study* (Oxford: Oxford University Press, 2018); Adam Ployd, *Augustine, the Trinity, and the Church: A Reading of the Anti-Donatist Sermons* (Oxford: Oxford University Press, 2015), esp. pp. 7, 144–184; Anthony Briggman, *Irenaeus of Lyons*

terms "power causality" and then "power theology" to name this philosophical grammar, used among patristic authors, both Latin and Greek, from Origen and Tertullian to the first Nicene Council, and in authors diverse as Origen, Hilary of Poitiers, and Gregory of Nyssa.[23] Barnes's term "power causality" involves a set of interrelated notions that provided certain characteristic terms and rules—a philosophical grammar—for ancient debate about divine and natural order. These notions provide the criteria for my attempt to characterize Roman imperial discourses in Latin and demonstrate their relationship to early Latin Christian thought. What Barnes calls "the technical sense of power" describes a common notion that makes it possible to compare claims across sectarian boundaries (e.g., Stoic, Epicurean, Christian) of religious and philosophical discourse.

According to Barnes, power causality entails four interrelated notions that developed out of ancient medicine and mixture theory. First and foremost, ancient medical writers conceived of "a power [δύναμις]" as an irreducible and individual material cause—fundamentally, as the "capacity of an existent to affect." As Barnes explains, "This *capacity to affect* is understood in three related ways. First, δύναμις is the capacity of an existent to affect insofar as it exists. . . . What is meant by 'to exist' is in large part the capacity to affect or to be affected."[24] This foundational notion necessitates a second. Any given "δύναμις is that *capacity* that is peculiar to an existent . . . that causal capacity, which follows not simply from the fact of existence, but from the *identity* of the existent. Fire, to take a famous example, has the δύναμις of heat, because . . . the δύναμις of heat follows specifically from what fire is."[25] This kind of causality Barnes terms "*X from X*," or

and the Theology of the Holy Spirit (Oxford: Oxford University Press, 2012); Mark Delcogliano, "The Interpretation of John 10:30 in the Third Century: Anti-Monarchian Polemics and the Rise of Grammatical Reading Techniques," *Journal of Theological Interpretation* 6.1 (2012): pp. 117–138; Carl Beckwith, *Hilary of Poitiers on the Trinity: From De Fide to De Trinitate* (Oxford: Oxford University Press, 2009); Andrew Radde-Gallwitz, *Basil of Caesarea, Gregory of Nyssa, and the Transformation of Divine Simplicity* (Oxford: Oxford University Press, 2009); Ayres, *Nicaea and Its Legacy*.

[23] My study relies on Barnes because his account of "power causality" provides the clearest point of reference for characterizing continuities between the Latin authors who interest me. However, there are actually two modern scholarly trajectories developing ancient δύναμις-causalities of which readers should be aware—Barnes and his influence in early Christianity, but also Anna Marmodoro developing from the work of Richard Sorabji in philosophy. See Anna Marmodoro, *Forms and Structure in Plato's Metaphysics* (Oxford: Oxford University Press, 2022), esp. Chapter 3, "Plato's Forms as Powers," pp. 65–82. These trajectories occasionally intersect, as in *Divine Powers in Late Antiquity*, ed. Anna Marmodoro and Irini-Fotini Viltanoiti (Oxford: Oxford University Press, 2017). In a more contemporary philosophical mode, Anna Marmodoro, *The Metaphysics of Powers: Their Grounding and Their Manifestations* (New York: Routledge, 2010). Earlier, Richard Sorabji, *Matter, Space, and Motion: Theories in Antiquity and Their Sequel* (Ithaca, NY: Cornell University Press, 1988).

[24] Michel R. Barnes, "One Nature, One Power: Consensus Doctrine in Pro-Nicene Polemic," *Historica, Theologica et Philosophica, Critica et Philologica* 29 (1997): p. 205.

[25] Barnes, "One Nature, One Power," p. 206.

"like from like," causality and documents its broad currency in early Christianity. It is the idea that the activity of any given product manifests the cause and thus makes the identity of that cause evident in its action.[26] Such a notion of specific causal capacities named from their effects led to a debate about how to understand the true identity of complex existents as diverse as bread, rabbits, and humans. Namely, which particular capacity disclosed the identity of an existent in which a multiplicity of powers (heat, cold, swiftness, reason) were evident? The question led to a third "sense of δύναμις as . . . the different capacities that are not exclusive to an existent. For example, fire has the δύναμις of being ever-moving, but so does intelligence."[27] By this distinction, ancient writers understood that complex existents contained a plurality of powers operating in union. The union of such powers in a complex entity was termed a "nature (*physis*, *natura*)," and this notion produced the phrase "power and nature" as a technical formula indicating the very identity or essence of a thing.[28] The fourth and final notion inherent to power causality is its empiricist epistemology. Because a power discloses an existent's identity through its effect, discourses based on a common notion of δύναμις held that the definition of a thing could be achieved by working backward from its effect to its nature.[29] Observing heat, one could discern the fact of fire and its character as a heating thing. As shall be seen, this presupposition is evident in claims about divinity ranging from Cicero's vision of Romulus to Tertullian's Christology. It is basic to Roman exemplary discourse after Cicero and permeates Latin discourse about deified heroes and the *virtus* of Christian martyrs.

The contributions of Ando and Barnes suggest that modern historians of antiquity, and particularly of Christianity, have substantially overlooked the mutual influence of technical theological and public political discourse in imperial Rome. Their accounts intersect in Tertullian (d. 220 A.D.). Ando identifies Tertullian's use of political metaphors at *Apol.* 24.3 and *Prax.* 2.3–5 as evidence of the "daily onslaught of Roman images" propagating the imperial vision of a "*singulare et unicum imperium.*"[30] Ando regards such language as an "analogy with the terminology and representatives of imperial domination."[31] And yet, like most historians of Latin trinitarian theology, Barnes points to the same texts and language as not mere analogy but rather as foundational source for Latin

---

[26] Barnes, *Power of God*, pp. 31–32, 56ff., 105ff.

[27] Barnes, "One Nature, One Power," p. 206.

[28] Michel R. Barnes, "Power and Nature as a Formula," pp. 37–44, in Michel R. Barnes, *The Power of God: Dynamis in Gregory of Nyssa's Trinitarian Theology* (Washington, DC: Catholic University of America Press, 2000).

[29] Harold W. Miller, "*Dynamis* and *Physis* in *On Ancient Medicine*," *American Philological Association* 83 (1952): pp. 184–197, quoted in Barnes, *Power of God*, p. 39.

[30] Tertullian, *Prax.*, 3, cited in Ando, *Imperial Ideology*, p. 42.

[31] Ando, *Imperial Ideology*, pp. 42–43.

62 ROMAN VIRTUE IN THE EARLY CHRISTIAN THOUGHT OF LACTANTIUS

trinitarian theology in the first six centuries of Christianity.[32] The intersection of their work suggests that patrologists have mainly treated trinitarian theology as a discourse abstracted from its imperial context, while historians have not fully considered the relationship between elite Roman discourse about divinity and early Christian attempts to articulate their Christian understanding. For that reason, this chapter traces the history of Latin philosophical and political discourse centered on the term "power" (δύναμις, *virtus, potestas, vis*) with a view to its historical context and political concerns. Doing so will allow us to better appreciate the relationship between Latin trinitarian thought and the Roman sources that early Latin Christians used, while also shifting the conceptual and textual horizon that governs modern scholarly approaches to Lactantius.

Epicurean *Virtus*: The Power and Nature of the Soul

The earliest clear occurrence of the technical sense of power in Latin literature appears in Lucretius's (d. 50s B.C.) *De rerum natura*.[33] A philosophical epic, the poem belongs to that era "of unsurpassed philosophical upheaval in the Greco-Roman world," when Roman intellectuals began to rethink Rome's traditional ideals by drawing upon Greek thought.[34] Lucretius offers the most radical attack upon traditional notions of *virtus* prior to Lucan's *Pharsalia*. He argues that Rome's mistaken religious notions are the cause of its upheaval. By his account, religion causes a fear of death, which men aim to escape through the glory of violence put on display. In traditional Roman fashion, he couches his argument as a true adherence to the *mos maiorum*. Lucretius claims that the martial ideal of *virtus* departs from Rome's ancient *mores*: "One man [it moves] to violate modesty [*pudorem*], another to break the bonds of friendship [*amicitiae*], and in the height of passion to revolt against piety [*in summa pietatem evertere suasu*]."[35] By rejecting martial *virtus, De rerum natura* attacks the theological underpinnings of Rome's traditional order. Lucretius redefines *virtus* in philosophical terms.[36]

In contrast to this martial *virtus, De rerum natura* dramatizes Epicurus as a paradoxical sort of hero, who liberates humanity by conquering the false notions that spur men to battle. Lucretius draws upon Epicurean thought to argue that death brings simply a dissolution of the soul into its physical elements. Much as

---

[32] Barnes, *Power of God*, pp. 94–173.
[33] See David Sedley, *Lucretius and the Transformation of Greek Wisdom* (Cambridge: Cambridge University Press, 1998), p. 62.
[34] Sedley, *Lucretius and the Transformation of Greek Wisdom*, pp. 62–93.
[35] Lucretius, *Nat. r.*, 4.82–84, in *Lucrèce: De La Nature I*, ed. Claude Rambaux (Paris: Les Belles Lettres, 1990). Cf. 5.43, 5.73.
[36] Lucretius, *Nat. r.*, 2.37–46, 53.

POWER AND *VIRTUS* 63

Sallust would promote the "*animi virtus*" of kings, Lucretius praises Epicurus's "*vivida vis animi*" as an "*animi virtus*" conquering in a battle with false religion:

> When human life lay shamefully before all eyes / sprawled upon the earth, crushed by the heavy burden of religion / which showed its head from the regions of heaven / threatening mortals from above by its terrible visage / a Greek, a mortal man, first dared to raise his eyes in defiance, first to stand against it. / Neither the stories of the gods, nor lightning, nor the rush of threatening / heavens constrained him, but so much more he roused the *virtus* of his mind [*animi virtutem*] and first desired . . . to break the bolts of nature's doors. / Thus did the vital power of his mind [*vivida vis animi*] conquer [*pervicit*] and proceed far beyond the world's flaming walls. / In mind and soul [*mente animoque*] he journeyed over every vast expanse / whence as victor [*victor*] he reports to us what is able to come into existence [*possit oriri*] and what cannot, and by what reason there is in each thing a defined power [*finita potestas*] and deep inherent end. / Thereby, religion trampled under foot is crushed in turn; his victory makes us equal to heaven.[37]

Lucretius inscribes a philosophical ideal onto the old heroic canvas. It is not Aeneas, nor Romulus and Marcellus, but Epicurus, whose *virtutes* raise humanity to the plane of deity. Epicurus wanders, Odysseus-like, over the earth and wages war before the flaming walls, not of Troy but of the cosmos. Storming heaven, he travels not on foot, but by the *virtus* of his mind and soul (*animi virtutem*), which is otherwise termed "the power belonging to reason [*sit haec rationi potestas*]."[38] Lucretius's philosophic hero storms the gates of a once mysterious universe to conquer the gods and heaven (*compressit caelum*). As Whitmarsh observes, "His victory consists in mastery of scientific fact."[39] Lucretius makes Epicurus a theomach, whose "power of reason" overcomes Rome's military dreams and the religious notions that sustained them.

Lucretius redescribes Epicurus in Roman heroic terms precisely to redistribute heroic honors from the battlefield to the Garden. His effort relies on the vocabulary of "power and nature" and the underyling discourse of power causality. Lucretius's term "*finita potestas*" translates the older Greek notion of "powers" as specific material causes whose activities are synonymous with existence (*possit oriri*). He has no deeper vocabulary for saying what is. Lucretius

---

[37] Lucretius, *Nat. r.*, 1.62–79. Cf. *Nat. r.*, 5.43, which counts Epicurus among the gods, and *Nat. r.*, 5.73, for gigantomachy.

[38] Lucretius, *Nat. r.*, 2.37–46, 53.

[39] Timothy Whitmarsh, *Battling the Gods: Atheism in the Ancient World* (New York: Knopf, 2015), p. 173; Pradit Chauduri, *The War with God: Theomachy in Roman Imperial Poetry* (Oxford: Oxford University Press, 2014), pp. 56–63.

invokes Empedocles, Democritus, and Epicurus as his sources for the thought.[40] Later lines use all of the remaining notions inherent in power causality, as Barnes defined them. Lucretius explains every complex entity as a mixture of powers. Lucretius uses *potestas*, *vis*, and *natura* to render Epicurean physical theories:

> Within nature [*in natura*] there is nothing / which is composed of a single element [*exo uno genere*] / nor anything which does not exist by a mixture of seeds [*seminum*]. / By the many potencies [*potestates*] a power possesses [*vis*], it shows that it contains in itself many kinds of principals / and many diverse forms [*plurima principiorum in sese genera ac varias docet esse figuras*].[41]

Lucretius's juxtaposition of *semina*, *vis*, and *potestates* reveals that his fundamental concept of nature relies on the basic conceptualities of mixture theory. He presents any given existent as a cooperation of powers located "*in natura*." Even his distinctively Epicurean term *seminum* is a more technical term designating "*potestates*" and "*vis*"—which is to say that whatever a *seminum* is, it is a power. The innumerable potential combinations of powers bring about the various kinds of existents that people experience in nature.[42] Lucretius's terms "seeds" and later "atoms" articulate the basic notion of a material cause operating according to its distinctive identity (*finita potestas*). Behind the technical vocabulary of *elements*, *principles*, and *forms* stands the notion of specific material causal capacities.

Lucretius reveals the intellectual geneology of his Epicurean thought as he elaborates his Epicurean physical theory as an argument for the mortality of the soul.[43] As Barnes observed, ancient medicine had developed "standard examples of . . . powers, [which] were hot, cold, wet, dry, sweet, sour, acidic, salty."[44] Lucretius defines the soul in these same elemental terms. His poetry reveals the underlying notions of a developing Latin philosophical lexicon:

---

[40] See Barnes, *Power of God*, pp. 26ff. Lucretius's veneration of Empedocles is notable. Empedocles was an early pioneer of the idea that there are four powers called elements, which combined to make the basis for all kinds of natures. Empedocles preceded Democritus and the atomists because he "did not believe in the absolute unity of true being." See also Myrto Garani, *Empedocles Redivivus: Poetry and Analogy in Lucretius* (New York: Routledge, 2007).

[41] Lucretius, *Nat. r.*, 2.583–587. Cf. Barnes, *Power of God*, pp. 44–47: "The point is repeatedly emphasized in *On Ancient Medicine* that no power acts alone since no power exists alone in isolation."

[42] Cf. Lucretius, *Nat. r.*, 1.72ff., 1.584ff., 5.82, 6.58ff. Exact parallels come as indirect questions, as at *Nat. r.*, 6.64–67, "*quid queat esse, quid nequeat, finita potestas denique cuique quondam sit ratione atque alte terminus haerens.*"

[43] For introduction to Epicureanism, see *The Oxford Handbook of Epicurus and Epicureanism*, ed. Phillip Mitsis (Oxford: Oxford University Press, 2023).

[44] See Barnes, *Power of God*, p. 31.

POWER AND *VIRTUS* 65

The primordial principles [*primordia principiorum*] rush around intermingled /
such that no single one can be separated, nor does any power [*potestas*] become
divided from the rest. Rather, even as many, they exist as the power of one body
[*quasi multae vis unius corporis extant*]. / Just as in the common flesh of any
kind of animal there is smell and a specific color and taste, and nevertheless, out
of all these there is one complete mass of body, / so also, heat, and air, and the
blind power [*potestas*] of wind / create one nature [*creant unam naturam*], when
mixed along with that motive / force [*vis mobilis*], which distributes to each from
itself the beginning of motion [*initium motus ab se*], / the sense-bringer whence
the first movement is born in the flesh. For deep down this nature [*natura*] lies
hidden and subsists below, / nor is there anything below this in our body, / and
so it is itself the soul of the whole soul [*anima est animae proporro totius ipsa*].[45]

Lucretius's description of the soul develops technical Latin vocabulary to communicate the Hippocratic notion in which a nature (*natura*) denotes a unity of
powers operating in union (*creant unam naturam*). Lucretius uses the term *vis*
to describe an uncaused capacity of initial motion that itself consists in a combination of individual material powers (*potestates*). That underlying capacity
(*vis*) he designates as "soul." As the lines continue, it becomes evident that
Lucretius has no term more basic than power (*vis, potestas*) for speaking about
elemental being:

Just as in our members and our whole body a force of mind [*vis animi*] and a
power of soul [*animaeque potestas*] lies hid / intermingled in our bodies because it is created from a few small powers, so also in you this unnamed force
[*nominis haec expers vis*] lies as made [*facta*] of minute bodies, and so is the
soul of the whole soul and rules in the whole body [*animae quasi totius ipsa
proporrost anima et dominatur corpore toto*].[46]

David Mehl explains that these lines "describe the mixture of the components
and the effects caused by different proportions. Lucretius declares first that the
components are mixed in such a way that one cannot be separated from the
others and that together they exist as one force, although the fourth component originates motion."[47] Put otherwise, Lucretius seems to identify *vis* as the

---

[45] Lucretius, *Nat. r.*, 3.263–275. Cf. 3.240–255.

[46] Lucretius, *Nat. r.*, 3.275–281. For Epicurean "*minima*," see David Konstan, "Atoms" in *The
Oxford Handbook of Epicurus and Epicureanism*, ed. Phillip Mitsis (Oxford: Oxford University
Press, 2020), pp. 59–80. For the Epicurean referents Lucretius attempts to capture by *anima* and *an-
imus*, see David Mehl, "The Intricate Translation of the Epicurean Doctrine of ΨΥΧΗ in Book 3 of
Lucretius," *Philologus* 143.2 (1999): p. 283.

[47] This is not to disagree generally with David Mehl, "The Intricate Translation of the Epicurean
Doctrine of ΨΥΧΗ," pp. 272–287.

66 ROMAN VIRTUE IN THE EARLY CHRISTIAN THOUGHT OF LACTANTIUS

material of what a *natura* is and *potestas* as the term for specific capacities or elements (e.g., fire) inherent in that nature. He represents the unity of the *natura* as consisting in the inseparability of the *potestates*. And, important for later discourse, Lucretius conceives of this *vis* and *potestates* as the basic content of the term *anima*. That is, the notion of power explains what *anima* means, but *anima* does not explain *vis*. Because his notion is materialist, Lucretius regards the soul as entirely knowable. There is no distinction between the power and the soul's very identity. The *natura* simply is a union of material causes.

Lucretius's argument is a good place to observe the process by which Latin philosophy would attach ethical value (*virtus*) to the physical notion of force or power (*vis*, *potestas*), and the context that motivated such a shift. *De rerum natura* is not attempting new scientific advances. Its concerns are social and political. Lucretius argues from the identification of material powers that the soul is mortal. In his thinking, that recognition of mortality undermines the ideology that inspired Roman elite rivalry with all its catastrophic consequences. In his thinking, a better account of the powers of nature renders fear of death or desire for eternal glory inane.

Lucretius thus calls upon Hellenistic philosophy to provide a materialist foundation for his vision of political order.[48] His concern motivates a lexical shift in the term *virtus*. Lucretius redefines *virtus* by narrowing its signification to a precise causal notion, which allows him to make immortality the product not of martial courage but the "power belonging to reason [*haec rationi potestas*]."[49] *Virtus* becomes synonymous with the activity by which that *potestas* rules the greater body. Lucretius wishes that this same *animi virtus* could master (*dominatur*) the body politic as well. In his thinking, a change in the underlying physics produces a change in moral vision. Notably, neither Lucretius nor his readers would regard him as confusing the meaning of *virtus*, since even martial *virtus* had been conceived as a cause.[50] Rather, Lucretius uses Epicurean philosophy to narrow and specify the kind of cause that *virtus* is and thus exclude notions he regards as false and dangerous.

After Lucretius, Cicero's *De natura deorum* witnesses to Epicurean thought at Rome. His character Velleius relies upon the vocabulary of power causality to reinterpret traditional Roman religion in a distinctively Epicurean mode. Velleius couches Epicurean philosophy in causal terms that take *vis* as the underlying cause of all things. He names a "supreme capacity of infinity [*summa vis infinitatis*]," which he regards as a worthy object of contemplation (*magna ac*

---

[48] Lucretius, *Nat. r.*, 6.1138–1286. Cf. Cicero, *Fin.*, 1.64, in Marcus Tullius Cicero, *On Ends*, trans. H. Rackham, Loeb Classical Library 40 (Cambridge, MA: Harvard University Press, 1914).

[49] Lucretius, *Nat. r.*, 2.37–46, 53.

[50] See Chapter 1, this volume. Compare Lucretius's *dominatur* here to *dominatu* in the speech of Balbus, *Nat. d.*, 2.29.

diligenti contemplatione dignissima est), but one that should not be designated as god in any sense implying a providential capacity. Still, he says that "in that power it must be understood that nature exists [*in qua intellegi necesse est eam esse naturam*]."[51] By the phrase "*in qua*," Velleius explains that *vis* represents the substance of what is meant by *natura*. Nature is a bundle of causal capacities united in an underlying power. Velleius uses this doctrine to reject the Stoic notion of providence.[52] He cannot distinguish between such material *vis* and *natura* or, perhaps better, existence itself.[53] He trades philosophical claims in causal terms.

As Velleius continues, he presents power causality as a common language of philosophical discourse among Stoic and Epicurean schools in the Late Republic. His comments suggest the precise point at which he disagrees with his Stoic interlocutor. Their positions rely commonly upon the terminology of "power and nature," but Velleius sees no need to number conscious oversight of human affairs (*sollertia*) among the fundamental capacities of nature (*infinitatis vis*). He draws support from other thinkers by presenting a taxonomy of positions offered in terms of power:

> Anaxagoras, who received his teaching from Anaximenes, was the first who thought that a manner [*modum*] and description [*descriptionem*] of all things should be given and described as the power and reason of an Infinite Mind [*mentis infinitae vi ac ratione dissignari . . . voluit*] . . . Strato, who is called "the naturalist" [*physicus*], thinks that every divine power [*omnem vim divinam*] has been seated in nature [*in natura*], which holds the causes [*causas habet*] of generation, growth, and diminution, but lacks any sense perception or form [*omni et sensu et figura*] . . . Zeno, moreover, as I come now to your people, Balbus, thinks that the natural law is divine and that this power [*eamque vim*] has its proper function [*obtinere*] in commanding what is right and forbidding the opposite.[54]

Velleius's description provides a genealogy of philosophical positions that opposed each other in the Roman world. He presents each of their claims as an

---

[51] Cicero, *Nat. d.*, 1.50 in *Cicero: De natura deorum*, ed. Otto Plasberg and Wilhelm Heinrich Ax (Stuttgardiae: Teubner, 1980). Cf. Cicero, *Nat. d.*, 1.54, and Lucretius, *Nat. r.*, 3.262, for *atoms* as *potestates* and *vires*. I will treat *De natura deorum* more fully below, but include Velleius here in order to conclude discussion of the Epicurean position.

[52] Cicero, *Nat. d.*, 1.54; Emidio Spinelli and Francesco Verde, "Theology," in *The Oxford Handbook of Epicurus and Epicureanism*, ed. Phillip Mitsis (Oxford: Oxford University Press, 2023), pp. 94–117, suggest reasons to consider that Velleius's so-called atheism might be unfair, a lingering legacy of Stoic critique, in which case, we should take Lucretius as opposing not "theology," which he has, but rather *religio*, which he rejects (pp. 101–102).

[53] Barnes, "One Nature, One Power," p. 205.

[54] Cicero, *Nat. d.*, 1.35–1.37. Cf. *Nat. d.*, 1.25–1.43. Cf. 1.26. Cf. Lucretius, *Nat. r.*, 1.35.

68   ROMAN VIRTUE IN THE EARLY CHRISTIAN THOUGHT OF LACTANTIUS

interpretation of what "the power" is—the capacity of an infinite mind, a capacity for generation without sensible faculties, even a natural law, which operates to guide moral action. "Reason" itself is a kind of *vis*. This is not to reduce Velleius's Epicurean position to the views he rejects but rather to identify the point of agreement that makes his objection intelligible. Velleius rejects not the causal language and logic of Anaxagoras, Strato, and Zeno, but their interpretiation of its fundamental capacity.[55] Underlying consensus about the basic terms and logic actually enables him to disagree in clear terms.[56] Velleius thus disputes the Stoic view on three grounds. First, he accepts Epicurean atomic theory as a sufficient explanation for the appearance of rational arrangement. Hence, he views any interpretation of the *vis infinitatis* as rational or providential as unneccessary, given his underlying physical theory. As a result, he does not regard immortality as the end of politics.[57] Set in the context of Cicero's treatise, the whole argument depends upon the assumption of a shared language and logic that makes it possible for Velleius to reject a political ethic oriented toward immortality.[58]

Ciceronian *Virtus*: a Technical Vocabulary

The political and intellectual significance of Marcus Tullius Cicero needs no introduction. Like Lucretius, he sought in philosophy a rational foundation to shore up Rome's failing *virtus*. Claude Moatti summed it up well: "Against the disorder born of crisis . . . Cicero calls [Roman society] to Reason: it is Reason, which will allow him simultaneously to rethink tradition and authority, organize knowledge according to logical methods useful for the City, and define a true program of civic education necessary for the formation of the political leader."[59]

---

[55]   See Marmadoro, *Forms and Structure in Plato's Metaphysics*, pp. 12–34, 62ff., for a discussion of Anaxagoras's influence on Plato's power ontology. Especially given his review of Anaxagoras, Velleius's speech looks like a good example of debate over "an ontology comprising only powers," which she calls the *Eleatic Principle.*

[56]   This point is consistent with R. J. Hankinson, "Explanation and Causation," in *The Cambridge History of Hellenistic Philosophy*, ed. Keimpe Algra, Jonathan Barnes, Jaap Mansfeld, and Malcolm Schofield (Cambridge: Cambridge University Press, 1999), p. 499, noting that Epicurean and Stoic arguments often did involve underlying agreements: "Epicurus accepts the basic causal principles of conservation that underlie Stoic physics, since total annihilation and creation *ex nihilo* are impossible."

[57]   John M. Cooper, *Pursuits of Wisdom: Six Ways of Life in Ancient Philosophy from Socrates to Plotinus* (Princeton, NJ: Princeton University Press, 2012), on the Epicureans, pp. 226–305.

[58]   Cicero, *Nat. d.*, 1.1–2, frames the dialogue as a question about how to secure justice and piety for the *res publica* in general, and makes *cultus deorum* foundational to political community.

[59]   Claude Moatti, "Tradition et Raison chez Cicéron: l'émergence de la rationalité politique à la fin de la République romaine," *Mélanges de l'Ecole française de Rome Antiquité* 100.1 (1988): pp. 385–430. See also Claudia Moatti, *The Birth of Critical Thinking in Republican Rome*, trans. Janet Lloyd (Cambridge: Cambridge University Press, 2015). Also Yelena Baraz, *A Written Republic: Cicero's Philosophical Politics* (Princeton, NJ: Princeton University Press, 2012).

POWER AND *VIRTUS* 69

Cicero composed the most influential philosophical corpus in Latin literature. In order to realize his political vision, he studied with major figures of his day, especially Antiochus of Ascalon and Philo of Larissa. Cicero's letters and dialogues also remain a primary source for the Stoicism of Posidonius and Panaetius.[60] In addition, Cicero translated Aratus's Stoic *Phaenomena* and had direct contact with Plato's dialogues.[61] Cicero's well-known debt to Antiochus and Philo helps to explain his inevitable contact with philosophical notions of "power and nature" influenced by Hippocratic medicine. Although as a translator, Cicero had direct access to Plato's writings, the philosophy of Antiochus and Philo expressed (and influenced) a more recent culture of "medical eclecticism," which developed in Rome and Alexandria in the first century B.C., and especially in the aftermath of Mithridates's siege of Athens in 88 B.C.[62] As Myrto Hatzimichali has recently shown, since the turn of the first century B.C., Alexandrian doctors had "attempted [a] synthesis and combination of rival views from the other three systems [Rationalism, Empiricism, and Methodism]."[63] These "eclectic doctors" applied Hippocratic principles not only in medical treatment but also in epistemology, grammar, historiography, theology, and physical theory; they used the term "eclectic" not in a pejorative sense, but to name their intent to find the best outcome in thought and medicine for the sake of their art.[64] In the process, they

[60] *P. A. Brunt: Studies in Stoicism*, ed. Miriam Griffin and Alison Samuels (Oxford: Oxford University Press, 2013), pp. 180–242.

[61] For an overview of Cicero's philosophical career and influences, see Jonathan Barnes, "Antiochus of Ascalon," pp. 51–96, in *Philosophia Togata II: Plato and Aristotle at Rome*, ed. Jonathan Barnes and Miriam Griffin (Oxford: Clarendon Press, 1999). Carlos Lévy, "Cicero and the New Academy," in *The Cambridge History of Philosophy in Late Antiquity*, ed. Lloyd Gerson (Cambridge: Cambridge University Press, 2015). Further, *Philosophia Togata II: Plato and Aristotle at Rome*, ed. Jonathan Barnes and Miriam Griffin (Oxford: Clarendon Press, 1999). John Dillon, *The Middle Platonists: 80 B.C. to A.D. 220* (Ithaca, NY: Cornell University Press; reprint 1996), uses Cicero extensively to reconstruct Middle Platonism. For Cicero's translation of Plato, recently, *Aristotle, Plato, and Pythagoreanism in the First Century B.C.: New Directions for Philosophy*, ed. Malcolm Schofield (Cambridge: Cambridge University Press, 2013), esp. pp. 187–275, for essays by Sedley, Annas, and Gildenhard.

[62] For discussion and review of the common view reported by Strabo and Plutarch that Sulla's capture and subsequent removal of Aristotle's library in 84 B.C. renewed eclectic Aristotelianism in revolutionary Rome, see Jonathan Barnes, "Roman Aristotle," in *Philosophia Togata II: Plato and Aristotle at Rome*, ed. Jonathan Barnes and Miriam Griffin (Oxford: Clarendon Press, 1999), pp. 1–69, who does not utterly dismiss the history.

[63] See Myrto Hatzimichali, *Potamo of Alexandria and the Emergence of Eclecticism in Late Hellenistic Philosophy* (Cambridge: Cambridge University Press, 2011), pp. 20–33, "medical eclecticism." Also, Rebecca Flemming, "Antiochus and Asclepiades: Medical and Philosophical Sectarianism at the End of the Hellenistic Era," in *Antiochus of Ascalon*, ed. David Sedley (Oxford: Oxford University Press, 2012), pp. 55–79. Flemming also places Antiochus of Ascalon in the medical context (pp. 55, 65ff.) and describes the increasing influence of Asclepiades and the medical arts in Scribonius Largus, Pliny the Elder, and Celsus, who claimed that medicine was the genesis of philosophy (Celsus, *De medicina*, Pr. 6–9). Also, Rebecca Flemming, *Medicine and the Making of Roman Women: Gender, Nature, and Authority from Celsus to Galen* (Oxford: Oxford University Press, 2000).

[64] Hatzimichali, *Potamo of Alexandria*, p. 16, "The language of eclecticism . . . was widely used in philosophical, medical, and theological works to indicate a choice of the 'good' ideas of one's

70 ROMAN VIRTUE IN THE EARLY CHRISTIAN THOUGHT OF LACTANTIUS

created an intellectual culture in which "a process of codification and systematization of past achievement was prioritized . . . This is the atmosphere within which developments in Alexandrian philosophy took place in the first century B.C."[65]

Hatzimichali places Antiochus of Ascalon in Alexandria and Rome, as a leading influence upon this eclectic philosophical culture.[66] Notably, Cicero's letters and dialogues are the major source for Hatzimichali's account, which contributes to a growing consensus about the interpenetration of philosophical, medical, and rhetorical traditions in the first century.[67] Cicero's philosophical corpus reflects the eclectic approach of his major teachers, whose efforts were shaped by the same tides of Roman imperial politics that concerned him. Civic ambition also informed Cicero's approach to philosophical writing as a service to the Republic. In that service, he aimed not primarily to pronounce his own narrow view but to create a tradition of philosophical discourse in the Latin language that would entice his Roman peers.[68] Cicero thus coined much of what became the Latin philosophical lexicon in works that became widely read and used as the basis of elite education in later schools of rhetoric and law. All of the major Latin Christian writers from Tertullian to Augustine presume a considerable knowledge of Cicero on the part of their interlocutors.

By dramatizing real philosophical figures (e.g., Varro, Velleius, Balbus, et alii), Cicero invites the reader into conversations shaped by his own aims but which also witness to the elite intellectual climate of his day; the boundary between

---

predecessors." For a broader portrait of philosophical and medical interchange in Alexandria and Rome, see also Nutton, *Ancient Medicine*, pp. 130–141.

[65] Hatzimichali, *Potamo of Alexandria*, p. 33.

[66] See David Leith, "Medicine," in *The Oxford Handbook of Roman Philosophy*, ed. David Konstan (Oxford: Oxford University Press, 2023), pp. 379–397, noting that "cross-fertilization [between Hippocratic medicine and philosophy] was to persist after Greek medicine was transplanted to Rome. From the Late Republic on, interactions between medicine and philosophy were principally mediated by the medical *haireseis*, or 'sects' as they are conventionally called."

[67] E.g., *Aristotle, Plato, and Pythagoreanism in the First Century B.C.: New Directions for Philosophy*, ed. Malcolm Schofield (Cambridge: Cambridge University Press, 2013); John M. Cooper, *Knowledge, Nature, and the Good: Essays on Ancient Philosophy* (Princeton, NJ: Princeton University Press, 2004), pp. 10–46. A. A. Long, "Stoic Psychology," in *The Cambridge History of Hellenistic Philosophy*, ed. Keimpe Algra, Jonathan Barnes, Jaap Mansfeld, and Malcolm Schofield (Cambridge: Cambridge University Press, 1999), pp. 604, 607, for the influence of Hippocratic literature: "The boundaries of medicine and philosophy remained fluid, even if, because of the lack of evidence, it is almost always impossible to identify the exact direction of these flows and currents between philosophy and medicine." Earlier, *Ancient Medicine in Its Socio-Cultural Context*, vol. 2, *Papers Read at the Congress Held at Leiden University, 13–15 April 1992*, ed. H. F. J. Horstmanshoff, Philip J. van der Eijk, P. H. Schrijvers (Boston: Brill, 1995).

[68] See Elizabeth Rawson, *Cicero: A Portrait* (London: Bristol Classics Press, 1983), pp. 203–229. More recently, Andrew Lintott, *Cicero as Evidence: A Historian's Companion* (Oxford: Oxford University Press, 2008), pp. 215–253.

POWER AND *VIRTUS*   71

literature and history is porous and often transgressed.[69] Cicero's characters trade claims about the true nature (*natura*) of the Divine Power (*vis divina*), of human *virtus* (*virtus humana*), and of the natural world (*ordo rerum*); they share a philosophical vocabulary and logic but offer significantly different interpretations. Debates often turn on the technical sense of power. In this respect, Cicero's dialogues attest to a broader philosophical conversation that was reshaping Roman society in a period when Romans were concerned with reconciling their traditional understanding of the gods with growing discontent over Rome's civic ideal and new Hellenistic philosophical influences. His works became a fundamental touchstone for later elite Roman social and political discourse. And, although Syme did not think that any political philosophy distinct to Cicero directly informed the political program of Augustus, even he acknowledged in Augustan ideology "the resurgence of phrases and even of ideas, that were current in the previous generation."[70] Hence, in his Tacitean way, Syme acknowledged that "Augustus exploited with art and with success the traditional concepts and the consecrated vocabulary of Roman political literature" for which Cicero remains our best source, even if only because "the speeches of his peers and rivals have all perished."[71] The importance of Cicero's writings, in this sense, is manifest not only in literature but in the real political discourse of the Empire.[72] Because Cicero's works attest to a broad reliance on the technical sense of power, which has gone mainly overlooked, the following sections trace Cicero's translation of technical notions of "power" from his early rhetorical works to his later philosophical and political treatises.

Early Rhetoric: Power and Nature in *De Inventione*

Cicero's *De Inventione* (c. 86–83 B.C.) was written just after Sulla's siege of Athens caused the scattering of intellectuals that sent Philo and Antiochus to Rome and Alexandria. Cicero's earliest published treatise, it reflects his early education in

---

[69] See Jed W. Atkins, *Cicero on Politics and the Limits of Reason: The Republic and Laws* (Cambridge: Cambridge University Press, 2013), pp. 1–20. Because Cicero writes dialogues, which purport some verisimilitude to the historical positions of their dramatized figures, determining which speaker (e.g., Varro, Velleius, Balbus, et alii) represents Cicero himself can be a knotty problem. For my purposes, what matters is to see the way Cicero's texts witness to a shared discourse that enables a range of philosophical positions to be taken in a broader conversation about the foundations of divine and human order. Yet also, it is possible to trace a coherent theological vision across speakers by paying careful attention to the philosophical locus under discussion.

[70] Syme, *Roman Revolution*, p. 319.

[71] Syme, *Roman Revolution*, p. 319.

[72] Undoubtedly, Cicero's influence was indirect through the numerous Stoics who served in the imperial administration and certainly not exclusive; see P. A. Brunt, "Stoicism and the Principate," in *P. A. Brunt: Studies in Stoicism*, ed. Miriam Griffin and Alison Samuels (Oxford: Oxford University Press, 2013), pp. 275–309.

72   ROMAN VIRTUE IN THE EARLY CHRISTIAN THOUGHT OF LACTANTIUS

Greek rhetoric and philosophy.[73] It is a valuable source for characterizing the fundamental referents of his philosophical lexicon.[74] This early work develops a technical rhetorical vocabulary in which the technical language of "power and nature" and its underlying causal models play a central role. Although it is not possible or necessary to trace a specific medical source, it is notable that Cicero's language and logic strip away the materialist presuppositions of power causality but reflect its underlying causal assumptions. Cicero thereby distinguishes abstract rhetorical categories while defining the practice of law and oratory by analogy to medicine. In this context, Cicero offers an early definition of *virtus* that his later works would correct, amplify, and dramatize.

Cicero's early use of the technical sense of the term "power" is evident from the very beginning of *De inventione*, which suggests an awareness of the influence of medicine in his thought. Cicero prefaces the work by classifying oratory (*eloquentia artificiosa*) as a part of political science (*ratio civilis/scientia civilis*), but he rejects the idea that political science "is wholly comprehended in the power and artifice of the orator [*rhetoris vi et artificio contineri magnopere*]."[75] Cicero then distinguishes oratory from political science by the distinct function (*officium*) of this power, which he can also term as a faculty (*facultas*): "The function of eloquence [*officium eius facultatis*] seems to be to speak in a manner suited to persuade an audience; the end [*finis*] is to persuade by speech."[76] Cicero relates *facultas* to *finis* as a cause to its effect, and amplifies the explanation with a medical analogy: "In the case of the function we consider what is to happen [*in officio quid fieri*], in the case of the end [*in fine*], what result should be produced [*quid effici*]. For example, we say that the function of the physician is to treat the patient in a manner suited to heal him, the end is to heal by treatment."[77] In Cicero's more concrete terms, function and

---

[73] Guy Achard, *De l'invention* (Paris: Belles Lettres, 1994), and also H. M. Hubbell, *De Inventione. De optimo genere oratorum. Topica* (Cambridge, MA: Harvard University Press, 1949); A. Corbeill, "Rhetorical Education in Cicero's Youth," in *Brill's Companion to Cicero: Oratory and Rhetoric*, ed. Y. L. Too (Leiden: Brill, 2002), pp. 23–48. The precise date is estimated to fall between 84 and 83 B.C.

[74] Notably, A. A. Long, "Cicero's Plato and Aristotle," in *Cicero the Philosopher: Twelve Papers Edited and Introduced by J. G. F. Powell*, ed. J. G. F. Powell (Oxford: Clarendon Press, 1995), p. 39, objects to the habit of studying "the philosophic works of Cicero's later years ... in isolation from books that he wrote earlier, not only *De re publica* and *De legibus*, but also *De inventione* and *De oratore*." See also John Dugan, "Cicero's Rhetorical Theory," in *The Cambridge Companion to Cicero*, ed. Catherine Steel (Cambridge: Cambridge University Press, 2015), pp. 25–28; John Dugan, *Making a New Man: Ciceronian Self-Fashioning in the Rhetorical Works* (Oxford: Oxford University Press, 2005).

[75] Cicero, *Inv.*, 1.6 in Cicero, *De Inventione*, trans. H. M. Hubbell (Cambridge, MA: Harvard University Press, 1949; reprint, 1993), "*et ab eis qui eam putant omnem rhetoris vi et artificio contineri magnopere dissentimus.*" Cf. Cicero, *Inv.*, 1.27.41, "*facultates sunt aut quibus facilius fit aut sine quibus aliquid confici non potest.*" I use Hubbell's translation because in rendering Cicero's terms into a technical idiom for oratory, his translation illuminates the way *vis* and *virtus* undergird technical discussions.

[76] Cicero, *Inv.*, 1.6.

[77] Cicero, *Inv.*, 1.7.

end relate as *power* to *product*. Oratory is a capacity that belongs to political science, but it is one distinct capacity among several, one power in the nature of political science. His reference to medical treatment makes an apt analogy, perhaps because Cicero is aware that his basic empirical notion is traceable historically to Empiricist arguments in Hellenistic philosophy and in Plato.[78] Whatever the historical genealogy, Cicero knowingly applies causal models drawn from Greek medicine and physical theory to define oratory in terms of immaterial causal relations.

Cicero soon uses the term "power" (*vis*) to designate mutually exclusive abstract categories of rhetoric. *Vis* names the irreducible content of a topic as distinguished from others. For example, he explains that "a definitional issue [*constitutio definitiva*]" inquires about "the force of a term [*vis nominis*] ... defined in words," while a "qualitative issue [*constitutio generalis*]" examines "what kind of thing it is [*qualis res sit*] because the dispute concerns the the value and nature of the act [*de vi et de genere negotii*]."[79] Hubbell renders Cicero's "*de vi et de genere*" as "the value and nature." Beneath his elegant choice lies a concrete medical notion—in the search for definition, one examines the power of a thing.[80] Before approaching a case, the orator must observe its "power and nature" in order to find the remedy effective in each legal situation.[81] The line introduces two important concepts for Latin discourse. First, Cicero's phrase, *vis nominis*, echoes Plato's use of δύναμις to indicate "the sense or meaning of the word or name itself."[82] To name something means to identify the distinctive power that communicates its identity. Second, Cicero connects the notions of power and identity. His empirical test of the hypothesis casts the orator and lawyer as a kind of doctor performing a diagnostic task.

The remaining notions associated with power causality are evident as the work unfolds. Cicero relies upon the notion of a plurality of powers that combine to form a more singular complex existent. His remarks use the technical sense of power and its underlying philosophical grammar to distinguish issues at law. This distinction uses the notion of a power as an individual existent, which is exclusive of other powers and revelatory of a topic's nature:

---

[78] See also Cicero, *Inv.*, 1.7.

[79] Cicero, *Inv.*, 1.10. Cicero is here using *genus*, not *natura,* but Hubbell's translation is warranted by Cicero's meaning and his later usage. Cf. Cicero, *Inv.*, 2.37.110: "*omnino autem qui diligenter omnium causarum vim et naturam cognoverit.*"

[80] One possible explanation for this analogy is the influence of Asclepiades of Bythinia on Antiochus of Ascalon's epistemology; see David Leith, "Medicine," in *The Oxford Handbook of Roman Philosophy*, pp. 381ff.

[81] Dugan, "Cicero's Rhetorical Theory," pp. 27–28, explains that this passage reflects "status theory," which he says, "represents the orator-in-training with an elaborate menu that categorized various likely oratorical challenges he might face and offered suitable responses to those problems."

[82] See Barnes, *Power of God*, pp. 70–76, on "The Cratylus and the Linguistic Sense of Δύναμις."

74   ROMAN VIRTUE IN THE EARLY CHRISTIAN THOUGHT OF LACTANTIUS

No issue or sub-head of an issue can have its own scope and also include the scope of another issue [*potest simul et suam habere et alterius in se vim continere*], because each one is studied simply by itself and in its own nature [*una quaeque ex se et ex sua natura simpliciter*], and if another is added [*altera assumpta*], the number of issues is doubled [*numerus duplicatur*], but the scope of any one issue [*vis constitutionis*] is not increased [*augetur*]. Therefore, this issue, which we call the qualitative issue, seems to us to have two subdivisions, the legal and equitable.[83]

What Hubbell translates as "scope" is literally "the power [*vim*]," which Cicero defines as mutually exclusive from any other "power [*vim*]." One "power" cannot contain the "power" of another "*in itself* [*in se*]," since power indicates, by definition, what a thing is. Substituting the traditional powers of Hippocratic and later Hellenistic physical theory for Cicero's types of issues, one could say that when both "the hot" and "the cold" are present, the number of powers is doubled, but cold does not augment hot because their natures are exclusive.[84] Barnes's characterization of Plato aptly describes this line: "[Cicero] has stripped away the materialist assumptions of Hippocratic power causality," while preserving the underlying logic and terminology.[85] He adapts medical and elemental language to rhetorical and legal categories.

In later passages, Cicero uses the tell-tale formula *vis et natura* to distinguish a range of issues. In the process, he draws analogies between the orator/lawyer and the doctor. Hubbell's translation, once again, replaces Cicero's concrete language with technical oratorical terms. As a translation, it both clarifies Cicero's meaning and masks his underlying idiom. Cicero says, "In the next place, let us consider the essence and nature [*vim et naturam*] of the syllogism."[86] Cicero then describes the lawyer's task. He advises the attorney to show his client lacked motive for a crime by considering "what is the power and nature [*vis et natura*] of this emotion [*affectus*]," which supposedly motivated the crime. Thus, "[the advocate] will weaken [*infirmabit*]" the case of the prosecutor and strengthen his own.[87] As the word *infirmare* suggests, Cicero's empirical test of the subject

---

[83]   Cicero, *Inv.*, 1.14–15.

[84]   See Barnes, *Power of God*, p. 29. See also R. J. Hankinson, "Explanation and Causation," in *The Cambridge History of Hellenistic Philosophy*, ed. Keimpe Algra, Jonathan Barnes, Jaap Mansfeld, and Malcolm Schofield (Cambridge: Cambridge University Press, 1999), pp. 507–508, which notes, "For a more full-blooded empirical attitude to the business of causation and explanation we need to turn to the medical schools, indeed principally to the school known as the Empiricists.... Diocles may well be the first to point out the pitfalls of explanatory dogmatism, while echoing the anti-theoretical empiricism of the Hippocratic treatise, *On Ancient Medicine*."

[85]   Barnes, "One Nature, One Power," p. 208.

[86]   Cicero, *Inv.*, 1.57.

[87]   Cicero, *Inv.*, 2.25. Barnes, *Power of God*, p. 29, explains medical diagnosis as a process of observing the powers operative in a disease and seeking to balance excessively strong powers by

reposes upon an analogy with medical diagnosis.[88] In the mid-50s B.C., Cicero's *De oratore* again uses the "power and nature" formula to define and distinguish legal issues. There, Cicero will still criticize the poor diagnoses of orators who use the wrong form, "not knowing [*ignari*] that all controversies can be referred to the power and nature of a general classification [*ad universi generis vim et naturam referri*]."[89]

Cicero uses the same medical models to define the virtues and their unity. *De inventione* 2.157–159 contains a well-known definition. He describes three classes of things that should be sought (*genera*) and distinguishes them from "their opposites" (*contraria*), much as the Hellenistic elemental theories understood powers as paired with their opposites—hot-cold, wet-dry, etc.[90] Cicero explains that the *honestas*, like "virtue" itself, is a *power* (*vis*), and one distinguishable from other "powers," such as "the useful [*utilitas*]," and even opposite powers (*contraria*), like "the repulsive [*turpitudo*]" and "the not-useful [*inutilitas*]."[91] Cicero's philosophical grammar is medical, but the topic is moral and immaterial: "There is something which draws us to itself by its own merit [*sua vi*]," he says using the Latin *vis*, "not capturing us by any prospect of gain, but drawing by its own dignity [*sua dignitate*]. To this class belong *virtus*, knowledge, and truth."[92] As said by Lucretius, *vis* designates the most basic explanatory term for explaining what the *honestas* is in causal terms—namely, a power that attracts for its own sake, irrespective of any product beyond itself.

Cicero uses this causal theory of *virtutes* as combined powers to articulate his famously influential account of the unity of the virtues, first in *De inventione* and later in *De finibus*.[93] In context, Cicero is explaining that a lower category of good is desirable because of what it produces (*fructum*).[94] The remark leads to a general definition of virtue in which the same assumptions that governed

introducing their opposites. Cicero's discussion at 2.25–27 describes a legal procedure that operates by close analogy to medicine.

[88] Cf. Long, "Stoic Psychology," in *The Cambridge History of Hellenistic Philosophy*, pp. 604–613.

[89] Cicero, *Orat.*, 2.133 in Marcus Tullius Cicero, *De oratore, with introduction and notes by Augustus S. Wilkins* (Cambridge: Cambridge University Press, 1895).

[90] Barnes, *Power of God*, p. 31. Also, Richard Sorabji, *Matter, Space, and Motion*, pp. 79–105. See David Sedley, "Hellenistic Physics and Metaphysics," in *The Cambridge History of Hellenistic Philosophy*, ed. Keimpe Algra, Jonathan Barnes, Jaap Mansfeld, and Malcolm Schofield (Cambridge: Cambridge University Press, 1999), pp. 355–409: "In listing the four elements—earth, air, fire, and water—the Stoics place themselves in a tradition which by their day included Empedocles, Plato, and Aristotle."

[91] Cicero, *Inv.*, 2.157.

[92] Cicero, *Inv.*, 2.157. Hubbell's translation, modified. Cf. Cicero's *dignitas* with Plato's *preseibeia* at *Republic* 509B. See Barnes, "One Nature, One Power," p. 208. Also, Barnes, *Power of God*, pp. 51–59. Cicero's use of the terms *vis* and *dignitas* to describe the *honestas* looks like a debt to Plato.

[93] Cicero, *Inv.*, 2.157.

[94] Cicero, *Inv.*, 2.158.

76 ROMAN VIRTUE IN THE EARLY CHRISTIAN THOUGHT OF LACTANTIUS

Hellenistic physical theory are used to explain *virtus* as a cause compounded with other powers:

> We shall call honorable [*honestum nominabimus*] anything which is sought in whole or in part on account of itself. Now, since it has two parts [*partes*], one of which is simple [*simplex*], the other compounded [*coniuncta*], we will consider the simple part first. Everything in this class is included under one power and name [*una vi atque nomine amplexa*], *virtus*. For *virtus* is a possession of the mind [*animi habitus*] agreeing, as it were, with nature and reason. Therefore, once all its parts are recognized, there shall have been examined the entire power of a simple *honestas* [*tota vis erit simplicis honestatis considerata*]. The *honestum* has four parts: prudence, justice, fortitude, and temperance.[95]

Cicero's description lays the foundation of a developing Latin philosophical grammar that reconciles diversity with unity by building claims about immaterial human capacities (i.e., virtues) upon claims about capacities in a nature. Three features of his argument deserve observation because they persist in later Latin discourse. First, Cicero closely associates the notion of a name (*nominabimus*) with the act of identifying the specific power (*virtus*). Second, these powers (*virtutes*) operate by combination—*simplex* or *coniuncta*—with other distinct powers. Third, a single name—*virtus, simplex honestas*—may contain a plurality of distinguishable "parts," when understood as the compounded (*coniuncta*) elements of a complex existent. On that logic, Cicero calls *virtus* a cause seated in the mind and orients his conception teleologically.

The same causal models are evident in Cicero's discussion of *virtus* in his later dialogues, especially in *De finibus*, where speakers all use some form of physical theory and draw analogies with medicine and biology to articulate their differing opinions about *virtus*. At *Fin.* 1.42, for instance, the Epicurean argues that just as in "the science of the doctors [*medicorum scientiam*]," we value the art because it is "the cause of good health [*bonae valetudinis causa*]," so we should evaluate "wisdom [*sapientia*]" and "*virtus*" in terms of their effects (. . . *si nihil efficeret*).[96] At *Fin.* 3.73–74, a Stoic voice roots his account of the "*virtutis vis*" in his "physics," and later explains that "nature avails [*natura valeat*]" to cultivate justice (cf. *Inv.*, 2.156–160). A rebuttal criticizes Stoic claims "about the power of *virtus* [*de virtutis vi*] . . . that it is able to cause happiness in itself [*ut beatum per se efficere possit*]," before using medical and horticultural analogies to elucidate the problem.[97] In terms profoundly comparable to

---

[95] Cicero, *Inv.*, 2.159. My translation.
[96] Cicero, *Fin.*, 1.42.
[97] Cicero, *Fin.*, 4.32.

Inv. 2.156–160, the language of Piso at *Fin.* 4.59 describes the *honestas* as something "whose power is so great [*tantam vim esse honestatis*], and so surpasses and excels beyond all other things that it cannot [*possit*] be drawn away by any penalties or rewards."[98] Later, Piso describes a scale that moves from natural capacities of the body to the mental powers by drawing an analogy with biological principles. Like the body, "the *animus* must . . . lack none of its powers [*de virtutibus*] . . . and there is also a *virtus* in each of the senses [*in sensibus virtus*]," which allows each sense to perform its function.[99] In this statement, *virtus* indicates not an ethical quality, but psychological capacities, for there are "many *virtutes*" of the mind, which is "the *princeps* of the soul and its parts."[100] Piso thus distinguishes two "*genera*" of such powers. Some "are begotten in us by nature involuntarily," while others, "since they are placed in the will, we usually name more properly as '*virtutes*,' because their exceeding preeminence is unto the praise of souls."[101] These and other passages amply demonstrate that Cicero's philosophic dialogues elucidate and differentiate forms of *virtus* using a philosophical idiom that relies on Hellenistic physical theories. In that respect, his work witnesses to a philosophical conversation in Rome, which conducted its debate about *virtus* using the philosophical grammar provided by Hellenistic theories of "power and nature" and the philosophical grammar those theories presumed.

Virtus: Political Theology in Cicero

Between 55 and 51 B.C. Cicero was suffering political marginalization after Pompey the Great had renewed his pact with Caesar and Crassus at the Lucca Conference.[102] Having read and circulated Lucretius's *De rerum natura* in 54 B.C., Cicero set himself to writing an alternative political theory that would also offer a new and philosophically grounded account of Roman *virtus*.[103] Cicero seems to have been discontented with Lucretius's atheological vision and its implication

---

[98] Cicero, *Fin.*, 4.59.

[99] Cicero, *Fin.*, 5.36.

[100] Cicero, *Fin.*, 5.36.

[101] Cicero, *Fin.*, 5.36.

[102] See Rawson, *Cicero: A Portrait*, pp. 131–163.

[103] See Cicero, *Ad q. fr.*, 2.9.4 in Marcus Tullius Cicero, *Letters to Quintus and Brutus; Letter Fragments; Letter to Octavian; Invectives; Handbook of Electioneering*, ed. and trans. D. R. Shackleton Bailey, Loeb Classical Library 462 (Cambridge, MA: Harvard University Press, 2002), for his remarks on Lucretius. See Sedley, *Lucretius and the Transformation of Greek Wisdom*, pp. 1–2. Cicero's writings form a coherent corpus written in two bursts of energy in 55–51, and later 46–43 B.C. His later texts address questions raised in early dialogues. See Malcolm Schofield, "Writing Philosophy," in *The Cambridge Companion to Cicero*, ed. Catherine Steel (Cambridge: Cambridge University Press, 2013), pp. 73–87.

78 ROMAN VIRTUE IN THE EARLY CHRISTIAN THOUGHT OF LACTANTIUS

for political order.[104] His works *On the Orator, Republic,* and *Laws* aim to reconcile traditional Roman "manliness" (*virtus*) with philosophic notions. Cicero distinguishes *virtus* as that particular power which operates in the activity of politics, and he groups Rome's iconic heroes—both martial and ethical—under this larger category. In so doing, Cicero narrows his use of *virtus* to a precise technical notion, which clarifies the meaning of *virtus* and thus also renders it more flexible. This allows Cicero to reconcile Rome's martial ideals with a teleological and theological vision of politics. In the process, Cicero provides rational terms for explaining the relationship between Rome's traditional pantheon and Hellenistic philosophical accounts of a single Divine Nature, whose power is mediated in the actions of great Roman figures. As Momigliano put it, what emerges from Cicero's writing is a "fully religious interpretation of politics," which understands human *virtus* as a mediation of the ordering capacities of *Nature* understood as rational and divine.[105]

Republic and Laws

Like Lucretius, Cicero saw the need to reconstruct Roman "manliness" in a coherent philosophical way. Rather than reject Roman tradition, Cicero attempts to reconcile Roman "manliness" (*virtus*) with Hellenistic philosophic excellence (ἀρετή). His opening to the *Republic* signals this project with a parade of historical figures that begins with famous warriors (Marcellus, Q. Maximus, Scipio Africanus) but reaches its zenith in the austere philosophic figure, Marcus Cato, "a man well-known and new, who like an exemplar [*quasi exemplari*], leads all of us, who desire these same things, to industry and *virtus* [*ad industriam et virtutem*]."[106] By placing Cato at the head of Rome's traditional heroes, Cicero gives philosophical orientation to the old Roman self-image without simply jettisoning the tradition in Epicurean fashion. In the next lines, Cicero interprets this historical pass-in-review with a thesis that juxtaposes defense of the state with ethical self-mastery: "I set down [*definio*], then, this one claim: *natura* has given to the human species [*generi*] so much need for *virtus* [*tantam necessitatem virtutis*] and such love for defending the common welfare [*ad communem salutem defendendam*] that this power [*ut ea vis*] has conquered all

---

[104] For *Republic* as anti-Epicurean, see Matthew Fox, *Cicero's Philosophy of History* (Oxford: Oxford University Press, 2007), p. 105; also Walter Englert, "Epicurean Philosophy in Cicero's *De re publica*: Serious Threat or Convenient Foil?" *Ethics and Politics* 16.2 (2014): pp. 253–266.

[105] Arnaldo Momigliano, "The Theological Efforts of the Roman Upper Classes in the First Century BC," in *Roman Religion*, ed. Clifford Ando, pp. 157–161. He makes this comment specifically of the *Republic*, but it applies to Ciceronian thought as a whole.

[106] Cicero, *Rep.*, 1.1. For Cicero's reconciliation of traditional "manliness," see Chapter 1, this volume.

POWER AND *VIRTUS*   79

the blandishments of pleasure and leisure [*voluptatis otioque vicerit*]."[107] Cicero's thesis provides a corrective to the Republican ideal of "manliness" while also staking out a position in opposition to Epicurean retreat from politics. He uses martial rhetoric to describe ethical tasks, while implying that self-mastery is the prerequisite for public service. The claim makes *vis* the term that explains what *virtus* is; whatever *virtus* means, *virtus* is a *power*. Cicero gives "this power" (*ea vis*) a specific activity of overcoming the Epicurean ideals of pleasure and leisure. And he associates this power (*ea vis*) with a *natura*, which presumably contains many others. Cicero thus gathers the various kinds of *virtus* under the single activity of statecraft: "The supreme activity [of *virtus*] is the governance of the state [*civitatis gubernatio*], and the fulfillment [*perfectio*], not in speech, but in fact [*reapse*] of all those things which [philosophers] drone on about [*personant*] in their corners."[108]

By orienting human *virtus* to statecraft, Cicero defines political governance as an imitation of the Divine Nature. He argues that statecraft inculcates justice, loyalty, and equity, as well as civic, religious, and familial pieties (*Rep.*, 1.3–6). Later remarks connect this activity to God's work in governing the universe. Cicero recapitulates his opening definition but replaces the phrase *natura* with the more archaic *numen deorum*: "There is nothing [*nulla res*] in which human *virtus* approaches nearer to the divine power of the gods [*ad numen deorum*] than in the founding of new states and the preservation of those already founded [*civitates aut condere novas aut conservare iam conditas*]."[109] These remarks set the agenda for a theological account of political order that Cicero would articulate and debate in two later stages—first in the *Republic* and *Laws* (55–51 B.C.), and second, in his late philosophical texts (46–43 B.C.). That theological account reinterprets traditional Roman religion in monotheistic terms, establish an exemplary relationship between political and cosmic order, and articulate a rational account of apotheosis to ground Rome's traditional mythologies. *Republic* and *Laws* outline this theological discourse, while later dialogues ponder its central themes and define its terms.

Scipio Africanus serves as the primary voice of the *Republic*'s political theology.[110] His discourse elaborates the doctrine of Cicero's prefatory remarks. Scipio begins with a monotheistic explanation of the traditional gods, one that

[107] Cicero, *Rep.*, 1.1.10–14; Barnes, *Power of God*, pp. 21–22.
[108] Cicero, *Rep.*, 1.2.15–19.
[109] Cicero, *Rep.*, 1.12.23–25. Cf. Cicero, *Rep.*, 3.4.10–17, which strengthens the same point, also in Cicero's own voice: "*ut incredibilis quaedam et divina virtus exsisteret.*"
[110] Recognizing the eclectic nature of Cicero's personal commitments, I take Cicero-Scipio-Marcus (*De legibus*) as representing a coherent doctrine of *virtus*. *Rep.* 1.1–12 delivers a doctrine in Cicero's voice; Scipio unfolds that doctrine in Stoic fashion, and Marcus will do so as well with reference to Chryssipus. See Dillon, *Middle Platonists*, p. 79, "Scipio's doctrine cannot be positively identified as Antiochian, but Antiochus could certainly have accepted it." One need not be a Stoic in matters of epistemology to advocate a teleological vision of politics.

80   ROMAN VIRTUE IN THE EARLY CHRISTIAN THOUGHT OF LACTANTIUS

relies upon political metaphors: "We rightly take up from [Aratus] the first principles of saying, what all men, learned and foolish alike, agree upon: there is One King of gods and men [*unus rex*]."[111] Scipio then evokes some notion of *numen* to reconcile this One God with Rome's traditional religious rites:

> If, because of their benefit to human life [*ad utilitatem vitae*], the rulers of states mandated [*constituta sunt*] the beliefs that there is One King in heaven, who "by his nod," as Homer says, "moves all Olympus," and likewise that the same One [*unus*] is King and Father of all, there is great authority and many witnesses . . . that all nations have agreed by the decrees of their leaders [*decretis videlicet principuum*] that there is nothing better than a king, since all think that the gods are ruled by the divine power of One King [*unius regi numine*].[112]

Scipio's defense of monarchy begins a process by which Cicero takes up traditional terms like *numen* and *rex* in order to give them precise theological definition. The reference to Homer associates traditional Greco-Roman deities to a monotheistic notion.[113] Cicero projects that understanding into the past in the figure of Scipio, who represents the philosophical view as a consensus doctrine of traditional Roman society. The terms *mens* and *numen* confirm that Scipio's account is actually a philosophical reinterpretation: "If, however, we have learned that these [beliefs] were established in the error of ignorant people and are fairy-tale fictions [*fabularum similia*], let us listen to those common teachers of the learned . . . those who by exploring the nature of things have learned that this whole world [is ruled] by mind [*mente*] . . ."[114] The text breaks off, but Scipio's point is apparent. Civic custom and philosophical speculation assert with one voice that there is one God, who governs all things. By representing this doctrine as a presupposition of civic religion, Scipio assimilates the traditional "divine power of the gods [*deorum numen*]" to the philosophic conception of divinity (*mens, unus rex*).

The comments of "Marcus," Cicero's avatar in *De legibus*, provide additional vocabulary that helps to interpret what Scipio means by *numen*. Marcus interprets such language according to a philosophical lexicon that makes *vis* explanatory of the other terms: "A preface on what is right [*iuris exordium*]," he says, "should be drawn from the law; for law is indeed [*enim*] the power of

---

[111] Cicero, *Rep.*, 1.56.1–4, "*ut rite ab eo dicendi principia capiamus, quem unum omnium deorum et hominum regem esse omnes docti indoctique consentiunt.*"

[112] Cicero, *Rep.*, 1.56.6–18. Cf. Vergil, *Aen.*, 1.664–666.

[113] For the term "monotheistic," see *One God: Pagan Monotheism in the Roman Empire*, ed. Peter van Nuffelen and Stephen Mitchell. Also, *Monotheism between Pagans and Christians in Late Antiquity*, ed. Stephen Mitchell and Peter van Nuffelen. Earlier, *Pagan Monotheism in Late Antiquity*, ed. Polymnia Athanassiadi and Michael Frede.

[114] Cicero, *Rep.*, 1.56.6–18.

nature [*naturae vis*], that mind and reason [*mens et ratio*] of the prudent man [*prudentis*], the canon of right and wrong [*iuris et inuriae regula*]."[115] Consistent with Cicero's usage in *De inventione*, these lines make *vis* the most basic unit of definition, one that explains the other terms. He thus makes the *naturae vis* (cf. *Rep.*, 1.1) a form of *lex* that he identifies as *mens et ratio*. Shortly hereafter, Marcus reduces the notions of *lex* and *mens* to their most basic elemental idea of power by saying that "all nature is ruled by the power [*vi*] of the immortal gods, or by nature [*natura*], or reason [*ratione*], or *virtus* [*virtute*], or mind [*mente*], or divine power [*numine*], or whatever other word I might use."[116] The passage is telling because it takes terms for "power" as interpretive of traditional religious language. Marcus renders the "*numen deorum*" (as in *Rep.*, 1.56) as the singular "*vis deorum immortalium*" and makes such a phrase synonymous with the obviously philosophic notions of a single *mens*, *virtus*, and *vis naturae*. The argument grounds the unity of the *unus rex* in the notion of a unitary causal capacity.

On this basis, Marcus makes *virtus* the principle of humanity's likeness to and community with God. He says that human beings "obey this heavenly pattern [*descriptionem*], the Divine Mind, and All-powerful God [*praepotenti deo*], such that this whole world [*universus hic mundus*] must be considered [*existimanda sit*] one great State [*civitas*] of gods and human beings."[117] This notion of a common *virtus* means that in some sense, human beings are like gods or divine. Marcus's comments provide a rational basis for thinking about *apotheosis*: "*Virtus* is the same in humanity and God [*virtus eadem in homine ac deo est*] and in no other species [*genere*] besides; *virtus* moreover is nothing other than a nature [*natura*] perfected and led to its height [*ad summam*]. Humanity, therefore, has a certain likeness [*similitudo*] to God [*est igitur hominis cum deo similitudo*]."[118] The definition identifies *virtus* as a capacity that both God and human beings share. Human beings become divine insofar as they approach the height of humanity's potential. Although the doctrine is explicitly couched in Stoic terms, it expands the argument Cicero made in his own voice at *Rep.* 1.12.

---

[115] Cicero, *Leg.*, 1.19, "*a lege ducendum est iuris exordium; ea est enim naturae vis, ea mens ratioque prudentis, ea iuris atque inuriae regula.*" Jed Atkins, *Cicero on Politics and the Limits of Reason*, pp. 33–35, shows that Marcus takes up a definition of natural law articulated in the *Republic*, not by Scipio, but rather by Laelius, and warns against too easily identifying either one with Cicero. Still, Dillon, *The Middle Platonists*, pp. 77–80, notes that "Antiochus' theory of politics and natural law did not differ from that of contemporary Stoicism." It is consistent to read Scipio and Marcus in agreement on this point, irrespective of any question about what the historical Cicero thought. Dillon also shows that Marcus's discussion at 1.22 is drawn from Chrysippus, whose Stoic thought would agree with Scipio. In the end, the language of these passages indicates that a broadly Stoic position argued against an Epicurean one.

[116] Cicero, *Leg.*, 1.21. Cf. Cicero, *Rep.*, 1.55–56.

[117] Cicero, *Rep.*, 1.22.

[118] Cicero, *Rep.*, 1.25.

82 ROMAN VIRTUE IN THE EARLY CHRISTIAN THOUGHT OF LACTANTIUS

Marcus's Stoic definition of *virtus* reasserts, for the sake of argument, a theological view that Scipio puts in narrative form. His theory likens political and heavenly order.[119] As Atkins explains, "Scipio draws attention to the constant movements that appear to characterize both planets and constitutions."[120] He presents the three types of constitution as having "revolutions [*orbes*] and something like cycles [*quasi circuitus*] of changes."[121] Scipio uses this analogy to identify the unique function and power of political leadership:

> It is of the wise man [*prudentis*] not only to recognize [*cognasse*] them, but even in governing the commonwealth to foresee [*prospicere*] them as they are suspended in their orbits [*inpendentis*], directing their course [*moderantem cursum*]; and thus holding [their course] in his own power [*in sua potestate retinentem*] is [the function] of a sort of great citizen, an almost divine man [*magni cuisdam civis et divini paene est viri*] . . . and so the fourth kind of republic is a moderated and combined [*moderatum et permixtum*] from the other three.[122]

Cicero's genitives—*prudentis, magni civis, divini viri*—identify this activity of political moderation as the mark or task of a wise and nearly divine citizen. His use of *in sua potestate* certainly refers to political authority, but the notion of politics rests upon a cosmological metaphor that presupposes an underlying physical theory. So, the wise and divine citizen uses his *potestas* to form a harmonious compound (*moderatum et permixtum*), which is a mixture of elements. The language of this passage echoes throughout the *Republic* and is eventually applied specifically to the activity of God in Scipio's *Dream*. In other words, Scipio describes the *prudens, princeps*, or *divinus vir*, as one who does for terrestrial order what God accomplishes for the cosmos generally. In that respect, the *divinus vir* exercises a divine power.

Scipio uses this ideal vision of the statesman to rehabilitate the traditional story of Romulus's divinization and thus to confirm his portrait of divine leadership in the Roman past while also shoring up the traditional narrative.[123] Romulus

---

[119] On the analogy with cosmic order more broadly, see van Nuffelen, *Rethinking the Gods*, pp. 101–121.

[120] Atkins, *Cicero on Politics and the Limits of Reason*, pp. 47–80, esp. 54. Atkins shows that "the *Dream* not only follows naturally after, but also plays an important role in completing the main line of argumentation in *De re publica* . . . that the science of astronomy frames the dialogue's entire investigation in the nature of politics."

[121] Cicero, *Rep.*, 1.44.

[122] Cicero, *Rep.*, 1.44.

[123] Cole, *Cicero and the Rise of Deification at Rome*, p. 88, "Cicero creates an august Republican genealogy for contemporary religious speculations by drawing on the authority of a Republican poet well known to Cicero's elite audience: Ennius. Ennius was not only the peerless singer of the *mos maiorum* . . . [but] he also translated Euhemerus' work on the apotheosis of early kings and benefactors for a Roman audience."

POWER AND *VIRTUS*   83

embodies Cicero's redefinition of *virtus* understood as a power. Scipio recalls the traditional story that "while it was dark, although nature snatched Romulus away to where all people go [*ad humanum exitum*], *virtus* is said to have raised him to heaven."[124] Following his account of the mixed constitution, Scipio takes up this Romulus story again, but refashions it according to a rationalized theological understanding. Scipio recounts Romulus's activities in founding Rome. He says Romulus exercised *providentia* by choosing a location that "embraced the advantages of maritime cities while avoiding their vices . . . by placing his city on the shore of a river that flows year-round and calmly into the sea."[125] This foresight is a kind of providence that provides evidence of a divine quality: "He seems to have divined [*divinasse*] that this city would one day offer itself as a home for the greatest Empire."[126] Scipio then presents Romulus as a kind of demiurge in terms that evoke Cicero's translation of Plato's *Timaeus* and his own ideal orator. Romulus had "the native defenses of his City plainly marked out and planned in his mind [*animo notata planeque cognita*]."[127] And the early kings, who followed him, built the City's walls with wisdom [*sapientia*], *virtus*, loyalty [*fides*], and justice [*iustitia*].[128] Romulus laid further plans "for confirming the new state [*ad firmandum novam civitatem*]" by securing wives from among the Sabine women.[129] As a supreme statesman, he presented himself as a model of *pietas* toward the gods and his people, much as Augustus's Shield would boast a few years later.[130] In that Romulus served "the great health of the State [*magna cum salute rei publicae*]," he demonstrated the claim of Cicero's prologue—that *virtus* is exercised in the founding and securing of the commonwealth.[131]

Scipio uses this account of Romulus's activities to justify the traditional story of his divinization and thus explain apotheosis. Scipio offers a striking contrast to Livy's diffident reportage: "When Romulus had ruled for thirty-seven years and had finished these two outstanding foundations . . . since he was nowhere to be found [*non comparuisset*] after a sudden eclipse of the sun, it was thought that he had established himself among the number of the gods."[132] Scipio then

---

[124] Cicero, *Rep.*, 1.25, "*quibus quidem Romulum tenebris etiamsi natura ad humanum exitum abripuit, virtus tamen in caelum dicitur sustulisse.*"

[125] Cicero, *Rep.*, 2.10.1.

[126] Cicero, *Rep.*, 2.10.5.

[127] Cicero, *Rep.*, 2.11.9–10, "*animo notata planeque cognita?*" Cf. Cicero, *Div.*, 1.17 in Marcus Tullius Cicero, *De divinatione: De fato; Timaeus. Ottonis Plasberg schedis usus* (In aedibus B. G. Teubneri, 1965) where, speaking of the courses of the stars, he says, "*omnia iam cernes divina mente notata.*"

[128] Cicero, *Rep.*, 2.11.12, "*tum etiam reliquorum regum sapientia definitus ex omni parte.*" Cf. *Rep.*, 2.29–38.

[129] Cicero, *Rep.*, 2.11.12. Cf. Cicero, *Rep.*, 1.1 and 1.12.

[130] See Chapter 1, this volume.

[131] Cicero, *Rep.*, 2.15–16. Scipio's "*ad firmandum novam civitatem*" echoes the phrase "*virtus . . . ad communem salutem defendendam*" in the prologue. The whole portrait of Romulus embodies the definition.

[132] Cicero, *Rep.*, 2.17.4–6.

84 ROMAN VIRTUE IN THE EARLY CHRISTIAN THOUGHT OF LACTANTIUS

justifies the claim by recalling Romulus's *virtus*: "This belief [*quam opinionem*] no mortal was ever able to attain without the extraordinary glory of *virtus* [*sine eximia virtutis gloria*]," he says.[133] Scipio then supports Julius Proculus's testimony with remarks that expose the technical undergirding of his thought. Scipio enacts an old medical procedure. He diagnoses, as it were, Romulus's divinity by observing the power expressed in his activities: "The power of character and virtue [*vis ingenii atque virtutis*] was so great in [Romulus], that what had never before been believed about any mortal was believed concerning him and on the basis of Julius Proculus, a rustic no less."[134] Whereas Livy would leave the reader on a discordant note, Scipio uses Romulus's *virtus* as epistemic justification (hence, *divinasse, divinius*). His divinity constitutes an exceedingly great display of that *virtus* which distinguishes humanity's likeness to god. In the end, Scipio defends the traditional tale by rationalizing it.

Scipio projects this exemplary figure into the past so as to confirm Rome's traditional self-image, while redefining its central term. His explanation of Romulus leads to an account of Rome's early kings, which attributes to them all the philosphic virtues: "Even though they were rustics, our [ancestors] saw that *virtus* and royal wisdom [*sapientia regia*], not lineage, should be considered."[135] Romulus's successor, Numa Pompilius, then appears as a legislator sowing loyalty (*fides*) and justice (*iustitia*) among his people, through institutions that implant religion (*religio*) and lenience (*clementia*). By such training (*quibus rebus institutis*), Pompilius inculcated humanity (*humanitas*) and gentleness (*mansuetudo*) among the early Romans. Scipio's story reinforces Rome's traditional narrative of ancestral *virtus* while dramatizing Cicero's claim that *virtus* constitutes a power operative in human beings and his vision of the ideal ruler, who holds an intermediary place within the larger cosmic hierarchy.

The crowning expression of Cicero's vision of apotheosis occurs at the conclusion of *Republic* 6. In his mysterious *Dream*, Scipio ascends into one of the heavens where he learns of "that Highest God who burns and contains the others."[136] He sees that the sun is "the leader [*dux*], *princeps*, and moderator [*moderator*] of the other heavenly lights [*reliquorum luminum*], the mind [*mens*] and temperance [*temperatio*] of the world, one so great that he illumines and fills all things by his own light."[137] This sun, whom he calls *princeps*, oversees a plurality of deities each having its distinctive place and function. The vision offers an archetype for Scipio's politics. The statesman has his own place within

---

[133] Cicero, *Rep.*, 2.17.7–8. Cf. 1.1. The latter passage evokes the earlier one with key words *tanta, virtus, vis*, and the *ut + subj.* construction. Cf. Cicero, *Nat. d.*, 2.60, "*vis inest maior aliqua.*"
[134] Cicero, *Rep.*, 2.20.2–11.
[135] Cicero, *Rep.*, 2.23–24.
[136] Cicero, *Rep.*, 6.17.6.
[137] Cicero, *Rep.*, 6.17.14.

POWER AND *VIRTUS* 85

this larger order, in which the powers of the Highest God operate differently but in union and for the sake of the greater commonwealth. His moderation of the heavens creates a musical *concordia* to which all political orders aspire.[138]

Scipio ultimately unifies the heroic and philosophical ideals of *virtus* in a theology that justifies and promulgates the notion of a divinized human.[139] He relies upon the technical sense of power to explain the precise way in which a human may be divine. In the voice of the elder Africanus, Cicero points to Scipio's activities: "Know then that you are a god, if indeed a god is one who has strength [*viget*], who feels, who remembers, who has foresight, who so rules [*regit*], moderates [*moderator*], and moves that body in which he has been placed, as that first God [*princeps Deus*] does this whole world."[140] Here, the soul of the man who exercises his faculties toward the security and peace of the state exercises therefore divine powers. That action wins the statesman a reward—his own divinization and participation in the realms above.[141] Scipio is a god because he performs divine actions by excercising his divine capacity. Cicero's later philosophical treatises take up and articulate this thought in technical terms.

Cicero's Philosophica

Between June and December of 45 B.C., Cicero reformulated his *Lucullus* and *Catulus* (May 45) into the text now called *Academica*. The following year, he composed *De natura deorum* and then mourned through his *Tusculanae disputationes*. It was the period of Caesar's dictatorship, when "Cicero sought distraction from a political situation he could do nothing about, and from the personal grief occasioned by the death of his daughter Tullia in February of 45."[142] Cicero viewed writing philosophy as a lesser form of political participation. In that moment, it was the only political activity available to him.[143] His philosophic triad delves into questions implied in *Republic* and *Laws*. The dialogues attempt to articulate the premises that underpin several different accounts of divinity, both of the One God that governs all things, as well as the

---

[138] Cicero, *Rep.*, 6.18. Cf. *Rep.*, 2.69.1–4, "*Harmonia* in song is *concordia* in a state."

[139] Dillon, *The Middle Platonists*, p. 100, remarks, "This is a remarkable adaptation of the old, heroic view, according to which the good man in a *moral sense* had no part in the Isles of the Blessed, but rather the famous warrior." Dillon connects this to *Leg.* 2.28, where "again we find a distinction made between the general run of souls, which are all immortal, and those of the 'great and good,' which are *divine*."

[140] Cicero, *Rep.*, 6.26.10–14. Cf. Cicero, *Tusc.*, 1.60–70.

[141] Cicero, *Rep.*, 6.18, "*quod docti homines nervis imitati atque cantibus aperuerunt sib reditum in hunc locum.*"

[142] J. G. F. Powell, "The List of Cicero's Philosophical Works," in *Cicero the Philosopher: Twelve Papers*, ed. J. G. F. Powell (Oxford: Clarendon Press, 1995), p. 5.

[143] Schofield, "Writing Philosophy," in *The Cambridge Companion to Cicero*, p. 74.

86   ROMAN VIRTUE IN THE EARLY CHRISTIAN THOUGHT OF LACTANTIUS

potential divinity or divinization of human beings. In the process, Cicero's dramatic figures witness to several positions by which one might reconcile the traditional pantheon with a monotheistic doctrine of God, while articulating a theology of divinization that would apply not only to exemplary leaders but also to lost family. In these dramatic conversations, power causality provides a philosophical grammar and technical vocabulary in which various speakers exchange views on divinity, immortality, and the soul.

At *Acad.* 1.24–29 Cicero's character, Varro, articulates a cosmology that represents the eclectic approach of Antiochus of Ascalon.[144] His elaborate statements, Dillon explains, are "a blend of Platonic and Stoic doctrine . . . the first extant development of what will henceforth become Middle Platonic physical theory."[145] Varro presents his synthesis within the framework of an anti-skeptical philosophical historiography. His language overlaps with that of Lucretius, but Varro denies the Epicurean theory that there is any indivisible element, and he accepts the claim that the primary power of nature is immaterial and providential, and therefore can be termed as "God." In the process of Varro's speech, Cicero develops technical vocabulary that persists in later Latin writers, both Christian and non-Christian.

Varro begins by explaining the Old Academy's analysis of any given existent as a product (*res efficeretur*), produced by the combination of an active cause (*efficiens*) and passive matter (*quasi huic se praebens*).[146] His remark describes fundamental being as a relationship between causes and products. Varro uses the term *vis* as a synonym for this active cause:

> [The Old Academy] held that there is power [*vim*] in that which is causative [*efficienti*], and in that which is caused a kind of matter [*materiam quondam*]. Nonetheless, both are in each thing, since matter itself could not hold together if it were contained by no power [*nulla vi*], and neither could there be power [*vim*] without any matter (for there is nothing which is not compelled to exist in some place). But that which is produced from both, they already called "body" [*corpus*] a kind of "quality" [*quandam qualitatem*].[147]

---

[144] Varro is understood to have followed Antiochus. See Brad Inwood, "Antiochus on Physics," in *Antiochus of Ascalon*, ed. David Sedley (Oxford: Oxford University Press, 2015), p. 195; Jonathan Barnes, "Antiochus of Ascalon," in *Philosophia Togata I: Essays on Philosophy and Roman Society*, ed. Miriam Griffin and Jonathan Barnes, pp. 82–83; Dillon, *The Middle Platonists*, p. 8; J. Glucker, *Antiochus and the Late Academy* (Göttingen: Vandenhoeck & Ruprecht, 1978).

[145] Dillon, *The Middle Platonists*, pp. 81–82. Also, Giuseppe Cambiano, "Philosophy, Science and Medicine," in *The Cambridge History of Hellenistic Philosophy*, ed. Kemp Aleigra et alii (Cambridge: Cambridge University Press, 2005), pp. 610–611, places a theory of "common and specific signs" at *Acad.* 2.34 in contact with medical epistemologies traced to Hippocrates through Galen et alii. Cf. Barnes, *Power of God*, pp. 49–50.

[146] Cicero, *Acad.*, 1.24.

[147] Cicero, *Acad.*, 1.24 in Marcus Tullius Cicero, *On the Nature of the Gods; Academica*, trans. H. Rackham (Cambridge, MA: Harvard University Press, 1933).

POWER AND *VIRTUS* 87

Varro's statement includes vocabulary that also appeared in Lucretius, even though Varro's position differs fundamentally. Varro is evidently working with the notion of specific material powers because he conceives of *vis* as inherent in a *materia* that allows *vis* to exist, as he says, "in some place." David Sedley's suggestion that Cicero's *materia* should be translated as *natura* seems to be supported by the likeness of "*vis et materia*" in Varro's statement to the more common phrase "*vis et natura*" already seen in Cicero's vocabulary. If that is correct, then Varro here uses *materia* to distinguish any material from immaterial *naturae*.[148] Hence, Varro uses the terms *corpus* and *qualitas* to distinguish a third kind of existent, which is the product of *vis* and *materia*, when combined. *Qualitas* refers, apparently, to immaterial products and *corpus* to material ones.[149]

Varro's thought draws upon Plato's appropriation of Hippocratic power physics for discourse about non-material causality. The textual point of reference is Plato's *Theaetetus*.[150] As Barnes explains, Plato had already come to realize that the active and passive powers must be of the same nature and thus also "that the unity of pairs of powers must be reflected in a corresponding terminology."[151] Plato's *Theaetetus* developed a theory of "dependent pairs" wherein "the power of sight depends upon the power of being seen [etc]."[152] To express this correspondence of nature, *Theatetus* 182d supplies the term ποιότης to signify a "third entity" which corresponds neither to the active power (i.e., the object perceived) nor to the passive power (i.e., the sensing organ), but rather to the

[148] David Sedley, "The Origins of Stoic God," in *Traditions of Theology: Studies in Hellenistic Theology, Its Background and Aftermath*, ed. Dorothea Frede and André Laks (Leiden: Brill, 2002), pp. 41–84, argues that Varro's *materia* may be Cicero's rendering of οὐσία: "when Cicero speaks of it as 'a kind of matter' ('*materia quaedam*') this could very well be translating οὐσία τις rather than ὕλη τις. . . . According to the *Timaeus* (35a, 37a–b), there are two kinds of οὐσία of which the world-soul is constituted, and about which it thinks. Bodies, or γιγνόμενα, possess an οὐσία which is μεριστή and σκεδαστή, a 'divisible' and 'scattered' kind of being, while unchanging things possess οὐσία γιγνόμενα, an 'indivisible (or undivided)' kind of being (37a–b)."

[149] Hatzimichali, *Potamo of Alexandria*, pp. 110–117 takes *Acad.* 1.24–29 as an Antiochean report and "not an entirely consistent account of quality because quality is described both as the product of force and matter . . . and as a force acting upon (shaping) unqualified matter." If, however, Sedley was right to consider *materia* as a rendering of οὐσία, then Varro's ambiguity might be clarified by Barnes's account of "power and nature" and the Platonic background. See also Sorabji, *Matter, Space, and Motion*, pp. 90–93. For *quality-powers*, see Barnes, *Power of God*, pp. 56ff. and 79ff., where Plato is said to give quality-powers an immaterial signification.

[150] See Carlos Lévy, "Cicéron, le moyen platonisme et la philosophie romaine: À propos de la naissance du concept latin de *qualitas*," *Revue de métaphysique et de morale* 57.1 (2008): pp. 12–13, identifying *Theaetetus* as the source for the term ποιότης translated by Cicero as *qualitas*. Also, Sedley, "Origins of Stoic God," p. 59. For this passage as a major instance in the development of "power theology," see Barnes, *Power of God*, pp. 78–80, for the conceptual correspondence as power causality.

[151] Barnes, *Power of God*, pp. 78–79.

[152] Plato, *Theaetetus* 156d, in Barnes, *Power of God*, p. 78, quoted in Barnes to emphasize the connection between Cicero's text and power ontology/theology as a concept. Varro draws upon a work that Barnes has shown to be central in the theological appropriation of Hippocratic power causalities.

88   ROMAN VIRTUE IN THE EARLY CHRISTIAN THOUGHT OF LACTANTIUS

product of these two powers in union. By this logic, Plato develops an account of non-material existents from materialist power causality. Varro uses the term *qualitas* to express this Platonic notion in Latin.

As Varro continues to elaborate his cosmology he uses the term *qualitates* as a translation of the Greek plural ποιότητας, which appears in Cicero's text.[153] Varro defines two kinds of "qualities [*qualitates*]," some being "primary [*principes*]" and others resulting from their combination (*ex his oratae*). The former he calls "of one sort and simple [*unius modi et simplices*]," while "various others" are "compound [*multiformes*]."[154] What "simple and one kind" means is defined by the theory of elemental powers. Like Lucretius, Varro evokes, "air . . . fire, water, and earth are primary [*principes*]; from them are born the forms [*figurae*] of animate beings [*animantium*] and of those things which are begotten [*gignuntur*] from the earth."[155] He can term these primary powers "beginnings [*initia*]" and even "elements [*elementa*]."[156] Still, *elementum* designates a power that is not combined and is not a product in any sense. As Varro explains, "Air and fire have a power of production [*vim efficiendi*], while the other parts, water and earth, have a force of receiving and suffering [*vim . . . patiendi*]."[157] By contrast, complex natures (*materiae* and later, *naturae*) refer to the combinations of such powers, "bodies" or "qualities," which are products or manifestations (*species*) of their causal powers.[158]

Varro uses this account of combined powers to explain the term "God" in a statement that puts the Stoic theory of cosmic harmony into Latin and gives it clear terminology.[159] He quickly passes over Aristotle's notion of a "fifth genus [*quintum genus*]," and then explains the Old Academy's belief "that underpinning all these [*subiectam omnibus*] is a sort of nature [*quamdam materiam*] that has no manifestation [*sine specie*] and is lacking any quality [*carentem ulla qualitate*]."[160] This "sort of nature" contains the infinite capacity "to receive all things and be changed in all ways and in every part," and thus is the source of all

---

[153] Cicero, *Acad.*, 1.25. Cicero proudly and self-consciously invents his technical terms in this passage.

[154] Cicero, *Acad.*, 1.26.

[155] Cicero, *Acad.*, 1.26. Cf. Lucretius, *Nat. r.*, 2.583–587, fn. 33.

[156] Cicero, *Acad.*, 1.26.

[157] Cicero, *Acad.*, 1.26.

[158] Richard Sorabji, *Matter, Space, and Motion*, pp. 81–87.

[159] See M. Jason Reddoch, "Cicero's *De Divinatione* and Philo of Alexandria's Criticism of Chaldean Astrology as a Form of Artificial Divination," *Dionysius* 32 (2014): p. 5. Cicero uses the terms *sympatheia* at *Div.* 1.7, 2.33–35, and renders it as *cognatio naturalis, concentus, consensus*; *convenientia, coniunctio naturae, continuatio, conunctio naturae*, to translate it. However, *Div.* 1.7 likens "natural divination" to medical arts in a discussion that clearly explains divination as an activity of identifying the nature of powers from their effects.

[160] Cicero, *Acad.*, 1.27. As far as I can tell, this passage coins the terms *species* and *qualitas* as technical terms denoting the effect or product of a specific causal capacity for the Latin philosophical lexicon. Both terms later feature in Seneca and Tertullian. See Carlos Lévy, "Ciceron, Le Moyen Platonisme, et La Philosophie Romaine," pp. 14–20.

POWER AND *VIRTUS* 89

generation.[161] Such a nature he names as a form of "that power [*illa vis*], which we have called *qualitas*" and its products therefore as "qualified [*qualia*]."[162] Designating this *vis* as *qualitas* seems to be Varro's way of defining it as immaterial. The linguistic derivation of *qualia* from *qualitas* reflects the *X from X* causal relationship between this immaterial power and its products. Varro's thought is like Lucretius's in that he locates this *vis* "underneath" all the others, in some sense.[163] Still, Varro understands this foundational *vis* as immaterial and ultimately divisible. Such an immaterial power explains the term "God," in his thinking:

> Moreover, the parts of the world are all those things present within [this power] and are held together by a sentient nature [*natura sentiente*], in which there is perfect reason [*ratio perfecta*], which is the same sempiternal. . . . They call this power the soul of the universe [*animum mundi*], and also mind [*mentem*] and perfect wisdom [*sapientiamque perfectam*], which they call "God" [*deum*].[164]

Varro's remarks develop a more precise account of such terms as reason (*ratio*), wisdom (*sapientia*), and mind (*mens*), which were so important for the political theology of *Republic* and *Laws*. Such terms designate specific capacities, or *partes mundi*, seated within "God"—the ultimate power of generation, which is not simple (*simplex*) but rather an immaterial compound (*multiformis*). Because the *vis efficiendi* contains the powers of reason, wisdom, and mind, it is "a kind of providence that grasps [*procurantem*] especially heavenly things, but then those things on earth which pertain to human beings."[165] He concludes by giving this Power a range of mythic titles such as, "*Necessity* . . . sometimes also *Fortune*, because it causes [*efficiat*] many unforeseen and unlooked for [events]."[166] *Acad.* 1.24–29 thus develops terms for a theology that was nascent in Cicero's corpus from an earlier period.[167]

A year after composing Varro's discourse, Cicero drafted his most influential discussion of theology at Rome. In *De natura deorum*, the Stoic figure Balbus offers an orthodox Stoic understanding of divinity. Balbus's speech allows us to distinguish the Stoic from Antiochian positions while recognizing their mutual opposition to an Epicurean philosophy. In that respect, Balbus augments

---

[161] Cicero, *Acad.*, 127. Beyond Sedley's argument, that *materia* indicates a "nature" is evident here from the thought itself. Varro describes an existent that holds a combination of powers in itself and expresses those powers in various actions. That thought is, by definition, an *ousia* in Greek mixture physics.

[162] Cicero, *Acad.*, 1.28.

[163] Cf. Lucretius, *Nat. r.*, 3.265–275.

[164] Cicero, *Acad.*, 1.28.

[165] Cicero, *Acad.*, 1.28–29.

[166] Cicero, *Acad.*, 1.27–29.

[167] On Cicero's philosophical involvement, see Baraz, *Cicero's Philosophical Politics*, pp. 137–139.

Varro's argument by using a Stoic doctrine of God as the intellectual basis for reinterpreting the traditional Roman *cultus deorum*. Balbus defines *virtus* in causal terms, which use the technical sense of power to provide a theological justification for divinizing Rome's traditional heroes. His speech represents ideas well-disseminated among the Roman upper classes under the principate and, in that respect, witnesses to a Stoic theological discourse that elite Romans were gradually adopting ever more broadly in the the century prior to Christianity.[168] The context is not insignificant. As Michael Koortbojian observes, "*De natura deorum* was composed at the very moment when Julius Caesar's increasingly unprecedented honors commenced—honors that would culminate, ultimately, in his divinization" by the Senate in 42 B.C.[169] If Cicero objected to the action, his dialogue witnesses nonetheless to ideas he had been developing from an early period. Somewhat ironically, his works helped to establish the intellectual preconditions for legitimizing a political figure (Julius Caesar) and political order (the principate) that Cicero himself rejected.[170]

Like Varro, Balbus presupposes the common language of power causality (or, rather, mixture physics). He differs, however, in seeing the "power of heat [*vim caloris*]" which permeates the elements as "the original generating power [*vis generans*]" of the cosmos.[171] He eventually names that "heat [*calor*]" as "soul [*animus*]," which makes the world "animate [*animantem mundum*]."[172] What Varro termed as an immaterial and infinitely divisible *qualitas*, Balbus names as the element of fire. Balbus argues from the all-pervasive presence of heat that a single *natura* embraces the entire universe.[173] In this respect, his notion is material.

[168] P. A. Brunt, "Stoicism and the Principate," *Papers of the British School at Rome* 43 (1975): pp. 7–35, "Stoicism permeated the writings of authors like Virgil and Horace, who professed no formal allegiance to the sect, and became part of the culture that men absorbed in their early education." See also Brent D. Shaw, "The Divine Economy: Stoicism as Ideology," *Latomus* 44.1 (1985): pp. 16–54.

[169] See Michael Koortbojian, *The Divinization of Caesar and Augustus: Precedents, Consequences, Implications* (Cambridge: Cambridge University Press, 2013), p. 4. Koortbojian regards Cotta as Cicero's avatar and thus says, "Cicero clearly had qualms about the entire matter and his skepticism in general should be regarded as an index of his views concerning Caesar in particular." I regard Cotta as Cicero's epistemological avatar, but Balbus as representing the cosmological theory that Cicero would accept, if he had to choose.

[170] Cole, *Cicero and the Rise of Deification at Rome*, shows that Cicero was the principal source for the translation of Hellenistic notions of kingship into Rome and the Latin idiom, and not even primarily in his philosophical treatises. Since the 80s B.C., Cicero's many public speeches had been articulating a philosophical basis for understanding leaders as divine.

[171] Cicero, *Nat. d.*, 2.23–24, *passim*. Cf. Barnes, *Power of God*, p. 30, fn. 14, noting "the strong religious understanding attached to fire consistently through the history of Greek thought . . . as the fundamental element underlying all existence."

[172] Cicero, *Nat. d.*, 1.31–32. On the Stoic fire, see Ricardo Salles, "Ἐκπύρωσις and the Goodness of God in Cleanthes," *Phronesis* 50.1 (2005): pp. 56–78. Also, Sorabji, *Matter, Space, and Motion*, pp. 86–87, suggests that Stoics could equate fire and air interchangeably as "active elements . . . call[ed] spirit," thus making spirit a term for both. Although his sources are later than this text of Cicero, the ambiguity may suggest why Varro and Balbus could differ so narrowly: fire and air were thought to be on the boundary between material and immaterial reality.

[173] Cicero, *Nat. d.*, 2.28.

He names *natura*, which "is not without sense or reason [*non sine sensu atque ratione*]," as something that is not "solitary nor simple [*solitaria nec simplex*], but conjoined and connected with something else [*alio iuncta atque conexa*]"; it "contains [*continet*]" other powers within itself.[174] What Balbus defines is a compound nature understood as materially existing in the element of fire.

Balbus's argument hinges on the notion that any given *natura*, which contains a plurality of powers must have a specific power that expresses its unique identity. Such a compound nature (*natura ... conexa*) has in it some "governing principle" [*principatus*], he argues, translating the Greek "ἡγεμονικὸν" into Latin.[175] Balbus names this *principatus* as the power of reason. Using this logic, he traces his account of any given *natura* to the theory of a cosmic divine nature:

> So, in that which is [*in quo sit*] the governing authority [*principatus*] of all nature there must be that which is best of all [*omnium optimum*] and of the highest rank [*dignissimum*] in respect to its power and dominion over all things.... So it follows that the world is wise and that nature [*eam naturam*] which holds all things in its embrace [*naturamque eam quae res omnes complexa teneat*] is excellent by the perfection of reason [*perfectione rationis excellere*]. Therefore, the world is god and every power of the world [*omnemque vim mundi*] is contained in the divine nature [*natura divina*].[176]

Translators often recognize the language of political authority in Balbus's statement at the expense of its underlying ontology.[177] Doing so is not incorrect, but it does obscure the causal notions that anchor his argument. Balbus's description of the ruling part as "*potestate dominatuque dignissimum*" seems to evoke Plato's description of the Good at *Republic* 509b, which characterized the Good as a transcendent cause.[178] Plato explains that "the Good is not the nature itself [οὐκ οὐσίας ὄντος τοῦ ἀγαθοῦ], but even surpasses the nature in rank and power [ἀλλ' ἔτι ἐπέκεινα τῆς οὐσίας πρεσβείᾳ καὶ δυνάμει ὑπερέχοντος]."[179]

---

[174] Cicero, *Nat. d.*, 2.29. Cf. *Nat. r.*, 2.352, Also see Barnes, *Power of God*, pp. 36–37, where the same concept appears in the Hippocratic context.

[175] Cicero, *Nat. d.*, 2.29.

[176] Cicero, *Nat. d.*, 2.30.

[177] E.g., Cicero, *On the Nature of the Gods, Academics*, trans. H. Rackham (Cambridge, MA: Harvard University Press, 1933), "most deserving of authority and sovereignty over all things." Joseph B. Mayor and J. H. Swainson, *Cicero: De natura deorum with Introduction, Notes, and Commentary*, vol. 2 (Cambridge: Cambridge University Press, 1883; reprint, 2010), p. 119, "most worthy of authority and lordship over all things."

[178] See *Nat., d.*, 2.32, where Balbus names and discusses Plato explicitly.

[179] Plato, *Rep.*, 509b. See Barnes, *Power of God*, pp. 87–89. The Greek πρεσβεία, like the Latin *dignitas*, refers properly to the "rank" or position of a person within a social hierarchy. Balbus's "*potestate dominatuque dignissimum*" approximate Plato's "πρεσβείᾳ καὶ δυνάμει" both in vocabulary and construction. A bit later, Balbus's *excellere* would nicely render ὑπερέχοντος, and Balbus explicitly evokes Plato in the next paragraph.

92   ROMAN VIRTUE IN THE EARLY CHRISTIAN THOUGHT OF LACTANTIUS

Balbus evokes that traditional concept here. He thinks that the power of reason is "supremely worthy in power and authority" over the others and that through reason, then, the cosmos itself is divine.

Balbus's account of the *natura divina* allows us to describe his opposition to Velleius and characterize the slight distinction between his position and Varro's. All sides agree that some infinite power underlies and sustains all things. They differ on the description of its identity.[180] Whereas Velleius denied his "*infinitatis vis*" any power of "*sollertia*," Balbus sides with Varro in naming *ratio* as that specific power, which makes the cosmos divine and the sense of being endowed with provident rationality. Distinct from Varro, Balbus thinks of "fire" as the material substance of "the divine nature [*natura divina*]."[181] And he locates reason within it. Balbus thus defines the significant term *natura divina*, along with philosophic *virtutes* (or, even more precisely, *qualitates*), such as wisdom and reason, as powers contained within divine nature.

The political implications of these divergent appropriations of power causality appear as Balbus continues. Like Scipio in *Republic*, Balbus interpets Rome's traditional religion in terms of his Stoic philosophical theology. The notion that specific powers disclose their nature in their effects comes to reconcile the plurality of Rome's traditional pantheon with the monotheistic doctrine just articulated. Balbus identifies each of Rome's traditional deities as specific manifestations of the power of a single and supreme godness. His comments recall the close association of a "power" and its "name," observed already in *De inventione*:

> With good cause, the wisest men of Greece and our ancestors set up and named many other natures of gods [*multae aliae naturae deorum*] on the basis of their great benefits [*ex magnis beneficiis eorum*]. For they knew that whatever confers great usefulness upon the human race did not happen without the divine goodness [*sine divina bonitate*] toward humanity. Hence, whatever was born from God [*illud quod erat a deo natum*], they would designate [*nuncupabant*] by the name of a god itself [*nomine ipsius dei*]. This is why we call corn "Ceres," and wine "Liber," as Terence says, "without Ceres and Liber, Venus is weak [*friget*]." So then, that thing [*res ipsa*], in which there is present some greater power [*in*

---

[180] See also Luke Gelinas, "The Stoic Argument *Ex gradibus entium*," *Phronesis* 1.1 (2006): pp. 52–73, arguing that "the existence of god and the nature proper to god, are in some important sense inseparable," but claims it should be "constru[ed] as an argument aimed at establishing the nature of the deity."

[181] Dillon, *The Middle Platonists*, p. 82, thinks Varro's nod to Aristotle's "*genus quinque*" shows discomfort with the Platonic theory and points to *Fin.* 4.12 as evidence Varro preferred a version of the Stoic fire.

qua vis inest maior aliqua], is so named, that the power itself [*ea ipsa vis*] is called a god [*deum*].[182]

Balbus explains traditional mythologies in the rational terms of power causality. He introduces a plurality of "natures of gods [*multae deorum naturae*]," whose worship he founds on ancestral precedent. Balbus distinguishes these natures by their *beneficia*, which might also be termed *effects* in bare causal language. Each benefit discloses the identity of the nature (*naturae*), from which it is "born." Hence, what results is a distinctive "name" that expresses the distinct identity of the power, which redounds from "the divine goodness," and is manifest in the effect. Each name designates "a god." The image of Venus losing power (*friget*) without the attendance of Liber and Mercury dramatizes Balbus's theory, which presents "the divine nature" as a compound (*complexa*) that is "conjoined" with other powers. Balbus's "god" is a compound of many parts (*partes*), which are not transmutable one into the other.

Balbus uses this philosophical theology to articulate the precise sense in which personified deities and exemplary human figures may be called gods. Gesturing to the immediate political context, he applies this doctrine to the most significant monuments of Roman *virtus* in Republican history. The narrative constitutes both an explanation of Rome's traditional politics and a justification for philosophic redefinition of *virtus*. Balbus continues:

> Consider the temple of Virtue [*Virtus*], the temple of Honor [*Honos*] restored by M. Marcellus, and likewise of Wealth, Safety, Harmony [*Concordia*], Liberty, Victory; because the power [*vis*] of all these things was so great that it could not possibly be exercised without God, the thing itself [*res ipsa*] obtained the name of the gods [*nomen deorum*]. . . . Hence, the gods who produced various benefits were set up because of the magnitude of their benefits [*ex utilitatum igitur magnitudine*], and by those aforementioned names, that power [*vis*] in each god is declared.[183]

---

[182] Cicero, *Nat. d.*, 2.60–66. Cf. Cicero, *Div.*, 1.6.12, "*Est enim vis et natura quaedam . . . aliquo instinctu inflatuque divino futura praeniuntiat.*" I have translated "God" and "a god" in order to capture what I think Balbus is saying. He gives *bonitas divina* as a general principle of which the gods represent specific manifestations. I take *bonitas divina* as a synonym for *natura divina*, above. We find then *providentia/deum/divina bonitas* as the ultimate cause of *beneficia*, which can be realized under a plurality of names. Furthermore, I note the similarity of two key lines to Plato's *Rep.* 509b, which Barnes makes foundational to the non-material appropriation of power causality for a teleological account of God. Cicero applies this schema to the practice of divinization.

[183] Cicero, *Nat. d.*, 2.61. See J. R. Fears, "The Theology of Victory at Rome: Approaches and Problems," *Aufstieg und Niedergang der Römischen Welt* 17.2 (1973): pp. 736–825, uses this passage to explain the cult of virtues: "A specific condition or quality . . . is recognized as the operation of a characteristic and peculiar divine power, which is designated by the condition or quality it produces. *Concordia* is the godhead which establishes *concordia*; *Pax* is the godhead which establishes *pax*; [etc.]." What Fears identifies is more technically describable as a form of *X from*

94 ROMAN VIRTUE IN THE EARLY CHRISTIAN THOUGHT OF LACTANTIUS

By his reference not only to Ceres and Hercules, but also to abstract deities and Republican heroes, Balbus interprets ancestral religion in the terms of a monotheistic account of the divine nature. He pointedly mentions, not just any religious praxis, but significant public icons of the Roman ideal of *virtus*.[184] In that respect, his comments augment Cicero's own remarks at *Rep.* 1.1–2. Both passages assimilate heroic to philosophic *virtus* by explaining it as a causal capacity oriented teleologically toward God.

The final section of Balbus's statement applies this same notion to human beings. Balbus explains the divinization of exemplary leaders with precisely the same language that he applied to Rome's traditional deities, like Hercules. Power causality justifies divinization of heroes:

> What is more, the common custom of human beings has permitted [*suscepit*] that by fame and will they may raise men into heaven for their outstanding benefits [*viros beneficiis exellentis*]. Thus, Hercules, Castor and Pollux, Aesculapius, Liber and . . . even Romulus [were deified]. Since their souls remain and enjoy eternity, rightly were they called "gods," for they were best [*optimi*] and everlasting [*aeterni*].[185]

This statement shows what it means "to be a god" in Roman theological terms. When read in context of the whole passage, it is apparent that human beings are divinized "because of their benefits [*beneficiis excellentis*]" in the same way that gods are named "on the basis of their great benefits [*ex magnis beneficiis*]." As Balbus interprets them, "gods" are natures through which the divine goodness operates to bestow its benefits. Imperial claims to divinization could thus operate on the same rational grounds as any other claim about divinity in Roman terms.

In the summer of 44 B.C., a grieving Cicero would return to this doctrine, which is traceable in his thought back to Scipio's *Dream* and the text of *Republic* 6. Cicero's *Tusculans* argue that the soul is both eternal and divine and that divine honors can therefore be paid to departed persons. Cicero's comments reinforce the argument of the *Republic* by setting this claim in direct contradiction to

---

X causality. McDonnell criticizes Fears for relying on literary sources to describe Roman religion as it existed socially, but Myles McDonnell, *Roman Manliness*: Virtus *and the Roman Republic* (Cambridge: Cambridge University Press, 2006), p. 90, observes this very concept in a fragment of Varro, where the term *virtus* appears: "*ita Virtus, quae dat virtutem, Honor, qui honorem, Concordia, quae concordiam, Victoria, quae dat victoriam.*"

[184] Cole, *Cicero and the Rise of Deification at Rome*, pp. 155–156, "Balbus drops some respected Roman names: Marcellus, Fabius Maximus, and also A. Atilius Catalinus, a man who is often mentioned with special reverence in Cicero's texts (*Tusc.*, 1.13, 1.110; *Fin.*, 2.116). Most of the human-generated divinities to which he refers carry positive connotations from the religious prescriptions of the *De legibus* (2.19, 2.28) . . . This list is identical to the one Cicero uses at *De legibus* 2.19."
[185] Cicero, *Nat. d.*, 2.62.

POWER AND *VIRTUS* 95

Epicurean philosophy. He translates a lengthy passage of Plato's *Phaedrus*: "This is the unique [*propria*] nature and power of the soul [*natura animi atque vis*], which since, out of all things, it is the one which moves itself, has not been born [*nec nata est*], and is eternal [*aeterna*]."[186] The statement that the soul moves itself directly opposes Lucretius's argument at *Nat. r.* 3.262 that the soul is dissolved with its material atoms. By translating *Phaedrus*, Cicero adduces Plato in rebuttal of Lucretius's Epicurus.

Tusc., 1.62–64 contradicts the Epicurean notion of the soul's dissolution. Cicero uses an alternative understanding of the power of the soul to emphasize its potential for divinization and to legitimize the notion of divinizing humans beings because of their evident *virtus*.[187] Cicero asserts of the soul that "what this power [*illa vis*] is and whence it comes should be understood."[188] He denies that a material explanation can account for powers such as memory, foresight, and imagination. The soul may be material in some way, but it is not simply matter. While maintaining his formal Academic commitments, Cicero opts decisively for the argument that human beings have a divine nature: "Certainly it is not [made] from the heart, or the blood, or the brain, or of atoms. . . . If it is made of breath [*animae*] or fire [*ignis*], I know not."[189] Cicero nonetheless makes a determined, if qualified, judgment: "If I could affirm anything else on such a difficult matter . . . I would swear that the soul is divine."[190] He justifies this preference by observing the power of the soul in its effects: "Just as you recognize God from his works [*ex operibus eius*], so from the memory of events, and discovery, and speed of motion, from all the beauty of virtue, recognize that the power of the mind is divine."[191] This argument justifies human divinity by applying to the soul a classic argument for God's existence and identity. Cicero uses it to justify a shrine and public cultus for his deceased daughter, Tullia. Just as Romulus could be divinized for *virtus*, the power of her nature deserves divine honor.

Cicero's discussion in the *Tusculans* also emphasizes that Cicero's thinking, in terms of power causality, developed with reference to his own earlier writings. *Tusc.* 1.54–70 draws specifically upon his own earlier corpus. Cicero's self-reference shows that his later vote in favor of a theological and teleological account of the divine power relied upon the same philosphical discourse first articulated in his political works, *Republic* and *Laws*. Cicero's justification of

---

[186] Cicero, *Tusc.*, 1.54 in Marcus Tullius Cicero, *Tusculan Disputations*, trans. J. E. King, Loeb Classical Library 141 (Cambridge, MA: Harvard University Press, 1927), quoting *Phaedrus* 245: "*Nam haec est propria natura animi atque vis, quae si est una ex omnibus quae se ipsa moveat, neque nata certe est et aeterna est.*" Cf. Cicero, *Rep.*, 6.28.15–19.

[187] Martin van den Bruwaene, *La Théologie de Cicéron* (Louvain: Bibliothèque de l'Université, 1937), pp. 216–220.

[188] Cicero, *Tusc.*, 1.60.

[189] Cicero, *Tusc.*, 1.60, "*Non est certe nec cordis nec sanguinis nec cerebri nec atomorum.*"

[190] Cicero, *Tusc.*, 1.60.

[191] Cicero, *Tusc.*, 1.70. Cf. Cicero, *Rep.*, 6.2.

96   ROMAN VIRTUE IN THE EARLY CHRISTIAN THOUGHT OF LACTANTIUS

Tullia's apotheosis has a direct textual relationship with his vision of the deified Scipio. *Tusc.* 1.67 repeats a famous passage of Scipio's *Dream*:

> Therefore there is a certain distinct [*singularis*] nature and power [*natura et vis*] of the soul that is distinguished from other common and well-known natures. Thus, whatever feels [*sensit*], whatever is wise [*sapit*], whatever lives [*vivit*], whatever exercises strength [*viget*] is heavenly and divine on account of it and is necessarily an eternal thing. Nor can God himself, who is understood by us, be understood in any other way than as a certain mind [*Mens*] unbounded and free, separated from every mortal compound [*concretione*], conscious of everything, self-moving and endowed with all movement eternally. The human mind is of this same kind and out of this same nature.[192]

Cicero's reliance upon his own earlier discussion (and his translation of Plato in that discussion) confirms the historical genealogy of his thought and the persistent influence of technical notions of "power and nature" throughout his corpus. Between the *Republic* of 53 B.C. and the *Tusculans* of 43 B.C., Cicero amplified and reinforced notions of divinity first made fundamental to his politics in the early dialogues. If Cicero was at first diffident about the finer points of physical theory, he seems in his later grief to have accepted a notion of divine providence articulated in terms of power theology.[193] That conception of power marks the difference between Ciceronian and Epicurean *virtus*. Their accounts of fundamental reality produce divergent notions of God, the soul, and human society. One rejects teleology; the other makes *virtus* the supreme reward of a deified statesman.

After Cicero: Imperial Theology Revisited

Cicero's thinking about power theology might be considered a mere philosophical or literary exercise, were it not for the clear influence of his ideas in later generations. The philosophical theology Cicero's texts precisely articulate can be found again in various epic, panegyrical, and philosophical sources, which were

---

[192] Cicero, *Tusc.*, 1.67.

[193] Contra Arnaldo Momigliano, "The Theological Efforts of the Roman Upper Classes in the First Century BC," in *Roman Religion*, ed. Clifford Ando, pp. 157–161. Momigliano argued that Cicero changed his religious opinions between the early *Republic* and the later *De natura deorum* and *De divinatione*. His argument rests on the judgment that Cotta represents Cicero's own voice and, likewise, that the skeptical position of *Div.* 2 expresses Cicero's true feelings. My point, by contrast, is that a coherent theological ontology is discernible in these dialogues. Cicero's account of the divine monarchy at *Rep.* 1.56 and 6.28, again at *Leg.* 1.21, at *Nat. d.* 2.60–62 and then at *Tusc.* 1.54–70 uses the same theological grammar. And Cicero recalls his own earlier works (e.g., *Rep.*, 6.28, quoting *Phaedrus*, again appears at *Tusc.*, 1.54.).

POWER AND *VIRTUS*   97

used to construct the imperial office for later generations. Whether this is because Cicero himself developed original ideas or because his thought witnessed to a philosophical culture makes no difference. His rhetorical and philosophical corpus created technical vocabulary that later authors deeply involved with the construction of imperial Roman ideology inherited and appropriated. Both Vergil and Seneca are prominent heirs to Ciceronian thought and vocabulary. Both interpret the traditional Roman gods as specific causal capacities that manifest themselves in various actions or power. Vergil's whole mythology of the gods, in this respect, can be read as a philosophical allegory.[194] Seneca, even more explicitly, updates the Ciceronian understanding of divinization as represented by Balbus and in the *Tusculans*. And Seneca does so not only in philosophical treatises but also in works written for and used by the Emperor Nero. Vergil and Seneca notably approach the world of early Christianity, and in that sense, witness to a form of imperial theology that Latin Christian apologists would critique not long after. Although this section does not offer a complete study, I will conclude by observing that major proponents of imperial Roman ideology echoed the philosophical theologies transmitted to the Roman world and into a Latin idiom by Cicero's philosophical dialogues.

Vergil's *Aeneid*

It would be strange to begin any exploration of imperial Roman philosophical theology with any text other than Vergil's *Aeneid*; its importance for the Augustan order and for later theological discourse needs no introduction. That Vergil knew the technical sense of power as an individual causal capacity, and even as a medical term, is evident from his description of Iapyx, the physician, who "that he might bear away the fates of a sick parent / preferred to know the powers of herbs [*potestates herbarum*] and their use for healing / and to engage arts without glory."[195] Beyond this literal medical reference, Vergil dramatized traditional divinities by describing them as powers, and he shows an awareness

---

[194] See John Stevens, "Platonism and Stoicism in Vergil's *Aeneid*," in *Platonic Stoicism—Stoic Platonism: The Dialogue between Platonism and Stoicism in Antiquity*, ed. Christoph Helmig and Mauro Bonazzi (Leuven: Leuven University Press, 2008), p. 87, arguing that "the Aeneid is organized around the principles of both [Platonic and Stoic] schools: its structure reflects Platonic soul division; its movement and purpose reflect Plato's theories of erotic and epistemological progress in the two versions of the doctrine of forms, and Stoic moral progress in its doctrine on the passions; its action is shaped by Stoic doctrines of fate and human agency; and its audience response theory originates in the Platonic dialogue and allegory of Republic, as well as in the Stoic theory of virtue and moral progress. Vergil answers Plato's challenge to Homer by showing that poetry fortified by philosophy is capable of educating, and need not inflame the emotions but can teach self-mastery over them."

[195] Vergil, *Aen.*, 12.395–396.

of the philosophical grammar that underlies discourse about "power and nature" in the broader environment. Vergil says, for instance, that "the power of the heavens commands [*caelestum vis iubet*]," using the term *vis* to name the principle of unity in the pantheon. He also uses *potestas* as a divine title, as when Aeneas prays, "Oh father, Oh eternal power over affairs and men! [*o pater, o hominum rerumque aeterna potestas!*] / for what else is there that we can now implore?"[196] Again, Stoic influence is apparent, when Aeneas cries out to his "*All-powerful Father* [*pater omnipotens*], in whom there is [*cui ... infit*] the first power of all things [*rerum cui prima potestas / infit*]."[197] The lines not only differentiate a "first power [*prima potestas*]," from others, but locate that power "within [*infit*]" God, just as Balbus does in Cicero.[198] Later, Vergil's portrait of the relationship between Venus and Mercury presumes the traditional *X from X* relationship of powers and their products described by Michel Barnes as so important for later Christian theological discourse. Venus names her relation to Mercury through the notion of identical powers: "My Son, *my powers* [*meae vires*], my great power [*magna potentia*], as a suppliant, I beg your divinity [*numen*]."[199] In this conversation, Venus's genetic relationship to Mercury is reduced to that of a power and its product. In this context, the terms *vis* and *potentia* provide technical content for the more ancient term *numen*. Vergil thus uses power (*vis, potestas*) as the most basic marker for being, understands powers both collectively and individually, and recognizes that one power communicates its identity in its effect.

Like Cicero's Balbus and *Dream of Scipio*, Vergil articulates a theology predicated upon the notion of divine "power," which justifies a doctrine of divinization located at the heart of *Aeneid* 6 and of the Augustan narrative of imperial divinization. Anchises explains to Aeneas how certain great souls become divine using the clear terms of a physical theory that illuminates Vergil's broader idiom. In the key passage, Aeneas looks down at a plain of souls who, "like bees in a meadow on a bright summer's day / settled upon many flowers," and seem to be waiting.[200] He then poses the question of reincarnation: Anchises, "O father, are we to believe that certain lofty souls [*sublimis animas*] go from here to heaven [*ad caelum*] and then return again to weighty bodies?"[201] The unity and

---

[196] Vergil, *Aen.*, 10.100. Cf. *Aen.*, 1.616, "*quae vis immanibus applicat oris,*" *Aen.*, 10.545. Aeneas's question echoes of Marcus's search for a term at Cicero, *Leg.*, 1.21.

[197] Vergil, *Aen.*, 10.15.

[198] *Nat d.*, 2.58–60.

[199] Vergil, *Aen.*, 1.655. Vergil names the same two deities that Balbus discusses at *Nat. d.*, 2.58–2.60.

[200] Vergil, *Aen.*, 6.706–709. The simile of the bees is, for Vergil, a central political metaphor. It appears again at *Aen.* 12.584–593, also in *Georgics* 4.51–89, where bees and their king represent a harmonious society. See Andre Stipanovic, "Bees and Ants: Perceptions of Imperialism in Vergil's *Aeneid* and *Georgics,*" in *Insect Poetics*, ed. Eric C. Brown (Minneapolis: University of Minnesota Press, 2018). Also, Wolfgang Polleichtner, "The Bee Simile: How Vergil Emulated Apollonius in His Use of Homeric Poetry," *Goettinger Forum fur Altertumswissenschaft* 8 (2005): p. 115–160. It appears earlier in Plato's *Republic* 8.

[201] Vergil, *Aen.*, 6.722–723.

POWER AND *VIRTUS* 99

plurality of the bees serves as an analogy of the soul, which Anchises will explain in terms of Hellenistic (Stoic) physical theory.[202] He answers that some souls return to bodies, while certain very great ones are purified to their most divine element. His technical terms can all be found in the Ciceronian philosophical corpus:

> At their beginning [*principio*], the heaven and earth [*caelum ac terras*] and the watery expanse and the shining orb of the moon and the stars of the Titans / spirit [*spiritus*] inwardly sustains and mind [*mens*] infused through the joints [*per artus*] / moves through the entire mass [*totam . . . molem*] and mixes itself with the great body [*magno se corpore miscet*] / thence the kinds of people and beasts [*hominum pecudumque genus*] and the lives of flowing things. / It is a fiery vigor [*igneus est ollis vigor*] and those seeds have their origin in heaven [*et caelestis origo / seminibus*], so long as harmful bodies do not encumber or earthly joints and limbs impede.[203]

Vergil's choice of language allows us to understand his work as an epic statement of more technical Hellenistic philosophical cosmologies.[204] Vergil's Anchises describes the cosmos in clear Stoic terms as a body mixed with *spiritus*. He says that *spiritus* blows through that body as its foundational element (*principium*), the material substance of *mens*.[205] *Spiritus* he identifies with the power of fire (*igneus vigor*) and locates it in individual substances—using the Lucretian term *seminum*—that allow *igneus vigor* to be compounded in complex bodies. Like Varro, Balbus, and Lucretius, Anchises's doctrine is distinguished neither by its vocabulary nor by the notion of powers as compounded, but rather by Anchises's assertion that the cosmos is infused with a rational potency. His statement disseminates a theology predicated on notions of power and nature to a wide Roman audience.

---

[202] Nicholas Horsfall, *Virgil, Aeneid 6: A Commentary* (Berlin: De Gruyter, 2013), p. 477, notes "the analogy of the bee as a human soul awaiting rebirth. . . . The literary potential of bees in a complex text such as this is remarkable, for at 710, we will discover that V.'s bees are *also* to be understood as to some degree portentous."

[203] Vergil, *Aen.*, 7.25–730.

[204] For philosophical allusions in this passage, see Horsfall, *Virgil, Aeneid 6: A Commentary*, pp. 485–487. Horsfall cites the *Somnium Scipionis* as the first point of reference for *Aen.* 7.24–25 and remarks, "It has never been clear to me why there should be such reluctance to admit Cic[ero] as an author read by V[ergil], with pleasure (he can hardly have disdained *Somn.*) and indeed profit." Cf. *Tusc.*, 1.56–1.57, *Rep.*, 6, *Phaedrus*, 245 et alii.

[205] Horsfall, *Aeneid 6: A Commentary*, p. 485, takes "*principio*" temporally, as "first off." However, Vergil's line echoes too nearly of Genesis for the allusion to be ignored. Given that, philosophically, he is locating *spiritus* as the foundation of the other elements, I take his term as playing on the same ambiguity of the term *arche* in Greek and in LXX Genesis. Notably, Jan Bremmer, "Virgil and Jewish Literature," *Vergilius* 59 (2013): pp. 157–164, argues that Isaiah 7:14, Genesis, and the *Sibylline Oracles* are all known in Rome; he suggests that 1 Enoch may have influenced *Aeneid* 6. Admittedly, the rest of my analysis is not vitiated by dissent from this rendering.

100 ROMAN VIRTUE IN THE EARLY CHRISTIAN THOUGHT OF LACTANTIUS

Anchises's account of the world soul provides a basis for his depiction of life after death. Anchises describes the rational power—*mens/spiritus*—as the supreme power in human beings, which remains after the body's other powers are removed. The lexical frame of reference is medical. He articulates a process in which our "darkened bodily prison [*carcere caeco*]," infected by all sorts of "evil [*malum*]," and "crime [*scelus*]," and "sicknesses [*pestes*]" is "exercised by pains [*exercentur poenis*]," that lead to their cleansing, even purgation[*exuritur igni*].[206] As a result, "we each suffer our own souls [*quisque suos patimur manis*]; then we are sent through the expanse of Elysium / and a few of us obtain the happy fields," in a long period of purification that leaves only our "pure ethereal sense [*purumque reliquit aetherium sensus*] and the fire of simple gold [*atque aurai simplicis ignem*]."[207] Vergil does not neglect philosophical vocabulary. He can use *manis*, but redefine it by the terms *anima, sensus, mens*, and *spiritus* somewhat interchangeably. Each is a way of denoting the rational capacity located in the expansive element of fire, which is the simple and active power that moves all things [*totam ... mollem ... agitat*].[208] The divine soul preserves its distinctive power (*sensus*), but separated from every other encumbering element becomes "simple [*simplicis*]." This is true for "a few lofty souls," while the rest return to an embodied state, apparently to try again.[209] By placing this theology in the mouth of Anchises, immediately prior to his prophecy of Augustus's rise (6.785ff.), Vergil makes this account of divinity the basis for his Augustan political theology.

Vergil's metaphysical language also explains his use of *virtus*. In the *Aeneid, virtus* almost always bears the heroic sense of martial and therefore physical strength, but such a connotation is built upon his underlying physical theory.[210] Vergil locates *virtus* physically as something visible "in the comely body [*pulchro in corpore*]" of Euryalus. He can also use technical terms when challenging anyone having "virtue and spirit present in their breast [*virtus animusque in pectore praesens*]," and associate *virtus* with power and heat, as when he says that Acestes "returns keener [*acrior*] to the fight and wrath stirs his force [*vim*] / also shame fires his powers [*pudor incendit vires*] along with conscious *virtus*."[211] Later, Vergil sings the "*virtus* stirred for war [*bello vivida virtus*]" in a line that echoes Lucretius's "*vis vivida animi*."[212] The collective plural *vires* along with the

---

[206] Vergil, *Aen.*, 6.742.

[207] Vergil, *Aen.*, 6.746–747.

[208] On Stoic fire and cosmic conflagration see Barnes, *Power of God*, p. 30, fn. 28, recalls "the strong religious understanding attached to fire consistently through the history of Greek thought. . . . [It is] understood as the fundamental element underlying all existence."

[209] Vergil, *Aen.*, 6.747–751. Cf. For *simplex* see Cicero, *Nat. d.*, 2.28–2.30, *Acad.*, 1.24–29.

[210] See McDonnell, *Roman Manliness*, pp. 14ff.

[211] Vergil, *Aen.*, 5.454–455.

[212] Vergil, *Aen.*, 5.752, 11.386, "*vivida virtus.*"

POWER AND *VIRTUS* 101

verbal forms (*incendit . . . ardens*) reflect the underlying notion of fire as the active element operating within the unified compound of a body. Vergil can also cast claims about *virtus* as relations between a cause and its product, as when Hercules says: "to extend fame by deeds [*famam extendere factis*], this is the work of *virtus* [*hoc virtutis opus*]."[213] The lines preserve a model of physical causation, but expand causality to the immaterial product of *fama*. Like Piso (*Fin.*, 5.36–37), Vergil can also equate physical and emotional powers: "There burns a great shame [*aestuat ingens . . . pudor*] and madness in a single heart combined [*uno in corde . . . mixto*] with grief [*luctu*], and love stirred by furies [*furiis agitatus amor*] and conscious *virtus*."[214] The line nicely articulates the way *virtus* could represent both heroic courage and an ethical quality. *Amor*, *pudor*, and *virtus* all operate as powers in a compounded heart/mind; the underlying physical theory actually sustains the moral notion. As Vergil put it, "Luck and *virtus* are mixed into one [*fors et virtus miscentur in unum*]."[215]

Two generations after Vergil, Seneca witnesses to the continuing influence of power causality on Roman philosophical and political theology. His works reflect a standardization of the Latin philosophical vocabulary, while his nearness to the emperor attests to the interpenetration of philosophical and political discourses in Rome. Writing during the first decades of Christianity, Seneca's discussions of theological and ethical matters range widely.[216] He repeats more than one of Cicero's Stoic formulations. Seneca closely associates the notions of power, effects, and names. He argues against the Epicurean refusal to name the *vis naturae* as *Deus*, and he updates claims seen in Cicero's account of the virtues at *De inventione* 2.157–160 and in Balbus's philosophical theology at *Nat. d.* 2.58–60.

Two significant passages in Seneca reveal the continuation of Ciceronian language for Stoic discourse in the Augustan era. The first comes from Seneca's remarks about *virtus* in *Ep.* 66. Seneca addresses the question of "how goods can be equal, if their condition is threefold [*quomodo possint paria bona esse, si triplex eorum condicio est*]."[217] It is the same basic question addressed by Cicero's

---

[213] Vergil, *Aen.*, 10.466.

[214] Vergil, *Aen.*, 12.666. Cf. *Aen.*, 12.908, the death of Turnus, where *virtus* is juxtaposed with *vires* as a failing capacity: "*non lingua valet, non corpore notae / sufficiunt vires, nec vox aut verba secuntur: sic Turnus, quacumque viam virtute petivit, successum dea dira negat.*" Cf. McDonnell, *Roman Manliness*, p. 388, observing that after Augustus, "an Augustan poet [could] extol the *pudicitia* of an Emperor's wife by praising her *virtus.*"

[215] Vergil, *Aen.*, 12.713. Vergil, *The Aeneid*, trans. Robert Fitzgerald (New York: Random House, 1990), tries to capture the physical and martial/ethical sense of the line as "prowess [*virtus*] merged with luck in the fighting power [*virtus*] of each."

[216] Susanna Braund, "Seneca *Multiplex*: The Phases (and Phrases) of Seneca's Life and Works," in *The Cambridge Companion to Seneca*, ed. Shadi Bartsch and Alessandro Schiesaro (Cambridge: Cambridge University Press, 2015), pp. 15–29.

[217] Seneca, *Ep.*, 66.5–6 in *Seneca, Epistles*, vol. 2, *Epistles 66–92*, trans. Richard M. Gummere, Loeb Classical Library 76 (Cambridge, MA: Harvard University Press, 1920). For introduction to Seneca's *Epistles* 58, 65, and 66, see Inwood, "Seneca, Plato, and Platonism: The Case of Letter 65," in *Platonic*

attempt to reconcile the plurality of virtues like prudence, justice, fortitude, and temperance under a single category called *virtus*. Seneca responds with a florid description of the capacities of a superlative soul, one perfectly adapted to any and every activity. He concludes by offering a vivid doctrine of *virtus*:

> Such a soul is *virtus*. This is its countenance [*facies*]. Though it may present itself in a single aspect [*unum . . . aspectum*] and show itself whole [*semel tota se ostendat*], its manifestations [*species*] are many . . . into various qualities [*qualitates*] it is converted once it is fashioned [*figurata*] according to the shape [*ad . . . habitum*] of what it would accomplish [*actura*]. Whatever it touches, it transforms into its own likeness and colors by soaking in itself. . . . And so its power [*vis eius*] and magnitude cannot increase, since for the greatest thing, there can be no growth. You will find nothing righter than the right, nothing truer than the true.[218]

Seneca's question contains the central problematic of what would become trinitarian theology among Christians—how can we maintain a conceptual unity, given that we acknowledge plurality? Seneca answers the question by claiming that *virtus* can assume a number of appearances (*species, qualitates*), which change their form according to the circumstance in which they are manifest. The one power is simply "converted [*convertitur*]" into various "*qualitates*"—the product required to perfectly accomplish a particular effect. And yet, *virtus* applied to a lesser thing is no less *virtus* itself.[219]

Given the close association of *virtus* with divinity, it is no surprise to find that the above doctrine of *virtus* also provides a logic for Seneca's understanding of the traditional Roman pantheon. In *De beneficiis*, Seneca articulates a doctrine of God that relies on the relationship between *virtus* and its effects. "However you may wish," Seneca writes, "You will rightly adapt to him [*illi*] names [*nomina*] containing a given power and effect of heavenly things [*vim aliquam effectumque caelestium rerum continentia*]: his titles [*eius appellationes*] can be as numerous as his rewards [*possunt esse quot munera*]."[220] This thinking explains

---

Stoicism—Stoic Platonism: The Dialogue between Platonism and Stoicism in Antiquity, pp. 149–168. Arguing that Seneca has direct access to multiple dialogues of Plato and Cicero *inter alii*, Inwood says that "Seneca's letters are much more plausibly to be taken as evidence for the nature of the living philosophical environment in which he worked and as evidence for the oral conduct of philosophy in Rome in his day."

[218] Seneca, *Ep.*, 66.7–8.
[219] For more on this, see Jason M. Gehrke, "*Singulare et Unicum Imperium*: Monarchianism and Latin Apologetic in Rome," in *New Narratives for Old: The Historical Method of Reading Early Christian Theology. Essays in Honor of Michel Barnes*, ed. Anthony Briggman and Ellen Scully (Washington, DC: Catholic University of America Press, 2022), pp. 142–163.
[220] Seneca, *Ben.*, 4.8.2 in *Seneca, Moral Essays*, vol. 3, *De Beneficiis*, trans. John W. Basore, Loeb Classical Library 310 (Cambridge, MA: Harvard University Press, 1935).

POWER AND *VIRTUS*   103

the plurality of names of divinities, each one understood as a manifestation of one fundamental power. It is notable that Seneca says each name "contains" a power, which is titled from its effect. Seneca applies this thought to explain the traditional gods:

> This is how [*hunc*] our school [*nostri*] considers Father Liber [*Liberum patrem*] and Hercules and Mercury: because [God] is the parent of all [*omnium parens*], in him has been found primarily [*primum*] the power of seeds [*seminum vis*], which is ready to nourish life through pleasure [*vitae consultura per voluptatem*]. [Thus we name him]—Hercules, because his power is unconquered [*qui vis eius invicta sit*], when it has been let loose in the works it produces [*lassata fuerit operibus editis*] and returns into fire [*in ignem*]; Mercury, because there is reason deep within him, along with number and order and knowledge [*quia ratio penes illum est numerusque et ordo et scientia*]. And wherever you turn, there you will see him rushing toward you; nothing escapes from him [*ab illo vacat*], he fills all his works [*opus suum ipse implet*].[221]

Seneca's remarks develop a theological vocabulary already evident in Cicero. The association of *nomen* and *vis* is typical of the technical sense of power, which Seneca, naturally, takes as the irreducible term for what exists. *Vis* names the reality of any divine title, and each title exists to specify the character that is unique to the given power. Likewise, each title denotes a distinctive capacity, which is compounded in a common nature. As he continues, Seneca thus emphasizes the unified reality underlying such *nomina*. Where Balbus spoke of specific powers combined and dispensed by "the Divine Goodness," Seneca emphasizes the oneness of God even more strongly:

> Therefore, you accomplish nothing, O most ungrateful of mortals, when you say that you are not [*negas*] in debt to God [*deo debere*], but rather to Nature, because there is no *Natura* without God, nor God without *Natura*. Each is one and the same [*sed idem est utrumque*]; the difference is in their function [*distat officio*]. If, what you received from Seneca, you say you owe to Annaeus or Lucius, you do not change the creditor [*creditorem*], but his name [*nomen*], since even if you had spoken his first-name [*praenomen*] or last name [*nomen*], or his personal name [*cognomen*], he would still have been that same person [*idem . . . ille esset*]. So then, call him Nature, fate, fortune: all these are names of the very same God [*omnia eiusdem dei nomina sunt*], who exercises his own power in various ways [*varie utentis sua potestate*]. Likewise, justice [*iustitia*], uprightness [*probitas*], prudence [*prudentia*], fortitude [*fortitudo*], frugality

---

[221] Seneca, *Ben.*, 4.8.1.

[*frugalitas*] are all goods of the same soul [*unius animi bona sunt*]; whichever of them pleases you, it is the soul that pleases.[222]

Seneca's argument makes the notion of mind [*animus*] the unifying reality behind any given divine power and thus assimilates the mythical powers such as *Fortuna* to one divine mind and its activity. In this respect, also, the philosophic virtues are understood as powers, but the presupposition of their unity and interpenetration emphasizes the divine unity. He has no way of distinguishing God from any given power in which God operates. Seneca can distinguish only the rightly adapted name. And because this deity *"fills his work,"* Seneca has no apparent way to distinguish God from the world in which divine action is manifest.

Seneca's account of God in *On Benefits* contains the theological assumptions that sustain his political theology as well. Although slightly earlier, Seneca's *On Clemency* uses the same philosophical theology to articulate Nero's divinity and his role in the cosmos. The treatise notably attests to the way Augustan discourse attributed a sort of canonical status to the works of Vergil and Cicero.[223] Seneca opens with an invocation of Zeus's "nod [*ad meum nutum*]" that echoes of Cicero's *Rep.* 1.56.[224] Like Hercules, Nero receives titles that name his specific powers: "many names [*congnomina*] are given to honor," such as *Augustus, Magnus, Felix,* "we have titled him [*appellivamus*] *pater patriae* so he might know that *patria potestas* has been given to him."[225] Although the legal category *patria potestas* preceded Stoic theology, the association of *nomen* and *potestas* interprets political authority according to a naturalistic philosophical grammar (*Inv.*, 2.157, *Rep.*, 6.15–18). Seneca grounds this theology in references to Vergil and Cicero. He calls Nero the *animus* and *spiritus vitalis* of the body and cites the famous ancient analogy of the bees in the text of Vergil's *Georgics*: "When their king is safe, all have one mind [*rege columni mens omnibus una*] / with him lost they break faith."[226] Vergil's metaphors explain what is meant by the emperor's

---

[222] Seneca, *Ben.*, 4.8.2.

[223] Malcolm Schofield, "Seneca on Monarchy and the Political Life: *De Clementia, De tranquillitate animi, De otio,*" in *The Cambridge Companion to Seneca*, ed. Shadi Bartsch and Alessandro Schiesaro (Cambridge: Cambridge University Press, 2015), pp. 68–82. Schofield notes that *De clementia* "was part of the publicity of the new [Neronian] regime" and informed speeches penned by Seneca, which Nero himself delivered.

[224] Seneca, *Clem.*, 1–2 in *Seneca, Moral Essays*, vol. 1, *De providentia; De constantia; De ira; De clementia*, trans. John W. Basore, Loeb Classical Library 308 (Cambridge, MA: Harvard University Press, 1928).

[225] Seneca, *Clem.*, 1.14.2. Cf. Identical language at *Ben.*, 4.8.1–2. See also Ando, *Imperial Ideology and Provincial Loyalty*, pp. 402–403, who connects Seneca and Pliny's addresses to Nero and Trajan with Tertullian's *Apologeticum* 34.1–2.

[226] Seneca, *Clem.*, 1.14.2. Also, *Clem.*, 19, again elaborates the bees metaphor. Cf. *Georgics*, 4.212, *Aen.*, 6.720–724.

POWER AND *VIRTUS* 105

power to preserve the harmonious action of the people. Seneca hopes Nero will surpass the other parts of the body politic by his supreme exercise of that rational faculty that rules in the body of nature (cf. *Aen.*, 6.720–730; *Nat. d.*, 2.30–32). Such imperial activity produces a unity, such that "this oneness [*unitas*] and this interweaving [*contextus*] of the great empire shall burst forth [*dissiliet*] into its many parts [*in multas partes*]."[227] Constant allusions to medicine anchor such cosmological language, along with the textual tradition that Seneca's works reflect.[228] *On Clemency* evokes medicine by its analogy of a body: "Just as Caesar has need of his powers, so [the body] needs a head."[229] Such rhetoric anticipates a clear evocation of Scipio's *Dream*: "You are the soul of your republic [*tu animus rei publicae tuae es*], and she your body [*illa corpus tuum*]."[230] By couching philosophical arguments as literary references, Seneca identifies Nero's regime as the continuation of a Roman tradition.

Underlying Seneca's account of the imperial office is a concept of the cosmic harmony and the Empire's special role in its maintenance. Seneca interprets *virtus* as a power compounded in the imperial body. His comments again echo of Cicero: "Although the *virtutes* have a harmony [*virtutibus inter se concordia*] among themselves, nor is any one better or more noble than another [*melior aut honestior*], nevertheless a particular one may be better adapted [*aptior*] for certain persons."[231] Seneca uses *virtutes* to signify a plurality of individual capacities that combine in the imperial nature. Seneca thus identifies *clementia* as the distinctive capacity that distinguishes Nero's regime in its continuation of what Ando termed the "Augustan charisma."[232] Just as *Ben.* 4.7–8 would explain, whether you call the emperor Octavius, or Tiberius, or Nero, the divine power remains the very same; only the quality is distinguished.[233] Ando was right to see more than analogy and metaphor in such ideological language. Seneca relies upon a philosophical theology traceable to Hellenistic discourses, which undergird political philosophy and theology in the early empire.

---

[227] Seneca, *Clem.*, 4.4. Cf. Balbus's *naturae perfectio* at Cicero, *Nat. d.*, 2.28–29. Cf. "*in multas partes*," Cicero, *Acad.*, 26–27.

[228] Seneca, *Clem.*, 3. Also, *Clem.*, 9, Livia's advice to Augustus; *Clem.*, 17: seek a "soothing medicine and a physician," etc.; *Clem.*, 24, where executions are to a king as funerals are to a physician.

[229] Seneca, *Clem.*, 4.3.

[230] Seneca, *Clem.*, 5.2.

[231] Cf. Seneca, *Ep.*, 66.7–8

[232] Ando, *Imperial Ideology and Provincial Loyalty*, pp. 27–33, 45, "Despite the passage of such a law, the Julio-Claudian emperors clearly derived their authority from Augustus: his charisma retained force after his death above all through its incarnation as a divinity, *Victoria Augusti.*"

[233] Cf. *Clem.* 5.3's *aptior* to *aptabis* at *Ben.* 4.8.1–2. Likewise, *Clem.* 12.3's claim that "a tyrant differs from a king by his deeds [*a rege factis distat*], not by his name [*non nomine*]," echoes the causal logic of *Ben.* 4.8.

Conclusion

In the century that divided Cicero (d. 43 B.C.) from Seneca (64 A.D.), the Roman political order fundamentally changed. Epitomized at Pharsalus (48 B.C.), Rome's civil wars inspired Cicero's and Lucretius's massively influential works of epic, theology, and politics. As the Republic fell and Augustus rose, Vergil's *Aeneid* and *Georgics* drew upon them. His poetry provided literary ammunition for continuing conflict over the new Roman order. Ovid, Seneca, and Lucan each took positions that were different in their criticism, but no less harsh. In the process, Augustan art refashioned Rome's ancient self-image to fit the new imperial forms. The philological expansion of the traditional term *virtus* to encompass not only martial force (*virtus*) but also ethical perfections (*virtutes*) and divine power (*virtus divina*) resulted from this social and intellectual conflagration, which remade the Roman political order. By the end of the first century, Latin philosophical discourse had developed a stable set of technical terms for debate about the meaning of *virtus* and its relationship to the fundamental order of the world. Classical Roman philosophical discourse closely associated the terms power (*vis*) and name (*nomen*) in order to designate a thing's identity and relationship to its cause. When distinguishing particular powers from the irreducible force of the cosmos, the term *vis* usually explained the others (e.g., *virtutis vis,* but not *viris virtus* or *potestatis virtus*).

A basket of synonyms for power (*vis, virtus, potestas, potentia*) soon emerged out of ancient medicine and physical theory for use in conversations as wide as law, rhetoric, metaphysics, and political philosophy. Latin philosophy used the term *natura* or *naturae* because no power was thought to act alone. *Natura* designated the compound of powers operating in union and located within a complex existent, whether plants, animals, humans, or gods. The phrase *vis et natura* translated the technical formula designating the very identity of a thing or concept. The cosmos itself was conceived as one grand *Natura*. When emphasizing its providential capacity, Stoics could term *Natura* as God (*Deus*), or employ a range of traditional titles (*appellationes*) in order to emphasize a particular divine capacity. Platonists used the same language, but conceived of reason (*rationis perfectio*) as immaterial and above *Natura*, rather than seated within the power of fire, which imbues everything. Epicureans rejected the power of providence (*providentia*) and accounted for material nature by their atomic theory, which was itself a theory of powers combined in a nature.

Such physical theory accounts for the apparent multivalence of the Latin term *virtus*. In human beings, *virtus* came to serve as the technical term for individual capacities that human beings share with *Natura/Deus* on account of their reason but which lower animals do not possess. Hence, Latin authors could use *virtutes* in the plural and speak of a *concordia* of the *virtutes* among themselves. In this respect, the physical and the political were fundamentally alike. In a person, *virtutes* might be thought to cohere and require balance and harmony, just as the fundamental powers needed proper combination in order for mind and body to thrive. Cicero thus coined the term *qualitas* to distinguish immaterial capacities that remained inseparable from the elemental powers. An author could use *virtus* as a summary term for qualities (*qualitates*) like justice, prudence, and clemency because such *qualitates* were understood as subsisting in the human nature. Stoics like Seneca seem to have located such capacities physically in the powers of heat and air, where Platonists would regard *virtus* as immaterial. Still, all agreed that *virtus* was a cause that distinguished humanity from other natures and demonstrated humanity's likeness to the gods. In this respect, Augustan thinking about *virtus* extended the traditional assumptions of Late Republican society.

The belief that "deep down," as Lucretius put it, power was indivisible, created two fundamental assumptions in Latin philosophical theology. The first is that the unity of any given nature consists in the unity of its powers. Between Cicero and Seneca, Latin texts do not postulate a single all-competent power, but rather a single nature which contains all specific powers within itself. This conceptualization is both shared and debated across a range of positions reflected in a broad array of literature—from the philosophical works of Cicero and Lucretius, to the poetic vision of Vergil, the historical arguments of Sallust, and the orthodox Stoic epistles and treatises of Seneca. The second assumption is that while natures contain a plurality of powers operating in union, there is no identity more basic than a given power, such that to identify a power is to name a thing rightly. In Latin philosophical discourse—a conversation that spans across several literary genres—terms like *nomen* and *appellatio* refer to the word one uses to identify a thing in terms of its causal capacity.

The philosophical conversation documented above created an articulate theological language for expressing claims about divinity in the Roman Empire after Augustus. The notion of a plurality of powers operating in union allowed Romans to understand their traditional pantheon in theological terms, while enabling innovations that responded to historical and intellectual changes in Roman life. Romans could include deified figures within the pantheon by naming their actions as the effects of a power that could only be called divine, and whose ultimate unicity was not in question. At the same time, the notion of abstractly distinguishable *qualitates* allowed emperors to distinguish their particular regimes without undermining their ostensible continuation of the Augustan charisma. For that political tradition, Vergil's and Cicero's works assumed a quasi-canonical status, as they provided a literary and philosophical basis for imperial claims. More to the point, Latin philosophical theology served as a constant point of reference for imperial ideology, and the imperial opposition to Christianity would inspire a Christian response that couched itself in these common terms. All sides shared a literary and philosophical tradition which provided terms and logic for another phase of Roman theological discourse, when Latin-speaking Roman Christians began defending their place in the Roman Empire by initiating a new Christian era of Roman discourse about *virtus*.

3

Virtus in Early Latin Christian Apologetic

> The power of inborn character and *virtus* [*vis ingenii atque virtutis*]
> was so great in [Romulus], that what had never before been believed
> about any mortal was believed concerning him and from [the re-
> port] of Julius Proculus, a rustic no less.
>
> —Cicero, *Republic*, 2.17

The preceding reconstruction of classical Roman discourse about *virtus* casts light upon the early Latin Christian writers whom Lactantius named as his principal influences.[1] Revisiting their thought is necessary because much in the modern evaluation of Lactantius's relationship to early Latin Christianity presupposes judgments about Latin Christian apologetic and its relationship to third-century Latin theology as a whole. Modern scholarship has tended to characterize Latin apologetic as concerned primarily with the rhetorical embellishment of a theological content derived mainly from Greek and Jewish sources.[2] Rather than developing Christian theology, the apologists are thought to have been concerned mainly with the construction of a Christian identity in response to "pagan" opposition.[3] As a result, modern narratives often emphasize the cultural binaries of "Christian" and "pagan" in a way that tends to simplify the dialectic of early Latin apologetic engagement with "pagan" ideas. What results is a somewhat obscured portrait of the relationship between early Latin Christians, their own cultural-intellectual inheritance, and

---

[1] See Introduction, this volume.

[2] Manlio Simonetti, "The Beginnings of Latin Theological Investigation in the West," in *History of Theology: The Patristic Period*, trans. Matthew J. O'Connell, ed. Angelino Di Perardino and Basil Studer (Collegeville, MN: Liturgical Press, 1997), pp. 204–224. Also, Michael Fiedrowicz, *Apologie im frühen Christentum: die Kontroverse um den christlichen Wahrheitsanspruch in den ersten Jahrhunderten* (Paderborn: F. Schöningh, 2000), p. 62. Earlier, Paul Monceaux, *Histoire Littéraire de L'Afrique du Nord: histoire littéraire de l'afrique chrétienne depuis les origines jusqu'à l'invasion arabe*, vol. 1 (Paris, 1901), pp. 500–510.

[3] E.g., Simon Price, "Latin Christian Apologetics: Minucius Felix, Tertullian, and Cyprian," in *Apologetics in the Roman Empire: Pagans, Jews, and Christians*, ed. Mark Edwards, Martin Goodman, and Simon Price (Oxford: Oxford University Press, 1999); Marcia Colish, *The Stoic Tradition from Antiquity to the Middle Ages* (Leiden: Brill, 1985), pp. 30–31. "Minucius simplifies considerably the task of disarming [his] opposition, while at the same time making it possible for himself to present his apology in a graceful and elegant style. This rhetorical decision makes it unnecessary for him to address the serious philosophical questions raised by a revealed theology as such or by the paradoxes of the central dogmas of Christianity."

Roman Virtue in the Early Christian Thought of Lactantius. Jason M. Gehrke, Oxford University Press.
© Oxford University Press 2025. DOI: 10.1093/9780197667781.003.0004

the contributions of that inheritance to the Christian development of doctrine. Insofar as Lactantius's thought arises from his reading of Latin apologetic, understanding him requires us to reconsider the Latin apologists' engagement with Roman literature and, in turn, their influence upon third-century Latin Christian thought.

The early development of Latin Christian theology (i.e., 180–325 A.D.) was inseparable from Latin Christian engagement with classical Roman literature and the political reality of Roman imperial self-representation. Driven in part by the Christian memory of persecution, political concerns were a central factor that motivated and shaped the Christian reading of classical Roman sources. Often, educated Roman converts to Christianity had to justify their beliefs and their continuing position within a political order that was publicly represented in religious terms. Those terms dictated the original problematic addressed by the Latin apologists prior to Lactantius. Their task was to explain how the person and work of Jesus Christ modified classical Roman thinking about divine and human order, which considered Christianity as incompatible with traditional Roman society. Christian apologetic efforts developed theological discourses that would come later to inform Latin trinitarian theology. Of course, Greek Christians also faced this challenge, but the Latin apologists brought a set of formative concerns that reflected their initiation into Roman literary and political traditions, which had shaped philosophical debate in Latin language of the Roman Empire.

This chapter will demonstrate three major points about the role of Latin apologetic in early Latin Christianity. First, the Latin apologists positioned themselves in continuity with earlier Roman arguments about *virtus* by assuming a tradition of Republican criticism of the Principate, which was familiar to educated Romans. Criticisms first formulated by Vergil, Livy, and Lucan come to provide a basis for the apologetic claim that Christian virtue is more consistent with Rome's own purported ideals than any imperial reconstruction. Second, in their arguments about the character and meaning of *virtus*, the Latin apologists represented Christ as the supreme *exemplum virtutis*, whose example corrected and ultimately superseded traditional Roman heroes. Third, this apologetic effort exercised a decisive influence on the development of Latin trinitarian theology. The apologists' trumpeting of Christ's example first led Latin Christians to express Christian doctrine in causal terms taken over from classical Roman authors like Cicero, Vergil, and Seneca. Certainly, the fact that all the principal Latin Christian writers shared a Roman education made their use of Latin philosophical language natural, perhaps inevitable. Still, the polemical context decisively shaped their earliest doctrinal constructions; and that polemical concern is never fully left behind, even in later intra-Christian arguments. As a result, Latin Christian opposition to classical Roman ideologies of the empire constituted an original field of theological discourse, which established a basic grammar for third-century Latin Christian theological discourse.

The *Octavius*: Strategic Contradiction Revisited

The *Octavius* of Minucius Felix provides the major point of departure for my account of early Latin theology because the dialogue is representative of early Latin apologetic. Although the precise date is disputed, scholars locate the *Octavius* in a period between 197 and 250 A.D., and probably between 212–247. It is generally viewed as a witness to the social atmosphere of the Severan era.[4] The *Octavius* has, moreover, a close relationship to Tertullian's *Apologeticus*, since one of the documents drew much upon the other.[5] Since Carl Becker's analysis, most agree that Tertullian wrote first. In that respect, *Octavius* reflects the argumentative strategy of Latin Christianity's greatest third-century author and the state of Latin Christian apologetic in the half century prior to Lactantius. Finally, Minucius directly informed both Cyprian and Lactantius, who lifted both arguments and citations from his work.[6] The *Octavius* captures a tradition.

A foundational element of the early Latin apologetic tradition appears in the *Octavius*'s consistent references to Cicero and Augustan literature. By those references, the *Octavius* dramatizes a forensic debate that aims to rebut elite Roman objections to Christianity.[7] Minucius Felix evokes the dramatic setting of Cicero's philosophic dialogues in order to situate the debate as an extension of earlier Roman conversations. The character Caecilius Natalis combines Cicero's Velleius and Cotta, while the character Octavius assumes the Stoic position of

---

[4] Jonathan Powell, "Unfair to Caecilius? Ciceronian Dialogue Techniques in Minucius Felix," in *Severan Culture*, ed. Simon Swain, Stephen Harrison, and Jas Elsner (Oxford: Oxford University Press, 2007), p. 179. Powell follows T. R. Glover and Gerald H. Rendall, "Introduction," in Minucius Felix, *Octavius*, trans. T. R. Glover and Gerald H. Rendall (Cambridge, MA: Harvard University Press, 1931), and Robin Lane Fox, *Pagans and Christians* (New York: Harper Collins, 1986), pp. 300–301.

[5] Scholarly consensus cedes the priority to Tertullian, see Beaujeu, "Introduction," xliv–lxvii, in Jean Beaujeu, *Minucius Felix: texte, introduction, commentaire* (Paris: Les Belles Lettres, 2002). Carl Becker, *Der Octavius des Minucius Felix* (Munich: Beck, 1967). Also, Gilles Quispel, "A Jewish Source of Minucius Felix," *Vigiliae Christianae* 3.2 (1949): pp. 113–122, and Jean Daniélou, *The Origins of Latin Christianity,* trans. David Smith and John Austin Baker (Philadelphia: Westminster Press, 1977), p. 161, prefer Minucius Felix. The argument is redoubled in Gilles Quispel, "African Christianity before Minucius Felix and Tertullian," in *Gnostica, Judaica, Catholica. Collected Essays of Gilles Quispel,* ed. Johannes van Ort (Leiden: Brill, 2008), pp. 389–459. For a summary of scholarship, see Chapot, "Les grandes orientations des travaux sur l'*Octavius* de Minucius Felix. Remarques sur trente ans de bibliographie," *Vita Latina* 150 (1998): pp. 18–28.

[6] Lactantius, *Inst.*, 5.1.21–28.

[7] Christian Noack, "Der *Octavius* des Minucius Felix: Ein interreligiöser 'Rechstreit' unter Freunden zur Beurteilung der römischen und christlichen *religio*," *Spes Christiana* 17 (2006): pp. 7–20, esp., p. 9.

112 ROMAN VIRTUE IN THE EARLY CHRISTIAN THOUGHT OF LACTANTIUS

Scipio and Balbus; Minucius himself moderates.[8] Minucius's literary form is not merely rhetorical imitation. The form of the dialogue contains an essential element of the argument over the Roman ideal of *virtus*.[9] Caecilius embodies an Augustan imperial reconstruction of Roman tradition, while Octavius presents Christian communities as better heirs of their Roman ancestors. Unifying all three voices is a subversive rhetorical strategy that Minucius takes over from his classical sources. Each of his dramatic figures evokes well-known criticisms written into Augustan literature. Making those criticisms explicit, Minucius subverts imperial ideology and presents Christians as the true Roman heirs of Republican liberty.

Minucius's subversion of imperial theology begins with Caecilius. He purports to represent Epicurean and Academic views but actually displays Minucius's own criticism of pagan inconsistencies. By juxtaposing those inconsistencies with references to Cicero and Vergil, Minucius allows Caecilius's speech to undermine itself. Caecilius's first textual allusion is to *De rerum natura* 1.51–55.[10] He opens by striking an Epicurean note that attacks the Stoic doctrine of providence, which Scipio, Balbus, and later Vergil's Anchises had placed at the foundation of the Augustan narrative.[11] Drawing language from Lucretius and Velleius, Caecilius repeats the signature Epicurean doctrine that the human soul is a bundle of material powers:

> Every person and animal which is born, inspired, or raised up exists as a compound [*voluntaria concretio est*] of elements having a will, and every person and animal is divided, resolved, dissipated back into them again. So without any maker, nor judge, nor author, all things flow back to their source and resolve into themselves.[12]

---

[8] Recently, Hervé Inglebert, *Les Romains Chretiens Face a L'Histoire de Rome: Histoire, Christianisme, et romanites en Occident dans l'Antiquite tardive* (Paris: Institut d'Etudes Augustinennes, 1996), p. 115: "[Minucius Felix] références sont grèces ou romaines, et Cicéron est son modèle stylistique et philosophique." Rendall, "Introduction," in *Minucius Felix, Octavius*, pp. 308–315. The *Octavius* influenced Cyprian's literary settings as well. Cf. *Oct.*, 1.4 and 2.3; *Ad Demetrianum*, 25; *Ad Donatum*, 1.

[9] Scholars have often presented Minucius as a "compiler" while downplaying the argumentative strategy that organizes his selection. E.g., Beaujeu, "Introduction," xliv–lii. Likewise, Claudio Moreschini and Enrico Norelli, *Histoire de la littérature chrétienne antique grecque et latine: de Paul à l'ère de Constantin* (Genève: Éditions Labor et Fides, 1995), p. 421; Rendall, "Introduction," p. 313: "It is the work of a trained rhetorician, a product of the Roman schools of rhetoric and law." Monceaux, *Histoire Litteraire de L'Afrique Chrétienne*, pp. 488–489.

[10] Minucius Felix, *Oct.*, 5.7.24 in *Octavius Texte établi et traduit par Jean Beaujeu* (Paris: Les Belles Lettres, 1964). Cf. Lucretius, *Nat. r.*, 51–55.

[11] See Chapter 2, this volume.

[12] Minucius Felix, *Oct.*, 5.8. Cf. *Nat. r.*, 3.262ff. Daniélou, *Origins of Latin Christianity*, p. 199, takes this as a "clear statement of the Stoic conception of the cyclical movement of nature . . . [200] Caecilius' attitude is therefore deliberately skeptical, not Epicurean, even though it is Stoicism which he wishes chiefly to criticise." Caecilius is making, however, the Epicurean argument for atheism based on the mortality of the soul. He sets the Epicurean argument in the context of Stoic cyclic

VIRTUS IN EARLY LATIN CHRISTIAN APOLOGETIC 113

Caecilius alludes to Lucretius's argument that the soul is a bundle of material powers that are dissolved at the end of life. Lucretius made that argument foundational to his assault on the Roman gods; Caecilius uses it to attack the Stoic doctrine of providence. So, *Oct.* 5 provide a catalog of withering criticisms. Caecilius names capricious nature and unjust fortune as evidence that no divinity concerns itself with the affairs of men.[13] He contradicts the claim of Scipio in *Rep.* 1.56 by claiming that "if the world were governed [*regeretur*] by divine providence [*mundus divina providentia*], by the authority of some divine power [*alicuius numinis auctoritate*] . . . Phalaris and Dionysius would not have merited a kingdom."[14] Providence undermines human freedom, he argues. Caecilius's sharp argument and forceful rhetoric provides a vivid backdrop for the backpedaling that follows:

> Since either *Fortune* [*Fortuna*] is certain or *Nature* [*Natura*] uncertain, how much more venerable and better to take up the priesthood of truth [*antistitem veritatis*], the instruction [*disciplinam*] of the ancestors, to worship received religions [*religiones traditas colere*], gods whom you were taught to fear [*inbutus es timere*] by your parents more than to know intimately [*familiarius*]; to adore, not to render judgment about the divine powers [*de numinibus*], but to believe in those forebears [*prioribus*], who in a rustic age, in the very birth times of the world [*rudi saeculo in ipsius mundi natalibus*] deserved to have gods, who were either lenient [*faciles*] towards them, or were kings [*reges*].[15]

In the context of Epicurean arguments, Caecilius's recitation of the traditional Augustan creed looks like mere lip service. He seems to lack the courage of his convictions. Having laid out a penetrating case against providence, he finishes by confessing the central doctrine of Rome's political self-identification in its Augustan reconstruction. But this comes only *after* Caecilius's evident Epicureanism, which preemptively undermines his purported belief. This strategy plays out even at the grammatical level. When he says, "If the world were

theory in order to expose a false uniformity. Simon Price explains that Minucius stages "a dispute between leaders of the three philosophical schools . . . [but] simplifies the dialogue by having only two speakers, not three." Simon Price, "Latin Christian Apologetics: Minucius Felix, Tertullian, and Cyprian," p. 120. The reference to Lucretius, *Nat. r.*, 1.51–55 sets the stage, onto which Minucius ushers this ambiguous hybrid figure. Caecilius can seem both Epicurean and Stoic because the context is not simply Stoicism but rather Roman imperial theology, which accepted Stoic and Epicurean positions, but not Christian. Minucius highlights that contradiction.

[13] Minucius Felix, *Oct.*, 5.8–13.
[14] Minucius Felix, *Oct.*, 5.12. Cf. Cicero, *Rep.*, 1.56. Caecilius is not just arguing against providence, but against the Ciceronian rendition of providence that had come to inform so much of Roman political theology.
[15] Minucius Felix, *Oct.*, 6.1.6.

114 ROMAN VIRTUE IN THE EARLY CHRISTIAN THOUGHT OF LACTANTIUS

governed by divine providence, by the authority of some divinity [*si mundus divina providentia et alicuius numinis auctoritate regeretur*]," Caecilius is actually rewriting Scipio's support for ancestral precedent as a condition contrary to fact.[16] Caecilius gestures to Phalaris and Dionysius, but his claim that if divine providence exists, then men are not raised to divinity by their virtue applies no less to Roman emperors; if they are elevated by providence, the virtue is not theirs. In either case, the strategy is subversion. Despite the argument, Caecilius retreats to a hybrid creed that represents no philosophical school; it rather critiques them all.

Caecilius's subversion of Stoic providence sets the stage for his invocation of imperial Rome's signature doctrines. He proceeds to boast in a series of literary *exempla*, which concludes with a reassertion of Anchises's prophecy at *Aen.* 6.796: "Thus, their empire [*imperium*] extended beyond the path of the sun and the very ocean's bounds, so long as they exercised a religious *virtus* in warfare [*religiosam virtutem in armis*] and fortified the city with sacred rites, chaste virgins, and the many offices and titles of the priests."[17] His lines capture again the central elements of Rome's imperial ideal.[18] The phrase *"religiosam virtutem in armis"* recalls the Vergilian redefinition of *virtus*, which had associated traditional martial *virtus* (i.e., the middle-Republican sense) with Augustan *pietas*. Again, Caecilius evokes this prophecy only after a speech that rejects its

[16] Compare *Oct.* 5.12 with *Rep.* 1.56. Caecilius says, *"quod si mundus divina providentia et alicuius numinis auctoritate regeretur."* The three key terms *auctoritas, numen,* and *regere* evoke Scipio's claim that philosophy and ancient wisdom assent to the idea of one God. However, Caecilius rephrases the claim as a contrary-to-fact condition that makes it a backhanded advocacy. He argues that since philosophers do not have any true account of the gods, Romans should keep pretending to believe their parents. The claim actually attacks Scipio's original argument. In *De re publica*, Scipio defended ancestral wisdom by arguing for its late provenance and recent confirmation by philosophical doctrines of providence (*Rep.*, 1.56, *Leg.*, 1.21, *Resp. har.*, 19). Other people developed fables during "[*Rep.*, 2.18] less erudite ages [*minus eruditis . . . saeculis*]," Scipio says, but Rome was founded after scientific learning. Caecilius is upholding tradition by a reason that contradicts the claim. Romans should adhere to their ancestors because they lived "[*Oct.*, 6.1] in a rustic [*rudi saeculo*] and primitive age." Ostensibly voicing Scipio's own theology, Caecilius contradicts the critical subpremise of his argument (*Oct.*, 5.4.8). He does it systematically. For example, at *Oct.* 8.7– 10, Caecilius evokes Cicero's appellation for Socrates, *"princeps sapientiae,"* ostensibly invoking Cicero and the philosophical tradition as an authority for his position. However, Caecilius ties the appellation to Laelius' Academic axiom that "what is above us does not concern us." In its original context, the honorific is spoken by Balbus (*Nat. d.*, 2.157), who marshals Socrates in support of the Stoic doctrine that the gods reward human beings for virtue. Caecilius repurposes the quotation in order to oppose Balbus's own position and thus to reject the philosophical basis of the providence that Vergil's prophecy of Augustan peace requires.
[17] Minucius Felix, *Oct.*, 6.2. Cf. Vergil, *Aen.*, 6.796, "*iacet extra sidera tellus / extra anni solisque vias.*" See H. E. Butler, *The Sixth Book of the Aeneid: with Introduction and Notes* (Oxford: Basil Blackwell, 1920), pp. 1, 3. Butler calls Book 6 "the very heart of the poem viewed as the National Epic of Rome, the *Gestae populi Romani* as it was sometimes known in ancient times . . . But when we reach Anchises, the whole spirit of the poem changes . . . Suddenly, there dawns on us the vision of the grandeur of Rome, and a deeper note is sounded than any Roman poet had sounded before or should sound again."
[18] See Hervé Inglebert, *Les Romains Chretiens Face a L'Histoire de Rome*, p. 110.

VIRTUS IN EARLY LATIN CHRISTIAN APOLOGETIC   115

foundational presuppositions. He exalts the *mos maiorum* as an exemplary but malleable standard. His recitation of the Vergilian ideal simply specifies the political theology he undermines. It is a strategy of contradiction worthy of Vergil himself.

Minucius intensifies this subversion of the imperial theology in the Christian figure Octavius, who is cast as the defender of traditional Roman ideals. Octavius offers a catena of Stoic philosophical axioms taken from Cicero's *De natura deorum*.[19] Through them, he defends providence against Epicurean and skeptic views, which Cicero denounced as dangerous to the *res publica*. The Christian thus defends a founding doctrine of Cicero's political philosophy:

> We are not able to explore and investigate this question [of human nature] without an inquiry into the universe as a whole. For they are so deeply involved, connected, interdependent that unless you have carefully laid out your understanding of divinity [*ut nisi divinitatis rationem diligenter excusseris*], you will be ignorant of humanity as well [*nescias humanitatis*]. Nor can you properly [*pulchre*] manage civil society, unless you acknowledge this common city [*civitatem*] of the entire world, especially since we differ in this respect from the beasts . . . that speech and reason, by which we know, sense, and imitate God have been given to us.[20]

Minucius casts the Christian Octavius as defender of a Ciceronian political theology. Both the content of Octavius's argument and his literary references to Roman sources are relevant to his position. Octavius assumes the role of Cicero's Balbus and takes center stage as the authentic Roman, who upholds received tradition. In so doing, Minucius casts Caecilius as the dangerous Epicurean that Cicero had warned against, while offering the Christian as a pillar of the Roman civic order.

In this context, Octavius begins to seed the philosophical portion of his argument with key allusions to the critical voices of Augustan literature. He invokes them in order to recast his position as a correction of the problems their criticisms had acknowledged. Rhetorically, this allows Minucius to represent Christians as opposing, not Rome itself, but rather the false construction of Rome pitted against his Christian community. His evocation of Lucan's *Pharsalia* 1.92–96 reveals this posture. Octavius continues his defense of providence in terms borrowed from Lucan's famous line:

---

[19] Minucius Felix, *Oct.*, 17.1. Cf. Vergil, *Aen.*, 6.724–750, *Rep.*, 1.1–12, *Leg.*, 2.19–21, 23, etc. See Beaujeu, "Introduction," xxxi–xxxiii, identifies both the material and content of chapters 5, 17, 18, and 19 as taken from Cicero's *De natura deorum*.

[20] Minucius Felix, *Oct.*, 17.2–27.

116   ROMAN VIRTUE IN THE EARLY CHRISTIAN THOUGHT OF LACTANTIUS

Or since there is no doubt about providence, maybe you think we must ask whether the heavenly kingdom is governed by the imperial will of one or many [*utrum unius imperio an arbitrio plurimorum caeleste regnum gubernetur*]? This question is not much work for someone who reflects on earthly kingdoms, which also provide *exempla* for heaven [*Rep.*, 1.19]. "When did society in government [*regni societas*] either begin in good faith or depart without bloodshed [*cum fide coepit aut sine cruore discessit*]?" I set aside the Persians choosing their kings by augury from the whinnying of horses, and likewise I pass over the Thebans' dead fables. The story about the twins [quarreling] over a kingdom and a cottage is well-known [*Phars.*, 1.192]. The wars of "the father-in-law" and "the son-in-law" [*Aen.*, 6.826–830] were spilled out over the whole world, and the fortune of a great empire did not admit of two men.[21]

Minucius anchors his Christian defense of providence upon carefully selected allusions to Republican criticisms of the imperial regime. The first allusion evokes the Ciceronian claim that statecraft must be predicated upon a theology of divine and human order. As we have seen, in *Rep.* 1.56, Scipio takes the heavenly realms as the *exemplum* of an ideal politics.[22] Octavius's second allusion criticizes the Augustan realization of that politics in the words of *Pharsalia* 1.192–196. Lucan's critical historiography establishes the prism for Minucius's diagnosis of the political problem.[23] Octavius thereby reminds his audience of its own ambivalence toward the imperial ideology. A final allusion—which is originally contained in Lucan's lines—responds to Caecilius's reading of *Aen.* 6.795. Octavius rebuts Caecilius's Vergilian reference with his own allusion to *Aen.* 6.826–830. In the terms of modern scholarship, Minucius elevates Vergil's ambivalent voice in order to undermine the pro-Augustan Vergil.[24] The literary rebuttal produces Octavius's own true claim: providence is true, but the Augustan construction of providence is a false myth propagating a false virtue—just as Romans have known all along.

Octavius's counter-exegesis of Vergil sets the stage for his broader critique of Augustan *virtus*. He makes a series of literary references that rely upon the broader ambivalence toward Augustan *virtus* preserved in Roman literature. Others' diffident remarks provide material for his apologetic argument. The pattern begins at *Oct.* 20.2, as Octavius responds to Caecilius with an allusion to Cicero's *Republic* once again:

---

[21] Minucius Felix, *Oct.*, 18.5–6.

[22] See Chapter 2, this volume.

[23] Cf. Lucan, *Phars.*, 1.92–96, "*Nulla fides regni sociis, omnisque potestas / Inpatiens consortis erit. gentibus ullis / Credite nec longe fatorum exempla petantur: / Fraterno primi maduerunt sanguine muri. / Nec pretium tanti tellus pontusque furoris / Tunc erat: exiguum dominos commisit asylum.*"

[24] See Richard Thomas, *Virgil and the Augustan Reception* (Cambridge: Cambridge University Press, 2001), esp. pp. 25–55.

VIRTUS IN EARLY LATIN CHRISTIAN APOLOGETIC   117

For if the world is governed by providence and "by the nod of one god" [*Rep.*, 1.56], naïve antiquity, taken captive and delighted by its own fairy-tales, should not drag us into the error of agreement [*consensus*], since it is refuted by the opinions of their own philosophers, who also possess a great authority of judgment and antiquity.[25]

Octavius responds to Caecilius by repeating a phrase gleaned from *Rep.* 1.56–57. That repetition exposes Caecilius's backhanded praise of Roman tradition for the skepticism it really was (*Oct.*, 5.4.8) by showing that Caecilius's praise of antiquity was in fact a condescension. Simultaneously, the remark subverts Caecilius's Augustan reading of Scipio by offering a Christian critique of *Rep.* 1.56. Even Cicero had acknowledged the possibility that Roman accounts of divinization lacked any firm basis: "If, however, we have learned that these [beliefs] were established in the error of ignorant people and are fairy-tale fictions [*fabularum similia*], let us listen to those common teachers of the learned."[26] Octavius emphasizes that acknowledgment in order to pit the philosophers against the Roman ancestors. In so doing, he separates Roman antiquity from its sanitized Ciceronian narrative. Octavius thereby accepts a real doctrine of providence but rejects the manifestation of that doctrine in the imperial political theology.

The same tactic also allows Octavius to use Ciceronian Euhemerism to his advantage. Both Ennius and Cicero had used Euhemerus to explain and justify the divinization of heroic monarchs.[27] Minucius turns their praise into proof that Rome's gods were merely mortal: "Read the historians and philosophers! You will see this and agree. As Euhemerus argues, it was either for the merits of their virtue or rewards [*ob merita virtutis aut muneris*] that men were held as gods."[28] In this context, Octavius invokes Livy's ambivalent characterization of Proculus's "very obscure tale [*perobscura fama*]," and his remark, "How amazing that there was so much confidence [*fides*] in that man as he spoke."[29] In Minucius, Livy's skepticism becomes a full-throated accusation of perjury: "[All the gods died], unless perhaps you fashion them as gods after death, as Romulus *by the perjury of Proculus* . . . and other kings, who are consecrated not in confidence of their divinity [*ad fidem numinis*], but in honor of their deserved power [*ad honorem emeritae potestatis*]."[30] Cicero argued that the merits of *virtus* elevate good men to the divinity. Minucius says those virtues reveal their mere humanity. This

---

[25] Minucius Felix, *Oct.*, 20.2. Cf. Cicero, *Rep.*, 1.56.

[26] Cicero, *Rep.*, 1.56. For Latin text, see Chapter 2.

[27] See Chapter 2, this volume.

[28] Minucius Felix, *Oct.*, 21.1. Cf. Tertullian, *Apol.*, 11.23 in Tertullian, Minucius Felix, *Apology; De Spectaculis*; T. R. Glover and Gerald H. Rendall: "*multo verius quam apud vos adseverare de Romulo Proculi solent.*"

[29] Livy, *Liv.*, 1.58. Cf. Lucan, *Phars.*, 1.16.4: "*Mirum quantum illi viro nuntianti haec fides fuerit.*"

[30] Minucius Felix, *Oct.*, 21.9.5–7. Cf. Lactantius, *Inst.*, 1.15.62.

118   ROMAN VIRTUE IN THE EARLY CHRISTIAN THOUGHT OF LACTANTIUS

retort is characteristic of the Latin apologetic strategy. At the plainest level, Minucius seems to argue that kings cannot be gods because they die. In fact, he is arguing that the Romans do not believe their kings are gods and never truly have. Octavius thus turns an argument that legitimized Augustan ideology into a justification for rejecting it. The strategy is probably inherited from Tertullian's *Apologeticus*. Both Cyprian and Lactantius, in their turn, recycle the argument.[31]

Octavius's method supports a final criticism of the Augustan myth of self-definition that the Christians oppose. By juxtaposing notions of *virtus* with *religio* and *pietas*, Minucius targets the Augustan transformation of *virtus* from a martial quality into Vergilian piety: "But nevertheless, [you will say] that this very superstition [*ista ipsa superstitio*] is what gave to the Romans their Empire [*Romanis dedit*], increased and founded it, since they grew powerful not so much by *virtus* as by religion and piety [*tam virtute quam religione et pietate pollerent*]."[32] His comment attacks the shift from an ideal of *virtus* as "manliness" to a notion of philosophical "excellence" and piety, which Augustanism required. Minucius exposes that reformulation of *virtus* by evoking the Romans' ancient diffidence in terms borrowed from Juvenal's *Satire* 8:

> Indeed! A distinguished and noble Roman justice [*iustitia Romana*] was divinely consecrated from the very cradles of the nascent empire [*ab ipsis imperii nascentis incunabulis*]! Were they not assembled from the beginning in criminality and fortified by the terror of their brutality? For the first plebiscite was gathered from a refugee camp [*nam asylo*]: from degenerates, criminals, the incestuous, murderers and traitors. And so that Romulus himself could outdo his own people in criminality, he committed parricide [*parricidium fecit*].[33]

Silver Age cynicism animates all these lines. Octavius adopts Juvenal's denunciation of Roman elites touting their *virtus* for political gain. In what follows, he reminds the audience of the well-known facts: the Roman ancestors kidnapped their wives and made war on their in-laws. And just as true Roman *virtus* was brute force even more than military courage, the transformation of *virtus* into *pietas* simply whitewashed Roman history.[34] Octavius thus concludes with a

---

[31] Cf. Cyprian, *Quod idola*, 4; Lactantius, *Inst.*, 1.15–20; 1.15.29–33; 2.6.13–16.

[32] Minucius Felix, *Oct.*, 25.1.17; Lactantius, *Inst.*, 4.6.1–5 uses this same vocabulary to describe Christ. Also, Tertullian, *Apol.*, 25.14–15. See Eberhard Heck, "Minucius Felix und Der Römische Staat: Ein Hinweis zum 25 Kapitel des 'Octavius,'" *Vigiliae Christianae* 38 (1984): pp. 154–164.

[33] Minucius Felix, *Oct.*, 25.2. Cf. Juvenal, *Sat.*, 8.20–25 in *Juvenal and Perseus*, ed. and trans. Susanna Morton Braund, Loeb Classical Library 91 (Cambridge, MA: Harvard University Press, 2004): "*nomen, ab infami gentem deducis asylo.*" See Robin Bond, "The Augustan Utopia of Horace and Vergil and the Imperial Dystopia of Petronius and Juvenal," *Scholia: Studies in Classical Antiquity* 19 (2010): pp. 31–52. Also, Livy, *Liv.*, 1.8–9 provides a point of reference for this story.

[34] Minucius Felix, *Oct.*, 25.3–4.

VIRTUS IN EARLY LATIN CHRISTIAN APOLOGETIC   119

Sallustian judgment uniformly repeated by the Latin Christian apologists: "So then, whatever the Romans keep, worship, or possess, is the spoil of their audacity. . . . The Romans are not so great because they were religious, but rather because of their shameless sacrilege."[35] The whole argument is a page from Lucan's rhetorical playbook. Octavius unmasks the shifting of Roman *virtus* as an Augustan manipulation. So much for the myth of sacred antiquity.

Minucius's Redescription of Roman *Virtus*

Octavius's criticism of Augustan *virtus* makes room for a Christian answer to the central question of Roman politics: what is *virtus* and what *exempla* model it? He offers a typically Latin Christian answer: *patientia* is the supreme *virtus*, and the Christian Scriptures and martyrs are the supreme sources of its revelation. This claim ultimately attributes Roman *virtus* to the Christian communities even as, in good Roman fashion, Octavius redescribes Roman *virtus* in Christian terms and offers his new account of *virtus* as the realization of the Romans' own ancient ideals.[36] In that respect, the *Octavius* is typical of the Latin Christian apologetic strategy. The apologists do not simply reject "pagan Rome," but rather extend the deep Roman impulse to present Christian virtue as a continuation of what was authentic in their own Roman traditions.

Octavius redefines Roman *virtus* by juxtaposing traditional Roman *exempla* with Christian martyrs, who truly fulfilled the austere demands of an age before Caesars. Both his claims and rhetoric communicate the idea: "Because we feel and endure [*sentimus et patimur*] the human vices of the body, it is not a punishment, but military training [*non poena, militia*]." Christians practice the "discipline of *virtus* [*disciplina virtutis*]," in both mind and body. That discipline is consistent with good Roman traditions of martial and agrarian virtue: "In fact, all your brave heroes [*viri fortes*], whom you preach as examples [*in exemplum*], flourished because they were celebrated for their hardships."[37] So, Christian martyrs carry forward a tradition Romans always valued.

Octavius layers his portrait of the Christian martyrs with multiple levels of historical and rhetorical allusion. He lifts his rhetoric from Seneca's—a Neronian

---

[35] Minucius Felix, *Oct.*, 25.5–6. Cf. Minucius Felix, *Oct.*, 25.6–7. See also, Tertullian, *Apol.*, 25.15; Lactantius, *Inst.*, 1.18.8–10, 15.

[36] See Kapust, *Republicanism, Rhetoric, and Roman Political Thought*, pp. 55–61, for remarks on the technique of "redescription." Minucius's "redescription" is positive in that he praises Christian *virtus*, but the term is apt insofar as his rhetoric shifts the true content of language in order to redefine terms. Minucius's method is Sallustian in that sense Sklenář observes: Sklenář, "The Language of Sallustian Morality," pp. 211–217. As for Sallust, so for Minucius: the *mos maiorum* provides a malleable and duplicitous standard.

[37] Minucius Felix, *Oct.*, 36.8.17. Cf. Lactantius, *Inst.*, 5.13.12–14.

120 ROMAN VIRTUE IN THE EARLY CHRISTIAN THOUGHT OF LACTANTIUS

author—portrait of Cato, the Republican hero, in order to liken Christian martyrs to the heroes of Republican liberty.[38] The same passage continues:

> What a beautiful sight [*pulchrum spectaculum*] it is to God, when a Christian is confronted with pain, when threats and punishments and torments are piled up against him, when laughing he treads down [*inculcat*] the uproar of death and the horror of butchered flesh [*carnificis*], when he arouses [*erigit*] his own liberty [*libertatem*] against kings and princes [*reges et principes*], and approaches God alone, to whom it belongs, when victorious he insults the one who spoke the verdict against him![39]

Octavius's praise actually describes Christian martyrs as the political and moral heirs of the Younger Cato. The message comes inter-textually. Seneca had described Cato's suicide as a "sight worthy to God [*spectaculum dignum deo*]," which is "more beautiful [*pulchrius*]" than any other earthly action.[40] Octavius invokes that rhetoric to describe the condemned Christian. His argument thus operates on both historical and literary planes. Cato was the last heroic opponent of Caesar, and Seneca wrote about the Cato of history in preparation for his own suicide at the command of Nero, Caesar's heir. By lifting such language, Octavius reconstructs Christian martyrdom as the extension of Cato's and Seneca's conflict with Roman emperors.[41] Just as Cato had opposed "the control of one man [*in unius dictionem*]" and, by his noble suicide, "ma[de] wide the road for liberty [*latam libertati viam faciet*]," so also, Christian martyrs witness not only to the truth of their faith but also of their claims upon Roman tradition and *virtus*.[42]

Octavius's invocation of Seneca is followed by an elaboration of virtues that claims for Christians all the best qualities attributed traditionally to the Roman ancestors. He moves from bravery (*fortitudo*) to the traditional Roman concern with sexual morality. He emphasizes Christian modesty (*pudor*) and the practice of keeping only one wife (*unius matrimonii*) both in mind and body. He trumpets Christian sobriety (*pudica, sobria*) and the moral symmetry of Christian speech and Christian actions (*casto sermone . . . corpore*).[43] In emphasizing each,

---

[38] Beaujeu, *Minucius Felix*, p. 157: "Minucius est inspiré des deux textes de Sénèque, pour opposer le héros chrétiens à ces héros *calamitosi*." Also, Christiane Ingremeau, "Minucius Felix et ses 'sources': le travail de l'écrivain," *Revue des Études Augustiniennes*, 45 (1999): pp. 11–13.

[39] Minucius Felix, *Oct.*, 37.6.

[40] Seneca, *Prov.*, 3.9.1. Cf. Tacitus, *Ann.*, 15.52–54.

[41] For Seneca's literature in the Neronian context see G. O. Hutchinson, *Latin Literature from Seneca to Juvenal: A Critical Study* (Oxford: Clarendon Press, 1993). Also, J. P. Sullivan, "Petronius, Seneca, and Lucan: A Neronian Literary Feud?" *American Philological Association* 99 (1968): pp. 453–467, is particularly attentive to the politics involved.

[42] Seneca, *Prov.*, 3.10. These words come from the mouth of Cato, in Seneca's portrait.

[43] Minucius Felix, *Oct.*, 30.5.9. Cf. Livy, *Liv.*, 1.57. What Minucius actually does in these lines is name all the failings of Lucretia's husband in the story by claiming Christians accomplish what the ancient exemplar could not.

VIRTUS IN EARLY LATIN CHRISTIAN APOLOGETIC   121

Octavius counters anti-Christian rumor-mongering. And at a deeper level, his response lays claim to the austere mores of aristocratic Republican society.[44]

Octavius's moral argument culminates in a passage that not only claims Roman virtues for Christians but also reinvests those virtues with a content taken from St. Paul. In so doing, he weaves together a tapestry of allusions that take up, once again, the satire of Lucan's *Pharsalia* 1.92–96, in order to correct them in the Pauline vision of faith, hope, and love. Paul's description of Christian brotherhood fulfills the ideals that Lucan had unmasked as a farce:

> So also, we do not show ourselves by a little mark on our bodies, as you think, but easily by the sign of modesty [*modestiae*] and by our refusal to harm others [*innocentiae*]: we delight in mutual love [*amore diligimus*]—something you are pained by—because we do not know how to hate [*odisse non novimus*]. And we call one-another brothers [*fratres*]—something you envy—as people of God, the One Parent [cf. Cicero, *Leg.*, 1.25ff], and companions in faithfulness [*consortes fidei, Phars.*, 1.92], coheirs in hope [*coheredes spei*]. But you do not ... recognize one-another as brothers, unless for the sake of parricide [*ad parricidum*].[45]

Octavius's description of Christian virtue rewrites Roman political ideals according to the Pauline vision of Christian brotherhood. Octavius's *"unius dei parentis homines"* glosses Cicero's vision of the human soul akin to God in *Leg.* 1.25.[46] By calling Christians *"consortes fidei,"* Minucius redeploys the language of *Phars.* 1.92 but positively and thus presents Christians as having achieved the very qualities to which Roman heroes could only pretend. Octavius's reference to *Phars.* 1.92, however, contains another allusion. The line is flanked by the phrase *"amore diligimus"* and the epithet *"coheredes spei."* Lucan had used *consortes fidei* to criticize the failures of Augustan morality. Octavius thus borrows Lucan's terms to represent the Pauline triad of faith, hope, and love.[47]

---

[44] On *pudor, castitas, pudicitia*, see Rebecca Langlands, *Sexual Morality in Ancient Rome* (Cambridge: Cambridge University Press, 2006). Also Catherine Edwards, *The Politics of Immorality in Ancient Rome* (Cambridge: Cambridge University Press, 1993). For the ideal of single marriage, see Susan Treggiari, *Roman Marriage: Iusti Coniuges from the Time of Cicero to the Time of Ulpian* (Oxford: Oxford University Press, 1991), esp. pp. 216–218, 233–236. For sobriety as a traditional virtue, see Brigette Ford Russell, "Wine, Women, and the *Polis*: Gender and the Formation of the City-State in Archaic Rome," *Greece and Rome* 50.1 (2003): pp. 77–85. For *castitas* in aristocratic society, Jacqueline M. Carlon, *Pliny's Women: Constructing Virtue and Creating Identity in the Roman World* (Cambridge: Cambridge University Press, 2009).

[45] Minucius Felix, *Oct.*, 30.8.2.

[46] Cicero, *Leg.*, 1.23–26, especially 1.25.

[47] 1 Cor. 13:13. The *Vetus Latina* has the terms *fides, spes*, and *caritas*. Cf. Tertullian, *Pat.*, 12.9–10 in Jean-Claude Fredouille, *Tertullien: De la patience: "permanent fides spes dilectio, fides quam Christi patientia induxit, spes quam hominis patientia expectat, dilectio quam deo magistro ptientia comitatur."*

122 ROMAN VIRTUE IN THE EARLY CHRISTIAN THOUGHT OF LACTANTIUS

Octavius uses this corrected notion of *virtus* to critique pagan sacrifice and its role in determining political citizenship. His argument plants the seed of an enduring political ethic in Christianity. It is neither blood-offering nor blood-kinship, he argues, but the virtues of innocence (*innocentia*), justice (*iustitia*), and piety (*pietas*) that define a Roman: "These are our sacrifices [*nostra sacrificia*]. These are the sacred rites of God [*sacra*]," he argues.[48] If that is true, then it is not the Christians abstaining from blood sacrifice, but rather the imperial power demanding blood that disturbs the peace of God and breaks with ancient Roman ideals. Octavius makes this claim by asserting Christian *virtus* over and against false imperial rites. In this respect, his argument uses a strategy of political assertion based on *virtus* which was by then as ancient as Marius and Sulla:

> Are you born to nobility? Do you praise your ancestors? Nevertheless, we are all born from an equal stock [*pari sort nascimur*], distinguished alone by *virtus* [*sola virtute distinguimur*]. We, therefore, who are measured by your habits and modesty [*moribus et pudore*], rightly abstain from your evil pleasures, pomp, and public shows. We know the origin of these rites and we condemn their guilty pleasures [*noxia blandimenta*].[49]

Alongside direct allusions to Juvenal's *Satire* 8, something of Marius's opposition to the *nobiles* can be heard in Octavius's argument.[50] The passage completes an act of redefining not only *virtus*, but the basis of political citizenship. Neither blood kinship nor shared ritual legitimize membership in the political community but rather the inheritance of virtue, which Octavius has defined in Christian terms. *Pietas* and *fides* remain, along with justice understood according to Paul's vision. The martial quality of *virtus* has been redirected as *patientia*, whose social function is intensified.

Octavius legitimizes this transformation of Roman ideals by a very traditional Roman recourse to exemplary narrative. He finds in the martyrs' *exempla* evidence of divine power and favor. Octavius once again opposes the Christian martyrs to Roman heroes:

> You yourself raise unfortunate men to heaven. . . . But how many of our people have endured not only their right hand, but their whole bodies to be burned, incinerated [*cremari*], without a single cry. . . . Shall I compare these men with

---

[48] Minucius Felix, *Oct.*, 32.3.2: "*Igitur qui innocentiam colit, deo supplicat; qui iustitiam, deo libat; qui fraudibus abstinet, propitiat deum; qui hominem periculo subripit, optimam victimam caedit. Haec nostra sacrificia, haec dei sacra sunt: sic apud nos religiosior est ille qui iustior.*" Cf. Cicero, *Nat. d.*, 2.71.

[49] Minucius Felix, *Oct.*, 37.10. Cf. Juvenal, *Sat.*, 8.

[50] Cf. Juvenal, *Sat.*, 8.

Mucius or with Aquilius or Regulus? By an inspired forbearance [*patientia*], our boys and young women make sport of pain, tortures [*tormenta*], irons and all manner of earthly punishments. Do you not understand, O miserable people, that no one can either wish to experience such punishment without reason, nor be able [*nec possit*] to endure torture without God?[51]

Octavius here argues that the martyrs' demonstration of physical endurance in the face of death demonstrates a divine power operative in them. That argument relies upon the traditional logic of Roman exemplary discourse and its underlying theological assumptions. When he says that "no one *is able* [*nec possit*] to endure [*sustinere*], without God," he appropriates Roman thinking about *virtus*: it is a quality that reflects the divine power sustaining the virtuous hero.[52] Hence, Octavius proves that the martyrs are "*nec possit . . . sine deo*" and that they are "*inspirata*" by reference to their *virtus*, in this case, *patientia*. Octavius thus also juxtaposes the martyrs and Roman heroes. It is the same argument Cicero and Livy had used to justify Romulus's divinization.[53] Simultaneously, Octavius's account implies that forbearance (*patientia*) is the supreme *virtus*. This account fits neatly into a broader North African Christian tradition, which offers the *patientia* of Christ as a revelation of God's character and an exemplar for Christian life and action.[54]

Virtus: From Apologetic to "Trinitarian" Theology

Underlying Minucius's rhetorical work is a body of technical language and philosophical premises (i.e., a theological grammar) inherited from the same classical Roman discourses he criticizes. Minucius articulates his ideal of *patientia* and its underlying account of the divine nature by engaging with Cicero, Vergil, and Seneca.[55] In the process, he comes to rely upon the technical sense of power

[51] Minucius Felix, *Oct.*, 37.3.19–37.7. Cf. Lactantius, *Inst.*, 5.13.13–15, which takes up and intensifies this attack. See Jochen Walter, *Pagane Texte und Wertvorstellungen bei Laktanz* (Goettingen: Vandenhoeck and Ruprecht, 2006), p. 91.

[52] See also Hervé Inglebert, "Les héros romains, les martyrs et les asccètes: Les *viritutes* et les préférences politiques chez les auteurs chrétiens latins du IIIe au Ve siècle," *Revue d'Études Augustiniennes et Patristiques* 40.2, pp. 305–326.

[53] See Chapter 2, this volume.

[54] See Kossi Adiavu Ayedze, "Tertullian, Cyprian and Augustine on Patience: A Comparative and Critical Study of Three Treatises on a Stoic-Christian Virtue in Early North African Christianity" (Unpublished dissertation, Princeton, NJ: Princeton Theological Seminary, 2000): "Though in three extant treatises Tertullian, Cyprian, and Augustine, present the virtue of patience as a gift of God." Like many, Ayedze skips Lactantius.

[55] Contra Jean Daniélou, *The Origins of Latin Christianity*, trans. David Smith and John Austin Baker (Philadelphia: Westminster Press, 1977), pp. 189–208. Daniélou works with a hard distinction between philosophical theology and traditional Roman religion that obscures his analysis of

124 ROMAN VIRTUE IN THE EARLY CHRISTIAN THOUGHT OF LACTANTIUS

(*virtus, vis, potestas*, etc.) and its underlying philosophical grammar. In this respect, *Octavius* witnesses to an original problematic that drove theological production in the Latin context. Latin Christians first articulated their account of the divine nature as a form of apologetic in response to the political ideology they confronted. Their apologetic arguments simultaneously came to inform doctrinal controversy among various "Christian" groups. In this case, the ideal of virtue to which *Octavius* witnesses and the theological grammar that sustain its arguments extend into foundational works of Latin trinitarian theology and Christian ethics. Even Tertullian's mature doctrinal treatises retain this original apologetic and political concern.

The character Octavius uses Vergil and Augustan literature not only to criticize the imperial theology but also to articulate his own view of the divine nature. That affirmation begins with his defense of a Christian view of God's oneness. Octavius argues that God is uniquely one, in such a way that the traditional deities do not share in the divine power. He advances the argument through references to Vergil. Just after his critical allusion to *Aen.* 6.826–830, Octavius affirms a Vergilian simile: "Consider other things: bees have one king [*rex unus apibus*], flocks have one [leader]. There is one guide [*unus rector*] among the herds."[56] The image comes from Vergil's famous simile of the bees in *Aen.* 6.724 and the *Georgics*.[57] Octavius then offers a Christian interpretation of the image:

> Do you believe that the Highest Power in heaven [*in caelo summam potestatem*] is divided and that the whole majesty of that true and divine empire is torn apart [*scindi veri illius et divini imperii totam maiestatem*], although it is clear that God, the Parent of all, has neither beginning nor end … ? He existed for himself even before the world [*qui ante mundum fuerit sibi ipse*], and commands all

---

Octavius's numerous references to classical Latin sources. For Daniélou, Cicero and Seneca provide merely rhetorical quotations, functionally useful for apologetic, but not theological, sources to be engaged, corrected, and redeployed.

[56] Minucius Felix, *Oct.*, 18.7. Daniélou, *Origins of Latin Christianity*, pp. 190–191, attempts to parse Octavius's language according to a priori categories, "Christian" versus "classical." He notes that the term "'*maiestas*,' which means 'transcendence,' and the word '*potestas*,' meaning sovereign authority" are examples of some Latin terms that "were adopted very quickly by Christians writing in Latin." Daniélou traces such usage to 1 Clement's translation of LXX terminology and distinguishes these terms from *parens* and *imperium*, labeled as "classical rather than Christian words." He says that "the three terms *verbum, ratio*, and *virtus* … also go back to early Christian usage … [while] the word *ratio* introduces a Stoic note." Daniélou does not discuss why these terms and not others were taken over "very early." As a result, Daniélou's glosses tend to isolate Minucius's "Christian" language from its formative cultural context. Use of Roman language is mere rhetorical assertion of ideas drawn from Greek and Jewish apologies.

[57] Eleanor Winsor Leach, "'Sedes Apibus': From the *Georgics* to the *Aeneid*," *Vergilius* 23 (1977): pp. 2–16. Also, Vergil transposes *Georgics* 4.220–228 at *Aen.* 1.430–436, where the simile serves to describe the busy life of the Carthaginian kingdom. It a fundamental Vergilian metaphor and found at the center of his Augustan prophecy.

VIRTUS IN EARLY LATIN CHRISTIAN APOLOGETIC   125

things of every kind by his word, arranges them by his reason, makes them perfect by his power [*verbo iubet, ratione dispensat, virtute consummat*]?[58]

Octavius's exegesis of the Vergilian simile of the bees affirms the idea of "*unus rex*" as a single power, but then insists that such a *potestas* cannot be divided or apportioned among a plurality of divine powers. In literary terms, we could say that he affirms the Vergilian simile, but corrects the Ciceronian power theology that interprets it.[59] Designating God by the terms *potestas, ratio,* and *virtus,* Octavius argues that even Romans believe God is one: "What shall I make of this *consensus omnium?* . . . Even those who named 'Jove' as *princeps,* are deceived by the name [*fallunter in nomine*], but they agree concerning the One Power [*de una potentia consentiunt*]."[60] This notion of "power" constitutes, for Octavius, a point of agreement between Christian and traditional pagan accounts of divinity.[61] And yet, Octavius also corrects Cicero, since his God is not a portion of the cosmos; the *summa potestas* cannot be divided. Octavius thus affirms the language of Cicero's theology, while objecting to Cicero's understanding of God's oneness.

Octavius continues to oppose Caecilius's Epicurean position by appropriating Vergilian arguments for his own Christian claims. In the process, he draws upon divine titles that persist in Latin Christian theology—*mens* and *spiritus.* When Vergil presented bees as an *exemplum* of the ideal human society, he pointed to a notion of *spiritus* and *mens:* "Bees have a share of the divine mind [*apibus mentis divinae partem*] and draught of the aether," he wrote, "For [a] God imbues all things—lands, the vast expanse of the sea and the deep heaven."[62] Vergil's lines conclude with a promise of the soul's soaring return to God in language evocative of Scipio's *Dream.*[63] Vergil's statement provides a basis for Octavius's explanation of the soul's immortality. He connects *Aen.* 6.724–730 to *Georgics* 4.220–228 in order to express his Christian belief. His lines and argument reappear in every Latin apologist:

> Does not the Mantuan Maro [Vergil] openly, plainly, and truly say, "from the beginning [*principio*], a spirit flies within, a mind [*mens*] poured out stirs the heavens and the earth," and all the other parts of the world, and thence also .

---

[58]   Minucius Felix, *Oct.,* 18.7.

[59]   Cicero, *Leg.,* 1.21 and *Rep.,* 1.56, for *maiestas, potestas, ratio, imperium.*

[60]   Minucius Felix, *Oct.,* 18.11. Cf. Vergil, *Aen.,* 2.688–692: "*Iuppiter omnipotens,*" *Aen.,* 2.488–490. On "*consensus omnium,*" Cicero, *Nat. d.,* 1.15. Daniélou, *Origins of Latin Christianity,* p. 193, observes that Tertullian's *Apol.* 17.4–6 and *Anim.* 2 both use this argument from the *consensus omnium,* but he does not consider the Vergilian mediation or its significance.

[61]   Cf. Tertullian, *Apol.,* 17.10. Lactantius, *Inst.,* 1.8.2–3, 1.5.11.

[62]   Vergil, *Grgcs.,* 4.220–222.

[63]   Cf. Cicero, *Rep.,* 6.17.6.

126 ROMAN VIRTUE IN THE EARLY CHRISTIAN THOUGHT OF LACTANTIUS

humans, sheep, and any other animate creature? Likewise, in another place, he calls this divine mind and spirit God [*mentem divinam et spiritum deum*]. These are his words: "For God imbues all things, both the earth and flowing seas and the high heaven, whence [come] human beings and animals, rain and lightning. How do we then say any different, when we call [*praedicatur*] God *mens* and *ratio* and *spiritus*?"[64]

Octavius's references again invoke Vergil's Augustan theology as a source for the Stoic doctrine of the eternal soul, found here at *Georgics* 4.225–228.[65] Minucius's approach thus accepts the language of Roman political theology as an adequate medium for his Christian thought, and presents the argument as a competition over the Roman heritage. Minucius's technical language arises from that argument and its foundational texts.

As Octavius proceeds, he makes it clear that the technical sense of power unifies his use of terms such as *ratio*, *mens*, and *spiritus*. Like Tertullian, Octavius specifies the notion of power he assumes by referring to Hellenistic philosophical positions, as they were mediated through Cicero's *De natura deorum*.[66] "Speusippus" he observes, called God "animate power [*vim animalem*]," while Aristotle used the terms "one power [*unum potestatem*]," but also "mind [*mentem*]" and even "the world [*mundum*]." Octavius then recognizes that "Zeno and Chryssipus have a multiplicity of statements, but all return to the oneness of providence [*ad unitatem providentiae*]." He concludes by affirming that Plato's account "of god, both his actions and names [*de deo et rebus ipsis et nominibus*]," such as when the Timaeus calls God, "parent of the world [*mundi parens*], artist of the soul [*artifex animae*], maker of the heavens and the earth [*caelistium terrenorumque fabricator*]," most closely approximates the truth, and all these resolve, for him, into a notion of some "incredible power [*incredibili potestate*]."[67] In a single lengthy sentence, Minucius lifts his whole doxography of

---

[64] Minucius Felix, *Oct.*, 19.2. See Tertullian, *Apol.*, 17.5–6, *Anim.*, 2, 5, in *Quinti Septimi Florentis Tertulliani De Anima*, trans. J. H. Waszink (Leiden: Brill, 2010). *Marc.*, 1.10 in Tertullian, *Adversus Marcionem*, ed. and trans. Ernest Evans (Oxford: Clarendon Press, 1972); Lactantius, *Inst.*, 1.5.11, 7.3.5.

[65] See Nicholas Horsfall, *Aeneid 6: A Commentary* (Berlin: Walter de Gruyter, 2013), p. 454. On these lines, "Readers must always have been struck by a singular, dominating counterpoint in these vv., between (a) the strongly Lucretian language and (b) the content, 'Orphic,' Platonic and Stoic ... In part, V. *naturally* uses Lucretian language when writing about philosophy ... [I]ts *generic suitability overrides any conflict* of philos. Appropriateness ... (2) Cic. *Somnium Scipionis*. It has never been clear to me why there should be such reluctance to admit Cic. as an author read by V. with pleasure (he can hardly have disdained *Somn.*) and indeed profit; cf. *Vergilius* 41 (1995), 55–56, against the excessive skepticism of J. G. F. Powell." Daniélou notes that "this passage is entirely Posidonian (i.e., Ciceronian) tradition. The phrase 'all things are full of God' can be found in Cicero (*Leg.*, 2.11.26)." Horsfall, *Aeneid 6: A Commentary*, Appendix A, discusses the Ciceronian influence of this phrase on Vergil, but makes no judgment on the question of the authenticity of the lines.

[66] Cf. Cicero, *Nat. d.*, 1.33–37, *Acad.*, 24–28.

[67] Minucius Felix, *Oct.*, 19.4–7.

VIRTUS IN EARLY LATIN CHRISTIAN APOLOGETIC   127

Hellenistic positions from Cicero, in order to present Christianity as the completion of ancient philosophic tradition:

> Our own positions as well: for we know God, and we call him "Parent of All" and never do we preach in public except when being interrogated. I set down the opinions of nearly all the philosophers, to whom is the glory of having designated One God by many names [*deum unum multis designasse ... nominibus*] so that either one may think Christians are now philosophers or that philosophers always were Christians.[68]

By couching his Christian position as the extension of power theologies recorded in Cicero, Octavius embraces the technical terminology of his sources while using their language to correct the pagan defense of traditional Roman divinities developed in those sources.[69] He affirms a Platonic and immaterial notion of God, not least because that notion defines God as creator. And yet, it is not simply philosophy, but philosophy mediated in Cicero's argument, that Octavius affirms. Since the power is one, God must also be one. Part of the argument lies in Octavius's concern for the traditional Roman association of powers and names, that is, divine titles.[70] Like his sources, Octavius accepts the common correlation of *nomen* and *potestas*, but again he uses shared assumptions about the unity of *potestas* to reject pagan titles.[71] *Oct.* 18.11 and 19.2 both exclude the title given by philosophers and Roman literature, even while accepting the usefulness of *potestas* as a term to indicate the divine oneness.

Minucius justifies his notion of God as "one power" by drawing upon the distinctive argument from causal relations contained in older Latin power theologies.[72]

---

[68] Minucius Felix, *Oct.*, 19.7.

[69] Minucius Felix, *Oct.*, 19.8. This will become a standard argument in later Latin theology.

[70] Cicero, *Nat. d.*, 2.58–60; Seneca, *Ben.*, 4.7–8, *Nat. q.*, 2.45–46 in Seneca, *Natural Questions*, vol. 1, Books 1–3, trans. Thomas H. Corcoran, Loeb Classical Library 450 (Cambridge, MA: Harvard University Press, 1971); *Clem.*, 5.

[71] Vincenz Buchheit, "Virgil und Thales bei Minucius Felix," *Rheinisches Museum für Philologie* 149.3–4 (2006): pp. 350–358, opposes the idea that "The pagan texts [such as *Ecl.* 4] have the same place as the *doctrina christiana*" in the works of the Latin apologists. He argues that "hasty, generalizing judgments about the alleged identity, symbiosis, and coincidence of pagan and Christian discoveries of the truth ... are untenable in the case of Minucius Felix [Eilfertige Pauschalurteile über die angebliche Identität, Symbiose, Koinzidenz von paganer und christlicher Wahrheitsfindung ... sind auf Minucius nich anwendbar]." Behind Minucius's uses of pagan authors, unmistakably Christian doctrines and sources are evident. In the end, Buchheit wants to "free Minucius from the *odium* of semi-paganism [von dem Odium eines semipaganus befreien]." I do not mean to attribute "semi-paganism" to Minucius but rather to reject the utility of such a category. The distance between Minucius and his "pagan" friends is no greater or lesser than the distance between Minucius and any other theological thinker. Put differently, the category "pagan" does not automatically disclose the content of Minucius's agreement or disagreement with another writer on any specific locus of theology.

[72] See Chapter 2, this volume.

128   ROMAN VIRTUE IN THE EARLY CHRISTIAN THOUGHT OF LACTANTIUS

He argues that the divine nature is revealed through the effects of God's action.[73] This explains, among other things, why Christians have no need for images. The language of his argument echoes throughout later Latin Christian theology: "On this basis, we believe in God since we can feel him [*sentire*], though we cannot see him [*videre*]. In his works [*in operibus eius*] and in all the movements of the world, we recognize his present *virtus* [*virtutem eius praesentem*]: in thunder, flashes and lightning, etc."[74] By this description, Octavius distinguishes the direct knowledge of God (*videre*) from the form of experience that nonetheless confirms Christian belief: Christians do not experience the invisible God directly, but they recognize the unity of God from God's work (*in operibus*).

Minucius's description provides Octavius's theology with a definitively Ciceronian genealogy. The quoted lines are from Cicero's *Tusc.* 1.70—the passage of Cicero's late corpus that relied upon *Rep.* 6 and Cicero's own translation of Plato's *Phaedrus*.[75] As Octavius continues, he imports Cicero's language: "As also with the human mind: although you do not see it [*eam videas*], but as you recognize God from his works [*agnoscis deum ex operibus eius*], so from our memory of events, from imagination, from all the beauty of *virtus*, recognize that the power of the mind is divine [*omnique pulcritudine virtutis vim divinam mentis agnoscito*]."[76] Octavius's citation of Cicero confirms that when Minucius uses the term "power" to speak of God, he means to evoke the larger complex of physical and epistemological notions contained in power theology. Second, by alluding to Cicero, he embraces the social and historical location of his power theology in the Roman tradition of political and moral philosophy.[77] The apologist thus situates his theology as a constructive intervention in more ancient Roman debates about the relationship between the divine nature and political order. He regards Christianity as containing the ultimate account of the divine power, and he presents

---

[73] Daniélou, *Origins of Latin Christianity*, pp. 197–198, where Daniélou observes the Platonic background to Minucius's theology, which "makes frequent reference to Stoic physics, while rejecting the theology associated with it . . . This preoccupation with the subjective element emerges for the first time in Minucius, is expressed more systematically by Tertullian, and reaches its fulfillment in the work of Augustine. The *Octavius* is, therefore, valuable as evidence of the first beginnings of this movement in Christian thought."

[74] Minucius Felix, *Oct.*, 32.4: "*Immo ex hoc deum credimus, quod eum sentire possumus, videre non possumus. In operibus enim eius et in mundi omnibus motibus virtutem eius semper praesentem aspicimus, cum tonat, fulgurat, fulminat, cum serenat.*" See Seneca, *Nat. q.*, 2.22–24 for power causality in storms and lightning.

[75] See Chapter 2, this volume.

[76] Cicero, *Tusc.*, 1.70. Cf. *Rep.*, 6.26, where the same powers of the mind justify the claim that "you are a god." Beaujeu takes this passage as a reference to Xen., *Mem.*, IV.3.13–14, which he cites at length. He notes that Clement of Alexandria, Theophilus of Antioch, and Cyril of Alexandria all cite Xenophon. Given the textual argument presented earlier, it seems better to say that the passage of Xenophon demonstrates just how broad and deeply penetrating the idiom of *power* had become in pre-Christian philosophical theology.

[77] Minucius Felix, *Oct.*, 20.14. Cf. *Oct.*, 32.2ff.

VIRTUS IN EARLY LATIN CHRISTIAN APOLOGETIC   129

Christian *patientia* as a public demonstration of that account in the lives of Christian people.

As already noted, Minucius Felix inherited much from Tertullian, who composed his *Apologeticus* in response to the same Ciceronian arguments.[78] Tertullian's discussion adds, however, an original explanation of the Christian God, which marks the starting point of Latin trinitarian theology. *Apologeticus* 21.10 opens with a parallel to *Oct.* 18.7, the claim that God "arranges all things by his reason [*ratione*], makes them perfect by his power [*virtute*]."[79] In the same line, Tertullian proceeds to introduce an account of the unity of the Godhead:

> Before I explain his substance, let the quality of his birth [*qualitas nativitatis*] be understood. We have already said that God arranged this entire universe [*universitatem mundi*] by his word [*verbo*], reason [*ratione*], and power [*virtute*]. But also among your own wise men it is established that the maker of the whole is seen as *Logos*, that is speech [*sermonem*] and reason [*rationem*]. Zeno determines that this one is the Maker [*factitatorem*] who fashioned all things in an orderly arrangement [*dispositione*]; and that the very same one is called *Fate*, and *God*, and *Mind of Jove*, and *Necessity* of all things.[80]

Earlier commentators noted that Tertullian's theology here is influenced by the apologies of Justin Martyr, Athenagoras, and Theophilus.[81] However true, in its Latin context, Tertullian borrows terms from Cicero and Seneca. His first lines borrow a term of distinctly Ciceronian coinage (*qualitas*) and are replete with references to Cicero's *De natura deorum*. Tertullian uses that Ciceronian vocabulary to articulate Christ's birth within the context of this apologetic argument, which aims to liken the Christian explanation of biblical titles for the Son to accepted philosophical theologies.[82] Furthermore, Tertullian's reference to divine

---

[78] Ernest Evans, *Tertullian's Treatise against Praxeas: The Text, Edited with an Introduction, Translation and Commentary* (London: S.P.C.K., 1948), p. 58. Translations modified from Evans. "In the early work, the *Apologeticus*, Tertullian had already, for a pagan audience, expressed the doctrine of the Incarnation in terms which in his later treatises were to need no correction, but only explanation and scriptural justification." By contrast, Simon Price, "Latin Christian Apologetics: Minucius Felix, Tertullian, and Cyprian," p. 121, minimizes this passage: "The *Apology* has a longer discussion of Christian theology, but again only incidentally to its argument."

[79] Tertullian, *Apol.*, 21.10. Joseph Moingt, *Théologie trinitaire de Tertullien. histoire, doctrine, méthodes*, 3 vols. (Paris: Aubier, 1966), pp. 874–875, notes in passing apologetic context: "Following the Apologists, Tertullian had used this idea to explain for pagans the very pure origin of the Son of God in his *Apologeticus* 21."

[80] Tertullian, *Apol.*, 21.10. Cf. Minucius Felix, *Oct.*, 19; Lactantius, *Inst.*, 1.5, *passim*.

[81] J. P. Waltzing, *Apologétique de Tertullien: Commentaire* (Paris: Belles Lettres, 1931), pp. 144–145. Daniélou, *Origins of Latin Christianity*, pp. 357–359, treats this passage under the heading *gradus* noting that Tertullian first introduces the idea, "in his *Ad Nationes* ... to prove that, whatever transformations the pagans believe take place in a piece of wood for it to be made into an idol, the final stages must be linked to the original substance."

[82] On *qualitas* in Cicero, see Chapter 2, this volume, especially discussion of *Acad.*, 25–26, and Seneca, *Ep.*, 66.

130 ROMAN VIRTUE IN THE EARLY CHRISTIAN THOUGHT OF LACTANTIUS

appellations—*Fate, God, Mind of Jove*—along with his argument that the divine titles represent "the same" power, uses a vocabulary found not only in Zeno but also in Seneca's argument at *Ben.* 4.7–8. Seneca's claim that the titles *Nature*, or *Fate*, or *Fortune* "are all names of the same God exercising his power in various ways [*omnia eiusdem dei nomina sunt varie utentis sua potestate*]," echoes in Tertullian's reference to traditional Roman philosophical theologies.[83]

In this context, Tertullian also first accepts the Stoic notion that *spiritus* is the material substance of the divine nature, in which God's powers inhere. For the sake of his opposition to persecution, Tertullian couches his whole argument as an affirmation of a Stoic philosophical theology that Cicero and Seneca had made acceptable to the imperial order long ago:

> Cleanthes gathered these [things] into spirit, which permeates the whole, he says. And we, moreover, by the same speech [*sermone*] and reason [*ratione*], and power [*virtus*] through which we said that God ordered all things, also write that spirit is a proper substance [*propriam substantiam*], which contains his speech in the act of pronouncing; and to which is present reason [*ratio*] in the act of arranging, [by which] his power [*virtus*] exercises control in making perfect.[84]

Tertullian's emphatic pronouns (*apud vestros . . . et nos atque*) highlight the fact that in this context, he turns to the technical sense of power to assert that his monotheistic doctrine is compatible with other philosophical theologies acceptable in Roman political society.[85] This political and apologetic argument leads Tertullian to introduce Christological formulae that persist in his own later Latin trinitarian arguments. At *Apol.* 21, Tertullian proceeds to define the relationship between Father and Son using analogies that would become standard in later Latin authors:

> Just as a ray [*radius*] is stretched forth [*porrigitur*] from the sun, a share [*portio*] from the highest, the sun will be in the ray, because a ray of the sun is a substance not separated but extended [*extenditur*]. So also spirit from spirit, and god from god, is reckoned as light from light. Just as the parental vine [*matrix materiae*] remains whole and unbroken, even if you borrow many offshoots of its kind [*qualitatis*], so also what has proceeded from god is god, and son of god, and both one. Just as "spirit from spirit" and "god from god" has made a second number, but in standing not condition [*gradu non statu*], so also he has

---

[83] Seneca, *Ben.*, 4.7–8, *Quaetiones Naturales*, 2.45–46.

[84] Cf. Tertullian, *Apol.*, 21.11. Cf. *Nat. d.*, 1.36; in the larger context, *Nat. d.*, 25–29, 32–37.

[85] Michel R. Barnes, *The Power of God: Dynamis in Gregory of Nyssa's Trinitarian Theology* (Washington, DC: Catholic University of America Press, 2001), pp. 103–111.

VIRTUS IN EARLY LATIN CHRISTIAN APOLOGETIC   131

not withdrawn [*recessit*] from the parent tree [*matrice*] but proceeded from it [*processit*]. This ray of god, therefore, just as it was always being preached in the past [*retro*], after descending [*delapsus*] into a certain virgin and being fashioned in her womb as flesh, is born as a person mixed with God. Flesh endued with spirit is nourished, grows, speaks, learns, acts [*operatur*] and is Christ.[86]

Tertullian's use of *X from X* causal models in this argument is notable for its context and content.[87] Immediately following his references to Cleanthes (via Cicero and Seneca), these metaphors serve to distinguish the Christian understanding of Christ's relationship to the Father from pagan theologies of the pantheon. Earlier in the treatise, Tertullian reviewed the same parade of deities that appear in *De natura deorum* 2.58–62 and in Seneca's *Ben.* 4.7–8, while noting that Romans "distribute [to their gods] powers and stations [*potestates et stationes*]," which came from "the Great God."[88] The imperial theology represents variously named deities as holding a number of "lower stations." This point distinguishes the imperial explanation from Tertullian's account of the Son. Tertullian shares the *X from X* causal model that Cicero and Seneca had applied to the traditional gods. In *Apol.* 21.12, however, he says the Christian doctrine "has made in mode a double number, yet in sequence not in status [*gradu non statu*]."[89] His metaphors explain this point. As the product of the Father's power, the Son has a different position—i.e., that of effect rather than cause—but obtains the same "status." The point distinguishes Tertullian's thought from the imperial position attested at *Apol.* 9.1–2 because it means that the Son has the same "status" as "the Great God." Still, *Apol.* 21.10–12 explains the divine titles as names for "the same [*eundem*]" Power, according to a grammar inherited from Cicero and Seneca. Hence, his apologetic work led him to express trinitarian theology in ways that draw upon the Roman imperial theology itself.

The Christological language and concerns of Tertullian's *Apologeticus* appear again in his later and better-known doctrinal arguments, where apologetic concerns remain, even if on the periphery. Written around 206 A.D., Tertullian's treatise, *De patientia,* was composed after *Apologeticus* (c. 198 A.D.) and before the anti-Monarchian arguments of *Adversus Praxeas* (c. 211–213 A.D.). In *De patientia*, Tertullian connects his Christology to a notion of ideal *virtus* as *patientia*, which echoes in the *Octavius*. He says that "a living and heavenly instruction [*disciplinae vivae et caelestis*]—and not some pretention [*adfectatio*] of canine level-headedness [*aequanimitatis*]—shows that God himself is the model [*exemplum*] of our patience."[90] A shot at Cynic philosophy, Tertullian's reference

---

[86] Tertullian, *Apol.*, 21.12–13.
[87] For the term "X from X," see Barnes, *Power of God*. See Chapter 2, this volume.
[88] Tertullian, *Apol.*, 9–11. *Prax.*, 8–10.
[89] Tertullian, *Apol.*, 21.12.
[90] Tertullian, *Pat.*, 2–3.

132   ROMAN VIRTUE IN THE EARLY CHRISTIAN THOUGHT OF LACTANTIUS

to "canine level-headedness" shows that he still feels the need to address pagan theologies, even in such a Christian meditation.[91] Tertullian introduces this language to resolve the conundrum of how Christians come to know the divine *exemplum*: "This appearance [*species*] of the divine *patientia*, as it appears so far away, may be considered among those things high above us [*de supernis*]."[92] Given that God's nature is "so high above us," he asks then, "what is that *patientia*, which has been grasped by human beings upon the earth, even *grasped by the hand*?" [1 John 1:2]. His response recycles the argument of *Oct.* 37.2. To answer this question, Tertullian introduces a statement that would become axiomatic in later Latin Christian accounts of the person and work of Christ:

> The one hidden in the form of a person imitated nothing of humanity's impatience [*impatientia*]. . . . From this most especially, oh Pharisees, you should have recognized the Lord. No human being could have achieved such patience! Such great and remarkable evidence—whose magnitude is, among the nations, a reason to scorn the faith, but among us its very definition and basis [*ratio et structio*]—proves [*probant*] not only by his words in teaching [*non sermonibus modo in praecipiendo*], but also by the Lord's passions in suffering [*passionibus domini sustinendo*], that for those to whom it has been given to believe, patience is God's nature [*patientiam Dei esse naturam*], the effect and excellence of some inborn property [*effectum et praestantiam ingenitaecuisdam proprietatis*].[93]

The above lines introduce a parallelism between Christ's "words in teaching" and "works in suffering" that appears again in Cyprian, Lactantius, and later writers. Tertullian's description of *patientia* as a *proprietas* and *effectum* proceeding from God is technical language that refers to the Son's generation.[94] That Christology is used here to address a characteristically Roman question, which Minucius (*Oct.*, 37.2–3) also shared: On what basis can human beings recognize the character of divine *virtus*, and therefore God? Tertullian offers a typically Roman answer: Christ's works are evidence (*documenta*) that reveal God's *virtus* in the

---

[91] Jean-Claude Fredouille, *Tertullien: De la patience*, pp. 65, 126. The term *canina* is a pejorative directed at the Cynics.

[92] Tertullian, *Pat.*, 3.1. Cf. 1 John 1:1–5. This is a Johannine reference.

[93] Tertullian, *Pat.*, 3.10–11. We might reasonably translate "*effectum et praestantiam*" as "effect and capacity, or quality" since *praestantia* also appears in naturalistic contexts to name the distinctive effects of particular herbs. Cf. Pliny, *His. Nat.*, 27.41, "*vulneribus sanandis tanta praestantia est, ut carnes quoque, dum cocuntur, conglutinet addita.*" Also, Cicero, *Fin.*, 5.12, "*deinde id quoque videmus, et ita figuratum corpus, ut excellat aliis, animum que ita constitutum, ut et sensibus instructus sit et habeat praestantiam mentis, cui tota hominis natura pareat.*" Later, Seneca, *Ben.*, 7.14.1, "*Quaedam eius condicionis sunt, ut effectum praestare debeant; quibusdam pro effectu est omnia temptasse, ut efficerent.*" See Nicole Guenter Discenza, "Power, skill and virtue in the Old English 'Boethius,'" *Anglo-Saxon England* 26 (1997): pp. 81–108.

[94] See Joseph Moingt, *Théologie trinitaire de Tertullien, histoire, doctrine, méthodes* (Paris: Aubier, 1966).

VIRTUS IN EARLY LATIN CHRISTIAN APOLOGETIC   133

same way that an effect manifests its causative power.[95] Hence, Christ reveals the divine nature through his works—through the spectacle of his *patientia*, which proves not only that Christ is the Lord, but that *patientia*, not martial force or violence, is the kind of *virtus* characteristic of divinity. The argument uses a language and logic well-known from earlier Roman and Latin philosophical discourses. And yet, in this context, such language supports a Christian vision of the divine nature and an ethic grounded in Christ's revelation through his Incarnation. Gesturing to Christ's passion, Tertullian concludes by emphasizing that Christ's own works reveal the true character of *virtus*: "This is the definition [*ratio*], this the training [*disciplina*], these are the works [*opera*] of true and heavenly patience."[96] While Tertullian's phrase "these are the *opera*" expresses the "genetic" relationship between a power and its product that had been fundamental to Latin arguments about divinity since Cicero, he uses that very traditional Latin logic to name Christ's incarnate works as the true account of whatever the *virtus* of *patientia* means.

The influence of earlier apologetic conversations upon Tertullian's doctrinal formulae is also evident in his later discussions of the divine titles and of the unity of the Father and Son. Tertullian takes up and repeats the same arguments, for instance, in his anti-Monarchian treatise *Against Praxeas*.[97] He opens by restating much of *Apol.* 21.10–12. He explains that God is

> three, however, not in condition but in standing [*non in statu sed in gradu*], not in substance but in form [*nec substantia sed forma*], not in power but in manifestation [*non in potestate sed in specie*], still one substance [*substantia*] and one condition [*status*] and one power [*virtus*], because there is one God, by whom these conditions, and forms, and manifestations [*species*] are assigned under the name [*in nomine*] of the Father, Son, and Holy Spirit.[98]

This famous passage restates the language of Tertullian's position at *Apol.*, 21.10–12, but Tertullian seems to have become more sensitive to the problem raised by using Seneca's language to say that the title Father and Son refer to the "same"

[95] On *proprietas*, see Frederic Chapot, *Virtus Veritatis: Langage et Vérité dans l'oeuvre de Tertullien* (Paris: *Collection des Études Augustiniennes*, 2009), pp. 190–191, who notes "the word *proprietas*, expresses conjointly the substantial specificity of an existent [d'une réalité], which makes it be no other thing, and its own identity, by which it is not able to be confused with anything else." Cf. Barnes, *Power of God*, pp. 104–107.

[96] Tertullian, *Pat.*, 16.1.4, "*Haec patientiae ratio, haec disciplina, haec opera, caelestis et verae scilicet.*"

[97] Barnes, *Power of God*, p. 103. Barnes introduces his lengthy discussion, "Tertullian uses *power* (often *potestas*, but also *virtus*) in doctrinal formulations in which the sense is 'one power, one substance.'" See also, Michel Barnes, "Latin Trinitarian Theology," in *The Cambridge Companion to the Trinity*, ed. Peter C. Phan (Cambridge: Cambridge University Press, 2011), pp. 70–84.

[98] Tertullian, *Prax.*, 2. Evans's translation, modified. Cf. *Tusc.*, 1.70, *Oct.*, 32.4.8, *Ben.*, 4.8.2.

134 ROMAN VIRTUE IN THE EARLY CHRISTIAN THOUGHT OF LACTANTIUS

power. Tertullian rejects the Senecan idea that God's power is simply "converted" into various forms.[99] That notion leaves precious little room for the idea that the Son is a "*res substantiva*," as Tertullian is arguing.[100] The language of Cicero's Balbus and Seneca's discussion at *Ben.* 4.7–8 is also evident in *Praxeas*'s discussion of the divine names. *Prax.* 6.1, for instance, uses the traditional Roman association of *potestas* and *nomen* to explain various biblical titles for the Son: "In the Scriptures, this *power* [*vis*] and this arrangement of the divine understanding [*sensus*] is also shown under the name of Wisdom [*in nomine Sapientiae*]."[101] Tertullian's thought reflects the ancient Latin correlation of power and name— *vis* and *nomina*—that Cicero and Seneca applied to Rome's traditional divinities. That usage also reveals a significant element of the argument between Tertullian and his Monarchian opponents. Apparently, both agree that in the Son's divine titles there is "one and the same power," but Tertullian insists that because that power redounds from God, it must be a real substance capable of distinct existence. Although the issue has shifted, the terms of classical Roman arguments about the divine power and names provide common language for the discourse.[102] Hence, Tertullian reasserts and expands upon the metaphors of light, of the tree, and of parental generation, which appear in *Apol.*, 21.12–13. At *Against Praxeas* 8, those metaphors come to explain the unity and distinction of Father and Son:

> Nor shall I hesitate to say that the fruit is the son of the root, and the river the son of its source, and a ray of light the son of the sun, for every source is a parent [*origo parens*] and everything that is brought forth from a source is an offspring. So much more is the Word of God, who also in an exact sense has received the name of Son. Still, the fruit is not cut off from the root, nor the river from the spring, nor the ray from the sun, any more than the Word is cut off from God. Therefore, according to the form of these examples, I profess that I say that God and his Word, the Father, and his Son, are two: for the root and the fruit are two things, but conjoined; and the spring and the river are two manifestations, but undivided; and the sun and its ray are two forms, but they cohere. Everything that proceeds from something must of necessity be another beside that from which it proceeds, but it is not for that reason separated from it.[103]

[99] See Seneca, *Ep.*, 66. Chapter 2, this volume.
[100] Tertullian, *Prax.*, 26.6–7.
[101] Tertullian, *Prax.*, 6.1. My translation.
[102] Much of this argument has also appeared in Jason M. Gehrke, "Singulare et Unicum Imperium: Monarchianism and Latin Apologetic in Rome," in *New Narratives for Old: The Historical Method of Reading Early Christian Theology*, ed. Anthony Briggman and Ellen Scully (Washington, DC: Catholic University of America Press, 2022), pp. 142–162.
[103] Tertullian, *Prax.*, 8. Evans's translation, adapted.

Tertullian's famous account of the unity and distinction of Father and Son is typically Latin in its reliance upon the technical sense of power and upon the genetic analogy of a cause and its product. What matures in *Praxeas*, however, is Tertullian's insistence upon the real distinction of the Son as an expression of the Father's power. Whereas in early works, his argument emphasized the conceptual communicability of classical accounts of the divine nature and his own Christian position, in *Against Praxeas*, he corrects a potential error arising from his earlier apologetic statements. Hence, where *Apol.*, 21.12–13 emphasized the oneness of the divine power, *Against Praxeas* takes pains to ensure the real distinction of that power's manifestations under the names of Father, Son, and Spirit.

Against Praxeas also defends the unity of Father and Son by including an argument from the Son's demonstration of divine power. Because the Son performs the works of the Father, the Son reveals the Father's nature. The same vocabulary and logic seen in Scipio's discussion of Romulus, in Cicero's divinization of Tullia, in Seneca's *De Beneficiis*, and also in Minucius Felix's explanation of the Christian martyrs reappears in that justly famous argument. Tertullian addresses the same question of how the divine nature is made evident to human beings that Cicero had so often treated. At *Rep.* 2.20, for instance, Cicero's character Scipio explained that "the power of character and *virtus* [*vis ingenii atque virtutis*] was so great in [Romulus], that what had never before been believed [*credidissent*] about any mortal was believed [*crederetur*] concerning him and from [the report] of Julius Proculus, a rustic no less."[104] Cicero's comment argues that Romulus's divinization can be believed because his mighty deeds demonstrate a power that can only be regarded as divine. Tertullian's account of the Father and Son uses the same assumptions and language: "Through the works [*opera*] then the Father will be in the Son and the Son in the Father. And so through [their] works, we understand that the Father and Son are [*esse*] One. He [John] kept pressing this point in order to bring us to see that two should be believed albeit in one power [*in una virtute*] because otherwise the Son could not possibly be believed in unless two is believed."[105] Tertullian's reliance upon the public demonstration of divine *virtus* echoes a sentiment as old as Roman politics. Christians know Christ to be one with the Father because they see the Father's power manifest in Christ's mighty deeds. Just as Balbus distinguished the nature of the *divina bonitas* by observing its benefits toward humanity, so Tertullian recognizes the divine nature of Christ from the power his works reveal.[106] Although grounded in his reading of John 10:38–41, it is a traditional

---

[104] Cicero, *Rep.*, 2.20. See Chapter 2, this volume.
[105] Tertullian, *Prax.*, 22. Evans, pp. 164–165.
[106] Chapter 2, this volume.

136 ROMAN VIRTUE IN THE EARLY CHRISTIAN THOUGHT OF LACTANTIUS

Roman way of thinking, which here provides the grammar for Tertullian's Christology.

This traditional Roman notion illuminates what is perhaps the most famous statement made in *Against Praxeas* about the unity of the Father and Son revealed in the actions of Christ. Tertullian writes that "the Father, therefore, abiding in the Son through the works of [his] powers [*opera virtutum*] and the words of his teaching [*verba doctrinae*], is seen through those things through which he abides and through him in whom he abides; and on the basis of this very property [*proprietate*] of each person, he says then: *I am in the Father and the Father is in me*."[107] The remark contains the same juxtaposition of Christ's words and deeds that Tertullian had made in *Pat.* 3—the works of his *virtutes* and the *verba* of his teaching manifest the divine *virtus* in which the Father dwells. Notably, Tertullian refers here to the "*opera virtutum*." Evans rendered this line: "abiding in the Son through works of power and words of doctrine."[108] One could fairly render it, "by the works of his virtues." In any case, Tertullian uses here a theological argument that borrowed terms from Ciceronian philosophy and originated in the apologetic context. It had already informed his meditation on Christ's example in *De patientia*, and now comes to distinguish his mature Christology from the errors of *Praxeas*. In that journey, a classical Roman theological grammar passed from the ancient theater of Roman political competition into conflicts between Christian and non-Christian Romans, and later, into early trinitarian controversy. Traveling that road, the technical sense of power came to provide the basis for a Christian transformation of Rome's martial ideals of *virtus* in the humility of Christ's passion. As shall be seen, Tertullian's parallelism—*the works of his powers* and the *words of his teaching*—are foundational to the whole Latin tradition of Christology, ecclesiology, and moral thought.

Christian *Patientia* in Cyprian

The greatest Latin cleric of the third century, Saint Cyprian of Carthage, built a coherent moral theology from the apologetic and Christological tradition he received from Tertullian and Minucius Felix. Cyprian's tenure as bishop of Carthage (246–258 A.D.) was marked by famine, persecution, and controversy.[109] Harried by circumstance, his major treatises and letters respond to specific challenges of his troubled time. Despite their occasional character,

---

[107] Tertullian, *Prax.*, 22.25–30. Following Ernest Evans's translation.

[108] Ernest Evans, *Tertullian's Treatise against Praxeas*, p. 169.

[109] For brief introduction to North African Christianity, see François Decret, *Early Christianity in North Africa*, trans. Edward Smither (Eugene, OR: Cascade Books, 2009), pp. 46–82. See also Michael M. Sage, *Cyprian* (Cambridge, MA: Philadelphia Patristic Foundation, 1975).

VIRTUS IN EARLY LATIN CHRISTIAN APOLOGETIC   137

Cyprian's writings express a coherent theological vision grounded in Tertullian's explanations of the divine nature revealed in Christ's public example. Cyprian uses Christological and apologetic elements of early Latin theology to develop an image of Christ as a moral exemplar and teacher, whose works confirm his divine character and reveal to humanity the true character of eternal life.

As is well known, Cyprian wrote his greatest theological treatise, *De unitate ecclesiae*, in response to the schism of Latin Christianity that occurred in the aftermath of the Decian Persecution. Bishops who disagreed over how to deal with the problem of the "lapsed" (*lapsi*)—baptized Christians, who either made sacrifice or compromised with imperial authorities in some way—denied Cyprian's authority in Carthage and set up a rival communion in both North Africa and Rome. The conflict provoked Cyprian's most enduring statement of the nature of the Church and its unity. His argument for the inviolable unity of the Church draws pervasively upon the logic and metaphors of Tertullian's *Adversus Praxeas*. Cyprian opens with a lament at the schism, which evokes the Johannine light and Christ's healing ministry. He asks what else the devil would do than create schism, "after having been cast down by the advent of Christ, after light has come to the nations, and saving light has come to sustain people in need of care, so that the deaf might receive the hearing of spiritual grace, the blind might open their eyes to God, the weak might receive the healing that is eternal; that the lame might run to the church and the mute pray with clear voices."[110] Cyprian's lament combines Johannine light imagery with the synoptic portrait of Christ's healing ministry drawn from Matthew 11:5. In his understanding, Christ's historical healing and teaching provides the content of what John's Gospel represents through the image of light shining upon humanity.

Cyprian places John's image of light on an ethical and political plane by interpreting that light as expressed in Christian actions toward the world. The metaphor of light comes to express the unity of the Church itself in Cyprian's larger argument. Cyprian cites Matt. 16:18 as evidence that while all the apostles were equal in both honor and power, Christ named Peter as the rock in order to show that the episcopate itself is founded in unity. He explains this unity within the plurality of bishops by drawing on a logic taken over from *Against Praxeas*:

> And we who are bishops and preside in the Church must firmly cling to and defend this unity, and so shall we prove that the episcopate itself is one and undivided [*unum atque indivisum*]. Let no one deceiving the brotherhood by a lie corrupt the true faith by deceit and disloyalty [*praevaricatione*]. There is but one episcopate a part of which is held by each one and yet remains whole [*in solidum*]. The Church is one, and yet is spread out more widely by the increase

---

[110] Cyprian, *De unitate*, 3.

of her fecundity. Just as there are many rays of the sun, but one light [*lumen unum*], and many branches of a tree, but one tree founded on its steadfast root, and as also many rivers descend from a single source [*cum de fonte uno rivi plurimi defluunt*], even when the multiplicity seems to be diffused by the abundance of riches pouring itself out, nevertheless the unity is preserved in its source [*in origine*]. Separate a ray of the sun from the body, and the unity of light still accepts no division. Break off a branch from a tree, and the broken part will not be able to grow again. Cut off a river from its source and the severed portion dries up. So the Church, suffused with the light of God, spreads forth its rays of light through the entire world. Nevertheless, there is one light, which is poured out in every place, though the oneness of the body is not separated [*nec unitas corporis separatur*]. The abundance of her wealth extends over the whole earth; she pours out rivers flowing forth evermore widely, and yet, there is one head and one source [*unum tamen caput est origo una*], one mother overflowing with offspring in her fertility: we are born from her, nursed from her milk, animated by her spirit.[111]

Cyprian's description of the Church's oneness is a barely reworked repetition of Tertullian's argument for the unity of God in *Apol.* 21 and *Prax.* 8. Each of Cyprian's central metaphors—light, the ray from the sun, the branch from a tree—appears in *Against Praxeas* 8, where they express the possibility of a real distinction within the context of an undivided unity of Father and Son.[112] Tertullian describes every source as a kind of parent, just as Cyprian draws deeply on the image of maternity. When Cyprian says light cannot be divided, any more than a branch can be cut off from its root, he simply repeats Tertullian's argument for the unity of the Father and Son in order to emphasize the destructive character of schism. Tertullian's Christology thus provides the foundation of Cyprian's ecclesiology. He grounds the unity of the Church in the unity of Father and Son. John 10:30—"I and the Father are one"—and 1 John 5:7—"And the three are one"—provide the scriptural basis for Cyprian's argument that the unity of the Church exists as a direct reflection of the divine unity. Both are one because the divine power is undivided: "And does anyone believe that this oneness, which comes from the divine strength [*unitatem de firmitate venientem*] and coheres in the heavenly sacraments can be divided in the Church and separated by the divorce of opposing wills?"[113] Cyprian's evocation of the sacraments makes a critical distinction. He traces the Church's unity back to its ultimate source in the Father and Son, but makes it clear that the Church is not immediately involved in any

[111] Cyprian, *De unitate*, 5.
[112] See Tertullian, *Apol.*, 21 and *Prax.*, 8.
[113] Cyprian, *De unitate*, 6.

VIRTUS IN EARLY LATIN CHRISTIAN APOLOGETIC 139

Father-Son relation exclusive to the Godhead. Its possession of divine power is sacramentally mediated. Still, because the Church is the offspring of a divine power mediated by the Incarnation through the sacraments, Cyprian can use Tertullian's Christological metaphors to describe the Church's own unity. This also explains his ultimate conclusion: any schismatic body cuts itself off from its own source, like a stream separated from its own source. Schism is, by this logic, not simply wrong or invalid, but impossible.

Written a few years after *De unitate*, Cyprian's short treatise, *On Good Works and Mercy*, extends his ecclesiological use of the *source-stream-flow* metaphor to economic and social doctrine. In the process, Cyprian cultivates a vocabulary to describe the Incarnate Christ as a teacher of virtue, who gives precepts for Christian life. This subject becomes the occasion for an economic teaching drawn out of Lk. 12:33 and Matt. 6:19–21:

> In the gospel, the Lord, the doctor of our life [*doctor nostrae vitae*] and teacher of eternal salvation [*magister aeternae salutis*], brings to life his faithful people and counsels those now enlivened unto what is eternal [*in aeternum*]. Among his divine mandates and heavenly precepts [*inter sua mandata et praecepta caelestia*], he mandates and prescribes [*mandat et praecipt*] nothing more often than that we should do mercy, that we should not sit upon our earthly possessions but "store up heavenly treasures." "[Lk. 12:33] Sell," he says, "all your things and give mercy." Again, he says, "[Matt. 6:19–21] Do not wish to establish [*condere*] your treasures upon the earth, where moth and rust destroy, where thieves break in and steal."[114]

Cyprian's citation of Matt. 6:19–21 and Lk. 12:33 emphasizes Christ's pedagogical role as central to his ministry in the Incarnation. Describing Christ's words as "heavenly precepts and mandates [*praecepta caelestia et mandata*]," he uses the equivalent verbs *praecipit* and *mandat*, to introduce citations of Christ from

---

[114] Cyprian, *De opere et eleemosynis*, 7: "*Itaque in euangelio dominus doctor uitae nostrae et magister salutis aeternae uiuificans credentium populum et uiuificatis consulens in aeternum inter sua mandata diuina et praecepta caelestia nihil crebrius mandat et praecipit quam ut insistamus eleemosynis dandis nec terrenis possessionibus incubemus sed caelestes thesauros potius recondamus. Vendite, inquit, res uestras et date eleemosynam, et iterum: nolite uobis condere thesauros super terram, ubi tinea et comestura exterminat et ubi fures effodiunt et furantur.*" Cf. *Inst.*, 6.12.32–37. Bowen and Garnsey, *Institutes*, p. 358, fn. 49, also notes the connection with Cyprian's *De opere et eleemosynis*, 9, "Unlike in L. 37 below, [Cyprian] allows no compromise." However, Cyprian's ethic is a matter of debate. See Christopher M. Hays, "Resumptions of Radicalism: Christian Wealth Ethics in the Second and Third Centuries," *ANRW* 102. Bd. S (2011): esp. pp. 267–272, who argues that Cyprian advocated "radical renunciation [which] is something that goes beyond almsgiving, but [does] not require a monastic pooling of possessions." For fuller discussion and bibliography, see Christopher M. Hays, *Luke's Wealth Ethics: A Study in Their Coherence and Character* (Tübingen: Mohr Siebeck, 2010).

140 ROMAN VIRTUE IN THE EARLY CHRISTIAN THOUGHT OF LACTANTIUS

the Gospels. Cyprian also calls Christ *magister aeternae salutis* and *doctor vitae* to portray Christ as a supreme teacher of moral wisdom.

Cyprian derives from the teaching of Jesus a doctrine that takes God's activity in creation as the authority for his moral and economic teaching. Cyprian teaches that created goods should be shared equally without respect to wealth or social status and urges the congregation at Carthage to imitate the apostolic Church, whose "original mentality was strong in greater virtutes [*primordia maioribus virtutibus viget*]" when the new faith of the believers was still "glowing with the warmth of faith."[115] Cyprian urges Christians to imitate the apostolic Church by adopting a unity of mind and purpose that results from their common knowledge of eternal life:

> Let us consider, beloved brothers, what the people of believers [*credentium populus*] did under the Apostles . . . when having torn up and sold their earthly patrimony they transferred their estates to that place where they might reap the fruit of an eternal possession, and building homes there they began to live eternally . . . [As Acts 4:32 says], "Then the crowd of believers was acting with one soul and mind [*anima ac menta una*], nor was there among them any distinction and no one measured himself on the basis of his possessions, but rather they held all things in common."[116]

Cyprian's argument depends on a distinction between the earthly and heavenly, which presumes that the former passes away and the latter endures. He urges that wealth be used to win souls for the Church and claims that good parents provide not for their children's temporal needs, but for their eternal ones.[117] On that logic, he advocates a unity that erases, within the community of Christians, any kind of social status derived from wealth. Cyprian grounds the teaching in an argument that God means the whole human race to enjoy creation equally. His explanation again deploys the metaphor of light taken over from Tertullian's Christology:

> This truly is to become a son of God by a spiritual birth. This is [what it means] to imitate the *aequitas* of God the Father by a heavenly law [*caeleste lege*]. Whatever is of God is common in our use; and no one is shut out from His heavenly benefits and gifts, as if any part of the human race [*omne humanum genus*] might not enjoy the divine goodness and largesse equally. *For equally the day brings light, the sun shines, the rain falls, and the wind blows; for those*

---

[115] Cyprian, *De opere et eleemosynis*, 25.
[116] Cyprian, *De opere et eleemosynis*, 25.
[117] Cyprian, *De opere et eleemosynis*, 18–24.

who sleep, there is one sleep; the light and splendor of the stars is common to all [*communis*]. By this example of equity [*exemplo aequitatis*], he who though a landowner on earth shares his goods with the brotherhood [*cum fraternitate*], is an imitator of God the Father for his offering is free and just [*communis et justus est*].[118]

Cyprian introduces the vocabulary of *aequitas* as a term defined by God's action in creation. In this case, it is not Christ's Incarnation, but God's creating gift that defines justice among human beings, although Cyprian's argument for equality does reiterate the metaphor of light coming from God. In this case, however, Cyprian refers to the sun's created light rather than the Johannine illumination in order to ground his moral doctrine in the Father's own "*exemplum aequitatis*." Although Cyprian refers to creation, this language of *aequitas* is not divorced from Cyprian's thinking on the Incarnation. Rather, Cyprian has read the creation in terms of the Incarnation and has applied an account of the divine nature revealed in Christ's specific work to all of God's action toward humanity. Cyprian then makes the jump from description to prescription by a typically Roman exemplary logic: since Christians imitate the deity they worship, they treat the entire human race [*omne genus humanum*] equally by giving one and the same gifts to everyone, as God does. Cyprian thus names *aequitas* as a "heavenly law" that Christians keep when they are "spiritually born."

Heavily influenced by Tertullian's *De patientia*, Cyprian's treatise *De bono patientiae* reflects the broader diffusion of Roman virtue discourse in Latin Christian theology.[119] When Cyprian opens his discourse promising "to speak of patience [*de patientia*] . . . in order to proclaim its advantages and benefits [*utilitates et commoda*]," he takes the typically Latin and Ciceronian correlation of *virtus* and *beneficia* (*utilitates, commoda, beneficia, munera*) as a point of departure; *beneficia* relates to *virtus* as product to power.[120] Cyprian follows Tertullian by grounding Christian *virtus* in his Latin account of the divine "power and nature." To the Christian Church as a whole, Cyprian applies language Tertullian developed to articulate the relationship between the Father and the Son:

---

[118] Cyprian, *De opere et eleemosynis*, 25. "*Hoc est natiuitate spiritali uere Dei filium fieri, hoc est lege caelesti aequitatem Dei Patris imitari. Quodcumque enim Dei est in nostra usurpatione commune est, nec quisquam a beneficiis eius et muneribus arcetur quominus omnehumanum genus bonitate ac largitate diuina aequaliter perfruatur. Sic aequaliter dies luminat, sol radiat, imber rigat, uentus adspirat, et dormientibus somnus unus est, et stellarum splendor ac lunae communis est. Quo aequitatis exemplo qui possessor in terris reditus ac fructus suos cum fraternitate partitur, dum largitionibus gratuitis communis ac iustus est, Dei Patris imitator est.*" Cf. Lactantius, *Inst.*, 5.14.15.

[119] Cyprian, *Á Donat et La vertu de patience: introduction, traduction et notes de Jean Molager* (Paris: Éditions Du Cerf, 1982), pp. 140–155, which compares the texts of Cyprian and Tertullian systematically.

[120] Cyprian, *Bon. pat.*, 1.

142 ROMAN VIRTUE IN THE EARLY CHRISTIAN THOUGHT OF LACTANTIUS

By a heavenly instruction we learn a patience [*patientia*], which we offer back to God in spiritual obedience as slaves and worshippers. Indeed, we share this power [*virtus*] with God. There [*inde*], patience begins; there its brightness and dignity [*claritas et dignitas*] find their source [*caput*]. The origin and magnitude [*origo et magnitudo*] of patience proceed [*procedit*] from God its author [*auctore*]. Humanity must love what is dear to God: the divine majesty [*maiestas divina*] entrusts to us the good it loves. If God is to us both Father and Lord, let us pursue the patience of the Lord and the Father equally. For just as it is necessary that servants be obedient, it is wrong for sons to be degenerate.[121]

D'Alès summarizes Cyprian's thought well, when he says, "The Christians, who profess wisdom, not in words, but in acts, have learned their patience [*la patience*] in the school of God himself [*à l'école de Dieu même*]."[122] Cyprian's lines imitate Tertullian's *Pat.* 3.10 but also develop further technical vocabulary. The terms *origo, procedit,* and *virtus,* as well as *maiestas divina,* are drawn from trinitarian theological discourse.[123] Framing that language, Cyprian invokes the Christological parallel of Christ's "words and deeds" that Tertullian uses in his own meditation on *patientia* (*Pat.,* 3) and in his later influential argument about the Son's revelation of the Father (*Prax.,* 22). Cyprian applies Tertullian's thought to the Church more broadly: it is now the *opera* of Christians that reveal a *patientia* mediated by the Son's display, which redounds from the Father its head [*caput*] and source [*origo*]. The *virtus* that marks the Son's unity with the Father also indicates the Christian's unity with God. Cyprian does not think that Christians somehow participate directly in the relationships of Father, Son, and Spirit exclusive to the divine nature. Rather, he argues that the Son's mediation of divine *virtus* in the Church and through the sacraments unites every Christian with one another and with God.

Cyprian develops his vision of Christian life into a fully articulated ethic over the course of his treatise. Such terms as lenience [*lenis*], long-suffering [*patiens*], and meekness [*mitis*] augment his core emphasis on *patientia*.[124] Roman exemplary logic remains operative, as he invokes these qualities as evidence of Christ's divinity and thus an example for humanity. Again, Cyprian grounds his parallel between "words and deeds" Christologically:

---

[121] Cyprian, *Bon. pat.*, 3. Cf. Tertullian, *Pat.*, 3.

[122] A. D'Alès, *La Théologie de Saint Cyprien* (Paris: Beauchesne, 1922), p. 352.

[123] E.g., *auctor, caput,* and *origo* are all titles of the Father in Novatian, *Trin.* 31. See Daniel Lloyd, *Ontological Subordination in Novatian of Rome's Trinitarian Theology* (Milwaukee, WI: Unpublished dissertation, Marquette University, 2009). Tertullian, *Prax.*, 7.1 uses *procedit* of both the Son and Spirit. *Claritas* and *dignitas* reflect Tertullian's causal metaphors at *Apol.* 21 and *Prax.* 2.

[124] Cyprian, *Bon. pat.*, 5: "*Atque ut plenius intellegere possimus, fratres dilectissimi, quia patientia Dei res est et quisque lenis, patients et mitis est Dei patris imitator est; cum in evangelio suo Dominus praecepta in salute daret et divina monita depromens ad perfectum discipulos erudiret, posuit et dixit*" [Matt. 5].

Nor did Jesus Christ our Lord and God teach this . . . only with words, but fulfilled it in deeds [*verbis docuit, sed impleuit et factis*]. The one who also had said he descended for this purpose, "that he might do the will of his Father," among the marvels of his virtues by which he expressed proof of his divine majesty [*inter cetera mirabilia virtutum quibus indicia*], he kept also his Father's patience in the course of his tolerance.[125]

When he says that Christ's *tolerantia* and *patientia* take primary place among the "*mirabilia virtutum*" by which Christ expressed the "*indicia divinae maiestatis*," Cyprian presupposes the causal relationship between a power and its effects.[126] He understands *patientia* as a "virtue" because it is a "power of action," or, more technically speaking, a capacity to produce effects that disclose the power consistent with God's nature. This logic supports Cyprian's redefinition of justice in accordance with Christ's example: "That man so just, so innocent—in fact, he who is justice itself and itself is innocence [*ille iustus, immo innocentia ipse et ipse iustitia*]—is reckoned among the criminals. The Truth is oppressed by false witnesses; he is judged who shall come to judge and the Word of God [*Dei sermo*], silent, is led to the slaughter."[127] Because he takes Christ's passion as the manifestation of God's power—i.e., the kind of work that God's *virtus* produces—Cyprian redefines the *virtus* of justice as manifest in willing acceptance of humiliation. Because he accepts the grammar of Tertullian's Christology, Cyprian inverts the Roman vision of *virtus* as a martial quality; he defines *virtus* on the basis of the works not of Romulus or Scipio Africanus, but of Jesus Christ.

After a lengthy quotation from Matthew 5, the above passage concludes by applying Tertullian's Christological logic to the Church's collective actions. For Cyprian, Christian works display God's *virtus* in the world and restore a divine image lost in Eden: "If the forbearance of God the Father abides in us, then the divine likeness which Adam lost by sin is manifested and shines bright [*luceat*] in our actions [*in actibus nostris*]," he argues.[128] Through this, God attributes to Christian actions the power of realizing a blessedness [*felicitas*] that was formerly given only to divine emperors and the gods themselves: "What glory it is to become like God, what a great and marvelous blessedness [*qualis et quanta felicitas*] to have in our powers [*in virtutibus*] that which is equal to the divine praise!"[129] The thought is formally indistinguishable from Tertullian's teaching that the Father and Son abide in one another through the works of the Son, which

[125] Cyprian, *Bon. pat.*, 6.
[126] Cyprian, *Bon. pat.*, 5.
[127] Cyprian, *Bon. pat.*, 7.
[128] Cyprian, *Bon. pat.*, 5.
[129] Cyprian, *Bon. pat.*, 5.

144 ROMAN VIRTUE IN THE EARLY CHRISTIAN THOUGHT OF LACTANTIUS

display the Father's power. A final passage completes his meditation invoking the causal metaphors that explain the Son's generation:

> Let us hold fast with complete observation to the patience, by which we remain in Christ and are able to come with Christ unto God. This patience, rich and manifold, is not confined in narrow borders nor compelled within a small space [*brevibus terminis*]. The power of patience [*patientiae virtus*] ranges widely; its fruitful abundance redounds from the font of a single Name [*ubertas eius et largitas de unius quidem nominis fonte*], but it pours in rushing veins through many paths of glories [*sed exundantibus venis per multa gloriarum itinera diffunditur*]; nor is anything in our actions able to proceed to the highest praise, unless from there [*inde*] we receive the firmness of its perfection [*firmitatem*].[130]

Like Tertullian, Cyprian grounds this Christology in his reading of John: "Let us who follow in Christ's saving footsteps walk by Christ's example [*exemplo*], just as the Apostle John instructs: 'He who says he is in Christ must remain in Christ and walk as Christ walked.'"[131] Christ's public example of *patientia* fills Cyprian's vision of the Christian life. His moral theology is trinitarian theology applied.

It was a close reading of John that originally inspired Tertullian's Christological axiom, and Cyprian follows in his footsteps by developing the logic of imitation on the basis of John's Gospel. He thus builds his ecclesiology on the foundation of Tertullian's Christology, out of which he also develops a moral vision of Christians as people walking in the "footsteps of Christ."

Conclusion

Third-century Latin theology began in apologetic works that adopted a typically Roman and Ciceronian approach: early Latin Christians imitated their ancestors' example (i.e., *mos maiorum*) while redefining, once again, the meaning of Roman virtue. To do so, the Latin apologists combined both philosophical and rhetorical strategies. Rhetorically, their arguments operated by systematically reasserting the oblique and ambivalent criticisms found in Augustan

---

[130] Cyprian, *Bon. pat.*, 20. Cf. Cyprian, *Unit.*, 5. Where the same trinitarian language expresses the unity of the Church: "*Sic et ecclesia, domini luce perfusa, per orbem totum radios suos porrigit, unum tamen lumen est quod ubique diffunditur nec unitas corporis separatur; ramos suos in uniuersam terram copia ubertatis extendit; profluentes largiter riuos latius spandit, unum tamen caput est et origo una, et una mater fecunditatis successibus copiosa: illius fetu nascimur, illius lacte nutrimur, spiritu eius animamur.*"

[131] Cyprian, *Bon. pat.*, 9.

literature to contradict imperial accusations against Christians. They appealed to a long-standing Roman tradition that regarded the imperial ideology as a destruction of Roman Republican traditions. That rhetorical method speaks to the nature of Latin Christianity's earliest engagement with Roman thought and culture. Latin apologetic does not simply reject Rome, but rather criticizes the imperial ideology while laying claim to an older Republican tradition of opposition to the principate. This rhetorical strategy is predicated upon a substantial theological argument. The apologists represent Christian teaching in the terms of power theology in order to redefine *virtus* according to the example of Jesus. In that effort, the apologists usher the technical sense of power (*virtus, vis, potestas*) into Latin trinitarian and moral discourse through their engagement with Cicero, Vergil, and Seneca. They do so in order to engage in the long Roman tradition of political debate predicated upon the notion of *virtus*.[132] In the process, the Latin apologists elevate "patience" (*patientia*) as the supreme *virtus* on the basis of Christ's humiliation, which is offered as the final *exemplar virtutis*. What results is a distinctive Christian iteration of Roman virtue discourse that arises from the North African tradition of Latin Christianity and comes to animate Christian thinking on the divine nature, the character of the Church, and the moral order of the Christian life. As shall be seen, this tradition constitutes the principal source of Lactantius's arguments, the basis of his trinitarian theology, and the content of his moral thought.

[132] For power theology in Tertullian, see Barnes, *Power of God*, pp. 100–120. Also, Michel R. Barnes, "Latin Trinitarian Theology," in *The Cambridge Companion to the Trinity*, pp. 70–83. Earlier, Joseph Moingt, *Théologie trinitaire de Tertullien. histoire, doctrine, méthodes*, 3 vols. (Paris: Aubier, 1966). Jules Lebreton, *Les Origines du Dogme de La Trinité*, 2 vols. (Paris: Beauchesne & Co. Éditeurs, 1910).

4

Virtus: The Power of God in Lactantius

> From this most especially, oh Pharisees, you should have recognized
> the Lord. No human being could have achieved such patience! Such
> great and remarkable evidence . . . proves [*probant*] not only by the
> words of his teaching, but also by the Lord's passions in suffering
> that patience is God's nature, the effect and excellence of some in-
> born property [*ingenitaecuisdam proprietatis*].
>
> —Tertullian, *On Patience*, 3

Lactantius's few self-referential comments provide vital information about his sources and influences. Especially important are the remarks at *Inst.* 5.1.22–25, where he places himself in an apologetic tradition as the successor to Tertullian, Minucius Felix, and Cyprian. Scholars have mainly used the passage to explain Lactantius's apologetic method. He aimed to improve upon the earlier Latin writers by arguing from pagan sources. By concealing his reliance upon Scripture, he aimed to lead educated pagans to reconsider their false judgments about Christianity.[1] Understanding this methodology is fundamental to reading Lactantius well. However, Lactantius does not only criticize his predecessors. His comments indicate his own breadth of reading in Latin Christian apologetic, pastoral, and doctrinal treatises; they also demonstrate that Lactantius understood himself as the heir to the Latin Christian apologetic tradition. Hence, Lactantius praises Minucius Felix's skill in thought and literary art; he regrets only that the *Octavius*'s argument is incomplete. Lactantius's claim that Tertullian was "skilled in every sort of writing," suggests that he knew Tertullian's works broadly; he criticizes only Tertullian's uneven style and rudeness. Cyprian receives abundant praise for his fame, clarity of expression, and theological

---

[1] Both Jochen Walter and Blandine Colot argue that Lactantius aims to lead pagan readers back to the Scriptures by subtly insinuating scriptural claims into his text, even though scriptural claims determine his real thinking. According to Walter, *Pagane Texte und Wertvorstellungen bei Laktanz* (Goettingen: Vandenhoeck and Ruprecht, 2006), p. 65, "Lactantius wanted to introduce his non-Christian reader gradually and in a consciously instrumentalized connection to non-Christian or extra-Christian discourse (toward Christianity [*zum Christentum*])." For Colot, *Lactance: Penser la conversion de Rome au temps de Constantin* (Firenze: Leo Olschki Editore, 2016), p. 41, Lactantius's rhetorical art is "a form in which the biblical text could become very subtly and very progressively delivered to the reader along with an argument constructed so as to lead the reader to comprehend the message found therein."

Roman Virtue in the Early Christian Thought of Lactantius. Jason M. Gehrke, Oxford University Press.
© Oxford University Press 2025. DOI: 10.1093/9780197667781.003.0005

learning; Lactantius regrets only that Cyprian preferred to preach rather than debate. He discussed "God's sacred mystery" and spoke things suitable only for the initiated.[2] Lactantius thus reviews his predecessors not primarily to call them inadequate, but to identify his debt to the tradition he defends. Although the *Divine Institutes* draws upon a wide range of texts and authors, Lactantius identifies third-century Latin Christian writers as the primary influence in his formation as a Christian and as an apologist.

A fundamental marker of Lactantius's debt to early Latin Christian theology is his reliance upon the technical sense of "power" (*virtus, potestas, vis*). Like his predecessors, Lactantius employs a common philosophical grammar predicated upon broadly held notions of power and nature, while also departing from classical Roman interpretations whenever they disagree with early Latin Christian understandings of the "power of God." Recognizing the philosophical underpinnings of Lactantius's argument is the first step toward understanding his theology as a whole. Hence, the next three sections explore the technical discourse that underpins his arguments. The first section examines his criticism of philosophical arguments about the highest good in order to show that Lactantius understands *virtus* in terms of causal relations built upon the technical sense of power. Recognizing the causal logic inherent in his language clarifies our reading both of Lactantius's polemic and of his doctrinal theology. The chapter then proceeds to examine Lactantius's doctrine of God in order to demonstrate the continuity of his understanding with Tertullian, Cyprian, and Novatian. A third and final section reexamines Lactantius's critique of the Roman gods, in light of the proceeding. Lactantius does not offer merely moral or ad hominem polemics. Rather, he argues that philosophical interpretations of the pantheon are self-defeating because they violate their own basic axioms. Lactantius's doctrine of God is expressed in the course of this critique, which clears the ground for the Christological narrative that follows in *Institutio* 4.

Virtus: Power Causality Revisited

Lactantius discusses *virtus* throughout the *Divine Institutes*, but the philosophical presuppositions of his usage are most evident in a relatively compressed passage at *Inst.* 3.7–12, where he criticizes the Stoic idea that *virtus* is the highest good.[3] His discussion relies heavily upon Cicero, whose vocabulary for causes, power, and so forth shaped nearly all Latin arguments about the true power and

[2] Lactantius, *Inst.*, 5.1.22.
[3] Lactantius, *Inst.*, 3.8.1–2.

148　ROMAN VIRTUE IN THE EARLY CHRISTIAN THOUGHT OF LACTANTIUS

nature of *virtus*.[4] His usage is typical of what Michel Barnes called "the technical sense of power."[5] The first element of "power causality" appears in his reliance upon causal language. Lactantius understands that classical definitions explain what *virtus* is by saying what it causes: "The Cynics say that *virtus* itself [*virtutem ipsam*] is to be praised because it effects pleasure [*quod sit efficiens voluptatis*]."[6] The term *efficiens* indicates the causal notion that underlies the argument. Whatever *virtus* is becomes apparent by the *effect* it produces. The next line uses *potestas* to define the irreducible content of the term: "The highest good cannot cause anyone to be blessed [*efficere quemquam beatum*], unless it shall always have been in its power [*in ipsius potestate*]."[7] Again, to be "*in eius potestate*" is Lactantius's way of naming an existent in causal terms. This statement, like many others, reveals that Lactantius's broader applications of the term *virtus* contain an irreducible causal content. *Virtus* is a power—or, rather, some kind of power is the operative thing in *virtus*.

As the argument proceeds, Lactantius presupposes the second and third elements of power causality. He uses the term "power" (*vis* and *virtus*) to designate individual causes, and he takes each "power" as revealing the identity of an existent in its effects. Both points are evident from his interrogation of the Stoic definition of the highest good, which pairs the terms *vis* and *significatio*: "Why does he prefer to say that knowledge rather than wisdom is the highest good, since the meaning and power is the same [*significatio ac vis eadem*]?"[8] The Ciceronian pairing of "meaning and power [*significatio ac vis*]" shows that Lactantius is using "power" as indicative of identity.[9] Moreover, his argument presupposes that power is the true marker of an existent: Lactantius's point is that knowledge and wisdom are simply two names for the same "power." He soon characterizes the relationship between *virtus* and the highest good as that of a power to its product: "*Virtus* itself is not the highest good, but the effector and mother [*effectrix ac mater*] of the highest good, since no one is able to approach the highest good without *virtus* [*quoniam perveniri ad illud sine virtute non potest*]."[10] In this argument, the term

---

[4] See Cicero, *Fin.*, 5.23 and 2.19 cited at *Inst.*, 3.7.7–8. See Heck and Wlosok, *Index Locorum*, in *Divinarum Institutionum Libri Septem*, fasc I–IV, ed. Eberhard Heck et Antonie Wlosok (Berlin: DeGruyter, 2005–2011), p. 766.

[5] See Chapter 2, this volume. Michel R. Barnes, *The Power of God: Dynamis in Gregory of Nyssa's Trinitarian Theology* (Washington, DC: Catholic University of America Press, 2001).

[6] Lactantius, *Inst.*, 3.8.9.

[7] Lactantius, *Inst.*, 3.8.14, quoted in Eberhard Heck and Antonie Wlosok, *Divinarum Institutionum Libri Septem*.

[8] Lactantius, *Inst.*, 3.8.30. Cf. *Inst.*, 2.9. Lactantius presents this definition as a correction of Cicero.

[9] Cf. Cicero, *Div.*, 1.12 also characterizes divinization as an observation of powers analogous to medical procedure: "*est enim vis et natura quaedam, quae tum observatis longo tempore significationibus, tum aliquo instinctu inflatu que divino futura praenuntiat.*" *Div.*, 2.124: "*enim divina vis quaedam consulens nobis somniorum significationes facit.*"

[10] Lactantius, *Inst.*, 3.8.32. Lactantius is engaging, in these passages, the debate at Cicero, *Fin.*, 5.77–79, as Heck and Wlosok note. *Fin.*, 5.78 couches the debate about the highest good as a question

VIRTUS: THE POWER OF GOD IN LACTANTIUS   149

effectrix specifies *virtus* as the agent of a causal relationship, while the term *mater* uses a genetic metaphor to characterize that causal relationship between *virtus* and its offspring. In this vein, Lactantius presupposes the notion that powers can be plural and indicate a plurality of specific causes: "If this is true, there is need for another *virtus* [*altera virtute*], in order to arrive at that *virtus* [*ad eam virtutem*] which is called the highest good [*summum bonum*]."[11] The distinction between *virtus* and *altera virtus* is not a redundancy. Lactantius is working with the notion of individual causes. The whole argumentative procedure conveys the legacy of medicine in philosophical discourse, insofar as Lactantius assumes that careful observation of powers and their effect is the procedure by which one discerns the identity of things.[12]

Lactantius expands upon the above distinction between *virtus* and *altera virtus* by discussing the distinctive product of *virtus* as a power, in terms taken over from Cicero. Textually, Lactantius plays with language and arguments found in Cicero's *Inv.* 1.6–7 and in his arguments at *De finibus* 5. Lactantius uses those passages to reject the idea that *virtus* itself can be the highest good. He says:

> If it is not possible to attain any good except through labor [cf. *Fin.*, 5.77–79], it appears that *virtus* is the means by which one arrives [at the highest good], since the power [*vis*] and function [*officium*] of *virtus* lies in undertaking labors and bringing them to completion. Now then, by definition, the highest good cannot be anything by which one arrives at something else. However, since they did not know what *virtus* causes or what it aims for [*quid efficeret virtus aut quo tenderet*], but found nothing more noble [*honestius*] than it, they stopped at the name of *virtus* itself [*in ipsius virtutis nomine*], which, they said, ought to be desired without promise of further advantage, so that they might establish as a good for themselves that which required a good.[13]

These lines build an argument about the highest good entirely upon the grammar of a power causality, and in the technical language of Cicero's philosophical thought. Not only does Lactantius draw directly upon the Ciceronian texts that introduced power causality for Latin discourse, but the logic of his argument

---

of "how great" the power of *virtus* is. The whole discussion is conducted in terms of degrees of power. Cf. *Fin.*, 5.77, which also discusses *virtus* in causal terms: "'*Utrum igitur tibi,*' inquit, '*non placet virtutisne esse tantam vim ut ad beatum vivendum se ipsa contenta sit . . . volo in virtute vim esse quam maximam.*'"

[11] Lactantius, *Inst.*, 3.8.35.
[12] This method of interrogation continues at length over the extended argument. Cf. *Inst.*, 3.8.11–15.
[13] Lactantius, *Inst.*, 3.8.36. Lactantius is here using the term *officium* in the sense of *product* as at Cicero, *Inv.*, 1.6–7, 2.159–160.

150   ROMAN VIRTUE IN THE EARLY CHRISTIAN THOUGHT OF LACTANTIUS

is predicated upon the shared body of assumptions transmitted by Cicero and later Latin philosophers to Christian argument. As confirmation of the point, Lactantius uses the signature phrase "power and nature" to summarize the very definition of what *virtus* cannot be: "If [*virtus*] cannot be blessed, because its power and nature [*vis et natura*] lies in the endurance of evils, it cannot then be the highest good."[14] His use of the technical formula confirms the philosophical origins of his argument.

The fact that power causality animates Lactantius's language of *virtus* explains how he can readily move between what might seem like distinct senses—one moral, one causal—of the term with no confusion. There is no contradiction because the moral sense of *virtus* relies upon the causal logic taken over from ancient elemental theories. The unity of these two notions in Lactantius's typically Latin thinking is most evident as his argument develops. Lactantius asks, "What is that on account of which we are born; what does virtue effect [*quid efficiat virtus*]?"[15] His answer relies upon the elemental theory mediated by Cicero and later Stoic thought: "There are two from which humanity is constituted [*homo constat*], soul and body [*animus et corpus*]. The soul has certain distinctives [*propria*]; the body does as well, while some are common to both. *Virtus* is one of them."[16] This sentence describes the human as a compound (*coniunctio*) and sets the notion of *virtus* into the context of a Stoic mixture theory traceable to Seneca and Cicero.

On that foundation, Lactantius can collapse the distinction between bravery and philosophical excellence, a move that has troubled many translators and philologists. Lactantius continues: "For the sake of distinction, when referred to the body it [*virtus*] is termed 'strength [*fortitudo*].' Since then strength underlies each one [*utrique subiacet fortitudo*], the idea of a contest is proposed for each one, and so for each, a victory results from that contest."[17] This line effectively equates philosophical excellence and martial bravery by making both the expression of a single causal capacity. *Virtus* animates both mental and physical activities because it is, in the end, a power. Hence also, at both physical and mental levels, *virtus* is the agent in a causal relationship—in this case, "victory." Unlike modern translators, and most modern interpreters, Lactantius does not see a strong distinction between martial prowess and ethical perfection. He sees mental and physical *virtus* as expressions of a power born within the compound that is human nature.

What makes this theory of *virtus* coherent, for Lactantius, is the Stoic physical theory that he presumes and shares with earlier Latin writers. Lactantius

[14]   Lactantius, *Inst.*, 3.8.11.
[15]   Lactantius, *Inst.*, 3.12.1.
[16]   Lactantius, *Inst.*, 3.12.1–3.
[17]   Lactantius, *Inst.*, 3.12.2.

VIRTUS: THE POWER OF GOD IN LACTANTIUS   151

explains the difference between mental and physical *virtus* by the difference in their material substances:

> Since it is solid and touchable, the body necessarily comes into conflict with what is solid and comprehensible [*cum solidis et comprehensibilibus confligat*]. Likewise, since it is tenuous and invisible [*tenuis est et invisibilis*], the soul engages with such enemies as cannot be seen and touched. What then are the enemies of the soul if not passions, vices, sins [*cupiditates vitia peccata*]? If *virtus* shall have conquered and put them to flight, the soul is spotless and pure.[18]

When Lactantius says that "the soul" engages with intangible and invisible enemies "because it is tenuous," he relies upon the common principle of ancient elemental theories that "like affects like."[19] Elementally speaking, he understands "philosophical virtue" as a capacity common to the whole nature called human because that nature exists as a compound of *corpus* and *animus*. Underlying this definition is a Stoic physical theory as old as Cicero and Seneca. Seneca, for instance, conceived every power of nature as attributable to *spiritus*, which he could use as a synonym for *animus* understood as a material element compounded of fire and air.[20] Hence, for Lactantius, "*virtus* of mind [*virtus animi*]" is the power of the soul to struggle against immaterial opponents, just as the "*virtus* of body [*virtus corporis*]" is the power animating physical bodies in battle. Still, physical *virtus* embodies a form of the struggle for life, which is ultimately governed by the mind. In every case, *virtus* is the same cause—which is to say, power. The connection of physical and mental *virtus* is enabled by Lactantius's underlying physical theory.

Lactantius's consistent understanding of *virtus* in terms of power causality rests on the presupposition that immortality, not *virtus* itself, is the highest good. He derives a definition of *virtus animi* by observing its expression in physical *virtus*. The logic of that argument therefore also reflects the *X from X* principle that cause produces its likeness in its effect. Lactantius thinks that by considering the physical manifestation of *virtus*, he can discern the nature of *virtus* as a power to preserve life, which is active even in non-physical contests. Lactantius says:

> Where then can we learn what the strength of the mind effects [*quid efficiat animi fortitudo*]? Clearly, from the thing connected with and similar to it [*ex coniuncto et pari*], which is to say, by comparison with the strength of the body

---

[18]   Lactantius, *Inst.*, 3.12.2–3.
[19]   See Chapter 2, this volume.
[20]   Seneca, *Nat. q.*, 2.45–46.

[*corporis fortitudo*]. Now then, when it comes into any conflict or contest, what else does it seek from its victory than life [*quam vitam petit*]? ... What then is the difference between the contest of the body and of the mind [*animi*] unless it is that the body seeks temporal life, and the mind eternal life? If then *virtus* is not blessed in itself, since, as I have said, ... its whole power [*tota vis*] is in fighting off evils ... [and] since its labors taken up and sustained even unto death cannot be without a reward [i.e., product] ... what else remains except that the thing which despises all earthly things causes something heavenly [*caeleste aliquid efficiat*]. ... Therefore, the blessed life is the reward of *virtus*, if *virtus* ... causes the blessed life [*ergo virtutis praemium beata vita est, si virtus ... beatam vitam facit*]. *Virtus* then is not to be sought ... for its own sake, but for the sake of the blessed life, which necessarily results from *virtus* [*quae virtutem necessario sequitur*].[21]

Lactantius's account of *virtus* as a "power" that brings about the happy life reveals two assumptions about his elemental theory. The first is that mental and physical powers exist as compounds of a single nature, since he says they exist in "conjunction [*coniunctio*]." The second is that he accepts the "like from like principle," a point evident in his claim that the effect of *virtus* reveals its true character. That principle explains why Lactantius thinks he can move from the observation of the effect of a bodily power to a judgment about the activity of a mental power—both seek to cause life. This argument establishes the fundamental premise of Lactantius's moral theory, which holds "eternal life" as the supreme good that defines and orders any exercise of *virtus*. His argument also clarifies the relationship between "moral excellence" and "power," which has plagued so many translators of Lactantius, and indeed, of Latin philosophical and theological literature.[22] Lactantius understands both power and virtue as causal capacities. He ascribes to the *animus* an ultimate end that reveals and expresses an immaterial dimension of the daily struggle for life, which is lived in the body. The argument therefore establishes a primary axiom of Lactantius's moral thought: *virtus* is the capacity that produces and sustains life, in all its dimensions. That axiom underpins his redefinition of both divine and human *virtus* throughout the *Divine Institutes*.

Against the Gods: Lactantius on the Divine Nature

Lactantius's doctrine of God and his criticism of Rome's traditional deities prove to be two sides of the same coin, because Lactantius articulates his constructive

[21] Lactantius, *Inst.*, 3.12.4–8, 12–13.
[22] See Chapter 1, this volume.

theology within the context of his critical arguments. Both components of his thought rely upon the same technical sense of power and reflect the common understanding of power causality in the Latin philosophical and theological tradition. Throughout both his critical and constructive discussions, divine *virtus* denotes that causal capacity by which one God creates and governs the cosmos. Parallel to the terms *potentia* and *potestas*, *virtus* signifies what Lactantius insists must be the unique and undivided person of God.[23] He understands the divine nature in Platonic terms as fundamentally transcendent, ineffable, and beyond power, but he also accepts the traditional idea that God's power signifies God's existence through its effects. In this, Lactantius extends a Latin tradition of apologetic and theology evident in Tertullian, Minucius Felix, Cyprian, and Novatian. And he frames his Christian definition of God as a criterion that simultaneously exposes the historic devotion to the Roman pantheon as false worship of human weakness.

Lactantius begins his argument by establishing the oneness of God. He asserts with Minucius Felix that whatever the title "God" indicates, it must be the title of a complete and undivided power—a power that contains all possible capacities.[24] To make this claim, Lactantius asks "whether the world is ruled by the power of one god [*potestate unius dei*] or many."[25] The term *virtus* appears as a synonym of *potestas* in this context. All rational people, he argues, know that "there is One, who both founded and controls all things by the same power [*virtute*] by which he founded them [*qui et condiderit omnia et eadem qua condidit virtute moderetur*]."[26] He plainly understands *virtus* in causal terms, since he uses *virtute* in the ablative case with transitive verbs (*condidit, moderetur*) and as a synonym for *potestas*. His claim makes *virtus* the agent in a causal relation. God creates by means of *virtus*.

Lactantius then uses his definition of God as a "perfect power [*virtus perfecta*]" to reject the Ciceronian philosophical account of Rome's gods that his opponents advocate. Consistent with Seneca and earlier Stoic usage, Lactantius makes *potestas* the irreducible content of the term *mens*: "God, moreover, who is eternal mind [*mens aeterna*], is in every part [a being] of perfect and consummate *virtus*. If that is true, he is necessarily one. Absolute virtue [*virtus*] and power [*potestas*] retains its distinctive strength [*propriam firmitatem*]."[27] Lactantius' claim that

---

[23] The terms *persona* and *natura* both appear in the larger context of this discussion in Lactantius. See *Inst.* 1.3.9–10 (see below): "*Virtutis autem perfecta natura in eo potest esse...*" *Inst.*, 4.29.11: "*Cum duas personas proposuisset, Dei regis, id est Christi et Dei patris, qui eum post passionem ab inferis excitavit.*"

[24] Cf. Minucius Felix, *Oct.*, 18–19, which uses the same argument about the *nomen* of *Deus*.

[25] *Inst.*, 1.3.1–2, "*utrum potestate unius dei mundus regatur anne multorum.*" Cf. *Rep.*, 1.55–56.

[26] Lactantius, *Inst.*, 1.3.2.

[27] Lactantius, *Inst.*, 1.3.4. Cf. Aloys Grillmeier, *Christ in the Christian Tradition*, vol. 1, *From the Apostolic Age to Chalcedon (451)*, 2nd ed. (Oxford: Mowbrays, 1976), pp. 193ff. Grillmeier did not

154 ROMAN VIRTUE IN THE EARLY CHRISTIAN THOUGHT OF LACTANTIUS

God must be One if God's power is complete assumes the common doctrine of his tradition: "power" is the basic marker of existence, because the assertion that one power designates one entity makes power coextensive with being. He thus uses *virtus* and *potestas* as synonyms that designate God as a single and providential cause.[28] To this point, Lactantius's argument is quite characteristic of Latin philosophical theologies since Cicero, both Christian and pagan.

Lactantius's definition of the divine nature is the philosophical basis for his criticism of the Roman pantheon that follows. He argues that the oneness of God's power (*virtus, potestas, vis*) precludes any attempt to understand traditional deities as specific manifestations of diverse capacities located within the divine nature.[29] With this claim, he attacks the plurality of the Roman gods as evidence that each "god" is defined not by power, but weakness:

> If there are many gods, they will be weaker [*minus valebunt*], insofar as the others have as much as exists in each one. Therefore, the gods' virtues and powers [*virtutes et potestates deorum*] will accomplish less [*minus valebunt*], since each individual will lack, however much was in the others; so, the greater in number, the weaker they are.[30]

Two features of this claim show that power causality underlies the argument. The first is the juxtaposition of "*virtutes et potestates*," which makes the two terms synonyms. The second is Lactantius's use of the verb *valere*. The combination of terms means that *virtus*, like *potestas*, is understood according to the logic of a causal relationship. His argument presumes the primary sense of *virtus* as a causal capacity and a marker of existence, since his ultimate claim is that because of their lack of power, the Roman deities as "gods" do not exist. They were not deities, but rather humans embellished in Roman memory. On this basis, Lactantius proceeds to contrast the complete power of God with the Roman deities' all-too-human weaknesses: "The perfect nature of *virtus* [*virtutis autem*

---

address this text or consider Lactantius's arguments in *Inst.* 4 in light of it. He begins with Wlosok and works entirely in *Inst.* 4. Loi is aware of the terms *vis, virtus, potestas*, and *summa potestas*, but not the grammar of their usage in Lactantius or his predecessors. Loi is also aware that "*virtus Dei*" is a Christological title derived from 1 Cor. 1:24 but, again, did not know about the technical sense of power and thus could not perceive the theological grammar of Lactantius's representation of the divine nature. See Vincenzo Loi, *Lattanzio nella storia del linguaggio e del pensiero teologico pre-niceno* (Zurich: Pas-Verlag, 1970), pp. 73–75 and pp. 212–215.

[28] Cf. Cicero, *Leg.*, 1.21–22.
[29] For examples of such an attempt, see Cicero, *Nat. d.*, 2.29–60, Seneca, *Ben.*, 4.7–8. For Lactantius's work as opposition to "*Romideologie*," see Colot, *Penser la conversion de Rome*, esp. pp. 3–48.
[30] Lactantius, *Inst.*, 1.3.9–10.

natura perfecta] is able to exist in the one in whom it is whole [*in quo totum est*]. If then God is perfect [*perfecta*], as he must be, he can only be One, such that all things are in him."[31] The logic of his argument is evident enough: if any subordinate deities participated in the divine power, their existence would involve a partitioning of divine power. Conversely, complete power requires, proves, and constitutes God's oneness. Built on this premise, Lactantius's discussion resolves into a narrative that uses *virtus* and *vis* as interchangeable divine titles and insists that they can be applied only to a single being.[32] In the course of that discussion, he consistently places *virtus* in opposition to weakness (*imbecillitas*) and uses it as a synonym for *potestas*.

Lactantius develops his constructive account of the divine nature in this critical context by drawing upon a logic taken over from Tertullian's *Apol.* 23 and from Minucius Felix's use of alpha-privative divine titles at *Oct.* 19. The argument situates Lactantius's theological grammar within the unfolding Latin apologetic tradition and reveals the precise content of certain divine titles that will appear in his Christology:

> So then, the other gods will not be gods but satellites and ministers, whom that one greatest and powerful over all [*unus maximus et pollens omnium*] compels to their duties; and they will serve his reign. If all are not equal, then all are not gods. Nor is it possible that the same one can be servant and master. For if "God" is the name of the Highest Power [*nomen summae potestatis*], he ought to be incorruptible, complete, impassible, and subject to nothing.[33]

This passage demonstrates three points about Lactantius's notion of God. First, it is an example of his traditional theology and its sources. The critical claim that divided and unequal power demonstrates the falsity of Roman divinities is taken from *Apol.* 23 and from an apologetic tradition that Lactantius draws upon consistently. Second, by using the phrase "*unus maximus et pollens omnium*," Lactantius defines the very word "*Deus*" as the "name of supreme power [*nomen summa potestatis*]," in order to distinguish the divine nature from any other nature.[34] Third, by appending to the notion of "greatest power" the titles "incorruptible, complete, impassible, and subject to nothing," Lactantius situates his

---

[31] Lactantius, *Inst.*, 1.3.9–10.

[32] Lactantius argues this way at length. See *Inst.*, 1.3.9–11: "Why is it that the Highest Power over all things [*summa illa rerum potestas*], that Divine Strength, [*vis divina*] cannot be at the same time divided."

[33] Lactantius, *Inst.*, 1.3.23–24. Cf. Tertullian, *Apol.*, 23.1–3: "*Aut si eadem et angeli et daemones operantur quae et dei vestri, ubi est ergo praecellentia divinitatis, quam utique superiorem omni potestate credendum est?*"

[34] Loi, *Lattanzio*, p. 38.

notion of the divine nature in a Platonic rather than Stoic tradition of power theology. He relies here not only upon Tertullian, but upon later third-century accounts of the divine nature, particularly that of Novatian.[35]

Lactantius's argument up to this point is typical of Latin-language theological discourse in Roman North Africa of the third century. The use of power theology and a Ciceronian idiom was fundamental to both Christian and non-Christian discussions of divinity. In his work, *On the God of Socrates,* for instance, Apuleius termed God "the parent [*parens*], ruler, and author [*dominator . . . auctor*] of all things," one who is characterized by "an incredible and inexpressible majesty [*maiestatis incredibile . . . ineffabili*]."[36] Like Lactantius and the Latin Christian writers, Apuleius attributes his definition to Plato's *Timaeus* 28c. Minucius Felix used the same phrase, "*incredibili potestate*," to affirm in Ciceronian language that Plato spoke "more clearly [*apertior*]" than others when he entitled God as "parent of the world [*parens mundi*]" and "artist of the soul [*artifex animae*]" and "maker [*fabricator*] of the heaven and the earth."[37] And Novatian would later argue that "the eloquence of human speech expresses nothing equal to the power of his majesty," in a longer passage describing God as a being "of perfect power and majesty [*perfectae potestatis et maiestatis*]" and beyond all good.[38] Novatian also speaks of God as *aeternus, immortalis et incorruptibilis,* and argues that "all appearances of virtues are necessarily lesser than him, who is God, the Parent of all virtues [*parens virtutum*]."[39]

Lactantius literally echoes these positions. When he says, for instance, that "*Deus* is the title [*nomen*] of supreme power" and argues that "because he is incorruptible he is also eternal [*quia incorruptibilis est et aeternus*], and therefore the *potestas divina* cannot be divided," Lactantius employs the same Ciceronian vocabulary mediated by Latin Christian receptions of Platonic philosophical theology.[40] Like Minucius Felix and Novatian, he understands the divine nature itself as ineffable and transcendent, knowable only through its revelation in its works.

---

[35] Daniel Lloyd, *Novatian's Theology of the Son: A Study in Ontological Subordinationism* (New York: Fortress Academic, 2020).

[36] Apuleius, *De Deo Socratis*, 3.11 in Apuleius, *Apologia; Florida; De Deo Socratis*, ed. and trans. Christopher P. Jones, Loeb Classical Library 534 (Cambridge, MA: Harvard University Press, 2017).

[37] Minucius Felix, *Oct.*, 19.4–7. Cf. See *parens, artifex, fabricator* in *Nat. d.*, 1.35–37 and Book 2.

[38] Novatian, *De Trinitate*, 2.9–10. See Daniel Lloyd, *Ontological Subordination in Novatian of Rome's Trinitarian Theology* (Unpublished dissertation, Marquette University, 2009), pp. 48–49. Lloyd situates Novatian's account in terms of third century Latin Platonism and compares this passage of *Trin.* 2.9 to Apuleius.

[39] Novatian, *Trin.*, 2.

[40] Novatian, *Trin.*, 2.8: "*Et quid per singula quaeque percurens longum facio.*" Cf. Minucius, *Oct.*, 18.1: "*Longum est ire per singular.*" Much more, compare Cicero, *Nat. d.*, 1.35–37, 2.29–60, with Seneca, *Nat. q.*, 2.45–46, *Ben.*, 6.78, *Ep.*, 65–66 to Tertullian, *Apol.*, 21.10–12, Minucius Felix, *Oct.*, 18–19.

VIRTUS: THE POWER OF GOD IN LACTANTIUS   157

Because he relies upon this widely shared power theology, Lactantius also proceeds to define God in terms of the ancient causal relationship between a power and its products. Arguing that God must be a complete power, Lactantius presents *creatio ex nihilo* as the activity that reveals the character of God as "Giver of Life [*dator vitae*]," and therefore as evidence that God's power contains all capacities. This claim allows Lactantius to establish a distinction between God and the created order, while also setting up his moral argument about the character of the divine activity. To set the stage for the later argument, Lactantius contrasts God's power with human weakness:

> God will be of lesser power [*minoris potestatis*], if he makes from what is pre-made, for that is characteristic of humanity [*quod est hominis*]. A craftsman will build nothing without wood, because he does not have the power [*non potest*] to make wood for himself. "To not have power [*non posse*]" is characteristic of the weakness of humanity [*imbecillitatis humanitatis*]. God himself makes matter on his own, because he is able [*potest*]. Indeed "to be able [*posse*]" is characteristic of God, for if he is not able, he is not God. A person makes out of that which exists, because through mortality he is weak [*per mortalitatem imbecillus est*] and through that weakness [*per imbecillitatem*] characterized by a definite and delimited power [*definitae ac modicae potestatis*]. God, by contrast, makes out of that which is not, because through eternity he is strong [*fortis*] through the strength of his immense power [*per fortitudinem immensae potestatis*], which has no end or limitation [*fine ac modo careat*], just as the life of the Maker itself.[41]

These lines present God's capacity to create without aid or limit as the activity that distinguishes God from humans. Lactantius articulates the whole argument in terms of power causality.[42] He argues that the activity of creation without limit or constraint is that work that reveals God's power, and he names that capacity by the divine title, *dator vitae*. The title links divine power to a broader moral claim: where there is giving of life itself, there divine *virtus* is present. Again, the activity of giving life is the distinctive activity that manifests the character of the

---

[41] Lactantius, *Inst.*, 2.8.26–29. Lactantius's opposition between God's *potestas immensa* and humanity's *potestas definita ac modica* is a further mark of the technical discourse that animates this discussion. The notion of a *potestas finita* first appears in Lucretius, who argued against any notion of divinity. Lactantius is deploying the Lucretian language to make the point that any limited power is mortal, as Lucretius had said.

[42] Lactantius, *Inst.*, 2.8.17: "*Quod si fit, imperfectae utique virtutis est, et erit iam potentior iudicandus materiae institutor.*" Cf. Lactantius, *Inst.*, 2.8.20: "*Quam vim potuit habere nullo dante, quam naturam nullo generante? Si habuit vim, ab aliquo eam sumpsit.*" *Inst.*, 2.8.17: "*Quo igitur ab homine divina illa vis differet si, ut homo sic etiam Deus ope indiget aliena?*"

158 ROMAN VIRTUE IN THE EARLY CHRISTIAN THOUGHT OF LACTANTIUS

divine nature. This doctrine informs both Lactantius's attack upon traditional Roman deities and his later presentation of Christ.

Expounded at length at *Inst.* 2.8–9, Lactantius's argument from God's unlimited creative activity reveals the premises of his critical disagreement, which begins earlier at *Inst.* 1.3 with Stoic philosophical accounts of the pantheon. Lactantius shares with his opponents the foundational notion that there is a single God, who can be spoken of in terms of power and conceived in unity as reason, sense, and wisdom.[43] Like Tertullian and Minucius, he rejects pagan divinities by asserting that the *unus maximus et pollens* cannot distribute its capacities among a hierarchy of lesser divinities. That is, Lactantius asserts a doctrine of divine simplicity: "The nature of the eternal one is simple [*aeterni natura est simplex*]," he says, "and all things descend from it as from a source [*ex fonte*]."[44] Both premises reflect an argument and language also evident in Novatian. The earlier writer had argued that that God is "*sine origine*" because nothing is "more ancient than him [*antiquius*]."[45] Lactantius likewise defines the Father as "one, alone, free, highest God, lacking origin [*carens origine*], because he is the origin of all things,"[46] extending a terminology and logic derived from Novatian. Lactantius thus employs a classical theological idiom but does not simply restate a pagan theology. While accepting the logic and language of power theology, he rejects the notion that the divine nature can in any way be understood as a compound of individual capacities operating in unity. For Lactantius, the divine nature contains every capacity in itself, without participation or conglomeration by others. Divine simplicity distinguishes his position from the neo-classical theology of Diocletian's court.

The Divine Monarchy Revisited

The explanation of the divine nature that Lactantius develops at *Inst.* 1.2–3, and further specifies at *Inst.* 2.8–9, bookends an extended critique of traditional Roman theology that occupies *Inst.* 1.8–20. Like his Latin apologetic predecessors, Lactantius also exploits the Vergilian strategy of exposing contradictions in order to transform Roman criticism of the imperial ideology

---

[43] Lactantius, *Inst.*, 2.8.33. Lactantius explains in terms reminiscent of Scipio's *Dream* and the *Tusculans*: "*Potestas faciendia aliquid non potest esse nisi in eo quod sentit, quod sapit, quod cogitat, quod movetur*." Also, *Inst.*, 2.8.38–40: "*Qui quoniam sensu, ratione, providentia, potestate, virtute praeditus est, et animantia et inanima creare et efficere potest, quia mutationem non caperet, si fuisset.*" See Cicero, *Rep.*, 6.18, *Tusc.*, 1.60–75.

[44] Lactantius, *Inst.*, 2.8.32. Cf. Cicero, *Nat. d.*, 2.28.

[45] Novatian, *Trin.*, 9.4.

[46] Lactantius, *Inst.*, 4.29.12: "*unus est enim, solus, liber, deus summus, carens origine, quia ipse est origo rerum.*"

VIRTUS: THE POWER OF GOD IN LACTANTIUS   159

into explicit accusations. He usually does so by citing or otherwise lifting passages from Minucius Felix and Tertullian.[47] And we have already seen that his account of the divine nature draws on their apologetic writings. He also extends the Latin apologists' Euhemerist argument.

However, Lactantius contributes something fresh to the apologetic tradition by subjecting Rome's traditional deities to a systematic review based upon the causal assumptions of power theology. He says, "Because we follow God as our teacher of wisdom and leader in *virtus* [*doctorem sapientiae ac ducem virtutis*], we call all people to the heavenly food."[48] His point is that the Christian account of the divine nature provides the rational basis for exposing the evident human character of Rome's traditional deities.[49] In this case power theology, with its causal logic, sustains a criticism that might otherwise be merely ad hominem. If God's *virtus* is perfect, Lactantius reasons, any putative deity that displays weakness is disqualified from its claim to divine power. For Lactantius, weakness is demonstrated either by the incapacity to create or self-generate without limit, or by moral failure. Inability demonstrates an imperfect *virtus* and thus reveals the underlying humanity of a given figure.

Lactantius grounds his apologetic criticism of the Roman pantheon in the *X from X* principle that a power reveals its character in its effects. He thus proposes to the reader a contrast between God's true works of creation and preservation of life, and the Roman narratives of their divinities' quite different activities. In that proposal, Lactantius follows Minucius Felix's citation of *Timaeus* 28c and Tertullian's explanation of God at *Apol.* 21.10–12 in order to argue that the character of the Incomprehensible and Ineffable God can be discerned, nonetheless, through God's works:

How then does anyone think anything difficult or impossible for God, who pondered such great and marvelous works [*opera*] in his providence, established them by his virtue [*virtute constituit*], perfected them by his reason [*ratione perfecit*]; he who even now sustains them by his Spirit [*spiritu sustentat*] and governs them by his power [*potestate moderetur*], the Incomprehensible Ineffable One, known to none other than himself?[50]

---

[47] See Chapter 3, this volume. I will not review Lactantius's citation of so many critical quotations, since the reader found them already in Chapter 3. Here, I'll focus on the logic of Lactantius's argument.

[48] Lactantius, *Inst.*, 1.1.19. Cf. *Inst.*, 6.6.4. Both *virtus* and *wisdom* in Lactantius's above lines are Christological titles in 1 Cor. 1:24, but his rhetorical usage does not, from this text, allow a reader to claim Lactantius is citing 1 Cor. 1:24 here.

[49] The reference to inviting "all people" also foreshadows the connection between Lactantius's thinking about the divine nature and his ethical concerns. See Chapter 6, this volume.

[50] Lactantius, *Inst.*, 1.8.2. Cf. Minucius Felix, *Oct.*, 19.14, Tertullian, *Apol.*, 17.1, 21.10–11.

160 ROMAN VIRTUE IN THE EARLY CHRISTIAN THOUGHT OF LACTANTIUS

Lactantius lifts his description of God's *virtus, potestas,* and *ratio* from Tertullian, while also insisting upon God's incomprehensibility and ineffibility. That insistence allows him to accept and use Tertullian's apologetic argument, while also making sure to distinguish Latin Christian thinking from the Stoic notion of a World Soul that permeates the cosmos. In that respect, Lactantius relies on a traditional Latin Christian apologetic tactic. He argues that the "great and marvelous works" of creation reveal the character of a power that serves as a revelation of the transcendent divine nature.

Lactantius eventually applies this notion of God to his larger social and political project by repeating Tertullian's Euhemerist criticism of Rome's practice of divinization. He says that thoughtful people should consider not the mighty works of Rome's heroes, which resulted in claims to their divinity, but the equally evident facts of their incapacity: "If anyone considers what the works of God are [*quae sint Dei opera*], he will judge ridiculous all those things which people so foolishly marvel at. Indeed, these are not to be measured by their divine and mighty deeds [*divinis virtutibus*] . . . but by the weakness of their powers [*infirmitate suarum virium*]."[51] This method of judging the gods by both their *virtus* and *fragilitas* forms the logical spine of his extended criticism. His argument ranges widely but always pivots on this basic premise—that the acclaimed divinity of the gods can be falsified by the limited nature of their powers.[52] As shall be seen, this line of attack is the inverse of the positive argument for Christ's divinity, which Lactantius also inherited from Tertullian, Cyprian, and Novatian.[53] Of course, Lactantius's polemic often echoes the ambivalent tradition of Romans' criticism of the Augustan and imperial ideology.[54]

Lactantius's specific attacks on the traditional Roman gods all rely upon this method of judging the incomplete and compromised character of their powers in the light of God's complete power. He begins with the generation, criticizing the gods' derivation from other natures. Unlike God, whom Lactantius affirms with Novatian as "lacking origin," the traditional deities all have parents: "As I reflect upon so great a majesty, those who worship the gods seem to me blind, thoughtless, foolish, barely different from mute animals, since they believe that those begotten by the intercourse of man and woman could have had anything of divine *virtus* and majesty [*maiestatis*]."[55] The point is not a mere insult, but rather contains the argument that anything generated by parents is not

[51] Lactantius, *Inst.,* 1.9.6. See 1.8.8 and 1.15.2. He often repeats Tertullian's Euhemerist claim that the gods were merely kings.

[52] E.g., Lactantius, *Inst.,* 1.11.45 invokes Ennius's Euhemerism.

[53] See Chapter 5, this volume.

[54] See Chapter 3, this volume. Lactantius repeats many of the arguments of Minucius Felix and Tertullian. He refers to Minucius Felix by name at *Inst.* 1.11.55. He invokes Mars and Bellona at *Inst.* 5.10.15, the lie of Proculus at *Inst.* 1.15.32.

[55] Lactantius, *Inst.,* 1.8.3.

itself unoriginated; but God is "*carens origine*." The suggestion that people who do not see this are like animals is an expression of Paul's critique in the New Testament.[56] Lactantius believes that the worship of idols caused human beings to debase themselves in the worship of mere animals—a point he conveys by persistent reference to the *rectus status* theme, which he interprets in terms taken over from Rom. 1:23–32.

Lactantius's presuppositions about power and nature ground the argument. He believes that because humans failed to consider God's invisible power and Godhead—the divine *virtus* and *maiestas*, in Latin—they debased themselves in the worship of animals or other idols. This polemic contains a definite syllogism: given that *Deus* is the name of a supreme power, which is the origin, source, and cause of all other natures, the derivation of Rome's traditional deities from parents shows that they cannot be God themselves. As he says: "I seek a God whom nothing at all exceeds, who is the source and origin of all things [*qui fons et origo sit rerum*]."[57] Because they lack the power of self-generation, the gods' *virtus* is characteristic of human weakness and thus cannot be truly divine.

In a similar way, Lactantius rejects the Stoic glorification of Hercules by observing the hero's failure of the Stoics' own moral ideals. Lactantius rhetorically situates this criticism as a reference to Cicero and the mythology of Scipio Africanus as an ideal leader so as to attack imperial self-presentations going back from Diocletian to Caesar Augustus. Lactantius scoffs at Hercules's very human subjection to lust, for instance, which contradicts the firm Stoic principle that his *virtus* is unconquerable: "Very famous on account of his *virtus* [*ob virtutem clarissimus*], Hercules is considered a sort of Africanus [*quasi Africanus*] among the gods. Yet is it not said that in drunken licentious adulteries [*stupris adulteriis libidinibus*] he sinned against the very earth which he wandered and purged?"[58] This claim is not a simple moralism. It is a minor premise in an argument about the nature of divinity. Lactantius subjects Hercules to a standard of divinity laid out in the earlier chapters—a definition his interlocutors presumably shared. In contrast to what Lactantius had called God's "great and marvelous works," he says that "even those great and marvelous things [*magna et mirabilia*] which [Hercules] did accomplish should not be judged as of the sort [*talia*] that seem worthy of being attributed to divine powers [*ut uirtutibus diuinis tribuenda uideantur*]."[59]

Lactantius's use of the term *talia* in this line shows the underlying connection of ethical and elemental theories that run through his argument, and is essential to

---

[56] On *rectus status*, see Chapter 6, this volume.
[57] Lactantius, *Inst.*, 1.11.50.
[58] Lactantius, *Inst.*, 1.9.1–2. Cf. Lactantius, *Inst.*, 1.8.2.
[59] Lactantius, *Inst.*, 1.9.1–2.

162 ROMAN VIRTUE IN THE EARLY CHRISTIAN THOUGHT OF LACTANTIUS

understanding the nature of his claims.[60] He is pointing out not only the relative incapacity of the gods but also making a claim about the character and quality of those actions that humans regard as divine. His point is not only that these weak human works are not truly divine works but that the examples left by such weak beings cannot therefore be taken as exemplary of divinity or used as a norm for moral ends.

The same point arises from Lactantius's attack on Jupiter and Saturn. Recalling the *Triumph of Cupid*, he reminds the audience that Jupiter's exploits had already become a theme of mockery among Romans. Lactantius then identifies Jupiter's failed *virtus*, his *fragilitas*, as evidence that Jupiter was in fact merely a famous human king, not the supreme god he had been made into: " [One author] portrayed a parade in which Jupiter is led in chains before the chariot of the triumphant Cupid. Indeed anyone so absent of *virtus* [*virtutis est expers*], who is conquered by cupidity and evil lusts . . . is subject not to Cupid, but to eternal death."[61] These remarks again parallel Lactantius's early language about divinity: "If 'God' [*deus*] is the name of the highest power [*nomen summae potestatis*], he must be incorruptible, perfect, impassible, subject to nothing [*nulli rei subiectus*]."[62] This mortal-behaving Jupiter, by contrast, is "subject to passion and death [*morti subiectus est sempiternae*]." His *virtus* cannot be divine. Lactantius meditates rather at length on this contrast between divine *virtus* and Jupiter's various signs of weakness.[63] In a later telling remark, he uses the title *dator vitae* of God, as a contrast with Jupiter's comparatively feeble title, "helper."[64] Even Jupiter's name thus denotes a lesser power. Lactantius thus adopts and endorses the Stoic and Ciceronian procedure of naming gods from the character of their benefits, but by that logic he arrives at a harsh judgment: "Anyone who thinks he is merely 'helped by God' does not understand the divine benefits."[65] Anyone who recognizes the nature of God's power disclosed in

[60] See Elizabeth DePalma Digeser, *The Making of a Christian Empire: Lactantius and Rome* (Ithaca, NY: Cornell University Press, 2000), pp. 32–36; Marcia Colish, *The Stoic Tradition from Antiquity to the Middle Ages* (Leiden: Brill, 1985), p. 46. Commentators have often and rightly noted that Lactantius's attacks on Jupiter and Hercules amount to attacks upon the Tetrarchy because Diocletian and Maximian had taken the honorifics of Jove and Hercules. The point is not wrong, but is perhaps too narrow a construction. By attacking the Ciceronian and Stoic redescription of Hercules and the traditional gods, Lactantius is criticizing the imperial ideology in its post-Augustan incarnation. Emperors had long claimed Hercules as the ancestor of the Augustan line, and Lactantius takes aim at the total ideology.

[61] Lactantius, *Inst.*, 1.11.2–3: "*morti subiectus est sempiternae*."

[62] Lactantius, *Inst.*, 1.3.23.

[63] Cf. Lactantius, *Inst.*, 1.11.8. Jupiter's taking authority from Saturn proves the imperfection of his virtus: "*Atquin divinum imperium aut semper immutabile est, aut, si est mutabile, quod fieri non potest, semper utique mutabile est*." Also, *Inst.*, 1.11.14–16, *passim*, where Jupiter's subjection to the fates shows that he is "mortal, weak, nothing."

[64] Lactantius, *Inst.*, 1.11.16: "*Ipse autem furto servatus furtimque nutritus Ζεύς seu Ζήν appelatus est, non ut isti putant a fervore caelestis ignis vel quod vitae dator et animantibus inspiret animas, quae virtus solius dei* est."

[65] Lactantius, *Inst.*, 1.11.43. This remark comes in the critique of Saturn, which applies the same procedure at 1.11.50–1.12.1ff. Determining that Saturn too was a man with parents, Lactantius

VIRTUS: THE POWER OF GOD IN LACTANTIUS   163

its effects (*beneficia*) can see that the deeds of Jupiter are unequal to the perfect, simple, and life-giving *virtus* of God.

At *Inst.* 1.18, Lactantius brings his argument to bear upon Cicero's theology of divinization and the larger narrative of Roman virtue represented in *Nat. d.* 2.58–62. Lactantius here introduces a new element to his apologetic by implying that the Romans developed a false account of *virtus* because they derived their understanding from false *exempla*: "They say it is *virtus* which raises men into heaven, not that *virtus* which the philosophers talked about, which is placed in the goods of the mind, but this physical one called strength [*fortitudo*]. So, they believe Hercules merited immortality because strength was in him."[66] Lactantius critiques this exclusively physical *virtus* as in fact an inadequate power of violence by examining the deeds that make it manifest. In language culled from Minucius Felix he accuses the Roman theology of promoting an ultimately violent politics because it chose false *exempla* as its models for *virtus*:

> They think brave and bellicose leaders are placed within the fellowship of the gods and that the only path to immortality is by leading an army, devastating foreign property, destroying cities, sacking forts, butchering free people and subjecting them to slavery. The more they afflict, despoil, and kill, the more people think them noble and of high rank [*nobiliores ac clariores*]; captivated by their own crimes they impose the name of *virtus* [*nomen virtutis*] upon the appearance of empty glory [*inanis gloriae specie*]. . . . If this is the *virtus* which makes us immortal, I prefer to die than be the destruction of so many.[67]

The argument gives a precise philosophical form to the Latin apologists' traditional attack on Rome's violent history. Lactantius's discussion of *virtus* relies upon the same philosophical grammar that enabled Tertullian's Christology and Seneca's non-Christian theology of the divine benefits. By their works, Roman gods and emperors do give an appearance (*species*) of some power (*virtus*). That power, however, is a power of destruction inconsistent with the Highest Power, which creates and gives life. Relying on the wrong manifestations of power, the Romans came to value as *virtus* that which actually displays *fragilitas*. Paradoxically, this means that for Lactantius, violence itself—which appears to manifest power—became the supreme evidence and expression of a human

---

proposes to examine the power revealed in Saturn's deeds. After reviewing Saturn's marriage to his sister, fear of his own offspring, infanticide, and cannibalism, Lactantius, *Inst.*, 1.13.5, concludes the argument in terms of power theology: "*Postremo cur extitit vis aliqua maior quae illius vinceret potestatem?*"

[66] Lactantius, *Inst.*, 1.18.3. Cf. Cicero, *Nat. d.*, 2.62: "*Suscepit autem vita hominum consuetudoque communis ut beneficiis excellentis viros in caelum fama ac voluntate tollerent.*"
[67] Lactantius, *Inst.*, 1.18.8–10, 15. Cf. Lactantius, *Inst.*, 3.8.11–12; Minucius Felix, *Oct.*, 25.5.18–19.

164 ROMAN VIRTUE IN THE EARLY CHRISTIAN THOUGHT OF LACTANTIUS

weakness that Rome consecrated as divine. On this logic, Lactantius ultimately echoes the traditional Latin Christian reassertion of traditional Roman critiques of Augustan ideology:

> And so there is no *virtus* [*nulla virtus*] in anyone, since vices rule everywhere; no loyalty [*nulla fides*], since everyone snatches everything for himself; no piety [*pietas*], since avarice spares not even parents and cupidity overthrows even one's own kin with poison and the knife; there is no peace [*pax*], no harmony [*concordia*], since cruel wars rage in public, while private enemies foam for blood; no shame [*pudicitia*] where those drunk with lusts contaminate every sex and all parts of the body.[68]

These lines review all the traditional Roman virtues that Diocletian claimed to preserve and protect by his persecution. Lactantius argues, however, that the persecution is another manifestation of the true Roman error of supplanting real divinity with human weakness and vice. He argues that Rome's traditional account of *virtus* was empty, and he draws upon the philosophical theology of his Christian predecessors to do so. In place of the imperial image, Lactantius offers the person of Jesus Christ as the true model of *virtus*, who provides the true pattern of a new ideal politics.

Conclusion

Modern scholars have read and translated Lactantius's use of the term *virtus* without recognizing the philosophical grammar that Lactantius presupposed. Because of that oversight, scholars often regarded law and rhetoric as the sole frame of reference for understanding his critique of the traditional Roman gods; and they have likewise seen the use of *virtus* in his theology as evidence that Lactantius lacked a technical theological vocabulary by which to engage with the subtleties of Latin Christian theology in the third century. Recognition of the language and logic of power causality and its wide use in early Christianity enables a better historical account of Lactantius's arguments and their relationship to other early Christian writers. Although it is true that Lactantius echoed the moral criticisms of earlier apologists, that moral argument was predicated upon more fundamental philosophical assumptions about the character of divine power, about the relationship between power, understood as a cause, and moral order, understood as the demonstration of a divine capacity. Lactantius's moral criticism serves as a minor premise in a philosophical argument

---

[68] Lactantius, *Inst.*, 1.20.25.

predicated upon the broadly held assumptions of power causality. This same use of the technical sense of power for philosophical and theological arguments also animates his account of the divine nature and his Christology. As shall be seen, he identifies God in terms of *virtus* and *potestas*, not because he lacked deep theological understanding, but rather because he shared the language and logic of major third-century accounts of Christian theology and exegesis.

5

The Power of the Son

The Father, therefore, abiding in the Son through the works of [his] powers [*opera virtutum*] and the words of his teaching [*verba doctrinae*], is seen through those things through which he abides and through him in whom he abides."
—Tertullian, *Against Praxeas*, 24

Although he is innocent and just—even more, he himself is innocence, he himself is justice—he is placed on a level with criminals . . . Unto the very end, he bears all things with perseverance and constancy so that in Christ a full and perfect patience [*patientia*] might be consummated.
— Cyprian, *De bono patientiae*, 7

With notable exceptions, scholars have seen Lactantius's theology as idiosyncratic. They have often contrasted his "pedagogical" view of Christ saving through teaching with sacrificial or penal descriptions of the atonement, which seemed more profound and more typical of Christian writing. Scholars mainly explained such idiosyncrasy as the result of unreconciled tensions in sources Lactantius eclectically selected and could not ultimately reconcile.[1] In reevaluating Lactantius's apologetic method, however, recent work also invites a new historical account of his theological understanding.[2] As I will argue, the *Divine Institutes* constitutes a conceptual unity that attempts to express the inherent implications of God's revelation in Christ for classical Roman thinking

---

[1] See Elizabeth DePalma Digeser, *The Making of a Christian Empire: Lactantius and Rome* (Ithaca, NY: Cornell University Press, 2000) pp. 71–78. Digeser relies on Vincenzo Loi, *Lattanzio nella Storia del Linguaggio e del Pensiero Teologico Pre-Niceno* (Zurich: Pas-Verlag, 1970), and Antonie Wlosok, *Laktanz und die philosophische Gnosis: Untersuchungen zu Geschichte und Terminologie der gnostischen Erlösungsvorstellung* (Heidelberg: Carl Winter, 1960).

[2] E.g., Pierre Monat, *Lactance et la Bible: Une propédeutique latine à la lecture de la Bible dans l'Occident constantinien* (Paris: Études Augustiniennes, 1982); Jochen Walter, *Pagane Texte und Wertvorstellungen bei Laktanz* (Goettingen: Vandenhoeck und Ruprecht, 2006); Blandine Colot, *Penser la conversion de Rome au temps de Constantin* (Firenze: Leo Olschki Editore, 2016); Anthony Patrick Coleman, *Lactantius the Theologian: Lactantius and the Doctrine of Providence* (Piscataway, NJ: Gorgias Press, 2017), articles in *Studia Patristica* 127.24 (2021), and Mattias Gassman, *Worshippers of the Gods: Debating Paganism in the Fourth-Century Roman West* (Oxford: Oxford University Press, 2020).

Roman Virtue in the Early Christian Thought of Lactantius. Jason M. Gehrke, Oxford University Press.
© Oxford University Press 2025. DOI: 10.1093/9780197667781.003.0006

about divine and human order. Lactantius's effort begins with his early critique of Roman religion and philosophy, continues in his account of Christ's person and work, and concludes with a constructive argument that extrapolates a Christian account of the moral order from Christ's revelation of God. Christology occupies the central chapter of the *Divine Institutes* because Christ's person and work provide the new basis for thinking about the moral and political questions that most concern Lactantius, as an apologist.

Having cleared the ground in *Inst.* 1–3, the *Divine Institutes* thus turns to an apologetic development of traditional Latin Christological themes. *Institutio* 4, entitled *De vera sapientia*, promises to offer Christ as the revelation of genuine wisdom, as Lactantius makes Christology the source and starting point for all moral knowledge. He opens *Institutio* 4 by recapitulating his claim that human idolatry is the root of ignorance, vice, and violence. He then proceeds to express a "two-stage Christology," which first explains the pre-Incarnate existence of the Son, and then presents Christ's life, death, and resurrection according to a credal narrative pattern.[3] In his incarnate ministry, Christ reveals himself as the God-Man, who guides humanity on the path of eternal life through his ministry of healing and teaching. In his passion and death, Christ overcomes humanity's fear of death through his demonstration of divine patience, which brings the knowledge of eternal life. In his person and works, Christ thus reveals the divine nature and offers it as the eternal paradigm—Lactantius calls it the "*specimen*"—of right moral order.

In what follows, I argue that Lactantius's apologetic Christology is traditional in several overlapping ways. The first is its narrative purpose. *Institutio* 4 is an exemplary narrative that does with Christ what Lucretius had done with Epicurus, Cicero with Romulus and, later, Minucius Felix with Regulus and the martyrs: it provides a historical basis for making claims about *virtus*.[4] Second, Lactantius presumes the same technical sense of power and nature (*vis*, *potestas*, *virtus*) broadly evident in Latin writers since Cicero—and specifically evident in Tertullian, Cyprian, and Novatian. Most important, the Latin trinitarian concern with "sight" is the central Christological theme that organizes Lactantius's thought across these books. He expands upon Tertullian's programmatic claim that "the Father, therefore, abiding in the Son through the works of [his] powers [*opera virtutum*] and the words of his teaching [*verba doctrinae*], is seen through those things through which he abides and through him in whom he abides."[5] Lactantius understands Tertullian's point in the plain terms

---

[3] Monat, *Lactance et la Bible*, p. 177. Monat notes that Lactantius's account of the mission of the Word contains "exactly the fundamental structure of Matthew's Gospel, and one of the forms adopted by the ancient catechism."

[4] See Chapter 3, this volume.

[5] Tertullian, *Against Praxeas*, 24 .

168 ROMAN VIRTUE IN THE EARLY CHRISTIAN THOUGHT OF LACTANTIUS

Tertullian meant: God is seen in the acts of Jesus. As Michel Barnes explained, "From its beginning, Latin theology has an emphasis on 'sight' in trinitarian theology: our sight of the Son, of the Father in the Son, and the Son's sight of the Father," a concern that began in Tertullian's anti-Monarchian theology.[6] Lactantius's Christology is best understood as an apologetic development of that theme. Hence, we need to distinguish Lactantius's doctrine of "the sight of the Father in the works of the Son" from other theological developments of that theme. In past scholarship, fourth-century trinitarian doctrines of the "vision of God" have been mainly set within a neo-Platonic context of "noetic vision" such as we find in Augustine.[7] While noetic vision is one form of sight, it does not exhaust the intellectual work that the logic of "the sight of the Father in the Son's works" performs in Latin theology. Lactantius develops Tertullian's programmatic statement by attempting to name those works that render the power of God publicly visible and thus reveal Christ as the ground and source of a new "Christian moral philosophy that could compete with and override classical ethical systems."[8] Lactantius's thought does not exclude noetic vision, but it makes Christ's public and historical demonstration of divine power the basis for any knowledge of God.

Maxima Virtus Patria: The Son

Lactantius's Christology begins in earnest at *Inst.* 4.6–10. His account is most shaped by Tertullian, while his exegesis is guided by Cyprian.[9] Drawing on Ps.

---

[6] Michel René Barnes, "Latin Trinitarian Theology," in *The Cambridge Companion to the Trinity*, ed. Peter C. Phan (Cambridge: Cambridge University Press, 2011), p. 72. See also Stephen Waers, *Monarchianism and Origen's Early Trinitarian Theology* (Leiden: Brill, 2022). Also Jason M. Gehrke, "*Singulare et Unicum Imperium*: Monarchianism and Latin Apologetic in Rome," in *New Narratives for Old: The Historical Method of Reading Early Christian Theology. Essays in Honor of Michel René Barnes*, ed. Anthony Briggman and Ellen Scully (Washington, DC: Catholic University of America Press, 2022).

[7] E.g., Roland Teske, "St. Augustine and the Vision of God," in *Augustine: Mystic and Mystagogue. Collectanea Augustiniana*, vol. 3, ed. Frederick Van Fleteren, Joseph C. Schnaubelt, and Joseph Reino (Bristol: Peter Lang, 1994), pp. 287–308. I thank Michel Barnes for pointing out this important distinction between Lactantius's understanding and other "noetic" notions of the "sight" of God.

[8] Peter Garnsey, "Introduction," in *Lactantius: The Divine Institutes*, ed. Anthony Bowen and Peter Garnsey (Liverpool: Liverpool University Press, 2003), p. 35.

[9] As seen below, his reading of the Old Testament is guided by his use of Cyprian, though not exclusively. Lactantius also shows the influence of Theophilus of Antioch (*Inst.*, 1.7.7, 2.12.19, 3.20.15, 4.5.6). See Tertullian (below, and also Lactantius, *Index Locorum*, in *Divinarum Institutionum Libri Septem*, fasc I–IV, ed. Eberhard Heck et Antonie Wlosok [Berlin: De Gruyter, 2005–2011], p. 796), and Justin Martyr (*Inst.*, 4.18.22). See also R. M. Ogilvie, *The Library of Lactantius* (Oxford: Clarendon Press, 1978), pp. 88–96. The most important study of Lactantius's use of scriptural and traditional Christian sources is Monat, *Lactance et la Bible*. For Lactantius's evaluation of pagan sources, see especially Jochen Walter, *Pagane Texte*. Also, Alain Goulon, "Les Citations des Poètes Latins dans L'œuvre de Lactance," in *Lactance et son Temps: Recherches Actuelles: Actes du IV Colloque D'Etudes Historiques et Patristiques Chantilly 21–23 Septembre 1976*, ed. J. Fontaine and

33:6, Prov. 8, and Hebrews, Lactantius happily refers to Christ as God's Word, Wisdom, Spirit, and even as an Angel. Hebrews 1:1–7 influences the structure of the presentation, along with pivotal cues from Cyprian's *Ad Quirinum*.[10] The terms *doctor iustitiae* and *dux virtutis* also appear within the context of this account of Christ's work.[11] Lactantius grounds these Christological titles ontologically in the language of *virtus*. Prov. 8 and Heb. 1 are the basis of his opening remarks:[12]

> Therefore (as I said in the second book) God the Maker and Constitutor of the world [*machinator constitutorque rerum*], before he attempted this brilliant work of the universe, generated [*genuit*] a holy and incorruptible spirit [*sanctum et incorruptibilem spiritum*], whom he officially designated as his son [*nuncuparet filium*]. Although afterward he created countless others, whom we call angels, he nevertheless deemed this Firstborn alone worthy of the Divine Name [Heb. 1:4], as the one exercising [*pollentem*] the Father's *virtus* and majesty [*patria virtute et maiestate*, Heb. 1:3–4]. Moreover, not only do the

---

M. Perrin (Paris: Editions Beauchesne, 1978), pp. 107–157. In English, Jackson Bryce, *The Library of Lactantius* (New York: Garland, 1990). This is an unedited version of his 1973 dissertation. Also, R. M. Ogilvie, *The Library of Lactantius* (Oxford: Clarendon Press, 1978).

[10] Monat, *Lactance et la Bible*, p. 174, and McGuckin, "Lactantius as Theologian: An Angelic Christology on the Eve of Nicaea," p. 493, both identify elements of Hebrews 1 as important for Lactantius. Here, I place the whole passage Heb. 1:1–7 as the basis for his account of the preincarnate Son. *VL* Heb. 1:1–7 in *Vetus Latina. The Remains of the Old Latin Bible 25/2*, ed. Roger Gryson (Freiburg in Breisgau, 1983). The below lines of the *Vetus Latina* follow the A line and place significant variants in parentheses. The A line stops at verse 5, after which I use the D line. This reading is particularly important because we have no recognized use of Hebrews in Lactantius's known sources: "[1] *Multis partibus et multis modis ante deus locutus est patribus in prophetis.* [2] *postremo in his diebus locutus est nobis in filio quem posuit heredem omnium per quem etiam fecit et saecula* [3] *qui est splendor gloriae et imago [figura – J] substantiae eius gerens [ferens – D] omnia verbo virtutis suae purgatione peccatorum a se facta sedit in dextera excelsis tanto melior factus angelis quanto excellentius [differentius/differentior – V] nomen accepit [hereditavit – J].* [5] *cui enim dixit aliquando angelorum 'filius meus est tu ego hodie generavi te et iterum ego ero illi in patrem et ipse erit mihi in filium,'* [6] *deinde iterum cum inducit primogenitum in creatione dicit et 'adorent illum omnes angelos dei et* [7] *ad angelos quidem dicit qui facit angelos suos spiritus et ministros suos ignem urentum.'*" I place this observation at the beginning as a point of reference for what follows. It is not only the *choice* of key terms, but the use of key terms—*virtus, maiestas, verbum, ministerium, differentia[us], generare*—in a definite sequence that indicates Hebrews 1 as the scriptural basis of the passage. Lactantius first introduces the major movements of his narrative with a reference to the "scriptures" or "the prophets." The references easily gloss Heb. 1:1. He then designates the Son with the terms *virtus, verbum*, and *maiestas* that together suggest Heb. 1:3–4. As the argument unfolds, he notes a "*differentia*" which serves to distinguish the Son from the angels with a reference to Ps. 33(32):6. *Differentia* gently adapts the "*differentius*" of Heb. 1:4, while the assertion that the angels are created for ministry reflects Heb. 1:7, while "ministering spirits" captures the context all the way to Heb. 1:14.

[11] Lactantius, *Inst.*, 4.13.1.

[12] Cyprian, *Quir.*, 2.1. This comment does not negate the equally important fact that *Quir.* 2.1 entails a series of exegetical selections that shape the structure of Lactantius's presentation all the way to *Inst.* 4.9.

170 ROMAN VIRTUE IN THE EARLY CHRISTIAN THOUGHT OF LACTANTIUS

words of the prophets agree unanimously [Heb. 1:1], but even the preaching of Trismegistus and the predictions of the Sibyls show that he is the Son of the Most High and endowed [*praeditus*] with the supreme power [*maxima potentia*].[13]

These lines indicate the Son's status as God by showing that the Son bears the Name, which signifies the Son's possession of the Father's distinctive *virtus*.[14] Lactantius identifies the divinity of the Son and his unity with the Father by the terms *maxima potentia* and *pollentem patria virtute*. His terms take up the clear formula of earlier remarks. The juxtaposition of *virtus* and *potentia* make it certain that Lactantius's term *virtus* conveys a causal notion. It is a marker of the fact that what the Son does enacts a different power than what the angels do.[15]

---

[13] Lactantius, *Inst.*, 4.6.1–3. Pace Digeser, *Making of a Christian Empire*, pp. 70–73. Monat, *Lactance et la Bible*, pp. 168–174, sees the influence of Prov. 8 in this chapter and notes also Heb. 1:4 at 4.6.8. *Biblia Patristica* II notes Heb. 1:7. Additionally, Lactantius's association of a Wisdom Christology with the Name theology has a clear precedent in Tertullian, *Prax.*, 6.1: "In the Scriptures, this power [*vis*] and this arrangement of the divine mind [*sensus*] is also shown under the name of Wisdom (cf. *Inst.*, 4.8.11, where Lactantius pairs *virtus* and *sensus*)." Loi, *Lattanzio*, p. 213, fn. 37, refers *virtus* in this passage to 1 Cor. 1:24. René Braun, *Deus Christianorum: Recherche sur le vocabulaire doctrinal de Tertullien, seconde édition* (Paris: Études Augustiniennes, 1977), pp. 280–281, also attributes it to 1 Cor. 1:24 and Lk. 1:35, noting the currency of this meaning in "Justin et ses successeurs."

[14] Charles A. Gieschen, "The Divine Names in Ante-Nicene Christology," *Vigiliae Christianae* 57.2 (2003): pp. 115–158. Gieschen identifies the theology of the "secret name" with the Tetragrammaton and traces this notion from New Testament literature to Second Temple Jewish theology. See also J. A. McGuckin, *Researches into the Divine Institutes* (Unpublished dissertation, Durham University, 1980), p. 183. McGuckin points out that Lactantius derives this title from Heb. 1:3, and distinguishes Christ's status as a Name, "which no other except [the Father] knows. . . . Here the Epistle uses the distinction of the 'name Christ has inherited' as the measure of his essential superiority over the angels. In both Hebrews and the *DI* this distinguishing title is one of Sonship." Cf. *Inst.*, 4.7.4.

[15] Cf. Lactantius, *Inst.*, 2.8.4. Lactantius first introduces a very brief statement of the Son's generation amid the so-called dualistic passages, that were interpolated by a later redactor. Scholars generally agree that redactor was Lactantius himself, although the most recent editors acknowledge it is uncertain. Elizabeth DePalma Digeser, "Lactantius and Constantine's Letter to Arles: Dating the Divine Institutes," *Journal of Early Christian Studies* 2.1 (1994): pp. 33–52. See Heck and Wlosok, *Divinarum Institutionum Libri Septem*, vol. 1, xxxix; Also Eberhard Heck, *Die Dualistischen Zusätze und die Kaiseranrden bei Lactantius* (Heidelberg: Universitätsverlag, 1972). The passage is an early statement of what Loi has termed Lactantius's "cosmological dualism." (See Loi, *Lattanzio*, p. 270.) I begin with *Inst.* 4.6, however, because Lactantius says that the later passage is his full discussion. Still, I note that these early lines already employ the central metaphor of pre-Nicene Latin theology, "*like a river from its source.*" That phrase places "*virtutibus patris dei praeditus*" into a certain lexical context. *Virtus* means *power* and designates the Son's identity relative to the Father and in contradistinction from the "*alterum spiritum.*" Finally, it should be noted contra Wlosok that Lactantius's "dualistic passages" proceed from his understanding of reality in terms drawn from medicine. That is evident from *Inst.* 2.12.4–6, which evokes Empedocles, Lucretius, and Varro before explaining the "*quattuor elementa*" and their principles of opposition. Lactantius then says humanity was made "just as the world itself, [*ex bono et malo,*] *ex luce ac tenebris, ex vita et morte.*" Heck and Wlosok place "*ex bono et malo*" in brackets regarding the terms as a later addition. Wlosok's comment, *Laktanz und die philosophische Gnosis*, p. 191, fn. 28, that "die dualistische Tendenz des Lakt, die indem afrikanischen Manichäismus stammt soll," overlooks the wider use of Hellenistic theories of mixture in third-century Latin theology.

THE POWER OF THE SON   171

By designating the Son in terms of "power" Lactantius establishes the onto-logical unity of Father and Son in a traditional Latin theological vocabulary. The theological weight of this language is evident by comparison with two earlier passages. The first is *Inst.* 1.3.23–34. In Lactantius's argument against the tra-ditional Roman deities, the title "*maximus et pollens*" designated the Father's exclusive and unitary nature. In the Christological narrative, the same title attributes to Christ what it denied to the traditional gods—the Father's *virtus* and *potestas*.[16] Second, at *Inst.* 4.4.10–11, Lactantius reasserts his opposition to the traditional gods in a passage that so closely identifies the Father and Son that previous translators have seen it as referring only to the Father:

> The One and Only who ought to be worshipped [is] he who preceded Jupiter and Saturn, heaven itself, and the earth. The one who created heaven and earth before humanity is necessarily the one who fashioned humanity. He alone, who created, is worthy to be called Father [*vocandus est*]. He alone, who rules, is worthy to be designated [*nuncupandus*] as Lord—the One who holds the true and perpetual power [*veram et perpetuam potestatem*] of life and death. And if anyone does not adore him, he is a foolish slave. If anyone either flees from him or does not know his own Lord, he is also an impious son, since he either hates or does not know his own true Father.[17]

Although these lines might be taken as referring solely to the Father, Lactantius's language points to his account of the One God as Father and Son. The passage

[16] Loi, *Lattanzio*, p. 212. Lactantius's use of Prov. 8 and the notion of the Son as "spirit" belies the influence of Tertullian's *Adversus Praxean*. Loi showed this linguistically: "Si l'espressione *vox dei* in riferimento al Figlio non è attestata anteriormente a Lattanzio, la concezione teologica in essa implicita non è forse estranea a Tertulliano e ad altri pensatori anteriori." However, Loi continues: "La equivalenza stabilita da Lattanzio tra le espressioni *Verbum Dei* e *Vox Dei* conferma il carattere realisticamente antropomorfico della concezione lattanziana della generazione divina attraverso il processo della '*prolatio vocis ac spiritus*.'" Barnes, however, has shown that the use of Prov. 8 and Heb. 1 is a feature of the earliest Christian pneumatologies, which arise from the Jewish context. Tertullian and Origen, however, change this exegesis in the context of their anti-Monarchian argu-ment. (See Michel Barnes, "The Beginning and End of Early Christian Pneumatology," *Augustinian Studies* 39.2 (2008): esp. pp. 171–173, 184ff.) Lactantius's identification of the Son with Wisdom is a mark of that influence. For the anti-Monarchian context of Origen's theology, see Stephen Waers, *Monarchianism and Origen's Early Trinitarian Theology* (Leiden and Boston: Brill, 2022).

[17] Lactantius, *Inst.*, 4.4.10–11: "*Unus igitur ac solus coli debet qui Iovem, qui Saturnum, qui caelum ipsum terramque antecessit. Is enim necesse est hominem figuravit, qui ante hominem caelum terramque perfecit. Solus pater vocandus est qui creavit, solus dominus nuncupandus qui regit, qui habet vitae ac necis veram et perpetuam potestatem. quem qui non adorat, et insipiens servus est, qui dominum suum aut fugiat aut nesciat, et impius filius, qui suum verum paterum vel oderit vel ignoret.*" Cf. Bowen and Garnsey, p. 231: "Only a creator can properly be called father, and only a ruler, one who has a true and lasting power of life and death, can properly be named lord," *Ante-Nicene Fathers, Divine Institutes*, p. 104, "He alone is to be called Father who created us; He alone is to be considered Lord who rules." For the son-slave antinomy, see Cyprian, *Bon. pat.*, 3.43–45: "*Si dominus nobis et pater deus est, sectemur patientiam domini pariter et patris, quia et servos esse oportet obsequentes et filios non decet esse degeneres.*"

172   ROMAN VIRTUE IN THE EARLY CHRISTIAN THOUGHT OF LACTANTIUS

opens with the traditional Roman son and father, Saturn and Jupiter, and says that the gods of sky and earth (or agriculture) are inferior to the God who created "heaven and earth." Lactantius then supplants the false pairing with the true, by referring to "the one who creates" and the "one who rules." The two titles refer to the Father and Son, respectively. Hence also, the Father who creates is called upon; the Son who rules with *potestas perpetua* is "designated [*nuncupandus*]," in the way that Lactantius shortly hearafter says that the Father "designated [*nuncuparet*]" the Son as worthy of *virtus patria ac maiestas* (*Inst.*, 4.6.1–3). This language of power, especially guided by the exegesis of *Ad Quirinum*, marks Lactantius's theology as a point of continuity with the thought of Cyprian and Tertullian.[18]

Lactantius adds important comments about the name and title of the Son in the next lines. He explains that the Son is named Jesus and distinguishes this name from the title *Christus*. The latter term Lactantius calls the "*nuncupatio potestatis et regni*," in a phrase that echoes of "*nuncuparet filium*" and "*dominus nuncupandus*," above. The title *Christus* signifies *rex*, he says, "not because [the Son] would obtain this earthly kingdom, but a heavenly and eternal one."[19] The line gives to Christ the very ruling function that designates the one *dominus* in the earlier passage at *Inst.* 4.4.11 and anticipates Lactantius's characterization of the Son's rule in a later part of the narrative. After explaining that the Son was born twice—a passage treated below—Lactantius situates the Son relative to the "other angels." He then gives an account of the Son that follows the narrative sequence of Heb. 1:

How then did he produce [him]? First, the divine works [*opera divina*] can be neither known nor explained by anyone. Still, it has been safeguarded for us in the holy scriptures [Heb. 1:1] that the Son of God is the Word [*sermonem*] and that the other angels are the breath of God [*dei spiritus*, Heb. 1:3–4]. For a word [*sermo*] is breath [*spiritus*] brought forth with signification [*Prax.*, 8.5]. Nonetheless, since breath and an audible word are brought forth from different parts—for breath proceeds from the nostrils but speech from the mouth [Ps. 33:6]—there is a great difference [*differentia*, Heb. 1:4] between this Son of God and the other angels [4.8.11] . . . by so much more [than our words] must we believe that the Word of God remains forever attended [*comitari*] by the

---

[18] Cyprian, *Quir.* 2.1–4, lists all of the texts that were most significant in third-century Latin power theology and places them in an order of presentation that Lactantius employs. For the "son" versus "slave" rhetoric, see *Bon. pat.*, pp. 3–5.

[19] Lactantius, *Inst.*, 4.7.4: "*Christus non proprium nomen est, sed nuncupatio potestatis et regni . . .* [4.7.8] *utrolibet nomine rex significatur, non quod ille regnum hoc terrenum fuerit adeptus . . .*" Cf. Tertullian, *Apol.*, 3.5. Lactantius addresses the appellation Christus. Cf. Lactantius, *Inst.*, 4.14.15–20, 7.19.3–4. See Loi, *Lattanzio*, p. 231.

THE POWER OF THE SON   173

virtus and understanding [*sensus*], which it draws from the Father "like a river from its source" [*Prax.*, 8].[20]

These lines are typical of third-century Latin theology in two ways. First, Lactantius's distinction between the Son and the angels, along with his identification of the Son as the Word, is immediately supported by references to Ps. 33:6 and Ps. 44:2. Shortly hereafter, he quotes the Sibylline Oracle to illustrate the argument from pagan sources. The authoritative foundation of the argument, however, is the Scriptures, since Lactantius predicates his citation of the Sybillines upon a biblical passage.[21] Second, they rely upon the central causal metaphors developed in third-century Latin accounts of the relationship between the Father and Son. Lactantius's description of the Son as drawing "power [*virtus*]" and "understanding [*sensus*]" from the Father "like a river from its source" is an unmistakable restatement of Tertullian's central Christological metaphors at *Against Praxeas* 8. Hence, despite the apparent anthropomorphism of Lactantius's thought, it represents little more than a traditional state of Christian theological exegesis, one derived from the most prominent theologian of the previous generations.

Lactantius's definition of "an audible word brought forth with signification," along with the reference to the Son as *spirit* and the use of Prov. 8:22–31, also reflects his debt to Tertullian's *Praxeas* 8–9.[22] Comparing Lactantius's account

[20] Lactantius, *Inst.*, 4.8.6–9. Cf. Lactantius, *Inst.*, 4.8.11. Monat, *Lactance et la Bible*, p. 174, notes the close resemblance of this thought with Heb. 1:4, but finds that "Lactance n'est pas assez théologien pour établir nettement une distinction entre nature et function." McGuckin says, "In fact, Lactantius follows the angelic doctrine of Tertullian which interprets it as a description of a function rather than a nature and applies it within the context of a revelatory Logos-theology (McGuckin, "Lactantius as Theologian: An Angelic Christology on the Eve of Nicaea," p. 495). But Lactantius is following Tertullian's technical sense of power and the exegesis of Cyprian's *Ad Quirinum*. Aloys Grillmeier, *Christ in the Christian Tradition*, vol. 1, *From the Apostolic Age to Chalcedon (451)*, 2nd ed. (Oxford: Mowbrays, 1976), p. 194, praises Lactantius's use of Tertullian's *source-spring-flow* metaphor as superior to the *paterfamilias* discussion at *Inst.*, 4.29, but does not seem to see that both are rooted in Tertullian and co-exist as mutual analogies for the same fundamental notion of undivided power.
[21] Lactantius, *Inst.*, 4.6.5–6. See Monat, *Lactance et la Bible*, p. 176. His comments underscore the traditional character of this exegesis: "Or, l'enseignement sur le Verbe donne dans l'*Adversus Praxean* fait figurer, à côté des trois textes *Prov. 8,27/Ps. 33,2/Jn. 1,1–3*, qui constituent comme l'épine dorsale du dossier de Lactance." Lactantius does not quote Jn. 1:3 until *Inst.* 4.9.3, a chapter borrowed largely from *Prax.* 5.3.
[22] See Tertullian, *Prax.*, 8.5: "*haec erit* προβολήν *veritatis custos unitatis, qua prolatum dicimus filium a patre sed non separatum. protulit enim deus sermonem, quemadmodum etiam paracletus docet, sicut radix fruticem et fons fluvium et sol radium.*" Cf. Tertullian, *Apol.*, 21.11; Lactantius, *Inst.*, 4.6.8–9, "*nam sermo est spiritus cum voce aliquid significante prolatus.*" Cf. Section 3.3.1, above. See Loi, *Lattanzio*, pp. 215–216. On Tertullian, Joseph Moingt, *Théologie Trinitaire de Tertullien: Substantialité et Individualité* (Aubier: Editions Aubier-Montaigne, 1966), p. 243, compares this to Athenagoras and Theophilus as well. As both Loi and Moingt note, Tertullian draws this notion from Stoic physics. Lactantius accepts that language but he is not, as Lewis Ayres notes (*Nicaea and Its Legacy: An Approach to Fourth Century Trinitarian Theology* [Oxford: Oxford University Press, 2004], p. 74), "a materialist in Tertullian's [Stoic] sense (thinking of God as an infinitely diffuse intelligent matter)."

174 ROMAN VIRTUE IN THE EARLY CHRISTIAN THOUGHT OF LACTANTIUS

with Tertullian's shows the way Lactantius adapts the Latin Christian traditions he inherited. Lactantius's concern with the Son's position relative to the angels is traditional.[23] It is not, however, a concern of *Prax.* 8, where Tertullian defends the notion of "two," in an anti-Monarchian argument.[24] Lactantius opposes Monarchian theology, but two additional factors shape his presentation.[25] The first factor is his need to avoid self-contradiction. In his denunciation of the traditional gods he asserted that the One Power cannot be divided among a plurality of powers.[26] In that context, he repeated Tertullian's claim that such derivative powers would be mere "satellites and ministers of God."[27] In this later Christological passage, Lactantius thus forestalls the claim that he has reintroduced the very pluralistic doctrine he rejected. He distinguishes Christ from the angels by distinguishing between their respective *virtutes*.

Lactantius also chooses to situate the Son relative to the angels because it suits his apologetic aims. Although scholars have taken the choice as evidence of Lactantius's limited acquaintance with the Latin theologies of his period, discussion of the angels reflects the apologetic strategy that guides Lactantius's exegesis.[28] At *Inst.* 4.5.3–5, he justified his use of the Scriptures, even to the pagan audience, by repeating the traditional apologetic argument from prophetic fulfillment.[29] As he uses Cyprian's *Ad Quirinum*, then, Lactantius cites the Old

[23] Michel R. Barnes, *The Power of God: Dynamis in Gregory of Nyssa's Trinitarian Theology* (Washington, DC: Catholic University of America Press, 2001), p. 105: "Positioning the Son vis-à-vis the angels is an enduring central concern of Latin Christology: *virtus* language places some burden on this argument since ... Tertullian uses *virtutes* to mean angels, and the Son must be distinguished from these 'powers.'"

[24] Tertullian, *Prax.*, 8.5. See Joseph Moingt, *Théologie Trinitaire de Tertullien: Substantialité et Individualité*, pp. 989–990: "La raison expresse de cet enseignement métaphorique est donc de faire apparaître l'unité là même où la séparation semble se produire, dans l'acte où le Fils sort du Père, de monter que cette 'prolation'ou 'sortie'n'est pas une scission, mais une promotion (*promoveri ad fructum*), c'est-à-dire une génération dans l'indivision de la substance."

[25] See Lactantius, *Inst.* 4.29, where Lactantius rejects all the major third-century heresies and identifies himself as "Catholic."

[26] Furthermore, Tertullian, *Apol.* 23.12 says that the gods were in fact *demons*. Likewise, Tertullian, *Carn.* 14 says "the other gods are not gods but satellites and ministers." The apologists thus had already situated the gods relative to angels and demons by asserting that traditional Roman gods were demons.

[27] See Chapter 4, this volume.

[28] See J. A. McGuckin, "Lactantius as Theologian: An Angelic Christology on the Eve of Nicaea," p. 497. He argued that "the angel Christology of Lactantius, although strangely preserved up to the eve of the Arian crisis itself, which saw the final demise of this tradition in its attempted use as an argument against the deity of Christ, is fundamentally orthodox." McGuckin argued contra Loi, *Lattanzio*, p. 177, which viewed this material as further evidence of Lactantius's lack of theological sophistication and failure to distinguish the Son's nature. McGuckin cites also Grillmeier, *Christ in the Christian Tradition*, pp. 47–53, who said, "Judaistically conditioned Christology is predominantly functional, not ontological." McGuckin cites *Quir.* 2.5 ("*quod idem angelus et deus Christus*") as evidence for the patristic authority of this otherwise strange and archaic theology. The discussion shows the way scholars viewed Lactantius's theology as strange and archaic because they did not recognize its fundamental logic and technical terms.

[29] Lactantius, *Inst.*, 4.5.3–5, "Before I begin to speak about God and his works, I need to say a few things about his prophets, whose testimonies must now be used, even though I held off [*ne facerem*

THE POWER OF THE SON   175

Testament text Cyprian provides but narrates the New Testament theology that shapes Cyprian's exegesis.[30] Hence, Lactantius's comparison of Christ with the angels reflects the Johannine reference of the heading—"*Quod Christus idem sermo Dei*"—but his apology follows the sequence of passages below it. So, Lactantius cites Ps. 42:1 and Ps. 33:6. He skips the two following references, probably for reasons of their content. Then, in much the same way that Cyprian cites John 1:1 as the end of this prophetic development, Lactantius turns to the text of John 1:3 at *Inst.* 4.9, only after demonstrating Christ's identity from the Old Testament Scriptures. Like Cyprian, he makes Johannine theology the consummation of the historical promise. Both choices reflect Lactantius's concern to present a traditional theology (*Inst.*, 4.30) that would be also apologetically justifiable.

Lactantius continues at length to emphasize Christ's ontological difference from the angels by demarcating their respective powers and functions.[31] He follows the philosophical grammar of power causality by distinguishing the Son and the angels according to their function. Lactantius continues:

> For those breaths [Ps. 33:6] go out from God silently, because they were not created for bearing God's teaching, but for ministry [*ad ministerium*, Heb. 1:7, 1:14]. Although he is breath, still he proceeds as a word with vocalization and sound from God's mouth [Ps. 33:5–6], particularly for this reason, because he was going to use his word for the people. That is, because he would be [*futurus*] the master of God's teaching in order to convey the secret of heaven to humanity.[32]

temperavi] from doing this in previous books. Before all things [*ante omnia*], he who desires to comprehend the truth [Jn. 1:5, *veritatem studet comprehendere*] must pay attention not only to the words of the prophets, but even [their] time [in history] . . . so that he may know what future events they proclaimed and after how many years their prophecies were fulfilled."

[30] Cyprian, *Quir.* 2.1–4 is as much a theological arrangement making a doctrinal argument as it is a kind of *florilegium* of texts. Cyprian's *Testimonia* are just that—witnesses to Christ culled from the Old Testament prophets and arranged as a narrative of history read through the revelation of Jesus. The organization of *Quir.* 2.1–3 is a signature example of that method: "*Quod idem sit et sapientia et uirtus dei*: [1 Cor. 1:22–24]." The next heading, "*Quod sapientia dei christus, et de sacramento concarnationis eius et passionis et calicis et altaris et apostolorum, qui missi praedicauerunt*: [Pr. 9:1–6]." The next heading, "*Quod christus idem sit sermo dei*: [Ps. 42:6] '*In psalmo xliii: eructauit cor meum sermonem bonum, dico ego opera mea regi.*' [Ps. 33:6] *Item in psalmo xxxi: sermone dei caeli solidati sunt et spiritu eius omnis uirtus eorum.* [Ps. 107:20] *Item in psalmo cu: misit sermonem suum et curauit illos.* [Jn. 1:3] *Item in euangelio cata iohannem: in principio fuit sermo et sermo erat apud deum et deus erat sermo.*"

[31] Cf. Tertullian, *Carn.*, 14: "*Iam ergo ceteri dii non erunt sed satellites ac ministri.*"

[32] Lactantius, *Inst.*, 4.8.7–10. Monat, *Lactance et la Bible*, pp. 176, explains that "les longues explications sur le *Logos* contenues dans le chapitre suivant, comme les images destinées à faire comprendre la Prolation, sont proches de Tert. *Apol.* 21,10–14 d'une part et *Adv. Prax.* 7 d'autre part. Mais, dans ces passages, Tertullien est lui-même largement tributaire de Justin, Tatien, Athénagore et Théophile." Cf. Tertullian, *Prax.*, 24.10. Novatian, *Trin.*, 31.2, where Tertullian's language of *prolatio* appears alongside an emphasis upon the Son as revealer of *arcana* and *secreta Patris*. On Ps. 33:6 and

176 ROMAN VIRTUE IN THE EARLY CHRISTIAN THOUGHT OF LACTANTIUS

Studer and Loi used this passage and the following lines to argue that Lactantius presented the unity of the Father and Son in a merely moral sense. However, Lactantius follows the logical progression inherent in power theology and the exegesis of his predecessors.[33] Tertullian had argued that "through the works, we understand that Father and Son are [*esse*] One . . . [such that] . . . two should be believed albeit in one power [*in una virtute*]."[34] Lactantius recognizes the epistemological point that the two are *believed*. Tertullian worked deductively; Lactantius works back to Tertullian's position inductively, that is, historically. He first observes the distinct works of the Son and the angels. The angels perform one action—silent ministry—while the Son has another—teaching. Through their works, he discerns a "great difference [*magna differentia*]" between them. Lactantius then proceeds to draw the ontological conclusion that Christ and the angels exercise a different power and are, therefore, different in being:

> He spoke him first, that through him he might speak to us, and so reveal the word and will of God. Therefore, he is deservedly called the *Sermo* and *Verbum* of God, because God comprehended a vocal spirit proceeding from his own mouth, whom he had conceived not in a womb, but in [his] mind by some unthinkable virtue [*virtus*] of his own majesty and power [*inexcogitabili suae maiestatis virtute ac potentia*].[35]

Having first observed distinctive works, Lactantius ascribes to the Son a distinct *virtus* and *potentia*, which the angels do not have, namely, the very *virtus ac potentia* of the Father's own *maiestas*. The Son's power, notably, has the same appellation, "unthinkable," that belongs to God's own nature. Although the angels proceed from God, Christ alone is God's *maxima potentia*, the *virtus patria maiestatis*, which indicates his distinct identity. This is Lactantius's account of the divine unity: the Son is not just any particular power. He is the Father's supreme power (*maxima potestas*), the very power that designates the Father's exclusive nature.[36]

Ps. 104:30 as sources for theology of early Christian pneumatology, see Barnes, "The Beginning and End of Early Christian Pneumatology," pp. 171–172.

[33] Grillmeier, *Christ in the Christian Tradition*, p. 196. Relying on the work of V. Loi, Grillmeier emphasized the anthropomorphic terms: "This text, with its very anthropomorphic flavor and its parallels, gives us some idea of Lactantius's notion of the relationship of Father to Son in one God. But it should be noted that he speaks as an apologist and descends to the level of his audience. The anthropomorphisms are comparisons and analogies."

[34] Tertullian, *Prax.*, 22.13: "*Per opera ergo erit Pater in Filio et Filius in patre. Et ita per opera intellegimus unum esse Patrem et Filium. Adeo totum hoc perseverabat inducere ut duo tamen crederentur in una virtute quia aliter Filius credi non posset nisi duo crederentur.*"

[35] Lactantius, *Inst.*, 4.8.8–10.

[36] See Monat, *Lactance et la Bible*, p. 174, esp. fn. 68. Monat observes that this description of the angels as "breaths" is drawn from Ps. 1–3 (104.4) and the *Epistle to the Hebrews*. In the footnote, he

THE POWER OF THE SON   177

Lactantius's account of the Incarnation soon restates this logic. Borrowing an argument from Novatian, he says: "God's power [*virtus dei*] appeared [*apparuit*] from the works [*ex operibus*] he did, human frailty [*fragilitas*] from the passion he endured."[37]

Lactantius does not stop at the simple assertion of Christ's unity with the Father. He also makes a point to distinguish the specific identity of the Son. He explains that the Son is the very power of the Father, but in such a way that the Son has an existence proper to himself. Once again, the notion of *power* anchors both the Son's unity with the Father (*virtus*) and the Son's independent existence (*vigeat*). The above passage continues as follows:

> God comprehended a vocal breath [*spiritus*] proceeding from his own mouth, whom he had conceived not in a womb, but in [his] mind by the virtue and power of his own unthinkable majesty [*inexcogitabili suae maiestatis virtute ac potentia*] to be an exact copy [*in effigiem*], which is strong [*vigeat*] with a wisdom and sentience proper to itself [*proprio sapientia et sensu*]; then he fashioned his other breaths [*suos spiritus*] into angels.[38]

observes that Lactantius does give Christ the title *princeps angelorum*, but then proceeds to say: "Le titre qui lui est ainsi conféré désigne une *fonction* et ne préjuge nullement de sa *nature*." However, the designation of a function in Lactantius's argument entails the distinction of *power* and *nature*.

[37] Lactantius, *Inst.*, 4.13.4. Cf. Novatian, *Trin.*, 11.4, seems influential here: "*Quasi hominis enim in illo fragilitates considerant, quasi Dei virtutes non computant, infirmitates carnis recolunt, potestates divinitatis excludunt?*" Cf. *Inst.*, 1.9.6 and 2.8. Furthermore, Lactantius already applied these terms and their exact argument negatively—*fragilitas humana, infirmitas*—in the polemic against the Roman gods and in his definition of God via *creatio ex nihilo* See Chapter 4, this volume.

[38] Lactantius, *Inst.*, 4.8.9–10. On this passage, McGuckin acknowledged "the inarticulate state of Lactantius' pneumatology" and noted that it "has frequently been explained on the basis of theological incompetence (John A. McGuckin, "Spirit Christology: Lactantius and His Sources," *Heythrop Journal* (1983): pp. 144–145). He noted that Lactantius follows an exegesis derived from Tertullian. Barnes, "Beginning and End of Early Christian Pneumatology," p. 181, is helpful in this regard. Commenting on Tertullian's use of Ps. 33:6, Prov. 8 and Jn. 1:3 in connection with *Prax.* 26–27, Barnes explains the invention by Tertullian and Origen of a new theology of the Holy Spirit in response to Spirit-Monarchianism: "The creative activity of the 'Spirit' in such LXX passages is read through the interpretive lens of John 1:3 [e.g., *Inst.*, 4.9]: the Word or Spirit created all things. (This argument is expanded by the identification of the Word/Spirit with Wisdom: LXX testimonies to Wisdom's role in creation are taken to restate the doctrine announced in Ps. 33:6 and John 1:3.) . . . the key passages are now understood to refer to the pre-existent Son in support of a theology of his distinct and personal existence before and during His incarnation." *Inst.*, 4.6.1–3, 8–10 reflect this tradition. Monat rejected Loi's identification of John 1:3 in this passage (Monat, *Lactance et la Bible*, p. 174. Cf. Loi, *Lattanzio*, p. 161), but no one disputes Lactantius's use of Jn. 1:3 at *Inst.* 4.9, which adopts Tertullian's argument (*Prax.*, 5.2–3; Tertullian, *Apol.*, 21.10; Minucius Felix, *Oct.*, 19.10) wholesale. As Monat, *Lactance et la Bible*, p. 176, explains, "L'enseignement sur le Verbe donné dans l'Adversus Praxean fait figurer, à coté des trois textes Prov. 8,27/Ps. 33,2/Jn. 1,1–3, qui constituent comme l'épine dorsale du dossier de Lactance, un célèbre passage d'Isaie." Where then scholarship has seen a merely archaic theology, it seems better to say that Lactantius reflects the third-century development of an anti-Monarchian exegesis in Tertullian. That emphasis reflects his awareness of third-century heresies (cf. *Inst.*, 4.30) and his intent to forestall them, even through this apologetic presentation.

178   ROMAN VIRTUE IN THE EARLY CHRISTIAN THOUGHT OF LACTANTIUS

With this point, Lactantius corrects a weakness of Tertullian's theology in *Prax.*
11–16. Tertullian tends to describe the Son and Spirit as properties of the Father.
As a result, as Barnes explains, Tertullian "tends to collapse the distinction between property and product," whose causal relation is the basis of his own defense of the real existence of the Son.[39] Lactantius's presentation of the Son
forestalls such an ambiguity. His description of Christ as a "copy" or "image"
emphasizes that the notion of Christ as the Father's *virtus* does not undermine
the Son's real and independent existence. That emphasis represents a later phase
of theological debate among third-century Christians.[40]

Lactantius's reliance upon the technical sense of *virtus* in his Christology is
also reflected in the series of metaphors he uses to articulate the unity between
the Father and Son at *Inst.* 4.29. As noted above, earlier scholarship regarded
these metaphors as evidence of Lactantius's mediocre theological ability and
explained them by reference to his traditionally Roman preference for the

[39] Barnes, *Power of God*, pp. 105–106. See also Joseph Moingt, *Théologie Trinitaire de Tertullien:
Substantialité et Individualité*, pp. 345–350: "Le *Sermo* semble mis au rang des attributs intellectuels;
il est à Dieu ce que l'intellect est à l'ame, une fonction operative, un *ingenium*."

[40] Although definitive proof is lacking, in my opinion this passage may reflect the influence of
Origen, even if indirectly. *Inst.* 4.6.1–3, 4.8.6–10, and 4.9.1–3 should be read alongside *Prin.* 1.2.7–9.
Several things suggest this conclusion. The first item of note is Lactantius's exegetical basis. According
to Barnes, "Origen's use of *power* . . . is based upon an exegesis of 1 Cor. 1:24, Heb. 1:3, and Wis.
7:25. His unique contribution to trinitarian theology is to develop a new "Wisdom" account of the
Godhead based on these texts. . . . The use of these three scriptural texts together in mutual support
of a common exegesis of *power* becomes an indication of the influence of Origen on all sides in the
trinitarian controversies" (Barnes, *Power of God*, p. 111). Lactantius does not quote Wis. 7:25, but
the other two texts are both influential in his Wisdom theology of the Son. As Gábor Kendeffy has
shown, 1 Cor. 1:18–24 is fundamental to his critique and his larger presentation of Christ as Wisdom
(see Gábor Kendeffy, "*Velamentum Stultitiae*: 1 Cor. 1:20ff. and 3:19 in Lactantius's *Divine Institutes*,"
in *Invention, Rewriting, Usurpation. Discursive Fights over Religious Traditions in Antiquity*, ed.
J. Ulrich, A.-Chr. Jacobsen and M. Kahlos (Frankfurt am Main: Peter Lang, 2012), pp. 57–70;
Biblia Patristica finds allusions to 1 Cor. 1:24 at *Inst.* 4.9.1, 4.16.2 as well as *Epitome* 37.2 and 44.1).
Furthermore, Lactantius's use of Hebrews is not accounted for by any of his undisputed sources.
As John A. McGuckin explained, "All Lactantius's references to Hebrews are clearly independent
of the *Ad Quirium* which does not reproduce a single text from that source (John A. McGuckin,
"The Non-Cyprianic Scripture Texts in Lactantius' *Divine Institutes*," *Vigiliae Christianae* 36.2
(1982): p. 147). This absence prompts the search for a source (Antonie Wlosok, "Zur Bedeutung der
nicht-Cyprianischen Bibelzitate bei Laktanz," *Studia Patristica* 4.79 (1961): pp. 234–250). At *Prin.*
1.2.1, Origen introduces the Son by drawing on the same text of Prov. 8 that Lactantius uses above
(*Inst.*, 6.1–3, fn. 43). Origen uses the title "Wisdom" and concludes the paragraph by quoting 1 Cor.
1:24 in order to call the Son God's *power*, much as Lactantius begins (*Inst.*, 6.1–3) with Wisdom theology and then calls the Son the "*virtus patria maxima*." Origen uses Heb. 1:3 to distinguish the Son's
unique existence from the Father. Prompted by the phrase, "*figura expressa eius substantiae* [Heb.
1:3]," he elaborates using the image of "a statue [*statuta*]" exactly like that which it portrays, except
that the statue can be comprehended because it is not so immense as the original. Origen thus also
uses Heb. 1:3 along with the image of "*statuta*," a term that is effectively equivalent to Lactantius's
"*effigies*" above. Although *effigies* does also appear in *Prax.* 7.7, Lactantius's discussion at *Inst.* 4.8.8–
10 looks remarkably similar to the discussion at *Prin.* 1.2.9. The narrative progression is like the
progression at *Prin.* 1.2.7–9, and Lactantius uses an indistinguishable theological argument and an
exegesis for which previous scholarship has located no clear source. Hence, I suggest that Lactantius
may have corrected a weakness of Tertullian's theology by an argument indebted to Origen. But it is
not certain.

THE POWER OF THE SON   179

forensic and oratorical over metaphysical technicalities.[41] Lewis Ayres has already observed, however, that Lactantius's metaphors draw upon the *X from X* causality common in third-century Latin theology.[42] Ayres's suggestion points to the power theology that underlies the whole passage, which includes the legal imagery and the Roman notion of the *paterfamilias*. The legal imagery does not indicate a mere analogical understanding of the relationship between the Father and the Son because the imagery is grounded in a theological grammar operative throughout *Inst.* 4.[43]

At *Inst.* 4.29, Lactantius returns to the question of the Son's unity with the Father. The choice is reasonable given Lactantius's own earlier rejection of any kind of plurality in the Godhead. He is aware of the apparent contradiction that his Christology entails. Having narrated the person and work of the Son, he attempts one last time to articulate the Son's unity, with special attention to the burdens of his apologetic context. Lactantius begins by drawing on the ontological metaphors common to third-century Latin Christianity. He opens with terms derived from Tertullian: "Since then the Father makes the Son, and the Son the Father, each is one mind, one spirit, one substance: one a sort of gushing fountain, the other like a river flowing from it [*defluens ex eo rivus*]; one as the sun, the other as [*quasi*] a ray of light extended from the sun."[44] These analogies reflect the predominant language of the early Latin Christian tradition. They emphasize the singularity of *substantia*, but interpret the notions of *mens* and *spiritus* in terms of *virtus*. In this respect, the above lines repeat Lactantius's earlier assertion that "God, moreover, who is eternal mind [*mens aeterna*], is in every part [a being] of perfect and consummate *virtus* [*virtutis*]."[45] His first steps into the subject begin where Tertullian did.

Lactantius's early language shapes a moral element that emerges as his discussion of Christ continues. He describes the unity of the Father and Son as demonstrated in the *virtus* of *fides*. This portrait of the *fides* of the Father and Son echoes Minucius Felix's criticism of Roman emperors and also anticipates Lactantius's own subsequent moral arguments. His references to the Son's fidelity and the Father's love assume the notion, well-established at this point, that common actions indicate a common nature. Lactantius writes:

---

[41] E.g., Grillmeier, *Christ in the Christian Tradition*, p. 194. Referring to this analogy he remarks, "It has an advantage over the strong stress of the moral interpretation of the unity of Father and Son in pointing to the unity of substance in God, however incomplete the ideas associated with it may have been. When Lactantius uses the analogy of the *paterfamilias* in God, he is probably betraying his 'Roman connections.'"

[42] Ayres, *Nicaea and Its Legacy*, pp. 71–72.

[43] Despite my urging, Gassman, *Worshippers of the Gods*, p. 46, fn. 190, still thinks that "[Lactantius] never arrives at a clear description of the ontological position of the Son."

[44] Lactantius, *Inst.*, 4.29.4–5. Cf. Tertullian, *Apol.*, 21.13, Cf. Hippolytus, *Contra Noetum*, 11.1; Ayres, *Nicaea and Its Legacy*, p. 23.

[45] Lactantius, *Inst.*, 1.3.4. Cf. Tertullian, *Apol.*, 21.13.

180 ROMAN VIRTUE IN THE EARLY CHRISTIAN THOUGHT OF LACTANTIUS

Since he is faithful and dear to the Highest Father, he is not separated, just as a river is not separated from its source nor a ray from the sun, because the water of a source is in the river and the light of the sun in the ray. In the same way, the voice cannot be divided from the tongue nor power [*virtus*] from the hand or body. Since then the prophets call him the hand, power [*virtus*], and Word [*sermo*] of God, there is no distinction, because the tongue is the minister of speech and the hand in which is power [*virtus*] are individual parts of the body [*individuae sunt corporis portiones*].[46]

By emphasizing this oneness, Lactantius responds to any potential accusation of self-contradiction. His early polemic (*Inst.*, 1.3–24) maintained that a plurality of gods would produce a disunity of mind and therefore conflict within God. On that basis, Lactantius asserted that God must be of a single *mens* and *virtus*, as noted above. His emphasis upon Christ's fidelity responds to that early claim.[47] Lactantius's portrait of Christ's *virtus* develops the negative argument of the early *Institutes*, which itself presupposed the notion that a divinity is recognized through the actions of a divine figure. In great contrast to the traditional gods— or, better, to Lucan's emperor deities, whose failure of *fides* betrayed their mere humanity (*Phar.*, 1.192)—Christ's fidelity proves the divine *virtus* that operates in this man. Textually, then, Lactantius offers the moral argument only within the context of a power theology.

At this point, Lactantius finally introduces his well-known analogy drawn from Roman law in order to articulate his understanding of the unity of the Father and Son. By using this metaphor, he attempts not only to illustrate his theology but also to establish a referent for his later moral and political argument. Rhetorically, the following passage sets up the transition to Lactantius's arguments in *Inst.* 5–6. He explains:

Let me use a more fitting illustration [*propiore exemplo*]: When someone has a son whom he loves uniquely, who nevertheless is in the home and the hand of his father, although he allows [the son] the name and power of a master [*nomen*

---

[46] Lactantius, *Inst.*, 4.29.5. Cf. Cyprian, *Quir.*, 2.4, "*Quod christus idem manus et brachium dei.*" See also Anthony Briggman, *Irenaeus of Lyons and the Theology of the Holy Spirit* (Oxford: Oxford University Press, 2012), p. 105ff. on the "hands of God" motif in sources known to Lactantius.

[47] See Lactantius, *Inst.*, 1.3.6–9. See also *Inst.*, 4.29.9. It is the same argument as when Tertullian says that "[*Prax.*, 22.13] *Per opera intelligimus unum esse Patrem <et Filium>.*" Loi, *Lattanzio*, acknowledges the phrase, "*una mens, unus spiritus, una substantia,*" but reads Lactantius's description of Christ's *fides* and the Father's love (*carus*) against these terms: "Ma questo asserto è estenuato nel suo valore teologico dalla spiegazione datane poco dopo, secondo cui l'unità ha carattere morale, poiché essa è garantita dalla fidelità e dall'amore del Figlio al Padre; che anzi, l'argomento migliore Lattanzio lo trova nell'analogia con l'unità intercorrent tra il pater familias ed il suo unigenito secondo il diritto romano." However, the significance of *fides* is determined by prior epistemological judgments entailed in the logic of power theology. The term does not stand alone. It is flanked by analogies that ground *fides* in common *virtus*.

THE POWER OF THE SON   181

domini et potestatem], still under the civil law the household remains one and designates one master. Likewise, this world is the one household of God, both Father and Son, who single-mindedly [*unanimes*] oversee the world, one God, because one is as [*tamquam*] two and two as One.[48]

The problem Lactantius deals with by this juxtaposition of physical and legal notions is the same problem he attempts to navigate by the notion of Christ as a three-dimensional image (*effigies*). In both cases, he is looking for a way to maintain the unity of the Godhead and the distinction of the persons. These metaphors locate his account of unity within the same substantial tradition that characterizes the theologies of Tertullian, Novatian, and Cyprian. It is not simply a question of unreconciled tensions, or an argument of merely rhetorical force. Rather, Lactantius has formulated a typical third-century Latin presentation tailored to address a Roman world, whose Augustan notions of *virtus* he aims to correct. He thus responds to pagan theologies, while navigating third-century heresies. As will be seen, the moral hues that he writes into this portrait of divine society are intentional. They set up his later arguments about human nature and the rights of Christians under Roman law.

The Incarnation

Lactantius's claim that the Son is God because he bears the distinctive *virtus* and *potestas* of the Father necessitates an explanation of his Incarnation. Textually, Lactantius's account of the Incarnation is interlaced with his narrative of Christ's mission and ministry, and he returns to the Incarnation later when speaking of soteriology.[49] Apologetically, the account of the Incarnation justifies his claim that Christ, the human, can be identified as true God, despite Lactantius's own earlier arguments that the human parentage of Rome's deities belied their claims upon divinity. In the process, Lactantius also identifies known heresies and emphasizes the real humanity of the Son and his birth from the womb of Mary.[50] This account of the Incarnation shows that Lactantius aims to elaborate the traditional themes of early Latin theology in a manner calculated to support his larger apologetic aims.

Lactantius's most distinctive explanations of the Incarnation occupy two lengthy passages, *Inst.* 4.13.1–6 and *Inst.* 4.25.1–7. The latter passage recapitulates the former with important elaborations. Both reflect a two-stage Christology

[48] Lactantius, *Inst.*, 4.29.7.
[49] Lactantius, *Inst.*, 25.1.
[50] Ayres, *Nicaea and Its Legacy*, p. 74, sees Lactantius and Novatian as both responding to adoptionism.

182 ROMAN VIRTUE IN THE EARLY CHRISTIAN THOUGHT OF LACTANTIUS

common in third-century Christian thought, in which the Son is "born" first from the father in a pre-incarnate condition and "second" in the womb of the Virgin. The account serves to justify Lactantius's claim that Christ, unlike the traditional gods, is not derived from a merely human *virtus*:

> [The Father] wanted [the Son] to be born as a human, so that through all things he could prove to be like the Highest Father [*summo patri similis*]. Indeed, God the Father himself, the source and beginning of all things [*origo et principium rerum*], because he lacks parents, is quite rightly called "fatherless" and "motherless" by Trismegistus, because he is not procreated from anything else. Therefore, the Son had to be born twice so that he could be "fatherless" and "motherless" [*ut et ipse fieret ἀπάτωρ atque ἀμήτωρ*].[51]

At one time, Lactantius's invocation of Trismegistus served as proof of his meager theological reflection. The analogy seemed to show a reliance upon marginal sources, an inability to think theologically about the relationship between the Father and the Son, and thus was supportive of a larger narrative of Lactantius's status on the margins of early Christian thought.[52] In fact, the reference to Trismegistus begins an extended defense of the Son's real divinity, which is couched in terms taken from Cyprian, Minucius Felix, Tertullian, and Hebrews.[53] As P. Monat has shown, Lactantius's reference to Trismegistus actually restates a theology derived from Heb. 7:1–4, which presents Melchizedek as "a priest of the Most High God," and as a "King of righteousness [βασιλεὺς δικαιοσύνης] . . . fatherless [ἀπάτωρ], motherless [ἀμήτωρ], having neither beginning of days nor end of life, but likened to the Son of God he remains a priest forever."[54] Reliance on Hebrews is consistent, of course, with Lactantius's portrait of the first nativity, before the foundations of the world. It also advances the apologetic argument, since the belief that all the traditional Roman gods derived from human parents was central to Lactantius's polemic against the pantheon. By contrast, Christ appears without a genealogy.

---

[51] Lactantius, *Inst.*, 4.13.1–4.

[52] Contra Digeser, *Making of a Christian Empire*, p. 73, which says that "the terms ἀπάτωρ and ἀμήτωρ survive in no other Latin author, [while] the concept itself pervades the Hermetica." But, Monat, *Lactance et la Bible*, pp. 168–174, saw the influence of Prov. 9 in this chapter and noted also Heb. 1:4 at *Inst.* 4.6.8. The terms ἀπάτωρ and ἀμήτωρ appear in Hebrews as noted above, which no other Latin author uses. Moreover, the concept is present in any Christian author who regards the virgin birth as evidence of Christ's divinity. Digeser's argument is insufficiently careful. The same critique applies to her use of the Nicene phrase, "consubstantial nature" to equate the Hermetic and Lactantian notions of the divine unity.

[53] For the term "Catholic" as contradistinguished from third-century heresies, see *Inst.* 4.29. For Lactantius's description of his apologetic tradition, see *Inst.* 5.1.22.

[54] See Monat, *Lactance et la Bible*, pp. 188–189. Monat observes that the 1563 edition of Lactantius was the first to attribute his teaching to Heb. 7:1. McGuckin, *Researches into the Divine Institutes*, pp. 179–185.

THE POWER OF THE SON   183

Lactantius's appeal to Trismegistus is the first in a series of textual references that articulate Christ's real divinity and real humanity. To his assertion of Christ's divine parentage, Lactantius adds an explanation of Christ's divine-human substance, which is articulated in terms common to a trajectory of early Latin theology originating in Tertullian. Lactantius continues:

> For he was motherless in the first spiritual birth, because he was born without the service of a mother [*sine officio*], but generated by God the Father alone [*generatus est*]. In the second carnal birth, he was "fatherless," since he was procreated in a virginal womb without the service of a father [*sine officio patris*], so that bearing a mediating substance [*ut gerens mediam substantiam*] between God and humanity, he might be able to lead this fragile and weak nature of ours, as if by the hand [*quasi manu*], to immortality. He was made Son of God through spirit and of humanity through flesh, that is, both God and human [Rom. 1:3–4]. God's virtue appeared from the works he did [*Dei virtus in eo ex operibus quae fecit apparuit*], human frailty from the passion he endured [*fragilitas hominis ex passione quam pertulit*] . . . That he was both God and human, combined of both kinds [*ex utroque genere permixtum*], we learn from the prediction of the prophets.[55]

This dense paragraph reproduces a traditional Latin argument but leaves behind the specific exegesis that produced it. The allusion to Rom. 1:3–4 reflects a constant Pauline referent in Lactantius's thought.[56] As Monat notes, the phrase "*ex utroque genere permixtum*" and its parallel "*ex utroque genere concretus*" derive from Cyprian's *Ad Quirinum*: "That Christ is both human and God combined from each kind [*ex utroque genere concretus*], so that he might be a mediator between us and the Father."[57] Lactantius uses the same language. Likewise, his emphasis upon Christ's dual parentage reproduces an argument from Tertullian's *De carne Christi* 5.7–8, which concludes with the judgment that "the powers of spirit [*virtutes spiritus*] prove him to be God, while his sufferings [*passiones*] prove the flesh of humanity."[58] Novatian uses virtually identical language and logic:

---

[55] Lactantius, *Inst.*, 4.13.1–4. Cf. Lactantius, *Inst.*, 4.25.1–3. On Lactantius's citations from the prophets, see Cyprian, *Quir.*, 2.6, 2.10. For "*permixtum*" language, cf. Tertullian, *Apol.*, 21.11. Also, Anthony Briggman, "Irenaeus' Christology of Mixture," *JTS* 64.2 (October, 2013): pp. 516–555, gives the term *comixtio* and its cognates a prominent place in his demonstration that Irenaeus relied on a Stoic theory of blending in his Christology.

[56] Lactantius, *Inst.*, 4.13.3. Cf. Cyprian, *Quir.*, 2.11.1, "*Quod de semine david secundum carnem nasci haberet*." *VLD* Rom. 1:3–4, "*de Filio suo, qui factus est ei ex semine David secundum carnem, qui praedestinatus est Filius Dei in virtute secundum spiritum sanctificationis ex resurrectione mortuorum*." See Monat, *Sources Chrétiennes* 377, p. 112.

[57] Cyprian, *Quir.*, 2.10.1.

[58] Tertullian, *Carn.*, 5.7–8.

While indeed they consider the weaknesses of humanity [*hominis . . . in illo fragilitates*] in him, they do not also account [*computant*] for the powers of God [*Dei virtutes*]. They accept the infirmities of his flesh [*infirmitates carnis*], but reject the powers of his divinity [*potestates divinitatis*]. If then this evidence from the infirmities [*ex infirmitatibus*] of Christ leads to the conclusion that his humanity is proved from his weaknesses [*ex infirmitatibus*], proof of divinity in him evidenced by his powers [*ex virtutibus*] also leads to the conclusion that he may be called God on the basis of his works [*ex operibus*]. If then sufferings [*passiones*] show a human weakness in him [*humanam fragilitatem*], why do works not bear witness to the divine power [*divinam potestatem*] that is in him?[59]

Given the correspondence of expression and anti-heretical concerns, Novatian's comments provide context for Lactantius. As Daniel Lloyd remarks, "To combat Sabellian theology, Novatian claims that the Son's distinction from the Father is proved by His ability to enact the miracles/works of the Father."[60] Lactantius condemns the same groups. At *Inst.* 4.30, he condemns heretical sects "whether Phrygians, or Novatianists, or Valentinians, or Marcionites, or Anthropians, or however else they are named. . . . It is therefore only the Catholic Church which retains true worship."[61] Hence, Lactantius not only relies upon the Latin theology of his most prominent predecessors but makes a point to name and reject the major third-century heresies, while calling himself "Catholic." In all of these elements, his Christology is typical of the best in third-century Latin Christian writing.

Prior Latin theology also informs an image of Christ that scholars regularly contrast with other early Christian portraits. Lactantius connects Christ's divine status to his work as a revealer of *virtus* using the language of mediation. At *Inst.* 4.13.3, the key phrase is "*ut gerens mediam substantiam.*" Later, *Inst.* 4.25.5 elaborates: "Therefore, he was both God and human, established midway [*constitutus medius*] between God and humanity (hence the Greeks call him mediator [μεσίτην]) so that he might be able to lead humanity to God, that is, to immortality."[62] Lactantius easily found the term at *Quir.* 2.10.1 where the term

---

[59] Novatian, *Trin.*, 11.4.

[60] Daniel Lloyd, *Novatian's Theology of the Father and Son: A Study in Ontological Subordinationism* (New York: Fortress Academic, 2020), p. 151.

[61] Lactantius, *Inst.*, 4.30.10–11, "*Cum enim Phryges aut Novatiani aut Valentiniani aut Marcionitae aut Anthropiani seu quilibet alii nominator . . . Sola igitur catholica ecclesia est quae verum cultum retinet.*"

[62] Lactantius, *Inst.*, 4.25.5, "*Fuit igitur et Deus et homo, inter Deum atque hominem medius constitutus, unde illum Graeci μεσίτην vocant, ut hominem perducere ad Deum posset, id est ad immortalitatem.*" Digeser, *Making of a Christian Empire*, p. 73, treats this phrase as evidence of a "Christology that moves sharply in the direction of philosophical monotheism," which she regards as an effort to construct a Christology that would resonate with Porphyry, who "denied that Christ was the incarnate logos, but counted Christ as a pious immortal." The suggestion is untenable. Lactantius has already made clear that Christ is fully God and fully human and himself used logos-Christology

THE POWER OF THE SON 185

mediator appears. Two further Latin sources provide a clear precedent. In a quotation of 1 Tim. 2:5, Tertullian uses this notion at *De carne Christi* 15.11, the same text that shapes Lactantius's earlier discussion.[63] Moreover, Lactantius's statement refers in Latin to a "*substantia medians*," whereas the noun "*mediator*" appears in Greek. Along with the quotation from Hebrews, the comment suggests a larger trajectory of influence. The strongest antecedent seems to lie in Origen's *Prin.* 2.6. Origen's text is probably not directly in the background of Lactantius's comment, since *Prin.* 2.6 uses the notion of a mediating substance differently. Still, the lines provide a third coordinate, as it were, to survey Lactantius's position in the landscape of third-century Latin theology. Origen says:

> Thus, as we have said, the Godhuman [*Deushomo*] is born with this substance of soul mediating [*hac ergo substantia animae mediante*] between God and flesh (for it was surely impossible without a mediator for the nature of God to be mixed [*misceri*] with a body), since because of this mediating substance it was not contrary to his nature to assume a body. But then again, it was not contrary to nature that this soul [*illa anima*], being a rational substance, should possesses God, since into him, as we said above, all things had already been placed [*tota iam cesserat*], such as the Word, Wisdom, and Truth.[64]

It must be acknowledged that Rufinus's translation may not represent Origen's Greek text precisely. Nonetheless, Lactantius is in good company. The notion of a mediating substance explains the possibility of contact between divinity and humanity for both Origen and Tertullian; the same language appears in Cyprian and Novatian. Origen says that the soul, as rational substance, unites the divinity and humanity of Christ. Lactantius also attributes the humanity and divinity of Christ to these two substances, flesh and spirit: "Since [Apollo] confesses that he was mortal according to the flesh, it follows that he was God according to spirit, which we also affirm."[65] Lactantius interprets this point soteriologically. Because Christ is incarnated in a mediating substance, he is able to act as mediator.

---

explicitly (*Inst.*, 4.8.9). The idea that the phrase *media substantia* would nod to the very denial of such a status, which Lactantius has been at pains to prove, makes Lactantius needlessly incoherent. It would also require that somehow philosophical monotheists would neglect Lactantius's own earlier statements.

[63] Tertullian, *Carn.*, 15.2, defends Christ's true humanity before offering several witnesses to the biblical basis of that teaching, and concludes with a citation of Paul: "*Etiam Paulus apostolus: 'mediator dei et hominum homo christus iesus.'*" Lactantius uses the title *mediator* in the context of restating Tertullian's argument.

[64] Origen, *Prin.*, 2.6.106–114. Translation is my own. Cf. Lactantius, *Inst.*, 4.13.4 with Origen, *Prin.*, 2.6.

[65] Lactantius, *Inst.*, 4.13.12, "*Sed cum fatetur secundum carnem fuisse mortalem, quod etiam nos pradicamus, consequens est ut secundum spiritum Deus fuerit, quod nos adfirmamus.*"

186   ROMAN VIRTUE IN THE EARLY CHRISTIAN THOUGHT OF LACTANTIUS

Composed of both body and *spiritus*, Christ is ontologically capable of bringing humanity into contact with its own highest good.

The Mission and Ministry of Christ

Lactantius's representation of the Son's mission and ministry expands upon the Son's role as Lord and King in order to characterize him as the only true *exemplum* of Roman *virtus* and therefore the starting point for right thinking about moral and political order.[66] As Pierre Monat has shown, Lactantius's portrait is a distinctive rendition of the traditional Christian and biblical notion of Christ as King. The narrative reflects a pattern of catechesis also evident in Irenaeus and Justin Martyr, a pattern shaped by an early Christian reception of the synoptic Gospels, and "more precisely, Matthew's Gospel."[67] Lactantius frames the traditional notion by characterizing Christ as the supreme manifestation of traditional Roman ideals of *virtus*. Rhetorically, he extends a theological tradition traceable to Tertullian and Cyprian by characterizing ideal *virtus* in terms derived from Christ's own works.[68] Theologically, Lactantius turns the argument of *Against Praxeas* outward to address a public Roman audience.[69] So, his account of the Son's "first nativity" articulates the source and content of Christ's *virtus*, while the narrative of Christ's mission demonstrates his *virtus* in the history of his actions (*opera*). Lactantius's later arguments are hinged on this otherwise traditional Roman exemplary narrative, which provides a basis for public discourse about the character of divine *virtus* and its implications for morality and law.

At *Inst.* 4.10, Lactantius explains Christ's mission with a kind of credal summary statement. The passage casts Christ as one who founds temples and instructs people in justice: "From the beginning there went out a plan of God,"

---

[66] Lactantius's account of Christ follows a pattern dictated by the baptismal creed and the narrative of Matthew's Gospel. See Monat, *Lactance et la Bible*, p. 192; Monat, "Introduction," in *Lactance, les Institutions Divine IV*, p. 4.

[67] Monat, *Lactance et la Bible*, p. 184. "Dans les paroles de l'ange à Marie, telles que les rapporte Luc, l'annonce de la Royauté est immédiatement après la nativité non par une formule kérygmatique, mais par l'épisode souvent proches de Lactance, comme Irénee, Justin et Évagre, rappellent simultanément, à l'aide de ces mêmes textes, l'Incarnation et la Royauté. . . . Enfin, la phrase par laquelle Lactance ramène son lecteur au textede *Daniel* évoque le célèbre passage de *l'Épitre aux Phillipiens* sur la 'kenose'et l'exaltation du Christ, qui semble bien avoi figuré dans la liturgie avant même d'entrer dans l'Épitre."

[68] Contra Digeser, *Making of a Christian Empire*, pp. 74–75, who follows Michel Perrin, *L'Homme Antique et Chretien. L'Anthropologie de Lactance* (250–325) (Paris: Beauchesne, 1981), p. 453. Also Loi, *Lattanzio*, pp. 253ff.

[69] Lactantius, *Inst.*, 4.12.17 presents a citation of Ps. 109:1: "*in Psalmo CVIII*," which is drawn from *Quir.* 2.26. The next paragraph [18] cites Is. 45:1–3. However, Ps. 109(110):1 is also cited at Heb. 1:13. Lactantius is often reading the prophets through Hebrews' exegetical prism.

THE POWER OF THE SON   187

Lactantius says, "that as the end of the age drew near, God's Son would descend to earth to found a temple for God and teach justice."[70] Both actions satisfy the Ciceronian and Augustan template for Rome's ideal figures. The passage proceeds to specify the origin and character of the *virtus* that God's Son would exercise in his public actions "not however in angelic *virtus* or by heavenly power [*potestate caelesti*], but in the form of a human [*in figura hominis*] and in a mortal state."[71] The juxtaposition of *virtus* and *potestas* demonstrates again that Lactantius is speaking in terms of traditional Roman virtue discourse and the idiom of power theology, while the emphasis upon Christ's humanity is a mark of Lactantius's debt to Christian tradition. As he concludes, Lactantius specifically emphasizes the activity of Christ's *virtus*:

> After he had fulfilled his office [*magisterio functus fuisset*], he would be handed over into the hands of impious men and suffer death, so that when it had been mastered [*domita*] through his *virtus* [*per virtutem*], he might rise and offer humanity ... which he was bearing, the hope of conquering death and admit [humanity] to the rewards of immortality.

With the terms "*per virtutem*" and "*domita*," Lactantius rewrites the template for political victory by casting Christ in the role of a traditional Roman hero. This vision is paradoxical, of course, in that Christ demonstrates his power by his mortal death, but it nonetheless respects the ancient Roman logic that heroic demonstrations of *virtus* serve as evidence of the divinity of, or divine favor that rests upon, a leader. Martial, Augustus, or Diocletian could be praised in identical terms.[72] The claim that Christ bestows "immortality" also responds to Lactantius's own earlier criticisms of the Roman gods. Unlike the traditional gods, whose power was exercised in violence and death, Christ's deeds reveal a power to give life; this is consistent with the divine power of God, whom Lactantius earlier named as the "giver of life [*dator vitae*]."[73] Hence, Christ exercises what Lactantius had earlier called "the *virtus* of God alone."[74] Lactantius's argument at *Inst.* 3.12 stands behind this narrative. By bringing human beings to immortality, Christ acts as the only true guide toward the highest good. In that respect, he is not only a Sage, who teaches both in deed and word, but also a heroic figure, who restores his people to virtue in traditional Roman terms. In so doing, Christ also redefines the character of virtuous actions.

[70] Lactantius, *Inst.*, 4.10.1.
[71] Lactantius, *Inst.*, 4.10.1–2. Cf. Lactantius, *Inst.*, 4.12.15.
[72] Mamertinus, *Lat. Pan.*, 10.13.
[73] Mamertinus, *Lat. Pan.*, 1.16, "*vitae sit dator.*" Cf. *Inst.*, 4.8.10, "*sensus ac vitae dator.*" *Inst.*, 4.26.15, "*qui datorem uitae deum nescientes.*"
[74] Lactantius, *Inst.*, 1.17.16.

188 ROMAN VIRTUE IN THE EARLY CHRISTIAN THOUGHT OF LACTANTIUS

Lactantius supports this Roman vision of Christ by framing it in terms of biblical narrative. He reads the story of Moses in Ciceronian terms, in order to cast both Moses and Christ in the role of an ideal statesman. In Lactantius's account, both figures constitute a people by giving them a new law and example:

> Now, from the beginning [*a principio*], the origin of this mystery [*sacramenti origo*] needs to be told [*narranda est*]. Our ancestors [*maiores nostri*], who were princes of the Hebrews, after they had come to labor in famine and poverty, crossed into Egypt for the sake of grain. Dwelling in that place for a rather long time, they became subject to an intolerable yoke of servitude. After 430 years, God was moved with compassion for them. So, he led them out [*eduxit*] and freed [*liberavit*] them from the hand of the Egyptian king by his leader Moses [*duce Moyse*], through whom afterwards a law was given to them by God. In this leading [*eductione*], God showed them the *virtus* of his majesty [*virtutem maiestatis*].[75]

These lines resituate the traditional tropes of Roman political narrative into a biblical framework.[76] Moses assumes the role of Scipio Africanus, while the Hebrew people occupy the position normally imagined for the ancient Romans.[77] Thus, Lactantius tells a story of "our ancestors," who were "led out and freed" from a "king," by a leader who revealed divine *virtus* in his laws. Livy could not have put it better.[78] Like Moses, Christ would be sent as "doctor of *virtus* . . . a leader [*dux*], companion [*comes*], and teacher [*magister*]" of his new people.[79] Lactantius casts Christ in this Mosaic role saying that "God Most High, wanting to pass on his own religion, sent a doctor of justice [*doctor iustitiae*] from heaven in order to give new worshippers a new law in him and through him." In this respect, Lactantius applies Tertullian's Christological logic to the history of God's actions through Israel in order to provide a political lens for viewing Christ's own mission. The passage concludes in terms taken from Latin Christian meditations on patience: "[Christ's] marvelous works [*opera miranda*] were signs and evidence of his heavenly *virtus* [*caelestis indicia virtutis*]."[80] Through his works, Christ would not only reveal God's law but his own true divinity to the nations.[81] Both claims interpret Christ's public role in terms of the same ancient Roman political idiom traceable to Cicero, Seneca, and Tertullian.

---

[75] Lactantius, *Inst.*, 4.10.5–7; Cf. 4.14.1–4.
[76] See Chapter 1, this volume.
[77] Lactantius, *Inst.*, 4.10.9.
[78] Lactantius, *Inst.*, 4.10.19. Cf. Tertullian, *Adversus Iudaeos* 8, for Christ as "*dux venturus.*"
[79] Lactantius, *Inst.*, 4.11.14.
[80] Lactantius, *Inst.*, 4.15.1. Cf. Cyprian, *Bon. pat.*, 5, Tertullian, *Pat.*, 3.15.
[81] Tertullian, *Adv. Prax.*, 22.25–30. See Chapter 3, this volume.

THE POWER OF THE SON   189

Lactantius's portrait of the Son's mission culminates in a passage that presents Christ as receiving the power, title, honor, and imitation that Roman politics had ascribed to its deified leaders. The lines confirm that Lactantius aims to present Christ as the fulfillment of Augustan notions of virtue, in order to establish Christ's public example as the starting point for social and ethical discourse. The passage expresses a theology traceable to Phil. 2:5–11 in the idiom of Augustan ideological rhetoric:

And finally, on account of the virtue and faithfulness [*ob virtutem ac fidem*], which he showed to God on earth, 'a kingdom, and honor, and authority [*imperium*] have been given to him, and all tribes and people shall serve him, and his power is eternal and shall never pass away, and his kingdom shall not be shaken [Dan. 7:14].' This statement can be understood in two ways: even now he has a perpetual power [*perpetuam potestatem*], since all nations and tongues venerate his name [*nomen*], confess his majesty [*maiestatem*], follow his teaching [*doctrinam*], imitate his *virtus* [*virtutem imitantur*]. And so he has authority and honor [*imperium et honorem*], since all the tribes of the earth obey his precepts [*praeceptis eius obtemperant*]; but at the same time, afterward, when he comes again in shining power [*in claritate et potestate*] to judge every soul and restore the just to life, then truly will he take possession of the government of the whole earth. Then, when all evil has been rooted out of human affairs, as the poets say, the Golden Age, a just and peaceful time, shall arise.[82]

This passage places Christology in contraposition to Hellenistic ideals of kingship in their Augustan form. It opens with an epithet—"*e caelo delapsus*"—which Cicero had first used to insinuate Pompey's divinity and concludes with a distinctly Vergilian reference to the Golden Age, which Aeneas was supposed to have ushered into Latium.[83] The body of the paragraph is littered with the tropes of imperial panegyric and earlier Christian apologetic: Christ demonstrates

[82] Lactantius, *Inst.*, 4.12.19–21.

[83] Furthermore, Lactantius's use of the Golden Age complements his assimilation of imperial ideals to the person of Christ. Louis. J. Swift, "Lactantius and the Golden Age," *American Journal of Philology* 89.2 (1968): pp. 144–156. Swift offers a very good entré into the twentieth-century discussion of this Lactantian theme and corrects more extreme judgments. As an example, he quotes E. A. Isichei, *Political Thinking and Social Experience. Some Christian Interpretations of the Roman Empire from Tertullian to Salvian* (New Zealand: University of Canterbury Publications, 1964), who took the theme as evidence "of the incongruous fusion of two incompatible theologies . . . a good example of [Lactantius's] inconsistent and uncritical eclecticism." More probably, this theme, like Lactantius's epithets, opposes Christ to imperial pretensions to divinity. E.g., Vergil, *Aen.*, 7.620, "*tum regina caelo delapsa.*" See Spencer Cole, *Cicero and the Rise of Deification at Rome* (Cambridge: Cambridge University Press, 2014), pp. 40–43. Cicero uses this epithet, "*de caelo delapsus*," in the context "of singling out a specific quality as divine [*virtus*]," and presenting Pompey's *adventus* as the arrival of a "heaven sent savior." On the Golden Age, Louis. J Swift, "Lactantius and the Golden Age," pp. 144–156. Swift corrects more extreme judgments on Lactantius.

190   ROMAN VIRTUE IN THE EARLY CHRISTIAN THOUGHT OF LACTANTIUS

fides and *virtus*, in a manner that starkly contrasts with the infidelity of Lucan's Pompey and Caesar (*Phars.*, 1.192). Christ holds the *imperium, honor*, and *potestas perpetua*, which characterize the one true God. In a classic Roman role, Christ provides himself as an *exemplum virtutis*, which the people imitate as they confess his *maiestas*.[84] His government of the earth will bring an endless peace. Where Aeneas and his heirs failed, Christ succeeds by founding an eternal order through his *virtus*. Here again, Lactantius's Christology participates in the traditionally Roman method of asserting the public authority of an ideal figure by touting the divine *virtus* evident in his actions. Lactantius thus imposes Christ onto the Augustan tradition of political theology and rhetoric.

Lactantius's evidently Roman narrative of Christ is also sustained by a trajectory of early Christian exegesis that derived its Christology from the Pauline letters. His portrait of Christ as king is derived from Cyprian's exegesis, which offers an apologetic reconstruction of the biblical narrative read through the prism of Paul's famous hymn at Phil. 2:5–11. Although Lactantius never cites the hymn explicitly, Pierre Monat has argued that "the phrase by which Lactantius directs his reader to the text of Daniel evokes . . . [Phil. 2:5–11] . . . concerning the 'kenosis' and exaltation of the Christ, which seems to have figured much in the liturgy before even entering into the *Epistle*."[85] Still, the absence of a clear citation is striking, since the passage does appear commonly in Latin writers that Lactantius knew.[86] Monat's argument is strengthened by a further observation. *Inst.* 4.12–16 should be read against the background of Cyprian's heading and sequence of citations between *Quir.* 2.13 and 2.25.8. Under the heading at 2.13, Cyprian cites Zech. 3:4, followed by Phil. 2:5–11. He cites Wis. 12:2–12 after the next heading. Lactantius follows this exegesis by citing Dan. 7:13–14 (*Inst.*, 4.12.12), then Zech. 3:3–4 (*Inst.*, 4.14.6–9), and Wis. 2:12–22 (*Inst.*, 4.16.7–10). Lactantius thus replaces Cyprian's citation of Phil. 2:5–11 with his own citation of Dan. 7:13–14, to which Monat refers. The choice may be explained by the heading at *Quir.* 2.25.8: "That when he had risen, he would receive from the Father all power [*omnem potestatem*] and his power is eternal [*potestas eius aeterna sit*]: [Dan. 7:13]." Cyprian uses the vocabulary of Phil. 2:9, but supports that vocabulary by reference to Dan. 7:13. Lactantius enacts this reading in his more elaborate narrative. His description of Christ uses the vocabulary of *Ad Quir.* 2.13 and Phil. 2:5–11, even as he continues to draw biblical citations from the prophets for apologetic reasons. Dan. 7:13 thus takes the place of Phil. 2:5–11 in his account of the exaltation.

---

[84] For the imperial history of this language, see Chapter 1, this volume.

[85] Monat, *Lactance et la Bible*, p. 184.

[86] E.g., Novatian, *Trin.*, 22.12, Cyprian, *De bono patientiae*, 24. *Biblia Patristica* gives Lactantius, *Ep.*, 46.2, "*se ipse humilem fecit*," as a reference to Phil. 2:8.

THE POWER OF THE SON   191

The Works of Christ

Lactantius aims to validate his explanation of the Son's double-nativity and mission through the narrative of Christ's life and miracles. Tertullian's claim that "the Father, who abides in the Son through the works of his powers [*per opera virtutum*] and the words of his teaching, is seen through those [works]" is programmatic for the narrative. Having asserted the Son's power and divinity in the above sections, Lactantius aims to demonstrate this power and divinity through the narrative of Christ's *opera*. In so doing, he hopes to demonstrate the superiority of Christ's *virtus* to that of traditional Roman figures, while also rewriting the classical template for exemplary action. Where his early polemic disabused the Romans' dead kings of their claim to a "*virtus* that makes us immortal," Lactantius's later meditation on Christ's kingship trumpets the revelation of a *virtus* that brings immortality.[87] In narrating the history of Christ's life, Lactantius offers a new founding mythology for the people of God.

Lactantius's presentation of Christ's earthly works begins with the healing ministry. Beginning with the story of Christ's birth and baptism, Lactantius proves Christ's status as an exemplary monarch by recounting the benefits he dispenses to his people. "From that time [of his baptism]," Lactantius explains, "[Christ] began to exercise [*operari*] his great powers [*virtutes*], not by magic tricks, which show nothing true or reliable, but by a heavenly capacity and power [*vi ac potestate caelesti*]."[88] The preceding line places the nouns *virtus*, *vis*, and *potestas* in a causal relationship that makes *virtus* exercised in Christ's actions through the efficacy of *vis ac potestas*. Evident from the line is Lactantius's aim to observe the operation of Christ's *virtus* in Christ's actions, in order to present Christ's ministry as public evidence for his *virtus*. Hence, Lactantius proceeds to survey Christ's divine power manifested in his various actions: "His deeds of power [*virtutes eius*] were what Apollo called portentific [*portentificas*], because wherever he went he would restore the ill and feeble suffering from every kind of sickness."[89] Importantly, in his exercises of divine power, Christ not only demonstrates divinity but redefines the character of true *virtus* by offering a new and better model for imitation:[90]

> Nor is it a wonder that he did these marvels by his word and command [*verbo ac iussione*], since he himself was the Word of God sustained by a heavenly strength and power [*caelesti virtute ac potestate subnixum*]. And it was not enough that he returned strength to the weak [*vires imbecillis redderet*],

[87] Lactantius, *Inst.*, 1.18.15.
[88] Lactantius, *Inst.*, 4.15.6.
[89] Lactantius, *Inst.*, 4.15.6.
[90] See Chapter 5, this volume.

192 ROMAN VIRTUE IN THE EARLY CHRISTIAN THOUGHT OF LACTANTIUS

integrity to the crippled, health to the ill and unwell, unless he also raised the dead as if he was recalling them to life freed only from sleep.[91]

Lactantius's account of the healing ministry rewrites the classical image of ideal monarchy by casting Christ the King in the role of medical doctor. Lactantius even interprets the notion of Christ as the *Logos* in terms of *virtus*, since the significant fact of the Word is its power to heal by a mere act of speech. *Virtus* and *potestas* interpret *logos*, for Lactantius, but not the other way around. Lactantius's emphasis upon Christ's self-sacrifice continues in Lactantius's survey of Christ's other miracles, which validate his claim to royal power and authority. Lactantius sets the feeding of the five thousand in a royal frame: "The multitude began to follow him on account of his *virtutes et opera divina*."[92] When he tells of Christ walking on water, he evokes *Aen.* 10.764, saying, "He went after [the disciples] walking as if on solid ground, *not as the poets lie about [mentiuntur]* Orion who, treading in the sea with part of his body submerged, 'stands above the waives at his shoulder [*umero supereminet undas*].'"[93] Lactantius lifted these terms from a Vergilian simile that compares Christ to Mezentius, the famed enemy of Aeneas, "who carries himself in his heavy arms."[94] Christ outstrips both Mezentius and Orion, since what the lying poets saying of them is reported truly of Christ in the Scriptures. Lactantius makes the point through a rhetorical play on the verb *mentire*: "Perhaps the sacred letters lie [*mentiuntur*] when they teach that there was in [Christ] a power so great, he could compel even the winds to obey by his command [*imperio suo*], the seas to serve him, the dead to rise, the depths to heed [*inferos oboedire*]."[95] The Vergilian comparison turns Christ's walking on water into a royal advent. At the same time, Lactantius engages with the panegyrical notion of an imperial power so great that even the elements obey.[96] Christ is then a monarch, but his *virtus* heals and sustains human life, just as the *virtus* of God, the *dator vitae*, creates and gives life.

Since Cicero, Roman notions of virtue had assimilated martial and philosophical ideals into a single figure, and Lactantius's portrait is not different. As he moves from Christ's healing ministry to the passion, he makes *patientia* the supreme *virtus* and unites Christ's royal image with that of the ideal Sage. Lactantius's passion narrative evokes his earlier criticism of the ideal Sage in

---

[91] Lactantius, *Inst.*, 4.15.9.

[92] Lactantius, *Inst.*, 4.15.16.

[93] Lactantius, *Inst.*, 4.15.21.

[94] Vergil, *Aen.*, 10.768, "*talis se vastis infert Mezentius armis.*" For Lactantius's use of Vergil, see Jackson Bryce, *The Library of Lactantius.* Also, Alain Goulon, "Les Citations des Poètes latins dans L'oeuvre de Lactance," pp. 133–134. Goulon observes the way Lactantius uses texts to make a citation "*ad sensum*," but to preserve his rhetorical presentation.

[95] Lactantius, *Inst.*, 4.15.23.

[96] See Mamertinus, *Lat. Pan.*, X(2),11.1–3.

THE POWER OF THE SON   193

order to identify Christ as the historical manifestation of the Stoics' ideal figure. Earlier, at *Inst.* 3.27.6, Lactantius concluded his debate about the highest good with a not-so-subtle foreshadowing of the cross: "Therefore, the Sage [*sapiens*] is indeed blessed [*beatus*] even under torture: but that endurance [*illa patientia*] will make him perfectly blessed [*beatissimum*], only when he is tormented for the sake of faith [*pro fide*], for justice [*pro iustitia*], for God [*pro Deo*]."[97] At *Inst.* 4.15–16, Lactantius applies the same language to Christ's public suffering:

> I come now to the passion itself . . . so that I may show that this passion was undertaken with great and divine reason [*cum magna et ratione divina*] and that in it alone, *virtus* and truth [*veritas*], and wisdom [*sapientia*] are contained. Otherwise, even if the most blessed man [*beatissimus*] had lived on earth and ruled as king his whole life in supreme happiness [*in summa felicitate regnasset*], no wise person would ever have believed [*sapiens . . . credidisset*] either that he was God or judged him worthy of divine honor.[98]

Lactantius's repetition of key vocabulary at 4.15–16 reveals that the earlier discussion actually was a foreshadowing of Christ's passion. The terms *beatus/beatissimus* make Christ, in his passion, the historical subject of both passages. Hence also, the three prepositional phrases at *Inst.* 3.27.6—*pro fide, pro iustitia, pro deo*—foreshadow Lactantius's image of Christ as an ideal monarch "who rules his whole life in supreme happiness." Likewise, *felicitas* and *honor divinus* are attributes customarily attributed to emperors.[99] By setting those appellations in the context of Christ's passion, Lactantius rewrites the model of heroic kingship and philosophic virtue. In place of Rome's traditional image of conquering *virtus*, Lactantius presents Christ as the suffering monarch, who endures the world's evils in order to reveal that *patientia* is the true character of God. Quoting both Cyprian and Sallust, Lactantius thus makes the passion a demonstration of both *virtus* and justice:

> For indeed, among earthly things [*in rebus terrenis*], it is not possible for something to be venerable and worthy of heaven; but alone it is virtue [*virtus*], alone justice [*iustitia*], which can be judged a true, heavenly and perpetual good, because it is neither given to anyone nor taken away. Since Christ came to earth

[97] Lactantius, *Inst.*, 3.27.27, "*beatus est igitur sapiens in tormentis: sed cum torquetur pro fide, pro iustitia, pro deo, illa patientia doloris beatissimum faciet.*"

[98] Lactantius, *Inst.*, 4.16.2. For Lactantius's use of *honor* divinus, see William Van Andringa, "Rhetoric and Divine Honours: On the 'Imperial Cult' in the Reigns of Augustus and Constantine," *Collegium* 20 (2016): pp. 10–21. Cf. Mamertinus, *Lat. Pan.*, X(2), 3.1, "*sacratissime imperator, debeat honos vester divinis rebus aequari.*"

[99] See Chapters 1 and 4, this volume. Cf. Harod Mattingly, Edward Sydenham, and Percy Webb, *Roman Imperial Coinage*, vol. 1 and vol. 5B (London: Spink and Son, 1984).

194 ROMAN VIRTUE IN THE EARLY CHRISTIAN THOUGHT OF LACTANTIUS

equipped with this virtue and justice, or rather, because indeed *he himself is virtue and he is justice* [*De bono patientiae*, 7], he descended in order to teach it and to form humanity.[100]

Lactantius's emphasis upon the public and epistemic value of Christ's passion as a revelation of virtue arises from a tradition of Latin Christian reflection on the virtue *patientia*, which was theologically rooted in Tertullian's anti-Monarchian arguments. The phrase, "he himself is virtue and he is justice" is a citation from Cyprian's *De bono patientiae* 7. Earlier, Lactantius described Christ in terms taken from *De bono patientia* 5: "Even now [God] suffers [*patitur*] human beings to err and be impious against him [*adversum se*], while he himself is just and meek and patient [*iustus et mitis et patiens*]. For it can only be that in him, who is perfect *virtus*, there is also perfect *patientia*."[101] In so demonstrating *patientia* Christ displays his possession of the power of God. By this account, Lactantius inscribes a Christian narrative onto the traditional Stoic notion of the Sage, and thus redefines the Sage's *virtus*, not as mere self-mastery but as a forbearance of evils. Lactantius extends this exemplary logic to human beings generally. It is in keeping with Christ's role as "our leader in virtue" that human *virtus* proceed from Christ's example as an effect from its cause. Hence, at *Inst.* 4.19, Lactantius concludes by explaining that "[Christ] acquired life for us by overcoming death. Therefore, no other hope of immortality is given to a person unless he believes in him and takes up that cross, which must be carried and endured [*portandam patiendamque*]."[102] Notably, in leading humanity to immortality through *patientia*, Christ also brings humanity to its own highest good, as Lactantius had defined it. Again, Lactantius aims to characterize Christ as the one who has realized all philosophic ideals in himself.

Christus Orator Perfectus

Lactantius completes his exemplary narrative of Christ's mission and ministry by describing Christ as the one who reveals "a new and living law." After the story of Christ's ascension (*Inst.*, 21), two lengthy passages (*Inst.*, 22–24, 26–27) elaborate on this theme, which Lactantius frames in Mosaic terms: "God announced through that lawgiver [Moses] that he would send his own Son, that is, a living and present law [*vivam praesentemque legem*] . . . so that through him who

---

[100] Lactantius, *Inst.*, 4.16.3. See Cyprian, *Bon. pat.*, 7, Tertullian, *Pat.*, 3.10, Sallust, *Bel. Jug.*, 1.3.

[101] Lactantius, *Inst.*, 2.17.3. Cf. Cyprian, *Bon. pat.*, 5.

[102] Lactantius, *Inst.*, 4.19.11, "*Vitam enim nobis acquisit morte superata. Nulla igitur spes alia consequendae immortalitatis homini datur, nisi crediderit in eum et illam crucem portandam patiendamque susceperit.*"

THE POWER OF THE SON   195

was eternal, he might sanction an eternal law."[103] With this theme, Lactantius concludes his account of the Son's work on earth by framing Christ as the one true "perfect orator" of the Roman rhetorical tradition. Lactantius's portrait of Christ as the *perfectus orator* is a significant new contribution to third-century Latin Christian apologetic discourse; however, Lactantius develops his portrait by drawing upon perennial early Latin Christian themes.

Since Cicero's influential *Republic* and *Orator*, Roman rhetoricians had imagined an ideal orator as the supreme form of a political leader.[104] In the middle of the first century A.D., the famed school master Quintilian expressed this ideal in his manual for the training of elite Roman schoolboys. Quintilian describes an ideal figure: "We are here to instruct that perfect orator, who cannot exist unless he is a good man [*bonus vir*], and thus we demand not only a surpassing faculty [*facultas*] of speaking, but all the *virtutes* of the mind [*animi virtutes*]."[105] Quintilian goes on to makes his *orator perfectus* a divine figure and leader of the people. He describes "a man outstanding with the nature of a divinity [*cum ingenii natura*], as mentally endowed with all the most noble arts, as he is given over to human affairs, such as no antiquity ever knew, singular and perfect [*singularem et perfectum*] in every way, as ideal in thought as he is in speech."[106] Quintilian's insistence upon the correspondence between character, teaching, and action recalls Cicero's earlier vision of a divine figure, endowed with both philosophic wisdom and the *virtus* required to found and secure an ideal commonwealth.

Quintilian's description of an *"orator perfectus,"* who would need no instruction in the *"virtutis praecepta,"* supplies an obvious textual referent for Lactantius's description of Christ as "the new and living law" for humanity.[107] Lactantius uses the theme to address two major pagan objections to his account of Christ's person and work. Some deny that an immortal nature could subsist in a mortal one, Lactantius observes. These people claim that the Incarnation

---

[103] Lactantius, *Inst.*, 4.17.7 and 4.17.13, 21. See Francis Dvornik, *Early Christian and Byzantine Political Philosophy* (Washington, DC: Dumbarton Oaks, 1966), pp. 610ff. Dvornik connects this theme of Christ as *lex vivens* to older theories of Hellenistic Kingship. More recently, Julien Smith, *Christ the Ideal King: Culture, Context, Rhetorical Strategy, and the Power of Divine Monarchy in Ephesians* (Tuebingen: Mohr Siebeck, 2011), shows the influence of Hellenistic Kingship theory in the Epistle to the Ephesians.

[104] See Gary A. Remer, *Ethics and the Orator: The Ciceronian Tradition of Political Morality* (Chicago: University of Chicago Press, 2017). Also, Robert Dodaro, *Christ and the Just Society in the Thought of St. Augustine* (Cambridge: Cambridge University Press, 2008), pp. 19–24, for summary of Cicero's orator with a view to Lactantius and Augustine.

[105] Quintilian, *Inst. orat.*, 12.1.23 in Quintilian, *The Orator's Education*, vol. 1, *Books 1–2*, ed. and trans. Donald A. Russell, Loeb Classical Library 124 (Cambridge, MA: Harvard University Press, 2002). Quintilian proceeds to argue that this figure will be the best leader in war and peace and cites the famous simile at Vergil, *Aen.*, 1.151. Cf. *Inst. orat.*, 2.15.34, 2.16.11, 2.17.31.

[106] Quintilian, *Inst. orat.*, 12.1.25. Cf. Lactantius, *Inst.*, 4.23.9–10.

[107] Quintilian, *Inst. orat.*, 1.17. Cicero, *Rep.*, 5.5.

196 ROMAN VIRTUE IN THE EARLY CHRISTIAN THOUGHT OF LACTANTIUS

would be unworthy of God.[108] Second, some object that if Christ had been divine, he should have come openly in a public display of power consistent with classical Roman notions: "Everyone would have been ready to heed his heavenly precepts [*caelestibus praeceptis*], if the *virtus ac potestas* of the god prescribing them had approached these things."[109] Lactantius imagines his opponents posing the traditional objection of Roman *virtus*—if Christ is a god, let him prove it through *virtus*.[110] Lactantius promises to turn these two arguments on their head. With an echo of *Against Praxeas* 22–23, he claims that "never could he have been believed to be God, if these things which you dispute had not been done."[111]

Lactantius rebuts the two objections in a lengthy discussion that fuses elements of Tertullian's anti-Monarchian theology with tropes of the Roman rhetorical ideal. Tertullian had introduced a symmetry between Christ's works and words as public evidence of his divinity: "The Father, therefore, abiding in the Son through the works of [his] powers [*opera virtutum*] and the words of his teaching [*verba doctrinae*], is seen through those things, through which he abides," he argued.[112] Lactantius uses Tertullian's argument to frame Christ as the ideal orator. With an allusion to Cicero's definition of *virtus* at *De inventione* 2.157–159, Lactantius describes Christ as one "in whom the highest *virtus* and complete justice [*perfecta iustitia*] agree [*consenserit*] with the highest teaching and knowledge [*summa doctrinae et scientiae*]."[113] The claim adjusts Tertullian's pairing of *verba* and *opera* in order to trace a correspondence between *doctrina* and *virtus*. Lactantius then goes on to say that "Christ . . . passed on wisdom by his word and confirmed his doctrine by manifest *virtus* [*praesenti virtute*]. . . . For a teacher [*doctor*] sent from heaven must be perfect [*perfectus*] . . . [if he] is to instruct human life in the rudiments of *virtus* and form it for justice."[114] That work of providing public instruction in the foundations of virtue is the work of the ideal Roman orator. Lactantius replaces Tertullian's term *opera* with *virtus praesens* but does not alter its traditional logic, since evident *virtus* is seen only in an act [*opus*]. Much as *Pat.* 3 argued that the Jews should have known that Christ was God from the display of his *virtus*, *Inst.* 4.23–24 argues that the Romans should recognize that Christ is the true Sage and Perfect Orator because his words and

[108] Lactantius, *Inst.*, 4.22.1–2.
[109] Lactantius, *Inst.*, 4.22.3.
[110] Lactantius, *Inst.*, 4.22.5.
[111] Lactantius, *Inst.*, 4.22.6.
[112] Tertullian, *Prax.*, 22–23.
[113] Lactantius, *Inst.*, 4.23.9–10. Cicero, *Inv.*, 2.159: "*Nam virtus est animi habitus naturae modo atque rationi consentaneus.*" Loi, *Lattanzio*, pp. 262–264, regards Lactantius as making a moral argument. The conclusion is not wrong, but misses the point that any moral argument is grounded in a prior argument about power and activity.
[114] Lactantius, *Inst.*, 4.23.9–10.

THE POWER OF THE SON   197

deeds correspond perfectly.[115] Christ proves his teaching through actions that manifest its power, just as the power of his actions confirms his divinity.

Lactantius uses the portrait of Christ as an exemplary leader to articulate the public and political dimension of Christ's saving work. For Lactantius, Christ's public role addresses the fundamental obstacle to human *virtus*, namely, "this body of death (Rom. 7:24)." As seen earlier (*Inst.*, 3.7–12), Lactantius understands the body as the seat of the vices, as an impediment to man's knowledge of the highest truth and attainment of immortality through *virtus*.[116] In this respect, Lactantius locates the human body at the root of man's failed state. *Inst.* 4 opens, in fact, by describing the public and corporate vulnerabilities that result from embodiment. In lines built upon Paul's account of the fall in Romans 1:27–32, Lactantius laments that "the former status of the human race" has been lost, such that "the definition of humanity [*ratio humanitatis*]" has been forgotten, and so the happiness of humanity has been "changed [*mutata est*]," in the worship of "corrupted and breakable gods."[117] He goes on to explain that the perversity of embodied creatures seeking only the goods of their bodies created the idolatry and death that comes, as a result, upon all of humanity:

> What this perversity caused, what evils it produced, the thing itself declares. They were turned away from the Highest Good—which is blessed and ever-lasting [*ideo beatum ac sempiternum*], because it cannot be seen, touched, comprehended [*videri tangi comprehendi*], and from the virtues congruent with it, which are equally immortal. Fallen into those corrupted and breakable [Rom. 1:25] gods and desiring those things by which the body alone is adorned, sustained, delighted, people sought for themselves endless death with bodily gods and goods; for every body is subject to death [Rom. 7:24]. Injustice and impiety followed religions of this sort, as was bound to happen . . . for once they had scorned the eternal and incorruptible goods [Rom. 1:23–25], which humanity should alone desire, [people] preferred temporal and passing

---

[115] Cf. Tertullian, *Pat.*, 3.5–10. See Chapter 3, this volume.

[116] Lactantius, *Inst.*, 4.24.2–3. Lactantius locates the *materia* of the vices *in visceribus*: "*nam in homine interna et propria doctrina esse nullo pacto potest; nec enim mens terrenis visceribus inclusa et tabe corporis impedita aut comprehendere per se potest aut capere veritate, nisi aliunde doceatur. Et si maxime posit, summam tamen virtutem capere nequeat et omnibus vitiis resistere, quorum materia in visceribus continetur. eo fit, ut terrenus doctor perfetus esse non possit.*" At other places, this opposition is stated even more strongly: "[*Inst.*, 7.24.12] *quoniam homo ex rebus diuersis ac repugnantibus configuratus est, anima et corpore, id est caelo atque terra, tenui et conprehensibili, aeterno ac temporali, sensibili atque bruto, luce praedito atque tenebroso, ipsa ratio ac necessitas exigebat et bona homini proponi et mala, bona, quibus utatur, mala, quae uitet et caueat.*"

[117] Lactantius, *Inst.*, 4.1–3. *VLD* Rom. 1:23: "*et mutaverunt gloriam incorruptibilis dei in similitudinem imaginis corruptibilis hominis et volucrum et quadripedum et serpentium.*"

198 ROMAN VIRTUE IN THE EARLY CHRISTIAN THOUGHT OF LACTANTIUS

things.... Thus shadow and darkness comprehended human life, which once in former times was lived in the brightest light [John 1:4–5].[118]

Interwoven with allusions to Johannine literature, these lines provide a negative image of Lactantius's Christology. He frames the problem of sin as a corporate and political problem that arises from humanity's descent into the needs and vices of the mortal body. Human beings lost sight of their own immortality because the highest good could not be "seen, touched, comprehended," and their ignorance led to the strife and violence that arise from seeking to protect bodies that are always "subject to death." Because the body causes humanity's need for *virtus*, it is therefore the precondition of any virtuous action.

In Lactantius's thinking, the body's relationship both to sin and virtue explains why Christ had to become incarnate and how his passion amounts to the highest evidence that he is the figure that all of Roman history and tradition had sought. "The heavenly teacher," Lactantius says, "upon whom divinity bestows knowledge and immortality [bestows] *virtus* is necessarily perfect and complete [*perfectus et consummatus*]."[119] Such a teacher, however, can be perfect only if he can suffer because *virtus*, by definition, "is to patiently [*patienter*] endure pain for the sake of justice and duty ... not to fear death itself ... and to forbear an injury bravely."[120] Since *virtus* is agonistic, the one who would perfectly teach perfect *virtus* must participate in the combat: "Unless he is mortal, he cannot in any way provide an *exemplum* for humanity."[121] If *virtus*, by definition, struggles against moral and physical opponents that overcome embodied beings, Christ could save humanity from their sins only by taking on a body.

Lactantius is not for this reason working with a simplistic "dualismo antropologico," blaming the body for humanity's problems. He is, rather, using a fundamental early Christian theme as the basis of an apologetic and political theology. As Lactantius explains Christ's saving work, his discussions of the Incarnation at *Inst.* 4.24.9–11 and 13–16 imitate the dramatic *speech-in-character* of Rom. 7:1–14.[122] In these passages, Lactantius makes it clear that it

---

[118] *Inst.*, 4.3–5. Cf. Minucius Felix, *Octavius*, 17. Lactantius's bicolon echoes Minucius Felix.

[119] Lactantius, *Inst.*, 4.24.7.

[120] Lactantius, *Inst.*, 4.24.7–8.

[121] Lactantius, *Inst.*, 4.24.13, "*sin vero sit immortalis, exemplum proponere homini nullo modo potest.*" I am actually limiting the discussion here. Lactantius introduces a further premise to this argument, which is the necessity that the Teacher leave humanity its freedom and thus also preserve God's justice in judgment on the disobedient.

[122] Heck and Wlosok do not acknowledge Romans 7:1–14 at this point, but the *Biblia Patristica* does. I agree with the *Biblia Patristica* on logical and linguistic grounds. Lactantius's logic of sin in *Inst.* 4.2–3 is an oratorical restatement of Rom. 1:18–24 and Wis. 13–15. His construction is rhetorical imitation of the speech. For Rom. 7:1–14 as *speech-in-character*, see Robert Jewitt, *Romans: A Commentary* (Minneapolis: Fortress Press, 2007), p. 455. See also Stanley K. Stowers, *A Rereading of Romans: Justice, Jews, and Gentiles* (New Haven, CT: Yale University Press, 1994).

THE POWER OF THE SON   199

is not the mere fact of the body, but rather the fear of death which embodiment makes possible, that renders the body an impediment to virtue. The person subject to passion and death objects to the Immortal Teacher: "Indeed I want not to sin [*volo non peccare*], but I am overcome [*sed vincor*]; I am clothed indeed in this fragile and weak flesh. It is that [flesh] which lusts, which is angered, which suffers pain, which fears to die."[123] The phrase '*mori timet*,' emphasizes that fear of death is the catalyst of sin. It is not the body qua material, but rather as the precondition for fear of death, which makes the body an impediment to virtue. Lactantius emphasizes this at length:

> Someone will object: "You do not sin, because you are free from this body; you do not lust, because an immortal has no need. But I have need of these things in order to sustain this life. You don't fear death because it has no power over you. But I am mortal and I fear, because tortures [*cruciatus*] hurt me terribly and the weakness of the flesh cannot bear them."[124]

Lactantius thus marks fear of death as the psychological cause motivating bodily vices.[125] By his reasoning, the body's subjection to mortality creates *fear*, and fear incites sin and vice. That fear, moreover, is determined by right or wrong knowledge: humanity's fear of death arises from false worship, which obscures the knowledge of the true God and of immortality. Hence, Lactantius locates the vices in the body, but with qualification: it is the body's mortality that inspires the fear of death, which fear leads to a struggle for survival that only embodied beings can experience.

This relationship between the body, fear, and death explains how Lactantius conceives of the operation of Christ's role as *doctor virtutis* soteriologically. By suffering, dying, and rising, the Teacher provides a model that defeats humanity's fear of death by restoring to human beings their knowledge of their own immortal nature. In Pauline language, Christ addresses the terrified:

---

[123] Lactantius, *Inst.*, 4.24.9, "*volo equidem non peccare, sed vincor; indutus sum enim carne fagili et imbecilla. Haec est quae concupiscit, quae irascitur, quae dolere, quae mori timet.*"

[124] Lactantius, *Inst.*, 4.24.13–14, "*aliqus ac dicet: tu quidem non peccas, quia liber es ab hoc corpore, non conupiscis, quia immortali nihil est necessarium. Mihi vero multis rebus opus est ut tuear hanc vitam. Mortem non times, quia valere in te non potest, utrume que timeo, quia cruciatus mihi gravissimos inferunt, quos tolerare carnis infirmitas non potest.*"

[125] McGuckin, *Researches into the Divine Institutes of Lactantius*, pp. 462–463, points to Hebrews 2:9 and 2:14–15 as the source of Lactantius's theology of *fear of death*. He notes, furthermore, that this is the same text from which Lactantius draws his theology of Christ's "priesthood and mediatorship" (*Inst.*, 4.25.4). McGuckin also observes that Lactantius's work is not entirely absent of sacrifical language: "[He] speaks of Christ's death in sacrificial terms of the scriptural tradition." E.g., *Inst.*, 4.26.39, "*agnus enim candidus sine macula Christus fuit, id est innocens et iustus et sanctus.*" Also *Inst.*, 4.18.2, "*interfeci pro salute multorum.*" Contra Digeser, *Making of a Christian Empire*, pp. 73–75, which pushes Lactantius to the margins of Christian tradition by contrasting his vision of Christ as a teacher with the sacrificial language of other early Christian writers.

200   ROMAN VIRTUE IN THE EARLY CHRISTIAN THOUGHT OF LACTANTIUS

> But I bear this flesh, and nevertheless sin is not lord over me [*dominator*, Rom. 6:12] . . . Look, I too have a body, and still I fight against all lust . . . Look, pain and death have power over me [*in me . . . potestatem*], and these things which you fear, I overcome [*ea ipsa quae times vinco*], that I may make you victor over pain and death [*ut victorem te faciam doloris ac mortis*]. I go [*vado*] first through these things you claim cannot be endured; if you cannot follow the one teaching you, follow him who goes before you.[126]

Tertullian's perennial claim that Christ teaches "by the words of his doctrine and the works of his powers" again is manifest in the final line of the above quotation, as Lactantius presents a Christ that saves not only by "teaching you," but by "going before you." This dialogue between the sinner and the Teacher explains why Lactantius frames soteriology as an intellectual affair, although "intellectual" does not approach the powerful cooperation of teaching and imitation that Lactantius's exemplary notion entails. Insofar as sin arises not just from the body, but from the fear of death that a body brings, Christ's mortal body subjects him to death in the same way that humans are subject. That fact makes the *exemplar Christi* an effective response to the problem of sin. Lactantius summarizes the whole point in the chapter's final nod to power causality:

> He then who is the *vitae dux et iustitiae magister*, must be corporeal . . . so that his teaching may be full and perfect [*illius plena et perfecta doctrina*] and . . . likewise, he must endure the weakness of the flesh and body and receive in himself that *virtus* of which he is the Teacher so that he may teach it in both word and deed [*ut eam simul et verbis doceat et factis*]. Finally, he must be subject to death and all passions [*subiectum esse morti et passionibus cunctis*], since the works of *virtus* consist [*officia virtutis versantur*] in enduring passion and undergoing death.[127]

This statement leads directly to Lactantius's account of the Incarnation on the basis of Hebrews (*Inst.*, 4.25), noted above. Christ's humanity enables him to reveal *virtus* and make its true form communicable to the mortal human. In that respect, Lactantius understands the Incarnation as a precondition of Christ's work as the *orator perfectus*.

---

[126] Lactantius, *Inst.*, 4.24.17.

[127] Lactantius, *Inst.*, 4.24.19. Cf. Cicero, *Inv.*, 1.6–7, where Cicero uses *officium* in the context of his power causality. Bowen and Garnsey, *Institutes*, p. 268, translate: "since it is in the endurance of suffering and in enduring death that the requirements of virtue are excercised." Within this larger section, Lactantius emphasizes the element of divine judgment that this soteriology involves. Part of the purpose is to render humanity subject to obedience (*Inst.*, 4.24.18). Lactantius sees God limiting the divine power in order to preserve human freedom and thus also divine justice.

THE POWER OF THE SON   201

Lactantius predicates the various tropes of his Christology—Sage, King, *Orator Perfectus*—upon the Christological insights of third-century Latin Christianity. His reliance upon earlier Latin Christian writers becomes again evident in his exegesis of the passion and miracles of Jesus. Pierre Monat called Lactantius's reading a "spiritual" or "figurative" interpretation and found precedent for it in Origen.[128] Tertullian, however, is a more likely predecessor because Lactantius's reading of Christ's miracles apply Tertullian's Christological arguments. Lactantius begins by asserting that "the *ratio* of the cross must be explained [*ratio crucis reddenda*] and its power articulated [*vis ennarranda*]."[129] The remark explains, in principle, what Lactantius aims to do—identify the character of the power at work in Christ's actions in order to justify the Christian assertion of Christ's divinity on the basis of that power. Lactantius thus proceeds to use Tertullian's language in his exegesis: "[Christ's] sufferings were not empty [*inania*], because they had a great figure and meaning [*significationem*], just as those divine works which he did [*divina illa opera*]. Their power and potency [*vis et potentia*] availed even in the present, but declared things yet to come."[130] The terms *vis*, *significatio*, and *opera* advance the traditional Latin Christian argument that Christ's activity, especially in his suffering, reveals the form and character of the divine nature. Like Tertullian, Lactantius makes Christ's passion the greatest among many *opera* that disclose his divinity.[131] As he reviews the ministry of Jesus, he punctuates each miracle with an explanation of the power revealed in it:

> He opened the lights [*lumina*] of the blind: This is the heavenly *virtus* [*caelistis virtus*] that he returned light [*lucem*] to those not seeing. And in fact, in this action [*hoc facto*] he was signifying what would happen: that turning to the nations who did not formerly know God, he would illuminate the hearts of the unwise with the light of wisdom and *"open the eyes of their heart"* [Eph. 1:18], in order to contemplate the truth. . . . He laid open the ears of the deaf: Never before had this heavenly power [*vis illa caelestis*] been exercised [*operata est*]. It was declaring that those who knew nothing of the truth would hear and understand the divine words of God. . . . He returned the tongues of the mute

---

[128] Monat, *Lactance et la Bible*, pp. 229–238: "Si, aux yeux de Justin et surtout de Tertullien, l'Ancien Testament dans ses divers épisodes désigne le Christ d'une manière cachée, voici que, pour Lactance, les événements racontés par le Nouveau Testament prennent en même temps valeur figurative: ils ne sont plus seulement réalisation des prophéties, mais deviennent *signes* du salut en Jésus Christ. A l'instar d'Origène, mais sans s'inspirer directement de lui, Lactance invite ses lecteurs à une *anagôgè*, interprétation spirituelle des événements de la vie du Christ."

[129] Lactantius, *Inst.*, 4.26.1.

[130] Lactantius, *Inst.*, 4.26.3.

[131] E.g., Tertullian, *Pat.*, 3.14, "*Haec patientiae ratio, haec disciplina, haec opera, caelestis et verae scilicet.*"

202   ROMAN VIRTUE IN THE EARLY CHRISTIAN THOUGHT OF LACTANTIUS

to eloquence: Amazing even as it was powerful [*potentia*]. Still, there was another meaning [*significatio*] in this power [*huic virtute*], which was showing what would happen: that those recently ignorant of heavenly things, when the doctrine of divine wisdom had been acquired, would speak of God and of the Truth. For he who does not know the definition of divinity [*rationem divinitatis*] is dumb and mute, even if he is the most eloquent of all."[132]

Whatever the value of describing Lactantius's exegesis as spiritual, the underlying grammar of Lactantius's argument is certain from the causal language he uses. His reading is a straightforward application of Tertullian's claim that the divine power of God "abides in the Son through the words of his teaching and the works of his powers."[133] Lactantius punctuates each miracle with an exclamation that identifies the specific power at work in Christ's action. On the basis of that power, Lactantius identifies Christ and his works as the very definition of what a god is (*ratio divinitatis*). More than just identify the fact of divine *virtus*, Lactantius's exegesis develops the meaning of each action in terms of the broader biblical narrative, and especially in terms of Paul's mission to the Gentiles. As Monat observed, Lactantius's reference to the "*eyes of their heart,*" alludes to *VL* Eph. 1:18.[134] Even more significantly for what is to come, Lactantius reads these *opera* not only as a demonstration of Christ's divinity, but as a model of the kind of speech and action divinity performs. The power of the Father, the *dator vitae*, is shown in the actions of the Son, who saves and heals his people, while refashioning the Roman vision of exemplary virtue, permanently. Lactantius's reading of Christ's miracles comes to a crescendo in his explanation of the cross itself. His explanation connects the power and meaning (*vis, significatio, ratio*) of the cross to Christ's mission as the new and living law (*lex nova et vivens*). The cross becomes, for Lactantius, the highest demonstration of that divine activity, which reveals God's character:

> When God decided to set humanity free, he sent a Teacher of *virtus* as his ambassador [*legavit*], who would form humanity in saving precepts [*praeceptis salutaribus*] unto innocence and open the way of justice by his outstanding

---

[132] Lactantius, *Inst.*, 4.26.4–8. Cf. *Inst.*, 4.26.8–26 continues at length. Notably, *Inst.* 4.26.19–22 says the bitterness of the passion shows what *virtus ipsa* is and provides its *specimen* and *exemplum*. This kind of exegesis becomes a tradition in Latin theology. See Andrew Harmon, *Image and Virtue in Ambrose of Milan* (Unpublished dissertation, Marquette University, 2017), p. 89, "For Ambrose, the Son's *opera* . . . point beyond themselves to their ultimate invisible realities. Since the works themselves demand further interpretation, they constitute something of a divine pedagogy, which serves to train audiences to see something beyond the seen works themselves." See also Wlosok, *Laktanz und die philosophische Gnosis*, pp. 256–257 on Lactantius's "*Erleuchtungsaussagungen.*"

[133] Tertullian, *Prax.*, 22–23.

[134] Monat, *Lactance et la Bible*, p. 229–238.

THE POWER OF THE SON   203

works and deeds [*praestantibus operibus factisque*]. By walking in them, a person following his own Teacher would come to life eternal. He then was incarnated and clothed in a garment of flesh . . . that he might offer *virtutis exempla* and enticements to humanity. But when, in all these actions of life he had provided a model [*specimen*] of justice, that he might transmit to humanity contempt of pain and endurance of death [*mortis patientiam*]—for *virtus* is made perfect and consummate in them—he came into the hand of an impious nation . . . Thus, he endured torments and beating and thorns. Afterward, he did not refuse even death, so that humanity, compelled by that leader [*illo duce*], might triumph over death with its chain of terrors.[135]

Lactantius's term *specimen* fixes the image of Christ's *patientia* as the final and definitive model of virtue for the Christian era. As noted earlier, commentators have usually regarded this account of Christ's saving work as idiosyncratic by contrasting it with the idea of sacrifice and substitutionary atonement.[136] Lactantius's language, however, makes it evident that his account of Christ relies specifically upon the early Latin Christian defense of Christ's real divinity, which was first articulated by Tertullian and then applied broadly in the third century to articulate the meaning of Christ's works and to uphold Christ as an account of the true character of God and of the Christian life in imitation of God in Christ. What explains Lactantius's theology, then, is not any attempt to unite Hermetic theory with Christian *praxis*.[137] Rather, the *Divine Institutes* articulate Christ in terms of his *virtus* and *opera* because Lactantius aims to demonstrate, among the pagans, the very claims Tertullian argued, theologically, against the Monarchians. Both authors were engaged in controversy about the true nature of Jesus's life as a public demonstration of his divinity. Lactantius emphasized the political and moral implications of that Christian claim at even greater length, but the fundamental insight that Christ's passion reveals the true character of divine power is first recorded in Tertullian's influential meditation *De patientia*. Lactantius derives his account of ideal justice from the Latin Christian tradition Tertullian set in motion.

---

[135] Lactantius, *Inst.*, 4.26.24–28.

[136] Loi, *Lattanzio*, p. 270, "La redenzione operata dal Cristo è presentata anche quale liberazione dal peccato; ma questo liberazione non è concepita come une remisione o un riscatto del peccato attraverso il sacrificio della Croce, bensì come una purificazione attraverso l'insegnamento della *iustitia* e della *virtus*, e attraverso lésempio del Cristo. . . . L'argomentazione prende l'avvio dalla constatatazione del dualismo antropologico, per cui la *caro* è la fonte prima è la sede del peccato, in contrapposizione allo *spiritus* che tende alla immortalità beata."

[137] Aloys Grillmeier, *Christ in the Christian Tradition*, p. 191: "With a *tour de force*, Lactantius sought to create a link between Christian reality and Hermetic theory: the Hermetic doctrine of revelation is declared to be a 'prophecy' of Christianity."

Conclusion

The preceding review of Lactantius's Christology justifies a new set of starting points for scholarly analysis of his thought. Lactantius's theology is fundamentally traditional when compared with other influential Latin Christian writers. The grammar of his thought and argument is most profoundly shaped by Tertullian's *Against Praxeas* and the treatises of both Tertullian and Cyprian on the virtue of *patientia*. His exegesis is guided by the judgments evident in Cyprian's testimonies *Ad Quirinum*. Most of Lactantius's seemingly peculiar decisions, especially his juxtaposition of Christ and the angels and his omission of explicit references to Phil. 2:5–11, can be explained by his reliance on the theological arrangement of Cyprian in combination with his own apologetic purposes. He also shows awareness of weaknesses in Tertullian's account of the Son's real existence, which may explain his choice to express the Son's real existence in terms that evoke arguments traceable to Origen; his explanation of Christ's dual natures echoes language found also in Novatian. Lactantius uses all the traditional metaphors of early Latin trinitarian theology, and he consciously makes a point to locate himself on the landscape of third-century doctrinal controversies by rejecting heretical movements and identifying his teaching with the "Catholic Church," in a statement that echoes Cyprian's *De unitate*.[138] Ultimately, his thought belongs to the early Latin tradition of "one power, one nature" arguments, and his distinctive apologetic framing of that theology is extrapolated from the traditional Latin concern to explain the "sight of the Father" in the Son and before the world.

Lactantius's account of the Son is traditional but not merely repetitive. He develops distinctive applications of the argument from Christ's power and works that confront Rome's ideal figures with the specific image of Christ. In that respect, Lactantius extends the Latin apologetic tradition and its criticism of Roman exemplary virtue by deriving a new account of *virtus* from Christ's new and better exemplar. Lactantius redescribes ideal kingship in terms of Christ's healing ministry, transforms the Sage's wisdom in Christ's endurance of sin and suffering, and realizes Quintilian's *orator perfectus* in the image of Christ as *doctor virtutis* and *magister iustitiae*. Lactantius develops that image theologically out of Paul's epistle to the Romans when he presents sin as caused by fear of death, which comes as the consequence of humanity's collective ignorance of eternal life—an ignorance brought about by idolatry. Rooted in the text of Romans 1:26–32 and John 1:1–5, such a diagnosis is the key premise that explains Lactantius's soteriology. Christ's word and example reveal the truth of a new law and living law, which draws all of humanity into God's saving work.

---

[138] Lactantius, *Inst.*, 4.30. Cf. Cyprian, *Unit.*, 5.

THE POWER OF THE SON 205

Lactantius's soteriological notion of Christ as teacher expresses the symmetry of Christ's "words and deeds," which Tertullian had made so central to his Christology and Cyprian took up as the organizing axiom of his Christology, ecclesiology, and moral thought. Lactantius develops that tradition to present Christ's person and work as a new point of departure for Roman reflection on the foundations of Roman life.

6

Virtus Revealed in Christ

This is the definition [*ratio*], this the training [*disciplina*], these are the works [*opera*] of true and heavenly patience.

—Tertullian, *On Patience*, 16

When God decided to set humanity free, he sent a Teacher of *virtus* as his ambassador [*legavit*], who would form humanity in saving precepts [*praeceptis salutaribus*] unto innocence and open the way of justice by his outstanding works and deeds [*praestantibus operibus factisque*].

—Lactantius, *Inst.*, 4.16

Many have noted that Lactantius's *Divine Institutes* can be divided into two parts. The first critiques classical Roman religion and philosophy (*Institutiones* 1–3), while the second offers an apologetic exposition of Christian doctrine, which begins with Christology (*Institutiones* 4–7) and culminates in Lactantius's vision of eternal life (*Institutio* 7: *De vita beata*).[1] Scholars have traditionally found these parts uneven.[2] They often regarded Lactantius's grasp of philosophy as eclectic and his Christology lacking in substance and precision, but saw his defense of religious conscience, his critique of imperialist warfare and violence, and his traditional concern for the poor as forward-thinking contributions.[3] Such

[1] See Oliver Nicholson, "Lactantius: A Man of His Own Time?" *Studia Patristica* 127.24 (2021): p. 169.

[2] Anthony Bowen and Peter Garnsey, "Introduction," in *Lactantius: The Divine Institutes*, ed. Anthony Bowen and Peter Garnsey (Liverpool: Liverpool University Press, 2003), p. 35; Earlier, Pierre de Labriolle, *The History and Literature of Christianity: Tertullian to Boethius*, trans. Herbert Wilson (New York: Barnes and Noble, 1968), p. 208. For de Labriolle, Lactantius was a man of mainly unreconciled tendencies. "As a theologian, he does not count." And yet, "What is perhaps the most novel trait in Lactantius is the really profound sense which he possesses of the moral efficaciousness and of the renovation which [Christianity] has brought to the soul of mankind." Also, Aloys Grillmeier, *Christ in the Christian Tradition*, vol. 1, *From the Apostolic Age to Chalcedon (451)*, 2nd ed. (Oxford: Mowbrays, 1976), pp. 190–206.

[3] Tom Hughson, "Social Justice in Lactantius' Divine Institutes: An Exploration," in *Reading Patristic Texts on Social Ethics: Issues and Challenges for Twenty-First Century Christian Social Thought*, ed. Johan Leemans, Brian J. Matz, and Johan Verstraeten Reading (Washington, DC: Catholic University of America, 2011), pp. 185–205. Robert Louis Wilken, *Liberty in the Things of God: The Christian Origins of Religious Freedom* (New Haven, CT: Yale University Press, 2019), pp. 7–24. Elizabeth DePalma Digeser, *The Making of a Christian Empire: Lactantius and Rome* (Ithaca, NY: Cornell University Press, 2000), pp. 111–114.

Roman Virtue in the Early Christian Thought of Lactantius. Jason M. Gehrke, Oxford University Press.
© Oxford University Press 2025. DOI: 10.1093/9780197667781.003.0007

VIRTUS REVEALED IN CHRIST   207

uneven praise made Lactantius something of an enigma, insofar as it required him to be doctrinally simple and confused but morally clear and sophisticated.[4] Lactantius himself constantly asserts that his moral theology relies directly upon his right understanding of the Divine Nature. For Lactantius, moral wisdom literally descends from its heavenly source, the God revealed in Christ. As an expression of that principle, *Institutiones* 5–6 offer a Christian account of justice and human society derived from Christ's *exemplar virtutis* characterized in *Institutio* 4.

Lactantius prosecutes his moral argument in these two books. *Institutio* 5 (*De iustitia*) and *Institutio* 6 (*De vera cultu*) address first the theory, and second the practice, of justice. This progression reflects the early Latin Christology that organizes Lactantius's argument.[5] When he says that Christ is believed to be God "because of this virtue and justice [*virtute ac iustitia*] by which he both taught and formed mankind... which he both taught and did [*docuit et fecit*]," he echoes the Latin theme of the "sight of the Father in the works of the Son," which originated in Tertullian's anti-Monarchian arguments and shapes all of Cyprian's theology.[6] The discussion that unfolds across *Institutiones* 5–6 reflects the parallelism of Tertullian's axiom. *Institutio* 4 presents Christ as a new *exemplum virtutis*, whose combined words and deeds provide a new and better account of divine power and virtue. Lactantius's narrative often designates Christ as the *praeceptor*, who "gives precepts [*praecepta dat*]" for living.[7] And Lactantius promises that he will "educate mortality in the precepts of justice [*praeceptis iustitiae*]. . . . Since there was no justice on earth, he sent a doctor of justice as a new and living law."[8] The following books attempt to make good on that promise. *Institutio* 5 extrapolates a theory of justice from Christ's public works and ministry, and from the vision of God's inner life that ministry reveals. *Institutio* 6 moves to the parallel element

---

[4] Although recent reappraisals have viewed Lactantius better, they focus mainly on his apologetic and narrative coherence. See Oliver Nicholson, "Lactantius: A Man of His Own Time?" p. 169. Also, Benjamin Hansen, "Preaching to Seneca: Christ as Stoic *Sapiens* in *Divinae Institutiones* IV," *Harvard Theological Review* 111.4 (2018): pp. 541–558, who traces very significant coherence in Lactantius's Christology, even while thinking little of Lactantius as a doctrinal theologian or reader of the Bible (e.g., Hansen, "Preaching to Seneca," p. 544).

[5] For rhetorical analysis of the thematic unity of *Institutiones* 4–7, see Blandine Colot, *Lactance: Penser la conversion de Rome au temps de Constantin* (Firenze: Leo S. Olschki, 2016), pp. 82–87, 107–111.

[6] See Lactantius, *Inst.*, 4.14.18, "*haec sunt duae viae dei in quibus eum ambulare praecepti, haec praecepta quae servanda mandavit.*" For Tertullian and Cyprian, see Chapter 3, this volume.

[7] See Lactantius, *Inst.*, 4.14.16, "*quae fuerint viae dei et quae praecepta eius, nec ambiguum nec obscurum est.*" Also, *Inst.*, 4.26.25, "*magistrum vertutis legavit in terram, qui et praeceptis salutaribus formaret homines ad innocentiam et operibus factisque praesentibus iustitiae viam panderet, qua gradiens homo et doctorem suum sequens ad vitam aeternam perveniret.*" *Inst.*, 4.23.1, "*praecepta dat* ... [23.2] ... *Si enim bona sunt quae praecipiuntur ... ipse praeceptis suis fidem detrahat levioremque doctrinam suam faciat [etc.]*"

[8] Lactantius, *Inst.*, 4.25.1–2, "*Deus summus [eum] mitteret ad erundiendam praeceptis iustitiae mortalitatem ... Nam cum iustitia nulla esset in terra, doctorem misit quasi novam legem vivam.*"

in the Latin Christological formula—"the words of his teaching"—as Lactantius represents his own practical ethics as an expression of Christ's teaching in the Gospels.

My exploration of Lactantius's thinking on justice traces the arc of his argument from theory to practice. Hence, this chapter explores the theoretical arguments of *Institutio* 5. In a wide-ranging critique of Cicero, Lactantius extrapolates a theory of justice from Christ's public example, and from a vision of God's inner life. Lactantius's theory can be distilled into four fundamental principles: (1) What is truly wise and good appears humble and foolish. (2) Virtue is not its own end but rather a power to achieve the true end, which is eternal life. (3) Justice is the *virtus* that causes persons to have the same nature and therefore equal status before God. (4) The activity of true justice—and the other virtues—is expressed in the activities of *pietas* and *aequitas* (*iustitia* = *pietas* + *aequitas*). *Pietas* refers to right worship of the true God; *aequitas* names the activity of loving other human beings because every person is a living "image and likeness of God [*simulacrum Dei*]."[9] As will be seen, *pietas* and *aequitas* formulate the example of Christ's own life into a theory of justice that provides the basis for Lactantius's critique of Cicero and Lucretius. Lactantius thus develops his foundational moral equation from the language and logic of Latin trinitarian theology and from the revelation of God's inner life revealed in Christ's life and ministry.

Wisdom and Foolishness in Lactantius

Lactantius grounded his moral theology in an epistemic principle that was already a central theme of his Christology. I will call this principle his "Pauline Rule." For Lactantius, true wisdom looks foolish; true virtue seems like weakness; true beauty is unattractive. As he puts it, "Justice has by its own nature a certain appearance of foolishness [*speciem stultitiae*]."[10] To support the point, he calls on Paul's teaching at 1 Cor. 3:19 and the words of Jesus. Paul says, "Just as human wisdom is the highest foolishness with God, so also the one who is conspicuous and exalted [*sublimis*] on earth will be humble and laid low [*abjectus*] before God."[11] Lactantius also cites the words of Jesus: "The one who exalts himself shall be humbled; he who humbles himself shall be exalted."[12] Allusions to

---

[9] Lactantius, *Inst.*, 6.12. For discussion of the *imago Dei* in Lactantius, see Chapter 7, this volume.

[10] See Chapter 3, this volume. For *species*, see Sen., *Ep.*, 66; Tert., *Pat.*, 3; Cyprian, *Bon. pat.*, 7, 20.

[11] Lactantius, *Inst.*, 5.15.8. Pierre Monat, *Lactance et la Bible: Une propédeutique latine à la lecture de la Bible dans l'Occident constantinien* (Paris: Études Augustiniennes, 1982), pp. 248–249, which takes these allusions as references to Cyprian, *Quir.*, 3.69 and *Bon. pat.*, 2.

[12] Lactantius, *Inst.*, 5.15.9.

both passages appear at the heart of his moral argument. For Lactantius, as for St. Paul and Jesus, the appearance of power and strength, which leads to earthly fame, contradicts the reality of true virtue, which is found in humility and suffering. This rule inverts the traditional Roman notion that divine *virtus* is seen in victory, whether through pleasing rhetoric or the public spectacle of power.[13] It also explains why moral philosophy, unaided by revelation, could never arrive at correct moral knowledge. The Divine Wisdom does not respect humanity's way of thinking.

Lactantius's assertion of his Pauline Rule at *Inst.* 5.15 is an initial indicator of the coherence of his theological vision grounded in Christology. The statement at 5.15 falls on a trajectory whose development begins in the opening lines of the *Divine Institutes* and culminates in Lactantius's moral argument. Lactantius consistently pairs criticism of humanity's moral ignorance with allusions to Christ in order to foreshadow the coming exposition of Christian revelation in the later books. Hence, *Institutes* 1.1–7 opens the entire work by making just this point: human beings have lacked moral knowledge. Lactantius's remarks are heavily laden with allusions to biblical prophecy of the Messiah:

> Because it was impossible for divine reason to become known to humanity on its own, God did not suffer [*non est passus*] humanity seeking the light of wisdom [*lumen sapientiae*] to wander so long [*diutius errare*] through inextricable darkness [*per tenebras inextricabiles*], lost without any result from his labor [*sine ullo laboris effectu vagari*], but rather God opened his eyes and made knowledge of the truth his own reward, in order to show [*monstraret*] that human wisdom is nothing and demonstrate [*ostenderet*] to one wandering and lost the way of pursuing immortality [*viam consequendae immortalitatis*].[14]

---

[13] See Chapter 2, this volume.

[14] Lactantius, *Inst.*, 1.1.6. Lactantius adapts here a Cyprianic exegesis. All of his terms can be found in citations of Isaiah and John. Cyprian, *Quir.*, 1.7.1, under the heading, "*Item quod essent amissuri lumen domini*," pairs Isaiah and John: "[Is. 2:3–5] *Apud esaiam: 'venite, ambulemus in lumine domini . . . Item in evangelio* [Jn. 1:9–10]: *'fuit lumen verum, quod inluminat omnem hominem veniens in hunc mundum. In hoc mundo fuit, et mundus per ipsum factus est, et mundus eum non agnovit.*" Later, under the heading, "[*Quir.*, 1.21.44–45] *Quod gentes magis in christum crediturae essent*," Cyprian pairs Is. 11:10 (also cited in Matt. 2:23) with Is. 9:1–2: "[Is. 11:10] *Et erit in illa die radix iesse, qui surget imperare omnibus gentibus: in illum gentes sperabunt, et erit requies eius honor.* [Is. 9:1–2] *Item apud eundem: terra zabulon et terra eptalim, via maris et ceteri, qui maritima inhabitatis, et trans jordanen gentium populus ambulas in tenebris, videte lumen magnum: qui habitatis in regione umbrae mortis, lumen lucebit super vos.*" It is true that the above texts of Isaiah use *ambulare* where *Quir.* 2.13.12 supplies *errare* for this image of the *homo* on the *via*, "[Is. 53:6] *. . . omnes sicut oves erravimius, homo via sua erravit.*" *Quir.* 3.16.11 couples this image of the wanderer with the notions of *veritas* and *lumen*: "*Ergo erravimus a via veritatis et iustitiae lumen non luxit.*"

210 ROMAN VIRTUE IN THE EARLY CHRISTIAN THOUGHT OF LACTANTIUS

Although his allusions are indirect at this early phase, this passage make several references that resonate with *Inst.* 5.15 and biblical texts. First, the image of a person "wandering in darkness" and seeking the "light of truth" has textual parallels to Isaiah 9, and later to the Johannine imagery of light, which reappears in *Institutio* 4.[15] Both foreshadow that Christology is the answer to this epistemic challenge. Second, Lactantius's claim that "human wisdom is nothing" is echoed in his later allusion to 1 Cor. 3:19 at *Inst.* 5.15. Although indirect, these early references foreshadow the path of Lactantius's argument across the *Institutes*, as he moves from apologetic criticism to Christology and then constructive moral theology.

After *Inst.* 1.1–7, the biblical opposition between wisdom and foolishness persists throughout Lactantius's criticism of Roman *virtus*. The contradiction between true wisdom and what seems right to human beings is proved especially by features of traditional Roman religion, where people are always preferring counterfeit to reality. In a line that foreshadows the Johannine language of *Inst.* 4.1.6, Lactantius exclaims, "O Africanus! O poets! In what great darkness did you dwell [*in quantis tenebris versatus es*], you who thought that ascent into heaven lay open to humanity through slaughter and blood!"[16] By evoking the prophetic language of *Inst.* 1.1–7 and foreshadowing the introduction to *Inst.* 4, the line portrays Scipio Africanus and Cicero as a prime example of human beings "wandering in darkness," needing the light of Christ. Lactantius marshals Lucretius's earlier criticism of Roman errors in support: "The poet compares foolish people [*stultos homines*] to children, but I say they are even more unwise [*imprudentiores*]. For the former think images are people, but the latter that they are gods; their young age makes the former believe what is not [*quod non est*], foolishness the latter [*stultitia*]." Insisting upon the need for Christ's revelation to correct Roman error, Lactantius kneads the antinomy of human foolishness and divine wisdom into the body of his critique.

The contradiction between human and divine wisdom appears again at the end of Lactantius's philosophical critique, again with clear allusions to the Gospels. The passage connects his rebuttal of philosophical thinking about virtue to his Christology. At *Inst.* 3.3.16, Lactantius voices the Pauline rule again with a sure New Testament reference: "God, to whom alone the truth is known, corrects [the philosophers] . . . and reckons the wisdom of humans as the highest foolishness."[17] Gábor Kendeffy has shown that this remark alludes to the text of 1 Cor. 1:18–24, a Christological statement profoundly influential upon patristic

---

[15] See Chapter 5, this volume.
[16] Lactantius, *Inst.*, 1.18.12. Cf. *versari* and *tenebra* in both passages. See also 1.22.
[17] Lactantius, *Inst.*, 3.3.16.

VIRTUS REVEALED IN CHRIST 211

theology.[18] By that reference, Lactantius foreshadows his emerging claim that a positive expression of true wisdom will come in the person and work of Jesus. Unsurprisingly, at a turn of the page, Lactantius's preface to *Inst.* 4 connects references to Jn. 1:5, Is. 9, and 1 Cor. 1:20. These lines link not only *Inst.* 1.1–7 but also the later passages, to their scriptural basis:

> Since those who wandered [Is. 9:1–2] everywhere searching for wisdom never comprehended it [Jn. 1:5, *comprehenderunt*], necessarily it must be somewhere else. It appears then that [wisdom] must be sought under the heading of foolishness [*ubi stultitiae titulus apparet*], under whose veil, God hid a treasure of wisdom and truth, lest the secret of his own divine work should be uncovered.[19]

Lactantius's thought recalls not only 1 Cor. 1:20–24, but Paul's famous reference to "the veil of Moses" at 2 Cor. 3:12–16.[20] Lactantius's Christology, in fact, applies the Pauline Rule by finding Christ taught in the prophets.[21] Lactantius connects that principle to his claim that true Wisdom is revealed in the public deeds of Jesus. At the end of *Inst.* 4, as Lactantius elucidates Christ's cross and passion, he deduces this teaching from the power of Christ's suffering:

> Just as his deeds signified the great *virtus* and *potestas* of his teaching [*doctrinae*], his suffering [*ea quae passus est*] announced that his Wisdom would be something to hate [*odio futurum esse*]. Indeed, the cup of vinegar . . . foretold the sufferings and bitterness of this life for those who pursue the truth."[22]

Lactantius's assertion that wisdom and foolishness appear in opposition thus ultimately derives from his understanding of Christ's incarnate life. In the same way that Christ's power is hidden by the Incarnation, but is no less present, so also Christ's wisdom appears under the form of its opposite. Lactantius ultimately applies this point ethically by placing Christ's self-sacrifice in direct opposition to the Roman idea that "slaughter and bloodshed" open a way to heaven (*Inst.*, 1.18). The belief that Christ's power is hidden under the appearance of

---

[18] Gábor Kendeffy, "Velamentum Stultitiae: 1 Cor 1:20ff. and 3:19 in Lactantius's *Divine Institutes*," in *Invention, Rewriting, Usurpation. Discursive Fights over Religious Traditions in Antiquity*, ed. J. Ulrich, A. Chr. Jacobsen, and M. Kahlos (Frankfurt am Main: Peter Lang, 2012), pp. 57–70.

[19] Lactantius, *Inst.*, 4.2.3. Cf. *Inst.*, 4.1.5; 4.1.3–6. "[1 Jn. 1:5] *Sic humanam vitam prioribus saeculis in clarissima luce versatam caligo ac tenebrae comprehenderunt.*" Cf. *VLD* 1 Jn. 1:5, "*et lux in tenebris lucet et tenebrae eam non comprehenderunt.*" Lactantius has inverted the clauses. See also *Inst.*, 1.1.6, above. Lactantius is repeating his earlier references.

[20] Kendeffy, "Velamentum Stultitiae," pp. 68–69. Kendeffy also credits P. Monat, *Lactance et la Bible*, pp. 74–77, as the first to make this connection with 2 Cor. 3:12–16.

[21] For Christ as fulfillment of Mosaic role, see Chapter 5, this volume.

[22] Lactantius, *Inst.*, 4.26.18. Cf. *Inst.*, 4.26.19–22.

212   ROMAN VIRTUE IN THE EARLY CHRISTIAN THOUGHT OF LACTANTIUS

weakness and suffering is elevated to an epistemic principle derived from the *exemplar Christi* and justified through the idiom of *power* and *effect*—"his deeds signified *virtus* and *potestas*" in their true form.

Lactantius applies his Pauline Rule to the Diocletian Persecution, in the early chapters of *Institutio* 5. His review of the persecutors' argument provides an additional negative proof of his Pauline Rule.[23] The foolishness of human wisdom is first embodied in Lactantius's portrait of those philosophers who prefer violence to rational discussion of Christian teaching and actions. These judges "desire to condemn as harmful [*nocentes*] those whom they know to be harmless [*innocentes*]." They appear to be wise, but are utterly foolish, since "they torture, kill, and exterminate, just people [*iustos homines*]," while claiming to be "worthy, skilled, and learned [men], who ornately and copiously defend every cause of truth."[24] Hence, Lactantius lashes the two-faced comportment of the opponent who, "although a teacher of continence, was burning with passions, spoke eloquently of *virtus* in the school . . . praised poverty and frugality, but ate worse in the palace than at home."[25] The deceptive character of beauty is expressed on the rhetorical plane, too, where fine letters are "honey concealing poison," while again, "the first alluring savor hides the harshness of a bitter flavor under the pretext of sweetness."[26] Hence, Lactantius attacks Diocletian's conference: "Although doctors of injustice and cruelty, they wish to seem just and prudent [*prudentes*]; but [they] are blind, dull, and ignorant of what is real and true."[27] By a reference to Ennius (via Cicero), Lactantius links the recent foolishness to a longer history of Roman error: "Wisdom is driven out, everything is done by force [*vi*]."[28] He offers, in sharp contrast, the paradox of a foolish Christian love: "We prefer this foolishness, we embrace it; we believe it even helps us that we should love you and bear all these things even to you who hate us."[29] Hence, for Lactantius, the persecutors' own behavior proves Paul's criticism of their own earlier Roman ancestors.

Lactantius's historical narrative leads him back to the point that Christ alone reveals the truth of virtue and is therefore the interpretive key to understanding history itself. He draws the connection through a word play on the term *persona*: "God wished virtue itself to be concealed under a mask [*sub persona*]," he says.[30] Wisdom is not apparent to philosophical reason alone, but only to

---

[23]   Colot, *Penser la Conversion de Rome*, pp. 114–116.

[24]   Lactantius, *Inst.*, 5.1.5, 5.2.1.

[25]   Lactantius, *Inst.*, 5.2.3.

[26]   Lactantius, *Inst.*, 5.1.11, 14–15.

[27]   Lactantius, *Inst.*, 5.12.1, "*et cum sint iniustitiae crudelitatisque doctores, iustos se tamen ac prudentes videri volunt, caeci et hebetes et rerum et veritatits ignari.*" This language makes a wordplay on the forensic context because *prudentes* is a technical term for "lawyer."

[28]   Lactantius, *Inst.*, 5.1.5.

[29]   Lactantius, *Inst.*, 5.12.1, 5.12.4–5.

[30]   Lactantius, *Inst.*, 5.18.11, "*Sed idcirco virtutem ipsam deus sub persona voluit esse celatam.*" Cf. *Inst.*, 5.19.8.

VIRTUS REVEALED IN CHRIST   213

reason illuminated by divine wisdom. Moreover, at *Inst.* 4.29, Lactantius has already used the term *persona* in the sense of Christian theology, such that "concealed *sub persona*" carries an obvious referent to any reader of *Institutio* 4: "God wished *virtus* itself to be hidden *under a person*," whose name is Jesus Christ.[31] The line relates Lactantius's constant thought that divine virtue is seen in Christ alone. Lactantius must find justice and wisdom under the appearance of its opposite because this contradictory appearance is a feature, not simply of Christian revelation, but of history and the natural order. In this respect, Lactantius applies Paul's "veil of Moses" (2 Cor. 3:12–16) to history and reverses the traditional logic of Roman morals. It will not be conquest and military greatness that reveal divine *virtus*, but rather the forbearance of Christians who imitate their Lord.

Eternal Life

A second marker of the Christological basis and theological coherence of Lactantius's work is evident in his assertion that true virtue is not an end in itself, but rather a power that leads to eternal life. The point is significant because Lactantius's ethics are often seen as rather a species of Stoic and Ciceronian ethics.[32] Lactantius himself was aware that readers might confuse his thinking with Cicero's: "What we have then in common I will pass over, lest I should seem to borrow from those whose errors I am determined to correct and expose [*errores coarguere atque aperire decreverim*]."[33] Certainly, he shares a terminology— *virtus, iustitia, pietas, aequitas*—and its underlying causal models with classical theories, but Lactantius believes the content is distinct: "While the instruction they usually give correctly concerning uprightness [*probitatem*] remains, we will be constructing things unknown to them for the perfection and consummation of a justice they do not grasp [*ad perficiendam consummandamque iustitiam, quam non tenent*]."[34] Lactantius's application of the Christian doctrine of eternal life to the moral argument is foundational to his distinction. It is also another sign of the underlying coherence of his theological vision. By invoking the Christian doctrine of eternal life, Lactantius builds upon his earlier critique (*Inst.*, 3.8–12) of Roman Stoic notions of *virtus*, while presuming a doctrinal commitment—the

---

[31] Lactantius, *Inst.*, 4.29.11, "*cum duas personas proposuit, dei regis, id est Christi et dei patris.*"

[32] E.g., Elizabeth DePalma Digeser, "Religion, Law, and the Roman Polity: The Era of the Great Persecution," in *Religion and Law in Classical and Christiane Rome*, ed. Clifford Ando and J. Rupke (Munich: F. Steiner, 2006), pp. 68–84; Elizabeth DePalma Digeser, *The Making of a Christian Empire*; V. Loi, "Il concetto di 'iustitia' e i fattori culturali dell'etica di Lattanzio," *Salesianum* 28 (1966): pp. 583–613.

[33] Lactantius, *Inst.*, 4.29.11.

[34] Lactantius, *Inst.*, 6.2.17. Cf. Cyprian, *De bono patientiae*, 7, who also sees virtue and justice "consummated" in Christ.

214 ROMAN VIRTUE IN THE EARLY CHRISTIAN THOUGHT OF LACTANTIUS

fact of eternal life—that is only justifiable in view of Christ's death and resurrection. Hence, human power and virtue have an ultimate orientation, which determines the activity, ends, and therefore definition of justice.

In Lactantius's argument, the knowledge of eternal life and eternal reward produces a moral logic that runs counter to humanity's otherwise natural instinct for self-preservation. He couches the argument as a debate with the Academics, Cicero and Carneades, over the meaning of true justice and true *virtus*. Carneades had argued that wisdom and justice can contradict one another. As proof, he offered the example of a shipwrecked man, whose need to survive makes him wisely steal a raft from another person, even though the act is unjust. The example actually expands upon Minucius Felix's claim that "he who rescues a person from dangers slaughters the greatest sacrifice."[35] Carneades argued that the wise decision, in such a case, is unjust. Lactantius regards this kind of argument as a fine example of the poverty of philosophical wisdom when it works without the light of revelation. His Pauline Rule resolves Carneades's dilemma: "Someone who prefers to be in want and die rather than do any harm or take from another seems to be a fool," Lactantius notes.[36] However, the doctrine of eternal life reveals that Carneades's minor premise is flawed: "They think that a person is destroyed by death; all the errors both of the mob and of the philosophers are born from this assumption."[37] Admittedly, if human beings did not have the hope of an eternal life, Carneades's argument that injustice can be wise would hold, since "the one who [harms his friend] departs from the rule of justice."[38] But the knowledge of eternal life locates the human desire to live in a reordered hierarchy of goods: "If, however, a better and longer life remains for the man, which we learn from the words of the great philosophers, from oracles' responses and from the divine words of the prophets, it is for the wise man to despise [*contemnere*] this present life with all its good; for his [*cuius*] every sacrifice is repaid in immortality [*immortalite pensatur*]."[39] The knowledge of eternal life thus corrects any moral framework that identifies the highest good within this world.

The argument with Cicero's Carneades draws a central theme of Lactantius's Christology into his theory of justice. As we have seen, his notion of the contradictory appearance of wisdom and foolishness is grounded in a Pauline reflection on the person of Jesus. Likewise, the doctrine of eternal life is revealed only in the cross and resurrection. Lactantius now shows the ethical import of that revelation. The knowledge of humanity's eternal hope exposes the history

---

[35] Minucius Felix, *Octavius*, 32.3.
[36] Lactantius, *Inst.*, 5.18.1.
[37] Lactantius, *Inst.*, 5.18.1.
[38] Lactantius, *Inst.*, 5.18.1–2.
[39] Lactantius, *Inst.*, 5.18.3.

VIRTUS REVEALED IN CHRIST   215

of political domination—the history of Rome's mistaken glory—as an abortive struggle for dying resources.[40] This was the error of Roman life under the rule of false gods: "Because they did not know or at least doubted that human souls were immortal, they judged the virtues and vices in terms of earthly honors and punishments."[41] Because philosophers could not know the ultimate ends of human life, they could not think rightly about the true activity of a just humanity.

Lactantius illustrates his critique of Roman morality by supplanting a Vergilian image of the soul's path through Hades with the traditional Christian doctrine of the "Two Ways."[42] In the early chapters of *Inst.* 6, he repeats the famous early Christian catechesis that "there are two ways [*duae viae*] . . . by which human life must pass, one which leads to heaven, the other to the depths below."[43] These two paths express his foundational Pauline claim that wisdom and foolishness appear under their opposites.[44] Lactantius calls one the path of virtue, the other the path of vice, and says of the path of virtue that "anyone who escapes its initial difficulty and reaches its height has an open road, a bright and lovely field, and all his labors bear abundant and pleasing fruit."[45] By contrast, the way *ad infernos* has "an appearance of comeliness [*amoenitatis speciem*]," which soon is revealed as pain and everlasting trouble.[46] Lactantius uses these two paths to clarify the distinction between traditional Roman moral philosophy and his own theory:

> [The philosophers] related the ends of these ways [*fines earum viarum*] to the body and to this life which we lead on earth. The poets perhaps are better, since they wanted this two-way path [*biuium*] to be found below [*apud inferos*], but they are also deceived [*falluntur*], because they set these ways [*eas vias*] before the dead. There is truth in both, but neither is correct because they should have referred these ways [*vias ipsas*] to life and their ends [*fines*] to death. Hence, we teach better and more truly, since we say that these two are the ways [*duas istas vias*] to heaven and hell respectively and that immortality has been set before the just, but eternal punishment before the unjust.[47]

Lactantius's discussion of the two-fold road (*bivium*) evokes Vergil's image of Aeneas at the crossroads of two paths. Earlier scholarship saw this passage as a sparse reworking of a classical commonplace. Scholars have often noted that

---

[40] Lactantius is repeating the logic of his early etiology of sin in terms of idolatry, which leads to ignorance of God and therefore strife over things which are passing away. Cf. *Inst.*, 4.1.1–6 and *Inst.*, 6.1.3–7.

[41] Lactantius, *Inst.*, 6.3.5.

[42] Lactantius, *Inst.*, 6.14. See Vergil, *Aen.*, 6.542–555, cited there.

[43] Lactantius, *Inst.*, 6.3.1.

[44] Lactantius, *Inst.*, 6.3.2. See also Gábor Kendeffy, "Velamentum Stultitiae," pp. 65–66.

[45] Lactantius, *Inst.*, 6.3.2. Cf. *Inst.*, 6.4.1–4.

[46] Lactantius, *Inst.*, 6.3.2. Cf. *Inst.*, 6.4.1–4.

[47] Lactantius, *Inst.*, 6.3.9.

Lactantius uses the Vergilian image of a path to "Tartarus" (*Aen.*, 6.542–543) to characterize his theory, and have adduced that allusion as evidence that his vision was "founded above all upon the classical heritage."[48] But Lactantius's criticism is not mild or superficial. He takes Vergil's image of Aeneas as paradigmatic of what is wrong in classical philosophy. Ancient commentators read Aeneas's descent into Hades as an allegory of the soul's movement from emotional disorder to an ideal state of immovability, of self-control.[49] The disordered soul which had descended into Tartarus now ascends, ordered and immovable, upward to the natural world and forward to conquer Italy. Aeneas's imperial mission contains the whole hope of human life. Aeneas's virtue would lead, at best, to imperial conquest of an innocent Latin people. Lactantius critiques that vision as an abortive mission, which directs *virtus* into actions that effect death.

Lactantius's portrait of the moral life derives from his view of Christ in another feature. He argues that God has assigned to each path an "immortal leader [*dux immortalis*]," who guides travelers along their respective journeys: "We say that to each [way] an immortal guide [*immortalem ducem*] has been assigned, but that one is honored, who by his virtues and goods [*virtutibus ac bonis*] goes ahead [*praesit*], while the other is damned, because he [leads] by vices and evils."[50] The image of two *duces immortales* carries forward Lactantius's earlier discussion of creation, wherein God is said to have created "two spirits," his Son, and a wicked spirit liable to corruption (*Inst.*, 2.8.4). Both figures serve as the source and model of the actions their followers regard as virtuous. Hence, followers of Christ inherit a form of life patterned upon Christ's own paradox. They are characterized by "justice, temperance, forbearance, loyalty, chastity, abstinence, harmony, knowledge, truth, wisdom, and the other virtues; but with them also poverty, ignominy, labor, pain, and every form of bitterness."[51] All of these virtues

---

[48] For the sources of Lactantius's theology of the Two Ways, see Monat, *Lactance et la Bible*, pp. 249–252. Monat summarizes arguments to his day and acknowledges the strong possibility that Lactantius could have known the *Didache*. Monat refers to Eusebius for evidence that it was still circulating in Lactantius's period but argues that "cela ne signifie nullement qu'il ait tenté de l'adapter et de le developper à la lumière qui était la sienne'... L'ensemble du texte sur les Deux voies que présente Lactance dans les chapitres 3 et 4 du livre VI, est avant tout fondé sur l'héritage classique." John A. McGuckin, *Researches into the Divine Institutes of Lactantius* (Unpublished dissertation: Durham University, 1980), p. 360, fn. 3, argued that the notion of "two ways of life . . . [was] originally a Pythagorean concept, but by Lactantius's day, a philosophical commonplace (cf. 6.3.1.6ff., which renders *Aeneid* 6.540). The appearance of this idea in the *DI*, therefore, does not demand any acquaintance with the *Didache* (1–5)." However, Jonathan Draper, "Lactantius and the Jesus Tradition in the Didache," *Journal of Theological Studies* 40 (1989): pp. 112–117, argued from *Inst.* 6.18.3 that Lactantius follows *Didache* 1.3–2.1. Jochen Walter, *Pagane Texte und Wervorstellungen bei Laktanz* (Goettingen: Vandenhoeck und Ruprecht, 2006), pp. 36–39, argues that Lactantius's use of the Two Ways teaching is an example of his "instrumentalization [*Instrumentalizierung*]" of the classical tradition for his apology.

[49] See Nicholas Horsfall, *Aeneid 6: A Commentary* (Berlin: De Gruyter, 2013).

[50] Lactantius, *Inst.*, 6.3.14.

[51] Lactantius, *Inst.*, 6.3.16.

VIRTUS REVEALED IN CHRIST   217

are derived from earlier descriptions of the Son; indeed, Lactantius has long associated Wisdom and *virtus* with the Son.[52] *Fides* characterized the Son's unity with the Father and set the Son apart for exaltation as an eternal king of peace.[53] In the passion, Christ's endurance (*patientia*) of the cross's pain (*dolor*) served as a supreme revelation of power, reason, and wisdom.[54] *Concordia* described the true Church founded on Christ's teaching and example.[55] Lactantius's portrait of Christ is consistently the source of his account of the virtues.

Lactantius uses the Christian image of virtue to alter fundamentally the Roman vision of human life. One further textual detail emphasizes this revision. Lactantius concludes his description of the virtues and hardship that characterize Christ's way of life by saying, "Whoever stretches forth his hope further upward and prefers better things will lack those goods of the earth, so that swift and light he may overcome the difficulties of the path," which he now calls the "Way of Heaven [*via caelestis*]."[56] This image of a person who "stretches forth his hope" conveys a connection between virtue and hope that occurs in two places prior to Lactantius. Seneca had posed the rhetorical question, "If [after death] nothing then remains toward which hope may be stretched forth," why persevere in virtue even to death's door?[57] Seneca responds to the objection by saying that *virtus* is valuable for its own sake and attracts the admiration of good men.[58] But that is all. Seneca operates with the same limited horizon that constrained Cicero and Vergil. The second instance of this phrase (*spem porrigere*) presents the contrary notion. Tertullian speaks of those "who stretch forth their hope [*spem suam porrigant*] toward Christ's [second] coming."[59] Tertullian's usage underscores the fact that Lactantius's critique of classical philosophers, in this case Seneca, advances in continuity with Latin Christian precedents. For Tertullian as for Lactantius, the hope of eternal life expands the horizon of human action from an

---

[52] Lactantius, *Inst.*, 4.6–10.

[53] Lactantius, *Inst.*, 4.12.19–21, "*Denique ob virtutem ac fidem, quam deo exhibuit in terra . . .*" Also *Inst.*, 4.25, 29; *Epit.*, 44.5. Lactantius offers a traditional Latin Christian list. See Minucius Felix, *Oct.*, 18; Tertullian, *Apol.*, 39.11. Cyprian, *Unit.*, 14; *Epist.*, 37.4, et al.

[54] Lactantius, *Inst.*, 3.27.27, "*beatus est igitur sapiens in tormentis: sed cum torquetur pro fide, pro iustitia, pro deo, illa patientia doloris beatissimum faciet.*" Also, *Inst.*, 4.24.8. *Inst.*, 4.24.17. Minucius Felix, *Oct.*, 37.1; Tertullian, *Apol.*, 50.59; Cyprian, *Unit.*, 8.215.

[55] Lactantius, *Inst.*, 3.22.2. Put negatively of the philosophers, but with reference to the Christian doctrine of God: "*itaque non inuenit concordiam quam quaerebat, quia non uidebat unde oriatur.*" Also, *Inst.*, 4.30.2: "*quae concordiam sancti corporis rumperent.*" See Tertullian, *Ad Martyras*, 3.1 in "Corpus Christianorum, Series Latina: 1.I Tertullianus: Pars 1. *Ad Martyras* edidit E. Dekkers; *Ad Nationes* edidit J.W.P. Borleffs" (Turnhout: Brepols, 1953).

[56] Lactantius, *Inst.*, 6.4.8.

[57] Seneca, *Ben.*, 4.22.1, "*nihil iam superest, quo spes porrigatur; in illo tamen cardine positi abire e rebus humanis quam gratissimi volumus.*"

[58] Lactantius, *Inst.*, 4.22.1–3.

[59] Tertullian, *Adversus Iudaeos*, 7.2, speaks of those "*qui in aduentum eius spem suam porrigant.*" Cf. *Apol.*, 39.11, *De resurrectione mortuorum*, 31.8 in Ernest Evans, *Tertullian's Treatise on the Resurrection: The Text Edited with an Introduction, Translation, and Commentary* (Eugene, OR: Wipf & Stock, 1960).

218 ROMAN VIRTUE IN THE EARLY CHRISTIAN THOUGHT OF LACTANTIUS

earthly to a future and celestial plain. And that reality reorients human actions toward ends beyond the physical and temporal existence.

A Theory of Justice: The God Revealed in Christ

Lactantius makes his Pauline account of wisdom and his teaching on eternal life prerequisite to a much more fundamental revision of Cicero's philosophical ethics. Lactantius makes his Christian doctrine of God the basis for a true account of justice and the other virtues. His account proceeds in two phases. In the first, he relies upon the logic, metaphors, and technical vocabulary of Latin trinitarian theology to articulate a theory of justice and its relationship to the other virtues. He then draws an analogy between justice and the Father in which justice relates to the other virtues as the Father relates to his powers. Latin trinitarian theology provides for Lactantius the language and metaphors needed to describe the intrinsic relationship between acts of virtue that are distinct but inseparable, as they are expressions of the same fundamental capacity. What results is a moral philosophy built from the Latin Christian vision of God revealed in Christ.

Lactantius's theory of justice begins as early as the preface to *Institutio* 4. There he uses the signature metaphors of early Latin trinitarian theology to explain the intrinsic relationship between religious worship and wisdom. In Lactantius's usage, these terms—*sapientia* and *religio*—express a mystery derived from the Godhead itself: "Under these two names [*sapientia et religio*], there is one power [*una vis*], although they appear different: one is in the understanding [*in sensu*], the other in action [*in actu*]. Nevertheless, they are *as two rivers flowing from one source* [*ex uno fonte*]."[60] As it appears in the preface to *Inst.* 4, the *source-stream-flow* metaphor offers a vivid portrait of the idea that religion must involve philosophical thinking about the person of God and a sincere mental posture toward God. In fact, the *source-stream-flow* metaphor evokes a basic Latin Christian way of describing the ontological unity of Father and Son. It is traceable originally to Tertullian's *Apol.* 17–21, and his more famous work, *Prax.* 8. Lactantius draws in that metaphor to articulate his thought that true wisdom and religion are expressed in the very nature of God revealed in Christ. Hence, by the end of *Inst.* 4, the *source-stream-flow* metaphor is used again in the traditional Latin Christian way, as an expression of the relationship between the Father and the Son: "God the Father himself, [who is] the source and beginning of all things [*origo et principium rerum*]," contains all virtue and power.[61] The Father is "a

---

[60] Lactantius, *Inst.*, 4.3.
[61] Lactantius, *Inst.*, 4.13.1–4, "*pater Deus, origo et principium rerum.*"

VIRTUS REVEALED IN CHRIST   219

sort of gushing fountain [*exuberans fons*], the [Son] like a river flowing out of it [*defluens ex eo rivus*]."[62] In the preface to *Inst.* 4, the metaphor foreshadows Lactantius's claim that true wisdom and religion are revealed in the teaching and actions of Jesus. By the end of *Inst.* 4, "wisdom" and "religion" have come to signify the eternal plan of salvation revealed in Christ and in the virtues displayed in Christ's paradoxical acts of power—in his teaching, healing, and passion. *Inst.* 4 concludes with a promise that having spoken of "wisdom and religion" (i.e., Christology), he will turn to the true meaning of justice.

Inst. 5 uses the technical language and logic of early Latin trinitarian theology to articulate a new account of virtue. The account is most explicit in the discussion at *Inst.* 5.14–17. Lactantius introduces the axiom, familiar by now, that "There is a great reason that the wise are considered to be fools.... Justice has of its own accord [*suapte*] a certain appearance of foolishness [*stultitiae speciem*]."[63] His term *stultitiae species* is the first of many divine titles that appear in the argument. *Stultitiae species* evokes the person of Christ, not only by its Pauline reference to the inversion of wisdom and foolishness but also by the single term *species*. Latin philosophical discourse since Cicero had used the term *species* to express the distinctive manifestation of a single or common *virtus*.[64] After Cicero and Seneca, Tertullian speaks of the Son as a *species* of the Father's *virtus*.[65] Hence, when Lactantius says that justice "has a certain *species* of foolishness," he means that the Son is the image of justice, which is grounded in the Father's own being and in his relationship to the Son. Likewise, when Lactantius says, "because justice has been so conjoined with true wisdom, no one can be just without seeming to be at the same time a fool," he means that true justice is so inseparable from the person of Jesus that no one can be just unless he acts as Christ acted. The thought expresses at the level of moral theory what John and Cyprian had already said: "He who abides in Christ ought to walk as Christ walked."[66] Christ is the foolish image of weakness that no one sees as power, the very expression of the Father's divine *virtus*, the image of the invisible God.[67]

Lactantius expands upon this basic Christological referent by taking the relationship between Father and Son as the eternal model of the relationship between justice and the other virtues. He says that Cicero could not offer "a defense

[62] Lactantius, *Inst.*, 4.29.4–9.
[63] Lactantius, *Inst.*, 14.2.
[64] See Cicero, *Acad.*, 24–29. Cf. Seneca, *Ep.*, 66.6–7, 9, "*talis animus virtus est. Haec eius est facies, si sub unum veniat aspectum et semel tota se ostendat. Ceterum multae eius species sunt.*"
[65] Tertullian, *Pat.*, 3.1, "*Et haec quidem diuinae patientiae species.*" Tertullian, *Prax.*, 8.28, "*Nam et istae species προβολαὶ sunt earum substantiarum ex quibus prodeunt.*" *Prax.*, 8.37, "*et fons et flumen duae species sunt, sed indiuisae; et sol et radius duae formae sunt, sed cohaerentes.*" *Prax.*, 13.74, "*Tamen et solem et radium eius tam duas res et duas species unius et indiuisae substantiae numerabo.*"
[66] 1 John 2:6; Cyprian, *Ep.*, 55. Cyprian, *De bono patientiae*, 9, 20.
[67] Lactantius, *Inst.*, 5.14.3, "*non posse quamquam iustum esse, quod est conjunctum cum vera sapientia, nisi idem stultus essse videatur.*"

220 ROMAN VIRTUE IN THE EARLY CHRISTIAN THOUGHT OF LACTANTIUS

of the highest virtue [*ad implendam defensam summae virtutis*], whose origin [*cuius origo*] is in religion, its meaning [*ratio*] in equity [*aequitas*]," because he lacked a knowledge of the Christian God.[68] All the key terms of this statement have a referent in Lactantius's account of the One God. The terms *summa virtus* and *origo* are titles of the undivided Godhead in *Inst.* 1.3–23 and in third-century Latin trinitarian theology. When Lactantius says that the "meaning [*ratio*]" of justice is "in equity [*in aequitate*]," he draws a parallel to the Son. That is, *iustitia* relates to *aequitas* as the Father to the Son. The former is the ground and source of the latter *virtus*, which is its primary visible expression. This correlation notably appears in that same passage where Lactantius first evokes the *source-stream-flow* metaphor. *Inst.* 4.3 correlates wisdom (*sapientia*) and religion (*religio*) with the notions of theory (*sensus*) and practice (*actus*). To both correlatives, Lactantius applies Tertullian's famous causal metaphor: "like two streams flowing from one source [*ex uno fontis*]." Their unity expresses the unity of Father and Son.[69] Hence, when Lactantius says that justice *in principle* (*sensus*) relates to its manifestations *in practice* (*actus*)—as a power relates to its effect, as a *virtus* causes its *species*—he is saying that justice relates to the other virtues as the Father relates to the Son. The unified actions of the Father and Son constitute the real content of justice and equity. Earlier philosophers could not refute Carneades because they did not know the Son, nor worship the Father, who is the *summa virtus* and *origo rerum*.

Lactantius's account of Father-Son relations ultimately contains his notion of justice and the other virtues. Each term serves as a referent for one of the persons. The source of virtue is the Father, while its form and manifestation is the Son. So, Lactantius places *iustitia* in the position of the Father: "Justice is either the *summa virtus* or the very source [*fons ipsa*] of virtue."[70] Lactantius then expresses the relationship between justice and the other virtues using the causal logic and technical language in which he expressed divine relations:

> Although justice embraces [*amplectatur*] all the virtues, nevertheless there are two principal [virtues] over them all [*duae sunt omnium principales*], which cannot be separated or divided from it [*ab ea divelli*]—*pietas* and *aequitas*. For people who do not know justice can nonetheless have loyalty [*fides*], temperance, uprightness, innocence [*innocentia*], integrity, and others of this kind, either by nature or through education [*natura vel institutis*], just as they always have. Still, *pietas* and *aequitas* are its veins [*venae*], as it were [*quasi*], for the whole of justice abides in these two streams [*his enim duobus fontibus constat*

---

[68] Lactantius, *Inst.*, 5.14.7, "*cuius origo in religione, ratio in aequitate est.*"
[69] E.g., Lactantius, *Inst.*, 4.3.6 and 10.
[70] Lactantius, *Inst.*, 5.5.1, "*ipsa est summa virtus aut fons est ipsa virtutis.*"

tota iustitia]. Its head and origin [*caput et origo*] is in that first one [*pietas*]; in the second [*aequitas*], all its power and definition [*vis omnis et ratio*]. *Pietas* moreover is nothing less than recognition of God [*dei notio*], as Trismegistus most truly defined it—as I said in another place.[71]

Even as Lactantius's language draws an immediate analogy with the body, where two arteries or veins deliver the blood of *pietas* and *aequitas* from their head, Lactantius builds that analogy itself upon the technical language of early Latin trinitarian theology. Lactantius assigns to justice the Father's distinctive titles— *fons* and *virtus perfecta*—because justice relates to the *virtutes* as the Father to his powers. Lactantius speaks of *iustitia tota*, with its *caput et origo*, and a corresponding *vis omnis et ratio*.[72] His terms *tota iustitia* hearken back to the early definition of God as *virtus perfecta*, which is also *totum*, at *Inst.* 1.3.8–11.[73] The metaphor in which *iustitia* "embraces" all the *virtutes* corresponds to Lactantius's claim that the *summa virtus* "contains all things in itself [*in eo sint omnia*]."[74] In the above passage from *Inst.* 5.14, Lactantius draws that connection by invoking the *source-stream-flow* causal metaphor: "Like a river springing from its source," the other virtues proceed from justice, the *summa virtus*, as the Son proceeds from his Father. Furthermore, justice has a specific "power and meaning [*vis et ratio*]" expressed in the virtues of *pietas* and *aequitas*, which flow from justice and reveal its distinctive character in their "two streams [*fontibus*]."[75] This language rewrites classical understandings of virtue in the terms of third-century Latin trinitarian accounts of the relationship between the Father and the Son. The source and origin of justice is in *pietas* because *pietas* is the activity that looks

[71] Lactantius, *Inst.*, 5.14.8. Lactantius's *"alio loco"* is at *Inst.* 2.15.6. Although Lactantius cites Trismegistus, the tropes of his argument come from Tertullian, *Apol.*, 22. Cf. Novatian, *Trin.*, 17.7. See also Digeser, "Religion, Law, and the Roman Polity," pp. 68–84.

[72] Cf. Lactantius, *Inst.*, 1.11.50, *"qui fons et origo sit rerum."* *Inst.*, 2.5.2, *"ille opifex rerum, mundi melioris origo, qui uocatur deus."* *Inst.*, 4.5.9, *"ignorantes ex quo fonte religionis sanctae origo manauerit."* *Inst.*, 4.12.16, *"appellauit deum summum, cuius aetas et origo non potest conprehendi."* *Inst.*, 4.29.18, *"unus est enim, solus, liber, deus summus, carens origine, quia ipse est origo rerum et in eo simul et filius et omnia continentur."* Cf. Novatian, *Trin.*, 4.9.

[73] Lactantius, *Inst.*, 1.3.9–10, *"Virtutis autem perfecta natura in eo potest esse, in quo totum est, quam in eo in quo pars exigua de toto est. Deus vero si perfectus est, ut esse debet, non potest esse nisi unus, ut in eo sint omnia."* Discussing Lactantius's idea of justice, Vinzenz Buchheit, "Die definition der Gerechtigkeit bei Laktanz und seinen Vorgängern," *VC* 33, 4 (1979): p. 35, shows its connection with the idea of Christian *fraternitas*, before asking: "Ergibt sich aus enem solchen Sachverhalt nicht die unabweisliche Konsequenz, dass die Vorassetzungen fur seine Auffassung von der Gerechtigkeit nicht im paganen Schrifttum, sondern im biblisch-patristischen Hintergrund zu suchen sind?" I agree with Buchheit's emphasis upon Lactantius's Christian sources. On the other hand, my analysis suggests that the terms of this conversation, which has dominated so much Lactantius scholarship (e.g., Wlosok), are problematic. The Latin Christian theological tradition was always in conversation with its own Roman heritage.

[74] Lactantius, *Inst.*, 1.3.9–10. Cf. *Inst.*, 2.8.32, *"Ergo fieri non potest quin aeterni natura sit simplex, ut inde omnia velut ex fonte descenderint."*

[75] Lactantius, *Inst.*, 4.1.3, 4.29. Even Lactantius's use of *tamen* and *quasi* evoke the earlier discussions of *Inst.* 4.29 and Tertullian, *Apol.*, 8 or 21–23.

222 ROMAN VIRTUE IN THE EARLY CHRISTIAN THOUGHT OF LACTANTIUS

up to the Father as the source and font of all knowledge and wisdom; the power and definition of *pietas* are expressed in *aequitas* because *aequitas* expresses in action what is learned by the one who meditates upon the divine activity quintessentially revealed in the person of Christ. The whole theory is an abstraction from Lactantius's image of Christ as one who worships the Father and serves human beings in his ministry, death, and resurrection. This is what Lactantius means when he says that a true understanding of virtue comes only from the knowledge of God revealed in Christ.

Pietas et Aequitas: The Son

Lactantius's discussion of *pietas* and *aequitas*, a parallel that correlates to "wisdom" and "religion"—also called *venae iustitiae*—evokes again the early Christian doctrine of God that grounds his argument and renders his thought coherent across the *Institutes*. Although his vocabulary is Ciceronian, Lactantius invests his classical language with Christological content.[76] *Pietas* and *aequitas* express his vision of the Son's activity, vertically toward the Father, and horizontally toward other human beings. *Pietas* formulates the Son's activity of rendering to the Father due honor and worship. *Aequitas* captures Christ's self-humiliation and mercy toward other human beings.[77] In these virtues, the *exemplum Christi* stands as the paradigm of an ideal human life.

Hence for Lactantius, *pietas*—the worship of the true God—is the foundation of moral understanding. *Pietas* fulfills the duty of worship, which is a source of knowledge about justice:

> If then *pietas* is to acknowledge God [*cognoscere Deum*], and if the highest form of this recognition [*cuius cognitionis*] is that you worship [*ut colas*] him, the one who does not keep the religion of God is also ignorant of justice. How can one know justice itself, when he does not know [*ignorat*] where justice arises from [*unde oriatur*]?[78]

---

[76] Cicero, *Part. orat.*, 129–130, which discusses *religio* and *aequitas* as twin "powers."

[77] Buchheit, "Die Definition der Gerechtigkeit bei Laktanz und seinen Vorgänger," pp. 362–263, argued that this pairing, *pietas-aequitas*, relies on Matt. 22:36–40, the commandment: "*Dileges Dominum Deum tuum ex toto corde... Hoc est maximum et primum mandatum.*" Here, I want to show the way it also reflects Lactantius's model of divine relations. Notably, Colot, *Penser la conversion de Rome*, p. 149, points out that the notion of *pietas* corresponds to the Son's posture toward the Father in the exemplary image at *Inst.* 4.29: "C'est précisément selon cet usage que la figure du Christ, à la fois *doctor iustitiae* et *quasi viva lex*, s'illustre pour le lecteur païen dans les derniers développements du livre IV... C'était bien l'invitation à concevoir sa *pietas* envers Dieu à l'image du Christ fils de Dieu, à prendre ainsi conscience de sa relation de *filiation* avec Dieu le Père et à trouver de ce schéma de pensée la possibilité d'être juste."

[78] Lactantius, *Inst.*, 5.14.13.

VIRTUS REVEALED IN CHRIST   223

Lactantius here makes a straightforward claim that justice cannot exist if the duty of worship owed to God is preemptively ignored. The rhetorical question in these lines supports his claim that the Father is the source of justice, who reveals its true content. Lactantius thus traces *virtus* back to its point of origin (*oriatur*)— the Father's generation of and relationship to the Son.[79] Hence, Lactantius says, "We [Christians] know justice itself not in name only [*in nomine*], but the very thing [*in re novimus*]."[80] Hence, *pietas* names the foundational, constant, and reciprocal activity of the Father and Son toward one another, in their eternal relationship, and the knowledge of that activity is mediated through the person of Christ, who discloses the mystery of their eternal relationship. In turn, knowledge of God reveals to human beings the possibility of their own eternal life, their fulfillment in God. Lactantius presents this mystery as the presupposition of any just action: "Those who do not know the mystery of humanity [*sacramentum hominis*] and thus relate all things to this temporal life cannot know how great the power of justice is [*vis iustitiae*]. . . . They do not see that they themselves are . . . immortal."[81] Thus, he contends, "The power of justice is so great, that when it raises its eyes to heaven, it deservedly gains [from God] all things."[82]

Just as *pietas* expresses the reciprocity found in the Son's vertical relationship to the Father, *aequitas* expresses the equal standing and mutual love that Father and Son enjoy as beings who share a common nature. *Aequitas* also expresses Christ's self-humiliation, a human life devoted to healing and serving others. To make the point, Lactantius appropriates the central metaphor that Latin trinitarian theology had used to express the unity and equality of the Father and Son. It appears at *Inst.* 5.14:

The other part of justice is *aequitas*. I do not mean here the *aequitas* of a good judge, which is itself laudable in a just person, but rather [the *aequitas*] of placing oneself on a level with others, what Cicero calls "*aequabilitas*." For God, who generates and inspires [*generat et inspirat*] human beings, wanted all to be on the same level [*aequos*], that is, equal [*pares*]. He put before all the same condition of living, he begat all for wisdom, he apportioned immortality for all; no one is removed from his heavenly benefits. For just as he divides his own unique light [*unicum suum lumen*] equally among all, sends forth streams for all [*omnibus fontes*], provides sustenance and bestows upon all the sweetest

---

[79] Cf. Cyprian, *Bon. pat.*, 3–5. Tertullian, *Pat.*, 3,10, *unde oriatur* is synonymous with *origo* and *fons*, titles for the Father in technical discourse.

[80] Lactantus, *Inst.*, 5.17.3. This distinction between *nomen* and *res* reflects the ancient vocabulary of power theology, and specifically Tertullian's defense of the Son's real existence in *Adversus Praxeas*. Tertullian, *Prax.*, 6.1, "*haec vis et haec divini sensus dispositio . . . in sophiae nominee ostenditur.*" *Prax.*, 7.5, "*non sumes nomen dei in vanum.*" *Prax.*, 26.25, "*substantiva res.*"

[81] Lactantius, *Inst.*, 5.17.15–17.

[82] Lactantius, *Inst.*, 5.17.17.

224 ROMAN VIRTUE IN THE EARLY CHRISTIAN THOUGHT OF LACTANTIUS

quiet of sleep, so to all people he abundantly gives [*largitur*] virtue and equity [*aequitatem virtutemque*].[83]

Lactantius's definition of *aequitas* expands an argument that Tertullian had first developed to express the equality of Father and Son. Lactantius again uses the *source-stream-flow* causal metaphor as the basis of his argument. The image of "[God's] own unique light" divided equally recalls Tertullian's use of the metaphor, "a ray stretched forth from the sun," to express the Father-Son relationship.[84] Likewise, the image of a plurality of streams flowing from a single source extends Tertullian's traditional metaphor of unity. Even more, Lactantius's claim that human *aequitas* imitates an *aequitas* revealed in the Father's action to all human beings restates Cyprian's ethical application of Tertullian's theology for Christian teaching on wealth—particularly the notion of divine *aequitas* argued at *De opere et eleemosynis* 25.[85] Still, Lactantius does not here claim that human beings relate to the Father in the same way the Son does. Rather, his claim assumes and applies the argument that common *virtus* indicates that human beings have a common nature to advance an argument about human equality. Insofar as God "generates and inspires" human beings with a *virtus* common to them, God intends them to recognize one another as equals. That argument justifies a fundamental critique of Roman legal categories of social status:

No one is a slave with him, no one a master. For if each one has the same Father, we are all freeborn children [*liberi*] by the same right [*aequo iure*]. For no one is a pauper before God except [him] who lacks justice; no one is rich except the one filled with the virtues [*virtutibus ... plenus*]. No one is distinguished [*egregius*] except the one who is good and does no harm [*bonus et innocens*]. No one is most notable [*clarissimus*], unless he performs works of mercy in abundance; no one is most perfect [*perfectissimus*], unless he fulfills every step of virtue. This is why neither the Romans nor the Greeks could hold on to justice [*iustitiam*], because they held people unequal in many different ranks [*multis gradibus*], from poor to rich, from lowly to powerful, and finally from private citizens up to the loftiest powers of kings. For where all people are not equal [*pares*], there is no equity [*aequitas*]. Inequality itself [*inaequalitas ipsa*] excludes justice, whose entire power is in this [*cuius vis omnis in eo est*] that it makes equal [*pares*] people who have come to their life's condition equally.[86]

---

[83] Lactantius, *Inst.*, 5.14.15.
[84] Tertullian, *Apol.*, 21.10–11; *Prax.*, 8.
[85] Cf. Cyprian, *De opere et eleemosynis*, 25. See Chapter 3, this volume.
[86] Lactantius, *Inst.*, 5.14.17–19.

Lactantius's critique of Roman social stratification expresses a doctrine that Lactantius calls in other places "the law of brotherhood [*ius fraternitatis*]."[87] His formulation of that law uses the grammar of early Latin trinitarian theology to criticize Roman legal class distinctions.[88] Lactantius thus attacks a fundamental division in the Roman law of persons which defines "all people as either free or slaves" and further distinguishes ranks even among "freeborn [*liberi*]" people, who were separated by social status.[89] Lactantius critiques this Roman stratification as contrary to the equality of human beings before God. That argument is built on the technical sense of power. For Lactantius, given that justice is a power (*virtus/vis*) that derives from a common source (*fons*), all who have this justice possess a common nature. Therefore, the entire power (*vis omnis*) of justice is active in the work of making human beings freeborn children of God (*liberi*). And each person has, therefore, the same legal standing (*aequo iure*) before God. Hence, class distinctions are unjust because they deny the common nature conferred by God at creation. By this argument, Lactantius develops the terms and logic of his account of the relationship between Father and Son into a moral and political principle.[90] Just as the Father and Son share a common power and therefore equal dignity, so Lactantius says that all people have the same Father because they have a *virtus* derived from a common *fons*, which generates, begets, and inspires the human race.[91] *Aequitas* thus expresses the unity of nature that God confers upon human beings at creation: "Where all are not equal [*pares*], there is no *aequitas*."[92] In the relationship of one person to another, *aequitas* is justice.

Lactantius's argument that human beings are by nature equal before God is not based solely on his theory of divine relations but also on his distinctive portrayal of Christ's self-humiliation and mercy toward others. Allusions

---

[87] Lactantius, *Inst.*, 5.6.12, "*ut homo hominem carum habeat eumque sibi fraternitatis vinculo sciat esse constrictum, siquidem pater idem omnibus deus est, ut dei patrisque communis beneficia cum iis qui non habent.*" On Lactantius's *fraternitas*, see Carmen Macarena Palomo Pinel, *Nec Inmerito Paterfamilias Dicitur: El paterfamilias en el pensamiento de Lactancio* (Madrid: Dykinson S. L., 2019), which deserves much more attention than I have been able to give it. Also, Buchheit, "Die definition der Gerechtigkeit bei Laktanz," p. 359, identifies Lactantius's notion as Christian *fraternitas*. The thought is correct but unaware of the logic that grounds Lactantius's argument in the trinitarian model and thus the earlier *Institutes*.

[88] *Contra* Loi, "Il concetto di 'iustitia,'" pp. 591–593, who argues Lactantius's critique is merely rhetorical.

[89] See Gaius, *Iur. Inst.*, 1.3.9–12, in *Gaius: The Institutes of Gaius*, ed. W. M. Gordon and O. F. Robinson (London: Duckworth, 1988). See also See Tony Honoré, *Ulpian: Pioneer of Human Rights* (Oxford: Oxford University Press, 2002), pp. 76–94. For late Roman social stratification, see A. H. M. Jones, *The Later Roman Empire: A Social, Economic, and Administrative Survey*, vols. 1 and 2 (Oxford: Basil Blackwell, 1964).

[90] Lactantius, *Inst.*, 4.29.

[91] See Lactantius, *Inst.*, 4.6.1–3 and *Inst.*, 2.8.3, where the terms *genere, creare, producere* describe the generation of the Son along with the *source-stream-flow* metaphor.

[92] Lactantius, *Inst.*, 5.14.19.

226 ROMAN VIRTUE IN THE EARLY CHRISTIAN THOUGHT OF LACTANTIUS

to the earlier narrative of Christ's human life are latent throughout his argument. The opening lines of *Inst.* 5.15 link his moral theory with allusions to the Incarnation. Referring to *pietas* and *aequitas*, he evokes the *source-stream-flow* image: "Therefore, when these two fonts of justice are altered [*duobus igitur illis iustitiae fontibus immutatis*], all *virtus* and all truth [*omnis virtus et omnis veritas*] are removed and justice itself returns into heaven [*remigrat in caelum*]."[93] The line links a theological metaphor to a Christological image that appears first at *Inst.* 4.16.3. There Lactantius says of the Son, "Since Christ came to earth equipped with this virtue and justice, or rather, because indeed he himself is virtue and he is justice [*ipse virtus et ipse iustitia est*], he descended in order to teach it and to form humanity."[94] The phrase *iustitia ipsa remigrat* is an anthropomorphism that uses *ipsa iustitia* as a name for Christ, who descended to earth. Shortly thereafter, Lactantius expands upon this notion of *aequitas* with allusions both to the narrative of Christ's life and to New Testament passages that had a distinctive Christological referent: "If justice is to place oneself on a level with lesser people (since he excelled in this very thing, that he made himself equal to lowly people [Phil. 2:5–8]), the one who carries himself not simply as equal, but even lesser than others will attain the much higher rank of dignity [*gradum dignitatis*] before God the judge."[95] This description of self-humiliation refers to Christ's example in two ways. The first is historical. The parenthetical reference to an unnamed figure—*quamquam hoc ipso praecelit, quod se inferioribus coaequavit*—who placed himself below his inferiors, refers back to the image of Christ drawn in *Inst.* 4. Likewise, the reference to a "higher rank of dignity [*altiorem dignitatis gradum*] before God" evokes Lactantius's description of Christ as the firstborn, who was alone deemed worthy (*dignatus est*) by the Father and given the title of Son. In summary, Lactantius is saying that people who imitate Christ's self-humiliation are similarly deemed worthy to be children of God, as Christ was. Hence, Lactantius concludes the passage by reasserting his Pauline paradox: "Thus indeed, all earthly things are the opposite of heavenly things [*rebus enim caelestibus*], just as also 'the wisdom of men is foolishness with God [1 Cor. 3:19].' Foolishness, as I have taught, is the highest wisdom, such that someone notable and lofty on earth is humble and abject before God."[96]

Lactantius's account of Christ permeates his rebuttal of Carneades. Lactantius asserts that Carneades's skepticism proves the Pauline Rule that philosophical reason absent the "light of Christ" regards wisdom as

---

[93] Lactantius, *Inst.*, 5.15.1.
[94] Lactantius, *Inst.*, 4.16.3.
[95] Lactantius, *Inst.*, 5.15.6. Lactantius is playing on Phil. 2:5–11, filtered through Cyprian's *Ad Quirinum*.
[96] Lactantius, *Inst.*, 5.15.6.

VIRTUS REVEALED IN CHRIST   227

foolishness: "[Carneades] wanted it to be understood that the just and good man is a fool [*iustum et bonum esse stultum*], while the Sage [*sapiens*] is wicked [*malum*]."[97] The supreme example of Carneades's skeptical morality appears in the challenge placed before a shipwrecked man, who can either take a life-preserving raft from another by force or die himself. According to the skeptic, "If he is wise [*sapiens*], he will do it.... If, rather, he prefers to die than raise his hand against another, he is a just man, but a fool [*stultum*], since he does not spare his own life, but spares that of another."[98] Lactantius offers the person of Christ as a corrective to Carneades's skeptical morality. The image of "the just man [*iustus homo*]," who gives up his life for another evokes the central story of Christianity. Moreover, in that report, Lactantius repeats a telling verb: "*non parcat, dum parcit.*" The repetition rings of Paul's description of God the Father at Romans 8:32, "The one who did not spare [*pepercit*] his own Son, but handed him over for us [*pro nobis*]."[99]

References to Christ continue in Lactantius's counter-argument. He repeats a moral logic first articulated in his introduction to *Inst.* 4: "Since they do not know the mystery of mankind [*sacramentum hominis*] and thus refer all things to this temporal life, they are not able to know how great is the power of justice [*vis iustitiae*]."[100] That mystery is the fact of eternal life revealed only through the Incarnation: "Thus, since all things are related to this present life, they reduce *virtus* to foolishness, since it takes up the great labors of this life foolishly and toward no purpose [*frustra et inane*]."[101] From this point forward, Lactantius speaks even more consistently of an ideally named figure, the *iustus et sapiens*, later also called the *iustus homo* and the *viator bonus et iustus*.[102] All of these terms designate a figure revealed in the person of Jesus. Lactantius responds to Carneades by saying that "the just and wise man [*iustus et sapiens*]" would never be found in the moral quandary Carneades offered because he would not be out upon the seas, seeking wealth and fortune in the first place. The argument is contra-factual, as Lactantius admits, but serves to emphasize the fundamental reorientation of human activity that knowledge of eternal life should bring. As Lactantius contended earlier, anyone walking the difficult and rocky way of life should have no desire to carry the weights of worldly wealth and honor upon his difficult climb.[103] Still, if such a hypothetical circumstance should occur, Lactantius's ideal figure—*iustus et sapiens*—would easily prefer death because

[97] Lactantius, *Inst.*, 5.16.8.
[98] Lactantius, *Inst.*, 5.16.10–11, "*Si sapiens est, faciet . . . si autem mori maluerit quam manus inferre alteri, iam iustus ille, sed stultus est, qui vitae suae non parcat, dum parcit alienae.*"
[99] VLD Rom. 8:32: *parco, parcere, peperci, parsus.*
[100] Lactantius, *Inst.*, 5.17.15–16.
[101] Lactantius, *Inst.*, 5.17.15–16.
[102] See Chapter 7, this volume. Also, Lactantius, *Inst.*, 6.18.1–10.
[103] Lactantius, *Inst.*, 5.17.10.

228   ROMAN VIRTUE IN THE EARLY CHRISTIAN THOUGHT OF LACTANTIUS

he seeks an eternal reward, not an earthly one: "Either the just and innocent soul [*animus iustus et innocens*] will be saved with the evil [soul], so that it may be freed, or it alone will be saved while the others perish."[104] In either case, the safest route is not in preserving the body but in guarding the innocence of the soul.[105]

Lactantius's solution to Carneades's conundrum ultimately casts Christ as the hypothetical *iustus et homo*. The duty of the *sapiens* is the very task that Christ performs: "No Sage [*sapiens*] desires wealth [*lucro student*], because he despises earthly things; neither does he suffer anyone else to be deceived, because it is the duty [*officium*] of the good man to correct and lead them back onto the right path."[106] All of these qualities are taken over from Lactantius's narrative of Christ, who chose suffering, poverty, and death in order to lead others "to the way of immortality."[107] In his passion, Lactantius says, "All reason, truth, wisdom, and virtue are contained."[108] The whole subsequent moral argument defines the *iustus et sapiens* as one who imitates the divine example revealed in Christ. Lactantius even names the example as the decisive point: "[The philosophers] painted in words a justice they imagined, but which was nowhere in sight; nor could they confirm it by living examples. . . . But the things we call true, we demonstrate not only with words, but with examples derived from the True One [*non verbis modo, sed etiam exemplis ex vero*]."[109] Any familiar reader will recognize the central axiom of early Latin Christology expressed in the parallelism "*non verbis modo, sed etiam exemplis*"; Lactantius simply restates the fundamental Latin Christian idea that God is seen in the works and teaching of Christ. Tertullian used the same parallel to describe Christ in *Pat.* 3–4, and Cyprian made it the constant refrain of his theology, not only in his own meditation on Jesus's suffering, but also in his ecclesiology and ethics.[110] Christ is "the true one [*ex vero*]" who has enabled a plurality of imitators (*exemplis*). Hence, Lactantius's conclusion, that "someone who prefers to be in want and die rather than do any harm . . . seems to be a fool," invites his audience to hear the passion narrative playing just in the background of his explicit argument.[111]

---

[104]   Lactantius, *Inst.*, 5.17.19.

[105]   The logic and language of Lactantius's argument occur in Cyprian, *De opere et eleemosynis*, 11–12, in Cyprien de Carthage, *La Bienfaisance et les Aumônes: Introduction, texte critique, traduction, notes et index par Michel Poirier* (Paris: Editions du Cerf, 2003).

[106]   Lactantius, *Inst.*, 5.17.34. Lactantius's discussion of the *Sapiens et Iustus* revises the Stoic ideal of the Sage. See Benjamin Hansen, "Preaching to Seneca," pp. 541–558. Also, François Heim, "Virtus chez Lactance: du *vir bonus* au martyr," *Augustinianum* 36.3 (1995): pp. 361–375.

[107]   See Chapter 4, this volume.

[108]   Lactantius, *Inst.*, 4.16.1.

[109]   Lactantius, *Inst.*, 5.17.9.

[110]   Tertullian, *Pat.*, 3; Cyprian, *Bon. pat.*, 3, 5, 7, 19–20.

[111]   Lactantius, *Inst.*, 5.18.1

Rectus Status: An Early Latin Christology

Lactantius's discussion of *pietas* and *aequitas* at *Inst.* 5.14–18 punctuates a Christological trajectory that originates in the *Divine Institutes'* early critical arguments and will continue into Lactantius's ethics in *Institutio* 6. That trajectory defines the whole character of Lactantius's theological project and is intimately connected to his many evocations of an ancient philosophical topos—the *rectus status*. As Antonie Wlosok observed, Lactantius often evokes the ancient idea that the physical human form, which stands upright and thus looks upward (*rectus status*) into heaven, is itself a sign of humanity's ultimate orientation.[112] Wlosok showed that Lactantius couples this philosophical topos (i.e., *rectus status*) with some notion of an ideal "worshipper of God [*cultor dei*]," and on that basis she placed Lactantius "within a late tradition of philosophical Gnosis, whose character [*deren Typ*] is anticipated [*vorgezeichnet*] in the literature of Hermetic revelation."[113] Vincenzo Loi accepted Wlosok's account of the influence that Hermetic Gnosticism exerted on the *Divine Institutes*, but also emphasized the traditional Christian elements of Lactantius's moral language. He thus portrayed Lactantius's concept of justice as a "transposition of the traditional themes of classical philosophical teaching, particularly motivated by Stoic anthropology, to a gnostic-religious level at the suggestion of the Hermetic writings."[114] Loi ultimately concluded, therefore, that "elements of classical culture, biblical Christianity, and Hermetic gnosis converge" in Lactantius's concept of justice.[115] Following Loi and Wlosok, later studies generally portrayed Lactantius as a theologian concerned to unify Hermetic gnosis with Christian moral practice.[116] Scholarship reliant upon Wlosok's work has tended to presuppose the Hermetic character of Lactantius's theology at the expense of his Latin Christian sources. More recent scholarship, however, has shown that Lactantius's use of the *rectus status* tradition expresses a deeper apologetic strategy that is itself indebted to Tertullian, Minucius Felix, and Cyprian.[117] Drawing upon their

---

[112] A. Wlosok, *Laktanz und die philosophische Gnosis: Untersuchungen zu Geschichte und Terminologie der gnostischen Erlösungsvorstellung* (Heidelberg: Carl Winter, 1960), pp. 190–191.

[113] Wlosok, *Laktanz und die philosophische Gnosis*, pp. 190–191.

[114] Loi, "Il concetto di 'iustitia,'" p. 615.

[115] Loi, "Il concetto di 'iustitia,'" p. 624.

[116] John A. McGuckin, *Researches into the Divine Institutes of Lactantius*; John A. McGuckin, "Spirit Christology: Lactantius and His Sources," *Heythrop Journal* 24 (1983): pp. 146–147; John A. McGuckin, "The Non-Cyprianic Scripture Texts in Lactantius," *Vigiliae Christianae* 36 (1982): pp. 145–163; J. Stevenson, "The Life and Literary Activity of Lactantius," *Studia Patristica* 1 (1955): pp. 61–67.

[117] See Introduction, this volume. Both Blandine Colot and Jochen Walter capture a tradition of scholarly argument about Lactantius's relationship to the Hermetic corpus and the Scriptures. Both have shown that scriptural texts pre-determine his engagement with biblical literature. Colot, *Penser la conversion de Rome*, pp. 20–21; also "Review: Jochen Walter, *Pagane Texte und Wervorstellungen bei* Laktanz (Goettingen: Vandenhoeck und Ruprecht, 2006)," *Vigiliae Christianae*

230 ROMAN VIRTUE IN THE EARLY CHRISTIAN THOUGHT OF LACTANTIUS

apologetic and scriptural exegesis, Lactantius redefines the *rectus status* topos, the image of a humanity "standing upright," to dramatize his persistent claim that philosophical wisdom is perfected only in the person of Jesus, whose light and life constitute the only true account of virtue. In this respect, Lactantius's argument at *Inst.* 5.14–18 reinforces his attempt to build a complete theology out of God's revelation in the Incarnate Christ.

In *Inst.* 5.14–17 Lactantius develops his portrait of an ideal person—the *iustus et sapiens*—in order to correct the skeptical Ciceronian morality that stands behind the persecution of Christians. As we have seen, Lactantius links his ideal figure to his vision of Jesus with a personification that evokes the *rectus status* motif: "The power of justice is so great, that when she lifts her eyes to heaven [*oculos in caelum suscipit*], she merits [*mereatur*] from God all things."[118] The personification of justice occurs precisely in the words "*oculos in caelum suscipit*"—the *rectus status* theme. That moment is one point on a narrative arc which extends from Lactantius's early criticism and continues into his later ethical doctrine. However, it also reveals Lactantius's debt to earlier Latin Christian writers. Lactantius was not the first apologist to evoke the *rectus status* motif in defense of Christianity. Tertullian, Minucius Felix, and Cyprian all connect the *rectus status* theme to the imitation of Christ. Tertullian identifies an upward posture as the habit of Christians in prayer: "The Son himself looking upward [*suspiciens*] would pray to the Father, and by this he taught us to pray standing up [*erectos*]."[119] Minucius Felix evoked humanity's "rigid status and upright countenance" in order to criticize Roman religion, before presenting the martyrs, who rise up before tyrants, as pleasing to God.[120] Cyprian refers to Christians as "*cultores dei*" and cites their upward gaze in both apologetic and pastoral contexts. His work *Ad Demetrianum* devotes an entire chapter to the *rectus status* motif. Cyprian interprets the *rectus status* as confirmed by Paul's moral criticism in Romans:

> Why do you humble yourself [*humilias*] and bend over for false gods . . . and bow to dumb images [*simulacra*] . . . God made you upright [*rectum*], and while other animals . . . are pressed upon the earth, your status is elevated [*sublimis*

---

63 (2009): pp. 189–210. Walter, *Pagane Texte und Wertvorstellungen bei Laktanz*, pp. 152–172. Also, Monat, *Lactance et la Bible*, remains fundamental.

[118] Lactantius, *Inst.*, 5.17.17.

[119] Tertullian, *Prax.*, 23. Cf. *Apol.*, 30. Cyprian, *De opere et eleemosynis*, 24. Minucius Felix, *Oct.*, 37. This is not a programmatic usage, but it does appear in context of the same larger argument against Roman religion and imperial worship.

[120] Minucius Felix, *Oct.*, 17.2, "*quod illa prona in terramque vergentia nihil nata sint prospicere nisi pabulum, quibus vultus erectus, quibus suspectus in caelum datus est, sermo et ratio, per quae deum adgnoscimus sentimus imitamur.*" *Oct.*, 17.11, "*vultus erecctus, oculi in summo velut in specula constitute.*" *Oct.*, 37.1, 37.7.

status]. To heaven and to his own God his face is lifted up [*vultus erectus*]. Lift your eyes [to heaven] and seek [*quaere*] God in the heights [*in supernis*]. Raise your heart suspended to high and heavenly places [*ad alta et caelestia*]. Why do you stretch yourself out in the fall of death with the serpent whom you worship [Rom. 1:23]? Why do you fall into the ruin of the devil through him and with him [Gen. 3]? Keep to the high place [*sublimitatem*] where you were born. Persevere as you were made by God. With the rising of your face and body [*cum statu oris et corporis*] stand up your soul [*animam*]. That you may acknowledge God [*cognoscere deum*], know first yourself [*cognosce*] . . . Believe in Christ, whom the Father sent to give us life and heal us.[121]

This statement of Cyprian places the *rectus status* theme into a rhetorical and theological form that Lactantius precisely reproduces. Both the language of Cyprian's comments and the logical progression of his argument about the *rectus status* topos reveal Lactantius's debt to *Ad Demetrianum* 16. Cyprian's first claim is that humanity's "upright stance" indicates that worshipping images is inappropriate for humans. Second, he asserts that the relationship between humanity's "upward posture" and God's location "above" means that self-knowledge is the beginning of knowledge of God. Therefore, third, Cyprian urges Demetrianus to "seek God [*quaere*]" on high, and he contrasts this upward-looking search with downward-looking mortal fate. In a glancing reference to Rom. 1:23–25, Cyprian warns that death comes from worshipping serpents. Cyprian thus frames salvation as a return to humanity's high birthplace (*sublimitas*) and to an original created form. That form he elsewhere identifies with the imitation of Christ's virtue, *patientia*. Christians, he says, "being slaves and worshippers of God [*servi et cultores dei*] learn patience from heavenly instruction [*magisteriis caelestibus*]."[122] The line attributes the title "*cultor dei*" (which also appears in *Ad Demetrianum*) to Christians, who are defined as people taught from heaven by the example of the incarnate Christ. In both treatises, then, the description of Christians as "*cultores dei*" connects Cyprian's apologetic argument about humanity's upward gaze to his pastoral theology, which urges Christians toward the imitation of Christ.

Lactantius precisely reproduces the language and logic of Cyprian's exhortations.[123] As an image of Christ, the *rectus status* theme appears first at

---

[121] Cyprian, *Demet.*, 16 in *Cyprien de Carthage, À Démétrien: Introduction, texte critique, traduction et commentaire par Jean-Claude Fredouille* (Paris: Editions du Cerf, 2003). For "*cultor dei*," see *Demet.*, 12, 17, 20. Also, *Quir.*, 3.14, *Mort.*, 12.238, *Demet.*, 17, 20, *Bon. pat.*, 3.35, *De mortalitate*, 14, as a description of the martyr: "What sublimity [*sublimitas*] to stand upright [*stare rectum*] amid the ruins of the human race rather than lying prostrate with those who have no hope in God."

[122] Cyprian, *Bon. pat.*, 3.35.

[123] Lactantius, *Inst.*, 5.1.20–22.

232 ROMAN VIRTUE IN THE EARLY CHRISTIAN THOUGHT OF LACTANTIUS

Inst. 2.18.6, in the transition from Lactantius's criticism of Roman religion to his critique of philosophic virtue. The early passage is replete with latent reference to the Pauline letters, and it repeats Cyprian's logic exactly:

> Whoever strives [*nititur*] therefore to keep [*tueri*] the mystery of mankind and to obtain an account of his own nature, will lift himself from the dirt [*ab humo*] and with mind uplifted [*mente erecta*] stretch forth [*tendat*] his eyes into heaven. Let him not seek [*quaerat*] God under his own feet ... but let him seek [*quaerat*] God on high [*in sublimi*], in the highest place [*in summo*] ... wherever there is an image [*simulacrum*], there is no religion [*religio*]. ... Thus, what is true must be preferred to all false notions and earthly things trampled under foot that we may obtain heavenly things [*calcanda terrena ut caelestia*]. ... Whoever prostrates his own soul, whose origin [*origo*] is from heaven, to deep and lowly places [*ad inferna et ima*] falls to the place where he cast himself down. He cannot hold [*tendere*] on to the memory of his own definition and standing [*rationis ac status*] without always striving toward things above [*ad superna*].[124]

Antonie Wlosok cited *Inst.* 2.18 and its counterpart at *Epit.* 20, as evidence that "Lactantius's 'cultor dei' precisely expresses the image of the pious gnostic, above all, according to the portrait of Asclepius."[125] However, Cyprian's exegesis and terminology animate the entire portrait. Lactantius repeats language—*ab humo, simulacra, mens erecta*—readily apparent in *Demet.* 16, a treatise he certainly knew and read. Moreover, *Inst.* 2.18 also restates the same theological argument that Cyprian had attached to the *rectus status* theme. Lactantius urges human beings to make a rational movement from the fact of their upright stance to the knowledge of their immortal origin, and on that basis to turn from false worship to the worship of Christ. Moreover, the end of *Inst.* 2.18 contains insinuations of Col. 3:1–2, which appear to be mediated by Cyprian's *Quir.* 3.11. Lactantius's opposition between *terrena* and *caelestia*, along with his use of forms of *tendere*, echo the heading of Cyprian's *Quir.* 3.11: "That ... one must think only upon heavenly and spiritual things [*caelestia tantum et spiritalia*] and not attend [*adtendere*] to the age."[126] The heading is clearly shaped by Pauline theology, since beneath the heading, Cyprian's scriptural catena includes Col. 3:1–2: "Therefore, if you have been raised together [*consurrexistis*] with Christ, seek those things which are above [*quae sursum sunt, quaerite*], where Christ is. Be wise about those things which are above [*quae sursum sunt, sapite*], not things on earth [*super*

---

[124] Lactantius, *Inst.*, 2.18.1, 4–5.
[125] Contra Wlosok, *Laktanz und die philosophische Gnosis*, p. 221.
[126] Cyprian, *Quir.*, 3.11.1.

terram]."[127] Cyprian's grouping of Col. 3:1–2 beneath a heading that draws a dichotomy between "earthly" and "heavenly" provides obvious precedent for Lactantius's use of the same language. Lactantius embellishes the language, but his phrase *oculos ... tendat in caelum*, his use of *tendere*, and his term *caelestia* reflect Cyprian's *adtendere* and the *caelestia-spiritalia* opposition. Additionally, Lactantius's use of *quaerat* two times echoes the double imperatives (*quaerite/sapite*) of Col. 3:1–2. Hence also, when *Epit.* 20.9 redacts *Inst.* 2.18.5, both the terms *sursum* and *quaerere* of Col. 3:2 reappear: "For this reason a person is called ἄνθρωπος, because he looks above and ... seeks [*quia sursum spectet ... quaerit*] the true God with face and eyes lifted up."[128] Perhaps, Lactantius's "*quia sursum spectet*" evokes, by homophony, the Pauline "*quae sursum sunt.*"[129] Though Lactantius's usage is always indirect, by allusion, the preponderance of terms that appear, along with the sense he attaches to them, justifies the suggestion that Col. 3:1–2 mediated by Cyprian stands behind Lactantius's evocation of the *rectus status* theme at *Inst.* 2.18.

Alongside allusions to Col. 3:1–2, *Inst.* 2.18.6 concludes with a more apparent reference to Paul's account of sin and idolatry in Rom. 1:22–32. Cyprian alluded to the same text at *Demet.* 16. In Lactantius, the allusion presents the ideal "worshipper of God" as the inverse of a sinful humanity defined in terms of Romans 1:23–32. Lactantius says: "Whoever does this plainly, this is the wise person [*hic sapiens*], this is the just one [*hic iustus*], this is the human [*hic homo*]; and he will be judged worthy of heaven [*caelo dignus iudicabitur*], because his own Parent will acknowledge him, not as earthly [*humilem*] and cast to the ground like a four-footed beast, but standing upright [*stantem potius ac rectum*] as He made him."[130] Lactantius's phrase "*hic homo, hic sapiens, hic iustus*" is the first assertion of an ideal figure, who becomes fully described only in the latter argument at *Inst.* 5.14–18. The phrase gives an early outline of Lactantius's ideal worshipper of God and contains language that Lactantius sharpens and recapitulates in the course of his argument. In that respect, these lines mark the starting point of a narrative trajectory that is threaded throughout the rest of his

---

[127] *Inst.*, 3.11.53. Cf. Col. 3:1–2. Cf. *VLD* [Au. s Dol. 17,6] Col. 3:1–2. Augustine uses *tendere* along with a citation of Col. 3:1–2 to urge his readers to look up and not be curved: "*Erigere a curvedine tua, noli terram sapere. Resurrexisti cum Christo, ille in caelo est: ad illum te tende et curvus non eris.*" Prior to Augustine, *Epit.*, 20.4 uses the same language: "*quodsi sursum oculos suos tollerent ac deum intuerentur, qui eos ad aspectum caeli suique excitauit, numquam se curuos et humiles facerent terrena uenerando.*" Cf. Tertullian, *De ressurectione carnis*, 23.15. Citing Col. 3:1–2: "*Ita animo ostendit resurgere, quo solo adhuc possumus caelestia adtingere, quae non quaereremus nec saperemus si possideremus.*"

[128] Lactantius, *Epit.*, 20.9.

[129] Cf. Cyprian, *De zelo et livore*, 14: "*Si filii dei sumus, si templa eius esse iam coepimus, si accepto spiritu sancto sancte et spiritaliter uiuimus, si de terris oculos ad caelum sustulimus, si ad superna et diuina plenum deo et christo pectus ereximus, non nisi quae sunt deo et christo digna faciamus.*" Also, Cyprian, *Ep.*, 11.7.

[130] Lactantius, *Inst.*, 2.18.5–6.

234 ROMAN VIRTUE IN THE EARLY CHRISTIAN THOUGHT OF LACTANTIUS

work. At *Inst.* 2.18.6, this ideal *iustus homo* is a simple inversion of Paul's vision of fallen humanity at Romans 1. Paul writes:

> Though claiming to be wise [*sapientes*], they became foolish, and exchanged the glory of the incorruptible [*incorruptibilis*] God for the likeness of an image [*in similitudinem imaginis*] of corruptible [*corruptibilis hominis*] humanity, birds, four-footed animals [*quadrupedum*], and serpents. . . . Those who refused to have God in their knowledge . . . although they knew the justice [*iustiam*] of God . . . are deemed worthy of death [*digni sunt morte*].[131]

Lactantius's allusions to Romans 1:22–32 are suggested by his use of the terms *sapiens, iustus, quadrupedis,* and *dignus,* within the context of a statement that inverts Paul's judgment. Romans 1 describes people who think they are "wise [*sapientes*]," but despise "justice [*iustitia*]" because they worship the images of "four-footed beasts [*quadrupedum*]." Lactantius describes the inverse: because this person worships God, he is truly "wise" and "just," unlike the "four-footed beasts," and so "will be judged worthy [*dignus iudicabitur*]," not of death, but heaven.[132] This ideal simply retraces and accentuates Paul's logic.

As the narrative progresses, however, Lactantius sharpens this ideal and its exegetical basis, first at *Inst.* 3.27 and then in the Christological narrative of *Inst.* 4. Lactantius's next statement of the *rectus status* theme appears in the transition from his criticism of the Stoic Sage in *Inst.* 3 to his exposition of Christ's person and work. *Inst.* 4.1.1–6 recapitulates all the Cyprianic language and logic of *Inst.* 2.18.6, including Lactantius's reference to Rom. 1:23–32. Lactantius laments that "the former status of the human race [*status*]" has been lost, such that "the definition of humanity [*ratio humanitatis*]" has been forgotten, and so the happiness of humanity was "changed [*mutata est*]," in the worship of "corrupted and breakable gods."[133] The terms *veritas, corruptos,* and *mutata est* recapitulate *Inst.* 2.18's allusions to Rom. 1:22–32.[134] Lactantius furthermore calls this miserable status "*indignum*," the opposite of the term "*dignum*" declared by God upon "the just man" at 2.18.6.[135] Naming this problem *perversitas,* Lactantius abstracts a vision

---

[131] *VLD* Rom. 1:22–23, "*Dicentes enim se esse sapientes, stulti facti sunt. Et mutaverunt gloriam incorruptibilis Dei in similitudinem imaginis corruptibilis hominis et volucrum et quadrupedum et serpentium.*"

[132] Lactantius, *Inst.,* 2.18.6. Cf. Rom. 1:32. *Biblia Patristica* II gives *Inst.* 2.5.5–6, 2.6.1, and 2.18.3 as allusions *ad sensum* to Rom. 1:22–23. *Inst.,* 2.3.18, "*qui se sapientes non esse fateantur . . . qui sapientiam professi stultitiam potius exhibent.*" *VLD* Rom. 1:22, "*dicentes se esse sapientes stulti facti sunt.*"

[133] Lactantius, *Inst.,* 4.1–3. *VLD* Rom. 1:23, "*et mutaverunt gloriam incorruptibilis dei in similitudinem imaginis corruptibilis hominis et volucrum et quadripedum et serpentium.*"

[134] *Biblia Patristica* cites this passage as a reference to Rom. 1:25. McGuckin, *Researches in the Divine Institutes of Lactantius,* pp. 256–257, argued that Lactantius's language of *corruptible-incorruptible* "reproduces scriptural doctrine" attributable to Paul.

[135] Lactantius, *Inst.,* 4.1.3.

of sin from the physical image of a person bent over rather than standing upright. Theologically, he makes idolatry the foundation of human ills, as Romans 1 also does. This reassertion of Cyprian's argument connects the *rectus status* theme to a Christological narrative that unifies the *Divine Institutes*. From beginning to end, the work asserts that Christ's person and work is the source and form of wisdom and justice.

By restating the *rectus status* theme, *Inst.* 4.1 presents Christology as the answer to a problem rooted in false worship, which is of course Lactantius's fundamental critique. *Inst.* 4.2–6 sharpens the argument by wedding Pauline references to Johannine imagery of light. In the passage that follows, Lactantius evokes Romans 1, but adds allusions to 1 John 1:1–3 and John 1:5. Just as *Inst.* 2.18 inverts Paul's judgment, Lactantius likewise inverts a Johannine narrative of Christ's work to explicate the problems of sinful humanity. The image of fallen humanity amounts to a photographic negative of Lactantius's positive Christology:

> What this perversity caused, what evils it produced, the thing itself declares. They were turned away from the Highest Good—which is blessed and everlasting [*ideo beatum ac sempiternum*], because it cannot be seen, touched, comprehended [*videri tangi comprehendi*], and from the virtues congruent with it, which are equally immortal. Fallen into those corrupted and breakable [Rom. 1:25] gods and desiring those things by which the body alone is adorned, sustained, delighted, people sought for themselves endless death with bodily gods and goods; for every body is subject to death. Injustice and impiety followed religions of this sort, as was bound to happen, for once they had scorned the eternal and incorruptible goods [Rom. 1:23–25], which humanity should alone desire, [people] preferred temporal and passing things. . . . Thus shadow and darkness comprehended human life, which once in former times was lived in the brightest light [Jn. 1:4–5].[136]

In these lines, Johannine referents appear first in the words "*videri tangi comprehendi*." The problem that the true God cannot be "seen, felt, touched," evokes the tripartite formula of 1 John 1:2: "What we have seen [*vidimus*] with our eyes, what we have looked upon [*perspeximus*], what our hands have touched [*contractaverunt*] concerning the Word of life." Lactantius imitates John's phrase, but replaces *perspicere* with *comprehendere*. John 1:5 accounts for that replacement. At *Inst.* 4.1.6, Lactantius plays on the ambivalence of *comprehendere*—to understand or to overcome—in a phrase that rewrites John 1:4–5: "*sic humanam vitam prioribus saeculis in clarissima luce versatam caligo*

---

[136] Lactantius, *Inst.*, 4.3–5. Cf. *Octavius*, 17. Lactantius's tricolons echo Minucius Felix, *Oct.*, 17.

236 ROMAN VIRTUE IN THE EARLY CHRISTIAN THOUGHT OF LACTANTIUS

ac tenebrae comprehenderunt."[137] The implied claim is evident: lost in the darkness that overcame human life, humanity did not comprehend Christ.

Lactantius's above reference to John 1:5 foreshadows a Christological claim that the continuing discussion states explicitly. When he eventually narrates the earthly ministry of Christ, Lactantius describes Jesus with the same Johannine language: "The eyes of those whose lights were blind and in deepest darkness [*in altissimis tenebris*], he restored to their pristine sight [*pristinum aspectum*]."[138] The notion of a "*pristine*" light refers back to the "*in prior ages*" of the earlier passage; Christ's work reverses the earlier condition of darkness and violence. Hence also, Lactantius's concluding summary of Christ's person and work combines references to Rom. 1 and John 1:5. Immediately following a citation of Is. 42:6, Lactantius says: "Although before, blind and locked in the prison of foolishness [*stultitiae*], we were sitting in darkness [*in tenebris*] not knowing God or the truth [*ignorantes deum et veritatem*], we were illuminated by him, who adopted us by his own testament and brought us freed from evil chains and led into the light of wisdom into the inheritance of a heavenly kingdom."[139] Arriving immediately after a direct citation, Lactantius offers these lines as a commentary on Is. 42:6, and as a summary of the argument in *Inst.* 4.21. The lines also repeat Lactantius's references to Rom 1:22–32—*stultitia, ignorantes deum et veritatem*—combined with allusions to John 1:5—*in tenebris, in lucem sapientiae*. In so doing, his narrative of Christ provides the answer to the human problem that he captured with the *rectus status* theme at *Inst.* 2.18 and 4.1.1–6.

Lactantius's comments on Is. 42:6 also have a precedent in Cyprian. The citation of Is. 42:6 comes from *Quir.* 2.7, whose heading states: "That Christ would come as the illuminator and savior of the human race."[140] Under that heading, Cyprian groups Is. 42:6 with other texts and then comments: "Whence [*unde*] in the Gospel according to John, the Lord says: 'I am the light of the world.'"[141] Cyprian thus interprets Is. 42:6 through the exegesis of John's Gospel. Lactantius does the same thing. He cites Is. 42:6 (*Inst.*, 4.20.12) and then comments on the verse (*Inst.*, 4.20.13) with allusions to John and Paul. Cyprian's exegesis once again provides the theological lens through which Lactantius reads the *rectus status* theme and attributes to it a Christological significance common in early Latin theology. The whole theme takes up the same thread Lactantius introduced in his opening lines at *Inst.* 1.1–7: "Because truth . . . cannot be comprehended

---

[137] Lactantius, *Inst.*, 4.1.6. I think Lactantius enacts this thought syntactically by separating the accusatives and placing *caligo ac tenebrae* at the end, thus enveloping the former period of human life in the darkness.

[138] Lactantius, *Inst.*, 4.15.1.

[139] Lactantius, *Inst.*, 4.21.1.

[140] Cyprian, *Quir.*, 2.7.1. Heck and Wlosok, *Divinarum Institutionum Septem Libri, fasc.* 2, sees *Quir.* 2.7 behind the citation of Is. 42:6 at *Inst.* 4.20.

[141] Cyprian, *Quir.*, 2.7.14.

[*comprehendi*] by human faculties alone ... God did not suffer [*non passus est*] humanity seeking the light of wisdom [*lumen sapientiae*] to wander [*errare*] lost in inextricable darkness" anymore.[142] Along with the verb *passus est*, the language of the prologue is the language of *Inst.* 4 and of Lactantius's Christology. Likewise, the image of a person wandering in darkness recalls the Old Testament imagery in Isaiah, which Cyprian so often interprets through a Johannine lens. Lactantius's prologue thus begins painting a Christological portrait that becomes progressively more vivid in the course of his work.

Alongside scriptural allusions that anchor Lactantius's use of the *rectus status* theme in New Testament exegesis, his later descriptions of the Sage and of Christ sharpen the image of the "*cultor dei*" expressed at *Inst.* 2.18.5–6. The later passages identify Christ as the paradigmatic *cultor dei* by systematically attributing to Christ the virtues and wisdom of the Sage. By that attribution, Lactantius gradually transforms the *rectus status* from a philosophical and apologetic commonplace into a Christological paradigm.

As noted earlier, Lactantius connects the *rectus status* theme to his Christology at *Inst.* 2.18.5–6. The passage concludes with an abstract image of the Sage—*hic sapiens, hic iustus, hic homo*—who reappears most notably in the refutation of Carneades that occupies *Inst.* 5.14–18.[143] Between *Inst.* 2.18 and the much later account of justice at *Inst.* 5.14–18, Lactantius progressively fashions that figure to fit his image of Christ. After *Inst.* 2.18.6, the *iustus et sapiens* first reappears at *Inst.* 3.27.12, where Lactantius says: "The Wise Man [*sapiens*] is happy [*beatus*] then even under torture [*in tormentis*]: but when he is tortured for faithfulness [*pro fide*], for justice [*pro iustitia*], for God [*pro deo*], this endurance of pain will make him supremely happy [*beatissimum*]."[144] The connection with *Inst.* 2.18 is evident from the term *sapiens*, and the context. *Inst.* 3.27 refers to the same abstract type. Lactantius's debate with the Stoic Sage sharpens that abstraction by attributing to it the Christian virtues of justice, fidelity, and patience. These are the same virtues that Lactantius and his apologetic forebears constantly attribute to Christians alone.[145] Lactantius then subsumes both passages (*Inst.*, 2.18.5–6, *Inst.*, 3.27) in his explanation of the Son. For example, in narrating the Son's first birth, Lactantius explains: "This first-born alone was deemed worthy [*dignatus est*] of the title of the divine name."[146] The term *dignatus est* applies to the Son the declaration of "dignity" promised to the upward-looking "worshipper of God" at *Inst.* 2.18.5–6. The Son receives just what *Inst.* 2.18.5 promised to the true worshipper of God, the Sage, who looks upward to his heavenly Parent. It is the

[142] Lactantius, *Inst.*, 1.1–7.
[143] Hansen, "Preaching to Seneca," pp. 541–558.
[144] Lactantius, *Inst.*, 3.27.12.
[145] *Patientia: Inst.*, 4.24–26, 5.9–13. *Fidelis: Inst.*, 4.14, 4.29, 5.1.26, 5.5.11, 5.19.29.
[146] Lactantius, *Inst.*, 4.6.3.

238　ROMAN VIRTUE IN THE EARLY CHRISTIAN THOUGHT OF LACTANTIUS

same *dignitas* that Lactantius's *iustus et sapiens* earns from God, when he makes himself equal to those beneath him (*Inst.*, 5.16). Lactantius eventually applies the virtues outlined in his criticism of the Sage (*Inst.*, 3.27) to Christ in his suffering and passion:

> I come now to the passion itself . . . so that I may show that this passion was undertaken with great and divine reason [*cum magna et ratione divina*] and that in it alone, virtue [*virtus*], and truth [*veritas*], and wisdom [*sapientia*] are contained [*Inst.*, 1.1–7]. . . . For even if the most blessed one [*beatissimus, Inst.*, 3.27] had been on the earth and had ruled through his whole life in the highest happiness, no wise man [*sapiens, Inst.*, 2.18.6, 3.27] would have believed that he was God or judged him worthy [*diuino dignum iudicasset*] of divine honor. . . . For nothing among earthly things [*in rebus terrenis*] can be venerable and worthy of heaven [*caeloque dignum*], but virtue alone.[147]

This account of the cross epitomizes Lactantius's prior arguments. Here again, the terms *beatissimus* and *sapiens* refer back to the Sage at *Inst.* 3.27.12. Likewise, the phrases "judged him worthy" and "worthy of heaven" repeat exactly Lactantius's description of the "*cultor dei*," who has come to adopt the form of the suffering Christ. Two chapters later, Lactantius applies the virtues of the Sage to the same human Christ: "Because he remained *fidelis* . . . he received the *dignitas* of an eternal priesthood . . . and the *nomen* of God."[148] As a "priest," the earthly Christ is also a "worshipper," and his *dignitas* is the one given to the Son in his first birth, whose was alone "deemed worthy [*dignatus est*]" of God's power and name.[149] The terms *dignitas* and *dignatus est* repeat Lactantius's promise at *Inst.* 2.18.6 (*caelo dignum iudicatur*), while Christ's faithfulness and wisdom identify him as the Sage of *Inst.* 3.27. The string of verbal allusions associates the person of Christ himself with Lactantius's development of the ideal human being, whom he describes according to the *rectus status* theme (*Inst.*, 2.18). The whole narrative builds up to *Inst.* 5.14–18, where Lactantius describes a new paradigm for human righteousness illuminated by the revelation of God in Christ. By this theme, Lactantius makes Christ the paradigm of all wisdom, worship, and virtue (*Inst.*, 4.8, 4.16).[150] Such constant reference to Jesus unifies the *Divine Institutes* and marks the coherence of its argument.

---

[147] Lactantius, *Inst.*, 4.16.1–3.

[148] Lactantius, *Inst.*, 4.18.20.

[149] Lactantius, *Inst.*, 4.6.

[150] Several OT citations also portray Christ with the formul *iustus homo* of *Inst.* 2.18.6. Cf. *Inst.*, 4.16.7. Wis. 2:12–22, "Solomon *in libro Sapientiae his verbis usus est*: '*Circumveniamus iustum, quoniam insuauis est nobis et exprobrat nobis peccata legis*.'" Later, "[*Inst.*, 4.18.25] *David quoque in Psalmo XCIII*: '*captabunt animum iusti et sanguinem innocentem condemnabunt*.'"

Conclusion

More than forty years ago, V. Buchheit argued that Lactantius's description of *pietas* and *aequitas* translates Christ's famous double-love commandment into a Ciceronian idiom.[151] For Buchheit, the conceptual parallel between two duties, one owed to God and the other to humanity, expresses Christ's command to love God and neighbor. The textual referent was evident from Lactantius's redaction of his *Institutes* at *Epit.* 29.5–6, which replaces the term *aequitas* with the distinctly Christian *caritas*: "Justice itself is bound up in two duties [*duobus officiis obstricta*]: one we owe to God as Father, the other to humanity as brother.... We must know what we owe to God, and what to humanity. To God, namely *religio*, to humanity *caritas*."[152] Lactantius elaborates the same thought at *De ira dei* 14.3–5 and summarizes the idea with the distinctive phrase: "*in his enim duobus tota iustitia consistit.*"[153] Buchheit placed the phrase "*in his enim duobus*" into a pattern of progressively developing allusions to Christ's words in Matt. 22:36–40. That pattern begins at *Inst.* 5.14–15 and the conceptual parallel of two duties, one owed to God and another to humanity. When at *Epit.* 29.5–6, Lactantius inserts the term *caritas*, he betrays the distinctly Christian notion of "love" that animates his idea. The phrase "*in his enim duobus*" is later lifted from Christ's own assertion that his double-love commandment captures the entire law and the prophets: "*In his duobus mandatis universa lex pendet et prophetae.*"[154] Buchheit revealed the exegesis that informed Lactantius's argument. This chapter reveals the theological structure that determines Lactantius's exegesis. Whatever the rhetorical form of his argument, Lactantius presents Christ's public life and teaching as the basis for a new account of human society illuminated by the Incarnation. In his vertical relationship to the Father and his horizontal relationship to other human beings, Christ reveals the true character of the divine nature and provides, in his Incarnation, a final and eternal *exemplum virtutis*. The fact that Lactantius's notion of justice develops from his understanding of the divine nature resolves any need to determine if Lactantius's notion of justice was authentically Christian, or some amalgamation of variously Ciceronian, Stoic, and Gnostic ideas.[155] Rooted in the words of Christ, Lactantius develops his central moral equation (*iustitia = pietas + aequitas*) from Christ's *exemplum*, which asserts that the inner life of the Christian God is the eternal model for right relations among beings of identical nature and therefore dignity.

---

[151] Vinzenz Buchheit, "Die Definition der Gerechtigkeit bei Laktanz und seinen Vorgängern," pp. 356–374, who demonstrates that Lactantius's definition of justice remains consistent across his works (*Inst.*, 5.14. and 6.10.2; also *Ep.*, 29.5–6, 54.6–9, 55.1 and *Ira.*, 14.4–5).

[152] Lactantius, *Epit.*, 29.5–6.

[153] Lactantius, *Ira.*, 14.3–5. See Buchheit, "Die definition der Gerechtigkeit bei Laktanz," pp. 362–363.

[154] Matt. 22:40, cited in Buchheit, "Die definition der Gerechtigkeit bei Laktanz," p. 363.

[155] For this argument, see the Introduction, this volume.

7

Virtus: Christ's Precepts of Justice

In the Gospel, the Lord, the instructor of our life [*doctor nostrae vitae*] and teacher of eternal salvation [*magister aeternae salutis*], brings to life his faithful people and counsels those now enlivened unto what is eternal [*in aeternum*]. Among his divine mandates and heavenly precepts [*inter sua mandata et praecepta caelestia*], he mandates and prescribes [*mandat et praecipit*] nothing more often than that we should do mercy, that we should not sit upon our earthly possessions but "store up heavenly treasures" [Lk. 12:33]. "Sell," he says, "all your things and give mercy." Again, he says [Matt. 6:19–21], "Do not wish to establish [*condere*] your treasures upon the earth, where moth and rust destroy, where thieves break in and steal."

—Cyprian, *De opere et eleemosynis,* 7

Institutio 5 (*De iustitia*) narrates Lactantius's foundational moral equation (*iustitia = pietas + aequitas*) on the basis of Christ's public example and of the vision of God's inner life that example reveals. *Institutio* 6 (*De vero cultu*) elaborates the practical implications of that moral vision.[1] Relying upon the now traditional Latin division of Christ's *opera* into his "actions in suffering" and "words in teaching," which together constitute a "sight of the Father," Lactantius develops a moral theology shaped profoundly by Cyprian's exegesis. He presents that moral theology as a true account of the natural law, which classical philosophy had only dimly perceived.[2] Although Lactantius refers interchangeably to *officia*, *mandata*, and *praecepta iustitiae*, his discussion turns on the Ciceronian terms *pietas* and *aequitas*.[3] Under the heading of *pietas*, *Inst.* 6.2–9 mounts a critique of Ciceronian morality, which presents Christ as superior to Cicero and the tradition he represented. A shift to *aequitas* at *Inst.* 6.10 then inaugurates Lactantius's positive account of the divine and human order. Advocating Christian views of

---

[1] For rhetorical analysis of *Institutiones* 5 and 6, see Blandine Colot, *Lactance: Penser la conversion de Rome au temps de Constantin* (Firenze: Leo S. Olschki, 2016), pp. 82–87, 107–111, who explains them as a kind of literary diptych.
[2] See Chapter 5, this volume.
[3] E.g., *Inst.*, 4.26.27, 6.9.15, 6.10.2, 6.18.3, *Ep.*, 54.4–5, 68.2.

Roman Virtue in the Early Christian Thought of Lactantius. Jason M. Gehrke, Oxford University Press.
© Oxford University Press 2025. DOI: 10.1093/9780197667781.003.0008

VIRTUS: CHRIST'S PRECEPTS OF JUSTICE 241

wealth, emotion, violence, and sexuality, Lactantius reintroduces the Ciceronian language of *humanitas* and *patientia* in order to invest Cicero's moral vocabulary with a content derived from Christ's life and ministry, as recounted in the preceding narratives of *Inst.* 4–5. *Humanitas* and *patientia* thus appear as two manifestations of a single *aequitas* that expresses God's beneficent character toward human beings. *Humanitas* expresses the mutual piety, love, and goodwill revealed in the inner life of the Father and Son, and it becomes the fundamental virtue of human society remade in God's image. Lactantius thus also uses *humanitas* as a synonym for *misericordia*; he derives its meaning from Luke's Gospel. *Patientia* likewise comes to signify the long-suffering disposition adopted by those who take Christ as their supreme model of virtue. Both terms express Christ's famous double-love commandment in its various implications and manifestations (Matt. 22:36–40).[4] By these formulations, *Institutio* 6 works to supplant Ciceronian morality with a Christian account of the divine and human order derived from the example and words of Jesus.[5]

My aim in this final chapter is to reveal the theological character of Lactantius's ethics as a critical engagement with the classical tradition, one that draws upon third-century Latin Christian exegesis of Scripture. To that end, this chapter first establishes Lactantius's critical position relative to classical moral philosophies represented by Cicero and Lucretius. It then proceeds to show that Lactantius's notion of *humanitas* is derived from his vision of relations between the Father and Son articulated in *Institutes* 5 and 6. Lactantius advocates the imitation of a divine model known only from the life of Jesus. Hence, he extrapolates his idea of *humanitas* from the *Divine Institutes'* earlier account of the mutual *pietas* that Father and Son have toward one another. This redefinition of *humanitas* is grounded exegetically in early Latin Christian exegesis of the Gospels, and especially in the work of Cyprian. Proceeding to the idea of *aequitas*, the discussion explores Lactantius's reading of the Synoptic Gospels—mainly Matthew and Luke—in order to demonstrate the exegetical basis of his teaching on wealth, emotion, killing, and marriage. Although he reviews a mainly traditional set of practices, Lactantius gives them new justification and systematic unity by grounding them in his Christian understanding of the divine nature and representing them as a complete account of the natural law. Ultimately, the discussion expresses the theoretical implications of Lactantius's fundamental notion of Christ's revelatory mission: "God Most High sent [him] to instruct mortality in the precepts of justice . . . Since there was no justice on earth, he

---

[4] See Vinzenz Buchheit, "Die Definition der Gerechtigkeit bei Laktanz und seinen Vorgängern," *Vigiliae Christianae* 33 (1979): pp. 356–374.

[5] Peter Garnsey, "Introduction," in Lactantius, *The Divine Institutes*, trans. Anthony Bowen and Peter Garnsey (Liverpool: Liverpool University Press, 2003), p. 35.

242 ROMAN VIRTUE IN THE EARLY CHRISTIAN THOUGHT OF LACTANTIUS

sent a teacher of justice as a new and living law."[6] Lactantius thus takes Christ's example and teaching as the foundation of an ethical system aimed to replace Ciceronian morality with a wisdom revealed in the Christian tradition.

Christ or Cicero: Lactantius's Critical Position

In the early chapters of *Institutio* 6, Lactantius again represents himself as the heir to Minucius Felix and the third-century Latin apologists. Recapitulating his fundamental assertion that *religio* and *sapientia* must be joined in a worship-informed knowledge of the true God, Lactantius identifies Christ as the source of his own moral arguments. His brief review interprets the *sapientia-religio* dyad as pointing to the God of early Latin trinitarian theology. In the process, Lactantius distinguishes his ideas from the Epicurean and Ciceronian philosophies that *Institutio* 6 criticizes. Hence, Lactantius opens by restating his belief that true worship is the foundation of virtue and the first activity of justice because worship is due to God.[7] This recapitulation evokes the Johannine imagery of *Institutio* 4 and the notion of humanity's *rectus status*. The remarks position Lactantius's ethics as an expression of his Christology: "Just as we said in Book 2, the meaning [*ratio*] of heaven is in the mind, and of earth in the body. Those who do not know the goods of the mind seek the goods of the body and so 'dwell in darkness and death [*in tenebris ac morte versantur*]', which come of earth and body because life and light are from heaven [*quia vita et lumen a caelo est*]."[8] The rhetoric of these remarks names Christ and the Gospels, rather than Cicero and the philosophical tradition, as the source of the argument that follows. The reference to people "dwelling in darkness" recalls the central Johannine image of Christ as the "light of the world," the image with which Lactantius introduces his Christology in *Inst.* 4 and, indeed, the entire *Divine Institutes* at *Inst.* 1.1–3. He concludes the section with a familiar Latin apologetic rhetoric: "This is the religion of heaven, which is established not on the basis of corrupt things, but from the virtues of the soul which itself comes from heaven. And true worship is that

---

[6] Lactantius, *Inst.*, 4.25.1–2, "*Deus summus [eum] mitteret ad erundiendam praeceptis iustitiae mortalitatem . . . Nam cum iustitia nulla esset in terra, doctorem misit quasi novam legem vivam.*" Compare to Cyprian, *De opere et eleemosynis*, 7, in Cyprien de Carthage, *La Bienfaisance et les Aumônes*, intro., texte critique, trad., notes et index par Michel Poirier (Paris: Éditions du Cerf, 1999).

[7] Carmen Macarena Palomo Pinel, "The Survival of the Classical Idea of Justice in Lactantius's Work," *Studia Patristica* 80 (2019): pp. 173–182, shows that Lactantius's *pietas-aequitas* equation is indebted to the Roman law and connected to his related terms *ius humanitatis* and *ius fraternitatis*. Cf. Carmen Macarena Palomo Pinel, *Nec inmerito Paterfamilias Dicitur: El Paterfamilias en el Pensamiento de Lactancio* (Madrid: Dykinson, S. L., 2017), esp. pp. 95–137.

[8] Lactantius, *Inst.*, 6.1.10–12, "*nam sicut in secondo libro docuimus, caeli ratio in animo, terrae autem in corpore est. qui bona neglegunt animi, corporis appetunt, in tenebris ac morte versantur, quae sunt terrae autem in corpore est, quia vita et lumen a caelo est.*"

VIRTUS: CHRIST'S PRECEPTS OF JUSTICE   243

in which the mind of the worshipper offers itself to God as the spotless victim."[9] Minucius Felix had said it before in practically the same words.[10] By evoking Minucius and John's Gospel, Lactantius identifies himself as an advocate of Latin Christianity. The next several chapters confirm this point.

Lactantius means to represent an early Christian apologetic critique of classical Roman ethics, but his significant points of agreement with Cicero have sometimes obscured the revision he intended. He understood the potential for confusion and thus made a point to forestall misapprehension, first at *Inst.* 6.2.15–18 and again at *Inst.* 6.8.11–13.[11] In these passages, references to Christ bookend biting critiques of Lucilius and Cicero. First, he promises that if pagan philosophers can offer moral guidance, much more "can he who has been illuminated by God give true precepts [*et inluminati possumus vera praecipere*]."[12] The Johannine claim to illumination again positions Lactantius as the representative of Christ's teaching, and the reference to "teaching true things [*vera praecipere*]" recalls Lactantius's portrait of Christ as the *praeceptor iustitiae*. Lactantius thus promises "to perfect and bring to completion a justice which [the philosophers] do not grasp."[13] Both remarks frame the argument of *Institutio* 6 as an attempt to surpass and correct classical philosophy in the light of Christ's revelation. The latter passage (*Inst.*, 6.8.11–12) comes after Lactantius's critique of Lucilius and his exposition of the Two Ways doctrine. In this position, his argument reaffirms the distinction between Christ and Cicero. Lactantius thus praises Cicero's *De Re Publica* 3 as a matchless description of the *lex naturale*, but uses that praise to present Cicero only as the supreme example of human understanding falling short of Wisdom: "If he had truly seen the power and definition of the Holy Law [*legis sanctae vim et rationem*], so that he could have known and explained in what precepts the Holy Law itself consists, he would have performed the duty not of a philosopher, but of a prophet." Some have thought the comment pays Cicero a quasi-oracular honor.[14] In fact, he is construing Cicero as the best of the ignorant: "What [Cicero] could not do, must be done by us, to whom that law has been handed down by God, the one Teacher and Commander [*Magister*

---

[9] Lactantius, *Inst.*, 6.2.13–14. Pace Vincenzo Loi, "Il concetto di iustitia e i fattori culturali dell'etica di Lattanzio," *Salesianum* 28 (1966): pp. 613–614.

[10] Minucius Felix, *Oct.*, 32.3.2. See Chapter 3, this volume.

[11] Lactantius's Two Ways teaching and his critique of Lucilius—whom he (probably wrongly) identifies as the source of Cicero's *De officiis*—occupy the chapters intervening between 6.2 and 6.11.

[12] Lactantius, *Inst.*, 6.2.16.

[13] Lactantius, *Inst.*, 6.2.17–18.

[14] Lactantius, *Inst.*, 6.8.11. See F. Heim, "*Virtus* chez Lactance: Du *bonus vir* au Martyr," *Augustinianum* 36 (1996): pp. 361–366, "Il compare Cicéron avantageusement aux auteurs chrétiens initiés à la vraie foi et pourtant inferieurs à Cicéron dans la compréhension de la loi naturelle." Also, Christiane Ingremeau, "Lactance et la Justice: du Livre 5 au Livre 6 des *Institutions Divines*," in *Regards sur le monde antique. Hommages à Guy Sabbah*, ed. M. Piot (Lyon: Presses Universitaires de Lyon, 2002), p. 45, "Le texte de Cicéron est, on le voit, reçu comme quasi prophétique." Loi, "Il concetto di 'iustitia,'" p. 586, "Essa fu già intuita da Cicerone, il quale, quasi per divina ispirazione."

244 ROMAN VIRTUE IN THE EARLY CHRISTIAN THOUGHT OF LACTANTIUS

et Imperator] of all."[15] By invoking the Christological titles *Magister et Imperator*, Lactantius juxtaposes Christ and Cicero as alternative sources of moral knowledge. Cicero represents the classical Roman order while Christ is named as the source of a teaching mediated by early Christian tradition.[16]

Between the above statements at *Inst.* 6.2 and 6.8, Lactantius takes pains to distinguish his own positive ethics from the ideas and language of Ciceronian morality that his thought will partially employ. Following his critique of Lucilius at *Inst.* 6.6.25, Lactantius cites a key passage of Cicero. *De officiis* 3.69 argues that "there is an association [*societas*] that at its furthest extent unites all to all," and which contains a law to which positive law should conform.[17] Cicero then concedes a weakness, which Lactantius seizes upon: "'But we,' [Cicero] says, 'have no solid and expressed image of the true and genuine justice [*veri iuris germanaeque iustitiae solidam et expressam effigiem*], and we work with only shadow and images, if only we followed them!'"[18] Lactantius cites the comment to expose a contradiction in Cicero's position, and even more because the term *expressam effigiem* has a unique place in his own theology. At *Inst.* 2.12.10, Lactantius had already placed Cicero's vocabulary into a Christological context. There, he explains that there is found in living humanity the "*effigies expressa*" of a "*societas*" between heaven and earth.[19] This living image stands in sharp contrast to the dead images of Rome's traditional gods, which are only "*effigies* of dead men."[20] The former is a true, the latter a false, "image of God" on earth. The true image subsequently appears again at *Inst.* 4.8.9, where the term *effigies* designates the Son's status as the pre-incarnate expression of the Father's mind: "God comprehended a vocal spirit . . . whom he had conceived not in a womb, but mentally [*in mente*] by some unthinkable *virtus* of his majesty and power into an *effigiem* [*in effigiem*], which lives on its own understanding and wisdom."[21] Begotten of the Father, Christ is the *effigies* of the Father's *mens* produced by his *virtus* and so also the manifestation of Wisdom.[22] As such, Christ is also the *nova lex*, the eternal image of the *lex naturale*, the *effigies* of *virtus*, which Cicero had sought. When then Lactantius advocates his idea of *humanitas* as "'that true and genuine justice,' of which you [Cicero] claim to have 'no firm and expressed

[15] Lactantius, *Inst.*, 6.8.12.
[16] Cf. *Inst.*, 4.23, which called Christ "the new and living law."
[17] Cicero, *On Duties,* trans. Benjamin Patrick Newton (Ithaca, NY: Cornell University Press, 2016), p. 150.
[18] Lactantius, *Inst.*, 6.6.25 citing Cicero, *Off.*, 3.69.
[19] Lactantius, *Inst.*, 2.12.10.
[20] Lactantius, *Inst.*, 2.17.6.
[21] Lactantius, *Inst.*, 4.8.9. See Chapter 4, this volume. Lactantius uses *effigies* to express the *figura* and *imago* of VLD Heb. 1:3, "*qui est splendor gloriae et imago [figura – J] substantiae eius gerens [ferens – D] omnia verbo virtutis.*" Both *imago* and *figura*, translate the Greek: "ὃς ὢν ἀπαύγασμα τῆς δόξης καὶ χαρακτὴρ τῆς ὑποστάσεως αὐτοῦ, φέρων τε τὰ πάντα τῷ ῥήματι τῆς δυνάμεως."
[22] Lactantius, *Inst.*, 4.8.9. See Chapter 5, this volume.

VIRTUS: CHRIST'S PRECEPTS OF JUSTICE   245

image [*expressam effigiem nullam*]," he states by allusion an otherwise straight-forward claim that Christ is the revealed image of the moral order Cicero only dimly perceived.[23] As the Father's *effigies expressa*, Christ becomes the *nova lex vivens* in what "he both taught and did."[24]

Lactantius ties his moral argument to his doctrine of the divine nature at two other places in these chapters. The most important statements are at the heart of his criticism of Lucilius's doctrine of *virtus*, which Lactantius (incorrectly) takes as a condensed statement of Cicero's ethics in *De officiis*.[25] Lactantius presents Lucilius as evidence of the way classical philosophy erred because it lacked a true account of eternal life with God. His fundamental point is that philosophers could not on their own find the true source of virtue. At the conclusion of this argument, Lactantius uses the Two Ways teaching to redirect his reader to the Christian God:

> This Way, moreover, which is the way of Truth, Wisdom, Virtue, and Justice— for all of which there is one source [*fons unus*], one power [*una vis*], one seat [*una sedes*]—this Way is simple [*et simplex est*] and on it we all walk as one with equal minds [*paribus animis*] in supreme concord [*summa concordia*] and wor-ship God. It is narrow because *virtus* has been given to the few, and hard because one cannot come to that high and supreme good without difficulty and labor.[26]

In their immediate context, these lines complete Lactantius's description of the Two Ways teaching and immediately precede (yet another) restatement of the *rectus status* theme.[27] More profoundly, Lactantius's use of the technical lan-guage of Latin trinitarian theology again identifies the Christian God as both the object of any philosophical activity and the source of moral knowledge. The terms *fons*, *vis*, and *simplex* are all traditional terms that designate the oneness of the divine nature.[28] And in Cyprian's theology, those terms identify the Father

---

[23] Lactantius, *Inst.*, 6.11.13, "*haec est 'vera illa et germana iustitia, cuius solidam et expressam effigiem nullam tenere vos' dicis*."

[24] Lactantius, *Inst.*, 4.2, 4.16, 4.24.

[25] For Lucilius, see Lactance, *Institutions Divines Livre VI, Introduction, texte critique, traduction, notes et index par Christiane Ingremeau* (Paris: Éditions du Cerf, 2007), pp. 391–392.

[26] Lactantius, *Inst.*, 6.7.9. See Chapter 5, this volume. Cf. Lewis Ayres, *Nicaea and Its Legacy: An Approach to Fourth Century Trinitarian Theology* (Oxford: Oxford University Press, 2004), pp. 70–71.

[27] Lactantius's terms *angusta, via, difficultate, gradiamur* again echo Cyprian's description of the Christian life as a walk in the footsteps of Christ. Cf. Cyprian, *Fort.*, 11.61, noting *angusti*, "*angusti itineris difficultate gradiantur*." Also, Cyprian, *Bon. pat.*, 9, noting *via salutis, gradiamur, exem-plum Christi*, "*Quodsi et nos, fratres dilectissimi, in christo sumus, si ipsum induimus, si ipse est salutis nostrae uia, qui christum uestigiis salutaribus sequimur per christi exempla gradiamur, sicut iohannes apostolus instruit dicens: qui dicit se in christo manere debet quomodo ille ambulauit et ipse ambulare*." See Chapter 3, this volume.

[28] See Chapter 6, this volume.

246 ROMAN VIRTUE IN THE EARLY CHRISTIAN THOUGHT OF LACTANTIUS

as the source of a *virtus* that Christ reveals in his incarnate life. Lactantius thus positions Christ's revelation of the Father as the object of true wisdom and religion (i.e., *sapientia-religio*).

Lactantius ultimately uses the *sapientia-religio* theme and his critique of Cicero in the early chapters of *Institutio* 6 (*Institutio* 6.2–8) to identify Latin Christianity as the source of true moral and philosophical wisdom. These passages exemplify a rhetorical procedure that persists throughout the rest of *Institutio* 6. The argument begins by recapitulating the *Divine Institutes'* organizing claim that true wisdom and religion can be found only in Christ. The point is made in terms that echo earlier Latin apologists such as at *Inst.* 6.1–3. Lactantius then devotes several chapters to a critical argument conducted on philosophical grounds, before returning at *Inst.* 6.8.11–12 to his positive Christian position. In the process, he indicates the source of his thought by redeploying the rhetoric of his own earlier Christology. The same pattern and rhetoric recur in the later chapters as well. Usually, the rhetoric evokes Christ's distinctive role as *praeceptor iustitiae* or *nova lex vivens*. To make the connection, Lactantius designates specific moral practices as *praecepta iustitiae* and uses phrases such as *Deus praecipit* or *Deus monet* to attribute a given *praeceptum* to Jesus.[29] Such language recalls the Christology of *Institutio* 4 and ultimately updates a Christological rhetoric traceable to Cyprian's treatises.[30] As shall be seen, this method allows Lactantius to advocate the ethics of Jesus without presenting his arguments narrowly as a form of biblical exegesis. In the process, he renders his portrait of Christ as the ideal human—*iustus ac sapiens, bonus vir*—progressively more vivid through a rhetoric predicated on Cyprian's exegesis.

Aequitas and *Humanitas*: The Society of Father and Son

From *Inst.* 6.10 onward, Lactantius elaborates his vision of justice in human society under the heading of *aequitas*. *Inst.* 6.10–14 develops Cyprian's doctrine of human equality to provide a foundation for the ethical duties in whose practice *aequitas* consists. Lactantius thus reintroduces the terms *humanitas* and *misericordia* as practical expressions of *aequitas*.[31] In this context, he affirms the apparently Ciceronian doctrine that man is a social animal, united to others by a

---

[29] See Pierre Monat, *Lactance et la Bible: Une propédeutique latine à la lecture de la Bible dans l'Occident constantinien* (Paris: Études Augustiniennes, 1982), p. 257. shows that while Lactantius's specific *texts* are difficult to identify, his thought is often traceable to early Christian tradition.

[30] See Chapter 3, this volume.

[31] Cf. Lactantius, *Inst.*, 5.6.4, "Since there was not even a footprint of justice, whose duties are *humanitas aequitas misericordia*." Christiane Ingremeau, *Institutions Divines* VI (Paris: Éditions du Cerf, 2007), p. 408, notes that *Inst.* 6.10–12 contains twenty-six appearances of the term *humanitas*, which appears only forty-six times in the *Institutes*.

VIRTUS: CHRIST'S PRECEPTS OF JUSTICE 247

natural affection. Lactantius corrects Cicero, however, by defining *humanitas* as an expression of the image of the Christian God, whose inner life constitutes the model of right relations among human beings. *Humanitas* makes every human being equal and thus requires that *misericordia* be shown to all. Introducing this point, Lactantius reasserts his basic notion of justice as rooted in a twin obligation:

> I have said what is owed to God. I will now say what must be rendered to the human being [*homini tribuendum est*]. Although whatever you render to the human being you render also to God, because the human being is the image [*simulacrum*] of God. The first duty of justice is to be joined with God and the second with humanity [*cum homine*]; the first is called *religio* and the second, *misericordia* or *humanitas*. It is the virtue [*virtus*] of the just worshippers of God because it alone contains the meaning [*rationem*] of our common life [*vitae communis*].[32]

Lactantius introduces *humanitas* and *misericordia* to express the shared "affection of *pietas* [*adfectum pietatis*]" that God gave to humanity in order to distinguish people from animals. As Buchheit notes, the coupling of *pietas* and *aequitas* as obligations to God and human beings expresses Christ's command to love God and neighbor (Matt. 22:36–40) in a Ciceronian idiom. *Humanitas* expresses the fact that all people belong to a single human family: "If we have all arisen from one man whom God made, we are certainly relatives [*consanguinei*]," he argues.[33] The language of inspiration and generation, which animates Lactantius's account of human equality at *Inst.* 5.14.16, reappears in this context: "And if we have all been inspired and animated by one God, what else are we than brothers, even more closely joined by the fact of our souls than those related by bodily generation."[34] Because the divine likeness in human beings is spiritual and consists in the knowledge and worship of God, Lactantius regards the bond of naturally born siblings as lesser than the one every human being shares with every other. Revealing this truth of *humanitas* was basic to the Son's mission as expressed in *Inst.* 4.[35]

Lactantius presents his economic teaching as the first of Christ's mandates in the Gospels. The claim that human beings are made in God's image provides the principled basis for Lactantius's defense of an early Christian practice of using

---

[32] Lactantius, *Inst.*, 6.10.1–3.
[33] Lactantius, *Inst.*, 6.10.6.
[34] Lactantius, *Inst.*, 6.10.6. Cf. *Inst.*, 6.10.19, "One man was made by God and by him the whole earth was filled with one human race."
[35] Cf. Lactantius, *Inst.*, 4.1–2. See Chapter 4, this volume.

248 ROMAN VIRTUE IN THE EARLY CHRISTIAN THOUGHT OF LACTANTIUS

wealth to aid the lowly. Christ teaches almsgiving in order to affirm the familial character of human society:

> For the sake of this familial bond [*ob necessitudinem germanitatis*] God teaches us to do not evil, but good. Moreover, what doing good really is, he himself prescribes [*praescribit*]: to aid the humble and belabored, to share food with those who have none. For since God himself is *pius*, he willed that we be a social animal [*animal nos voluit esse sociale*]. And so we ought to consider ourselves in other human beings . . . We do not deserve to be freed from danger, if we do not help; we do not deserve aid, if we ourselves deny it. Concerning this, the philosophers give no moral instruction [*praecepta*].[36]

Earlier in the *Institutes*, Lactantius used vocabulary that expressed Christ's role as Teacher of Justice; here he recalls this language in order to attribute the precept directly to Christ, claiming that "he himself prescribes [*idem ipse praescribit*]" the real meaning of "doing well [*bene facere*]."[37] Likewise, the terms *iustus, pius,* and *humanus* ground Lactantius's argument in his earlier account of *iustitia* and its twin tributaries, *pietas* and *aequitas,* which express Christ's revelation of the divine persons.[38] It is "because God himself is *pius*" that he gave human beings that "*adfectum pietatis,*" which makes them a "social animal," Lactantius says.[39] The disposition that moves human beings to care for one another is not a mere animal affection for creatures of like nature. Rather, the human *adfectum pietatis* manifests that same quality which moved the Father to send his Son: "Since [God] is *clemens* and *pius* toward his own, he sent him to the very people he had hated, that he might not close off from them the way of salvation."[40]

Lactantius's notion of *humanitas* expresses on the human plane a Christian understanding of God's affection revealed in the inner life of the Father and Son. *Humanitas* provides "what should be bestowed upon human beings [*quod homini tribuendum est*]" made in God's likeness in the same way that "the Father loves [*diligat*] the Son and bestows all things upon him [*ei omnia tribuat*] and the Son faithfully obeys the Father and wants nothing but what the Father wants." *Humanitas* means showing to human beings the same love that Father and Son share, because that love constitutes the image of God in human beings: "*Humanitas* must be kept if we want to call ourselves human. And what else is it to keep *humanitas* than to love [*diligere*] other human beings, because

---

[36] Lactantius, *Inst.*, 6.10.8.
[37] Lactantius, *Inst.*, 6.10.9. Cf. Lactantius, *Inst.*, 3.14–17, 4.14.18, 4.24.17.
[38] See Chapter 5, this volume.
[39] Lactantius, *Inst.*, 6.10.3 and 6.10.10.
[40] Lactantius, *Inst.*, 4.11.15. Cf. Hosea 1:6–10, 11, 14.

VIRTUS: CHRIST'S PRECEPTS OF JUSTICE 249

they are human and the same as we are?"[41] When people care for one another, and especially for the lowly, they manifest that specific quality that constitutes their status as "living images of God [*simulacra Dei viventia*]."[42] In this respect, Lactantius does not derive his idea of human affection from philosophical reflection on the natural order or from the literature of philosophic gnosis. Rather, his moral theology presents a third-century Latin Christian account of the divine nature as the basis for his account of human society.

Lactantius's understanding of the image of God and his ethic of care for the lowly distinguish his notion of *humanitas* from any classical doctrine. He knew well that Cicero defended human affection as the first cause of human society. Lactantius argues, however, that Cicero knew the fact of human affection but not its cause, true content, or practical expression. Hence, Lactantius positions his principle of *humanitas* as a critique of Epicurean and Stoic moral systems. He uses a single line from *De natura rerum* to confirm the point that human beings belong to a common family: "In this respect, Lucretius is not wrong when he says that 'we have all arisen from a heavenly seed and all have the father.'"[43] The remark is ironic praise, however, because Lucretius would never affirm Lactantius's Christian idea of a personal and providential God. The subsequent paragraphs thus introduce a later passage of Lucretius to condemn the Epicurean idea that human society depends upon a people's need for protection against hunger and violence.[44] People did not "first begin to build towns [*oppida*] when they saw that the multitude needed to be kept safe against the beasts!"[45] Lactantius does briefly acknowledge that Cicero and the Stoics rejected such Epicurean theories: "Others . . . said that *humanitas* was itself the reason that humans congregated because people naturally flee from solitude and seek community and society."[46] Still, he presents Cicero and Lucretius as ultimately in

---

[41] Lactantius, *Inst.*, 11.1.1, "*Conservanda est igitur humanitas, si homines recte dici velimus. id autem ipsum conservare humanitatem, quid aliud est quam diligere hominem, quia homo sit et idem quod nos sumus?*"

[42] See *Inst.*, 6.13.13. In a play on *excolere*: "If worshippers of the gods carefully honor [*excolunt*] *simulacra insensibilia* . . . how much more true and just is it to carefully honor [*excolere*] *viventia Dei simulacra*." Lactantius uses the terms *simulacrum* and *imago* interchangeably. He does not seem to make a strong distinction between "image" and "likeness." Rather, the term *simulacrum* contrasts dead idols with living humans.

[43] Lucretius, *Nat. r.*, 2.991 at *Inst.*, 6.10.7.

[44] Lactantius's critique of the Epicurean view of society engages Lucretius, *Nat. r.*, 5.990–1029. See Ingremeau, *Institutiones Divines* VI, pp. 407–408. See Kristina Meinking, "*Sic Traditur a Platone*: Plato and the Philosophers in Lactantius," in *Plato in the Third Sophistic*, ed. Ryan C. Fowler (Berlin: DeGruyter, 2014), p. 106. Commenting on *De ira Dei*, Meinking explains, "Lactantius targets specific philosophers with whom he finds the multitude of philosophers to be in disagreement. The result is to create the effect of a triangulation: philosophers who held the 'wrong' opinion are demonstrated to have done so by those who hold the 'correct' opinion (in Lactantius's estimation), and Lactantius provides himself the opportunity of criticizing or supporting each view."

[45] Lactantius, *Inst.*, 6.10.15–16.

[46] Lactantius, *Inst.*, 6.10.18.

250 ROMAN VIRTUE IN THE EARLY CHRISTIAN THOUGHT OF LACTANTIUS

agreement because of what they do not know: "One man was created by God and the entire earth was populated from him, and it was in the same way after the flood."[47] The point reveals why Lucretius and Cicero ultimately "say the same thing [*res eadem est*]," in Lactantius's view.[48] Although Cicero spoke richly of affection as the cause of human society, he had no idea that true *humanitas* means caring for every being equally—even the lowly—in order to honor the likeness of God in each person and restore the original bond between divine and human society that God intended at creation.[49]

As Lactantius expands upon the duties of *humanitas* in *Inst.* 10.11–13, progressively more explicit references to Cyprian and the Gospels reveal the Christian provenance of his doctrine. Lactantius first indicated his debt to Cyprian when he expressed the view that justice consists in *pietas* and *aequitas*. *Inst.* 5.14.16 evokes Cyprian's original argument for human equality by repeating verbatim Cyprian's claim that God's gifts of light, water, food, and sleep constitute an *exemplum aequitatis* for Christians to emulate.[50] Lactantius's critique of Cicero thus advocates a position that Lactantius derives from Cyprian's treatise, *On Almsgiving*. When, later, Lactantius argues that Cicero undermined his own principle by urging people to be judicious in their liberality, he positions *On Duties* 2.52–56 as representing the very advice Cyprian rebuked when he urged parents to provide for their children's souls rather than their bodies.[51] Lactantius furthermore represents his notion of *humanitas* as the true idea and basis for just action.[52] He concludes with a remark that simultaneously evokes Christ's words in the Gospels, Cicero's lament at *De officiis* 3.69, and Cyprian's *Almsgiving* 7:

> Cast away "those dark images and take hold of the true and express image of justice." Be generous "to the blind, the lame, the destitute" [Matt. 11:5; Lk. 14], who must die unless you are generous. They are worthless [*inutiles*] to human beings, but useful [*utiles*] to God, who keeps them alive [*in vita*], gives them breath [*spiritu*], and judges them worthy of light [*luce dignatur*].[53]

---

[47] Lactantius, *Inst.*, 6.10.19. Lactantius's references to "one man" and the "flood" suggest he has in mind the Genesis accounts of creation and flood, and thus the figures Adam and Noah.

[48] Lactantius, *Inst.*, 6.10.19.

[49] *Pace* Loi, "Il concetto di 'iustitia,'" pp. 589–591, the notion of *humanitas seu misericordia* is a consistent expression of Lactantius's doctrine of human equality, which is not a mere rhetorical device at *Inst.*, 5.14.7.

[50] See Chapters 3 and 5, this volume. Cf. *Inst.*, 5.14.16; Cyprian, *De opere et eleemosynis*, 7, 25; *De dono patientiae*, 3–4.

[51] Cyprian, *De opere et eleemosynis*, 9.

[52] Lactantius, *Inst.*, 6.11.13, "non enim 'idoneis hominibus' largiendum est, sed quantum potest non idoneis. Id enim iuste, id pie, id humane fit, quod sine spe recipiendi feceris." The terms *iustus, pius*, and *humanus* refer to Lactantius's vision of the divine nature. Also, see Monat, *Lactance et la Bible*, p. 254, who notes that the phrase *"recipiendi spes"* makes reference to Luke 6:35.

[53] Lactantius, *Inst.*, 6.11.18. Cf. *Inst.*, 5.14.6 and Cyprian, *De opere et eleemosynis*, 7.

VIRTUS: CHRIST'S PRECEPTS OF JUSTICE   251

This citation represents a vision of Jesus mediated by Cyprian's theology and exegesis. Lactantius's references to life [*vita*], breath [*spiritu*], and light [*lumen*] are a compressed allusion to Cyprian's doctrine of human equality grounded in God's *exemplum aequitatis,* which Lactantius first cited more fully at *Inst.* 5.14.16.[54] Paired with that allusion, his reference to "the blind, the lame, and the destitute" is an *ad sensum* citation of Christ's parable of the wedding feast, whose Lukan version Cyprian had cited at *Almsgiving* 13.[55] Lactantius also returns to Luke's Gospel on the next page, this time naming Christ as his source: "Likewise, God prescribes [*praescribit*] that when we prepare a meal, we invite to the dinner those who cannot call us back to return the favor [*revocare et vicem reddere*], so that no act of our life should be lacking in the reward of *misericordia.*"[56] Lactantius does not here cite a specific text of Luke but rather, like Cyprian, uses the phrase "*Deus praescribit*" to introduce a summary statement of Christ's teaching in the Gospel (Lk. 14:8–11).[57] A more robust reference to the same passage concludes the argument: "They bury their goods in the earth because memory confers nothing upon the dead, nor are their works eternal. For either by some tremor of the earth they crumble and fall, or they are consumed by a chance fire, or demolished by some enemy's attack [*hostili aliquo impetu*] or at the least [*certe*] they become dilapidated by old age [*ipsa vetustate*]."[58]

Lactantius's criticism of the Roman culture of public benefactions rhetorically dresses up Christ's admonition to "lay up your treasures in heaven," familiar from the Gospels.[59] If there is any doubt, the argument concludes with a third reference to Luke 12:20/33: "Why hesitate to make passing and fragile goods eternal, to entrust your treasures [*thesauros tuos*] to God, where you would fear neither robber nor burglar, rust [*robigenem*] nor tyrant?"[60] This final remark repeats not

---

[54] See Chapter 3, this volume. Cf. *Inst.,* 6.11.18 to *Inst.,* 5.14.16 and Cyprian, *De bono patientiae,* 5 and 7, *De opere et eleemosynis,* 25.

[55] Monat, *Lactance et la Bible,* p. 254. Cf. Cyprian, *Ad Quirinum,* 3.1.133–139 under the heading "On Good Works and Mercy," Cyprian's last citation is to Luke 14:8–11: "Concerning this in the Gospel of Luke [14:8–11]: When you host a dinner or a meal, do not call your friends [*amicos*], nor your brothers [*fratres*] or neighbors [*uicinos*], nor the wealthy [*diuites*], lest by chance they invite you in return [*illi reinuitent te*] and it becomes a retribution against you [*fiet retributio tibi*]. When you host a dinner, call the homeless poor [*mendicos*], the disabled [*debiles*], the blind [*caecos*], the lame [*clodos*], and you will be happy [*felix eris*], for they have nothing to pay you back with [*retribuere tibi*], and so it will be returned to you in the resurrection of the just [*in resurrectione iustorum*]."

[56] Lactantius, *Inst.,* 6.12.3.

[57] See Chapter 3, this volume.

[58] Lactantius, *Inst.,* 6.11.24, "*bona sua in terra sepeliunt, quia nec memoria quidquam mortuis confert nec opera eorum sempiterna sunt, siquidem aut uno tremore terrae dissipantur et corruunt aut fortuito consumuntur incendio aut hostili aliquo impetu diruuntur aut certe vetustate ipsa dissoluta labuntur.*"

[59] *VLD* Luke 12:33. His use of the term *vetustas* recommends Luke 12:20/33 as an immediate textual referent. *VLD* has several variants for this verse, but all use the key terms *thesauros* and *vetescunt:* "*Date eleemosynam. Facite vobis sacculos, qui non veterescent thesaurum non deficientem in caelis, ubi fur non accedit, nec tinea consumit.*"

[60] Lactantius, *Inst.,* 6.12.35, "*Quid ergo dubitas bene collocare id, quod tibi forsan eripiet aut unum latrocinium aut existens repente proscriptio aut hostilis aliqua direptio? Quid verere fluxum fragile*

252 ROMAN VIRTUE IN THE EARLY CHRISTIAN THOUGHT OF LACTANTIUS

only Cyprian's exegesis, but even the rhetoric of *Almsgiving* 13, which concludes with a rhetorical question asking why people store earthly wealth at the expense of heavenly riches.[61]

As the discussion proceeds, Lactantius systematically reconstructs traditional Christian practices to show they express a Christian vision of virtue revealed in the life of Jesus. *Inst.* 6.12.15–31 elaborates Jesus's admonition to welcome the lowly by naming "works of mercy [*opus misercordiae*]" that express his doctrine of *humanitas*. V. Loi showed that the practices named reflect the deep imprint of early Christianity, but the fact that Lactantius constructs these practices as a direct expression of his third-century Christology has been mainly overlooked.[62] Lactantius alludes once more to Luke 14:12: "The home of the one who is just and wise should be open not to people of rank [*inlustribus*], but to the humble and downcast [*sed humilibus et abiectis*]."[63] To identify the *abjecti*, he specifies a list of "*officia iustitiae*" that early Christians regarded as good works. These include the ransom of captives (12.15, *captivorum redemptio*), protection and provision for impoverished widows and orphans (12.21, *pupillos et viduas destitutos et auxillio indigentes tueri atque defendere*), care for the sick (12.25, *aegros*), and burial of the dead (12.25, *peregrinorum et pauperum sepultura*). Lactantius attributes these practices to Christ's teaching. He says that care for widows, orphans, and the sick is "especially our work, since we have received the law, the words of God himself instructing us [*qui legem, qui verba Dei ipsius praecipientis accepimus*]."[64] The comment draws again on Cyprian's *Ad Quirinum* 3.113, which collects a catena of Old Testament mandates under the heading: "*Viduam et pupillos protegi oportere*."[65] Cyprian's passive infinitive *protegi* is an interpretive gloss on the collected texts, which do not use the verb. Lactantius seems to accept that gloss by describing the command as "guarding and defending orphans and widows."[66]

Lactantius attributes these practices not only to Christ's words but also to the example of his life in order to affirm and elucidate his foundational moral equation. As he says, "We [Christians] have received the law [*legem . . . accepimus*]

---

bonum facere sempiternum aut thesauros tuos custodi deo credere, ubi non furem praedonemque timeas, non robigenem, non tyrannum?" Heck and Wlosok, *Divinarum Institutionum*, pp. 584–585, refer this quote to Matt. 6:19–20 and Lk. 12:33; also Bowen and Garnsey, *Lactantius: The Divine Institutes*, p. 359.

[61] Cyprian, *De opere et eleemosynis*, 13.

[62] Loi, "Il concetto di 'iustitia,'" p. 606, who argues that "The depth of the influence of Christian teaching influenced on Lactantius is manifest in the very linguistic expression of his doctrine of *iustitia*." Loi shows that the phrases *opera iustitae*, *operari iustitiam*, *facere iustitiam*, and *operator iustitiae* all express distinctly septuagental and early Christian locutions.

[63] Lactantius, *Inst.*, 6.12.6.

[64] Lactantius, *Inst.*, 6.12.

[65] Cyprian, *Quir.*, 3.113.

[66] Lactantius, *Inst.*, 6.12.21.

VIRTUS: CHRIST'S PRECEPTS OF JUSTICE   253

instructing us," in the above passage.[67] All the actions Lactantius recommends imitate the ministry of Jesus. Care for the poor and sick is consistent with miracles enumerated in Lactantius's earlier summary of Christ's life and ministry (*Inst.*, 4.26). Likewise, by naming burial of travelers and the poor as "the last and greatest duty of piety [*pietatis officium*]," and by claiming that "the divine words command it to be done," Lactantius asserts the unity of his theory and practice.[68] He might have in mind the figure of Tobit, whom Cyprian cited favorably for his practice of burying the dead and giving alms.[69] It is notable that he later seems to give the Golden Rule in its negative form, following Tobit 4:15's influential command.[70] More important, Lactantius grounds this mandate in the doctrine of *humanitas:* "We will not suffer the form and workmanship of God [*figuram et figmentum Dei*] to lie in the open as a meal for wild animals and birds. We return it to the earth, whence it came," he argues. Reasserting this practice, Lactantius traces it to his own doctrine of the unity of human nature: "Even for a stranger, we will fulfill the duty [*munus*] owed to a family member [*necessariorum*], in whose absence, *humanitas* will draw near.... For justice really consists in this: what we do for our own families out of affection [*adfectum*], we do for strangers [*alienis*] through *humanitas*."[71]

Lactantius's doctrine of *humanitas* motivates a thorough defense of human emotion that comes immediately after his defense of almsgiving. As Christiane Ingremeau explains, *Inst.* 6.14–19 critiques "the four fundamental passions ... according to their traditional classification—desire (*cupiditas/ἐπιθυμία*), pleasure (*laetitia/ἡδονή*), fear (*metus/φόβος*), and grief (*maestitia/λύπη*)."[72] Lactantius regards the Stoic theory that emotions are a kind of sickness as a typical example of the way philosophers fell short of the truth because they had no clear account of the divine nature, whose affection for human beings and wrath at sin are a model for human affection as well. Lactantius thus argues that eliminating the emotions would eliminate virtue, given that virtue is a capacity to govern oneself

---

[67] Lactantius, *Inst.*, 6.12.22.

[68] Lactantius, *Inst.*, 6.12.26, "*tum divinae voces, quae id fieri iubent.*"

[69] See Monat, *Lactance et la Bible*, p. 258, who attributes this to Matt. 7:12, but regards Lactantius's negative form as a general nod to a common moral principle rather than any textual citation. Also Loi, "Il concetto di 'iustitia,'" p. 593. However, Chris L. de Wet, "The Book of Tobit in Early Christianity: Greek and Latin Interpretations from the 2nd to the 5th Century CE," *Teologiese Studies/Theological Studies* 76 (2020): pp. 1–13, shows that early Christians often cited the Golden Rule in its negative form from Tobit 4:15. Cf. Lactantius, *Epit.*, 55.3.

[70] See Lactantius, *Epit.*, 55.2–3, "*radix iustitae et omne fundamentum aequitatis est illud, ut non facias quod pati noils, sed alterius animum de tuo metiaris.*" Loi, "Il concetto di 'iustitia,'" p. 593, attributes this to Matt. 7:15. Cf. Tobit 12:13–14, cited at Cyprian, *Mort.*, 10 and Tobit 14:10–11, cited at *De opere et eleemosynis*, 5, 20.

[71] Lactantius, *Inst.*, 6.12.31.

[72] Christiane Ingremeau, *Institutions Divines* VI, pp. 413, *passim*. See also Gábor Kendeffy, "Lactantius on the Passions," *Acta classica Universitatis scientiarum Debreceniensis* 36 (2000): pp. 113–130.

in the face of desire, grief, pain, and suffering.[73] The Stoics undermine their own attempt to achieve virtue, which they claim to regard as the highest good.[74] The Peripatetics are only slightly better, he argues, because they believe the emotions should be moderated, rather than eliminated entirely. And yet, it would be immoderate to rejoice only a little in a very great good, and likewise wrong to be aggrieved only a little at a very great evil.[75] Lactantius's ultimate concern emerges in the conclusion to this critique:

> The whole matter ought to reside in this, that since the impetus of these emotions neither can nor should be removed, since it has been placed in us for the sake of duties that must be kept [*ad tuenda officia vitae*], it must rather be directed onto the right path, where even a runner has no risk of stumbling [*cursus offensione ac periculo careat*].[76]

The metaphor of a runner recalls Lactantius's fundamental image of the human being walking the path to eternal life. Just as people must direct their steps to the true path, so also the emotions must be guided toward the true Way.[77] If *virtus* is not an end, but a means to eternal life, then every emotion rightly directed can potentially produce virtue. This argument allows Lactantius to present the biblical idea of the "fear of God" as a source of great wisdom and virtue: "the highest fear is the highest *virtus*" because "anyone who fears God, does not fear" anything else.[78] Cyprian seems to lurk in the background here, since *Quir.* 3.20 claims that "the foundation and strength of hope and faith is fear."[79] As evidence, Cyprian collects scriptural passages commending the fear of God: "The fear of the Lord is the beginning of wisdom."[80] Lactantius commends this same "fear of God" as a source of *patientia*. As proof, he reprises Minucius Felix's encomium to the martyrs' heroic patience.[81] Their example proves a simple point: "Nothing else than the fear of God created this *virtus*."[82]

Lactantius defends emotion—fear and anger in particular—because he regards *humanitas* as the expression of God's image in humanity. By attempting

[73] Lactantius, *Inst.*, 6.15.1–7, "*quare nihil aliud dixerim quam insanos qui hominem, mite ac sociale animale, orbant suo nomine, qui euulsis adfectibus, quibus omnis constat humanitas, ad immobilem stuporem menti perducere volunt, dum student animum perturbationibus liberare et, ut ipsi dicunt, quietum tranquillumque reddere.*"

[74] Lactantius, *Inst.*, 6.15.

[75] Lactantius, *Inst.*, 6.16.1–5.

[76] Lactantius, *Inst.*, 6.16.11.

[77] Lactantius, *Inst.*, 6.17.12. Cf. *Inst.*, 1.1–2. See Chapter 6, this volume.

[78] Lactantius, *Inst.*, 6.17.4, "*sed simpliciter ostendam summum metum summam esse virtutem.*"

[79] Cyprian, *Quir.*, 3.20, "*fundamentum et firmamentum spei et fidei esse timorem.*"

[80] Cyprian, *Quir.*, 3.20, "*Psalmo CVIIII: Initium sapientiae metuere Deum.*"

[81] Cf. Minucius Felix, *Oct.*, 37 and Lactantius, *Inst.*, 6.17.2–8. Lactantius repeats Minucius's rhetoric: "*felix atque invicta patientia sine ullo gemitu pertulit.*" Cf. Tertullian, *Ad Nationes*, 2.2.

[82] Lactantius, *Inst.*, 6.17.9, "*hanc virtutem nihil aliud quam metus dei fecit.*"

to eradicate affective dispositions (*adfectus*), the Stoics deprive human beings of their distinctive quality as living images of God and thus undermine the basis of human society—*humanitas*: "What else can I call it but insane, when people deprive humanity, a mild and social animal, of its own name by uprooting the affections in which all *humanitas* consists," he argues.[83] The point is so important that Lactantius devoted an entire treatise to defending the claim that God has just emotions. *De ira dei* grounds his defense of emotion in the claim that God has just affections: "Goodwill [*gratia*], anger [*ira*], and compassion [*miseratio*] have their substance in God and that supreme and undivided power uses them rightly for the preservation of all things."[84] Although God lacks lust, fear, grief, envy, and other such vices, "those affections [*adfectus*], which arise from virtue [*qui sunt virtutis*]—anger against evil people, love for good people, compassion for the afflicted [*miseratos in adflictos*]—he holds properly as his own, as just and true, because they are worthy of the divine power."[85] Lactantius's thought ultimately makes *humanitas* an imitation of that divine disposition that Christ commanded and demonstrated in his own life. *Humanitas* keeps Christ's commandment to love God and neighbor: "God wants all people to be just, that is, to hold both God and humanity dear, which is to honor God as a parent, and to love humanity as brother, for in these two the whole of justice consists."[86]

Patientia: The Example of Jesus

Lactantius's critique of the Stoic theory of the passions effects a transition from his discussion of human society to his treatment of individual moral character. Lactantius uses the discussion to develop progressively an ideal *iustus homo*, which he lifts from the biblical narrative of Christ's prophetic ministry and passion. Lactantius develops that ideal from Christ's teaching and example in two ways. First, he advocates works of mercy, non-retaliation, and marital fidelity in an argument that synthesizes Christ's words in Matthew 5–7 and Luke 6:20–49—Christ's *Sermon on the Mount*. (Although Lactantius occasionally provides direct citation of the Gospels, his allusions mainly fall into a category Stefan Freund has described as "unmarked reproduction of contents or mental

---

[83] Lactantius, *Inst.*, 6.17.20.

[84] Lactantius, *Ira.*, 15.12, "*At vero et gratia et ira et miseratio habent in eo materiam recteque illis utitur summa illa et singularis potestas ad rerum conservationem.*"

[85] Lactantius, *Ira.*, 16.7.

[86] Lactantius, *Ira.*, 14.4, "*in his enim duobus tota iustitia consistit.*" See V. Buchheit, "Die Definition der Gerechtigkeit bei Laktanz," pp. 358–363. As Buchheit showed, "*in his enim duobus tota iustitia consistit,*" is lifted from Matt. 22:36–40, so that what he summarizes here under the terms *pietas* and *aequitas* is nothing else but Christ's double-love commandment, which contains "all the law and the prophets."

256 ROMAN VIRTUE IN THE EARLY CHRISTIAN THOUGHT OF LACTANTIUS

structures," whose source is evident only when compared to the background source.)[87] Lactantius's presentation reflects his debt to an exegetical tradition that received and interpreted the Synoptic portrait of Christ as a fulfillment of Old Testament prophecy. *Inst.* 6.18 updates that tradition and reasserts it as the basis for a human ideal, the *iustus homo*, which is an eternal paradigm derived from Christian reflection on the person of Jesus. Second, by grounding his ethical ideal in Christ's *Sermon*, Lactantius elevates *patientia* as the supreme virtue for life in the present age. Lactantius will eventually state the point explicitly in a description of the *iustus ac bonus vir* that looks backward to the passion of Jesus: "Thus *patientia* must be considered the highest *virtus*, since God was willing that the *iustus homo* be scorned as a fool, that he might obtain it."[88] *Inst.* 6 thus attempts to elaborate a foundational account of the moral and political order from Lactantius's vision of Christ.

Lactantius connects his positive moral argument to his vision of Christ by once again evoking the *iustus homo* in *Inst.* 6. "Let us then leave aside the philosophers," he says, "and return to our original proposal. Since God has sent the truth and revealed his wisdom from heaven [*veritas et caelitus sapientia*] to us alone, let us do what God our enlightener bids [*iubet inluminator noster deus*]: let us endure [*perferamus*] the labors of this life to the end by aiding one another, but not in any hoping that if we shall have done any good work, we will receive glory from it."[89] The notion of receiving knowledge from God and working without hope of temporal reward correlate to Lactantius's ethic of *humanitas*—the double-love of God and neighbor—but emphasize the subjective dimension of virtue and its supreme expression in *patientia*. Both ideas amount to an imitation of Jesus, as Lactantius's language also indicates. His Christological title "*Inluminator*" and reference to an exclusive "*veritas et caelitus sapientia*" both advert back to Christ as the source of *patientia*.[90] He proceeds to develop yet further the idea of the *iustus homo* from the scriptural narrative of Christ's person and work. As already noted, Lactantius evokes Isaiah when he says that "*patientia* must be considered the highest virtue . . . since God willed that the just man [*iustus homo*] be despised as a fool, in order to obtain it."[91] Lactantius later echoes Tertullian and Cyprian when he calls *patientia* "the one virtue [*una virtus*] opposed to all vicious affections [*opposite vitiis et adfectibus*]."[92] This

[87] Stefan Freund, "The Hidden Library of Lactantius," *Studia Patristica* 24 (2021): p. 193.
[88] Lactantius, *Inst.*, 6.18.30.
[89] Lactantius, *Inst.*, 6.18.1–2, "*Sed omittamus philosophos... Nos ergo, ut ad propositum revertamur, quibus solis a deo veritas revelata et caelitus missa sapientia est, faciamus quae iubet inluminator noster deus. Sustineamus, invicem et labores huius vitae mutuis adiumentis perferamus nec tamen, si quid boni operis fecerimus, gloriam captemus ex eo.*" Cf. Lactantius, *Ira.*, 18.3 reproduces this passage verbatim.
[90] See Chapter 4, this volume.
[91] Lactantius, *Inst.*, 6.18.30.
[92] Lactantius, *Inst.*, 6.18.32. Cf. Tertullian, *Pat.*, 1, 3, 14.

VIRTUS: CHRIST'S PRECEPTS OF JUSTICE 257

virtue enables the *iustus homo* to walk the path toward eternal life. The connection between Christ's own life and the Christian imitation of Christ becomes evident in the various synonyms Lactantius coins for this *iustus homo*. He calls his ideal figure "the true and just traveler [*viator ille verus ac iustus*]" walking the road to eternal life, and likewise names this figure, the *cultor dei*, in contrast to the pagan *cultores deorum*.[93] These titles distinguish the Christian, who follows in Christ's footsteps and imitates his patience, from the pagans' imitation of false gods. Lactantius's Two Ways doctrine and his portrait of Christ as opening the path toward eternal life stand behind these titles.[94]

Lactantius's description of the *cultor dei* is ultimately the description of someone who imitates Christ and follows Christ's teaching. Hence, just as Christ's example reveals *patientia* as the supreme *virtus*, so Christ's teaching in the Gospels is the source of his specific moral arguments elaborating the meaning of that virtue ethically. Lactantius describe his ideal figure by lifting moral precepts from Christ's *Sermon on the Mount*. He draws first upon Matt. 6:1–7:

> God admonishes us that the doer of justice [*operator iustitiae*] ought not be a boaster, lest he seem to have fulfilled the duty of *humanitas* not so much from a desire to obey heavenly mandates [*mandatis caelestibus*], as to impress and thus obtain a prize of glory [*pretium gloriae*], which he has taken, but never receive the reward [*praemium*] of a divine and heavenly wage. The other things which the worshipper of God [*cultor dei*] should do are easy once these virtues have been comprehended [*facilia sunt illis virtutibus comprehensis*].[95]

P. Monat recognized the inspiration of Matthew's Gospel animating Lactantius's classical rhetoric in these lines.[96] Monat cites Matt. 6:1 as the inspiration for Lactantius' idea but admits that Lactantius is echoing a principle rather than citing a text. The *Biblia Patristica* goes further, offering *Inst.* 6.18.3 as the only third-century Latin reference to Matt. 6:1–4.[97] What both sources recognize is that *Inst.* 6.18.3 provides a close paraphrase of Christ's thought while lifting key language from the Gospel narrative.[98] The pairing captures Jesus's critique of the

---

[93] Lactantius, *Inst.*, 6.18.6.

[94] E.g., Lactantius, *Inst.*, 1.1–3, *Inst.*, 2.18, *Inst.*, 4.1–3, *Inst.*, 6.2–4. See Chapter 6, this volume.

[95] Lactantius, *Inst.*, 6.18.3, "*Monet enim deus operatorem iustitiae non oportere esse iactantem, ne non tam mandatis caelestibus obsequendi quam studio placendi humanitatis officio functus esse videatur habeatque iam pretium gloriae, quod captavit, nec praemium caelestis illius ac divinae mercedis accipiat.*"

[96] Monat, *Lactance et la Bible*, p. 257. With these words, we are "bien dans le mouvance des propos par lesquels, chez Matthieu, s'ouvre l'enseignement du Christ sur les 'oeuvres."

[97] *Biblia Patristica: Index des Citations et Allusiones Bibliques dans La Littératures Patristique*, vol. 2, *Le troisième siècle* (origène excepté) (Paris: Éditions du Centra National de la Recherche Scientifique, 1986), p. 248.

[98] See Loi, "Il concetto di 'iustitia,' " p. 609, explains that this term is of exclusively Christian origin.

258 ROMAN VIRTUE IN THE EARLY CHRISTIAN THOUGHT OF LACTANTIUS

Pharisee, who "practices his justice before others, in order to be seen by them."[99] The contrast between a temporal *"pretium gloriae"* and a better *"praemium caelestis"* (also termed a *"merces divinus"*) likewise extends the field of allusions. The former phrase redirects Christ's critique of the Pharisees toward Rome's famous culture of glory-seeking while the latter recommends God's eternal judgment as the only true concern for the *iustus homo*.[100] Lactantius thus captures the contrast between divine and human sight in Matt. 6:1 and 4. His remark summarizes a point made earlier at *Inst.* 6.13.14:

> For if worshippers of the gods [*cultores deorum*] venerate dumb images [*simulacra insensibilia*] and confer upon them whatever precious things they have, although [the images] can neither enjoy those things or be grateful for them, how much more just and true [*iustius et verius*] is it to venerate the living images of God [*iustius est et verius viventia dei simulacra excolere*], that you may earn virtue? For just as they use whatever they receive and are grateful, so also God, "*in whose sight you shall have done good*" also will approve and deliver the reward of *pietas* [*mercedem pietatis*]?[101]

The paraphrase of Matt. 6:1–4 reveals Christ's admonition again as the source of Lactantius's moral vision. That admonition links the historical person of Jesus to the moral ideal of the *iustus homo*, whose description develops through these chapters. At *Inst.* 6.18.4–7, Lactantius says, "The other [precepts] that the worshipper of God [*cultor dei*] should observe are easy once these virtues have been comprehended."[102] He continues with a lengthy sketch that follows the logic and order of Christ's statements in Matthew 5–7 and Luke 6:20–49. Lactantius's portrait of the *iustus homo* begins with a command to speak the truth:

> [The *cultor dei*] should never lie so as to cheat or harm someone. Indeed, it is a crime for the one who desires truth [*qui studeat veritati*] to be false in any matter and so to walk away [*discedere*] from that truth which he pursues [*ab illa ab ipsa quam sequitur*]. On this path of justice and virtue [*in hac via iustitae virtutumque*] there is no place for falsehood. And so that true and just traveler

---

[99] Matt. 6:1 and 4: "*Attendite ne iustitiam [elemosinam] vestram faciatis coram hominibus ut videamini ab eis alioquin mercedem non habebitis apud Patrem vestrum qui in caelis est . . . ut sit elemosyna tua in abscondito et Pater tuus qui videt in abscondito reddet tibi.*"

[100] For *gloria* in Roman civic culture, see, e.g., Cicero, *Phillipics*, 14.34, who offers "glory" as consolation for families mourning loved ones: "*gloriae munus optimis et fortissimis civibus monumenti honore persolvitur, consolemur eorum proximos, quibus optima est haec quidem consolation.*" Also Vergil, *Aen.*, 6.767, names the "*Troianae gloria gentis.*" For critique, see Lucretius, *Nat. r.*, 2.2.37–54.

[101] Lactantius, *Inst.*, 6.13.14.

[102] Lactantius, *Inst.*, 6.18.4.

[ille viator verus ac iustus] will not say with Lucilius: "It is not my way to lie to a friend and family member [*homini amico et familiari*]," but even to an enemy and a stranger [*inimico atque ignoto*] he will deem it unworthy of himself to lie, so that his tongue the interpreter of his soul may not disagree with his understanding and thought [*sensu ac cogitatione*].[103]

Lactantius's use of *non mentiendum* echoes an exegesis also evident in Cyprian. His term *Veritas* in the above passage should be taken not only as a general reference to truthful speech, but as a specific allusion to Christ, who is the Word and the Truth. Cyprian's collection of *Testimonia* makes a similar set of exegetical moves. At *Ad Quirinum* 104, for instance, Cyprian glosses an Old Testament scripture with the same phrase: "*Non Mentiendum: Lying lips are an abomination to the Lord.*"[104] Cyprian glosses the text with the same verb (*mentire*) that appears above. Paul's admonition at Ephesians 4:25 might also inform Lactantius: "putting away deceit [*deponentes mendacium*], speak truth each one with his neighbor [*cum proximo suo*], since we are members of one another."[105] Lactantius's allusion to Lucilius's ethic of friendship in this context—"*homine amico et familiari*"—might be read fairly as a gloss on Paul's "*cum proximo suo*," at Eph. 4:25, especially since *Inst.* 6.18.33 later urges *patientia* with a sure citation of Eph. 4:26: "God instructs 'that the sun should not go down on our anger,' so that a witness against our fury may not escape."[106] Finally, Lactantius's insistence upon the symmetry of thought and speech echoes Matt. 5:37: "Moreover, let your *sermo 'est'* be '*est*' and '*non*,' *non*. For anything excessive comes [*abundantius*] from the evil one."[107] Whether summarizing one or all of these passages, the biblical insistence upon truth-telling stands behind Lactantius's ethic.

The derivation of Lactantius's *iustus homo* from the Gospel becomes more evident as Lactantius proceeds. Christ's *Sermon* shapes much of *Inst.* 6.18. Immediately following his point that the *iustus homo* is truthful, Lactantius reproduces the thought of Luke 6:32–36 with its condemnation of usury. *Inst.* 6.18.7–10 continues:

If he lends any money [*pecuniam si quam crediderit*], he will not take interest [*non accipiat usuram*], so that his reward may be uninhibited because he helped someone in need.... The *iustus homo* will never pass up the opportunity to aid someone financially [*aliquid misericorditer faciat*], nor will he pollute himself

---

[103] Lactantius, *Inst.*, 6.18.4–6.

[104] Cyprian, *Quir.*, 103.

[105] Lactantius, *Inst.*, 6.18.4, *VLD* Eph. 4:23–25, "*et induite novum hominem, qui secundum Deum creatus est in iustitia et sanctitate veritatis. Propter quod deponentes mendacium, loquimini veritatem unusquisque cum proximo suo [A-SS Elig 2 - cum fratre suo]: quoniam sumus invicem membra.*"

[106] Lactantius, *Inst.*, 6.18.33.

[107] *VLD* Matt. 5:37, "*sit sermo vester: est, est, non, non; quod autem abundantius est, a malo est.*"

260 ROMAN VIRTUE IN THE EARLY CHRISTIAN THOUGHT OF LACTANTIUS

with money-making of this kind [*in huiusmodi quaestu*].... He will not take a bribe [*munus*] from a poor man, so that if he stands surety for anything, it will be good for him, because he did it freely.[108]

Luke 6:32–36 contains a pattern reproduced in the above passages. Jesus first criticizes an ethic that prefers friends to others: "If you love those who love you, what favor will there be for you [*gratia vobis*]? For even sinners love those who love them."[109] Lactantius echoes this point when Jesus continues: "But truly love your enemies and do good to them [*beneficite*]; lend your money seeking nothing in return [*fenerate nihil desperantes*] and your reward [*merces vestra*] will be great [*multa*] in heaven, and you will be sons of the Most High, since he himself is kind [*suavis*] upon both the ungrateful and sinners [*ingratos et nequas*]."[110] Christ urges generosity to all people as an imitation of God's own character. Lactantius's progression from an ethic of friendship to an injunction against usury follows Christ's thought pattern.[111]

Lactantius's summary of Christ's command against usury expresses not only Christ's *Sermon* but also a Christological exegesis traceable again to Cyprian. *Ad Quirinum* 3.48–49, addresses the topic of usury by collecting the same Old Testament passages that Christ evokes in Luke 6:32–35. Cyprian thus represents Christ's teaching as a fulfillment of prophecy in a series of passages that describe a certain figure—the *iustus homo*. Cyprian says:

> We Must Not Lend at Interest [*Non Faenerandum*]
>
> In Psalm 13: "He has not given his money at interest [*faenori*], nor has.he taken bribes at the expense of the innocent [*super munera innocentes*], for the one who does these things shall not be raised into heaven. Also in Ezekiel, "For whoever would be a just man [*iustus erit homo*] shall not oppress a person; he will restore the debtor his pledge and he will not take a stolen thing." Also in Deuteronomy: "You will not lend to your brother at interest on your money [*usurum*] and interest on meals."[112]

Lactantius once again lifts his description of the *iustus homo* in this respect from Cyprian's Christological exegesis of the Old Testament. In the above passage,

---

[108] Lactantius, *Inst.*, 6.18.7–10.

[109] *VLD* Luke 6:32, "*Et si diligitis eos qui vos diligent quae erit vobis gratia nam et peccatores diligent diligentes se.*"

[110] *VLD* Luke 6:35, "*Veruntamen diligite inimicos vestros et benefacite et fenerate nihil desperantes et erite meces vestra multa in caelo et eritris fili Excelsi, quoniam ipse suavis est super ingratos et nequas.*"

[111] See Lactantius, *Inst.*, 6.11–12. For "*sine spe recipiendi*" as reference to Luke 6:35, see Monat, *Lactance et la Bible*, pp. 253–265.

[112] Cyprian, *Quir.*, 3.48.

Cyprian couples the term *munus* with forms of *faeneratio* in order to warn that taking profit through exploitation of the innocent comes at the cost of eternal life. Cyprian's reference to Ezekiel presents a certain *iustus homo* in the same language that Lactantius uses throughout *Inst.* 6.18.[113] Cyprian's very next heading connects this teaching to Luke 6:32–35:

> That Enemies Also Must Be Loved [*Inimicos Quoque Diligendos*]
> In the *Gospel according to Luke* [6:32], "If you love those who love you, what good is it to you. Even sinners love those who love them." Concerning this also in the Gospel according to Matthew: "Love your enemies [*Diligite inimicos*] and pray for those who persecute you, that you may be sons of your Father in heaven, who makes the sun to rise on the good and evil and rain to fall on the just and the unjust."[114]

Cyprian recognizes the prophetic background to Luke 6:32–35 and thus arranges Ezek. 18:5–9 as a confirmation of Christ's teaching. The arrangement is not a mere list of texts, but rather a theological interpretation of the text as a prophecy and confirmation of Christ's ministry. Cyprian's theological exegesis provides a tradition that inspires Lactantius's movement from an account of *humanitas* at *Inst.* 6.11–12 to a description of the *iustus homo* at *Inst.* 6.18. Lactantius's account of divine and human affection expresses a Christian vision of God's inner life, while his account of the *iustus homo* develops an ethical vision for humanity from earlier traditions of Latin exegesis that saw Christ as the fulfillment of God's plan for the world through Israel.

Lactantius's moral vision ultimately moves from Old Testament prophecy to New Testament fulfillment as he moves from economic teaching to deal with the problem of violence. Christ's *Sermon on the Mount* inspires his argument.[115] Lactantius frames his teaching of non-retaliation as an imitation of Christ's example grounded in the words of his teaching. His reading synthesizes texts of Paul, and Luke's Gospel:

> Let [the just man] respond with a blessing to the one cursing him [*maledicenti benedicto respondeat*]; "let no evil word proceed from the mouth [Eph. 4:29]" of the one who worships the Good Word [*ne verbum malum procedat ex ore hominis, qui colit verbum bonum*]. Rather let him be careful not to make an enemy by his own fault. And if it so happens that some violent person injures

---

[113] See Ingremeau, *Institutions Divines* VI, p. 402, which finds a debt to Ezekiel in Lactantius's critique of Cimon of Athens at *Inst.* 6.18.9. *Quir.* 3.48 is a likely inspiration for Lactantius's reading.

[114] Cyprian, *Quir.*, 3.48–49.

[115] See Chapters 3 and 5, this volume, for Cyprian as background. Cf. Cyprian, *Demet.*, 16; *Bon. pat.*, 5 and 7.

262 ROMAN VIRTUE IN THE EARLY CHRISTIAN THOUGHT OF LACTANTIUS

the good and just man [*bono et iusto homini*], let him bear it graciously and with moderation [*clementer ac moderate*] and let him not take revenge into his own hands [*ultionem suam non sibi adsumat*], but wait for God's judgment [*iudici deo reservet*]. Let him guard his innocence [*innocentiam*] always and everywhere; and this precept means not only that he himself does not harm another, but when harmed he does not seek revenge for himself [*inlatam sibi non vindicet*]. For indeed that greatest and most equitable judge holds court [*sedet*], as watchman and witness over all things. [The just man] will prefer him to any person, even to pass judgment in his own cause. . . . Thus it happens that the *iustus homo* is a contempt to all.[116]

Although Lactantius again masks his sources, those familiar with the New Testament will hear Christ's mandate, "Bless those who curse you and pray for those who abuse you," in Lactantius's admonition that the just man respond "to the one who curses him with a blessing [*maledicenti benedicto*]." The allusion to Luke 6:28 resonates with the most common pre-Vulgate renderings: "*Benedicite maledicentes vos, orate pro eis qui calumniantur vos.*"[117] The above paragraph also reproduces Christ's progression from wealth to non-retaliation in Luke 6:29–31: "To one who strikes you on the cheek, offer the other also, and from one who takes away your cloak do not withhold your tunic either. Give to everyone who begs from you, and from one who takes away your goods do not demand them back. And as you wish that others would do to you, do so to them."[118] Lactantius follows the progression of these verses when he addresses cursing and then non-retaliation immediately after his lengthy discussion of wealth based on Luke 6:35.

Lactantius's use of Luke 6:28 also echoes a portrait of Christ's passion developed in Cyprian's exegesis of the same passage. *Quir.* 3.39 collects references to 1 Peter 2:21–23, Luke 6:28, and the famous kenotic hymn of Phil 2:5–11. Under the heading, "That an *exemplum vivendi* is given us in Christ," Cyprian writes:

In the *Epistle of Peter* to the exiles: "Christ has suffered leaving for you an example, that you might follow in the footsteps of him who did not sin, nor was there deceit [*dolus*] found in his mouth: when he was cursed, he did not curse [*cum malediceretur, non maledixit*—Luke 6:28], when he suffered, he did not threaten; even more, he handed himself over to an unjust judge." Likewise, Paul

---

[116] Lactantius, *Inst.*, 6.18.10–13. Lactantius's citation of Eph. 4:29 reflects a textual tradition evident in *Shepherd of Hermas* 107.4, *VLD* [HER P 107, 4], "*nec ullam verbum malum de ore processit illorum.*"

[117] Luke 6:28.

[118] *English Standard Version* Luke 6:29–31. I have used a modern translation because the important point here is the progression of topics, not the precise verbal elements.

VIRTUS: CHRIST'S PRECEPTS OF JUSTICE   263

to the Philippians: "Who although established in the form of God [*in figura dei constitutus*] did not think it robbery [*rapinam*] that he was equal to God; but emptied himself taking the form of a slave [*formam serui accipiens*], and made in the likeness of a man [*in similitudine hominis*] was found human in appearance [*in habitu*]. He humbled himself and became obedient unto death, even the death of the cross. On account of which God exalted him and gave to him a name, that he might be above every name [*ut sit super omne nomen*], that in the name of Jesus every knee should bow, in both the heavens and the earth and the depths, and every tongue confess that the Lord Jesus is in the glory of God the Father [*quia Dominus Iesus in gloria est Dei Patris*]." Concerning this also in John's Gospel: "If I, your Lord and Master have washed your feet, you also ought to wash one-another's feet. For I have given to you an *exemplum*. As I have done, you do also."[119]

Cyprian's use of the phrase "*cum malediceretur, non maledixit*" interprets 1 Peter 2:21–23 as a restatement of Luke 6:28. The statement "he handed himself over to an unjust judge" invokes the passion narrative by affirming the negative of 1 Pet. 2:23, which says Christ "continued entrusting himself to him who judges justly."[120] Cyprian's "*iudici iniuste*" provides a reference by contrast for Lactantius's "*iudici deo*," above.[121] 1 Pet. 2:21–22 notably characterizes the Christian life using the same image of a person "walking in Christ's footsteps," which Lactantius invokes with his description of the "*viator iustus ac bonus*" who "does not depart from the truth he seeks."[122] Phil 2:5–11 situates Christ's willing self-humiliation as the eternal exemplar expressed in his incarnate life. Cyprian thus constructs Christian ethics, out of John's Gospel, according to a logic of imitation.

Cyprian and Lactantius both express the meaning of *patientia* through a Christological exegesis of the Old Testament prophets and the Pauline letters. This exegetical approach allows them to range widely through the Scriptures for evidence that Christ's humiliation is an *exemplum* for the Christian life. At *Inst.* 6.18.3, for instance, Lactantius couples his reference to Luke 6:28 with a citation of Eph. 4:29: "Let no evil word proceed from the mouth of the one who worships the Good Word."[123] The comment follows Cyprian by interpreting Eph. 4:29

---

[119] Cyprian, *Quir.*, 3.39. Edwina Murphy, "As Far as My Poor Memory Suggested: Cyprian's Compilation of *Ad Quirinum*," *Vigiliae Christianae* 68 (2014): pp. 541–542. The phrase "*In epistula Petri ad Ponticos*' in Book 3 [also at 3.36, 3.37] is similar to the phrase used by Tertullian in *Scorp.* 12," which suggests that *Ad quirinum* is a work arranged theologically that expresses a third-century Christian tradition of theological exegesis and catechesis.

[120] *English Standard Version* 1 Peter 2:23.

[121] Lactantius, *Inst.*, 6.18.11.

[122] Cf. *Inst.*, 6.18.5–7.

[123] Lactantius, *Inst.*, 16.18.12.

264   ROMAN VIRTUE IN THE EARLY CHRISTIAN THOUGHT OF LACTANTIUS

according to a theology of imitation. This reference is one of two direct citations of Eph. 4 in *Inst.* 6.18, since *Inst.* 6.18.32 concludes with a citation of Eph. 4:26. These two verses contain a Pauline ethical teaching that echoes Christ's *Sermon*:

> Be angry and do not sin: Do not let the sun go down on your anger [*Inst.*, 6.18.32]. Leave no place for the devil: If someone is robbed, let him not steal: rather, let him labor in doing good with his own hands, that he may provide the need for one suffering. Let no evil word proceed from your mouth.[124]

Lactantius interprets Eph. 4:26–29 according to his Johannine theology of Christ as "Word," as he emphasizes that Christian behavior should reflect the character of the *Word* Christians worship. Cyprian's citation of John 13:15–17 at *Quir.* 3.39 makes the same exegetical move.[125] The comparison seems to indicate that Lactantius gleaned not only specific biblical passages from *Ad Quirinum* but also his exegetical method. Hence, Cyprian's developed portrait of Christ's *exemplum* also informs Lactantius's teaching on non-retaliation. When Lactantius says "let him not take revenge into his own hands [*ultionem suam non sibi adsumat*], but wait for God's judgment [*iudici deo reservet*]," he repeats a doctrine found at *Quir.* 3.106. Under the heading, "That when an injury has been received *patientia* must be maintained and revenge [*ultio*] left to God," Cyprian says: "You shall not say: 'I will avenge myself on my enemy, rather wait on God, and you will be a help to yourself.' Again elsewhere [Deut. 32:35]: 'vengeance is mine [*mihi vindictam*], I will repay, says the Lord.'"[126] By associating *ultio* and *patientia*, Cyprian uses Deut. 32:35 to define and confirm *patientia*—the classic virtue of the Stoic Sage advocated in Lactantius and his Latin Christian predecessors. Cyprian's exegesis echoes in Lactantius's "*ultionem suam*," just as the phrase "*iudici deo reservet*" expresses Cyprian's "*Mihi vindictum*." Rom. 12:14–19 seems to have shaped Cyprian's citation, since Paul also cites Deut. 32:35 at Rom. 12:19: "Bless those who persecute and do not curse [*benedicite persequentibus vos: benedicite et nolite maledicere*]." The verse repeats the language of Luke 6:28 and so authorizes a later reader to consider Rom. 12:14 as an echo of Christ's

---

[124] *VLD* Eph. 4:26–29, "*Irascimini et nolite peccare: sol non occidat super iracundiam vestram. Nolite locum dare diabolo: qui furabatur, iam non furetur magis autem laboret, operandum manibus suis, quod bonum est, ut habet unde tribuat necessitatem patienti. Omnis sermo malus ex ore vestro non procedat: sed si quis bonus ad aedificationem fidei ut det gratiam audientibus.*" Cf. Lactantius, *Inst.*, 6.18.33. Lactantius's citation of Eph. 4:29 is closer to *Shepherd of Hermas* 107.4 *VLD* [HER P 107, 4] Eph. 4:29, "*nec ullam verbum malum de ore processit illorum.*" Several *Vetus Latina* manuscripts have a form of *tribuere patienti*, the same vocabulary Lactantius uses at *Inst.*, 6.10.1 "*quod homini tribuendum est.*"

[125] See also Cyprian, *Quir.*, 3.8.

[126] Cyprian, *Quir.*, 3.106.1–4, "*Item illic iniuria accepta patientiam tenendam et ultionem deo relinquendam ne dixeris: ulciscar me de inimico meo, sed sustine deum, tu tibi auxilio sit. Item alibi: mihi uindictam, ego retribuam, dicit dominus.*"

Sermon. A citation of Deut. 32:35 then appears at Rom. 12:19: "Do not defend yourselves, beloved, but leave place for God's anger [*date locum irae*], for it is written: *Mihi vindicta.*"[127] Lactantius's review of Luke 6:28 synthesizes Cyprian's theological judgment but leaves his exegesis to be investigated by readers seeking the sources of his wisdom. Like Cyprian, Lactantius views *patientia* as the supreme virtue: "*Patientia* is the one virtue [*una virtus*] opposed to all vices and affections [*opposita vitiis et adfectibus*]."[128] This view is rooted in his commitment to divine emotion and to his image of Christ's patience. *Patientia* ultimately reflects a view of the divine nature and the *exemplum Christi* that Lactantius receives from Tertullian and Cyprian. His work reflects that third-century Latin tradition, which took *patientia* as the presupposition for every kind of virtue.[129]

Patientia in Marriage and Killing

Two of Lactantius's most trenchant moral arguments immediately follow from his description of the *iustus homo* at *Inst.* 6.18. Immediately thereafter, Lactantius conducts a rapid review of the affections—anger, greed, lust—and of the pleasures of the five senses (*Inst.*, 6.19–23) in order both to define their good and divinely intended purpose, and to warn against their abuse. The discussion provides a series of caveats, as it were. In this context, Lactantius argues that human affections need not to be excised but rather redirected toward specific ends for which they were created. For Lactantius, *cupiditas* motivates the work of acquiring life's necessities; *libido* ensures the propagation of children; *ira parentum* preserves children from sin.[130] The argument leads him to two major claims about violence and sexuality. First, he forbids every form of killing human beings on grounds that the Fifth Commandment is absolute; Lactantius extends the prohibition even to military service. Second, he advocates a doctrine of chastity grounded in his notion that justice makes human beings equal. Both topics reveal the influence of Christ's teaching in his moral thought but also show the limits of his ethical vision. His critique of the Roman law of marriage is consistent with *Institutio* 5's argument for human equality (*Inst.*, 5.14.7–5.15.3), but he does not envision any end to marriage or sexual relationship between married people. Similarly, Lactantius's categorical rejection of killing is consistent with his ideal of the *iustus homo* (*Inst.*, 5.14–15, 6.18), but the later *Epitome* seems

---

[127] VLD Rom. 12:19, "*Non vosmetipsos defendentes, charissimi, sed date locum irae. Scriptum est enim, 'Mihi Vindicta, ego retribuam,' dicit Dominus.*"

[128] Lactantius, *Inst.*, 6.18.32. Cf. Tertullian, *Pat.*, 1, 3, 14.

[129] Lactantius, *Inst.*, 6.17.12, 6.17.20–22, 6.24.

[130] Lactantius, *Inst.*, 6.19. See Gábor Kendeffy, "Lactantius on the Passions," *Acta classica Universitatis scientiarum Debreceniensis* 36 (2000): pp. 113–130.

266   ROMAN VIRTUE IN THE EARLY CHRISTIAN THOUGHT OF LACTANTIUS

to reverse his condemnation of military service. That reversal has appeared to many as clear evidence of Lactantius's capitulation to the political imperatives of Constantine's rise and a remarkable departure from earlier Christian tradition. As will be argued below, however, both arguments reflect a theological development consistent with his early work and grounded in the conceptual imperatives of his early doctrinal understanding of the divine nature, received from the Latin Christian tradition.

Killing and Military Service

Lactantius's remarks on military service come in his review of the pleasures of the eyes (*Inst.*, 6.20.15–18). He affirms the philosophical view that ocular pleasure should direct human beings "to look upward" and to gaze upon the divine works, before devoting the chapter to a lengthy denunciation of the Roman games and theater.[131] His condemnation is a familiar theme of Christian apologetic, but Lactantius contributes to that tradition a new element. He argues that the spectacle of killing extinguishes *humanitas*: "Imbued with this custom they lay waste to *humanitas*."[132] In opposing even attendance at the games, Lactantius evokes Christ's interpretation of the commandments: "When God forbids killing [*cum occidere deus vetat*], he prohibits not only killing for personal gain [*latrocinari*], which is even illegal under the law, but also admonishes [*monet*] us against things human laws consider permissible."[133] It is clear from the *Epitome*'s redaction of this passage that Lactantius has the Ten Commandments in mind, since he lists the commandments against killing, adultery, and false testimony in their traditional sequence.[134] And yet in both places, Lactantius interprets the commandments according to Matt. 5:21, where Jesus contrasts the literal provision of positive law with the more strict intention of God.[135] As Cyprian records

---

[131] Cyprian is the actual source for his acceptance of this theme, see Chapter 3, this volume, and below. On Christian denunciation of the games, see Tertullian, *De spectaculis, Apologeticus*, Minucius, *Oct.*, 12.5, Cyprian, *Donat.*, 7ff.

[132] Lactantius, *Inst.*, 6.20.13.

[133] Lactantius, *Inst.*, 6.20.15.

[134] Lactantius, *Epit.*, 59.5–7, "*vetus praeceptum est non occidere ... item non adulterare ... eiusdem legis est falsum testimonium.*"

[135] That Lactantius has Christ's statement in mind is evident not only from Lactantius's choice of the verb (*occidere*), but also by the fact that *Quir.* 3.8 places Matt. 5:21 alongside Prov. 16:32 and Eph. 4:26 as a counsel of *patientia*. Under the heading, "That Anger Must Be Conquered Lest It Compel Sin," Cyprian gives: "As Solomon says in the *Proverbs*: 'Better is a patient man [*patiens*] than a strong one [*forti*]. For the one who contains his anger [*iracundiam*] is better than a man who takes a strong city.' Likewise: 'The foolish man announces his anger [*iram*] on the same day, but the cunning man hides his own dishonor.' Concerning this also, Ephesians [4:26]: 'Be angry and do not sin. Do not let the sun go down on your anger. You have heard it said of old, "You shall not kill [*occides*], for the one who kills shall be guilty in the judgment." But I say to you that everyone who is angry with his brother without cause will be guilty in the judgment [*reus erit iudicio*].'" As noted already, Eph. 4:26 is one

VIRTUS: CHRIST'S PRECEPTS OF JUSTICE   267

Matt. 5:21, "You have heard it said of old, 'You shall not kill [*occides*],' for the one who kills shall be guilty in the judgment. But I say to you that everyone who is angry with his brother without cause will be guilty in the judgment [*reus erit iudicio*]."[136] Christ thus draws a distinction between what the letter of the law permits and what is just in the view of eternal judgment. Lactantius echoes this principle when he extends the Fifth Commandment to military service: "And so it will not be permissible for the *iustus* to be a soldier, since his *militia* is justice itself [*ipsa militia*]."[137] By this comment, Lactantius means that the imitation of Christ is the *militia* of a Christian, since Christ's person and work is the revelation of justice in the world. Lactantius thus affirms Tertullian's traditional condemnation of capital punishment as a violation of the commandment—*non occides*: "There is no distinction between killing someone with a sword or a word," he argues, "since killing itself is prohibited [*occisio ipsa prohibetur*]."[138] What Lactantius adds to Tertullian's reading is a more expansive justification that grounds his readers' understanding of the commandment in the notion of *humanitas* defined according to Christ's example:

> In this precept of God [*in hoc dei praecepto*], there is no exception, since it is always a crime to kill the human being, whom God wanted to be a sacrosanct animal [*sacrosanctum animal esse voluit*]. And let no one think it permissible to smother newborn babies to death ... for God inspires souls for the sake of life [*inspirat ad vitam*], not death. But lest there be any crime with which they fail to dirty their hands, human beings deny to young and simple souls a light they do not themselves bestow![139]

Lactantius's description of the prohibition against killing as a *praeceptum Dei* and his phrase *sacrosanctum animale* adjusts the text of his earlier statement that God "wanted us to be a social animal [*animale nos voluit esse sociale*]," by replacing "*sociale*" with "*sacrosanctum*."[140] Likewise, his statement that "God inspires souls for life, not death" and his invocation of the "light" God gives to children alludes to Cyprian's doctrine of human equality expressed already above.[141] Lactantius thus reasserts his own earlier doctrine of *humanitas* as the

---

of two passages textually cited in *Inst.* 6.18. Lactantius here redescribes Christ's words in Matt. 5:21 following Cyprian.

[136] Cyprian, *Quir.*, 3.8.

[137] Lactantius, *Inst.*, 6.20.16.

[138] Lactantius, *Inst.*, 6.20.16. By this statement, Lactantius may have in mind only the use of courts to avenge private wrongs, since at *Inst.*, 6.12.21, he affirms the task of "good and just judges" when they perform their duty in a way consistent with divine law.

[139] Lactantius, *Inst.*, 6.20.16–17.

[140] See Lactantius, *Inst.*, 6.10.6–18.

[141] See Lactantius, *Inst.*, 5.14.6 and *Inst.*, 6.

268   ROMAN VIRTUE IN THE EARLY CHRISTIAN THOUGHT OF LACTANTIUS

basis for Christ's prohibition against killing. It is forbidden by divine command both on the grounds of the Fifth Commandment and Christ's promise that judgment is left to God.

If one grants that the *Epitome* should be given the same weight as *Divine Institutes*, then Lactantius seems later to have reversed his position on killing in order to affirm military service. Where *Inst.* 6.20 presents anger as a good for correcting children only, *Epit.* 56.4 recasts Lactantius's defense of anger in distinctly political terms and affirms the defense of one's own country. A single compressed paragraph reprising Lactantius's doctrine of emotion seems to recant *Divine Institutes*' critique of Roman imperialism and the argument that justice makes human beings equal:

> Just as bravery is good, if you fight for your country, but evil if against it, so also if you hold [the emotions] to their good purpose [*ad usus bonos*], they will be virtues, but if you use them for evil purposes [*ad usus malos*], they are called vices. Therefore, anger has been given by God for the correction of sinners [*ad coercitionem peccatorum*], that is, for the governance and discipline of subjects [*ad regendam subiectorum disciplinam*] so that fear might restrict licentiousness and curb audacity. But those ignorant of anger's limits become angry at their peers and even superiors [*paribus aut etiam potioribus*] and then leap into monstrous crimes, whence come slaughter and wars.[142]

Lactantius repositions just anger as a political emotion when he affirms its use by a martial analogy. Oliver Nicholson has pointed out that by illustrating the right use of anger with a reference to defensive warfare "Lactantius surely has in mind more the convictions of potential readers than his own."[143] Still, the contrast is striking. Where *Inst.* 6.20 restricted anger to the parental duty of restraining children from sin, *Epit.* 56 affirms the good use of "ruling subjects" and thus presupposes relationships of subordination. That presupposition seems to undermine Lactantius's doctrine of equality at *Inst.* 5.14 and thus also his very definition of justice as a virtue that makes human beings equal. A later paragraph confirms the accommodation. *Epit.* 59.5 redacts *Inst.* 6.20.15–17: "It is an old command '*not to kill* [*non occidere*]*,*' which should not be understood as forbidding only homicide, which even public laws condemn, but by this command it will not be permissible even to place someone in danger of death by a word, nor to kill or expose an infant, nor to damn oneself by a voluntary death."[144] Lactantius does retain the idea that it is wrong to cause someone's death by some

---

[142] Lactantius, *Epit.*, 56.5. See also tacit acceptances of military service at *Epit.*, 2.4, 33.5, and 61.2.

[143] Oliver Nicholson, "Lactantius on Military Service," *Studia Patristica* 24 (1993): p. 182, fn. 41.

[144] Lactantius, *Epit.*, 59.5.

VIRTUS: CHRIST'S PRECEPTS OF JUSTICE   269

verbal act, but he removes the more specific legal language of his earlier statement. The redaction renders his rejection of capital punishment ambiguous. He also retains his condemnation of infant exposure, suicide, and murder, but no mention of military service appears, and he entirely omits the broader point that the Fifth Commandment forbids killing categorically.

Scholars have often reviewed Lactantius's redaction of his earlier position with varying degrees of skepticism and disappointment. They often attribute the seeming *volte face* on the ethics of killing to the new relationship between Christianity and the Roman Empire brought about by Constantine.[145] "No doubt," Louis J. Swift presumed, "on the eve of full participation in the political life of the empire it was difficult for a Christian like Lactantius to look upon victories over persecutors with a wholly disapproving eye, even though those victories involved bloodshed."[146] Such broad gestures, however, favor psychological or contextual generalizations at the expense of significant theological and exegetical considerations. Lactantius's remark in the *Epitome* might be evidence of accommodation to Constantinian politics.[147] And yet, his acceptance of Constantinian politics might itself have been shaped by his theological commitments.[148] For instance, Christiane Ingremeau explains Lactantius's evolution with a sympathetic gesture to the Council of Arles in 314 A.D., which may have affirmed

[145] For most recent review of the debate and literature, see Phillip Wynn, *Augustine on War and Military Service* (Minneapolis: Fortress Press, 2013), 33–70, esp. 57–59.

[146] Louis J. Swift, "War and Christian Conscience: The Early Years," *Aufstieg und Niedergang der Römischen Welt* 23, 1 (1979): pp. 859–860, "But the larger dimensions of this attitude are clear.... The alignment of temporal and spiritual powers suggested by Lactantius's later remarks and the approval of war as a legitimate instrument of state became much more overt in the period after Constantine." Swift does note, however, that "[859, Fn. 101] there are some texts which do not fit in well with Lactantius' early pacifist positions [i.e., *Inst.,* 6.20.15–18]. See for example, 3.17.3, where Epicurus is criticized for forbidding the timid man to become a Soldier." Earlier, Vincenzo Loi, "I valori etici e politici della romanità negli scritti di Lattanzio," *Salesianum* 27 (1965): pp. 87–88, argues that the changes "derive from a conscious ideological revision worked by Lactantius." These were "completely new and adapted to the new climate of appeasement [*conciliazione*] between the Empire and Christianity." However, Oliver Nicholson, "Lactantius on Military Service," p. 177, observes that "the context of this straightforward disavowal of military service is not a discussion of political loyalties, it illustrates the moral danger of enjoying slaughter which made a Roman holiday." Nicholson further argues that Lactantius's apocalypticism "does not tell us if or when the heavenly warfare which is the perpetual duty of Christians should become military actions. What it does do is put Lactantius's ideas into a providential context," which might help to explain his identification of God's purposes with Constantine's military actions in the later *De mortibus.*

[147] Anthony Bowen and Peter Garnsey, "Introduction," in Bowen and Garnsey, Lactantius, *The Divine Institutes,* p. 48, "Lactantius, as a Christian convert, had not lost contact altogether with the *Romanitas* ... of which he had been a leading representative.... It was thus in principle possible that, when a second revolution in his circumstances occurred with the arrival of a Christian emperor ... he would seek ways of reconciling traditional Roman values ... with those of the newly evolving Christian state."

[148] Oliver Nicholson, "Lactantius: A Man of His Own Time?" *Studia Patristica* 25 (2021): p. 170, reminds us, "This is not an author, who can be dissolved into a series of sources or influences.... It is nowhere more marked than when Lactantius is writing from his own experience. He lived through the Great Persecution of 303–313, lost his job, and saw his former colleagues in the imperial household burned and thrown into the sea."

270   ROMAN VIRTUE IN THE EARLY CHRISTIAN THOUGHT OF LACTANTIUS

military service for Christians.[149] Ingremeau suspects that Lactantius could no longer "explicitly" condemn military service after an episcopal ruling, whatever his private belief.[150] Submission to conciliar judgment would be consistent with Lactantius's profession of loyalty to the "Catholic Church" and to "the true tradition [*veram traditionem*]" against all heresies.[151] By 314, however, it is possible that Lactantius was already under the spell of Constantinian victory, especially if one accepts Digeser's argument that Constantine's *Letter to Arles* borrows language from Lactantius's *Divine Institutes*.[152]

The *Epitome* reflects, however, a theological development that was necessitated by Lactantius's fundamental affirmation of God's wrath and eternal judgment. Even while Diocletian still reined, Lactantius had written at *Inst.* 2.17 that God allows both evil and good "that he might have some to punish and others to honor."[153] The point portrays God as a monarch, whose eschatological judgment "pours out his anger in heavenly power and virtue."[154] Lactantius thus criticizes those who claim that God does not get angry. He promises that "the task of discussing God's anger [*his locus de ira dei disserendi*] must be put aside for the time being because its material is rather substantial [*uberior*] and must be discussed more broadly in a proper work [*opere proprio latius exsequenda*]."[155] These early comments witness to two considerable factors. First, long before Constantine's triumph, Lactantius knew the complexity of his commitment to the idea that emotions are good and his belief that God could express emotion in perfect righteousness. Lactantius planned to develop a complete account of this position. Second, the fundamental idea of divine exemplarity—the claim that God's activity is a model for humanity—suggests that God's activity of eternal judgment would require a temporal analogue and come into tension with Lactantius's vision of *humanitas*.

Written between 313 and 316, after Constantine's victory at the Milvian Bridge and before his break with Licinius, *De mortibus persecutorum* and *De*

---

[149] See C. Munier, *Concilia Galliae a.314–a.506* (Turnhout: Brepols 1963), pp. 9–13. The Canon is uncertain however: "Concerning those who throw away their arms in peace, it pleases the council that they abstain from communion [*De his agitur etiam qui arma proiciunt in pace: placuit abstineri eos a communion*]." For discussion of this canon, see Wynn, *Augustine on War and Military Service*, 57–59.

[150] See Ingremeau, *Institutions Divines* VI, p. 417, who suggests that Lactantius's criticism of war persists in his remarks at *Epit.* 58, and the fact that Lactantius develops the eschatological theme of the *sancta militia* at *Inst.* 7.19.5 and in the *De mortibus*. See also Michel Perrin, *L'Homme Antique et Chrétien: L'Anthropologie de Lactance, 250–325* (Paris: Beauchesne, 1981), pp. 515–517.

[151] See Lactantius, *Inst.*, 4.30, denouncing the Phrygians, Novatianists, Valentinians, Marcionites, and Anthropians, before taking Cyprian's position: "*sola catholica ecclesia est, quae verum cultum retinet.*"

[152] Elizabeth DePalma Digeser, "Lactantius and Constantine's Letter to Arles: Dating the Divine Institutes," *Journal of Early Christian Studies* 2 (1994): pp. 33–52.

[153] Lactantius, *Inst.*, 2.17.1.

[154] Lactantius, *Inst.*, 2.17.2.

[155] Lactantius, *Inst.*, 2.17.5.

ira dei eventually provide the broader treatment of divine anger that Lactantius had promised. *De mortibus* offers an exegesis of history, in which Lactantius narrates the persecuting emperors' demise as evidence of God's providential care for Christians; God is the constant and ultimate agent of the persecutors' deaths.[156] Lactantius's argument is both triumphalist and consistent with his scriptural commitment to God's eternal judgment. *De ira dei* defends divine anger theologically by a distinction between "just anger for the correction of depravity [*ad pravitatis correctionem*]" and "fury or rage [*furor vel iracundia*]," which Lactantius condemns.[157] He thus affirms that God has just anger on analogy with judges, whose punishment of people who do harm (*nocentes*) is an imitation of God's example of anger at violations of the eternal law.[158] Critically, for Lactantius, this means that neither God nor judges "do harm" in their anger, since it is right to punish wickedness.[159] The political rhetoric of *Epit.* 56.5 restates the language of this discussion: "just as we must correct those subject to our power [*potestati nostrae subiectos*], so also God must correct the sins of the whole world."[160] Lactantius specifies the "subjects" he means, "slaves [*serui*], children [*liberi*], wives [*coniuges*], and students," in a comment apparently content with the legal status of slavery, despite his remarks at *Inst.* 5.14.7.[161] He regards this just correction as an expression of God's *exemplum humanitatis*—as a correlative of God's love for creation:

> Therefore, we rise up in punishment [*in vindictam*], not because we have been wronged, but that instruction may be preserved [*disciplina servetur*], behavior corrected [*mores corrigantur*], and licentiousness repressed. . . . This is just anger [*ira iusta*]; and as it is necessary in a person for the correction of depravity, it is also in God, from whom an example comes to humanity [*in deo a quo exemplum pervenit ad hominem*].[162]

This argument might reflect Lactantius's compromise with the comfort of Constantine's court (whether at Trier or Nicomedia). And yet, his comments

---

[156] Gianna Zipp, *Gewalt in Laktanz' De mortibus persecutorum* (Berlin: DeGruyter, 2021), pp. 235–253.

[157] Lactantius, *Ira.*, 17.18. Also, Oliver Nicholson, "Lactantius on Military Service," p. 180, "It is God's triumph which Lactantius celebrates, not that of any individual, not even Constantine."

[158] Lactantius, *Ira.*, 17.5–7.

[159] Lactantius, *Ira.*, 16.6, "There is a kindness even in anger itself." Cf. *Ira.*, 15.12, "Favor and anger and compassion all have their substance [*materiam*] in God, and that highest and singular power uses them rightly for the preservation of all things."

[160] Lactantius, *Ira.*, 17.18–19. Cf. *Epit.*, 56.5.

[161] Lactantius, *Ira.*, 17.15. Cf. Chapter 5. It should be observed that Lactantius is referring to domestic order here, where *Inst.* 5.14.7 criticized the classes (*egregius, clarissimus, perfectissimus*) of later Roman hierarchy.

[162] Lactantius, *Ira.*, 17.17–18.

attempt to resolve tensions present in his early theology. Lactantius rejected killing and military service on the basis of the scriptural promise of an eternal reward given to the just by God. That reward presupposed not only divine judgment but the claim that God has just emotions; and Lactantius presented divine emotion as the basis for *humanitas* itself. But this also means that Lactantius could not defend *humanitas* without defending God's role as a just judge, acting in anger at sin. Only injustice and indifference could allow the wicked ultimately to dominate the righteous. Hence, in Lactantius's thought, God's love requires and inspires just wrath against evil. The execution of that wrath does not harm but rather benefits even those against whom God acts.[163]

The treatise *De ira dei* thus expands the scope of just anger to include political relationships. The line of reasoning is consistent with the biblical portrait of God as a monarch, whose just governance provides an eternal example for human beings.[164] Held long prior to Constantine, this vision of God as the ruler of the universe inspires Lactantius's defense of anger in the *Institutes* as well as his theological development in *De ira dei* 15–18. The *Epitome* reflects that development. It is notable, in this respect, that Lactantius never makes an exception for personal self-defense. Soldiers defend the country, just as superiors correct inferiors—for the sake of justice, not for personal interest. Their judgment imitates God's own example, just as Christian *misericordia* imitates Christ.

It is neither possible nor desirable to disentangle Lactantius's theological development from his experience of the persecution and of Constantine's rise. And yet, the fact of Lactantius's political involvement and the influence of current affairs on him does not itself account for his theological judgments.[165] Lactantius's commitment to divine exemplarity meant that his vision of *humanitas* was, from the outset, in tension with his understanding of divine wrath and the concomitant idea of eternal judgment and reward—both notions foundational even to Lactantius's categorical rejection of killing. Thus, even if *Inst.* 2.17 does not name this tension specifically, Lactantius's early intention to explore divine anger more completely made his treatment of God's political and juridical role a predictable development in his theology. And because he regarded divine behavior as the model for justice in human life and society, Lactantius would always have had to find a place for the ethical expression, not only of God's loving disposition to save, but also of God's justice meted out toward the wicked. *De ira dei* resolves the tension by characterizing just wrath as an expression of God's affective disposition toward the creation: "There is a kindness even in anger itself."[166] At minimum,

---

[163] In this sense, Lactantius also anticipates ideas more fully developed by Augustine. See Phillip Wynn, *Augustine on War and Military Service* (Minneapolis, MN: Fortress Press, 2013).

[164] Lactantius, *Inst.*, 1.1–3. See Chapter 4, this volume.

[165] See Mattias P. Gassman, *Worshippers of the Gods: Debating Paganism in the Fourth Century Roman West* (Oxford: Oxford University Press, 2020), p. 45.

[166] Lactantius, *Ira.*, 16.6.

VIRTUS: CHRIST'S PRECEPTS OF JUSTICE   273

Lactantius's redaction of his position on military service is a consistent working out of tensions in his early theology. He could not have arrived at a different view of God's wrath, and therefore of legitimate authority, without altering the first principles that supported his own early doctrine of *humanitas*. Lactantius's acceptance of Constantine and soldiering must take into account this theological problem, which is inherent to Lactantius's concept of *humanitas*—his most profound contribution to early Latin theology.

Equality in Marriage

Lactantius's remarks on marriage reflect the same tension between an ideal ethic and an affirmation of mundane life as is evident in his argument about divine wrath and political rule. Although he acknowledges celibacy as a permissible and supremely delightful way of life, his comments on sexuality generally affirm Christian marriage.[167] Lactantius begins by repeating the traditional Christian teaching that sexuality was given by God for the sake of procreation.[168] The influence of Matthew and Romans is evident both from implicit allusions and direct citation.[169] He presents sexual behavior as a point of conflict between God and the Adversary. God created sexual desire as a catalyst for human life, while the Adversary, knowing "how great is the power of this desire [*quanta vis hiuis cupiditatis*]," tries to misorient that power by inserting "illicit desires [*inlicita desideria*]" in order to contaminate [*ut aliena contaminent*] the nature created by God.[170] His remarks lead to a renewed critique of sexual license, in which Lactantius introduces two scriptural allusions. The first is a faint echo of Romans 1:26: "[The Adversary] even pairs males with males and an unspeakable coitus [*nefandos coitus*] against nature and against the instruction of God is effected by some machination [*machinatus est*]."[171] The allusion to Rom. 1:26 is made evident by Lactantius's use of "*contra naturam*" as a description of homosexual practices, but the term "*in caeni gurgite demersit*" amplifies Rom. 1:24's "*inmunditiam*" as well. The following lines denounce adultery, pederasty, and

---

[167] Lactantius, *Inst.*, 6.23.37.

[168] Lactantius, *Inst.*, 6.23.2. Bowen and Garnsey, *Lactantius: The Divine Institutes*, p. 379, fn. 84, notes that his denunciation echoes Minucius Felix, *Oct.*, 28.10–11, Clem., *Strom.*, 2.18.88.4, 2.7.58.2, Just., *Apol.*, 1.29, Jos., *Ap.*, 2.199, and 2.202.

[169] See Monat, *Lactance et la Bible*, pp. 258–260.

[170] Lactantius, *Inst.*, 6.23.9. Lactantius thinks this especially true for men, who apparently struggle with sexual desire more than females.

[171] Lactantius, *Inst.*, 6.23.8, "*idem etiam mares maribus appliuit et nefandos coitus contra naturam contraque institutum dei machinatus est.*" Cf. *VLD* Rom. 1:26, "*Propterea tradidit illos Deus in passiones ignominiae: nam feminae eorum immutaverunt naturalem usum in eum usum qui est contra naturam.*" If the allusion seems tenuous, it is perhaps forgivable given that Lactantius elsewhere draws upon this text.

274 ROMAN VIRTUE IN THE EARLY CHRISTIAN THOUGHT OF LACTANTIUS

prostitution and conclude with a second reference to Paul: "Not only is it impermissible to approach the bed of another, but God prescribes and teaches [*deus praecipit docetque nos*] that we must abstain even from prostitution and casual intercourse [*publicis vulgatisque corporibus*], since when two bodies are engaged in sexual intercourse they become one body [*unum corpus efficere*]."[172] Lactantius's reference to "one body" evokes 1 Cor. 6:15–16.[173] On this basis, Lactantius trumpets the traditional vision of Christians as an ideal community characterized by self-mastery.[174] However, with this reference, Lactantius interprets the text through the lens of Christ's *Sermon*. The reference in 1 Cor. 6:15–16 to "one body" evokes Gen. 2:24, which appears elsewhere only at Eph. 5:31, and in Matt 19:5/Mk. 10:8. Thus, Lactantius attributes the teaching to Christ by his regular formula, as when he says "*deus praecipit docetque nos*."[175]

Lactantius points to Christ even more explicitly as the source of a superior law of marriage in the paragraphs that follow. He criticizes the common "definition of public law, where the woman alone is an adulteress, if she has another man [*alium*], while the husband is absolved from the crime of adultery even when he has many others."[176] Like infant exposure, suicide, and killing, the double-standard typifies his argument that human laws fall short of true justice because they are not founded in the teaching of Jesus.[177] Lactantius thus proceeds to evoke a superior mandate again with reference to 1 Cor. 6:15–16: "but the divine law [*divina lex*] joins two in matrimony, which is [*quod est*] 'into one body [*in corpus unum*]' by an equal right [*pari iure*], so that anyone who shares the bond of his body with others is an adulterer."[178] Much as Lactantius earlier used the phrase *deus praecipit* to introduce a citation of 1 Cor. 6:15–16, the key phrase *lex divina* introduces the term "*in corpus unum*," and thus refers the thought to New Testament teaching. Lactantius's comment brings that exegesis into connection with his idea of justice as equality, and with his vision of the Christian

---

[172] Lactantius, *Inst.*, 6.23.15, "*nec tantum alienis toris quaeque attingere non licet, verum etiam publicis vulgatisque corporibus abstinendum deus praecipit docetque nos, cum duo inter se corpora fuerint copulata, unum corpus efficere.*" Cf. *VLD* 1 Cor. 6:15–16, "*nescitis quoniam corpora vestra membra sunt Christi? Tollens ergo membra Christi faciam membra meretricis? Absit. An nescitis quoniam qui adhaeret meretrici, unum corpus efficitur? Erunt enim [inquit] '[Gen. 2:24] duo in carne una.*'"

[173] See Heck and Wlosok, *Divinarum Institutionum Libri Septem*, p. 625.

[174] Lactantius, *Inst.*, 6.23.19–22, "*sint omnes qui se discipulos dei profitebuntur ita morati et instituti, ut imperare sibi possint.*" For the apologists' redescription of Roman heroes, see Chapter 3, this volume.

[175] See Monat, *Lactance et la Bible*, p. 257.

[176] Lactantius, *Inst.*, 6.23.25, "*non enim sicut iuris publici ratio est, sola mulier adultera est quae habet alium, maritus autem etiamsi plures habeat, a crimine adulterii solutus est.*"

[177] For Lactantius's influence on Constantine's marriage legislation, see Judith Evans Grubbs, *Law and Family in Late Antiquity* (Oxford: Oxford University Press, 2000), esp. pp. 14–18, 88–94, 255–257.

[178] Lactantius, *Inst.*, 6.23.25, "*sed divina lex ita duos in matrimonium, quod est 'in corpus unum,' pari iure coniungit, ut adulter habeatur quisquis compagem corporis in diversa distraxerit.*"

VIRTUS: CHRIST'S PRECEPTS OF JUSTICE   275

community as a body of equals, noted already at *Inst.* 6.7.9. Likewise, his insistence upon an equal right [*pari iure*] reflects the claim that justice is manifest in *aequitas* and entails the leveling of social distinctions on the basis of quality beside *virtus*.[179] Lactantius brings that definition to bear upon the inequity of Roman marital law, as he rebukes the demand that women observe a chastity their husbands cannot perform: "It is wrong [*iniquum*] that you should compel what you yourself are not able to do," he argues.[180] Allusions to Christ's *Sermon* become more apparent in his defense of the point. Lactantius cites Quintilian to support the claim that male unchastity incites adultery on the part of women who either imitate the example or seek revenge.[181] As Lactantius fully develops his own position, his remarks interpret the words of Paul and Jesus according to the principle of equality and *humanitas* developed earlier:

> Let the habits of both become mutually familiar and let both bear the yoke [*iugum*, 1 Cor. 6:14] with equal spirits [*paribus animis*]. Let us consider ourselves in the other. For in this consists almost the whole of justice [*fere in hoc iustitiae summa consistit*], that "you not do to another anything that you would not wish to suffer from another" [Matt. 7:15, Tobit 4:15]. These are the things taught by God [*praecipiuntur a deo*] concerning continence.[182]

Lactantius's urging of equal continence pairs two closely related notions, which point to exegetical traditions that shape his reading of Jesus's words. The first notion is the humane idea of "considering ourselves in another," as being "almost the whole of justice [*fere iustitiae summa*]." Both phrases reassert the language of *Inst.* 6.10, where Lactantius redefines the Aristotelian claim that "man is a social animal" according to the principle of *humanitas*. As he put it, *humanitas* means "loving others because they are human and the same as we are," and likewise: "The meaning of justice consists in this: that what we do for our own families through affection is what we do for strangers through *humanitas*."[183] In the last line of the above passage, Lactantius identifies this principle with the Golden Rule, which he attributes to Jesus by the phrase *praecipiuntur a deo*. Lactantius's rendition of the Golden Rule is often attributed to Matt. 7:12, "Therefore, all those things which you wish others would do for you, you also, do them for others. This is indeed the law and the prophets."[184] Given the negative

---

[179] See Chapter 6, this volume.

[180] Lactantius, *Inst.*, 6.23.26–29, "*Iniquum est enim, ut id exigas quod praestare ipse non possis.*"

[181] Lactantius, *Inst.*, 6.23.29–32.

[182] Lactantius, *Inst.*, 6.23.32.

[183] Lactantius, *Inst.*, 6.10.6–18.

[184] *VLD* Matt. 7:12, "*Omnia ergo quaecunque vultis ut faciunt vobis homines bona et vos facite illis: haec est enim lex et prophetae.*" Lactantius has stated the phrase negatively, replacing *vultis* with *nolis*. He preserves the biblical *ut faciant* with *ut facias*.

276 ROMAN VIRTUE IN THE EARLY CHRISTIAN THOUGHT OF LACTANTIUS

form, however ("*do not do what you would not have others do*"), Lactantius may have Tobit 4:15 in mind, though his thought is no less clearly a reference to Christ's words.[185] Lactantius thus follows the above allusions with three well-documented citations of Matt. 19 and Matt. 5:

> Nevertheless, lest anyone think he can frame divine precepts for himself, so that all calumnies and occasion for crime might be removed, it is added that "whoever shall marry a woman divorced from her husband is an adulterer" [Matt. 19:9], and "the one who divorces his wife, except for the crime of adultery, commits adultery" [5:32]. For God did not wish the body to be separated and destroyed [Matt. 19:4]. Furthermore, not only must adultery be avoided, but even the thought, lest anyone look at another woman and lust in his mind [5:28].[186]

Lactantius's critique of the Roman law of adultery identifies Christ's teaching in the Scriptures as a revealed source of the divine and eternal law that corrects Roman positive law and history. This discussion of marriage may help to explain an apparent incongruity between his critique of Roman society—the rhetoric of equality at *Inst.* 5.14.7–15.3—and his apparent acceptance of traditional social distinctions. Somewhat paradoxically, it seems that by rooting his doctrine of equality in *virtus*, Lactantius believes that real equality can exist even in the presence of social, economic, or legal distinctions. Hence the husband and wife are one body, but their married status does not undermine their bodily distinction. Hence, Lactantius stresses that the husband should inspire a wife's *virtus* by his own example of continence, just as Christ provides an *exemplum virtutis* for all Christians. And yet, because *virtus* is a matter of the soul, justice can exist between people who occupy very different locations in the hierarchies of civil society. Hence, Lactantius acknowledges the order of the Roman household—even apparently the status of *servus*—while also criticizing Roman class distinctions (*Inst.*, 5.14.7–15.3). In both cases, justice in any given social structure depends upon the way a person uses their position for the sake of justice.

Medicina Paenitentia and the *Cultor Dei*

Lactantius seems to have recognized that by making Christ the eternal model for justice in human life, he presents the reader with an unattainable ideal. *Inst.* 6.24

---

[185] Cf. Lactantius, *Inst.*, 6.12.26.

[186] Lactantius, *Inst.*, 6.23.33. Monat, *Lactance et la Bible*, p. 259, attributes the statement to Matt. 5:23b and 19:9, but thinks Lactantius derived the citation from an intermediary source also used by Theophilus of Antioch.

VIRTUS: CHRIST'S PRECEPTS OF JUSTICE 277

thus concludes Lactantius's moral argument by returning to the topic of penitence first broached at *Inst.* 6.13.[187] He introduces the idea of an ascent in virtue that proceeds, step-by-step, along the path to eternal life. Lactantius's notion of an upward movement in virtue could seem like a thinly Christianized reiteration of an ancient philosophic gnosis—and some have argued the point.[188] Seated within the context of Lactantius's specific doctrine of repentance, the same discussion completes his Christian account of the *cultor dei* and cements the traditional character of his arguments. As scholars have noted, *Inst.* 6.24 contains a treasury of citations from Cicero and Seneca.[189] The two princes of Latin philosophy appear as witnesses to the fact that classical philosophers, ironically, knew of God's eternal law and yet never knew it rightly. Lactantius draws inspiration from Christ's *Sermon* and concludes his remarks with a signature statement of the *source-stream-flow* metaphor inviting his reader to the Scriptures. *Inst.* 6.24 thus collects the central tropes of Lactantius's work into a summary that leads to the Church door.[190] Read against the background of early Latin Christianity, Lactantius's doctrine of repentance offers Christian theology as the ultimate source of wisdom, and Christian liturgy as the true path to inward virtue.

In the context of his doctrine of repentance, Lactantius introduces a threefold notion of sin that correlates to three "steps" in virtue, which have seemed to some like a poor synthesis of Christian and gnostic ideas. Having discussed the righteousness of a just person, Lactantius urges Christians to heal the wounds of post-baptismal sin through good works of almsgiving: "Examine your conscience and heal its wounds [*medere vulneribus*] however much you are able," he says.[191] In this context, he introduces a three-part schema that describes both the burden of sin and Christian progress in holiness: "The cloak of the flesh [*indumento carnis*] weighs us down, and its weakness subjects us to a threefold dominion of sin in *deeds, words, thought*."[192] Regular attendees at any western liturgy will recognize the tricolon from the common liturgy of confession, but Lactantius

---

[187] See *Inst.*, 6.13 and *Inst.*, 6.24. The structure is notable. *Institutio* 6 concludes its discussions of *humanitas* and *aequitas* with remarks on penance.

[188] See Digeser, *The Making of a Christian Empire: Lactantius and Rome* (Ithaca, NY: Cornell University Press, 2000) pp. 78ff.

[189] *Inst.*, 6.24.12, 20, preserves three fragments of Seneca's *Exhortationes*. See Chiara Torre, "Seneca and the Christian Tradition," in *The Cambridge Companion to Seneca*, ed. Shadi Bartsch and Alessandro Schiesaro (Cambridge: Cambridge University Press, 2015), pp. 266–274; Przemyslaw Nehring, "The Authority of Seneca in Early Christian Argumentation," *Symbolae Philologorum Posnaniensium Graecae et Latinae* 37.3 (2017): pp. 161–163. Earlier, Stephen Casey, "The Christian Magisterium of Lactantius" (Unpublished dissertation: McGill University, 1972), pp. 48ff. Also, François Heim, "*Virtus* chez Lactance: du *vir bonus* au martyr," *Augustinianum* 36.2 (1996): pp. 361–376.

[190] Oliver Nicholson, "Lactantius: Man of His Own Time?" p. 169, notes that "he intended to take his readers only as far as the baptistery door, to get them onto the right path."

[191] Lactantius, *Inst.*, 6.13.5.

[192] Lactantius, *Inst.*, 6.13.5. It is a tricolon in the original: "*factis dictis cogitatione*."

278   ROMAN VIRTUE IN THE EARLY CHRISTIAN THOUGHT OF LACTANTIUS

seems to be the source of this language in Latin, rather than its recipient.[193] He correlates this triad to three steps walked *in via virtutis*: "The first step of virtue [*gradus virtutis*] is to abstain from evil deeds, the second, even from evil words, and the third, even from the thought of evil things. He who ascends the first has just enough; the second has perfect *virtus*, since truly he sins neither in deeds nor in words; but whoever ascends the third, will seem to have achieved likeness to God."[194] Cyprian and Apuleius may have each provided inspiration. Apuleius describes a person who "having gone through these things walks the way of virtue [*gradu virtutis*] with step secure and confident and having received a sure meaning for his life [*solidam vivendi rationem*] suddenly becomes perfect."[195] However, given the direct influence of Cyprian's *De lapsis* on Lactantius's doctrine of penitence at *Inst.* 6.24, as well as the pervasive influence of Cyprian's portrait of the Christian life as a walk in Christ's footsteps, Cyprian's comments at *Lap.* 3 also deserve mention: "The first title of victory is to confess the Lord when taken by the hands of the gentiles; the second step to glory [*ad gloriam gradus*] is to be reserved for the Lord, removed by a careful withdrawal [*cauta secessione*]."[196] Still, Lactantius's tripartite enumeration of the *gradus virtutis* also serves as a counterpart to his own earlier comments criticizing the three classes (*egregius-clarrissimus-perfectissimus*) of late Roman hierarchy: "Romans and Greeks never grasped justice because they held people unequal in many steps [*multis gradibus*]," he argues.[197] Lactantius's threefold *gradus virtutis* responds to that early criticism. The *gradus virtitus* supplants a social hierarchy predicated on wealth and birth with a hierarchy of inner virtue, which Lactantius interprets according to a Synoptic ethic mediated by Cyprian's exegesis.[198] *Inst.* 6.13 thus advocates persistent almsgiving (*opera misericordiae*) in accordance with Christ's words in Luke 6:32–35. Lactantius's comments complete his portrait of the *cultor dei* as a Christian who hears and obeys the teaching of Jesus. As is so

---

[193] See Patrick Sims-Williams, "Thought, Word, and Deed: An Irish Triad," *Ériu* 29 (1978): pp. 78–111, who traces the roots of a similar Irish formulation to its earliest sources in Ephrem and Gregory, who both post-date Lactantius: "The three steps which the ordained man steps . . . is the triad in which every man sins, that is in word, in thought, in deed, and it is the triad through which he is renewed again and . . . moved to the body of Christ." However, I have been unable to find Latin instances prior to Lactantius, although it appears after him in penitential contexts, e.g., Augustine, *Ep.*, 187, "*siue factorum dictorum cogitationumque nostrarum in illius lauacri mundatione deletis tamen*"; also, Augustine, *Serm.*, 56, "*quidquid uiuendo addidistis dictis factis cogitationibus: omnia dimittuntur.*" Later, Prudentius, *Prefationes in Bibliam Latinam*, 8.2.5, "*pro omnibus facinoribus meis siue actis siue factis, dictis, cogitationibus iniquis.*" Cassiodorus, *Expositio Psalmorum*, 1.128, 18.245, 32.279.

[194] Lactantius, *Inst.*, 6.13.5.

[195] Apuleius, *De platonis et eius dogmate*, 2.20, "*eum, qui per haec profectus fidenti et securo gradu virtutis via graderetur, adeptum solidam vivendi rationem repente fieri perfectum.*"

[196] Cyprian, *De lapsis*, 3.

[197] For discussion of Lactantius, *Inst.*, 5.14.18, see Chapter 6, this volume.

[198] Cf. Digeser, *Making of a Christian Empire*, pp. 64–91, interpreting *gradus virtutis* entirely through the Hermetic lens.

VIRTUS: CHRIST'S PRECEPTS OF JUSTICE   279

often the case, Lactantius's *gradus virtutis* is neither wholly separate from nor reducible to the thought of another.

Lactantius introduces the topic of penitence by returning to his central metaphor of a person walking a path to eternal life. The metaphor of a person wandering one of two roads harkens back to the Two Ways teaching and Lactantius's even more central image of the *cultor dei*: "No one should give up and despair of himself, if overcome by greed, or driven by lust, or deceived by error, or compelled by some power, he falls [*lapsus est*] onto the way of injustice. It is possible for him to be led back and freed, if he repents of his deeds, and turning to better things, makes satisfaction to God."[199] Without reference its Christian context, Lactantius might appear to fall back on a mere philosophical topos and some vague notion of illumination. *Inst.* 6.24.1–2, however, brings the image of the *cultor dei* walking a path to eternal life into connection with Cyprian's theology of repentance set out in *De lapsis*; Lactantius's use of the verb *lapsus est* is the first marker of his involvement in the more technical theological discourse. Cyprian taught that those who had lapsed after extended suffering could receive forgiveness and even rise to the martyr's glory; he cited Luke 6:22 and promised a reward of immortality even for them.[200] Cyprian condemned, however, those who capitulated without resistance in order to avoid suffering as fallen because of their love for earthly possessions. He thus urged his lapsed members to recognize the depth of their sin: "Open the eyes of your hearts . . . neither despairing [*desperantes*] the mercy of God, nor demanding immediate admission [to communion]."[201] He warns that "to the same degree that God, for the sake of his own *pietas* as Father, is indulgent and good [*indulgens et bonus est*], he is equally to be feared for the sake of his majesty as Judge."[202] In terms that use a medical metaphor, Cyprian further laments those who demand immediate readmission before a period of penance: "They do not seek the patience of health nor the true medicine that comes from penance. Penitence is driven from their hearts and the memory of the most weighty and extreme sin is taken away."[203] Cyprian's comments recall the fact that dealing with the problem of the lapsed had a particular purchase on early Latin Christianity.

Lactantius's comments reflect that Latin Christian struggle. He reproduces Cyprian's doctrine and language encouraging Christians not to "despair"

---

[199] Lactantius, *Inst.*, 6.24.1.

[200] Cf. Cyprian, *De lapsis*, 11–14.

[201] Cyprian, *De lapsis*, 35, "*oculos cordis aperite, nec desperantes misericordiam Domini nec tamen iam veniam vindicantes.*"

[202] Cyprian, *De lapsis*, 35.

[203] Cyprian, *De lapsis*, 15, "*quaerunt sanitatis patientiam nec veram de satisfactione medicinam: paenitentia de pectoribus excussa est, gravissimi extremique delicti memoria sublata est.*" Note the rhetorical effect of "*veram medicinam: paenitentia.*" This seems to be the first near association of the terms *paenitentia* and *medicina* in Latin literature prior to Lactantius.

280 ROMAN VIRTUE IN THE EARLY CHRISTIAN THOUGHT OF LACTANTIUS

(*desperet*) and promising that the one who "has lapsed" can receive mercy by repentance. The vocabulary of *De lapsis* multiplies, as Lactantius uses the analogy of human parenting to explain God's even greater mercy:

> If we are willing to take up again and support and embrace our own children, once we determine that they have repented of their faults and think that humbled and cast down they have been corrected, why should we despair and think that God's mercy [*clementiam dei*] is not able to be placated when we repent [*paenitendo*]? For our most indulgent [*indulgentissimus*] Lord and Parent promises that he will remit the sins of those who repent and blot out all the iniquities of him who begins to do justice once again.[204]

Lactantius's terms and logic repeat Cyprian's image of God as an "indulgent Father [*indulgens*]," who is lenient with his children. Lactantius does substitute *clementia* for *misericordia*, but the thought and image of God as a *paterfamilias* remains. Lactantius connects this idea to his central image of the *viator* walking the way to eternal life: "And so God, knowing our weakness opened the way of salvation for the sake of his own *pietas* so that the medicine of penitence [*medicina paenitentiae*] might come to aid in this dire need to which our weakness has been subjected."[205] By associating the three terms, *pietas*, *paenitentia*, and *medicina* with a promise that God is *indulgentissimus* in his role as Father, Lactantius precisely reproduces Cyprian's theology at *De lapsis* 15. Despite some rhetorical reworking, the doctrinal judgment belongs to Cyprian.

Lactantius uses this doctrine of Cyprian to reassert the person of Christ as a superior source of moral knowledge. His lines recall the earlier juxtaposition of Christ and Cicero at *Inst.* 6.8.11–12. Lactantius reminds his reader "that no one is able to hide from him, in whose sight we live. To the one from whom nothing is hidden, nothing can be secret," just as Jesus explains at Matt. 6:4.[206] This admonition introduces a greater exhortation that evokes the healing miracles summarized in Matt. 11:5: "Thus, it is better either to flee our own knowledge of our own conscience [*conscientiam*] or open our minds to drain the poison by

---

[204] Lactantius, *Inst.*, 6.24.4. Cf. *Inst.*, 6.20 and *Ira.*, 15–18, where the same language and logic appear: "*Si liberos nostros, cum delictorum suorum cernimus paenitere, correctos esse arbitramur et abdicatos abiectosque rursus tamen suscipimus foveumus amplectimur, cur desperemus clementiam veri patris paenitendo posse placari? Ergo dominus ac parens indulgentissimus remissurum se paenitentibus peccata promittit et obliteraturum omnes iniquitates eius qui iustitiam denuo coeperit operari.*"

[205] Lactantius, *Inst.*, 6.24.9, "*Et idcirco deus imbecillitatem nostrum sciens pro sua pietate aperuit homini portum salutis, ut huic necessitate, cui fragilitas nostra subiecta est, medicina paenitentiae subveniret.*"

[206] Lactantius, *Inst.*, 6.24.12, "*In cuius conspectu vivimus, nec si universos homines celare possumus, cui nihil absconditum, nihil potest esse secretum.*"

VIRTUS: CHRIST'S PRECEPTS OF JUSTICE   281

reopening our wounds. No one else is able to heal them except him alone who healed the crippled, restored sight to the blind, purified blemished bodies, raised the dead."[207] Lactantius had already given Christ's healing miracles a central place in his narrative of Christ.[208] *Inst.* 6.24, however, interprets Christ's ministry affectively: "He extinguishes the fire of lust, roots out lust, removes envy, sooths wrath, returns true and enduring health [*perpetuam sanitatem*]. All desire this medicine because the soul is troubled by a greater danger than the body and the care of inward hidden diseases must come first."[209]

Lactantius expands, in this context, upon the superiority of spiritual over bodily virtue. His comments reveal the difference between a philosophical view of inward virtue and the Christian practice that shapes Lactantius's thought. Lactantius calls *sanus*, not the physically strong person, but rather "the one who does not fix his eyes on another's happiness or marvel at his riches, who looks at another man's wife in holiness [*sancta*], hungers for nothing at all, desires nothing belonging to another, envies no one, hates no one, but rather is humble, merciful, kind, meek, humane. Peace abides in his soul."[210] This description of the "healthy soul" is a rapid synopsis of Christ's reading of the Decalogue in Matt. 5–7 and provides a clue to Lactantius's ultimate concern in *Inst.* 6.24. Lactantius uses this description to define his central thematic image of the *cultor dei* in terms provided by Christ's teaching. Hence, the same passage concludes with yet another assertion that it is Christ who reveals and defines the *cultor dei* more than any philosopher: "This one is the healthy person. He is the just one, the perfect one. Therefore, whoever obeys all these heavenly precepts, he is the true *cultor dei*, and his sacrifices are gentility of spirit, an innocent life, and good deeds."[211] Although Lactantius spent the preceding six *Institutiones* redefining the *cultor dei* according to Christ's example, this is his single most explicit assertion of his deep belief that the philosophical search for *virtus* must lead to the person of Jesus. Lactantius immediately brings that assertion back into connection with the natural law argument he made at the beginning of *Institutio* 6. Criticizing the "sacrifice of a dumb animal" he urges rather

> those things offered from the depth of the human heart. And so, onto that altar which is truly greatest and cannot be stained by shed blood because it

---

[207] Lactantius, *Inst.*, 6.24.23. Cf. *Inst.*, 4.15. Also, Cyprian, *De lapsis*, 15–17, for the rhetoric of sickness.

[208] See Lactantius, *Inst.*, 4.15.

[209] Lactantius, *Inst.*, 6.24.23.

[210] Lactantius, *Inst.*, 6.24.25.

[211] Lactantius, *Inst.*, 6.24.25, noting the rhetorical continuity with *iustus ac sapiens* or *iustus ac bonus*: "*Ille homo sanus, ille iustus, ille perfectus est. quisquis igitur his omnibus praeceptis caelestibus obtemperaverit, hic cultor est verus dei, cuius sacrifice sunt mansuetodo animi et vita innocens et actus boni.*" Cf. Vergil, *Aen.*, 8.270–272 for *ara maxima* and Cicero, *Leg.*, 1.18, 2.8.

282 ROMAN VIRTUE IN THE EARLY CHRISTIAN THOUGHT OF LACTANTIUS

is in the heart, there is placed justice, patience, faith, innocence, chastity, self-restraint [*abstinentia*]. This is the truest ritual [*ritus*], this is "the law of God" as Cicero called it, "clear and divine, which also commands what is upright and honorable and forbids the depraved and filthy."' Whoever is obedient to that most holy and certain law necessarily lives in a just and lawful way [*iuste ac legitime*].[212]

We have already noted that Lactantius's strong assertion that spiritual virtues surpass any animal ritual is traditional and derived from the arguments of Minucius Felix and Tertullian. Lactantius adds to that traditional argument the even stronger redefinition of Cicero's natural law according to the words of Jesus. The above passage juxtaposes its synopsis of Christ's *Sermon* with Cicero's language as a final expression of the point Lactantius made from the outset: Cicero knew the fact of a *lex naturale* but had no idea what it said. Jesus came to reveal its content *in praeceptis caelestibus* and prove their power by his example. Lactantius thus leads the reader back to the person and work of Christ, whom he has offered as the source of a moral knowledge grounded in a true account of the Father and Son. Hence, Lactantius's conclusion redeploys the *source-stream-flow* metaphor and the Christological rhetoric of John 1:5:

> "Of this Holy Law, I have put down only a few chapters [*pauca equidem capita*] because I promised to discuss only those things that relate to the highest point [*summum fastigium*] of virtue and justice. If anyone wishes to comprehend [*comprehendere*] all the rest, let him seek it from the source itself [*ex fonte ipso*], whence that stream [*rivuus iste*] has flowed to us."[213]

This passage concludes what is perhaps Lactantius's most original contribution to early Latin Christianity with a recapitulation of the *Divine Institutes*' central metaphors. His reference to "*pauca capita*" might be a coy allusion to the "*capitula*" of Cyprian's *Ad Quirinum*, though this is impossible to confirm.[214] The term *comprehendere* invokes our orator's inversion of John 1:5 at *Inst.* 4.1, while the *source-stream-flow* metaphor concludes where Lactantius began, with the claim that a true account of moral and political order requires a knowledge of the one true God.

---

[212] Lactantius, *Inst.*, 6.25.29.

[213] Lactantius, *Inst.*, 6.24.30–31.

[214] Cyprian, *Quir.*, 3, "*ut ad instruendum te excerperem de scipturis sanctis quaedam capitula ad religiosam sectae nostrae disciplinam pertinentia . . . collecta sunt a me quaedam praecepta dominica et magisteria divina quae esse et facilia et utilia legentibus possint, dum in breviarium pauca digesta . . . et frequenter iterantur.*"

Conclusion

Modern scholarship has generally viewed Lactantius's moral thought as the superior part of his contribution to the history of Christianity. That judgment is correct. His arguments about the character of the just society express his deepest concerns and contain his most original formulations. Previous scholarship missed, however, Lactantius's deep agreement with the third-century Latin tradition he claimed to represent. For all the Latin writers, Christ's life and ministry provided an image of the divine nature that altered classical accounts of the character of divine power and its implications for human action. Lactantius's contribution resides in his effort to specify the implications of that traditional Latin Christian teaching for ethics and politics in a comprehensive way that could address the most urgent matters of his day. That effort did not require him to leave behind specialist doctrinal formulations in favor of merely classical or Ciceronian moral reasoning. Rather, it meant naming and emphasizing the immediate implications of any theology of the divine nature for any argument about human beings and their life together. *Institutio* 6 is about that. Lactantius ultimately regards the life of God revealed by Christ as the ultimate vision of any society, and he attempts to rewrite the fundamental terms of classical moral thought in accordance with that revelation. This also means, for him, upending traditional thinking about the right use of wealth and sexuality, and thus also, it means taking Christ's teaching in the Scriptures as the ultimate source of moral knowledge. Lactantius has often disappointed by his apparent *volte face* on the question of violence. Even that development in his thought, however, reflects his commitment to divine love and to the scriptural narrative. Ultimately, Lactantius's most innovative, even modern insights, arise from his ancient and deeply traditional commitments. His moral theology, regarded as peculiar by so many, witnesses to the unity of early Latin theology in its engagement with classical thought and scriptural exegesis.

Conclusion

Since the late nineteenth century, scholars of Lactantius have labored under the assumption that his work is somehow strange. Although his putative idiosyncrasies furnished a wealth of material for debate, divergent perspectives rested on a deeper consensus, which mainly saw his *Divine Institutes* as a pastiche of conflicting intellectual impulses. At the turn of the twentieth century, Lactantius's readers saw him as passionate, but superficial. They thought he produced an outpouring of Ciceronian rhetoric uninformed by rigorous scriptural exegesis. He seemed to settle archaic theological anthropomorphisms uncomfortably alongside Stoic moral and political arguments. Though perhaps more than a dilettante, he was far less than a serious Christian theologian. A second generation of accounts showed more nuance. For mid-century scholars, Lactantius became, like his one-time teacher Arnobius, emblematic of an era when philosophically engaged pagans adopted Christianity but understood their new faith in mainly unconverted terms. By this account, Lactantius did not seem to convert *away* from pagan belief so much as *toward* Christian ritual and moral rigor. His writing reflects that hybrid religious experience, it was thought, since he attempts to ground Christian praxis in Hellenistic gnosis and thereby give Christianity a broad appeal to educated Romans of the administrative class like himself. Still, these scholars allowed that Lactantius's most enduring contribution was a new concept of religion that integrated intellectual and ritual commitments into a coherent notion, which would remain central to Christian thought, even into the modern age. For all its merits, this second-generation view still made Lactantius a quixotic sort of figure responding to political violence with quaint allusions to Cicero. Lactantius's feeble synthesis made him a strangely out-of-touch sort of advocate, more apt to encourage the initiated than persuade the adversary.

One formidable intervention aimed to explain Lactantius's idiosyncratic blend of pagan and Christian by a sensible gesture to politics. An orator, a former employee of Diocletian, an advisor to Constantine, Lactantius could be explained as a propagandist of Christian triumph—a professor of rhetoric who updated Rome's traditional theology of victory in service to the new regime. Although this account makes Lactantius relevant to ancient politics, it also raises the specter of a deep and cynical compromise of Christian teaching, since it implies that he tailored his theology to suit the needs of his favored prince,

Roman Virtue in the Early Christian Thought of Lactantius. Jason M. Gehrke, Oxford University Press.
© Oxford University Press 2025. DOI: 10.1093/9780197667781.003.0009

CONCLUSION 285

Constantine the Great. Certainly, Lactantius has had defenders arguing that his work could be harmonized with early, if archaic, expressions of Christian thought. Yet their arguments never captured the modern scholarly imagination, perhaps because even if modern readers could allow that he was merely behind-the-times, rather than ignorant or syncretistic, he seemed nonetheless an outlier to his own historical-intellectual moment. Hence, at the turn of this century, the most influential English-language study still identified Constantine's political priorities as the hermeneutical key to his theology. As the servant of a syncretistic Christian ruler who needed to defuse tension between pagans and Christians, Lactantius intermingled Christian and pagan authorities in order to promote a new ethic of toleration for Constantine's eclectically Christian regime. All of these views produced major contributions to our understanding of Lactantius. They also agreed, more and less explicitly, that he was some kind of anomaly, a useful representative of neither the Christianity he defended, nor the traditional Roman religion that he polemicized.

My aim, in this study, has been to overturn these assumptions by providing an integrated portrait of the development of classical Roman and early Latin Christian theologies, which shaped his understanding of the conflict be-tween Christian and pagan Romans. That theological development illuminates Lactantius's *Divine Institutes* as a late installment in a heated family fight about pressing issues of moral and political order; Lactantius took a Christian position, but the argument was fundamental to ancient Roman self-understanding. It was a debate that began in the late Republic and continued, more-or-less unbroken, into the early fifth century. (Augustine's *City of God* makes perhaps the closing argument in that occasionally violent domestic dispute.) From this perspective, Lactantius's *Divine Institutes* is not any kind of peculiar statement. It is rather the only attempt to give programmatic expression to third-century Latin Christian thinking about God's revelation in the person of Christ, and the deep implications of that revelation for Roman thinking about moral and political order.

Trained as an orator, catechized in the treatises of Tertullian and Cyprian, impressed by the example of Minucius Felix, Lactantius tried to overcome the occasional character of early Latin Christian writing. He understood Christian teaching as a species of ancient thought corrected and illuminated by God's reve-lation in Christ, communicated by the Apostles through the holy Scriptures. His work thus attempts to reveal the unity of third-century Latin theology from its critical apologetic to its constructive Christological and moral claims. This at-tempt at coherent arrangement necessarily combines theological texts and topics that would later develop into discrete fields of discourse (e.g., apologetic, trini-tarian theology, ethics). That programmatic quality means that what often seems eccentric in Lactantius is the very thing that makes him so traditional. Philosophy and apologetic, metaphysics and politics, historical narrative and scriptural exegesis—these were, for Lactantius and his Christian predecessors, a coherent body of discourse that emerged from the historical event of Christ's life and ministry. What Lactantius provides, therefore, is the closest thing we have to a complete synthesis of third-century Latin Christian thinking about the implications of Christianity for classical Roman views of God, nature, and political order.

Lactantius's *Divine Institutes* thus highlights the fact that early Latin Christianity was itself the product of classical Roman intellectual culture. What Mattias Gassman has written of later fourth-century figures is no less true of their third-century predecessors: "Devout Christians and devout pagans were ... inhabitants of the same society and participants in the same culture. Both naturally shared common attitudes and common ideas," which motivated serious disagreements that were "products of divergent beliefs and practices, not just polemical identity making."[1] Earlier readings of Lactantius stumbled over this point, as scholars attempted to sift the genuinely Christian from his presumptively naive, or merely apologetic use of pagan texts and language. That effort had the unfortunate consequence of reifying modern categories of "Christian" and "pagan," which then served as a prism for evaluating Lactantius's relationship to two alternatives imagined as necessarily binary. Subsequent scholarship, however, has allowed us to replace that anachronism with a clearer historical view. Classical philosophical and moral discourses provided a fund of technical concepts and language, as well as a shared history of discourse, which simultaneously motivated and enabled Christian apologetic and doctrinal development.

In this respect, the writings of Cicero must be regarded as a fundamental starting point for the development of Christian thought in the Latin context. His philosophical works created much of the Latin philosophical vocabulary, which informed the magnificently influential literature that appeared in Rome between Julius Caesar and the emperor Nero. Through that literature, classical Roman moral and theological discourses predicated upon what has been termed "the technical sense of power" came to influence Latin Christian thinking. Latin Christian apologetic ensured this fundamental development. In their efforts to explain Christianity and justify its place in the Roman order, the Latin apologists drew upon Roman philosophical and moral discourses. The result was a Latin Christian theological tradition created to address the basic misconceptions of classical Roman thinking, in part by reinvesting its fundamental grammar with a content derived from the person and work of Christ, as he was remembered in the Church and made the object of constant meditation in the daily practice of scriptural exegesis.

The deep political interest of classical Roman culture and the immediate problem of persecution thus endowed Latin Christianity with an urgent

---

[1] Mattias Gassman, *Worshippers of the Gods: Debating Paganism in the Fourth Century Latin West* (Oxford: Oxford University Press, 2020), p. 172.

interest in moral and political problems. *Divine Institutes* is emblematic of those concerns. Both scriptural teaching and Roman tradition had represented divinity as an object of imitation for the sake of training in virtue. Latin Christianity thus developed—from the example of Jesus—a profoundly reformed account of classical Roman virtue, one that inverted the fundamental presuppositions of ancient political culture. Rather than seeing political community as the product of family and ethnic relationships and warfare as a default state, Latin Christians argued that mutual love between human beings understood as fundamentally equal because they are created in the image of God, is the foundational principle of social order—a relation to be broken only for limited and justified reasons. Concomitantly, they developed from Christ's revelation a new account of virtue itself and sought to define right relations between human beings according to their Scriptural understanding of Christ's person and work. Patience, forbearance, and mercy thus became basic expressions of divine *virtus* in Latin Christian discourse, which offered the public and historical event of Christ's life, death, and resurrection as the basis for moral knowledge. Lactantius epitomized this Latin Christian tradition. Even when, late in his career, Lactantius admits the need for military force and judicial violence, his belief that God appoints legitimate authority to mete out both rewards and punishments arises from his traditional Latin commitment to a politics predicated upon the divine love. The recognition that divine love must include both just judgment and righteous anger marks his thought as a genuine development of both Latin Christian exegesis and classical political theory, rather than any kind of utopian simplification.

Recognition of the debt that early Latin Christian theology owes to classical Roman literature also provides a new starting point for reflection on Lactantius's contribution to Constantine's political program. Although he does not convey all the depths of Christian theology—a point Lactantius himself knew and intended—he offered, nonetheless, an original statement of the implications of Christian revelation for political rule. Insofar as he did influence Constantine—the extent and character of which influence remains a matter for discussion—Lactantius promoted a Christian view that was typical of Latin Christian writing in the third century. He attempted thereby to fashion Constantine's political vision by presenting Christ's example in suffering and his words in teaching as the ultimate source of political wisdom, the supreme object for any ruler's imitation. The first Christian to bear the burden of political rule, Constantine's self-representation as an imitator of Christ, as a worshipper looking up to God, may suggest Lactantius's enduring, if partial, influence upon the first Christian emperor.[2]

---

[2] For Constantine's public iconography, see Jonathan Bardill, *Constantine: Divine Emperor of the Christian Golden Age* (Cambridge: Cambridge University Press, 2012), chapter 2.

Bibliography

Primary Sources

Apuleius. *Apologia; Floria; De Deo Socratis*, edited and translated by Christopher P. Jones. Loeb Classical Library 534 (Cambridge, MA: Harvard University Press, 2017).

Brandt, S. and G. Laubmann. *L. Caeli Firmiani Lactanti Opera Omnia*. CSEL, vols. 19 and 27 (Leipzig: 1890–1897).

Cicero, Marcus Tullius. *De Divinatione, De Fato, Timaeus, Ottonis Plasberg schedis usus* (Stuttgart: In aedibus B. G. Teubneri, 1965).

Cicero, Marcus Tullius. *De Inventione*, translated by H. M. Hubbell (Cambridge, MA: Harvard University Press, 1949; reprint 1993).

Cicero, Marcus Tullius. *De natura deorum*, edited by Otto Plasberg and Wilhelm Heinrich Ax (Stuttgart: Teubner, 1980).

Cicero, Marcus Tullius. *De Officiis*, translated by Walter Miller. Loeb Classical Library 30 (Cambridge, MA: Harvard University Press, 2014).

Cicero, Marcus Tullius. *De optimo genere oratorum, Partitiones oratoriae, Topica. Recognovit Gulielmus Friedrich* (Stuttgart: In aedibus B. G. Teubneri, 1914).

Cicero, Marcus Tullius. *De Oratore, with Introduction and Notes by Augustus S. Wilkins* (Cambridge: Cambridge University Press, 1895).

Cicero, Marcus Tullius. *De Re Publica; De Legibus; Cato Maior de Senectute; Laelius de Amicitia*, edited by J. G. F. Powell (Oxford: Oxford University Press, 2006).

Cicero, Marcus Tullius. *Letters to Quintus and Brutus; Letter Fragments; Letter to Octavian; Invectives; Handbook of Electioneering*, edited and translated by D. R. Shackleton Bailey. Loeb Classical Library 462 (Cambridge, MA: Harvard University Press, 2002).

Cicero, Marcus Tullius. *On Ends*, translated by H. Rackham. Loeb Classical Library 40 (Cambridge, MA: Harvard University Press, 1914).

Cicero, Marcus Tullius. *On the Nature of the Gods; Academica*, translated by H. Rackham (Cambridge, MA: Harvard University Press, 1933).

Cicero, Marcus Tullius. *Philippics 1–6*, edited and translated by D. R. Shackleton Bailey, revised by John T. Ramsey, Gesine Manuwald. Loeb Classical Library 189 (Cambridge, MA: Harvard University Press, 2010).

Cicero, Marcus Tullius. *Pro Archia; Post Reditum in Senatu; Post Reditum Ad Quirites; De Domo Sua; De Haruspicum Responsis; Pro Plancio*, translated by N. H. Watts, Loeb Classical Library 158 (Cambridge, MA: Harvard University Press, 1923).

Cicero, Marcus Tullius. *Pro Sestio; In Vatinium*, translated by R. Gardner. Loeb Classical Library 309 (Cambridge, MA: Harvard University Press, 1958).

Cicero, Marcus Tullius. *Tusculan Disputations*, translated by J. E. King. Loeb Classical Library 141 (Cambridge, MA: Harvard University Press, 2014).

Creed, J. L., ed. *Lactantius: De Mortibus Persecutorum* (Oxford: Oxford University Press, 1984).

Cyprian. *Cyprien de Carthage, Ceux qui sont tombés*, introduction par Graeme Clarke et Michel Poirier (Paris: Éditions du Cerf, 2012).

Cyprian. *Cyprien de Carthage, A Démétrien: Introduction, texte critique, traduction et commentaire par Jean-Claude Fredouille* (Paris: Éditions du Cerf, 2003).

Cyprian. *A Donat et La vertu de patience: Introduction, traduction et notes de Jean Molager* (Paris: Éditions du Cerf, 1982).

Cyprian. *Cyprien de Carthage, La Bienfaisance et les Aumônes: Introduction, texte critique, traduction, notes et index par Michel Poirier* (Paris: Éditions du Cerf, 2003).

290 BIBLIOGRAPHY

Cyprian. *Cyprien de Carthage, L'unité de l'Église,* edited by Paul Mattei, Michel Poirer, and Paolo Siniscalco (Paris: Éditions du Cerf, 2006).

Cyprian. *Sancti Cypriani Opera Omnia.* Corpus Christianorum Series Latina 3A-F, edited by Robert Weber, Maurice Bevenot, Manlio Simonetti, Claudio Moreschini, Laetitia Ciccolini, and Paul Mattei (Turnhout: Brepols, 1972–2016).

Ennius, Quintus and Otto Skutsch. *The Annals of Q. Ennius* (Oxford: Oxford University Press, 1985).

Evans, Ernest. *Tertullian's Treatise against Praxeas: The Text, Edited with an Introduction, Translation and Commentary* (London: S.P.C.K., 1948).

Evans, Ernest. *Tertullian's Treatise on the Resurrection: The Text Edited with an Introduction, Translation, and Commentary* (Eugene, OR: Wipf & Stock, 1960).

Frakes, Robert M. *Compiling the* Collatio Legum Mosaicarum et Romanarum *in Late Antiquity* (Oxford: Oxford University Press, 2012).

Gaius. *Gaius: The Institutes of Gaius,* edited by W. M. Gordon and O. F. Robinson (London: Duckworth, 1988).

Horace. *Odes IV and Carmen Saeculare,* edited by Richard Thomas (Cambridge: Cambridge University Press, 2011).

Ingremeau, Christiane. *La Colère de Dieu* (Paris: Éditions du Cerf, 1982).

Justin. *Justin, Philosopher and Martyr: Apologies edited with introduction, translation, notes, and commentary on the text by Denis Minns and Paul Parvis* (Oxford: Oxford University Press, 2009).

Juvenal. *Juvenal and Perseus,* edited and translated by Susanna Morton Braund. Loeb Classical Library 91 (Cambridge, MA: Harvard University Press, 2004).

Lactantius. *Divinarum Institutionum Libri Septem,* fasc I–IV. Ediderunt Eberhard Heck et Antonie Wlosok (Berlin: De Gruyter, 2005–2011).

Lactantius. *The Divine Institutes,* edited and translated by Anthony Bowen and Peter Garnsey (Liverpool: Liverpool University Press, 2003).

Lactantius. *Epitome Institutionum Divinarum,* edited by Eberhard Heck and Antonie Wlosok (Teubner: Stuttgart, 1994).

Lactantius. *Lactance: Les Institutions Divines* VI, Introduction, texte critique, traduction, notes et index Christiane Ingremeau (Paris: Éditions du Cerf, 2007).

Livius. *Ab urbe condita.* Tomus I. Oxford Classical Texts Series. Edited by R.M. Ogilvie. Oxford: Oxford University Press, 1974. https://www.amazon.com/Ab-Urbe-Condita-Classical-Bks-1-5/dp/0198146612

Livius. *Ab urbe condita vols. I–VI, recognovit et adnotatione critica instruxt Robertus Maxwell Ogilvie and P.G. Walsh* (Oxonii: E Typographeo Clarendoniano, 1974–1999).

Lucan. *The Civil War (Pharsalia),* translated by J. D. Duff. Loeb Classical Library 220 (Cambridge, MA: Harvard University Press, 1928).

Lucan. *De Bello Civili,* edited by Paul Roche (Oxford: Oxford University Press, 2009).

Lucretius. *Lucrèce: De La Nature I,* edited by Claude Rambaux (Paris: Les Belles Lettres, 1990).

Lucretius. *On the Nature of the Universe: A Verse Translation by Sir Ronald Melville with Introduction and Notes by Don and Peta Fowler* (Oxford: Clarendon Press, 1997).

Mayor, Joseph B. and J. H. Swainson. *Cicero: De natura deorum with Introduction, Notes, and Commentary,* vol. 2 (Cambridge: Cambridge University Press, 1883; reprint, 2010).

McDonald, Sister Mary Francis. *The Minor Works* (Baltimore: Catholic University Press, 1965).

Minucius Felix. *Octavius Texte établi et traduit par Jean Beajeu* (Paris: Les Belles Lettres, 1964).

Monat, Pierre. *Institutions Divines. Livre I.* SC 326 (Paris: Éditions du Cerf, 1986).

Monat, Pierre. *Institutions Divines. Livre II.* SC 337 (Paris: Éditions du Cerf, 1987).

Monat, Pierre. *Institutions Divines. Livre IV.* SC 377 (Paris: Éditions du Cerf, 1992).

Monat, Pierre. *Institutions Divines. Livre V.* 2 vols. SC 204–205 (Paris: Éditions du Cerf, 1973).

Moreau, J. *De Mortibus Persecutorum.* SC 39 (Paris: Éditions du Cerf, 1954).

Novatian. *De Trinitate: Novatiani Romanae urbis presbyteri "De Trinitate" liber,* edited by W. Yorke Fausset (Cambridge: Cambridge University Press, 1909).

BIBLIOGRAPHY 291

Ovid. *Heroides*; *Amores*, translated by Grant Showerman, revised by G. P. Goold. Loeb Classical Library 41 (Cambridge, MA: Harvard University Press, 1914).

Perrin, Michel. *L'ouvrage du dieu créateur*, vol. 1. Sources Chrétiennes 213 (Paris: Éditions du Cerf, 1974).

Perrin, Michel. *L'ouvrage du dieu créateur, vol. 2*. Sources Chrétiennes 214 (Paris: Éditions du Cerf, 1974).

Quintilian. *The Orator's Education*, Volume I: Books 1–2, edited and translated by Donald A. Russell. Loeb Classical Library 124 (Cambridge, MA: Harvard University Press, 2002).

Sallust. *The War with Catiline*; *The War with Jugurtha*, translated by J. C. Rolfe, revised by John T. Ramsey (Cambridge, MA: Harvard University Press, 2013).

Seneca. *Epistles*, Volume II: *Epistles 66–92*, translated by Richard M. Gummere. Loeb Classical Library 76 (Cambridge, MA: Harvard University Press, 1920).

Seneca. *Moral Essays*, Volume I: *De Providentia; De Constantia; De Ira; De Clementia*, translated by John W. Basore. Loeb Classical Library 308 (Cambridge, MA: Harvard University Press, 1928).

Seneca. *Moral Essays*, Volume III: *De Beneficiis*, translated by John W. Basore. Loeb Classical Library 310 (Cambridge, MA: Harvard University Press, 1935).

Seneca. *Natural Questions*, Volume I: *Books 1–3*, translated by Thomas H. Corcoran. Loeb Classical Library 450 (Cambridge, MA: Harvard University Press, 1971).

Suetonius. *Suetonius, with an English Translation by J. C. Rolfe* (Cambridge, MA: Harvard University Press, 1997–1998).

Tacitus. *Annals: Books 13–16*, translated by John Jackson. Loeb Classical Library 322 (Cambridge, MA: Harvard University Press, 1937).

Tertullian. *Adversus Marcionem*, edited and translated by Ernest Evans (Oxford: Clarendon Press, 1972).

Tertullian. Corpus Christianorum, Series Latina: 1. I Tertullianus: Pars I. *Ad Martyras*, edidit E. Dekkers; *Ad Nationes* edidit J.W.P. Borleffs (Turnhout: Brepols, 1953).

Tertullian. *De la Patience, Introduction, texte critique, traduction et commentaire par Jean-Claude Fredouille* (Paris: Éditions du Cerf, 1984).

Tertullian. *Quinti Septimi Florentis Tertulliani De Anima*, translated by J. H. Waszink (Leiden: Brill, 2010).

Tertullian, Minucius Felix. *Apology*; *De Spectaculis*; *Minucius Felix: Octavius*, translated by J. R. Glover and Gerald H. Rendall. Loeb Classical Library 250 (Cambridge, MA: Harvard University Press, 1931).

Vergil. *Aeneis*, edited by Gian Biagio Conte (Berlin: Walter DeGruyter, 2009).

Studies of Lactantius

Adamik, Tamas. "Laktanz' Menschenbild." *Acta Antiqua Academiae Scientiarum Hungarica* 40 (2000): pp. 3–14.

Alimi, Toni. "Lactantius' Modern Concept of Religion." *Journal of Religious History* (2023): pp. 1–23.

André, Jan-Marie. "Lactance et l'idée stoicienne de justice." In *Valeurs dans le stoicisme. Du portique a nos jours*, edited by M. Soetard (Lille: Presses Universitaires de Lille, 1993).

Bardill, Jonathan. *Constantine: Divine Emperor of the Christian Golden Age* (Cambridge: Cambridge University Press, 2012).

Bender, Albrecht. *Die natürliche Gotteserkenntnis bei Laktanz und seinen apologetischen vorgängern* (New York: Peter Lang, 1983).

Brandt, S. "Über die Quellen von Laktanz' Schrift De opificio Dei." *Wiender Studien: Zeitschrift fur Klassiche* 13 (1891): pp. 225–292.

Bryce, Jackson. *Bibliography of Lactantius*. http://www.carleton.edu/curricular/CLAS/lactantius.bibli.htm.

Bryce, Jackson. *The Library of Lactantius* (New York: Garland, 1990; reprint, Harvard Dissertations in the Classics, 1974).

292 BIBLIOGRAPHY

Barnes, Timothy David. "Constantine's Speech to the Assembly of the Saints: Place and Date of Delivery." *Journal of Theological Studies* 52 (2001): pp. 26–36.

Barnes, Timothy David. "From Repression to Toleration: The Evolution of Constantine's Religious Policies." *Scripta Classica Israelica* 21 (2002): pp. 189–202.

Barnes, Timothy David. "Lactantius and Constantine." *Journal of Roman Studies* 63 (1973): pp. 29–46.

Buchheit, Vinzenz. "Cicero Inspiratus: Vergilius Propheta? Zur Wertung paganer Autoren bei Laktanz." *Hermes* 118 Bd., H.3 (1990): pp. 357–372.

Buchheit, Vinzenz. "Die Definition der Gerechtigkeit bei Laktanz und seinen Vorgänger." *Vigiliae Christianae* 33 (1979): pp. 356–374.

Buchheit, Vinzenz. "Goldene Zeit und Paradeis auf Erden (Laktanz *Inst.*, 5, 5–8)." *WJA* 4 (1978): pp. 161–185, and *Würzburger Jahrbücher für die Altertumswissenschaft* 5 (1979): pp. 219–235.

Buchheit, Vinzenz. "Juppiter alz Gewalttäter Laktanz (Inst. 5.6.6) Und Cicero." *Rheinisches Museum für Philologie*, Neue Folge, 125, Bd., H 3–4 (1982): pp. 338–342.

Buchheit, Vinzenz. "Laktanz und die Apolloorakel." *Hermes* 136. Jahrg. H 3 (2008): pp. 381–382.

Buchheit, Vinzenz. "Laktanz und seine '*Testimonia Veritatis*." *Hermes* 130. Bd. H.3 (3rd Qtr., 2002): pp. 306–315.

Buchheit, Vinzenz. "Der Zeitbezug in der Weltalterlehre des Laktanz (*Inst.* 5, 5–6)." *Historia: Zeitschrift für Alte Geschichte Bd. 28*, H. 4 (1979): pp. 472–486.

Cain, Andrew. "Gregory of Elvira, Lactantius and the Reception of the *De ira dei*." *Vigiliae Christianae* 64 (2010): pp. 109–114.

Cain, Andrew. "Three Further Echoes of Lactantius in Jerome." *Philologus* (2010): pp. 88–96.

Casey, Stephen. *The Christian Magisterium of Lactantius* (Unpublished dissertation, McGill University, 1972).

Cavalcanti, Elena. "Aspetti della strutturazione del tema della giustizia nel cristianesimo-antico (Lattanzio, *Divinae Institutiones*, V–VI.)." In *Atti dell'Accademia Romanistica constantiniana, VIII Convegno internazionale* (Perouse: Presses Universitaires de Perouse, 1990).

Champeaux, Arron. "Arnobe Lecteur de Varron." *Revue des Etudes Augustiniennes* 40 (1994): pp. 327–352.

Coleman, Anthony Patrick. *Lactantius the Theologian: Lactantius and the Doctrine of Providence* (Piscataway, NJ, Gorgias Press, 2017).

Colombo, Sisto. "Lattanzio e S. Agostino." *Didaskalion* 10, no. 2–3 (1931): pp. 1–22.

Colot, Blandine. "*Pietas*, argument et expression d'un nouveau lien socio-religieux dans le christianisme romain de Lactance." *Studia Patristica* 34 (2001): pp. 942–945.

Colot, Blandine. "Review: Pagane Texte und Wertvorstellungen bei Lactanz." *Vigiliae Christianae* 63, no. 2 (2009): pp. 189–194.

Conte, Gian Biagio. "The Strategy of Contradiction." In *The Poetry of Pathos: Studies in Virgilian Epic, Gian Biagio Conte*, edited by S. J. Harrison (Oxford: Oxford University Press, 2007).

Digeser, Elizabeth DePalma. "Casinensis 595, Parisinus Lat. 1664, Palatino-Vaticanus 161 and the 'Divine Institutes,' Second Edition." *Hermes* 127. Bd. H. 1 (1999): pp. 75–98.

Digeser, Elizabeth DePalma. "Citizenship and the Roman *Res Publica: Cicero and a Christian Corollary*." *Review of International Social and Political Philosophy* 6, no. 1 (2003): pp. 5–21.

Digeser, Elizabeth DePalma. "Lactantius." In *Great Christian Jurists and Legal Collections in the First Millenium*, edited by Philip L. Reynolds (Cambridge: Cambridge University Press, 2019).

Digeser, Elizabeth DePalma. "Lactantius and Constantine's Letter to Arles: Dating the *Divine Institutes*." *Journal of Early Christian Studies* 2 (1994): pp. 33–52.

Digeser, Elizabeth DePalma. "Lactantius, Porphyry, and the Debate over Religious Toleration." *Journal of Religious Studies* 88 (1994): pp. 129–149.

BIBLIOGRAPHY 293

Digeser, Elizabeth DePalma. *The Making of a Christian Empire: Lactantius and Rome* (Ithaca, NY: Cornell University Press, 2000).

Digeser, Elizabeth DePalma. "Religion, Law, and the Roman Polity: The Era of the Great Persecution." In *Religion and Law in Classical and Christian Rome*, edited by C. Ando and J. Rüpke (Munich: F. Steiner, 2006).

Digeser, Elizabeth DePalma. *A Threat to Public Piety: Christians, Platonists, and the Great Persecution* (Ithaca, NY: Cornell University Press, 2012).

Doignon, J. "Nos bons hommes de foi": Cyprien, Lactance, Victorin, Optat, Hilaire (*De Docr. Christ.* IV, 40, 61)." *Latomus* 22 (1963): pp. 795–805.

Draper, Jonathan A. "Lactantius and the Jesus Tradition in the Didache." *Journal of Theological Studies* 40 (1989): pp. 112–119.

Edwards, Mark. "The Flowering of Latin Apologetic: Lactantius and Arnobius." In *Apologetics in the Roman Empire: Pagans, Jews and Christians*, edited by M. Edwards Goodman and S. Price (Oxford: Oxford University Press, 1999).

Fabrega, V. "Die chiliastische Lehre des Laktanz." *Journal of Ancient Civilizations* 17 (1974): pp. 126–146.

Ferrini, Contardo. "Die juristischen Kenntnisse des Arnobius und des Lactantius." *Zeitschrift der Savigny-Stiftung für Rechtsgeschichte* 15 (1894): pp. 343–352.

Ferrini, Contardo. "Su le idee giuridiche contenute nei libri V e VI delle Instituzioni di Lattanzio." *Rivista internazionale di scienze sociali e discipline ausiliarie* 5 (1894): pp. 581–586.

Fischer, Joseph Anton. "Die Einheit der beiden Testamente bei Laktanz." *Münchener Theologische Zeitschrift* 1 (1950): pp. 96–101.

Fisher, Arthur L. "Lactantius' Ideas Relating Christian Truth and Christian Society." *Journal of the History of Ideas* 43, no. 3 (1982): pp. 355–377.

Fontaine, J. and M. Perrin, eds. *Lactance et son Temps: Recherches Actuelles: Actes du IV Colloque D'Etudes Historiques et Patristiques Chantilly 21–23 Septembre 1976* (Paris: Editions Beauchesne, 1978).

Fraisse, Anne. "Concilier la sagesse avec la religion (V, 1, 11). Analyse du prologue du livre V des *Institutions divines* de Lactance." *Vita Latina* 159 (2000): pp. 26–35.

Fredouille, Jeane-Claude. "Lactance historien des religions." In *Lactance et son Temps: Recherches Actuelles: Actes du IV Colloque D'Etudes Historiques et Patristiques Chantilly 21–23 Septembre 1976*, edited by J. Fontaine and M. Perrin (Paris: Editions Beauchesne, 1978).

Freund, Stefan. "Christian Use and Valuation of Theological Oracles: The Case of Lactantius' *Divine Institutes*." *Vigiliae Christianae* 60, no. 3 (2006): pp. 269–284.

Freund, Stefan. "The Hidden Library of Lactantius," *Studia Patristica* 24 (2021): pp. 183–196.

Freund, Stefan. "Lactanz und die Johannesoffenbarung." *Studia Patristica* 46 (2010): pp. 45–52.

Garnsey, Peter. "Lactantius and Augustine." In *Representations of Empire: Rome and the Mediterranean World*, edited by A. K. Bowman, H. M. Cotton, M. Goodman, and S. Price (Oxford: Oxford University Press, 2002).

Gaudemet, Jean. "Lactance et le droit romain." *Acta Archaeologica* 2 (1975): pp. 83–101.

Gerhardt, Martin. *Das Leben und die Schriften des Lactantius* (Erlangen: Verlag der Wissenschaften, 1924).

Gibson, Richard. "Lactantius on Anger." In *The Consolations of Theology*, edited by Brian S. Rosner (Grand Rapids, MI: Eerdmans, 2008).

Gill, Christopher. "The Emotions in Greco-Roman Philosophy." In *The Passions in Roman Thought and Literature*, edited by S. M. Braund and C. Gill (Cambridge: Cambridge University Press, 1997).

Goulon, Alain. "Lactance et les classiques:*Poetas dico ac philosophos (Inst. 1, 5, 2)*." *Vita Latina* 133 (1994): pp. 29–36.

Goulon, Alain. "Les Citations des Poètes Latins dans L'œvre de Lactance." In *Lactance et son Temps: Recherches Actuelles: Actes du IV Colloque D'Etudes Historiques et patristiques*

294 BIBLIOGRAPHY

Chantilly 21–23 Septembre 1976, edited by J. Fontaine and M. Perrin (Paris: Editions Beauchesne, 1978), pp. 107–157.

Grant, Robert M. "*Patristica* (Lactantius and Irenaeus)." *Vigiliae Christianae* 3 (1949): pp. 225–229.

Greer, Rowan A. "Cicero's Sketch and Lactantius's Plan." In *The Early Church in Its Context: Essays in Honor of Everett Ferguson*, edited by A. J. Malherbe, F. W. Norris, and J. W. Thompson (Leiden: Brill, 1998).

Grillmeier, Aloysius. "Sapiens-Religion—Religio-Sapientia: On the Christology of Lactantius." In *Christ in the Christian Tradition*, vol. 1, *From the Apostolic Age to Chalcedon (451)*, translated by John Bowden (London: Mowbrays, 1975).

Grossman, Christiane. "Die neutestamenschlichen Grundlagen der Gerechtigkeitsdefinition im 5. Buch der Institutionen des Laktanz. Eine Untersuchung zu *Inst.* V 8, 5–9." *Mittellateinisches Jahrbuch* 37 (2002): pp. 395–403.

Grossman, Christiane. "*Pietas est dei notio*: Eine Untersuchung zu Lact. *Inst.* V.14, 11f." *Mittellateinisches Jahrbuch* 39, no. 2 (2004): pp. 171–181.

Gryson, Roger, ed. *Vetus Latina. The Remains of the Old Latin Bible* (Freiburg in Breisgau: Herder, 1983).

Hays, Christopher M. *Luke's Wealth Ethics: A Study in Their Coherence and Character* (Tübingen: Mohr Siebeck, 2010).

Heck, Eberhard. "Constantin und Lactanz in Trier—Chronologisches." *Historia* 58 (2009): pp. 118–130.

Heck, Eberhard. *Die Dualistischen Zusätze und die Kaiseranreden bei Lactantius* (Heidelberg: Universitätsverlag, 1972).

Heck, Eberhard. "Die Dualistischen Zusätze und die Kaiseranreden bei Lactanz." *Studia Patristica* 13 (1975): pp. 185–188.

Heck, Eberhard. "Lactanz und die Klassiker. Zu Theorie und Praxis der Verwendung heidnischer Literatur in christlicher Apologetik bei Laktanz." *Philologus* 132 (1988): pp. 160–179.

Heck, Eberhard. "Nochmals: Lactantius und Lucretius. Antilucreziches im Epilog des lactanzischen Phoenix-Gedichts?" *International Journal of the Classical Tradition* 9, no. 4 (2003): pp. 509–523.

Heim, F. "L'influence exercée par Constantin sur Lactance: La théologie de la victoire." In *Lactance et son Temps: Recherches Actuelles: Actes du IV Colloque D'Etudes Historiques et Patristiques Chantilly 21–23 Septembre 1976*, edited by J. Fontaine and M. Perrin (Paris: Editions Beauchesne, 1978).

Heim, F. "*Virtus* chez Lactance: du *vir bonus* au martyr." *Augustinianum* 36, no. 2 (1996): pp. 361–376.

Hughson, Thomas. "Social Justice in Lactantius's *Divine Institutes: An Exploration*." In *Reading Patristic Texts on Social Ethics: Issues and Challenges for Twenty-First Century Christian Social Thought*, edited by Johan Leemans, Brian J. Matz, and Johan Verstraeten (Washington, DC: Catholic University of America Press, 2011).

Ingremeau, Christiane. "Quand un citoyen romain d'Afrique écrit: 'Nos ancêtres, les Hébreux . . .'" In *Les Grecs, Les Romains et nous. L'antiquité est-elle moderne?* edited by R. P. Droit (Paris: Le Monde, 1991).

Ingremeau, Christiane. "Lactance et la philosophie des Passions." In *Les apologistes chretiens et la culture grecque*, edited by B. Pouderon and J. Doré (Paris: Beauchesne, 1998).

Ingremeau, Christiane. "Lactance et la Justice: Du Livre 5 au Livre 6 des *Institutiones Divines*." In *Regards sur le monde antique. Hommages à Guy Sabbah*, edited by M. Piot (Lyon: Presses Universitaires de Lyon, 2002).

Ingremeau, Christiane. "Les Institutions Divines de Lactance: Une composition architecturale." *Vita Latina* 132 (1993): pp. 33–40.

Kahlos, Maijastina. "*Ritus ad solos digitos pertinens* (Lact., *Inst.* 5.19.29): A Caricature of Roman Civic Religion in Lactantius' *Institutiones Divinae*." In *Critique and Apologetics: Jews,*

BIBLIOGRAPHY   295

Christians, and Pagans in Antiquity, edited by Anders-Christian Jacobsen, J. Ulrich, and D. Brakke (Frankfurt am Main: Peter Lang, 2009).

Kendeffy, Gábor. "Lactantius as Christian Cicero, Cicero as Shadow-like Instructor." In *Brill's Companion to the Reception of Cicero* (Leiden: Brill, 2015).

Kendeffy, Gábor. "Lactantius on the Function of the Two Ways." *Studia Patristica* 46 (2010): pp. 39–44.

Kendeffy, Gábor. "Lactantius on the Passions." *Acta Classica Universitatis Scientiarum Debreceniensis* 36 (2000): pp. 113–129.

Kendeffy, Gábor. "*Velamentum Stultitiae*: 1 Cor 1:20ff. and 3:19 in Lactantius' *Divine Institutes.*" In *Invention, Rewriting, Usurpation. Discursive Fights over Religious Traditions in Antiquity*, edited by J. Ulrich, Anders-Christian Jacobsen, and M. Kahlos (Frankfurt am Main: Peter Lang, 2012).

Koch, H. "Cipriano e Lattanzio." *Ricerche Religiose* (1931): pp. 122–132.

Kotting, Bernhard. "*Endzeit Prognosen zwischen Lactantius und Augustinus.*" *Heythrop Journal* 77 (1958): pp. 125–139.

Lausberg, Marion. "Christliche Nächstenliebe und heidnische Ethik bei Laktanz." *Studia Patristica* 13 (1975): pp. 29–34.

Leadbetter, William Lewis. "Lactantius and Paideia in the Latin West." In *Ancient History in a Modern University*, vol. 2, *Early Christianity, Late Antiquity and Beyond*, edited by T. W. Hillard, R. A. Kearsley, C. E. V. Nison, and A. M. Nobbs (Sydney: W. B. Eerdmans, 1998).

Leonhard, Thomas. *Die Sapientia als Schlüsselbegriff zu den Divinae Institutiones des Laktanz: Mit besonderer Berücksichtigung seiner Ethik* (Freiburg Schweiz: Paulusdruckerei, 1959).

Lo Cicero, C. "Omnium Stoicorum acutissimus: Seneca filosofo in Lattanzio: Intertestualità e riscrittura." *Studi di filologia classica in onore di Giusto Monaco* 3 (1989): pp. 1237–1261.

Loi, Vincenzo. "Il concetto di 'iustitia' e i fattori culturali dell'etica di Lattanzio." *Salesianum* 28 (1966): pp. 583–625.

Loi, Vincenzo. "Il libro quarto delle *Divinae institutiones*: Fu da Lattanzio composto in Gallia?" *Mél. Christine Mohrmann: Nouveau recueil* (1973): pp. 61–79.

Loi, Vincenzo. "I valori etici e politici della romanità negli scritti di Lattanzio." *Salesianum* 27 (1965): pp. 65–132.

Loi, Vincenzo. *Lattanzio nella Storia del Linguaggio e del Pensiero Teologico Pre- Niceno* (Zürich: Pas-Verlag, 1970).

Mazlowski, Tadeuz. "The Opponents of Lactantius in Book VII." *California Studies in Classical Antiquity* 7 (1974): pp. 187–213.

McGuckin, John A. "The Christology of Lactantius." *Studia Patristica* 17, no. 2 (1982): pp. 813–820.

McGuckin, John A. "Lactantius as Theologian: An Angelic Christology on the Eve of Nicaea." *Journal of Early Christian Studies* 8, no. 4 (2000): pp. 495–511.

McGuckin, John A. "Legal Theology in the Western Fathers: Tertullian and Lactantius." In *The Ascent of Christian Law: Patristic and Byzantine Formulations of a New Civilization*, edited by J. A. McGuckin (Yonkers, NY: St. Vladimir's Seminary Press, 2012).

McGuckin, John A. "The Non-Cyprianic Scripture Texts in Lactantius' *Divine Institutes.*" *Vigiliae Christianae* 36, no. 2 (1982): pp. 145–163.

McGuckin, John A. *Researches into the "Divine Institutes" of Lactantius* (Unpublished dissertation, Durham University, 1980).

McGuckin, John A. "Spirit Christology: Lactantius and His Sources." *Heythrop Journal* 24 (1983): pp. 141–148.

Meinking, Kristina A. *Anger Matters: Politics and Theology in the Fourth Century CE* (Unpublished dissertation, University of Southern California, 2010).

Meinking, Kristina A. "Eusebius and Lactantius: Rhetoric, Philosophy, and Christian Theology." In *Eusebius of Caesarea: Tradition and Innovations*, edited by A. Johnson and J. Schott (Washington, DC: Center for Hellenic Studies, 2013).

296 BIBLIOGRAPHY

Meinking, Kristina A. "*Sic Traditur a Platone*: Plato and the Philosophers in Lactantius." In *Plato in the Third Sophistic*, edited by Ryan C. Fowler (Berlin: DeGruyter, 2014).

Micka, Ermin F. *The Problem of Divine Anger in Arnobius and Lactantius* (Washington, DC: Catholic University of America, 1943).

Monat, Pierre. *Lactance et la Bible: Une propédeutique latine à la lecture de la Bible dans l'Occident constantinien* (Paris: Etudes Augustiniennes, 1982).

Nicholson, Oliver. "Arnobius and Lactantius." In *Cambridge History of Early Christian Literature*, edited by F. Young, L. Ayres, and A. Louth (Cambridge: Cambridge University Press, 2004).

Nicholson, Oliver. "Broadening the Roman Mind: Foreign Prophets in the Apologetic of Lactantius." *Studia Patristica* 34 (2001): pp. 364–374.

Nicholson, Oliver. "*Caelum potius intuemini*: Lactantius and a Statue of Constantine." *Studia Patristica* 34 (2001): pp. 177–196.

Nicholson, Oliver. "Civitas quae adhuc sustentat omnia: Lactantius and the City of Rome." In *The Limits of Ancient Christianity: Essays in Honor of R. A. Markus*, edited by W. E. Klingshirn and M. Vessey (Ann Arbor: University of Michigan, 1998).

Nicholson, Oliver. "Flight from Persecution as Imitation of Christ: Lactantius' Divine Institutes IV,18,1–2." *Journal of Theological Studies* 40 (1989): pp. 48–65.

Nicholson, Oliver. "Hercules at the Milvian Bridge: Lactantius, *Divine Institutes*, I, 21,6–9." *Latomus* 43 (1984): pp. 133–142.

Nicholson, Oliver. "Lactantius: A Man of His Own Time?" *Studia Patristica* 127, no. 24 (2021).

Nicholson, Oliver. "Lactantius on Military Service." *Studia Patristica* 24 (1993): pp. 175–183.

Nicholson, Oliver. *Lactantius: Prophecy and Politics in the Age of Constantine the Great* (Unpublished dissertation, Oxford University, 1982).

Nicholson, Oliver. "The Source of the Dates in Lactantius' Divine Institutes." *Journal of Theological Studies* 36 (1985): pp. 291–310.

Ocker, Christopher. "*Unius Arbitrio Mundum Regi Necesse Est*: Lactantius' Concern for the Preservation of Roman Society." *Vigiliae Christianae* 40 (1986): pp. 348–364.

Ogilvie, R. M. *The Library of Lactantius* (Oxford: Clarendon Press, 1978).

O'Meara, Dominic J. *Platonopolis: Platonic Political Philosophy in Late Antiquity* (Oxford: Oxford University Press, 2003).

Penwill, John. "Does God Care? Lactantius v. Epicurus in the *De Ira Dei*." *Sophia* 43, no. 1 (2004): pp. 23–43.

Perrin, Michel. "Culture et foi chez Lactance (250–325). Quelques problems concernant la creation du monde et de l'homme." *Les Cahiers de Fontenay* 39–40 (1985): pp. 57–66.

Perrin, Michel. *De Opificio Dei* (Paris: Éditions du Cerf, 1974).

Perrin, Michel. *L'Homme Antique et Chrétien: L'Anthropologie de Lactance (250–325)* (Paris: Beauchesne, 1981).

Perrin, Michel. "L'image du stoicien et du stoicism chez Lactance." In *Valeurs dans le stoicisme. Du Portique à nos jours. Textes réunis en hommage à M. Spanneut*, edited by M. Läetard (Lille: Presses Universitaires de Lille, 1993).

Perrin, Michel. *Lactance: L'Ouvrage du Dieu le Créateur* (Paris: Éditions du Cerf, 1976).

Perrin, M. "Lactance et la culture grecque. Esquisse d'une problématique." In *Les apologistes chrétiens et la culture grecque*, edited by B. Pouderon and J. Doré (Paris: Beauchesne, 1998).

Perrin, Michel. "Lactance et la *ratio* romaine et chrétienne." In *En deça et au-delà de la ratio*, edited by V. Naas. (Lille: Éditeur du Conseil scientifique de l'Université Charles-de-Gaulle-Lille 3, 2004).

Perrin, M. "La revolution constantinienne vue à travers l'oeuvre de Lactance (250–325 ap. J. C.)." *Les Cahiers de Fontenay* 63–64 (1991): pp. 81–94.

Perrin, Michel. "Le Platon de Lactance." In *Lactance et son Temps: Recherches Actuelles: Actes du IV Colloque D'Etudes Historiques et Patristiques Chantilly 21–23 Septembre 1976*, edited by J. Fontaine and M. Perrin (Paris: Editions Beauchesne, 1978).

BIBLIOGRAPHY 297

Perrin, Michel and Jean-Louis Michel. "Rôle et function de la mythologie chez Lactance (env. 250–325), rhéteur, apologist et historien." *Pallas. Revue d'études antiques* 78 (2008): pp. 361–370.

Piccaluga, G. "Ius e Vera Iustitia (Lact. Div. Inst. VI 9.7). Rielaborazione cristiana di un valore assoluto della religione romana arcaica." *L'Etica cristiana dei secoli III e IV: Eredità e confronti: Studia Ephemeridis Augustinianum* 53 (1996): pp. 257–269.

Pichon, René. *Lactance: Etude sur le mouvement philosophique et religieux sous le regne de Constantin* (Paris: Éditions de l'Artisan,1901).

Pinel, Carmen Macarena Palomo. *Nec Inmerito Paterfamilias Dicitur: El paterfamilias en el pensamiento de Lactancio* (Madrid: Dykinson, S.L., 2017).

Pinel, Carmen Macarena Palomo. "The Survival of the Classical Idea of Justice in Lactantius' Work." *Studia Patristica* 80 (2019).

Pizzani, Ubaldo. "Osservazioni sulla genesi della theologia della storia in Lattanzio." *Augustinianum* 16 (1976): pp. 53–60.

Pouderon, B. and J. Doré, eds. *Les apologistes chretiens et la culture grecque* (Paris: Beauchesne, 1998).

Pricco, Salvatore. "Per una storia dell'oracolo nella tarda Antichità: Apollo Clario e Didimeo in Lattanzio." *Augustinianum* 29 (1989): pp. 351–374.

Quinn, Dennis P. "Roman Household Deities in Latin Christian Writers." *Studia Patristica* 44 (2010): pp. 71–76.

Roots, Peter A. *De Opificio Lactantii: A Reassessment of the Work of L. Caecilius Firmianus Lactantius* (Unpublished dissertation, Cambridge University, 1988).

Roots, Peter A. "The *De Opificio Mundi*: The Workmanship of God and Lactantius." *Classical Quarterly* 37, no. 2 (1987): pp. 466–486.

Sage, Michael M. *Cyprian* (Cambridge, MA: Philadelphia Patristic Foundation, 1975).

Schneweis, E. *Angels and Demons according to Lactantius* (Washington, DC: Catholic University of America, 1944).

Schott, Jeremy M. *Christianity, Empire, and the Making of Religion in Late Antiquity* (Philadelphia: University of Pennsylvania Press, 2008).

Shelton, W. Brian. "Lactantius as Architect of a Constantinian and Christian 'Victory over the Empire.'" *Rethinking Constantine: History, Theology, and Legacy*, edited by E. Smith (Eugene, OR: Pickwick, 2014).

Siegert, Julia. *Die Theologie des Apologeten Lactantius in ihrem Verhältnis zur Stoa* (Munich: Verlag der Bayerischen Akademie der Wissenschaften, 1933).

Simmons, M. B. *Arnobius of Sicca: Religious Conflict and Competition in the Age of Diocletian* (Oxford: Oxford University Press, 1995).

Speigl, Jakob. "Zum Kirchenbegriff des Laktanz." *Römische Quartalschrift für christliche Altertumskunde und für Kirchengeschichte* 65 (1970): pp. 15–28.

Stevenson, J. "Lactantius and the Hermetica. Review of *Laktanz und die philosophische Gnosis: Untersuchungen zu Geschichte und Terminologie der gnostischen Erlösungsvorstellung* by Antonie Wlosok." *Classical Review* 13, no. 1 (1963): pp. 80–81.

Stevenson, J. "The Life and Literary Activity of Lactantius." *Studia Patristica* 1 (1955): pp. 661–677.

Swift, Lewis J. "Lactantius and the Golden Age." *American Journal of Philology* 89 (1968): pp. 144–156.

Walter, Jochen. *Pagane Texte und Wertvorstellungen bei Lactanz* (Goettingen: Vandenhoeck & Ruprecht, 2006).

Winger, Wolfram. *Personalität durch Humanität: Das ethikgeschichtliche Profil christlicher Handlungslehre bei Lactanz: Denkhorizont-Textübersetzung-Interpretation-Wirkungsgeschichte* (Frankfurt am Main: Peter Lang Verlag, 1999).

Wlosok, Antonie. "Lactance (L. Caelius ou Cae(cil)ius Firmianus Lactantius)." In *Nouvelle Histoire de la Littérature Latine*, vol. 5, edited by R. Herzog and P. L. Schmidt (Paris: Éditions du Cerf, 1993).

298 BIBLIOGRAPHY

Wlosok, Antonie. *Laktanz und die philosophische Gnosis: Untersuchungen zu Geschichte und Terminologie der gnostischen Erlösungsvorstellung* (Heidelberg: Carl Winter, 1960).

Wlosok, Antonie. "Zur Bedeutung der nicht-Cyprianischen Bibelzitate bei Laktanz." *Studia Patristica* 4, no. 79 (1961).

Wlosok, Antonie. "Zur Gottesvorstellung bei Laktanz." In *Ermeneia. Festschrift Otto Regenbogen zum 60. Geburtstag* (Heidelberg: Carl Winter, 1952).

Wlosok, Antonie. "Zur lateinischen Apologetik der constantinischen Zeit (Arnobius, Lactantius, Firmicus Maternus)." *Gymnasium* 96 (1989): pp. 133–148.

Zarini, Vincent. "Lactance et Rome au livre V des *Institutions Divines*." In *Chartae caritatis. Études de patristique et d'antiquité tardive en homme à Yves-Marie Duval*, edited by B. Gain, P. Jay, and G. Nauroy (Paris: Institut d'Études Augustiniennes, 2004), pp. 69–81.

Zipp, Gianna. *Gewalt in Laktanz' De mortibus persecutorum* (Berlin: DeGruyter, 2021).

General Studies

Achard, Guy. *De l'invention* (Paris: Belles Lettres, 1994).

Amarelli, Francesco. *Vetustas-Innovatio: Un'antitesi apparente nella legislazione di Costantino* (Naples, IT: E. Jovene, 1978).

Ando, Clifford. *Imperial Ideology and Provincial Loyalty in the Roman Empire* (Berkeley: University of California Press, 2000).

Ando, Clifford. *Imperial Rome AD 193 to 284: The Critical Century* (Edinburgh: Edinburgh University Press, 2012).

Ando, Clifford. *Law, Language, and Empire in the Roman Tradition* (Philadelphia: University of Pennsylvania Press, 2011).

Ando, Clifford. *The Matter of the Gods: Religion and the Roman Empire* (Berkeley: University of California Press, 2008).

Ando, Clifford. "Pagan Apologetics and Christian Intolerance in the Ages of Themistius and Augustine." *Journal of Early Christian Studies* 4, no. 2 (1996): pp. 171–207.

Ando, Clifford. *Roman Religion* (Edinburgh: Edinburgh University Press, 2003).

Armstrong, Gail E. "Sacrificial Iconography: Creating History, Making Myth, and Negotiating Ideology on the Ara Pacis Augustae." *Religion and Theology* 15, no. 3/4 (June 2008).

Athanassiadi, P. and M. Frede, eds. *Pagan Monotheism in Late Antiquity* (Oxford: Oxford University Press, 2002).

Atkins, Jed. *Cicero on Politics and the Limits of Reason* (Cambridge: Cambridge University Press, 2013).

Ayedze, Kossi Adiavu. *Tertullian, Cyprian and Augustine on Patience: A Comparative and Critical Study of Three Treatises on a Stoic-Christian Virtue in Early North African Christianity* (Unpublished dissertation, Princeton Theological Seminary, 2000).

Ayres, Lewis. *Augustine and the Trinity* (Cambridge: Cambridge University Press, 2010).

Ayres, Lewis. *Nicaea and Its Legacy: An Approach to Fourth-Century Trinitarian Theology* (Oxford: Oxford University Press, 2004).

Bailey, Shackleton. "Nobiles and Novi Reconsidered." *American Journal of Philology* 107 (1986): pp. 255–260.

Balmaceda, Catarina. *Virtus Romana: Politics and Morality in the Roman Historians* (Chapel Hill: University of North Carolina Press, 2017).

Baraz, Yelena. *A Written Republic: Cicero's Philosophical Politics* (Princeton, NJ: Princeton University Press, 2012).

Barnes, Jonathan. "Antiochus of Ascalon." In *Philosophia Togata II: Plato and Aristotle at Rome*, edited by Jonathan Barnes and Miriam Griffin (Oxford: Clarendon Press, 1999).

Barnes, Jonathan. *Porphyry: Introduction* (Oxford: Clarendon Press, 2003).

Barnes, Jonathan. "Roman Aristotle." In *Philosophia Togata II: Plato and Aristotle at Rome*, edited by Jonathan Barnes and Miriam Griffin (Oxford: Clarendon Press, 1999).

Barnes, Jonathan and Miriam Griffin, eds. *Philosophia Togata: Essays on Philosophy and Roman Society* (Oxford: Clarendon Press, 1989).

BIBLIOGRAPHY 299

Barnes, Jonathan and Miriam Griffin, eds. *Philosophia Togata II: Plato and Aristotle at Rome* (Oxford: Clarendon Press, 1999).

Barnes, Michel R. "The Beginning and End of Early Christian Pneumatology." *Augustinian Studies* 39, no. 2 (2008).

Barnes, Michel R. "The Fourth Century as Trinitarian Canon." In *Christian Origins: Theology, Rhetoric, and Community*, edited by L. Ayres and G. Jones (London: Routledge, 1998).

Barnes, Michel R. "Irenaeus' Trinitarian Theology." *Nova et Vetera* 7, no. 1 (2009): pp. 67–106.

Barnes, Michel R. "Latin Trinitarian Theology." In *The Cambridge Companion to the Trinity*, edited by Peter C. Phan (Cambridge: Cambridge University Press, 2011), pp. 70–84.

Barnes, Michel R. "One Nature, One Power: Consensus Doctrine in Pro-Nicene Polemic." *Historica, Theologica et Philosophica* 29 (1997).

Barnes, Michel R. *The Power of God: Dynamis in Gregory of Nyssa's Trinitarian Theology* (Washington, DC: Catholic University of America Press, 2001).

Barnes, Timothy D. *Constantine and Eusebius* (Cambridge, MA: Harvard University Press, 1981).

Barnes, Timothy D. *Constantine, Dynasty, Religion, and Power in the Later Roman Empire* (Oxford: Wiley-Blackwell, 2011).

Barnes, Timothy D. "*Review: Christianity, Empire, and the Making of Religion in Late Antiquity* by Jeremy Schott." (Philadelphia: University of Pennsylvania Press, 2008). *Journal of Theological Studies* 61, no. 1 (2010): pp. 337–340.

Barnes, Timothy D. "Sossianus Hierocles and the Antecedents of the Great Persecution." *Harvard Studies in Classical Philology* 80 (1976): pp. 239–252.

Barnes, Timothy D. *Tertullian: A Historical and Literary Study* (Oxford: Oxford University Press, 1985).

Barret, Anthony. *Caligula: The Corruption of Power* (New Haven, CT: Yale University Press, 1998).

Beard, M., J. North, and S. Price. *Religions of Rome: A History*, 2 vols. (Cambridge: Cambridge University Press, 1998).

Beaujeu, Jean. *Minucius Felix: Texte, introduction, commentaire* (Paris: Les Belles Lettres, 2002).

Becker, Carl. *Der Octavius des Minucius Felix* (Munich: Beck, 1967).

Becker, Maria. *Die Kardinaltugenden bei Cicero und Ambrosius: De officiis* (Basel: Schwabe Verlag, 1994).

Beckwith, Carl. *Hilary of Poitiers on the Trinity: From "De Fide" to "De Trinitate"* (Oxford: Oxford University Press, 2009).

Behr, John. *The Way to Nicaea. The Formation of Christian Theology* (Crestwood, NY: St. Vladimir's Seminary Press, 2001).

Billows, Richard. "The Religious Procession of the Ara Pacis Augustae: Augustus' *Supplicatio* in 13 BC." *Journal of Roman Archaeology* 6 (1993): pp. 80–92.

Birley, Anthony. *Marcus Aurelius: A Biography* (London: Routledge, 2002).

Birley, Anthony. *Septimius Severus: The African Emperor* (London: Routledge, 1999).

Boersma, Gerald P. "The Logic of the Logos: A Note on Stoic Logic in *Adversus Praxean* 10." *Journal of Early Christian Studies* 22, no. 4 (2014): pp. 485–498.

Bolkestein, Hendrik. "Humanitas bei Lactantius: Christlich oder orientalisch?" In *Pisciculi: Studien zur Religion und Kultur des Altertums: Franz Joseph Dölger zum sechzigsten Geburtstage*, edited by W. R. L. G. E. K. Bär (Münster in Westfalen: Verlag Aschendorff, 1953), pp. 62–65.

Bond, Robin. "The Augustan Utopia of Horace and Vergil and the Imperial Dystopia of Petronius and Juvenal." *Scholia: Studies in Classical Antiquity* 19 (2010).

Bosworth, Brian. "Augustus, the *Res Gestae* and Hellenistic Theories of Apotheosis." *Journal of Roman Studies* 89 (1999): pp. 1–18.

Bousset, Wilhelm. *Kyrios Christos: A History of the Belief in Christ from the Beginnings of Christianity to Irenaeus*, translated by John E. Steely (Waco, TX: Baylor University Press, 2013).

BIBLIOGRAPHY

Bracht, Katharina. "Product or Foundation? The Relationship between the Doctrine of the Holy Trinity and Christology in Hippolytus' and Tertullian's Debate with Monarchianism." *Acta Patristica et Byzantina* 18 (2007): pp. 14–31.

Braun, René. *Deus Christianorum: Recherches sur le vocabulaire doctrinal de Tertullien*, 2nd ed. (Paris: Études Augustiniennes, 1977).

Braund, Susanna. "Seneca *Multiplex*: The Phases (and Phrases) of Seneca's Life and Works." In *The Cambridge Companion to Seneca*, edited by Shadi Bartsch and Alesandro Schiesaro (Cambridge: Cambridge University Press, 2015), pp. 15–29.

Bremmer, Jan. "Virgil and Jewish Literature." *Vergilius* 59 (2013): pp. 157–164.

Brennan, Tad. *The Stoic Life: Emotions, Duties, and Fate* (Oxford: Oxford University Press, 2005).

Brent, Allen. "The Political Theology of the Augustan Revolution: Cosmic Reconstruction." In *A Political History of Christianity*, edited by Allen Brent (New York: T&T Clark, 2009).

Briggman, Anthony. "Irenaus' Christology of Mixture." *Journal of Theological Studies* 84, no. 2 (2013).

Briggman, Anthony. *Irenaeus of Lyons and the Theology of the Holy Spirit* (Oxford: Oxford University Press, 2012).

Briggman, Anthony. "Measuring Justin's Approach to the Spirit: Trinitarian Conviction and Binitarian Orientation." *Vigiliae Christianae* 63, no. 2 (2009): pp. 107–137.

Brodd, Jeffrey and Jonathan L. Reed, eds. *Rome and Religion: A Cross-Disciplinary Dialogue on the Imperial Cult* (Atlanta: Society of Biblical Literature, 2011).

Brown, Peter. *Augustine of Hippo: A Biography* (Berkeley: University of California Press, 2000).

Brown, Peter. *The Body and Society: Men, Women, and Sexual Renunciation in Early Christianity* (Cambridge: Cambridge University Press, 1988).

Brown, Peter. *Power and Persuasion in Late Antiquity: Towards a Christian Empire* (Madison: University of Wisconsin Press, 1992).

Brown, Peter. *The Rise of Western Christendom: Triumph and Diversity, A.D. 20–1000* (Oxford: Wiley-Blackwell, 2013).

Brunt, P. A. "Stoicism and the Principate." *Papers of the British School at Rome* 43 (1975): pp. 7–35.

Bucur, Bogdan G. "The Angelic Spirit in Early Christianity: Justin, the Martyr and Philosopher." *Journal of Religion* 88, no. 2 (2008): pp. 190–208.

Buchheit, Vinzenz. "Virgil und Thales bei Minucius Felix." *Rheinisches Museum für Philologie* 149, nos. 3–4 (2006): pp. 350–358.

Burrows, Mark S. "Christianity in the Roman Forum: Tertullian and the Apologetic Use of History." *Vigiliae Christianae* 42 (1988): pp. 209–235.

Burrus, Virginia. *Begotten, Not Made: Conceiving Manhood in Late Antiquity* (Stanford, CA: Stanford University Press, 2000).

Butler, Harold E. *The Sixth Book of the Aeneid: with Introduction and Notes* (Oxford: Basil Blackwell, 1920).

Cambiano, Giuseppe. "Philosophy, Science, and Medicine." In *The Cambridge History of Hellenistic Philosophy*, edited by Kemp Aleigra et al. (Cambridge: Cambridge University Press, 2005).

Cameron, Avril. *Christianity and the Rhetoric of Empire: The Development of Christian Discourse* (Berkeley: University of California Press, 1994).

Cameron, Avril. *The Last Pagans of Rome* (Oxford: Oxford University Press, 2011).

Cameron, Avril. *The Later Roman Empire* (Cambridge, MA: Harvard University Press, 1993).

Carlon, Jacqueline M. *Pliny's Women: Constructing Virtue and Creating Identity in the Roman World* (Cambridge: Cambridge University Press, 2009).

Carroll, James. *Constantine's Sword: The Church and the Jews* (Boston: Houghton Mifflin Harcourt, 2002).

Casali, Sergio. "The *Bellum Civile* as an Anti-*Aeneid*." In *Brill's Companion to Lucan*, edited by Paolo Asso (Leiden: Brill, 2010).

BIBLIOGRAPHY 301

Caspary, Gerard E. *Politics and Exegesis: Origen and the Two Swords* (Berkeley: University of California Press, 1979).

Centre d'Analyse et de Documentation Patristiques, ed. *Biblia Patristica: Index des citations et allusions bibliques dans la littérature patristique.* Vol. 2, *Les auteurs latins* (Paris: Éditions du Centre National de la Recherche Scientifique, 1977).

Chadwick, Henry. *The Church in Ancient Society: From Galilee to Gregory the Great* (Oxford: Oxford University Press, 2001).

Chaplin, Jane D. *Livy's Exemplary History* (Oxford: Oxford University Press, 2001).

Chapot, Frederic. "A propos de quelques mots du vocabulaire de la propriété chez Tertullian." In *Antiquité tardive et Humanisme: De Tertullien à Beatus Rhenanus. Hommages à Francois Heim,* edited by Y. Lehmann, G. Freyburger, and J. Hirstein (Leuven: Turnhout, 2005).

Chapot, Frederic. "Les grandes orientations des travaux sur l'*Octavius* de Minucius Felix. Remarques sur trente ans de bibliographie." *Vita Latina* 150 (1998).

Chapot, Frederic. *Virtus Veritatis: language et vérité dans l'œuvre de Tertullien* (Paris: Institut d'Études Augustiniennes, 2009).

Charlesworth, Martin P. "The Virtues of a Roman Emperor: Propaganda and the Creation of Belief." *Proceedings of the British Academy* 23 (1937).

Chauduri, Pradit. *The War with God: Theomachy in Roman Imperial Poetry* (Oxford: Oxford University Press, 2014).

Christiansen, David James. *Character and Morality in the Sallustian Monographs* (Unpublished dissertation, University of Wisconsin-Madison, 1990).

Clark, Anna J. *Divine Qualities: Cult and Community in Republican Rome* (Oxford: Oxford University Press, 2007).

Clark, Elizabeth A. *History, Theory, Text: Historians and the Linguistic Turn* (Cambridge, MA: Harvard University Press, 2004).

Clark, Elizabeth A. *Reading Renunciation: Asceticism and Scripture in Early Christianity* (Princeton, NJ: Princeton University Press, 1999).

Cochrane, Charles Norris. *Christianity and Classical Culture: A Study of Thought and Action from Augustus to Augustine* (Indianapolis: Liberty Fund, 1940; reprint, 2003).

Cohn, Norman. *Cosmos, Chaos and the World to Come: The Ancient Roots of Apocalyptic Faith* (New Haven, CT: Yale University Press, 1993).

Cole, Spencer. *Cicero and the Rise of Deification at Rome* (Cambridge: Cambridge University Press, 2014).

Colish, Marcia. "Cicero, Ambrose, and Stoic Ethics: Transmission or Transformation?" In *The Classics in the Middle Ages, Papers of the Twentieth Annual Conference of the Center for Medieval and Early Renaissance Studies,* edited by A. Bernardo and S. Levin (Binghamton, NY: Center for Medieval and Early Renaissance Studies, 1990).

Colish, Marcia. *The Stoic Tradition from Antiquity to the Early Middle Ages 2: Stoicism in Christian Latin Thought through the Sixth Century* (Leiden: Brill, 1985).

Collins, John J. *Jewish Wisdom in the Hellenistic Age* (Louisville: Westminster John Knox Press, 2001).

Colot, Blandine. *Penser la conversion de Rome au temps de Constantin* (Firenze: Leo Olscki Editore, 2016).

Conte, Gian Biagio. "The Strategy of Contradiction." In *The Poetry of Pathos: Studies in Virgilian Epic,* edited by S. J. Harrison (Oxford: Oxford University Press, 2007).

Conte, Gian Biagio. *Vergilius Publius Maro: Aeneis* (Berlin: Walter DeGruyter, 2012).

Cooper, John M. *Knowledge, Nature, and the Good: Essays on Ancient Philosophy* (Princeton, NJ: Princeton University Press, 2004).

Cooper, John M. *Pursuits of Wisdom: Six Ways of Life in Ancient Philosophy from Socrates to Plotinus* (Princeton, NJ: Princeton University Press, 2013).

Cooper, Kate. *The Fall of the Roman Household* (Cambridge: Cambridge University Press, 2007).

302   BIBLIOGRAPHY

Copenhaver, Brian P. *Hermetica: The Greek Corpus Hermeticum and the Latin Asclepius in a New English Translation, with Notes and Introduction* (Cambridge: Cambridge University Press, 1992).

Corbeill, Anthony. "Rhetorical Education in Cicero's Youth." In *Brill's Companion to Cicero: Oratory and Rhetoric*, edited by Y. L. Too (Leiden: Brill, 2002), pp. 23–48.

Courtney-Murray, John. *We Hold These Truths: Catholic Reflections on the American Proposition* (Lanham, MD: Sheed and Ward, 1960).

Cox, Ronald R. *By the Same Word: Creation and Salvation in Hellenistic Judaism and Early Christianity. Beihefte zur Zeitschrift für die neutestamentliche Wissenschaft und die Kunde der älteren Kirche 145* (Berlin: Walter DeGruyter, 2007).

D'Alès, Adhémar. *La Théologie de Saint Cyprien* (Paris: Beauchesne, 1922).

D'Alès, Adhémar. *La Théologie de Tertullien* (Paris: Beauchesne, 1905).

Daniélou, Jean. *The Origins of Latin Christianity*, translated by David Smith and John Austin Baker (Philadelphia: Westminster Press, 1977).

Davis, Leo. *The First Seven Ecumenical Councils (32–787): Their History and Theology* (Collegeville, MN: Liturgical Press, 1983).

Decret, François. *Early Christianity in North Africa*, translated by Edward Smither (Eugene, OR: Cascade Books, 2009).

DelCogliano, Mark. "Eusebian Theologies of the Son as the Image of God before 341." *Journal of Early Christian Studies* 14, no. 4 (2006): pp. 459–484.

DelCogliano, Mark. "The Interpretation of John 10:30 in the Third Century: Anti-Monarchian Polemics and the Rise of Grammatical Reading Techniques." *Journal of Theological Interpretation* 6, no. 1 (2012): pp. 117–138.

De Labriolle, Pierre. *The History and Literature of Christianity: Tertullian to Boethius*, translated by Herbert Wilson (New York: Barnes and Noble, 1968).

De Labriolle, Pierre. *La réaction paienne: Étude sur la polémique antichrétienne du 1er au Vie siècle* (Paris: Édition du Cerf, 2005).

De Ste. Croix, G. E. M. "Aspects of the 'Great Persecution.'" *Harvard Theological Review* 47 (1954): pp. 75–113.

De Wet, Chris L. "The Book of Tobit in Early Christianity: Greek and Latin Interpretations from the 2nd to the 5th Century CE." *HTS Teologese Studies/Theological Studies* 76 (2020).

Dillon, John. "The Ideas as Thoughts of God." *Études Platoniciennes* 8 (2011): pp. 31–42.

Dillon, John. *The Middle Platonists: 80 B.C. to A.D. 220* (Ithaca, NY: Cornell University Press, 1977, reprint 1996), pp. 139–183.

Dillon, John and A. A. Long, eds. *The Question of "Eclecticism"* (Berkeley: University of California Press, 1988).

Dillon, John and A. A. Long, eds. "Ganymede as the Logos: Traces of a Forgotten Allegorization in Philo?" *Studia Philonica* 6 (1979–1980): pp. 37–40.

Discenza, Nicole Guenther. "Power, Skill and Virtue in the Old English *Boethius*." *Anglo-Saxon England* 26 (1997).

Dodaro, Robert. "Augustine's Revisions of the Heroic Ideal." *Augustinian Studies* 36, no. 1 (2005): pp. 141–157.

Dodaro, Robert. *Christ and the Just Society in the Thought of St. Augustine* (Cambridge: Cambridge University Press, 2008).

Douglas, A. E. "The Intellectual Background of Cicero's Rhetoric: A Study in Method." *Aufstieg und Niedergang der Römischen Welt* 1, no. 3 (1973): pp. 95–138.

Drake, H. A. *Constantine and the Bishops: The Politics of Intolerance* (Baltimore: Johns Hopkins University Press, 2002).

Droge, Arthur J. *Homer or Moses? Early Christian Interpretations of the History of Culture* (Tübingen: Mohr Siebeck, 1989).

Dugan, John. "Cicero's Rhetorical Theory." In *The Cambridge Companion to Cicero*, edited by Catherine Steel (Cambridge: Cambridge University Press, 2015), pp. 25–28.

BIBLIOGRAPHY 303

Dugan, John. *Making a New Man: Ciceronian Self-Fashioning in the Rhetorical Works* (Oxford: Oxford University, Press, 2005).

Dunn, Geoffrey D. "The Diversity and Unity of God in Novatian's *De Trinitate*." *Ephemerides Theologicae Lovanienses* 78, no. 4 (2002): pp. 385–409.

Dvornik, Francis. *Early Christian and Byzantine Political Philosophy* (Washington, DC: Dumbarton Oaks, 1966).

Dyck, Andrew R. *A Commentary on Cicero: "De Legibus"* (Ann Arbor: University of Michigan Press, 2004).

Earl, Donald. *The Moral and Political Tradition of Rome* (Ithaca, NY: Cornell University Press, 1967).

Eden, K. *Hermeneutics and the Rhetorical Tradition: Chapters in the Ancient Legacy and Its Humanist Reception* (New Haven, CT: Yale University Press, 2005).

Edmondson, Jonathan. *Augustus* (Edinburgh: Edinburgh University Press, 2009).

Edwards, Catherine. *The Politics of Immorality in Ancient Rome* (Cambridge: Cambridge University Press, 1993).

Englert, Walter. "Epicurean Philosophy in Cicero's *De re publica*: Serious Threat or Convenient Foil?" *Ethics and Politics* 16, no. 2 (2014): pp. 253–266.

Erskine, Anthony. "Cicero and the Shaping of Hellenistic Philosophy." *Hermathena* 175 (2003): pp. 5–15.

Etienne, Robert. *Le Culte imperial dans la peninsule iberique* (Paris: E. de Boccard, 1958).

Evans, Ernest. *Tertullian's Treatise against Praxeas: The Text, Edited with an Introduction, Translation and Commentary* (London: S.P.C.K., 1948).

Faust, Ulrich. *Christo servire libertas est* (Regensburg: A. Pustet, 1983).

Fears, J. Rufus. "The Cult of Virtues and Roman Imperial Ideology." *Aufstieg und Niedergang der Römischen Welt* 17, no. 2 (1986).

Fears, J. Rufus. "The Theology of Victory at Rome: Approaches and Problems." *Aufstieg und Niedergang der Römischen Welt* 17, no. 2 (1973): pp. 736–825.

Feeney, Denis C. *Caesar's Calendar: Ancient Time and the Beginning of History* (Berkeley: University of California Press, 2007).

Feeney, Denis C. *Literature and Religion at Rome: Cultures, Contexts, and Beliefs* (Cambridge: Cambridge University Press, 1998).

Feeney, Douglas. *The Gods in Epic: Poets and Criticism of the Classical Tradition* (Oxford: Oxford University Press, 1991).

Fiedrowicz, Michael. *Apologie Im Frühen Christentum: die Kontroverse um den Christlichen Wahrheitsanspruch in den Ersten Jahrhunderten* (Paderborn: F. Schöningh, 2000).

Fishwick, Duncan. "Genius and Numen." *Harvard Theological Review* 62 (1969): pp. 356–367.

Fishwick, Duncan. "The Imperial Cult in the Latin West: Studies in the Ruler Cult of the Western Provinces of the Roman Empire." *Epigraphica Pomponiana* 108, nos. 1–2 (1991): pp. 1–2.

Fishwick, Duncan. "The Inscription of Mamia Again: The Cult of the *Genius Augusti* and the Temple of the Imperial Cult on the *Forum* of Pompeii." *Epigraphica* 57 (1995): pp. 17–38.

Fishwick, Duncan. "The Name of the Demigod." *Historia* 24 (1975): pp. 624–628.

Fishwick, Duncan. "On the Temple of Divus Augustus." *Phoenix* 46, no. 3 (1992): pp. 232–255.

Fishwick, Duncan. "Prudentius and the Cult of Divus Augustus." *Historia* 39 (1990): pp. 475–486.

Fitzgerald, John T. *Passions and Moral Progress in Greco-Roman Thought* (New York: Routledge, 2007).

Flemming, Rebecca. "Antiochus and Asclepiades: Medical and Philosophical Sectarianism at the End of the Hellenistic Era." In *Antiochus of Ascalon*, edited by David Sedley (Oxford: Oxford University Press, 2012), pp. 55–79.

Flemming, Rebecca. *Medicine and the Making of Roman Women: Gender, Nature, and Authority from Celsus to Galen* (Oxford: Oxford University Press, 2000).

304 BIBLIOGRAPHY

Ford Russell, Brigette. "Wine, Women, and the *Polis*: Gender and the Formation of the City-State in Archaic Rome." *Greece and Rome* 50, no. 1 (2003).

Fox, Michael. *Cicero's Philosophy of History* (Oxford: Oxford University Press, 2007).

Fox, Robin Lane. *Pagans and Christians* (New York: Harper Collins, 1986).

Frede, Michael. "Stoics and Skeptics and Clear and Distinct Impressions." In *Skeptical Tradition* (Berkeley: University of California Press, 1983).

Fredouille, Jean-Claude. *Tertullien: "De la patience": Introduction, texte, critique traduction et commentaire* (Paris: Éditions du Cerf, 1984).

Frey, Martin. "Untersuchungen zur Religion und zur Religionspolitik des Kaisers Elagabal." *Historia Einzelschriften* 62 (1989).

Galinsky, Karl. *Augustan Culture: An Interpretive Introduction* (Princeton, NJ: Princeton University Press, 1996).

Galinsky, Karl. "Clothes for the Emperor." *Arion* 10 (January 2003).

Galinsky, Karl. *The Herakles Theme: The Adaptations of the Hero in Literature from Homer to the Twelfth Century* (Oxford: Blackwell, 1972).

Ganiban, Randall T. *Statius and Virgil: The Thebaid and the Reinterpretation of the Aeneid* (Cambridge: Cambridge University Press, 2009).

Garani, Myrto. *Empedocles Redivivus: Poetry and Analogy in Lucretius* (New York: Routledge, 2007).

Garthwaite, Dominik J. and P. A. Roche. *Writing Politics in Imperial Rome* (Leiden: Brill, 2009).

Gassman, Mattias. "Arnobius' Scythians and the Dating of *Adversus Nationes*." *Journal of Theological Studies* 72, no. 2 (2021): pp. 838–841.

Gassman, Mattias. *Worshippers of the Gods: Debating Paganism in the Fourth-Century Roman West* (Oxford: Oxford University Press, 2020).

Gehrke, Jason M. "*Singulare et Unicum Imperium*: Monarchianism and Latin Apologetic in Rome." In *New Narratives for Old: The Historical Method of Reading Early Christian Theology. Essays in Honor of Michael Barnes*, edited by Anthony Briggman and Ellen Scully (Washington, DC: Catholic University of America Press, 2022), pp. 142–162.

Gelinas, Luke. "The Stoic Argument *Ex gradibus entium*." *Phronesis* 1, no. 1 (2006): pp. 52–73.

Gelzer, Matthias. *The Roman Nobility*, translated by Robin Seager (Oxford: Blackwell, 1969).

Gerber, Chad Tyler. *The Spirit of Augustine's Early Theology: Contextualizing Augustine's Pneumatology* (Burlington, VT: Ashgate, 2012).

Gersche, H. *Die Vergottung Caesars*. Frankfurter althistorische Studien, Band 1 (Kallmünz: Lassleben, 1968).

Gerson, Lloyd P., ed. *The Cambridge History of Philosophy in Late Antiquity*, 2 vols. (Cambridge: Cambridge University Press, 2010).

Gieschen, Charles A. "The Divine Names in Ante-Nicene Christology." *Vigiliae Christianae* 57, no. 2 (2003): pp. 115–158.

Glucker, John. *Antiochus and the Late Academy* (Göttingen: Vandenhoeck & Ruprecht, 1978).

Goodman, Martin. *The Roman World: 44 BC–AD 180*, 2nd ed. (New York: Routledge, 2012).

Gowing, Alain. *Empire and Memory: The Representation of the Roman Republic in Imperial Culture* (Cambridge: Cambridge University Press, 2005).

Gowing, Alain. "Tully's Boat: Responses to Cicero in the Imperial Period." In *The Cambridge Companion to Cicero*, edited by Catherine Steel (Cambridge: Cambridge University Press, 2013), pp. 233–250.

Gradel, Ittai. *Emperor Worship and Roman Religion* (Oxford: Clarendon Press, 2002).

Grebe, Sabine. "Augustus's Divine Authority and Vergil's *Aeneid*." *Vergilius* 50 (2004).

Green, Peter. *The Poems of Exile: Tristia and the Black Sea Letters* (Berkeley: University of California Press, 2005).

Griffin, Miriam. *Seneca: A Philosopher in Politics* (Cambridge: Clarendon Press, 1992).

Griffin, Miriam and Alison Samuels, eds. *P. A. Brunt: Studies in Stoicism* (Oxford: Oxford University Press, 2013).

BIBLIOGRAPHY 305

Grillmeier, Aloys. *Christ in the Christian Tradition*, vol. 1, *From the Apostolic Age to Chalcedon (451)*, 2nd ed. (Oxford: Mowbrays, 1976).

Gros, Pierre. "Rites funeraires et rites d'immortalite dans la liturgie de l'apotheose imperiale." *Annuaire de l'école pratique des Hautes études, IV sect., Sciences hist & philol* (1965–66): pp. 477–490.

Grubbs, Judith Evans. *Law and Family in Late Antiquity* (Oxford: Oxford University Press, 2000).

Hagendahl, Harald. *Latin Fathers and the Classics: A Study on the Apologists, Jerome, and other Christian Writers* (Stockholm: Almquist & Wiksell, 1958).

Haimson, Ayelet Lushkov. *Magistracy and the Historiography of the Roman Republic* (Cambridge: Cambridge University Press, 2015).

Halsberghe, G. H. "Le Culte de Deus Sol Invictus à Rome au 3ᵉ siècle après J.C." *Aufstieg und Niedergang der Römischen Welt* 17, no. 4 (1984): pp. 2181–2201.

Hankinson, R. J. "Explanation and Causation." In *The Cambridge History of Hellenistic Philosophy*, edited by Keimpe Algra, Jonathan Barnes, Jaap Mansfeld, and Malcolm Schofield (Cambridge: Cambridge University Press, 1999).

Hannestad, Niels. *Roman Art and Imperial Policy* (Aarhus: University Press, 1986).

Hansen, Benjamin. "Preaching to Seneca: Christ as Stoic *Sapiens* in *Divinae Institutiones* IV." *Harvard Theological Review* 111, no. 4 (2018).

Hardie, Phillip. *The Epic Successors of Virgil: A Study in the Dynamics of a Tradition* (Cambridge: Cambridge University Press, 1993).

Hardy, Edward R. *Christology of the Later Fathers* (Philadelphia: Westminster John Knox Press, 1977).

Harl, Marguerite. *Origène et la fonction révélatrice du verbe incarné. Patristica Sorbonensia* 2 (Paris: Éditions du Seuil, 1958).

Harmon, Andrew. *Image and Virtue in Ambrose of Milan* (Milwaukee, WI: Marquette University, Unpublished dissertation, 2017).

Harries, Jill. *Imperial Rome AD 284 to 363: The New Empire* (Edinburgh: Edinburgh University Press, 2012).

Hart, Daryl G. *A Secular Faith: Why Christianity Favors the Separation of Church and State* (Chicago: Ivan R. Dee, 2006).

Hatzimichali, Myrto. *Potamo of Alexandria and the Emergence of Eclecticism in Late Hellenistic Philosophy* (Cambridge: Cambridge University Press, 2011).

Heck, Eberhard. "Minucius Felix und Der Römische Staat: Ein Hinweis zum 25 Kapitel des 'Octavius.'" *Vigiliae Christianae* 38 (1984): pp. 154–164.

Heijne, Camilla Hélena. *The Messenger of the Lord in Early Jewish Interpretations of Genesis* (Berlin: Walter DeGruyter, 2010).

Hellemo, Geir. *Adventus Domini: Eschatological Thought in 4th Century Apses and Catecheses* (Leiden: Brill, 1989).

Hill, Jonathan. "The Self-Giving Power of God: Dunamis in Early Christianity." In *Divine Powers in Late Antiquity*, edited by Anna Marmodoro and Irini-Fotini Viltanoiti (Oxford: Oxford University Press, 2017), pp. 127–140.

Honoré, Tony. "Ulpian, Natural Law, and Stoic Influence." *Legal History Review* 28 (2010): pp. 199–208.

Honoré, Tony. *Ulpian: Pioneer of Human Rights* (Oxford: Oxford University Press, 2002).

Hooker, Mischa Andre. *The Use of Sibyls and Sibylline Oracles in Early Christian Writers* (Unpublished dissertation, University of Cincinnati, 2007).

Horsfall, Nicholas. *A Companion to the Study of Virgil. "Mnemosyne"* (Leiden: Brill, 1995), pp. 268–272.

Horsfall, Nicholas. *Virgil, Aeneid 6: A Commentary* (Berlin: DeGruyter, 2013).

Horsfall, Nicholas. *Virgil, Aeneid 6*, vol. 2 (Berlin: DeGruyter, 2013).

Horsfall, Nicholas. *Virgil, Aeneid 7: A Commentary* (Oxford: Oxford University Press, 2000).

BIBLIOGRAPHY

Horstmanshoff, H. F. J., Philip J. Eijk, and P. H. Schrijvers, eds. *Ancient Medicine in Its Socio-Cultural Context*, vol. 2, *Papers Read at the Congress Held at Leiden University, 13–15 April 1992* (Boston: Brill, 1995).

Hubbell, H. M. *De Inventione. De optimo genere oratorum. Topica* (Cambridge, MA: Harvard University Press, 1949).

Hurley, Donna W. *An Historical and Historiographical Commentary on Suetonius' Life of Caius Caligula* (Atlanta: Scholars Press, 1993).

Hutchinson, Gregory O. *Latin Literature from Seneca to Juvenal: A Critical Study* (Oxford: Clarendon Press, 1993).

Ierodiakonou, Katerina. *Topics in Stoic Philosophy* (Oxford: Oxford University Press, 1999).

Inglebert, Hervé. "Les heros romains, les martyrs et les ascetes: Les *virtutes* et les preferences politiques chez les auteurs chretiens latins du IIIe au VI siecle." *Revue des Etudes Augustiniennes* 40 (1994): pp. 305–325.

Inglebert, Hervé. *Les Romains Chretiens Face a L'Histore de Rome: Histoire, Christianisme, et romanites en Occident dans l'Antiquite tardive* (Paris: Institut d'Études Augustinennes, 1996).

Ingremeau, Christiane. "Lactance et la Justice: Du Livre 5 au Livre 6 des Institutions Divines." In *Autour de Lactance: Hommages à Pierre Monat* (Besançon: Institut des Sciences et Techniques de l'Antiquité, 2003).

Ingremeau, Christiane. "Minucius Felix et ses "sources": Le travail de l'écrivain." *Revue des Études Augustiniennes* 45 (1999).

Inwood, Brad. "Antiochus on Physics." In *Antiochus of Ascalon*, edited by David Sedley (Oxford: Oxford University Press, 2015).

Inwood, Brad, ed. *The Cambridge Companion to the Stoics* (Cambridge: University Press, 2003).

Inwood, Brad, ed. *Ethics and Human Action in Early Stoicism* (Oxford: Oxford University Press, 1985).

Inwood, Brad. "Seneca, Plato, and Platonism: The Case of *Letter 65*." In *Platonic Stoicism: The Dialogue between Platonism and Stoicism in Antiquity*, edited by Mauro Bonazzi and Christoph Helmig (Leuven: Leuven University Press, 2007).

Ip, Pui Him. *Origen and the Origins of Divine Simplicity before Nicaea* (South Bend, IN: University of Notre Dame Press, 2022).

Isichei, Elizabeth Allo. *Political Thinking and Social Experience: Some Christian Interpretations of the Roman Empire from Tertullian to Salvian* (New Zealand: University of Canterbury Publications, 1964).

Jacobs, Andrew S. "'Let Him Guard Pietas': Early Christian Exegesis and the Ascetic Family." *Journal of Early Christian Studies* 11, no. 3 (2003): pp. 265–281.

Jacobson, Howard. *Ovid's Heroides* (Princeton, NJ: Princeton University Press, 1974), pp. 76ff.

Jaeger, Hasso. "The Patristic Conception of Wisdom in the Light of Biblical and Rabbinical Research." *Studia Patristica* 4 (1959): pp. 90–106.

Jewitt, Robert. *Romans: A Commentary* (Minneapolis: Fortress Press, 2007).

Johnson, Walter R. *Momentary Monsters: Lucan and His Heroes* (Ithaca, NY: Cornell University Press, 1987).

Jones, A. H. M. *The Later Roman Empire 284–602: A Social, Economic, and Administrative Survey, vols. 1 and 2* (Oxford: Basil Blackwell, 1964).

Judge, Edwin A. "Antike und Christentum: Towards the Definition of a Field. A Bibliographical Survey." *Aufstieg und Niedergang der Römischen Welt* 23, no.1 (1979): pp. 3–58.

Kapust, Daniel J. *Republicanism, Rhetoric, and Roman Political Thought: Sallust, Livy, and Tacitus* (Cambridge: Cambridge University Press, 2011).

Kemezis, Adam M. "Augustus the Ironic Paradigm: Cassius Dio's Portrayal of the *Lex Julia* and *Lex Papia Poppaea*." *Phoenix* 61 (2007).

Kennedy, Geoffrey. "Cicero, Roman Republicanism and the Contested Meaning of Libertas." *Political Studies* 14, no. 62 (2014): pp. 488–501.

Kerestes, Paul. "The Imperial Roman Government and the Christian Church I. From Nero to the Severi." *Aufstieg und Niedergang der Römischen Welt* 23, no. 1 (1979): pp. 247–315.

Kerestes, Paul. "The Imperial Roman Government and the Christian Church II. From Gallienus to the Great Persecution." *Aufstieg und Niedergang der Römischen Welt* 23, no. 1 (1979): pp. 375–386.

Kienast, Dietmar. *Augustus: Prinzeps und Monarch* (Darmstadt: Primus-Verlag, 2009).

Kolb, Frank. *Diocletian und die Erste Tetrarchie: Improvisation oder Experiment in der Organisation Monarchiser Herrschaft?* (Berlin: DeGruyter, 1987).

Konstan, David. "Atomis." In *The Oxford Handbook of Epicurus and Epicureanism*, edited by Phillip Mitsis (Oxford: Oxford University Press, 2020), pp. 59–80.

Koortbojian, Michael. *The Divinization of Caesar and Augustus: Precedents, Consequences, Implications* (Cambridge: Cambridge University Press, 2013).

Kuefler, M. *The Manly Eunuch: Masculinity, Gender Ambiguity, and Christian Ideology in Late Antiquity* (Chicago: University of Chicago Press, 2001).

Kuttner, Ann L. "'Ara Pietatis Augustae': Ein Geisterbau." *Rheinisches Museum für Philologie* 89 (1982): pp. 453–455.

Kuttner, Ann L. *Dynasty and Empire in the Age of Augustus: The Case of the Boscoreale Cups* (Berkeley: University of California Press, 1955).

Langlands, Rebecca. *Exemplary Ethics in Ancient Rome* (Cambridge: Cambridge University Press, 2018).

Langlands, Rebecca. *Sexual Morality in Ancient Rome* (Cambridge: Cambridge University Press, 2006).

Leach, Eleanor Winsor. "*Sedes Apibus*: From the *Georgics* to the *Aeneid*." *Vergilius* 23 (1977).

Lebreton, Jules. *Les Origines du Dogme de La Trinité*, 2 vols. (Paris: Beauchesne, Éditeurs, 1910).

Leith, David. "Medicine." In *The Oxford Handbook of Roman Philosophy*, edited by David Konstan, Myrto Garani, and Gretchen Reydams-Schils (Oxford: Oxford University Press, 2023), pp. 379–397.

Leithart, Peter. *Defending Constantine: The Twilight of an Empire and the Dawn of Christendom* (Downers Grove, IL: IVP Academic, 2010).

Lenski, Noel. *Constantine and the Cities: Imperial Authority and Civic Politics* (Philadelphia: University of Pennsylvania Press, 2016).

Levene, D. S. "Sallust's' 'Catiline' and Cato the Censor." *Classical Quarterly* 50, no. 1 (2000).

Lévy, Carlos. *Cicero Academicus. Recherches sur les "Académiques" et sur la philosophie cicéronienne* (Rome: École Française de Rome, 1992).

Lévy, Carlos. "Cicero and the New Academy." In *The Cambridge History of Philosophy in Late Antiquity*, edited by Lloyd Gerson (Cambridge: Cambridge University Press, 2015).

Lévy, Carlos. "Cicéron, le moyen platonisme et la philosophie romaine: À propos de la naissance du concept latin de qualitas." *Revue de Métaphysique et de Morale* 57, no. 1 (2008): pp. 5–20.

Lichtenberger, Achim. *Severus Pius Augustus: Student zur sakralen Reprasentation und Rezeption der Herrschaft des Spitimius Severus und seiner Familie* (Leiden: Brill, 2011).

Lilla, Mark. *The Stillborn God: Religion, Politics, and the Modern West* (New York: Vintage Books, 2008).

Linbeck, George. *The Nature of Doctrine: Religion and Theology in a Post-Liberal Age* (Louisville, KY: John Knox Press, 1984).

Lintott, Andrew. *Cicero as Evidence: A Historian's Companion* (Oxford: Oxford University Press, 2008), pp. 215–253.

Litchfield, Henry. "National Exempla Virtutis in Roman Literature." *Harvard Studies in Classical Philology* 25 (1914).

Littlewood, Joy R. *A Commentary on Ovid's "Fasti, Book 6"* (Oxford: Clarendon Press, 2006).

Lloyd, Daniel. *Novatian's Theology of the Son: A Study in Ontological Subordinationism* (New York: Fortress Academic, 2020).

308 BIBLIOGRAPHY

Lloyd, Daniel. *Ontological Subordination in Novation of Rome's Trinitarian Theology* (Milwaukee, WI: Marquette University, Unpublished dissertation, 2009).

Long, A. A. "Cicero's Plato and Aristotle." In *Cicero the Philosopher: Twelve Papers Edited and Introduced by J. G. F. Powell*, edited by J. G. F. Powell (Oxford: Clarendon Press, 1995).

Long, A. A. "Cicero's Politics in *De Officiis*." In *From Epicurus to Epictetus: Studies in Hellenistic and Roman Philosophy*, edited by A. A. Long (Oxford: Oxford University Press, 2006).

Long, A. A. "Roman Philosophy." In *The Cambridge Companion to Greek and Roman Philosophy*, edited by David Sedley (Cambridge: Cambridge University Press, 2003).

Long, A. A. "Stoic Psychology." In *The Cambridge History of Hellenistic Philosophy*, edited by Keimpe Algra, Jonathan Barnes, Jaap Mansfeld, and Malcolm Schofield (Cambridge: Cambridge University Press, 1999).

Long, Stephen D. *The Goodness of God: Theology, Church, and the Social Order* (Grand Rapids, MI: Brazos Press, 2001).

Lushkov, Ayelet Haimson. *Magistracy and the Historiography of the Roman Republic: Politics in Prose* (Cambridge: Cambridge University Press, 2015).

Lyne, R. O. A. M. *Further Voices in Vergil's Aeneid* (Oxford: Oxford University Press, 2006).

Martin, Jean-Pierre. *Providentia deorum: Recherches sur certains aspects religieux du pouvoir impérial romain* (Rome: École française, 1982).

MacCormack, Sabine G. *The Shadows of Poetry: Vergil in the Mind of Augustus* (Berkeley: University of California Press, 1998).

MacIntyre, Alasdair. *After Virtue*, 3rd ed. (Notre Dame, IN: University of Notre Dame Press, 2007).

MacRae, Duncan. *Legible Religion: Books, Gods, and Rituals in Roman Culture* (Cambridge, MA: Harvard University Press, 2016).

Mattingly, Harold, Edward Sydenham, and Percy Webb. *Roman Imperial Coinage*, vol. 5B (London: Spink and Son, 1984).

Markus, R. A. *Christianity and the Secular* (Notre Dame: University of Notre Dame Press, 2001).

Markus, R. A., W. E. Klingshirn, and M. Vessey. *The Limits of Ancient Christianity: Essays on Late Antique Thought and Culture in Honor of R. A. Markus* (Ann Arbor: University of Michigan Press, 1999).

Marmodoro, Anna and Irini-Fotini Viltanoiti, eds. *Divine Powers in Late Antiquity* (Oxford: Oxford University Press, 2017).

Marmodoro, Anna. *Forms and Structure in Plato's Metaphysics* (Oxford: Oxford University Press, 2022).

Marmodoro, Anna. *The Metaphysics of Powers: Their Grounding and Their Manifestations* (New York: Routledge, 2010).

Mastrocinque, Attilio. "Creating One's Own Religion: Intellectual Choices." In *A Companion to Roman Religion*, edited by Jörg Rupke (Oxford: Wiley Blackwell, 2011), pp. 378–392.

Mazzoni, Cristina. *She-Wolf: The Story of a Roman Icon* (Cambridge: Cambridge University Press, 2010).

McCruden, Kevin B. "Monarchy and Economy in Tertullian's *Adversus Praxean*." *Scottish Journal of Theology* 55, no. 3 (2002): pp. 325–337.

McDonnell, Myles. *Roman Manliness: Virtus and the Roman Republic* (Cambridge: Cambridge University Press, 2006).

McGowan, Andrew Brian. "God in Early Latin Theology: Tertullian and the Trinity." In *God in Early Christian Thought: Essays in Memory of Lloyd G. Patterson. Supplements to Vigiliae Christianae 94*, edited by L. G. Patterson, Andrew Brian McGowan, Brian Daley, and Timothy J. Gaden (Leiden: Brill, 2009).

McGowan, Andrew Brian. "Tertullian and the 'Heretical' Origins of the 'Orthodox' Trinity." *Journal of Early Christian Studies* 14, no. 4 (2006): pp. 437–457.

McGushin, Patrick. *C. Sallustius Crispus, Bellum Catilinae: A Commentary* (Lugduni Batavorum: Brill, 1977).

BIBLIOGRAPHY 309

Mehl, David. "The Intricate Translation of the Epicurean Doctrine of ΨΥΧΗ in Book 3 of Lucretius." *Philologus* 143, no. 2 (1999).

Miller, Harold W. "*Dynamis* and *Physis* in *On Ancient Medicine*." *American Philological Association* 83 (1952), pp. 184–197.

Milnor, Kristina. "Augustus, History, and the Landscape of the Law." *Arethusa* 40, no. 1 (2007).

Mitsis, Philip, ed. *The Oxford Handbook of Epicurus and Epicureanism* (Oxford: Oxford University Press, 2023).

Moatti, Claude. *La raison de Rome* (Paris: Sevil, 1997).

Moatti, Claude. "Tradition et Raison chez Cicéron: L'émergence de la rationalité politique à la fin de la République romaine." *Mélanges de l'Ecole Française de Rome Antiquité* 100, no. 1 (1988): pp. 385–430.

Moatti, Claudia. *The Birth of Critical Thinking in Republican Rome*, translated by Janet Lloyd (Cambridge: Cambridge University Press, 2015).

Moingt, Joseph. "Le problème du Dieu unique chez Tertullien." *Revue des Sciences Religieuses* 44, no. 4 (1970): pp. 337–362.

Moingt, Joseph. *Théologie trinitaire de Tertullien*, 4 vols. (Paris: Aubier, 1966).

Momigliano, Arnaldo. *The Conflict between Paganism and Christianity in the Fourth Century* (Oxford: Clarendon Press, 1963).

Momigliano, Arnaldo. "The Theological Efforts of the Roman Upper Classes in the First Century BC." In *Roman Religion*, edited by Clifford Ando (Edinburgh: Edinburgh University Press, 2003).

Monceaux, Paul. *Histoire littéraire de l'Afrique Chrétienne depuis les origins jusqu'à l'invasion arabe*, 7 vols. (Paris: E. Leroux, 1901–1923).

Moreschini, Claudio and Enrico Norelli. *Early Christian Greek and Latin Literature: A Literary History*, translated by Matthew O'Connell (Grand Rapids, MI: Baker Academic, 2005).

Moreschini, Claudio and Enrico Norelli. *Histoire de la littérature chrétienne antique grecque et latine: de Paul à l'ère de Constantin* (Genève: Éditions Labor et Fides, 1995).

Mueller, Hans-Friedrich. *Roman Religion in Valerius Maximus* (New York: Routledge, 2002).

Munier, Charles. *Concilia Galliae a.314–a.506* (Turnhout: Brepols, 1963).

Murphy, Edwina. "As Far as My Poor Memory Suggested: Cyprian's Compilation of *Ad Quirinum*." *Vigiliae Christianae* 68 (2014).

Murphy, Edwina. *The Bishop and the Apostle: Cyprian's Pastoral Exegesis of Paul* (Berlin/Boston: De Gruyter, 2018).

Mynors, R. A. B, C. E. V. Nixon, and Barbara Saylor Rodgers, eds. *In Praise of Later Roman Emperors: The Panegyrici Latini: Introduction, Translation and Historical Commentary* (Berkeley: University of California Press, 1994).

Narducci, Emanuele. *Lucano: Un'epica Contro l'impero: Interpretazione della Pharsalia* (Rome: Laterza, 2002).

Nehring, Przemyslaw. "The Authority of Seneca in Early Christian Argumentation." *Symbolae Philologorun Posnaniensium Graecae et Latinae* 37, no. 3 (2017).

Nelson, N. E. "Cicero's *De officiis* in Christian Thought: 300–1300." In *Essays and Studies in English and Comparative Literature 10* (Ann Arbor: University of Michigan Press, 1933), pp. 59–160.

Nicgorski, Walter. "Cicero's Focus: From the Best Regime to the Model Statesman." *Political Theory* 19, no. 2 (1991): pp. 230–251.

Noack, Christian. "Der *Octavius* des Minucius Felix: Ein interreligiöser 'Rechstreit' unter Freunden zur Beurteilung der römischen und christlichen *religio*." *Spes Christiana* 17 (2006): pp. 7–20.

Noonan, J. D. "*Sum Pius Aeneas*: Aeneas and the Leader as Conservator/σΩΤΗΡ." *Classical Bulletin* 83, no. 1 (2007): pp. 65–91.

North, Helen. *Sophrosyne: Self-Knowledge and Self-Restraint in Greek Literature* (Ithaca, NY: Cornell University Press, 1966).

310   BIBLIOGRAPHY

North. J. A., and S. R. F. Price. *The Religious History of the Roman Empire: Pagans, Jews, Christians* (Oxford: Oxford University Press, 2011).

Nutton, Vivian. *Ancient Medicine*, 2nd ed. (New York: Routledge, 2013), pp. 116ff.

Orr, David G. "Roman Domestic Religion: The Evidence of the Household Shrines." *Aufstieg und Niedergang der Römischen Welt* 16, no. 2 (1978): pp. 1557–1591.

Ortigues, Edmond. *Le Monothéisme. La Bible et les philosophes* (Paris: Hatier, 1999).

Osborn, Eric. *Clement of Alexandria* (Cambridge: Cambridge University Press, 2005).

Osborn, Eric. *Tertullian, First Theologian of the West* (Cambridge: Cambridge University Press, 1997).

Papandrea, James Leonard. *Novatian of Rome and the Culmination of Pre-Nicene Orthodoxy* (Eugene, OR: Pickwick, 2012).

Papandrea, James Leonard. *The Trinitarian Theology of Novatian of Rome: A Study in Third-Century Orthodoxy* (Lewiston, NY: Edwin Mellen, 2008).

Partoens, G., G. Roskam, and T. Van Houdt, eds. *Virtutis Imago: Studies on the Conceptualisation and Transformation of an Ancient Ideal* (Louvain: Peeters, 2004).

Pelikan, Jaroslav. *The Christian Tradition: A History of the Development of Doctrine*, vol. 1, *The Emergence of the Catholic Tradition (100–600)* (Chicago: University of Chicago Press, 1975).

Pépin, Jean. *Mythe et allégorie: Les origines grecques et les contestations judéo-chrétiennes* (Paris: Études Augustiniennes, 1976).

Petitfils, James. *Mos Christianorum: The Roman Discourse of Exemplarity and the Jewish and Christian Language of Leadership* (Tübingen: Mohr-Siebeck, 2017).

Pinel, Carmen Macarena Palomo. *Nec Inmerito Paterfamilias Dicitur: El paterfamilias en el pensamiento de Lactancio* (Madrid: Dykinson S. L., 2019).

Ployd, Adam. *Augustine, the Trinity, and the Church: A Reading of the Anti-Donatist Sermons* (Oxford: Oxford University Press, 2015).

Polleichtner, Wolfgang. "The Bee Simile: How Vergil Emulated Apollonius in His Use of Homeric Poetry." *Goettinger Forum fur Altertumswissenschaft* 8 (2005).

Potter, David. *Constantine the Emperor* (Oxford: Oxford University Press, 2012).

Pouderon, Bernard and Josephe Dore, eds. *Les Apologistes Chretiens et la Culture Grècque* (Paris: Beauchesne, 1998).

Powell, Anton. *Virgil the Partisan: A Study in the Re-integration of Classics* (Oakville, CT: Distributed in the USA by David Brown, 2008).

Powell, Jonathan. "Unfair to Caecilius? Ciceronian Dialogue Techniques in Minucius Felix." In *Severan Culture*, edited by Simon Swain, Stephen Harrison, and Jas Elsner (Oxford: Oxford University Press, 2007).

Powell, J. G. F., ed. *De re publica* (Oxford: Oxford University Press, 2006).

Powell, J. G. F., ed. *Cicero the Philosopher: Twelve Papers* (Oxford: Clarendon Press, 1995).

Press, Gerald A. *Development of the Idea of History in Antiquity* (Montreal: McGill-Queen's Press, 1982).

Price, Simon. "Latin Christian Apologetics: Minucius Felix, Tertullian, and Cyprian." In *Apologetics in the Roman Empire: Pagans, Jews, and Christians*, edited by Mark Edwards, Martin Goodman, and Simon Price (Oxford: Oxford University Press, 1999).

Putnam, Michael C. J. "Two Ways of Looking at the 'Aeneid.'" *Classical World* 96, no. 2 (2003): pp. 177–184.

Quinn, Kenneth. *Virgil's "Aeneid": A Critical Description* (London: Routledge & Kegan Paul, 1968).

Quispel, Giles. "African Christianity before Minucius Felix and Tertullian." In *Gnostica, Judaica, Catholica. Collected Essays of Gilles Quispel*, edited by Johannes van Ort (Leiden: Brill, 2008).

Quispel, Giles. "A Jewish Source of Minucius Felix." *Vigiliae Christianiae* 3, no. 2 (1949): pp. 113–122.

BIBLIOGRAPHY   311

Radde-Gallwitz, Andrew. *Basil of Caesarea, Gregory of Nyssa, and the Transformation of Divine Simplicity* (Oxford: Oxford University Press, 2009).

Radde-Gallwitz, Andrew. *Gregory of Nyssa's Doctrinal Works: A Literary Study* (Oxford: Oxford University Press, 2018).

Rawls, John R. *Theory of Justice* (Cambridge, MA: Belknap Press of Harvard University Press, 1999).

Rawson, Elizabeth. *Cicero: A Portrait* (London: Bristol Classics Press, 1983), pp. 203–229.

Rébillard, Éric. *Christians and Their Many Identities in Late Antiquity, North Africa, 200–450 CE* (Ithaca, NY: Cornell University Press, 2012).

Reddoch, M. Jason. "Cicero's *De Divinatione* and Philo of Alexandria's Criticism of Chaldean Astrology as a Form of Artificial Divination." *Dionysius* 32 (2014).

Rees, Roger. *Layers of Loyalty in Latin Panegyric AD 289–307* (Oxford: Oxford University Press, 2002).

Rees, Roger. *Latin Panegyric* (Oxford: Oxford University Press, 2012).

Remer, Gary A. *Ethics and the Orator: The Ciceronian Tradition of Political Morality* (Chicago: University of Chicago Press, 2017).

Rendall, Gerald H. "Introduction." In *Minucius Felix, Octavius*, translated by T. R. Glover and Gerald H. Rendall (Cambridge, MA: Harvard University Press, 1931), pp. 308–315.

Rives, James. "The Decree of Decius and the Religion of Empire." *Journal of Roman Studies* 89 (1999): pp. 135–154.

Rives, James. "Human Sacrifice among Pagans and Christians." *Journal of Roman Studies* 85 (1995): pp. 65–85.

Rives, James. *Religion and Authority in Roman Carthage: From Augustus to Constantine* (Oxford: Clarendon Press, 1995).

Rives, James. *Religion in the Roman Empire* (Malden, MA: Blackwell, 2007).

Roche, Paul. *Lucan: De Bello Civili* (Oxford: Oxford University Press, 2009).

Roller, Matthew. *Constructing Autocracy: Aristocrats and Emperors in Julio-Claudian Rome* (Princeton, NJ: Princeton University Press, 2001).

Roller, Matthew. "Exemplarity in Roman Culture." *Classical Philology* 99, no. 1 (2004).

Rowan, Clare. *Under Divine Auspices: Divine Ideology and the Visualization of the Imperial Power in the Severan Period* (Cambridge: Cambridge University Press, 2012).

Runia, David T. "Eudaimonism in Hellenistic-Jewish Literature." In *Shem in the Tents of Japhet: Essays on the Encounter of Judaism and Hellenism*, edited by James L. Kugel (Leiden: Brill, 2002).

Runia, David T. *Philo in Early Christian Literature: A Survey* (Leiden: Brill, 1993).

Rüpke, Jörg. *Religion in Republican Rome: Rationalization and Ritual Change* (Philadelphia: University of Pennsylvania Press, 2012).

Rüpke, Jörg. *Religion of the Romans*, translated and edited by Richard Gordon (Cambridge: Polity Press, 2007).

Russell, Brigette Ford. "Wine, Women, and the *Polis*: Gender and the Formation of the City-State in Archaic Rome." *Greece and Rome* 50, no. 1 (2003): pp. 77–85.

Russell, Daniel C. "Happiness and Agency in the Stoics and Aristotle." *Boston Area Colloquium in Ancient Philosophy* 24 (2008): pp. 83–125.

Saller, Richard P. *Patriarchy, Property and Death in the Roman Family* (Oxford: Oxford University Press, 1994).

Salles, Ricardo. "Ἐκπύρωσις and the Goodness of God in Cleanthes." *Phronesis* 50, no. 1 (2005): pp. 56–78.

Salzman, Michelle Rene, Marianne Sághy, and Rita Lizzi Testa, eds. *Pagans and Christians in Late Antique Rome* (Cambridge: Cambridge University Press, 2016).

Scanlon, Thomas F. *The Influences of Thucydides on Sallust* (Heidelberg: Carl Winter, 1980).

Scanlon, Thomas F. *Spes Frustrata: A Reading of Sallust* (Heidenheim: A. Druckenmüller Verlag, 1987).

312 BIBLIOGRAPHY

Scullard, Herbert H. *Early Christian Ethics in the West, from Clement to Ambrose* (London: Macmillan, 1907).

Schanz, Martin von. *Geschichte der römischen Litteratur bis zur Gesetzgebungswerk des Kaisers Justinian*, vol. 3 (Munich, 1922).

Scheid, John. *Quand faire cést croire* (Paris: Aubier, 2005).

Scheid, John. *Religion et piété à Rome* (Paris: A. Michel, 2001).

Scheid, John. *La religion des Romains* (Paris: A. Colin, 2003).

Scheid, John. *Rites et croyances dans les religions du monde romain* (Vandoeuvres-Genève: Fondations Hardt pour l'étude de l'antiquité classique, 2007).

Scheid, John. "Les sens des rites. L'exemple romain." In *Rites et croyances dans les religions du monde romain*, edited by J. Scheid (Vandoeuvres-Genève: Fondations Hardt pour l'étude de l'antiquité classique, 2007).

Schofield, Malcolm, ed. *Aristotle, Plato, and Pythagoreanism in the First Century B.C.: New Directions for Philosophy* (Cambridge: Cambridge University Press, 2013), pp. 187–275.

Schofield, Malcolm. "Seneca on Monarchy and the Political Life: *De Clementia, De Tranquillitate Animi, De Otio.*" In *The Cambridge Companion to Seneca*, edited by Shadi Bartsch and Alessandro Schiesaro (Cambridge: Cambridge University Press, 2015), pp. 68–82.

Schofield, Malcolm. "Writing Philosophy." In *The Cambridge Companion to Cicero*, edited by Catherine Steel (Cambridge: Cambridge University Press, 2013), pp. 78–87.

Sedley, David. *Antiochus of Ascalon* (Oxford: Oxford University Press, 2012).

Sedley, David, ed. *The Cambridge Companion to Greek and Roman Philosophy* (Cambridge: Cambridge University Press, 2003).

Sedley, David. "Hellenistic Physics and Metaphysics." In *The Cambridge History of Hellenistic Philosophy*, edited by Keimpe Algra, Jonathan Barnes, Jaap Mansfeld, and Malcolm Schofield (Cambridge: Cambridge University Press, 1999), pp. 355–409.

Sedley, David. *Lucretius and the Transformation of Greek Wisdom* (Cambridge: Cambridge University Press, 1998).

Sedley, David. "The Origins of Stoic God." In *Traditions of Theology: Studies in Hellenistic Theology, Its Background and Aftermath*, edited by Dorothea Frede and André Laks (Leiden: Brill, 2002), pp. 48–84.

Sharples, Robert W. *Peripatetic Philosophy, 200 BC to AD 200: An Introduction and Collection of Sources in Translation* (Cambridge: Cambridge University Press, 2010).

Shaw, Brent D. "The Divine Economy: Stoicism as Ideology." *Latomus* 44, no. 1 (1985): pp. 16–54.

Siecienski, A. Edward, ed. *Constantine: Religious Faith and Imperial Policy* (New York: Routledge, 2017).

Simon, Marcel. *Jewish Sects at the Time of Jesus* (Philadelphia: Fortress, 1980).

Simonetti, Manlio. "The Beginnings of Latin Theological Investigation in the West." In *History of Theology: The Patristic Period*, translated by Matthew J. O'Connell, edited by Angelino Di Perardino and Basil Studer (Collegeville, MN: Liturgical Press, 1997).

Sims-Williams, Patrick. "Thought, Word, and Deed: An Irish Triad." *Eriu* 29 (1978).

Sisson, Russell B. "Roman Stoic Pre-Creation Discourse." *Religion and Theology* 18 (2011).

Sklenář, R. "La République des Signes: Caesar, Cato, and the Language of Sallustian Morality." *Transactions of the American Philological Association* 128 (1998): pp. 205–220.

Sklenář, R. *The Taste for Nothingness: A Study of Virtus and Related Themes in Lucan's Bellum Civile* (Ann Arbor: University of Michigan Press, 2003).

Smith, J. Warren. *Christian Grace and Pagan Virtue: The Theological Foundation of Ambrose's Ethics* (Oxford: Oxford University Press, 2010).

Smith, Jonathan Z. *Drudgery Divine: On the Comparison of Early Christianities and the Religions of Late Antiquity* (Chicago: University of Chicago Press, 1990).

Smith, Julien. *Christ the Ideal King: Culture, Context, Rhetorical Strategy, and the Power of Divine Monarchy in Ephesians* (Tuebingen: Mohr Siebeck, 2011).

BIBLIOGRAPHY 313

Solodow, Joseph B. *The World of Ovid's Metamorphoses* (Chapel Hill: University of North Carolina Press, 1988).

Sorabji, Richard. *Emotion and Peace of Mind from Stoic Agitation to Christian Temptation* (Oxford: Oxford University Press, 2003).

Sorabji, Richard. *Matter, Space, and Motion: Theories in Antiquity and Their Sequel* (Ithaca, NY: Cornell University Press, 1988).

Sorabji, Richard. *The Philosophy of the Commentators, 200–600 AD: Psychology (with Ethics and Religion)* (Ithaca, NY: Cornell University Press, 2005).

Souter, Alexander. *A Glossary of Later Latin to 600 AD* (Oxford: Oxford University Press, 1949).

Spanneut, Michel. *Le stoïcisme des Pères de l'Église* (Paris: Seuil, 1957).

Spanneut, Michel. *Tertullien et les premiers moralistes africains* (Paris: Éditions du Cerf, 1969).

Spielberg, Lydia. "Language, Stasis and the Role of the Historian in Thucydides, Sallust and Tacitus." *American Journal of Philology* 138, no. 2 (2017).

Spinelli, Emidio and Francesco Verde. "Theology." In *The Oxford Handbook of Epicurus and Epicureanism*, edited by Phillip Mitsis (Oxford: Oxford University Press, 2023), pp. 94–117.

Steel, Catherine, ed. *The Cambridge Companion to Cicero* (Cambridge: University Press, 2015).

Sterling, Gregory E. "Philosophy as the Handmaid of Wisdom: Philosophy in the Exegetical Traditions of Alexandrian Jews." In *Religiöse Philosophie und philosophische Religion der frühen Kaiserzeit*, edited by Rainer Hirsch-Luippold, Herwig Görgemanns, and Michael von Albrecht (Tübingen: Mohr Siebeck, 2009).

Sterling, Gregory E. "Platonizing Moses: Philo and Middle Platonism." *Studia Philonica Annual* 5 (1993): pp. 96–111.

Sterling, Gregory E. "'The Queen of the Virtues': Piety in Philo of Alexandria." *Philonica Annual* 18: pp. 103–123.

Stevens, Edward B. "Aeneid 6.72ff. and Cicero's Hortensius." *Classical Weekly* 36, no. 8 (1942).

Stevens, John. "Platonism and Stoicism in Vergil's *Aeneid*." In *Platonic Stoicism—Stoic Platonism: The Dialogue between Platonism and Stoicism in Antiquity*, edited by Christoph Helmig and Mauro Bonazzi (Leuven: Leuven University Press, 2008).

Stevenson, J. "The Life and Literary Activity of Lactantius." *Studia Patristica* 1 (1955): pp. 61–67.

Stevenson, Tom. "Women of Early Rome as Exempla in Livy, *Ab Urbe Condita*, Book 1." *Classical World* 104, no. 2 (2011).

Stipanovic, Andre. "Bees and Ants: Perceptions of Imperialism in Vergil's *Aeneid* and *Georgics*." In *Insect Poetics*, edited by Eric C. Brown (Minneapolis: University of Minnesota Press, 2018).

Stout, Jeffrey. *Democracy and Tradition* (Princeton, NJ: Princeton University Press, 2004).

Stowers, Stanley K. *A Rereading of Romans: Justice, Jews, and Gentiles* (New Haven, CT: Yale University Press, 1994).

Strange, S. K. and J. Zupko, eds. *Stoicism: Traditions and Transformations* (Cambridge: Cambridge University Press, 2004).

Strasburger. "Novus Homo." *Realencyclopädie der Classischen Altertumswissenschaft* 17, no. 1 (1937).

Stroumsa, Guy. *Hidden Wisdom: Esotericism and the Roots of Christian Mysticism* (Leiden: Brill, 2005).

Studer, Basil. "La Soteriologie de Lactance." In *Lactance et son Temps: Recherches Actuelles: Actes du IVe Colloque d'Etudes Historiques et Patristiques, Chantilly 21–23 Septembre 1976*, edited by J. Fontaine and M. Perrin (Paris: Editions Beauchesne, 1978).

Sullivan, J. P. "Petronius, Seneca, and Lucan: A Neronian Literary Feud?" *American Philological Association* 99 (1968): pp. 453–467.

Sutherland, C. H. V. "Two 'Virtues' of Tiberius: A Numismatic Contribution to the History of His Reign." *Journal of Roman Studies* 28, no. 2 (1938).

Swift, Louis J. "War and Christian Conscience: The Early Years." *Aufstieg und Niedergang der Römischen Welt* 23, no. 1 (1979).

314   BIBLIOGRAPHY

Syed, Yasmin. *Vergil's Aeneid and the Roman Self: Subject and Nation in Literary Discourse* (Ann Arbor: University of Michigan Press, 2005).

Syme, Ronald. "Livy and Augustus." *Harvard Studies in Classical Philology* 64 (1959).

Syme, Ronald. *The Roman Revolution* (Oxford: University Press, 1939).

Syme, Ronald. *Sallust* (Berkeley: University of California Press, 1964).

Tarrant, Richard J. "Aspects of Virgil's Reception in Antiquity." In *The Cambridge Companion to Virgil*, edited by Charles Martindale (Cambridge: Cambridge University Press, 1997).

Taylor, Charles. *A Secular Age* (Cambridge, MA: Belknap Press of Harvard University Press, 2007).

Taylor, Joan E. "The Phenomenon of Early Jewish-Christianity: Reality or Scholarly Invention?" *Vigiliae Christianae* 44, no. 4 (1990): pp. 313–334.

Teske, Roland. "St. Augustine and the Vision of God." In *Augustine: Mystic and Mystagogue. Collectanea Augustiniana*, vol. 3, edited by Frederick Van Fleteren, Joseph C. Schnaubelt, and Joseph Reino (Bristol: Peter Lang, 1994), pp. 287–308.

Testa, Rita L. "Christian Emperor, Vestal Virgins and Priestly Colleges: Reconsidering the End of Roman Paganism." *Antiquité Tardive* 15 (2007): pp. 251–262.

Thomas, Richard. "Torn between Jupiter and Saturn: Ideology, Rhetoric and Culture Wars in the 'Aeneid.'" *Classical Journal* 100, no. 2 (2004).

Thomas, Richard. *Virgil and the Augustan Reception* (Cambridge: Cambridge University Press, 2001).

Torre, Chiara. "Seneca and the Christian Tradition." In *The Cambridge Companion to Seneca*, edited by Shadi Bartsch and Alessandro Schiesaro (Cambridge: Cambridge University Press, 2015).

Treggiari, Susan. *Roman Marriage: Iusti Coniuges from the Time of Cicero to the Time of Ulpian* (Oxford: Oxford University Press, 1991).

Trigg, Joseph Wilson. *Origen: The Bible and Philosophy in the Third-Century Church* (London: SCM Press, 1985).

Turpin, José. "Cicero *de Legibus* I–II et la religion romaine: Une interpretation philosophique à la veille du principat." *Aufstieg und Niedergang der Römischen Welt* 16, no. 3 (1986): pp. 1877–1908.

Van Andringa, William. "Rhetoric and Divine Honours: On the 'Imperial Cult' in the Reigns of Augustus and Constantine." *Collegium* 20 (2016).

Van den Bruwaene, Martin. "Influence d'Aratus et de Rhodes sur l'oeuvre philosophique de Cicéron." *Aufstieg und Niedergang der Römischen Welt* 4 (1974): pp. 428–437.

Van den Bruwaene, Martin. *La Théologie de Cicéron* (Louvain: Bibliothèque de l'Université, 1937).

Van der Blom, Henriette. *Cicero's Role Models: The Political Strategy of a Newcomer* (Oxford: Oxford University Press, 2010).

Van der Linden, Marcel and John Scheid. "Quand croire, c'est faire. Le problème de la croyance dans la Rome ancienne." *Archives de Sciences Sociales des Religions* 81 (1993): pp. 47–62.

Vander Waert, Paul A. "Philosophical Influence on Roman Jurisprudence? The Case of Stoicism and Natural Law." *Aufstieg und Niedergang der Römischen Welt* 36, no. 7 (1994): pp. 4851–4900.

Van Nuffelen, Peter. *Rethinking the Gods: Philosophical Readings of Religion in the post-Hellenistic Period* (Cambridge: Cambridge University Press, 2011).

Van Nuffelen, Peter and Stephen Mitchell, eds. *Monotheism between Pagans and Christians in Late Antiquity* (Leuven: Peeters, 2010).

Van Nuffelen, Peter and Stephen Mitchell, eds. *One God: Pagan Monotheism in the Roman Empire* (Cambridge: Cambridge University Press, 2010).

Van Oort, Johannes. *Jerusalem and Babylon: A Study into Augustine's City of God and the Sources of His Doctrine of the Two Cities* (Leiden: Brill, 1991).

Vasaly, Ann. *Livy's Political Philosophy: Power and Personality in Early Rome* (New York: Cambridge University Press, 2015).

BIBLIOGRAPHY 315

Veyne, Paul. "*Humanitas.* Les Romains et les autres." In *L'homme romain,* edited by A. Giardina, translated by M. Aymard and P. Chemla (Paris: Seuil, 2002).

Veyne, Paul. "Une evolution du paganism gréco-romain: Injustice et piété des dieux, leurs orders ou 'oracles.'" *Latomus* 45 (1986): pp. 259–283.

Vogt, Joseph. *Homo Novus, Ein Typus des roemischen Republik* (Stuttgart: W. Kohlhammer, 1926).

Vogt, Katja Maria. *Law, Reason, and the Cosmic City: Political Philosophy in the Early Stoa* (Oxford: Oxford University Press, 2008).

Volk, Katharina. *The Roman Republic of Letters: Scholarship, Philosophy, and Politics in the Age of Cicero and Caesar* (Princeton, NJ: Princeton University Press, 2021).

Von Albrecht, Michael. *Cicero's Style: A Synopsis* (Leiden: Brill, 2003).

Von Campenhausen, Hans F. *The Fathers of the Latin Church,* translated by Manfred Hoffman (London: A&C Black, 1972).

Von Harnack, Adolph. *History of Dogma,* vol. 3 (New York: Russell and Russell, 1958).

Waers, Stephen. *Monarchianism and Origen's Early Trinitarian Theology* (Leiden and Boston: Brill, 2022).

Wallace-Hadrill, Andrew. "The Emperor and His Virtues." *Historia: Zeitschrift fur Alte Geschichte* 30, no. 3 (3rd qtr., 1981).

Wallace-Hadrill, Andrew. *Rome's Cultural Revolution* (Cambridge: Cambridge University Press, 2008).

Waltzing, Jean Pierre. *Apologétique de Tertullien: Commentaire* (Paris: Belles Lettres, 1931).

Warde, Fowler. *Roman Ideas of Deity in the Last Century before The Christian Era: Lectures, 1914* (Whitefish, MT: Kessinger Publishing Reprints, 2007).

Weinstock, Stefan. *Divus Julius* (Oxford: Clarendon Press, 1971).

Wendt, Heidi. *At the Temple Gates: The Religion of Freelance Experts in the Roman Empire* (New York: Oxford University Press, 2016).

Wetzel, James. *Augustine and the Limits of Virtue* (Cambridge: Cambridge University Press, 1992).

Whitmarsh, Timothy. *Battling the Gods: Atheism in the Ancient World* (New York: Knopf, 2015).

Williams, Daniel H. "Constantine, Nicaea, and the 'Fall' of the Church." In *Christian Origins: Theology, Rhetoric, and Community,* edited by Lewis Ayres and Garth Jones (London: Routledge, 1998).

Wilken, Robert. *Aspects of Wisdom in Judaism and Early Christianity* (Notre Dame: University of Notre Dame Press, 1975).

Wilken, Robert. *Judaism and the Early Christian Mind* (Eugene: Wipf & Stock, 1971).

Wilken, Robert. *Liberty in the Things of God: The Christian Origins of Religious Freedom* (New Haven, CT: Yale University Press, 2019).

Winston, David and Gregory E. Sterling. *The Ancestral Philosophy: Hellenistic Philosophy in Second Temple Judaism.* Brown Judaic Studies (Atlanta: Scholars Press, 2001).

Wiseman, T. P. *New Men in the Roman Senate* (London: Oxford University Press, 1971).

Wolterstorff, Nicholas. *Justice: Rights and Wrongs* (Princeton, NJ: Princeton University Press, 2010).

Wynn, Phillip. *Augustine on War and Military Service* (Minneapolis, MN: Fortress Press, 2013).

Yoder, John Howard. *The Politics of Jesus* (Grand Rapids, MI: Eerdmans, 2004).

Young, Frances M. and Andrew Teal. *From Nicaea to Chalcedon: A Guide to the Literature and Its Background* (Grand Rapids, MI: Baker Academic, 2010).

Zanker, Paul. *The Power of Images in the Age of Augustus* (Ann Arbor: University of Michigan Press, 1988).

Index

For the benefit of digital users, indexed terms that span two pages (e.g., 52–53) may, on occasion, appear on only one of those pages.

Actium, Battle of, 40
Acts, Book of, 140
adoptionism, 181n.50
Aeneas, 34, 42–50, 63, 97–98, 189–90, 215–16
  ethical *virtus* of, 43
  failures/vice of, 43, 45–46, 48–49, 50
  martial *virtus* of, 44
  Ovid's account of, 50
  pietas of, 43–45, 48
  Vergil's criticism of, 45–49
  wrath of, 48–49
aequitas, 12–13, 20–21
  in Lactantius, 208, 213–18, 219–20, 221–22, 239, 240–41, 246–55, 274–75
Alexandria, 68–70, 71–72
Anaxagoras, 67–68
Anaximenes, 67
ancestors. *See mos maiorum*
Anchises, 46–50, 98–100, 112, 114–15
Ando, Clifford, 25, 31–32, 47, 56–59, 61–62
Antiochus of Ascalon, 68–70, 71–72, 79n.110, 86, 89–90
apologetic, Latin Christian, 20, 44n.92, 53, 107, 109–12, 117–19, 123–37, 141, 144–45, 146–47, 152–53, 155, 160, 163–64, 189–90
  and Lactantius, 4n.10, 7–8, 10, 17–18, 24–25, 146–47, 155–56, 158–59, 166–67, 174–75, 181, 198–99, 206–7, 242–43, 266–67
Apuleius, 156, 277–79
Aquilius, 122–23
Arianism, 15–16, 174n.28
Aristotle, 69n.62, 75n.90, 88–89, 126–27, 275–76
Arnobius, 2–3, 10
Asclepius, 232–33
Athenagoras, 129–30, 173n.22
Athens, 68–70, 71–72
Augustan literature, 32–53, 97–98, 110–11, 115, 144–45, 158–59
Augustine of Hippo, 70, 123n.54, 128n.73, 167–68, 195n.104

Augustus Caesar, 17–18, 24–26, 27, 31–32, 38–39, 40, 45, 46, 47–48, 49–50, 53, 70–71, 100, 106, 161, 187
  Altar of Peace, 28–29, 42–43
  Divi filius, 40, 57–58
  Shield of Virtus, 28–29, 31–32, 82–83
De ave phoenice (Lactantius), 6
Ayres, Lewis, 15, 17, 178–79

Balmaceda, Catarina, 24–25
baptism
  Lactantius on, 11–12
Barnes, Michel, 56, 59–60, 61–62, 63–64, 74, 87–88, 97–98, 147–48, 167–68, 173–74, 178
Becker, Carl, 111
Brandt, Samuel, 10
brotherhood (Christian), 121, 140–41, 225, 247, 254–55
Buchheit, Vinzenz, 12–14, 21–22, 239, 247

Casali, Servio, 49–50
Catholic Church
  in Lactantius, 174n.25, 182n.53, 184, 204, 269–70
Cato the Elder, 26–27, 29–30
Cato the Younger, 34, 35, 36–38, 52n.128, 78–79, 119–20
  suicide, 120
Christ, 1, 9–10, 17, 22, 53, 110, 131–32, 157–58
  ascension of, 194–95
  atonement, 166–67, 203
  baptism of, 191
  begotten, 132–33
  birth of, 129–31, 183, 191
  death of, 202–3, 211, 213–14, 221–22, 228
  deeds of, 135–37, 142–44, 176–77, 183, 186, 188, 191–94, 202–3, 206, 211
  dignitas of, 237–38
  exaltation of, 190
  exemplum virtutis, 18–19, 20–21, 22, 110–11, 123, 136–37, 142, 144–45, 163–64, 186, 189–90, 198, 202–3, 206–8, 239, 252–53, 263–65

318 INDEX

Christ (*cont.*)
forgiveness of, 280–81
God from God, 130–31
healing ministry of, 137, 191, 192, 201–2,
218–19, 223, 280–81
honor of, 189–90
humanity of, 181, 182, 183, 184, 186–87, 200
humility of, 190, 208, 223, 263–64
incarnation of, 18–19, 130–31, 132–33, 141,
181–86, 195–96, 200
justice and, 143, 186–87, 192–94, 196–97,
202–3, 206, 208
kingship, 172, 186, 189–90, 191, 192,
193, 216–17
light, 137–38, 201–2, 210, 226–27, 229–30,
236–37, 242–43
light from light, 130–31
logos, 192
maiestas, 189–90
Mary and, 130–31, 181
mediator, 183, 184–86
Melchizedek, 182
mercy of, 252–53
ministry of, 181, 186–90, 207–8, 221–22,
236, 252–53
Name, 237–38
natural law and, 18–19, 21
"new and living law," 194–96, 202, 204, 241–
42, 244–45, 246
obedience to Father, 248–49
opera virtutum—verba doctrinae, 132–33,
135–36, 142–43, 146, 166, 167–68, 196–
97, 200, 202, 207–8, 218–19, 240–41
orator perfectus, 194–203
passion of, 132–33, 136, 143, 144–45, 146,
176–77, 183–84, 187, 192–93, 194, 199,
200, 211, 216–17, 218–19, 228
patientia of, 123, 131–32, 143, 144, 146,
166, 192–93, 194, 203, 216–17,
231, 255–65
peace, 189–90, 216–17
precepts/mandates of, 139–40, 206, 207–8
rectus status and, 230, 231–32, 234–
35, 237–38
relation to Father, 18–19, 21, 130–31,
173, 216–17, 219–20, 223, 225, 241–
42, 246–55
resurrection of, 213–14, 221–22
.reveals Father, 20–21, 23, 123, 135–36, 141,
142, 143–44, 166–68, 202, 218–19, 221–
22, 229–30, 245–46
Sage, 187, 192–93, 196–97, 228, 238
species, 18, 219

spirit, 168–70, 173–74, 177
suffering of, 198, 211–12, 228, 237–38
teacher, 139–40, 175–76, 186–87, 188, 189,
193–94, 196–97, 198, 200, 202–3, 204,
206, 211, 218–19, 240, 241–42, 243–
44, 246
temple, 186–87
unity with Father, 133–34, 135–36, 138–39,
142, 171, 177
virtus, 1–2, 15–16, 18–19, 135–36, 139, 163–
64, 169–70, 172–73, 176–78, 183, 186–
87, 188, 189, 191, 193–94, 195–97, 200,
201–2, 206, 207–8, 212–13, 228, 229–30,
238, 245–46, 281
Wisdom, 133–34, 178, 211, 216–17, 218–19,
228, 238, 241–42, 244–45
Word of God, 168–69, 172–73, 175, 180, 185,
191–92, 264–65
Christian apologetic. *See* Latin Christian
apologetic
Christian love
caritas, 212, 239
diligere, 248–49
enemies, 260
Christian martyrs, 60–61, 119–20, 122–23,
167–68, 230, 254, 279
like Republican heroes, 119–20, 122, 123
Christology of Lactantius, 9, 14–15, 18, 20–21,
155, 164–65, 166–67, 168–81, 206–7,
209, 219–20, 229–38
angels and, 169n.10, 170, 172–77, 204
divine unity, 170–71, 176–77, 178–79, 180–
81, 218–19, 220, 223, 225
doctor iustitiae, 168–69, 188
dux virtutis, 168–69, 216–17
effigies, 178n.40, 180–81, 244–45
eternal life, 167, 214–15, 256–57
fides, 179, 180, 189–90, 192–93, 216–17
Incarnation, 176–77, 181–86, 198–99, 200,
211–12, 239
iustus homo, 227–28, 255–57, 258, 259
iustus et sapiens, 227–28, 230, 246
maiestas, 171–72
maxima potestas, 176–77
mediation, 184–85
mission and ministry, 186–90, 201, 225–26
moral knowledge, 167, 245–46, 280–81, 282
Name, 169–70
opera, 191–94
opera virtutum—verba doctrinae, 132–33,
135–36, 142–43, 146, 166, 167–68, 196–
97, 200, 202, 207–8, 218–19, 240–41
orator perfectus, 194–203

INDEX 319

passion, 198, 201, 202, 225–26, 238, 255–56, 262–63
rectus status, 229–38
rex, 172, 189–90, 201
Sage, 187, 201, 237–38
sight of the Father, 167–68, 207–8, 240–41
soteriology, 181, 185–86, 197, 198–99, 200, 203, 204, 218–19
traditional, 167–68, 173–75, 180–81, 183, 186, 194–95, 201, 204, 207–8
Veritas, 259
viator bonus et iustus, 227–28
virtus, 168–69, 171–73, 180, 198, 201, 238
Word, 172–73, 175, 176, 180, 264–65
Chryssipus, 79n.110, 81n.115, 126–27
Cicero, 8–9, 10–11, 14–15, 17–18, 19–20, 24–25, 32–33, 44–45, 55–56, 60–61, 68–97, 104–6, 107, 110–12, 115, 117–18, 123–24, 125, 126–27, 129–30, 131, 135–36, 144–45, 147–49, 150, 153–54, 156, 162–63, 167–68, 186–87, 188, 189–90, 210, 217–18, 219, 222, 223–24, 239, 276–77, 280–81
Academica, 85–91, 219
background of, 68–71
Balbus, 70–71, 89–91, 92, 94, 96–97, 98–99, 101, 103, 111–12, 114n.16, 115, 133–34, 135–36
bonitas divina, 93n.182
Carneades, 214–15, 219–20, 226–28, 237–38
Catalus, 85–86
cosmos, 84–85, 86, 88, 91–92
Cotta, 90n.169, 96n.193, 111–12
divinus vir, 82
expressam effigiem, 244–45
De finibus, 66–67, 75–77, 147–48, 149
God in, 77–78, 79–82, 84–86, 88–94, 95, 96, 107
De inventione, 71–77, 101, 149, 196–97
Lactantius's critique of, 208, 213–15, 218, 219–20, 226–27, 230, 240–47, 249–50, 282
law in, 71–72, 73, 74–75, 80–81
De legibus, 77–85, 121, 125
Marcus, 80–81, 82
medicine in, 71–72, 75, 76–77
mens, 80–81, 84–85, 96, 99–100, 104, 125, 126–27, 128–29, 153–54, 179, 180
De natura deorum, 66–68, 85–86, 89–94, 101, 115, 126–27, 129–30, 131, 163
natural law, 243–44, 282
nomen, 76, 92, 103, 106, 107, 127
numen, 80–81
De officiis, 244–45, 250

De oratore, 74–75, 77–78, 195
Partitiones oratoriae, 222
Philippics, 30
Piso, 76–77, 100–1
political theology of, 56, 72–73, 77–78, 85–86, 89, 92, 118–19
power causality in, 66–67, 73, 85–86, 90–93, 95–97, 149–50
Pro Sestio, 30
qualitas, 87–89, 102, 106–7, 129–30
De re publica, 30, 77–85, 94–95, 96, 116–17, 125, 195, 243–44
Scipio Africanus, 79–81, 82–84, 161
Scipio, 111–12, 113–14, 117
Somnium Scipionis, 84–85, 94–96, 98–99, 104–5, 125, 158n.43
teleology in, 76, 77–78, 94, 96
Tullia, 85–86, 95–96
Tusculanae disputationes, 85–86, 94–97, 128–29
unity of virtues, 75–76, 101–2
Varro, 70–71, 86–87, 89–91, 92, 99, 170n.15
Velleius, 66–68, 70–71, 92, 111–12
vis/power in, 73–76, 78–79, 80–81, 86–87, 88–91, 99
civil wars (Rome), 17–18, 32–33, 47, 53, 106
Cleanthes, 131
Clement of Alexandria, 16n.74, 128n.76
clementia, 28–29, 84, 105, 106–7
Colossians, Epistle to
3:1–2, 232–34
Colot, Blandine, 13–14, 21–22
Constantine, 1, 2–4, 5–6, 14–16, 22, 265–66, 269–73
Conte, Gian Biagio, 43, 49
conversion of Lactantius, 4–5, 10
1 Corinthians, Epistle to
1:18–24, 210–11
1:20, 210–11
1:20–24, 211
1:24, 153–54n.27, 159n.48, 170n.13, 178n.40
3:19, 210
6:14, 275
6:15–16, 273–75
13:13, 121n.47
2 Corinthians, Epistle to
3:12–16, 211, 212–13
cosmology, 104–5, 106
Council of Arles, 269–70
Crassus, 77–78
creation, 8, 99, 129, 140, 141, 152–53, 157, 216–17, 225
ex nihilo, 157, 158

320 INDEX

Crispus Caesar, 3–4
cultus deorum, 8, 9–10, 11–12, 53, 89–90. *See also* pantheon
Cyprian, 2–3, 7–8, 12–13, 17–19, 20, 21, 111, 117–18, 123n.54, 132–33, 136–44, 147, 152–53, 167–69, 174–75, 181, 182, 185–86, 190, 193, 204, 207–8, 219, 229–30, 234–35, 245–46, 250–51, 256–57, 259, 263–64
  aequitas in, 267–68
  On Almsgiving, 250–52
  bishopric, 136–37
  De bono patientiae, 141–42, 166, 194
  Christology, 136–37, 139–40, 141, 142, 144, 260–61, 262–63, 264–65
  cultor dei in, 231
  Ad Demetrianum, 230, 231, 232–34
  divine unity in, 138–39
  ecclesiology of, 137–39, 140, 144, 204, 228
  economic teaching of, 139, 140
  eternal life in, 140
  ethics of, 136–37, 140, 142, 144, 228
  exemplum aequitatis, 250, 251
  fear of God in, 254
  human equality in, 246–47
  influence on Lactantius, 144, 241–42
  justice in, 143
  De lapsis, 277–81
  De opere et eleemosynis, 144, 240
  politics of, 136–37
  Ad quirinum, 10, 168–69, 171–72, 174–75, 183, 190, 232–33, 236–37, 252, 254, 259, 260–61, 262–63, 264–65, 266–67, 282
  rectus status, 230, 232–33, 236–37
  schism, 138–39
  self-knowledge, 231
  De unitate ecclesiae, 137–38
  usury in, 260–61
Cyril of Alexandria, 128n.76

D'Alès, Adhémar, 142
Daniel, Book of, 190
  7:13–14, 189, 190
Decian Persecution, 137
Democritus, 59–60, 63–64
Deuteronomy, Book of, 260
  32:35, 264–65
Didache, 216n.48
Digeser, Elizabeth DePalma, 14–15, 269–70
dignitas, 91n.179, 142
Dillon, John, 86
Diocles, 74n.84
Diocletian, 2–3, 7–8, 31–32, 58, 158, 161, 187, 270

persecution, 3–4, 5–6, 13–14, 18, 164, 212
  Tetrarchy, 6, 25, 162n.60
divine favor, 28–29, 32, 42, 47, 57
  cause of victory, 25
  effect of *virtus*, 28–29, 32, 39, 44–45, 52–53
divine simplicity. *See* under God
divine titles, 125, 127, 133–34, 154–55, 162–63
divinization, 55, 58, 60–61, 79, 81, 84–86, 89–90, 93, 94, 95, 96–97, 98–99, 117–18, 160, 163, 189
  of Caesar, 89–90
  of Romulus, 42, 82–84, 109, 123, 135–36
  of Tullia, 95–96, 135–36
double-love commandment (of Jesus), 12–13, 239, 240–41, 247, 256–57
dualism
  of Lactantius, 9, 21–22

Edmondson, Jonathan, 40
Elysium, 100
Empedocles, 59–60, 63–64, 75n.90, 170n.15
emperor, 25, 57, 101, 113–14, 120, 163–64, 193
  deified, 51, 57–58, 180
  diffused power, 58
  divine favor, 57–58
  dynastic continuity, 57–58
  curator legum et morum, 25, 49–50, 57–58
  pater patriae, 25–26, 57–58, 104–5
  pietas of, 25
  power (=*virtus*) of, 58–59, 104–5
Empire (Roman), 70–71, 114–15, 118
empiricism, 60–61, 72–73, 74n.84
Ennius, 30, 82n.123, 117–18, 212
Ephesians, Epistle to, 195n.103
  1:18, 201–2
  4:25–26, 259, 263–64
  4:26–29, 264–65
  4:29, 263–64
  5:31, 273–74
Epicureanism, 59–60, 62–68, 76–79, 86, 89–90, 94–95, 96, 101, 106, 112, 112–13n.12, 113–14, 115, 125, 242–43, 249–50
  materialism, 67–68, 106, 112
Epicurus, 62–64, 167–68
Epitome (Lactantius), 232–33, 239, 265–67, 268, 269–71, 272
eternal life, 9–10, 18
  ethics and, 214–18
  knowledge of, 214–15, 227–28
  in Lactantius, 151–52, 184–85, 187, 191, 194, 199, 204, 206–7, 209, 213–18, 223–24, 227–28, 276–77, 279
ethics of Lactantius, 21, 152, 161–62, 166–67, 179, 180, 186, 189, 197, 207–14, 229–38

INDEX 321

abjecti, 252–53
adfectum pietatis, 247, 248
aequitas, 223–24, 225–26, 246–55, 268–69, 274–75, 276
almsgiving, 247–48, 252–53, 277–79
anger, 198–99, 266–67, 268–69, 271, 272, 280–81
body, 197–99, 235, 277–79
burial of dead, 252–53
chastity, 265–66
Christology and, 213–17, 225–26, 242–43, 245, 282
critique of classical Roman philosophy, 241–42, 243–44, 248, 249–50, 253–54, 277–79, 281
cultor dei, 256–57, 258–59, 276–82
cupiditas, 265–66
despair, 279–80
divine nature and, 246–49
emotion (defense of), 240–42, 253–55, 265–66, 268, 270
envy, 280–81
epistemology, 206–7, 208–9, 210, 212–13, 219–20, 223, 227–28, 236–37, 243–44
eternal life, 245, 256–57, 276–79
false worship, 199
fear of death, 198–99, 202–3, 204, 214, 268
fear of God, 254, 279
generosity, 250, 260
glory, 256–57, 277–79
gradus virtutis, 277–79
greed, 279
healing/health, 280–81
hospitality, 252
humanitas, 240–42, 244–45, 246–55, 256–57, 261, 266–68, 272–73, 274–76
ignorance, 209, 210, 211, 222, 227–28, 234–37, 242–43
image of God, 208, 247–50
indignum, 234–35
ira parentum, 265–66, 268–69
iustus homo, 255–57, 259–61, 265–66, 277–79, 281
justice, 206–7, 214–15, 218–22, 243–44, 246–47, 265–66, 268–69, 274–75, 281–82
killing, 241–42, 265–73
    capital punishment, 268–69
    military service, 265–73
    self-defense, 272
    suicide, 268–69
love, 260, 261
lying, 258–59
marriage and sexuality, 21, 240–42, 255–56, 265–66, 273–76

adultery, 273–75, 276
celibacy, 273–74
divorce, 276
homosexuality, 273–74
lust, 198–99, 200, 276, 279, 280–81
pederasty, 273–74
prostitution, 273–74
misericordia, 240, 246–47, 251, 255–56, 272, 281
natural law, 241–42
non-retaliation, 255–56, 261–62, 264–65
officia, 240–41
ordered society, 206–7
orphans, 252
pain, 199–200, 202–3, 237–38
patientia, 240–41, 254, 255–57, 265–66, 281–82
Pauline Rule, 208–9, 210–11, 212, 214–15, 218, 225–26
peace, 281
penitence (as medicine), 276–82
perversitas, 234–35
pietas, 222–23, 247
pleasure, 265–67
praecepta iustitiae, 240–41, 247–48
sanus, 281
Satan, 273–74
the sick, 252–53
sin, 198, 199, 204, 233–34, 277–79
    thoughts, words, deeds, 277–79
usury, 259–61
viator bonus et iustus, 227–28, 280
vice, 197–99
violence, 198, 240–41, 261–62, 264–65, 268
virtus, 276, 277–79, 282
wealth, 21, 227–28, 240–42, 247–48, 251–52, 259–60
widows, 252
Euhemerism/Euhemerus, 8, 82n.123, 117–18, 158–59, 160
Eusebius, 216n.48
exemplarity, 1–2, 9, 18–19, 26, 37, 38–39, 40–41, 60–61, 78–79, 84, 93, 114–15, 119, 122, 123, 141, 142, 161–62, 163, 186
Ezekiel, Book of, 260–61
    18:5–9, 261

faith, hope, and love, 121
fall of man, 197–98, 235
false worship, 9–10, 152–53
Fears, J. Rufus, 28–29
felicitas, 143–44
Flavius the Grammarian, 2–3

322 INDEX

founding of Rome, 40–41
  Livy's retelling, 40–41, 83–84
Freund, Stefan, 13–15, 255–56

Genesis, Book of, 8, 99n.205
  2:24, 273–74
  3, 230–31
gnosis, 276–79
God
  aequitas of, 140–41
  benefits/effects, 127–28, 140–41, 146, 152–
    53, 162–63, 223–24, 260, 261
  in Cicero, 79
  creator, 32, 127, 152–53, 156, 157–58, 159,
    169–70, 171–72, 225, 233–34
  dator vitae, 157–58, 162–64, 187, 192, 202
  emotions (just), 6, 254–55, 270, 271–72
  humanitas of, 271–73
  impassible, 155–56, 162–63
  incorruptible, 155–56
  ineffable, 156, 159
  inner life of, 207–8, 240–41, 246–
    47, 248–49
  judgment of, 6, 267–68, 270–73, 279
  knowledge of, 11–12, 20, 23, 127–28, 167–
    68, 247
  as light, 141, 223–24, 267–68
  love of, 179, 180n.47, 253–54, 270–73
  monarch, 272–73
  obedience to, 142
  oneness, 124, 153–56, 158, 171, 180, 219–20,
    224, 245–46
  Parent, 124–25, 127, 156, 233–34, 237–
    38, 254–55
  paterfamilias, 9, 15–16, 173n.20, 179n.41, 280
  patientia of, 131–33, 141
  power of,
    complete power, 153–56, 157, 159, 160–
      61, 221–22
    maiestas, 118–19, 161, 176–77, 188
    ratio, 125–27, 129, 130, 158, 159
    virtus, 81, 106–7, 124–25, 127–28, 129,
      132–33, 142, 143, 152–53, 157–58, 159,
      188, 218–19, 244–45
    vis/potestas, 77–83, 84–86, 88–94, 95, 96–
      97, 101–5, 106–8, 115, 116–17, 122–36,
      137–44, 147–64, 176, 245–46
    weakness of pantheon vs., 159–63
  providence, 89, 92, 96, 117, 124–25, 152–53
  relation to Son, 18–19, 21, 130–31, 173, 219–
    20, 223, 225, 241–42, 246–55
  revealed by Christ, 20–21, 23, 166–68
  source and origin, 161, 182, 218–19, 245–46

source-stream-flow, 130–31, 137, 138–39,
    173n.20, 173, 179, 180, 218–20, 221–22,
    224, 225–26, 276–77, 282
  spiritus, 125–27, 130
  unity with Son, 133–34, 135–36, 138–39, 142,
    171, 176–77
  will of, 176, 186–87
  wisdom of, 212–13
  works of, 127–29, 159, 161, 184
  wrath of, 253–55, 264–65, 270–73
gods, traditional Roman, 63, 70–71, 77–78, 79,
    92–94, 96–97, 102–3, 106, 113, 114n.16,
    117–18, 131, 133–34
  benefits/effects, 93n.182, 93, 94, 102–
    3, 162–63
  Ceres, 92–93, 94
  Cupid, 162–63
  Hercules, 28–29, 31–32, 41, 94, 100–1, 103,
    104–5, 161, 162n.60, 163
  household, 43
  images, 244–45
  Jupiter, 44–45, 49, 162n.60, 162–63, 171–72
  Lactantius's critique of, 147, 152–58, 159,
    160, 161, 162–63, 164–65, 171, 173–74,
    180, 181–82, 187, 210, 214–15, 231–
    32, 244–45
  Liber, 92–93, 103
  Mars, 40, 42–43
  Mercury, 93, 97–98, 103
  power/*vis* of, 96–99, 131
  Rome's founders and, 41
  "satellites and ministers," 155, 173–74
  Saturn, 46, 162–63, 171–72
  Venus, 45, 92–93, 97–98
  violence, 187
  virtus and, 55, 117–18, 163–64
  weakness (*fragilitas/imbecillitas*) of, 154–55,
    159, 160–64
Gregory of Nyssa, 59–60
Grillmeier, Aloys, 12, 15–16

Hatzimichali, Myrto, 68–70
Hebrews, Book of, 182, 184–85
  1, 171n.16, 172–73
  1:1–7, 168–69, 170n.13, 178n.40, 182n.52
  2:9, 199n.125
  2:14–15, 199n.125
Heim, François, 15–16
Hellenistic philosophy, 19, 31, 35, 55, 70–73, 74,
    77–78, 105, 126–27, 148–49
  Hippocratic medicine, 59–60, 65, 68–70,
    74, 87–88
  influence on Rome, 62, 105

INDEX 323

medical theory, 60–61, 64, 70, 71–73, 74–75, 83–84, 97–98, 100, 104–5, 106, 148–49, 170n.15

mixture theory, 8, 19–20, 56, 60–61, 63–64, 65–66, 74–77, 82, 86, 88, 90–91, 96, 98–99, 100–1, 106–7, 150–51, 152, 161–62

virtus and, 8, 19–20, 26, 33–34

heretical sects
Anthropians, 184
Marcionites, 184
Novatianists, 184
Phrygians, 184
Valentinians, 184

Hermes Trismegistus, 8, 13n.58, 169–70, 182–83, 220–21

Hermetic Gnosticism, 11–12, 182n.52, 203, 229–30, 232–33, 239

Hilary of Poitiers, 59–60

Holy Spirit, 9, 21–22, 159, 177n.38

Homer, 80

Honos et Virtus (temple), 26–27, 28–29, 93

hope, 217–18

Horace, 45–46, 47n.110

humanitas, 18–19, 84, 240–41, 244–45, 246–55, 257, 261, 266–67, 270, 272–73, 274–76

idolatry, 8, 160–61, 167, 197, 230–31, 232–35, 256–57, 258

immortality. *See* eternal life

imperial ideology/theology, 19, 20, 25–26, 44, 49, 55–56, 57–62, 70, 96–97, 107, 115, 116, 117, 144–45, 160, 162n.60, 189–90
Christianity and, 58–59, 131
criticism of, 19, 20, 51, 111–12, 115, 116, 124, 144–45, 158–59

imperium, 25, 35, 41, 44–45, 53, 96–97, 105–6, 114–15, 122, 124n.56, 130, 268
Aeneas and, 46, 47
Augustan narrative, 31–32, 42–43, 117–18
critique of, 37, 49–50, 53, 116, 179, 206–7
divine favor and, 44
reward for *virtus*, 35–36
self-presentation of, 110, 111–12, 113–14, 118, 161

Ingremeau, Christiane, 253–54, 269–70

De ira dei (Lactantius), 6, 239, 254–55, 270–71, 272–73

Irenaeus of Lyons, 186

Isaiah, Book of, 256–57
2:3–5, 209n.14
7:14, 99n.205
9, 210–11
9:1–2, 209n.14

11:10, 209n.14
42:6, 236–37
45:1–3, 186n.69
53:6, 209n.14

Israelites, 188

Jerome, 2–4, 9

1 John, Book of
1:1–3, 235
1:2, 235–36
2:6, 219
5:7, 138–39

John, Gospel of, 144, 242–43, 262–63
1:1, 174–75
1:1–5, 204
1:3, 174–75, 177n.38
1:4–5, 197–98, 235
1:5, 210–11, 235–36, 282
1:9–10, 209n.14
10:30, 138–39
10:38–41, 135–36
13:15–17, 264–65

John, St. the Evangelist, 135–36, 198, 210, 219, 242–43
light, Johannine, 137, 210, 235, 236–37, 242–44

Julius Caesar, 25, 27, 28–29, 36–37, 40, 47, 49–50, 52, 77–78, 85–86, 120, 189–90

Julius Proculus, 42, 83–84, 109, 117–18, 135–36

justice, 9, 12–13, 18–19, 28–29, 79, 84, 103, 106–7, 118, 122, 141, 143, 230, 237–38, 275–76
in Lactantius, 166, 193–94, 207–8, 218–22, 223, 245, 247
as *pietas* + *aequitas*, 208, 220–28, 239, 240–41, 248

Justin Martyr, 129–30, 186

Juvenal
Satires, 118–19, 122

Kendeffy, Gábor, 210–11

Koortbojian, Michael, 89–90

de Labriolle, Pierre, 11

Laelius, 114n.16

Larentia, 40–41

Late Republic, 17–18, 24–25, 27, 35, 53, 67, 70–71

Lavinia, 48–49

Lavinium, 28

Licinius, 5–6, 270–71

Livy, 38–42, 55, 83–84, 110–11, 117–18, 123, 188

324 INDEX

Lloyd, Daniel, 184
Loi, Vincenzo, 12, 176, 229–30, 252
Lucan, 49–50, 51–53, 55, 106, 110–11, 118–19
    Pharsalia, 51–53, 62, 115–16, 121,
        180, 189–90
Lucca Conference, 77–78
Lucilius, 243–45, 258–59
Lucretius, 8, 24–25, 42–43, 55–56, 62–70, 75,
        78–79, 86, 87, 88–89, 94–95, 99, 107,
        113, 167–68, 170n.15, 210
  ethics of, 66
  Lactantius' critique of, 241–42
  materialism, 66
  politics of, 66
  De rerum natura, 62–65, 77–78, 112, 249–50
Luke, Gospel of, 240–42, 261
  1:35, 170n.13
  6:20–49, 255–56, 258
  6:22, 279
  6:28, 262, 263–65
  6:29–31, 262
  6:32, 261
  6:32–36, 259, 260–61
  12:20/33, 251
  12:33, 139–40
  14:8–11, 251
  14:12, 252

Manichaeism, 31–32
Marc Antony, 40
Marcus Claudius Marcellus, 26–27, 63, 78–79, 93
Marius, 26–27, 28–29, 35, 122
Mark, Gospel of
  10:8, 273–74
Martial, 187
materia, 86–89, 89n.161, 106
Matthew, Gospel of, 186, 241–42, 261, 273–74
  2:23, 209n.14
  5, 143–44
  5:21, 266–67
  5–7, 255–56, 258, 275–76, 281
  6:1–4, 257–58, 280–81
  6:1–7, 257
  6:19–21, 139–40
  7:12, 275–76
  7:15, 275
  11:5, 137, 280–81
  16:18, 137
  19, 275–76
  19:4, 276
  19:5, 273–74
  19:9, 276
  22:36–40, 239, 240–41, 247

Maximian, 6, 162n.60
Maximin Daza, 6
McDonnell, Myles, 16n.72, 24–25, 28–29, 33–
    34, 93–94n.183, 100n.210
McGuckin, John, 12–13
Mehl, David, 65–66
Minucius Felix, 7–8, 17–19, 111–24, 132–33,
    135–37, 152–53, 156, 158–59, 163, 179,
    182, 214, 229–30, 242–43, 254, 282
  Caecilius Natalis, 111–15, 116–17, 125
  human freedom, 113
  Octavius, 111–23, 131–32, 146–47, 155
  providence, 113–14, 115–16, 117, 126–27
  rectus status, 230
Mithridates, 68–70
Moatti, Claude, 68–70
Momigliano, Arnaldo, 77–78
Monarchianism. *See* under Tertullian
Monat, Pierre, 12–13, 182, 183, 186, 190, 201,
    202, 257–58
De mortibus persecutorum (Lactantius),
    6, 270–71
mos maiorum, 27, 28–30, 34, 35–37, 38, 41–42,
    62, 93, 111–12, 113, 114n.16, 114–15,
    118–19, 119n.36, 120–21, 122, 144–45
Moses, 172–73, 188, 194–95, 212–13
Mucius, 122–23

natura, 60–61, 63–64, 65–67, 68–73, 74–75,
    76–77, 78–79, 80–81, 86–87, 88–89,
    90–91, 94, 96, 97–98, 99, 103–4, 106–7,
    113. *See also* under power, "power and
    nature"
natural law, 18–19, 67–68, 240–41, 281. *See also*
    under Cicero
Neoplatonism, 14–15, 167–68
Nero, 49–50, 51, 52, 53, 55, 96–97, 104–5, 120
Nicene Council, 59–60
Nicholson, Oliver, 21–22, 268–69
Nicomedia, 3–4, 271–72
nobiles, 27, 30, 122
Nock, Arthur Darby, 58
Novatian, 4–5, 15, 17–19, 20, 21, 147, 152–53,
    155–56, 158, 160–61, 167–68, 176–77,
    178–79, 181, 183, 185–86, 204
  De Trinitate, 20, 184
novi homines, 30
Numa Pompilius, 25–26, 84
Numitor, 41

Octavian. *See* Augustus Caesar
Odysseus, 63
De opificio dei (Lactantius), 5–6, 11–12

INDEX 325

Origen, 16n.74, 59–60, 171n.16, 178n.40, 201, 204
De Principiis, 184–86
Ovid, 8, 49–51, 106

Panaetius, 68–70
paterfamilias, 178–79. *See also* under God
patientia, 18–19, 20–21, 119, 122–23, 128–29, 132–33, 136–44, 146, 166, 188, 194, 204, 206, 231, 237–38, 240–41, 254, 255–65
   as *summa virtus*, 123, 131–33, 144–45, 192–93, 203, 255–57
Paul, Apostle, 7–8, 121, 183, 185n.63, 190, 197, 199, 202, 219, 230, 231–33, 261
1 Peter, Epistle of, 262–63
   2:21–23, 263
Philippians, Epistle to
   2:5–11, 189, 190, 204, 225–26, 262
Philo of Larissa, 68–70, 71–72
philosophy (Roman), 70, 101, 110, 147, 153–54
   and Lactantius, 147, 149–50, 206–7, 210–11, 212, 214–16, 240–41
   monotheism, 127, 130
   philosophical grammar, 56, 59–60, 70–71, 73, 75, 76–77, 85–86, 123–24
Pichon, René, 10, 11–12, 15–16
pietas, 12–13, 18, 28–30, 32, 34, 44–45, 78–79, 82–83, 114–15, 121, 122, 163–64
   established by emperor, 58, 78–79
   in Lactantius, 208, 221–28, 239, 240–41, 247
Plato, 59–60, 68–70, 72–73, 74, 75n.90, 82–83, 96, 101–2n.217, 128n.73, 152–53
   dependent pairs, 87–88
   God in, 127, 152–53
   Phaedrus, 94–95, 128–29
   Republic, 91–92, 93n.182, 128–29
   Theatetus, 87–88
   Timaeus, 126–27, 156, 159
Platonism, 86, 155–56
Pliny the Elder, 69n.63
Plutarch, 69n.62
pneumatology, 175–76n.32, 177n.38
political theology, 35, 39–40, 42–43, 57–58, 89, 100, 101, 104–5, 118, 126
politics (Roman), 22, 24–25, 30, 49–50, 55, 58–59, 70–71, 96–97, 106–7, 119, 135–36, 188, 214–15
   citizenship, 122
   constitutions, 82
   in Lactantius, 164, 166–67
   and religion, 5–6, 42, 82
Pompey the Great, 28–29, 47, 52, 77–78, 189–90
Porphyry, 184–85n.62

Posidonius, 68–70
power
   doctrine of God
      in Cicero, 77–82, 84–86, 88–94, 95, 96, 106–8
      in Cyprian, 137–44
      in Lactantius, 147–64
      in Minucius Felix, 115, 116–17, 122–29
   power causality, 59–60, 63–64, 66–67, 71–72, 73, 85–86, 87–88, 90–93, 95–97, 101, 125, 126–29, 130–33, 135, 141, 142–43, 144–45, 152–53
      in Cicero, 66–67, 71–72, 85–86, 90–91, 95–96, 149–50
      in Lactantius, 147–58, 159, 161, 164–65, 170, 175–76, 178–79, 180, 186–87, 200, 202
      in Lucretius, 62–66
      X from X causality, 60–61, 88–89, 93–94n.183, 97–98, 131, 151–52, 159, 178–79
   "power and nature," 60–61, 63–64, 67, 68–70, 71–72, 73, 74–75, 76–77, 96, 97–98, 106, 141, 149–50
      in Seneca, 96–97, 101–5, 106–8, 131, 133–34
      in Tertullian, 129–36
      in Vergil, 96–101, 107–8, 125
   "technical sense of power," 59–60, 62, 70–73, 84–85, 89–90, 96, 97–98, 103, 123–24, 126–27, 130, 135–36, 144–45, 164–65
      in Lactantius, 147–48, 152–58, 167–68, 178–79
   vis/potestas/virtus, 1–2, 17, 18–20, 30, 59–62, 63–72, 73–77, 78–79, 80–81, 82–84, 86–87, 89, 90–91, 92–93, 95, 96, 97–98, 100–1, 102–6, 107, 123–25, 127, 133–34, 141, 144–45, 147–48, 150, 151–52, 153–55, 208, 213–14
power theology. *See* power causality
Pre-Socratics, 59–60
prophets, 169–70, 183, 209
Proverbs, Book of
   8, 168–69, 170n.13, 171n.16, 177n.38
   8:22–31, 173–74
   9, 182n.52
Psalms, Book of
   13, 260
   33:6, 168–69, 173, 174–75, 177n.38
   42:1, 174–75
   44:2, 173
   109:1, 186n.69
Pythagorus, 216n.48

Q. Caedicius, 26–27
Q. Maximus, 78–79

326 INDEX

qualitas, 87–89, 90–91, 102, 106–7, 129–30
Quintilian, 195, 274–75
 orator perfectus, 195–97

reason, 67–70, 89, 90–92, 99–100, 104–5, 106, 115, 124n.56, 126–27
rectus status, 9–10, 11–12
 Christ and, 9–10, 230, 231–32, 234–35, 237–38
 cultor dei and, 229–30, 232–34, 235, 236, 237, 238
 in Lactantius, 160–61, 229–38, 241–43, 245–46
Regulus, 122–23
religio, 8, 9–10, 12, 63, 118, 247. *See also religio-sapientia* dyad
religio-sapientia dyad, 11–12, 17, 21–22, 218–20, 222, 242–43, 245–46
rhetoric, 2–3, 7–8, 9, 70, 111–12, 144–45, 195–97, 212
 Cicero and, 71–75
 of Lactantius, 9n.39, 13–14
Roman elite, 55–57, 61–62, 66, 70–71, 89–90, 111–12, 118–19, 122, 195
Roman games, 266–67
Roman identity, 24–25, 32–33, 38–39, 53, 55, 78–79, 84, 106
Roman law, 180–81, 274–76
Roman Republic
 decline and collapse of, 34, 38–39, 53, 68–70, 106, 144–45
Roman theater, 266–67
Romans, Epistle to, 204, 230
 1, 235, 236
 1:3–4, 183
 1:18–24, 198n.122
 1:22–23, 234
 1:22–32, 160–61, 197, 204, 233–35, 236
 1:23, 230–31
 1:23–25, 231, 235
 1:26, 273–74
 7:1–14, 198–99
 7:24, 197–98
 8:32, 226–27
 12:14–19, 264–65
Romulus, 25–26, 40, 42–43, 60–61, 63, 82–83, 84, 94, 95, 117–18, 135–36, 143
 Remus and, 40–42

Sabine women, 82–83
sacrifice, 48, 122
Sallust, 33–38, 55, 62–63, 107, 118–19, 119n.36, 193
 Bellum Catalinae, 36

sapientia, 9–10, 76–77, 89. *See also religio-sapientia* dyad
Scipio Africanus, 78–80, 92, 135–36, 143, 188, 210
Scribonius Largus, 69n.63
Second Coming, 217–18
Sedley, David, 87·
Senate, 25–27, 38, 40
Seneca, 24–25, 49–50, 53, 55–56, 96–97, 101, 102, 103, 104–7, 110–11, 119–21, 120n.41, 123–24, 129–30, 131, 133–34, 144–45, 153–54, 163–64, 188, 217–18, 219, 276–77
 De beneficiis, 102–3, 104–5, 129–30, 131, 133–34, 135–36
 De clementia, 104–5
 Epistulam 66, 101–2
 ethics, 101
 God, 103–5
 Stoicism, 101–2
 suicide, 120
 theology, 101, 104–5
 virtus in, 101–4, 105
Sermon on the Mount, 255–56, 257, 259, 260, 261, 264–65, 273–75, 276–77, 282
Servius, 45–46
Sicca Proconsularis, 2–3
Skepticism, 112–13n.12
slavery, 224, 270–71, 276
Socrates, 114n.16
Sossianus Hierocles, 7–8
soul, 64–66, 76–77, 85–86, 90–91, 94–95, 96, 98–99, 100, 112, 125, 156, 185–86
 divine, 95
 immortality of, 125
 in Lactantius, 150, 151, 152
 material, 112
 mortality of, 64, 66, 112–13n.12
Speusippus, 126–27
Stevenson, Tom, 40–41
Stoicism, 44–45, 59–60, 66–67, 68–70, 76–77, 81–82, 88–90, 92, 97n.194, 97–98, 99, 101, 104–5, 106, 107, 112–13n.12, 115, 124n.56, 130, 147–48, 150, 153–54, 155–56, 158, 161, 162–63, 173n.22, 192–93, 229–30, 239, 249–50
 eternal soul, 126, 160
 fire, 90–91, 92, 92n.181, 100, 100n.208
 highest good, 147–49
 passions, 253–56
 providence, 66–67, 112, 113
 Sage, 192–93, 194, 234–35, 237–38, 264–65
Strato, 67–68

INDEX

Studer, Basil, 15–16, 176
subordinationism, 184n.60
Suetonius, 40
Sulla, 28–29, 69n.62, 71–72, 122
Swift, Louis J., 269–70
Sybilline oracle, 7–8, 173
Syed, Yasmin, 42–43
Syme, Ronald, 33–34, 70–71
sympatheia, 88n.159

Tacitus
  Annals, 49–50
Ten Commandments, 266–67
  Fifth, 266–69
Terence, 92–93
Tertullian, 15, 17–19, 20–21, 59–60, 61–62, 70,
    111, 123n.54, 123–24, 126–27, 128n.73,
    129, 130–31, 136–37, 146–47, 152–53,
    158–59, 160, 167–69, 171–72, 176,
    178–79, 181, 182–83, 185–86, 188, 191,
    200, 217–18, 219, 224, 229–30, 256–57,
    264–65, 282
  Against Praxeas, 20, 131, 133–36, 137, 138–
    39, 142, 166, 172–73, 178, 186, 195–96,
    204, 218–19
  anti-Monarchian, 167–68, 173–74, 177n.38,
    194, 196–97, 203, 207–8
  Apologeticus, 111, 117–18, 129, 130–31, 133–
    34, 138–39, 155–56, 159, 218–19
  capital punishment, 266–67
  De carne Christi, 183, 184–85
  Christology of, 60–61, 129–30, 131–33,
    135–36, 138–39, 140, 143–44, 163–64,
    188, 201
  God in, 129, 138–39, 141, 143–44
  Lactantius's critique of, 7–8
  opera virtutum—verba doctrinae,
    132–33, 135–36, 142–43, 146, 166,
    167–68, 196–97, 200, 202, 207–8, 218–
    19, 240–41
  De patientia, 131–32, 136, 141–42, 146, 196–
    97, 203, 206, 228
  rectus status, 230
Tetrarchy, 6, 14–15, 162n.60
Theophilus of Antioch, 9, 128n.76, 129–30,
    168–69n.9, 173n.22
Thomas, Richard, 33n.38, 44n.89, 45,
    47n.107, 50
Tiberius Caesar, 38–39
1 Timothy, Epistle to
  2:5, 184–85
Tobit, Book of
  4:15, 252–53, 275–76

tradition (Roman), 13–14, 29–30, 32, 34, 36,
    68–70, 104–5, 114n.16, 115, 119–20, 122
  criticism of, 32–42, 52, 117
  virtus in, 34, 35
Trier, 3–4, 271–72
Trinitarian theology (Latin), 20, 59–60, 102,
    110–11, 123–36, 142, 144–45, 167–68,
    208, 218–20, 221–22, 223, 225, 228,
    242–43, 245–46
  imperial context, 61–62, 131
  in Tertullian, 130
"Two Ways" doctrine, 215–17, 243–44, 245–46,
    256–57, 279

Ulpian, 8

Valerius Maximus, 29–30
Venus Victrix, 28–29
Vergil, 9, 24–25, 32–33, 38–39, 42–50, 55,
    96–105, 107, 110–11, 112, 116, 123–26,
    144–45, 158–59, 192, 215–16, 217–18
  Aeneid, 42–49, 97–105, 106, 114–15, 116,
    124, 125, 192
  cosmology, 99
  counter-narrative in, 45–49
  Creusa, 45–46
  Dido, 44–45, 46, 50
  Georgics, 106, 124, 125, 126
  Golden Age, 189–90
  Pallas, 48–49
  post-Vergilian literature dialogue with,
    49–50
  Turnus, 45–46, 48–49, 101n.214
vice, 34, 35, 36, 37, 38–39, 40, 51, 62, 100, 119
  in Lactantius, 151, 163–64, 167, 197
  path of, 215
virtus
  aequitas and, 224
  altera virtus, 148–49
  Augustan Era, 116, 119, 181, 186–87,
    189, 208–9
  city name, 28–29
  divine favor and, 26–27, 28–29, 32–33, 39,
    52–53, 102–3
  eternal life and, 152, 213–14, 254
  ethical/moral excellence, 26, 30, 34, 35–36,
    44–45, 55, 66, 78–79, 118, 150, 151, 152
  Greek philosophy and, 8, 19–20, 26, 33–34
  highest good, 149
  lexical shift, 26, 28–29, 30–31, 32, 33–34, 53,
    55–56, 66, 78–79, 106, 114–15, 118–19,
    122, 136, 144–45, 152, 191
  likeness to God, 81, 83–84, 106–7, 142

328 INDEX

virtus (*cont.*)
"manliness," 1–2, 19–20, 24–25, 77–79, 118
martial, 24–25, 26, 27, 36–37, 52, 55, 62–63, 94, 100–1, 114–15, 118, 122, 150, 151, 192–93, 208–9
martyrs and, 123
path of, 215–17, 243–44, 245–46, 256–57, 279
patientia, 67, 123, 143
personified, 26–27
philosophical accounts of, 32–33, 52, 53, 62, 78–79, 84–85, 93, 94, 192–93
pietas, 35–36, 53, 118
in politics, 24–25, 35, 36, 77–78
"power" (*see* power)
rivalry over, 27, 28–29, 32–33, 35–36, 53, 118–19
suffering, 198
sustains life, 152
traditional ideal, 38, 55, 84, 120, 210
victory and, 26–27
vis (*see* power)
Volk, Katharina, 55

Walter, Jochen, 12–14, 21–22
Whitmarsh, Timothy, 63

wisdom
and foolishness, 208–13, 219 (*see also* Pauline Rule)
in Lactantius, 208–13, 214, 223–24, 237–38, 243–44, 245, 246, 276–77 (*see also* *sapientia*)
Wisdom, Book of
2:12–22, 190
7:25, 178n.40
12:2–12, 190
13–15, 198n.122
Wlosok, Antonie, 11–12, 229–30, 232–33
worship, 9–10, 17, 232–33, 245, 247
idolatry, 8, 160–61, 167, 197, 230–31, 232–35, 256–57, 258
as justice, 242–43
and wisdom, 218–19

X from X causality, 60–61, 88–89, 93–94n.183, 97–98, 131
in Lactantius, 151–52, 159, 178–79
See also power causality

Zechariah, Book of
3:4, 190
Zeno, 67–68, 126–27, 129–30